3rd Edition
Ventures 4
TEACHER'S EDITION

Gretchen Bitterlin ▪ Dennis Johnson ▪ Donna Price ▪ Sylvia Ramirez
K. Lynn Savage (Series Editor)

CAMBRIDGE
UNIVERSITY PRESS

CAMBRIDGE
UNIVERSITY PRESS

University Printing House, Cambridge CB2 8BS, United Kingdom

One Liberty Plaza, 20th Floor, New York, NY 10006, USA

477 Williamstown Road, Port Melbourne, VIC 3207, Australia

314–321, 3rd Floor, Plot 3, Splendor Forum, Jasola District Centre, New Delhi – 110025, India

79 Anson Road, #06–04/06, Singapore 079906

Cambridge University Press is part of the University of Cambridge.

It furthers the University's mission by disseminating knowledge in the pursuit of education, learning and research at the highest international levels of excellence.

www.cambridge.org
Information on this title: www.cambridge.org/9781108685177

© Cambridge University Press 2018

First published 2008
Second edition 2014
Third edition 2018
20 19 18 17 16 15 14 13 12 11 10 9 8 7 6 5 4 3 2

Printed in Great Britain by CPI Group (UK) Ltd, Croydon CR0 4YY

A catalogue record for this publication is available from the British Library

ISBN 978-1-108-44958-8 Student's Book
ISBN 978-1-108-45062-1 Workbook
ISBN 978-1-108-44947-2 Online Workbook
ISBN 978-1-108-44923-6 Class Audio CDs
ISBN 978-1-108-45054-6 Presentation Plus

Additional resources for this publication at www.cambridge.org/ventures

CONTENTS

TO THE TEACHER

What is *Ventures*?

Ventures is a six-level, four-skills, standards-based, integrated-skills series that empowers students to achieve their academic and career goals.

- Aligned to the new NRS descriptors while covering key English Language Proficiency, College and Career Readiness Standards, and WIOA requirements.
- A wealth of resources provide instructors with the tools for any teaching situation, making *Ventures* the most complete program.
- Promotes 21st century learning complemented by a suite of technology tools.

How Does the Third Edition Meet Today's Adult Education Needs?

- The third edition is aligned to the NRS' interpretive, productive, and interactive outcomes at each level.
- To help students develop the skills they need to succeed in college and the workplace, *Ventures* 3rd Edition offers a dedicated College and Career Readiness Section (CCRS) with 10 worksheets at each level, from Level 1 to Transitions (pages 136–155).
- Audio tracks and grammar presentations linked to QR codes can be accessed using smartphones (see page x), promoting mobile learning.
- Problem-solving activities added to each unit cover critical thinking and soft skills key to workplace readiness.
- More rigorous grammar practice has been added to Lessons B and C, and more evidence-based reading practice has been added to Lesson D.

What are the *Ventures* components?

Student's Book

Each of the core **Student's Books** contains ten topic-focused units, with five review units. The main units feature six skill-focused lessons.

- **Self-contained lessons** are perfectly paced for one-hour classes. For classes longer than 1 hour, additional resources are available via the Workbook and Online Teacher's Resources.
- **Review units** recycle and reinforce the listening, vocabulary, and grammar skills developed in the two prior units and include a pronunciation activity.

Teacher's Edition

The interleaved **Teacher's Edition** includes easy-to-follow lesson plans for every unit.

- Teaching tips address common problem areas for students and additional suggestions for expansion activities and building community.
- Additional practice material across all *Ventures* components is clearly organized in the *More Ventures* chart at the end of each lesson.
- Multiple opportunities for assessment such as unit, mid-term, and final tests are available in the Teacher's Edition. Customizable tests and test audio are also available online (www.cambridge.org/ventures/resources/).

Online Teacher's Resources
www.cambridge.org/ventures/resources/

Ventures Online Teacher's Resources offer hundreds of additional worksheets and classroom materials including:

- *A placement test* that helps accurately identify the appropriate level of *Ventures* for each student.
- *Career and Educational Pathways Worksheets* help students meet their post-exit employment goals.
- *Collaborative Worksheets* for each lesson develop cooperative learning and community building within the classroom.
- *Writing Worksheets* that help literacy-level students recognize shapes and write letters and numbers, while alphabet and number cards promote partner and group work.
- *Picture dictionary cards and Worksheets* that reinforce vocabulary learned in Levels Basic, 1, and 2.
- *Multilevel Worksheets* that are designed for use in multilevel classrooms and in leveled classes where the proficiency level of students differs.
- *Self-assessments* give students an opportunity to reflect on their learning. They support learner persistence and help determine whether students are ready for the unit test.

Workbook

The **Workbook** provides two pages of activities for each lesson in the Student's Book.

- If used in class, the Workbook can extend classroom instructional time by 30 minutes per lesson.
- The exercises are designed so learners can complete them in class or independently. Students can check their answers with the answer key in the back of the Workbook. Workbook exercises can be assigned in class, for homework, or as student support when a class is missed.
- Grammar charts at the back of the Workbook allow students to use the Workbook for self-study.

Online Workbooks

The self-grading **Online Workbooks** offer programs the flexibility of introducing blended learning.

- In addition to the same high-quality practice opportunities in the print workbooks, the online workbooks provide students instant feedback.
- Teachers and programs can track student progress and time on task.

Presentation Plus
www.esource.cambridge.org

Presentation Plus allows teachers to digitally project the contents of the Student's Books in front of the class for a livelier, interactive classroom. It is a complete solution for teachers because it includes the Class audio, answer keys, and the Ventures Arcade. Contact your Cambridge ESL Specialist (www.cambridge.org/cambridgeenglish/contact) to find out how to access it.

Ventures Arcade
www.cambridge.org/venturesarcade/

The Arcade is a free website where students can find additional practice for the listening, vocabulary, and grammar found in the Student's Books. There is also a Citizenship section that includes questions on civics, history, government, and the N-400 application.

Unit organization

LESSON A Listening focuses students on the unit topic. The initial exercise, **Before you listen**, creates student interest with visuals that help the teacher assess what learners already know and serves as a prompt for the unit's key vocabulary. Next is **Listen**, which is based on conversations. Students relate vocabulary to meaning and relate the spoken and written forms of new theme-related vocabulary. **After you listen** concludes the lesson by practicing language related to the theme in a communicative activity, either orally with a partner or individually in a writing activity.

LESSONS B AND C focus on grammar. The lessons move from a **Grammar focus** that presents the grammar point in chart form; to **Practice** exercises that check comprehension of the grammar point and provide guided practice; and, finally, to **Communicate** exercises that guide learners as

they generate original answers and conversations. These lessons often include a *Culture note*, which provides information directly related to the conversation practice (such as the use of titles with last names) or a *Useful language* note, which introduces useful expressions.

LESSON D Reading develops reading skills and expands vocabulary. The lesson opens with a **Before you read** exercise, designed to activate prior knowledge and encourage learners to make predictions. A *Reading tip*, which focuses on a specific reading skill, accompanies the **Read** exercise. The reading section of the lesson concludes with **After you read** exercises that check comprehension. In Levels Basic, 1, and 2, the vocabulary expansion portion of the lesson is a **Picture dictionary**. It includes a *word bank*, pictures to identify, and a conversation for practicing the new words. The words expand vocabulary related to the unit topic. In Books 3 and 4, the vocabulary expansion portion of the lesson uses new vocabulary from the reading to build skills such as recognizing word families, selecting definitions based on the context of the reading, and using clues in the reading to guess meaning.

LESSON E Writing provides practice with process writing within the context of the unit. **Before you write** exercises provide warm-up activities to activate the language needed for the writing assignment, followed by one or more exercises that provide a model for students to follow when they write. A *Writing tip* presents information about punctuation or paragraph organization directly related to the writing assignment. The **Write** exercise sets goals for the student writing. In the **After you write** exercise, students share with a partner.

LESSON F Another view brings the unit together with opportunities to review lesson content. **Life-skills reading** develops the scanning and skimming skills used with documents such as forms, charts, schedules, announcements, and ads. Multiple-choice questions (modeled on CASAS[1] and BEST[2]) develop test-taking skills. **Solve the problem** focuses on critical thinking, soft-skills, and workplace development. In Levels 1–4, **Grammar connections** contrasts grammar points and includes guided practice and communicative activities.

---

[1] The Comprehensive Adult Student Assessment System. For more information, see www.casas.org.
[2] The Basic English Skills Test. For more information, see www.cal.org/BEST.

SCOPE AND SEQUENCE

UNIT TITLE TOPIC	FUNCTIONS	LISTENING AND SPEAKING	VOCABULARY	GRAMMAR FOCUS
Welcome pages 2–5	■ Exchanging information ■ Discussing study habits and strategies	■ Listening to people talk about study habits and strategies ■ Asking about study habits and strategies ■ Talking about classmates' study habits and strategies	■ Study habits and strategies	■ past continuous and simple past ■ simple past and present perfect
Unit 1 **Personal information** pages 6–17 Topic: **Ways to be smart**	■ Describing personal strengths ■ Expressing opinions ■ Expressing agreement and disagreement	■ Asking about aptitudes ■ Discussing multiple intelligences ■ Giving opinions	■ Adjectives and adverbs ■ Multiple intelligences ■ Prefixes and roots	■ Nouns, verbs, adjectives, and adverbs ■ Noun clauses with *that* ■ *so* and *that*
Unit 2 **At school** pages 18–29 Topic: **Planning for success**	■ Inquiring about educational opportunities ■ Describing educational goals ■ Describing successful people	■ Asking about courses and classes ■ Discussing how to continue one's education ■ Discussing obstacles and successes	■ Education and careers ■ Educational requirements	■ The present passive ■ Infinitives after the passive ■ *be + supposed to* and *be + not supposed to*
Review: Units 1 and 2 pages 30–31		■ Understanding a conversation		
Unit 3 **Friends and family** pages 32–43 Topic: **Parents and children**	■ Discussing appropriate behaviors at home and school ■ Using polite forms of language	■ Asking about rules at home and at school ■ Asking questions indirectly ■ Talking about past events and experiences	■ Rules and expectations ■ Word families	■ Indirect *Wh-* questions ■ Indirect *Yes / No* questions ■ *say* and *tell* with reported speech
Unit 4 **Health** pages 44–55 Topic: **Stressful situations**	■ Discussing stress ■ Expressing necessity and lack of necessity ■ Making suggestions ■ Expressing past regrets	■ Asking about stress ■ Discussing ways to cope with stress ■ Giving advice about past actions	■ Stress and ways to cope ■ Suffixes	■ *should, shouldn't, have to, don't have to* ■ *should have* and *shouldn't have* ■ *must* and *may / might*
Review: Units 3 and 4 pages 56–57		■ Understanding a phone conversation		
Unit 5 **Around town** pages 58–69 Topic: **Community involvement**	■ Describing volunteer responsibilities ■ Describing a sequence of events ■ Describing repeated actions in the past and present	■ Asking about volunteer activities ■ Discussing personal experiences of volunteering or helping people ■ Discussing schedules	■ Volunteerism ■ Positive and negative words	■ Clauses with *until* and *as soon as* ■ Repeated actions in the present and past ■ Contrasting *used to* and *be used to*

READING	WRITING	LIFE SKILLS	PRONUNCIATION
■ Reading a paragraph about bad weather	■ Writing sentences about your partner	■ Discussing study habits and strategies for learning English	■ Pronouncing key vocabulary
■ Reading an article about multiple intelligences ■ Skimming to predict what a reading is about	■ Writing a descriptive paragraph about a primary intelligence ■ Using a topic sentence and supporting details	■ Using a dictionary ■ Reading and understanding a visual diagram	■ Pronouncing key vocabulary
■ Reading an article about an immigrant family ■ Scanning to find specific information	■ Writing a descriptive paragraph about a successful person ■ Using specific details such as facts, examples, and reasons	■ Using a dictionary or thesaurus to identify synonyms ■ Reading and understanding a chart about the location of vocational classes	■ Pronouncing key vocabulary
			■ -ed verb endings
■ Reading an article about barriers between generations ■ Noticing words that repeat to get an idea of what a reading is about	■ Writing an expository paragraph about a difference between generations ■ Using a transition within a paragraph	■ Using a dictionary ■ Reading and understanding a chart ■ Interpreting census bureau information	■ Pronouncing key vocabulary
■ Reading an article about stress ■ Relating the title and section heads to personal experience	■ Writing a descriptive paragraph about how to cope with stress ■ Using causes and effects to organize a paragraph	■ Reading and understanding a bar graph ■ Discussing stress in the workplace	■ Pronouncing key vocabulary
			■ Contrasting intonation of direct and indirect Wh- questions
■ Reading an article about volunteers ■ Using context clues to guess if the meaning of a word is positive or negative	■ Writing a descriptive paragraph about someone who made a difference ■ Making writing more interesting by including details that answer Wh- questions	■ Reading and understanding ads for volunteer positions ■ Discussing volunteer activities	■ Pronouncing key vocabulary

UNIT TITLE TOPIC	FUNCTIONS	LISTENING AND SPEAKING	VOCABULARY	GRAMMAR FOCUS
Unit 6 **Time** pages 70–81 Topic: **Time and technology**	▪ Expressing agreement and disagreement ▪ Giving opinions and reasons	▪ Talking about time-saving devices ▪ Discussing the advantages and disadvantages of technology	▪ Technology and time- saving devices ▪ Words with multiple definitions	▪ *although* ▪ Contrasting *because* and *although* ▪ *so* and *such*
Review: Units 5 and 6 pages 82–83		▪ Understanding a radio interview		
Unit 7 **Shopping** pages 84–95 Topic: **Buying and returning merchandise**	▪ Explaining problems with a purchase ▪ Discussing preferences ▪ Explaining mistakes ▪ Asking for information about store policies	▪ Asking about returning merchandise ▪ Asking about store policies ▪ Talking about shopping mistakes ▪ Describing people, places, and things	▪ Buying and returning merchandise ▪ Compound nouns	▪ *who, that* and *which* as the subject of an adjective clause ▪ *that* as the object of an adjective clause ▪ Clarifying questions
Unit 8 **Work** pages 96–107 Topic: **Success at work**	▪ Giving advice ▪ Making suggestions ▪ Explaining job responsibilities ▪ Describing the duration of an activity	▪ Discussing work schedules ▪ Talking about workplace problems and their solutions ▪ Asking questions about work experiences	▪ Job responsibilities and skills ▪ Prefixes and roots	▪ Contrasting present perfect and present perfect continuous ▪ Adjectives ending in *-ed* and *-ing* ▪ Polite requests and offers
Review: Units 7 and 8 pages 108–109		▪ Understanding a class lecture		
Unit 9 **Daily living** pages 110–121 Topic: **Saving our planet**	▪ Describing environmental issues and concerns ▪ Giving advice ▪ Making suggestions ▪ Describing actions one can take	▪ Asking questions about "saving our planet" ▪ Discussing causes and effects of environmental problems ▪ Discussing actions that could help the environment	▪ The environment ▪ Antonyms	▪ Present unreal conditional ▪ *since* and *so* ▪ Contrasting present real and present unreal conditionals
Unit 10 **Free time** pages 122–133 Topic: **Celebrations**	▪ Describing future possibility ▪ Describing actions based on expectations ▪ Expressing hopes and wishes ▪ Comparing customs and celebrations	▪ Asking about and comparing wedding customs ▪ Discussing possible and hypothetical holiday plans ▪ Talking about hopes and wishes	▪ Celebrations ▪ Words with multiple meanings	▪ Contrasting future real and future unreal conditionals ▪ *hope* and *wish* ▪ Tag questions
Review: Units 9 and 10 pages 134–135		▪ Understanding a street interview		

READING	WRITING	LIFE SKILLS	PRONUNCIATION
■ Reading a magazine article about the impact of technology ■ Reading first and last paragraph for main idea	■ Writing an expository paragraph about a time-saving device or activity ■ Using advantages and disadvantages to organize a paragraph	■ Using a dictionary ■ Reading and understanding a table ■ Discussing Internet use ■ Discussing survey results	■ Pronouncing key vocabulary
			■ Stressed and unstressed words
■ Reading a newspaper advice column about return policies ■ Recognizing synonyms in a reading	■ Writing a persuasive paragraph about shopping online ■ Using transition words such as *first, second, next, furthermore, moreover,* and *finally* to signal a list of reasons in a paragraph	■ Reading and understanding a returned-merchandise form ■ Talking about returning or exchanging merchandise	■ Pronouncing key vocabulary
■ Reading an article about hard and soft job skills ■ Reading an email cover letter to apply for a job ■ Recognizing quotations and reasons for using them	■ Writing an email cover letter to apply for a job ■ Including information about skills and experience in a cover letter	■ Using a dictionary ■ Reading and understanding a table about the fastest-growing occupations ■ Discussing work skills	■ Pronouncing key vocabulary
			■ Stressing function words
■ Reading a fable about how all things in life are connected ■ Asking questions to identify a cause-and-effect relationship	■ Writing a paragraph about an environmental problem ■ Using cause and effect to organize a paragraph	■ Using a dictionary or thesaurus ■ Reading and understanding a chart about reasons to "Save our planet" ■ Discussing ways to help the environment	■ Pronouncing key vocabulary
■ Reading an article about special birthday celebrations around the world ■ Using punctuation as a clue to meaning	■ Writing a descriptive paragraph about a favorite holiday or celebration ■ Concluding a paragraph by relating it to your personal life	■ Using a dictionary ■ Reading and understanding a recipe ■ Discussing traditional meals and recipes	■ Pronouncing key vocabulary
			■ Linking consonant-vowel sounds

CORRELATIONS

UNIT	CASAS Competencies	Florida Adult ESOL Low Beginning	LAUSD ESL Beginning Low Competencies
Unit 1 **Personal information** Pages 6–17	**0.1.2, 0.1.4, 0.1.5, 0.1.6, 0.2.1, 0.2.4, 4.1.7, 4.1.8, 4.4.2, 4.5.2, 4.5.5, 4.6.1, 4.7.3, 4.8.1, 4.8.2, 7.1.1, 7.1.4, 7.2.3, 7.2.4, 7.4.1, 7.4.2, 7.4.5, 7.4.9, 7.5.1**	5.01.01, 5.01.02, 5.01.03, 5.01.04, 5.03.06, 5.03.10, 5.03.11	A Course: I. 1b II. 5a VIII. 45 B Course: I. 1a, 1b, 1c II. 6a, 6b VIII. 35, 37, 38
Unit 2 **At school** Pages 18–31	**0.1.2, 0.1.5, 0.1.6, 0.2.1, 0.2.4, 2.3.1, 2.3.2, 2.5.5, 2.7.6, 4.1.4, 4.1.7, 4.1.9, 4.4.1, 4.6.1, 4.8.1, 4.8.2, 4.9.1, 6.0.1, 7.1.1, 7.1.4, 7.2.1, 7.2.2, 7.4.1, 7.4.2, 7.4.5, 7.5.1**	5.01.01, 5.01.13, 5.03.05, 5.03.06, 5.03.11, 5.03.12	A Course: II. 5a, 5b III. 11a, 11b, 11c, 15 VIII. 42, 43 B Course: II. 5, 9a III. 10a, 10b, 10c VII. 29 VIII. 35, 37, 38, 39
Unit 3 **Friends and family** Pages 32–43	**0.1.2, 0.1.3, 0.1.4, 0.1.5, 0.2.2, 0.2.4, 4.4.3, 4.8.1, 4.8.2, 6.0.1, 6.6.5, 7.1.1, 7.1.4, 7.2.1, 7.2.3, 7.5.1, 7.5.5, 7.5.6, 8.3.1, 8.3.2**	5.01.01, 5.01.03, 5.02.08, 5.03.06, 5.03.11, 5.05.01	A Course: I. 1b II. 5a, 6 B Course: I. 2 II. 5, 6a, 7 III. 11 VIII. 37, 38
Unit 4 **Health** Pages 44–57	**0.1.2, 0.1.3, 0.1.4, 0.1.5, 0.2.2, 0.2.4, 4.4.3, 4.8.1, 4.8.2, 6.0.1, 6.6.5, 7.1.1, 7.1.4, 7.2.1, 7.2.3, 7.5.1, 7.5.4, 7.5.5, 7.5.6, 8.3.1, 8.3.2**	5.01.01, 5.01.03, 5.03.06, 5.03.11, 5.05.01	A Course: I. 1b B Course: II. 6c VI. 27 VIII. 37
Unit 5 **Around town** Pages 58–69	**0.1.2, 0.1.5, 0.1.6, 0.2.4, 2.7.3, 3.1.3, 3.5.8, 3.5.9, 4.1.4, 4.8.1, 6.0.1, 7.1.1, 7.1.3, 7.1.4, 7.2.1, 7.2.2, 7.4.1, 7.4.2, 7.4.3, 7.5.1, 7.5.2, 7.5.5, 8.3.1, 8.3.2**	5.01.01, 5.02.07, 5.03.02, 5.03.06, 5.03.11	A Course: I. 1b VIII. 44 B Course: II. 6c III. 12, 13 VIII. 37, 40

For more details and correlations to other state standards, go to: www.cambridge.org/ventures/correlations

NRS Educational Functioning Level Descriptors	English Language Proficiency and College and Career Readiness Standards
Interpretive ▪ Determine the main idea and key details in a conversation about personal strengths. ▪ Determine the main idea and key details in a reading about multiple intelligences. ▪ Use *prefixes* and *roots* to determine the meaning of vocabulary related to personality types. ▪ Determine the main idea and key details in a diagram about left-brain and right-brain functions. **Productive** ▪ Deliver a short oral presentation that describes classmates. ▪ Compose a paragraph about and provide examples for one personality type. ▪ Report on an Internet research project to find careers that match a given personality type. **Interactive** ▪ Participate in conversations about aptitudes and intelligent types. ▪ Discuss men's and women's aptitudes in different areas of intelligence.	ELP Standards 1–10 Reading Anchors 1, 2, 4, 5, 6, 7, 8, 9, 10 Speaking & Listening Anchors 1, 2, 3, 4, 6
Interpretive ▪ Determine the main topic and key details in a conversation about future educational plans. ▪ Determine the main topic and key details in a written text about an immigrant family's success story. ▪ Use a dictionary or thesaurus to determine the meaning of vocabulary about planning for success. ▪ State an opinion and cite evidence to support it. **Productive** ▪ Write a paragraph that has a topic sentence, examples, and a concluding sentence about someone you know who is successful. ▪ Deliver a short oral presentation about a classmate's course registration. ▪ Report on a short research project about a class from an adult school or community college. ▪ Identify and use academic words in a reading about planning for success. **Interactive** ▪ Participate in conversations about planning for success. ▪ Discuss with a partner each other's writing about a person you know who is successful.	ELP Standards 1–10 Reading Anchors 1, 2, 4, 5, 6, 7, 8, 9, 10 Speaking & Listening Anchors 1, 2, 3, 4, 6
Interpretive ▪ Determine the main topic and key details in a conversation about a student's absence. ▪ Determine the main topic and key details in a written text about immigrant families. ▪ Use context clues to determine the meaning of vocabulary about friends and family. ▪ State an opinion and cite evidence to support it. **Productive** ▪ Write a paragraph about differences between you and your parents or you and your children that has a transition between the two parts of your paragraph. ▪ Deliver a short oral presentation about a classmate's life as a teenager. ▪ Report on a short research project about rules that children should follow at home. ▪ Identify and use academic words in a reading about parents and children. **Interactive** ▪ Participate in conversations about the teenage years. ▪ Discuss with a partner each other's writing about parents and children.	ELP Standards 1–10 Reading Anchors 1, 2, 4, 5, 6, 7, 8, 9, 10 Speaking & Listening Anchors 1, 2, 3, 4, 6
Interpretive ▪ Determine the main topic and key details in a conversation about advice for coping with stress. ▪ Determine the main topic and key details in a written text about stress. ▪ Use *suffixes* to determine the meaning of vocabulary about stressful situations. ▪ State an opinion and cite evidence to support it. **Productive** ▪ Write a paragraph about how you cope with stress giving three examples and details for each example. ▪ Deliver a short oral presentation about a classmate's situation that didn't go as planned. ▪ Report on a short Internet research project about how to cope with anxiety before and during a test. ▪ Identify and use academic words in a reading about stressful situations. **Interpretive** ▪ Participate in conversations about a situation that didn't go as planned. ▪ Discuss with a partner each other's writing about how to cope with stress.	ELP Standards 1–10 Reading Anchors 1, 2, 4, 5, 6, 7, 8, 9, 10 Speaking & Listening Anchors 1, 2, 3, 4, 6
Interpretive ▪ Determine the main topic and key details in a conversation about responsibilities for volunteer jobs. ▪ Determine the main topic and key details in a written text about a volunteer program for the blind. ▪ Use context clues to determine the meaning of vocabulary about community involvement. ▪ State an opinion and cite evidence to support it. **Productive** ▪ Write a paragraph about someone you know who made a difference in your life or someone else's life that includes specific details that answer *wh-* questions. ▪ Deliver a short oral presentation about a classmate's volunteer experiences. ▪ Report on a short research project about ways that people have helped you. ▪ Identify and use academic words in a reading about community involvement. **Interactive** ▪ Participate in conversations about volunteer experiences. ▪ Discuss with a partner each other's writing about someone who made a difference in your life.	ELP Standards 1–10 Reading Anchors 1, 2, 4, 5, 6, 7, 8, 9, 10 Speaking & Listening Anchors 1, 2, 3, 4, 6

UNIT	CASAS Competencies	Florida Adult ESOL Low Beginning	LAUSD ESL Beginning Low Competencies
Unit 6 **Time** Pages 70–81	0.1.2, 0.1.5, 0.1.6, 0.2.4, 1.1.3, 1.3.1, 1.4.1, 1.7.4, 2.1.1, 2.2.3, 4.5.1, 4.5.2, 4.5.5, 4.8.1, 6.0.1, 7.1.1, 7.1.4, 7.2.1, 7.2.3, 7.2.4, 7.2.5, 7.4.1, 7.4.2, 7.4.8, 7.5.1, 7.7.1	5.01.01, 5.01.02, 5.01.03, 5.03.02, 5.03.06, 5.03.11, 5.03.15	A Course: II. 5a B Course: II. 6a, 6b VIII. 37, 38
Unit 7 **Shopping** Pages 84–95	0.1.2, 0.1.3, 0.1.5, 0.1.6, 1.2.2, 1.3.1, 1.3.3, 1.4.1, 1.6.3, 1.7.1, 4.8.1, 6.0.1, 7.1.1, 7.1.4, 7.2.1, 7.2.3, 7.2.5, 7.4.2, 7.4.3, 7.4.8, 7.5.1	5.01.01, 5.03.02, 5.03.06, 5.03.11, 5.04.02, 5.04.09	A Course: IV. 21a B Course: VIII. 37
Unit 8 **Work** Pages 96–107	0.1.2, 0.1.3, 0.1.5, 0.1.7, 0.2.4, 2.3.1, 2.3.2, 2.4.1, 4.1.2, 4.1.6, 4.1.7, 4.1.8, 4.4.1, 4.4.2, 4.4.3, 4.4.4, 4.5.2, 4.5.5, 4.6.2, 4.7.3, 4.8.1, 4.8.2, 6.0.1, 7.1.1, 7.1.4, 7.2.1, 7.2.3, 7.2.7, 7.3.1, 7.3.2, 7.4.1, 7.4.2, 7.4.5, 7.5.1, 7.5.2, 7.5.6	5.01.01, 5.01.03, 5.03.02, 5.03.03, 5.03.06, 5.03.07, 5.03.11, 5.03.13	A Course: I. 4b VII. 34, 38a, 38b, 38c, 41 B Course: VIII. 37, 38, 41
Unit 9 **Daily living** Pages 110–121	0.1.2, 0.1.5, 1.4.1, 2.2.3, 2.3.3, 2.7.3, 4.8.1, 5.6.1, 5.7.1, 7.1.1, 7.2.1, 7.2.2, 7.2.6, 7.3.1, 7.3.2, 7.3.4, 7.4.2, 7.4.3, 7.5.1, 7.5.4, 8.3.1	5.01.01, 5.01.03, 5.02.02, 5.03.06, 5.03.11	B Course: II. 7 VIII. 37, 38
Unit 10 **Free time** Pages 122–133	0.1.1, 0.1.2, 0.1.5, 0.1.6, 0.2.4, 1.1.1, 1.1.5, 2.3.2, 2.5.7, 2.7.1, 2.7.2, 2.7.4, 4.5.2, 4.5.5, 4.8.1, 6.0.1, 7.1.1, 7.1.4, 7.2.1, 7.2.3, 7.2.4, 7.2.6, 7.4.1, 7.4.2, 7.4.4, 7.4.5, 7.5.1, 7.5.6	5.01.01, 5.01.03, 5.02.03, 5.03.06, 5.03.11	A Course: II. 5b B Course: II. 6b, 7, 9 VIII. 37, 38, 40

For more details and correlations to other state standards, go to: www.cambridge.org/ventures/correlations

NRS Educational Functioning Level Descriptors	English Language Proficiency and College and Career Readiness Standards
Interpretive ■ Determine the main topic and key details in a conversation about people's opinions about technology. ■ Determine the main topic and key details in a written text about the impact of technology. ■ Use context clues and parts of speech to determine the meaning of vocabulary about time and technology. ■ State an opinion and cite evidence to support it. **Productive** ■ Write a paragraph about a time-saving device that includes both advantages and disadvantages. ■ Deliver a short oral presentation about a classmate's time-saving device. ■ Report on a short Internet research project about a time-saving device you have or would like to have. ■ Identify and use academic words in a reading about time and technology. **Interactive** ■ Participate in conversations about time saving tools and devices. ■ Discuss with a partner each other's writing about a time-saving device.	ELP Standards 1–10 Reading Anchors 1, 2, 4, 5, 6, 7, 8, 9, 10 Speaking & Listening Anchors 1, 2, 3, 4, 6
Interpretive ■ Determine the main topic and key details in a conversation about returning merchandise. ■ Determine the main topic and key details in a written text about being a smart shopper. ■ Use *compound nouns* to determine the meaning of vocabulary about buying and returning merchandise. ■ State an opinion and cite evidence to support it. **Productive** ■ Write a paragraph that has transitions words to signal your list of reasons about why you should shop online. ■ Deliver a short oral presentation about a classmate's purchase. ■ Report on a short research project about the return policy for three stores. ■ Identify and use academic words in a reading about shopping. **Interactive** ■ Participate in conversations about a purchase you made. ■ Discuss with a partner each other's writing about shopping online.	ELP Standards 1–10 Reading Anchors 1, 2, 4, 5, 6, 7, 8, 9, 10 Speaking & Listening Anchors 1, 2, 3, 4, 6
Interpretive ■ Determine the main topic and key details in a conversation about a work problem and solution. ■ Determine the main topic and key details in a written text about job skills. ■ Use *prefixes* and *roots* to determine the meaning of vocabulary about success at work. ■ State an opinion and cite evidence to support it. **Productive** ■ Write a cover letter for a real or imaginary job that you are interested in that has at least two examples of your skills and experiences. ■ Deliver a short oral presentation about a classmate's experiences. ■ Report on a short Internet research project about how to write a good cover letter. ■ Identify and use academic words in a reading about success at work. **Interactive** ■ Participate in conversations about experiences. ■ Discuss with a partner each other's writing about their skills and experiences.	ELP Standards 1–10 Reading Anchors 1, 2, 4, 5, 6, 7, 8, 9, 10 Speaking & Listening Anchors 1, 2, 3, 4, 6
Interpretive ■ Determine the main topic and key details in a conversation about environmental problems and solutions. ■ Determine the main topic and key details in a written text about how all things are connected. ■ Use *antonyms* to determine the meaning of vocabulary about living green. ■ State an opinion and cite evidence to support it. **Productive** ■ Write a paragraph about an environmental problem in your city or community explaining the causes and their effects. ■ Deliver a short oral presentation about cause and effect relationships. ■ Report on a short research project about ways your school could be green. ■ Identify and use academic words in a reading about living green. **Interactive** ■ Participate in conversations about cause and effect relationships. ■ Discuss with a partner each other's writing about environmental problems.	ELP Standards 1–10 Reading Anchors 1, 2, 4, 5, 6, 7, 8, 9, 10 Speaking & Listening Anchors 1, 2, 3, 4, 6
Interpretive ■ Determine the main topic and key details in a conversation about differences in customs. ■ Determine the main topic and key details in a written text about special birthdays around the world. ■ Use context clues to determine the meaning of vocabulary about celebrations. ■ State an opinion and cite evidence to support it. **Productive** ■ Write a paragraph about your favorite holiday or celebration that has a conclusion that relates the celebration to your personal life. ■ Deliver a short oral presentation about a classmate's hopes for you. ■ Report on a short Internet research project about a holiday or celebration in another country. ■ Identify and use academic words in a reading about celebrations. **Interactive** ■ Participate in conversations about hopes and wishes. ■ Discuss with a partner each other's writing about favorite holidays and celebrations.	ELP Standards 1–10 Reading Anchors 1, 2, 4, 5, 6, 7, 8, 9, 10 Speaking & Listening Anchors 1, 2, 3, 4, 6

UNIT TOUR

The Most Complete Course for Student Success

- Helps students develop the skills needed to be college and career ready and function successfully in their community
- Covers key NRS and WIOA requirements
- Aligned with the English Language Proficiency (ELP) and College and Career Readiness (CCR) standards

The Big Picture

- Introduces the unit topic and creates an opportunity for classroom discussion.
- Activates students' prior knowledge and previews the unit vocabulary.

Unit Goals

Introduces the competencies students will learn.

UNIT 8 WORK

Lesson A Listening

UNIT GOALS
Identify problems at work and school **Describe** hard and soft skills
Provide solutions and identify consequences to those solutions

1 Before you listen
A What do you see?
B What is happening?

Yolanda

David

2 Listen

A **Listen** and answer the questions.
1. Who are the speakers?   2. What are they talking about?

B **Listen again.** Complete the diagram.

Yolanda's problem
1. _____   Possible solutions   4. _____
2. _____   3. _____
Yolanda's decision

3 After you listen

A **Read.** Complete the story.

| advice | close up | exhausted | negotiate | tasks |
| chart | deal with | initials | share | work (something) out |

Yolanda and David work at Daria's Donut Shop. Lately, David has been leaving work early, and Yolanda has to ___close up___ the shop by herself. Tonight, Yolanda is having coffee with her friends. She is _____. Her friends give her _____. Teresa thinks she should talk to her boss, but Yolanda wants to try to _____ things _____ with David first. Julie thinks Yolanda should make a _____ of their duties. Then she should _____ with David and decide who is going to do which _____. When they finish a task, they should write their _____ on the chart. If David isn't doing his _____ of the work, it will show in the chart. Then, Yolanda can show the chart to their boss and let her _____ the situation.

Listen and check your answers.

B **Discuss.** Talk with your classmates.

📖 Listen for and identify a work problem and possible solutions   UNIT 8   97

How to use a QR code

- Open the camera on your smartphone.
- Point it at the QR code.
- The camera will automatically scan the code. If not, press the button to take a picture.
* Not all cameras automatically scan QR codes. You may need to download a QR code reader. Search "QR free" and download an app.

3 Easy Ways to Access Audio

- Scan QR codes
- Download from *Ventures* Online Resources:
  www.cambridge.org/ventures/audio/
- Play from Class audio CDs

Every unit has two grammar lessons taught using the same format.

Grammar Chart

· Presents and practices the grammar point.
· Extra grammar charts online can be used for reference and give additional support.

Grammar Presentation

Animated presentations to watch on mobile devices using QR codes allow for self-directed learning and develop digital literacy.

Additional Grammar Activities

Ensures students have the chance to practice more grammar to meet the rigor of CCRS.

Natural Progression

Moves from controlled to communicative activities for students to ask and answer questions about familiar text, topics, and experiences.

Real-life Practice

Engages students and provides meaningful application of the grammar.

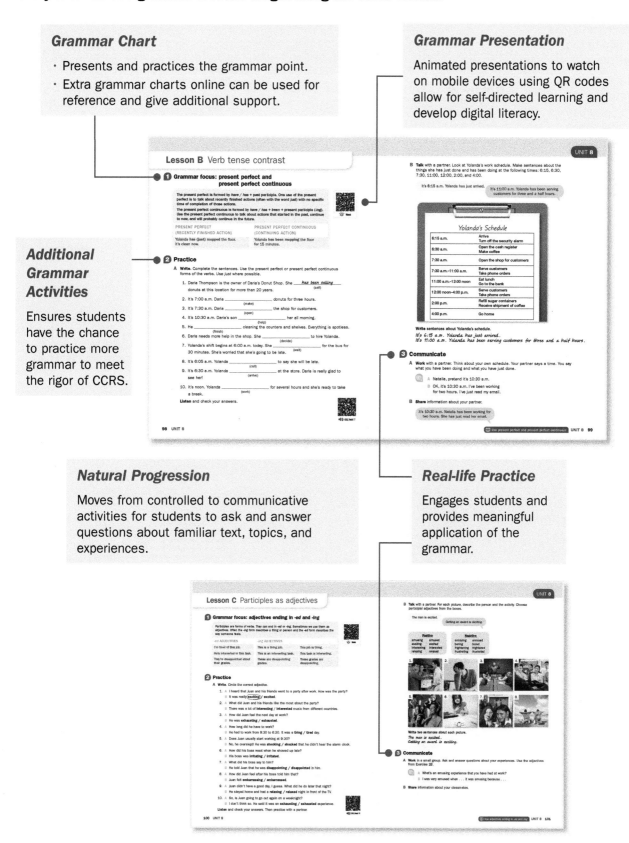

Reading

- Uses a 3-step reading approach to highlight the skills and strategies students need to succeed.
- Combines reading with writing and listening practice for an integrated approach to ensure better comprehension.
- Brings text complexity into the classroom to help students read independently and proficiently.

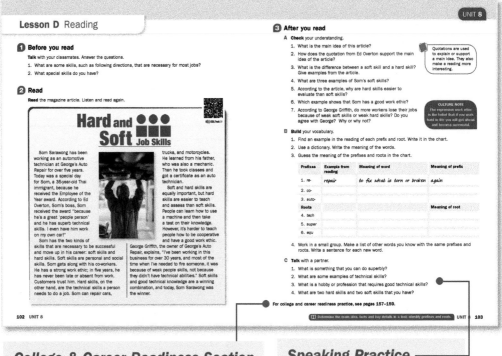

Writing

- Helps students develop a robust process-writing approach.
- Supports students to meet the challenges of work and the classroom through academic and purposeful writing practice.

College & Career Readiness Section

Builds critical-thinking skills and uses informative texts to help master the more complex CCR standards.

Speaking Practice

Helps students internalize the vocabulary and relate it to their lives.

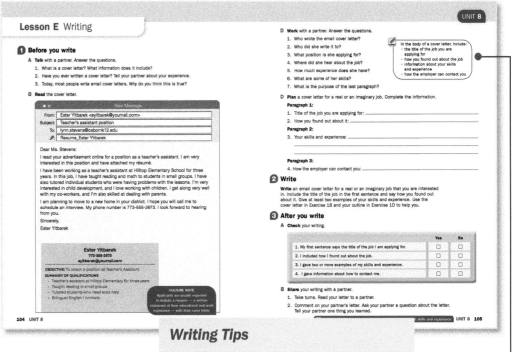

Writing Tips

Gives students confidence in writing with easy-to-follow writing tips and strategies.

Document Literacy

Builds real-life skills through explicit practice using authentic document types.

Grammar connections

Contrasts two grammar forms in a communicative way to help with grammar accuracy.

Test-taking Skills

Prepares students for standarized tests like the CASAS by familiarizing them with bubble answer format.

Problem-solving Activity

Covers critical thinking and soft skills – crucial for workplace readiness – and helps students meet WIOA requirements.

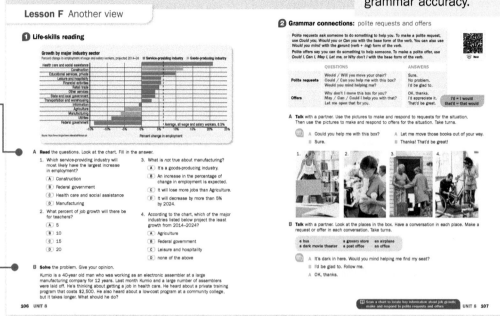

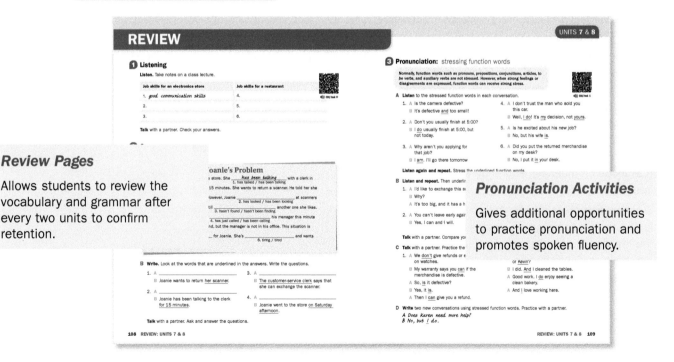

Review Pages

Allows students to review the vocabulary and grammar after every two units to confirm retention.

Pronunciation Activities

Gives additional opportunities to practice pronunciation and promotes spoken fluency.

FEATURES OF THE TEACHER'S EDITION

Introduction

The *Ventures* Teacher's Edition includes step-by-step teaching notes for each lesson. The teaching notes divide the lesson into six stages. Each lesson begins with a warm-up and review followed by a presentation stage. The practice, comprehension, application, and evaluation stages do not follow a strict sequence in the Teacher's Edition. They vary depending on the content of the lesson being presented.

Stages of a lesson

Warm-up and review Each lesson begins with a review of previous material and connects that material to the current lesson. Quick review activities prompt students' memories. Warm-up activities at the beginning of class introduce the new lesson. These activities may take many forms, but they are quick, focused, and connected to the new material to be introduced. A warm-up also helps teachers ascertain what students already know about the topic and what they are able to say.

Presentation During this stage of the lesson, the teacher presents new information, but it should not be a one-way delivery. Rather, it is a dynamic process of student input and interaction – a give-and-take between the teacher and students as well as among students. The teacher may give examples rather than rules, model rather than tell, and relate the material to students' experiences.

Practice It is important that students have enough time to practice. A comfortable classroom environment needs to be created so students are not afraid to take risks. Practice needs to be varied and interesting. There should be a progression from guided to independent practice. In the *Ventures* grammar lessons, for example, practice begins with mechanical aspects such as form, moves to a focus on meaning, and ends with communicative interactions.

Comprehension check Asking, "Do you understand?" is not enough to ascertain whether students are following the lesson. The teacher must ask concrete questions and have students demonstrate that they understand. In this stage, students are asked to repeat information in their own words. Students are also invited to come to the board or to interact with other students in some way.

Application A teacher must provide opportunities for students to practice newly-acquired language in realistic situations. These situations could be in class or outside of class. The important point is that students use what they have learned in new ways. In the grammar lessons, for example, the Communicate section asks students to role-play, interview, share information, or ask questions.

Evaluation An ongoing part of the lesson is to determine whether students are meeting the lesson objectives. This can be done formally at the end of a unit by having students complete the Self-assessment and then giving the unit test, but it can also be done informally toward the end of the lesson. Each lesson in the *Ventures* Teacher's Edition ends with a review and verification of understanding of the lesson objectives. Any in-class assignment or task can serve as an evaluation tool as long as it assesses the objectives. Having students complete Workbook pages can also serve as an informal evaluation to gauge where students may be having difficulty.

The following chart presents the most common order of lesson stages and suggests how long each stage could take within a one-hour class period.

Stages of the lesson	Approximate time range
Warm-up and review	5–10 minutes
Presentation	10–20 minutes
Practice	15–20 minutes
Comprehension check	5–10 minutes
Application	15–20 minutes
Evaluation	10–15 minutes

The Teacher's Edition includes:

- Interleaved Student's Book pages with answers
- Lesson objectives and step-by-step teaching instructions
- Expansion activities, extra teaching tips, and culture notes
- Activities to encourage learner persistence and community building
- Tests and games
- Ideas for multilevel classroom management
- Class audio listening scripts

LESSON A Listening

PRESENTATION

- Books open. Direct Ss' attention to Exercise 2A. Have Ss listen for the main ideas. Read the instructions aloud. Tell Ss that they are going to hear two different audio segments.
- **CD1, Track 25** Play or read the audio (see audio script, page T-178).
- Ask Ss if they understood everything in the listening exercise. Write any unfamiliar words on the board, and help Ss understand the meanings. Make sure that Ss understand the meaning of *unreliable*.
- Elicit answers to the questions. For example: *The speakers are Sara, Cindy (Sara's co-worker), Mr. Stanley (Sara's boss), and Mike (Sara's friend). In the first audio segment, Mr. Stanley asks Cindy where Sara is. Then, after Sara arrives, Mr. Stanley tells Sara that if she's late to work again, she'll be fired. In the second audio segment, Sara tells Mike about her nervousness as she waits to take her driving test.*
- Focus Ss' attention on Exercise 2B and read the instructions aloud. Tell Ss to listen and complete the chart based on the information they hear. Ask Ss what *symptoms* means. Elicit responses, such as: *Symptoms are signs of illness that a person might show or feel.*
- **CD1, Track 25** Tell Ss to listen for details about Sara's symptoms and Mike's advice. Model the task. Play or read the audio again. Pause the audio after Sara says in Part 2: *I'm so worried about losing my job, I can't sleep.* Ask a S to read the example written under Sara's symptoms (can't sleep). Tell Ss to listen and complete the chart. Then play or read the rest of the audio.
- **CD1, Track 25** Play or read the audio again. Ss listen and check their answers. Repeat the audio as needed.
- Write the numbers 1–6 on the board. Ask Ss to come to the board to write the answers. Have other Ss make corrections on the board as needed.

Learner persistence *(individual work)*
- **CD1, Track 25** Ss can listen to the audio for Exercise 2A and 2B at home for reinforcement and review. They can also listen to the audio for self-directed learning when class attendance is not possible.

PRACTICE

- Direct Ss' attention to Exercise 3A, and read the instructions aloud. Tell Ss that the story in this exercise is a summary of what happened in the pictures on page 44.
- Focus Ss' attention on the words or expressions in the word bank. Say each word and ask Ss to repeat. Correct pronunciation. Explain any new words.
- Model the task. Ask a S to read aloud the first two sentences in the story, including the example answer.

- Ss complete the exercise individually. Walk around and help as needed.
- **CD1, Track 26** Play or read the audio (see audio script, page T-179). Ss listen and check their answers. Repeat the audio as needed.
- Write the numbers 1–10 on the board. Ask Ss to come to the board to write their answers. Work with the class to correct any answers as necessary.

Learner persistence *(individual work)*
- **CD1, Track 26** Ss can listen to the audio for Exercise 3A at home for reinforcement and review. They can also listen to the audio for self-directed learning when class attendance is not possible.

APPLICATION

- Focus Ss' attention on Exercise 3B and read the instructions aloud.
- Ss complete the exercise in pairs. Help as needed.
- Ask several pairs to share their answers with the class.

Community building *(whole group)*
- Because Ss may face a wide range of stress-inducing situations, it is important to discuss resources in your community that may be available to help alleviate stress. If your program is affiliated with a college, find out what the college has to offer in the way of counseling or stress-management classes. Ask Ss if they can recommend any stress-reduction classes they may have taken. Compile a list of places in your community that offer such classes or techniques and distribute it to the class. Your local librarian may also be helpful in finding resources that you can pass on to Ss.

EVALUATION

- Direct Ss' attention to the lesson focus on the board. Ask individual Ss to look at the pictures on page 44 and make sentences using the words in Exercise 3A.
- Check off each part of the lesson focus as Ss demonstrate an understanding of what they have learned in the lesson.

More Ventures, Unit 4, Lesson A	
Workbook, 15–30 min.	
Multilevel Worksheets, 30–45 min.	www.cambridge.org/ventures/resources/
Collaborative Worksheets, 30–45 min.	
Student Arcade, time varies	www.cambridge.org/venturesarcade/

T-45 Unit 4

UNIT GOALS
Recognize causes of stress **Explain** strategies for coping with stress
Recognize the impact of stress on work

2 Listen

A Listen and answer the questions.
1. Who are the speakers?   2. What are they talking about?

CD1, Track 25

B Listen again. Complete the chart.

Sara's symptoms	Mike's advice
1. *can't sleep*	4. *think positive thoughts*
2. *can't eat*	5. *deep breathing*
3. *can't concentrate*	6. *meditate*

CD1, Track 25

3 After you listen

A Read. Complete the story.

anxiety	calm down	cope with	positive	techniques
breathing	concentrate	meditation	stressed out	tense

Mike is driving Sara to the Department of Motor Vehicles (DMV) to take her driving test. He notices that she's very ___*tense*___ (1). Sara says she's ___*stressed out*___ (2) because she was late to work again. She's worried that her boss will fire her if she's late one more time. She's so afraid of losing her job that she can't eat, she can't sleep, and she can't ___*concentrate*___ (3). Mike says that she has to ___*calm down*___ (4) if she wants to pass her driving test. He suggests three ___*techniques*___ (5) to help her ___*cope with*___ (6) her ___*anxiety*___ (7). One is deep ___*breathing*___ (8). The second one is thinking ___*positive*___ (9) thoughts, and the third one is ___*meditation*___ (10).

Listen and check your answers.

B **Discuss.** Talk with your classmates.
1. Do you ever feel stressed out? What makes you feel stressed out?
2. What helps you when you feel stressed out?

CD1, Track 26

📖 Listen for and identify causes of and advice for coping with stress **UNIT 4** **45**

END-OF-UNIT ACTIVITIES

Ventures provides several resources to help wrap up a unit:

The **Self-assessments** are available via the Teacher's Online Resources (www.cambridge.org/ventures/resources/). They can be used in several ways:

- To identify any needs for additional practice before the unit test.
- For portfolio assessment. Print out copies for each student and keep completed Self-assessments in a folder.
- For pre- and post-assessment. Print out two Self-assessments for each student. Have students complete one before beginning and another after finishing the unit.

The **Projects** are another useful tool and a fun way to wrap up a unit. They are available via the Teacher's Online Resources.

The **Unit Tests** are a third end-of-unit activity. They are available at the back of this Teacher's Edition. Customizable tests and test audio are available via a secure download site. Contact your Cambridge ESL Specialist (www.cambridge.org/cambridgeenglish/contact) for more information.

Class time guidelines

Ventures is designed to be flexible enough for use with one-, two-, and three-hour classes.

Component	One-hour class	Two-hour class	Three-hour class
Teacher's Edition	Follow lesson plan in Teacher's Edition		
Workbook	Assign as homework		Use in class
Student Arcade	Assign for lab or homework		
Online Teacher's Resource Room			Use Collaborative Worksheets in class

(Top row) Dennis Johnson, K. Lynn Savage; (bottom row) Gretchen Bitterlin, Donna Price, and Sylvia G. Ramirez. Together, the *Ventures* author team has more than 200 years teaching ESL as well as other roles that support adult immigrants and refugees, from teacher's aide to dean.

Gretchen Bitterlin has taught Citizenship, ESL, and family literacy through the San Diego Community College District and served as coordinator of the non-credit Continuing Education ESL program. She was an item writer for CASAS tests and chaired the task force that developed the TESOL Adult Education Program Standards. She is recipient of The President's Distinguished Leadership Award from her district and co-author of *English for Adult Competency*. Gretchen holds an MA in TESOL from the University of Arizona.

Dennis Johnson had his first language-teaching experience as a Peace Corps volunteer in South Korea. Following that teaching experience, he became an in-country ESL trainer. After returning to the United States, he began teaching credit and non-credit ESL at City College of San Francisco. As ESL site coordinator, he has provided guidance to faculty in selecting textbooks. He is the author of *Get Up and Go* and co-author of *The Immigrant Experience*. Dennis is the demonstration teacher on the *Ventures Professional Development DVD*. Dennis holds an MA in music from Stanford University.

Donna Price began her ESL career teaching EFL in Madagascar. She is currently associate professor of ESL and vocational ESL / technology resource instructor for the Continuing Education Program, San Diego Community College District. She has served as an author and a trainer for CALPRO, the California Adult Literacy Professional Development Project, co-authoring training modules on contextualizing and integrating workforce skills into the ESL classroom. She is a recipient of the TESOL Newbury House Award for Excellence in Teaching, and she is author of *Skills for Success*. Donna holds an MA in linguistics from San Diego State University.

Sylvia G. Ramirez is a Professor Emeritus at MiraCosta College, a teacher educator, writer, consultant, and a recipient of the California Hayward award for excellence in education, honoring her teaching and professional activities. She is an online instructor for the TESOL Core Certificate. Her MA is in education / counseling from Point Loma University, and she has certificates in ESOL and in online teaching.

K. Lynn Savage first taught English in Japan. She began teaching ESL at City College of San Francisco in 1974, where she has taught all levels of non-credit ESL and has served as Vocational ESL Resource Teacher. She has trained teachers for adult education programs around the country as well as abroad. She chaired the committee that developed *ESL Model Standards for Adult Education Programs* (California, 1992) and is the author, co-author, and editor of many ESL materials including *Crossroads Café*, *Teacher Training through Video*, *Parenting for Academic Success*, *Building Life Skills*, *Picture Stories*, *May I Help You?*, and *English That Works*. Lynn holds an MA in TESOL from Teachers College, Columbia University.

WELCOME

① Meet your classmates

A Look at the picture. What do you see?

B What are the people doing?

Teaching objectives
- Provide practice asking and answering questions about personal information
- Provide practice talking about study habits and strategies

WARM-UP AND REVIEW

- **Before class.** Write today's lesson focus on the board.
  Welcome unit:
  Exchange information
  Talk about study habits and strategies
- **Begin class.** Books closed. Say: *Welcome to English class.*
- Introduce yourself to the class. Write your name on the board. Point to it. Tell Ss your name and ask them to repeat it. Tell Ss where you are from and anything else of interest that you would like to add, for example: *I am married. I have two children and a dog. I love dancing, cooking, and eating. My lucky number is seven.*
- Ask Ss to introduce themselves to the class. Encourage them to say their names, where they are from, and anything else they would like to add.

Teaching Tip

If any Ss feel uncomfortable or unable to add extra information to their introduction, don't force them. Ss can share more information later as they become more familiar with you and with one another.

PRESENTATION

- **Books open.** Set the scene. Hold up the Student's Book. Direct Ss' attention to the pictures on page 2. Ask the question from Exercise **1A**: *What do you see?* Elicit and write on the board any vocabulary that Ss know, such as: *flash cards, students, books, tables, basketball.*
- Direct Ss' attention to Exercise **1B**. Read the question aloud: *What are the people doing?* Hold up the Student's Book. Point to the students in Picture 3. Ask: *What are they doing?* Elicit an appropriate answer, for example: *They're studying for a test together.*
- Ss in pairs. Have Ss continue the exercise by pointing to people in the picture and asking questions about what they are doing. Walk around and help as needed.
- Ask several pairs to ask and answer the questions for the rest of the class.

Expansion activity *(whole group)*

- Point to people in the picture and ask more questions, or encourage Ss to think of more questions to ask about the picture.
- Call on Ss individually, or put Ss in pairs to ask and answer additional questions, such as: *Who are they? Where are they? Take a guess: Where are they from? What have they been studying?*

COMPREHENSION CHECK

- Hold up the Student's Book. Ask Ss *Yes / No* questions about the people's actions in the picture. Use a variety of tenses. Encourage Ss not to answer with single-word answers, *Yes* or *No*, but to use short forms, such as: *Yes, she is. / No, she isn't. Yes, they are. / No, they aren't.*

  Point to Mark. Ask: *Has he been studying?* (Yes, he has.) Point to the students in Picture 3. Ask: *Are they eating dinner?* (No, they aren't. They're studying.)

Community building *(small groups)*

- Have small groups of classmates visit your school library or community public library. You can help Ss prepare for their library visit by inviting your school librarian or a librarian from your public library to visit your class to talk about the library's offerings. Work with Ss to prepare some questions for the librarian beforehand. Tell Ss that the purpose of their library visit is to become familiar with their library so they feel comfortable there and can go there to study, check out books, or speak with the librarian.
- While they are visiting the library, have Ss collect any useful information about your community (e.g., a community calendar of cultural events, a newsletter, announcements) that is available.
- Invite each group to present its findings to the class at a later date. Follow up with a general discussion of the benefits of your school or community public library.

WELCOME UNIT

WARM-UP

- Books closed. Write on the board: *study habits and strategies*. Ask Ss: *What is a habit?* Explain or elicit that a *habit* is something you do regularly, often without thinking about it. Offer examples of your own habits, such as: *I have a habit of waking up early when I'm nervous about a test. I have a habit of reading the newspaper online every morning before breakfast*. Ask Ss to give examples of their own habits.

- Ask: *What is a strategy?* Explain or elicit that a *strategy* is a planned series of actions used to achieve something. Ask Ss: What is your strategy for learning English? Elicit answers, such as: *taking English classes, writing new words in a journal, meeting with a conversation partner*.

PRESENTATION

- Books open. Direct Ss' attention to Exercise **2A**. Read the instructions aloud. Remind Ss that an *adjective* is a word that describes a person, place, or thing. Review the words in the chart. Define any words that are unfamiliar to Ss, and write them on the board. Have Ss repeat.

- ⊙ *CD1, Track 2* Play or read the audio (see audio script, page T-176). Ss listen and complete the exercise individually.

- Focus Ss' attention on the second part of Exercise **2A**. Read the instructions aloud.

- ⊙ *CD1, Track 2* Play or read the audio again. Ss listen and check their answers.

- Read each word in the chart and ask: *Was this word used in the conversation?* Elicit complete answers from the Ss: *Yes, it was.* or *No, it wasn't.* Make corrections as needed.

- Tell Ss to choose one adjective from the chart that they feel best describes them. Have Ss take turns saying *I am _____*. Ss repeat one another's answers turning the *I* pronoun into *he* or *she*. For example: *I am reliable.* ➔ *She is reliable.*

Learner persistence *(individual work)*

- ⊙ *CD1, Track 2* Ss can listen to the audio for Exercise **2A** at home for reinforcement and review. They can also listen to the audio for self-directed learning when class attendance is not possible.

PRACTICE

- Focus Ss' attention on Exercise **2B**. Read the instructions aloud. Review the words in the chart. Define any words that are unfamiliar to Ss, and write them on the board. Have Ss repeat.

- Ss complete the task individually. Walk around and help as needed.

- Direct Ss' attention to the second part of **2B**. Ss work in pairs to ask and answer the questions.

- Tell Ss you are going to ask the class each of the questions in the chart. Ss should raise their hands if their answer is *Yes, I do*. Ask each question, and encourage individual Ss who answer *yes* to share details about how they accomplished that particular study habit.

APPLICATION

- Direct Ss' attention to the instructions in **2C**. Read the instructions aloud. Ask a pair of Ss to read the dialog aloud. Ensure Ss understand the activity. Write *Yes, I do.* and *No, I don't.* on the board. Encourage Ss to use these answers as they talk with their classmates.

- Tell Ss to stand up and to pick up their books. Ask Ss to walk around the classroom interviewing their classmates about the items in the chart. Ss continue asking one another questions until they have completed the chart. Walk around and help as needed.

- Direct Ss' attention to the instructions in the second part of **2C**. Read the instructions aloud. Ask three Ss to read the example dialog. Encourage Ss to share information about their classmates with the class.

Teaching Tip

This exercise serves two purposes. It allows Ss to get to know each other, and it allows the teacher to find out on the first day of class how much English Ss already know.

EVALUATION

- Split the class into small groups. Direct Ss' attention to the chart on page 3. Ask each group to come up with two to three additional study habits or strategies students can develop in order to make learning easier.

- Listen and make sure that Ss ask and answer questions correctly.

- Check off each part of the lesson focus as Ss demonstrate an understanding of what they have learned in the lesson.

2 Study habits and strategies

A Listen. Check (✓) the adjectives, study habits, and strategies you hear.

☑ active   ☑ creative   ☑ outgoing   ☑ study in a group

☑ artistic   ☑ fun-loving   ☐ patient   ☑ study while moving

☐ confident   ☑ make vocabulary cards   ☐ reliable   ☐ use a dictionary

◀⑴ CD1, Track 2

Listen again. Check your answers.

B Read the list of study habits and strategies. Which ones have you tried?
Check (✓) your answers on the chart. Then tell a partner about your answers.

Do you ever . . .?	Yes, I do.	No, I don't.
1. make vocabulary cards	*Answers will vary.*	
2. use a dictionary to learn new words		
3. ask a stranger a question in English		
4. study English with a friend		
5. use a to-do list to organize your time		
6. try to guess the meaning of new words		

C Talk with your classmates. Complete the chart.

A Song-mi, do you watch TV in English every day?

B Yes, I do.

Find a classmate who . . .	Name
1. watches TV in English every day	*Answers will vary.*
2. asks questions when he or she doesn't understand something	
3. underlines important information in textbooks	
4. likes to sing songs	
5. speaks English at work	
6. sets goals for learning English	

Talk with your class. Ask and answer questions.

Who watches TV in English every day?

Song Mi does.

Manny does, too.

3 Verb tense review (past continuous and simple past)

A **Listen** to each sentence. Circle the verb form you hear.

1. listened — (was listening)
2. (heard) — was hearing
3. watched — (was watching)
4. (woke) — were waking
5. played — (was playing)
6. did — (were doing)
7. (drove) — were driving
8. (vacuumed) — were vacuuming

CD1, Track 3

Listen again. Check your answers.

> Use the simple past to talk about an activity that began and ended at a particular time in the past: *yesterday, last night, a few days ago, in 2016.*
> Use the past continuous to talk about an activity that was happening, but not completed, at a point of time in the past. Example: *I went to bed at 10:00. The phone rang at 10:30. I was sleeping when the phone rang.*

B **Read.** Complete the story. Use the correct verb form.

Last summer, my sister and I _____*drove*_____ from Tucson to Phoenix.
1. drive

On our way, it _____*was*_____ very windy, and there _____*were*_____
2. be   3. be

dark clouds in the sky. We _____*were traveling*_____ slowly when suddenly we
4. travel

_____*saw*_____ huge clouds of dust in the air. The sky _____*turned*_____
5. see   6. turn

brown, and we couldn't see anything. It _____*was*_____ very scary.
7. be

While we _____*were driving*_____, we _____*were looking*_____ for a place to turn
8. drive   9. look

off the road. Finally we _____*came*_____ to an exit and _____*got*_____
10. come   11. get

off the main road. We _____*went*_____ into a restaurant. The dust finally
12. go

_____*went*_____ away while we _____*were waiting*_____ at the restaurant.
13. go   14. wait

Listen and check your answers.

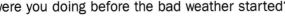
CD1, Track 4

C **Talk** with a partner. Ask and answer questions.

1. Talk about a time you were in bad weather. Describe the weather. Explain what happened.

2. What were you doing before the bad weather started?

3. What did you do while the bad weather was happening?

Teaching objectives
- Provide review of past continuous and simple past verb tenses
- Provide review of three uses of the present perfect

WARM-UP AND REVIEW

- Before class. Write today's lesson focus on the board.

  Welcome unit:
  Review past continuous and simple past verb forms
  Read and talk about bad weather

- Begin class. Books closed. Write the following questions on the board:

  Where were you last night?
  What were you doing there?
  What were you doing before you came to class today?
  What were you doing before you ate dinner last night?

- Point to the first question. Ask a S to tell you where he or she was last night, using the past tense. Elicit appropriate answers, such as: *I was at the movies last night.* Continue with the remaining questions.

- Write several answers on the board. There should be at least two answers per question on the board.

- Call on individual Ss to come to the board, underline the verbs, and identify the verb form (simple past or past continuous). Help Ss as needed.

PRESENTATION

- Books open. Direct Ss' attention to Exercise **3A**, and read the instructions aloud.

- ▶ *CD1, Track 3* Model the task. Play or read the audio for number 1 (see audio script, page T-176). Pause the audio after the first sentence. Write *listened* and *was listening* on the board. Ask: *Which verb should I circle?* (was listening.)

- Hold up the Student's Book. Say: *Listen and circle the correct verb form for the rest of the sentences.*

- ▶ *CD1, Track 3* Play or read the rest of the audio. Ss listen and complete the exercise individually.

- Focus Ss' attention on the second part of Exercise **3A**. Read the instructions aloud.

- ▶ *CD1, Track 3* Play or read the audio again. Ss listen and check their answers.

Learner persistence (individual work)
- ▶ *CD1, Track 3* Ss can listen to the audio for Exercise **3A** at home for reinforcement and review. They can also listen to the audio for self-directed learning when class attendance is not possible.

PRACTICE

- Direct Ss' attention to Exercise **3B** and read the instructions aloud.

- Model the task. Ask a S to read the first sentence aloud, including the example answer in number 1. Have the S read number 2 and fill in the correct verb form. Ask Ss: *Is the answer for number 2 correct?* Have Ss correct if needed.

- Ss complete the exercise individually. Walk around and help as needed.

- Direct Ss' attention to the second part of the instructions for Exercise **3B**.

- ▶ *CD1, Track 4* Play or read the audio again (see audio script, page T-176). Ss listen and check their answers.

- Write the numbers *1–14* on the board. Ask individual Ss to come to the board to write their answers. Ask other Ss if the answers are correct. Make corrections on the board as needed.

Learner persistence (individual work)
- ▶ *CD1, Track 4* Ss can listen to the audio for Exercise **3B** at home for reinforcement and review. They can also listen to the audio for self-directed learning when class attendance is not possible.

APPLICATION

- Direct Ss' attention to Exercise **3C**. Read the instructions aloud.

- Model the task. Ask for a volunteer to answer the first question. If any weather-related vocabulary words are new to students, write them on the board. Have Ss repeat.

- Ss work in small groups to complete the activity. Walk around and help as needed.

- Have several Ss ask and answer the questions for the rest of the class. Make sure that Ss use the correct verb form when responding to the questions.

WARM-UP AND REVIEW

- Write on the board: *simple past* and *present perfect*. Ask Ss: *What is the simple past?* Elicit answers, such as: *It's the verb tense we use to talk about something we completed in the past.* Ask Ss: *What is present perfect?* Elicit answers, such as: *It's the verb tense we use to talk about an experience we have had or something that started in the past and continues into the present.*

- Tell Ss that although both the simple past and present perfect can be used to talk about the past, each of them is used in different situations. Write simple past and present perfect on the board. Beneath them, write: *for / since* and *ever*. Ask Ss questions using the simple past or present perfect, for example: *How long have you lived in the United States? Have you ever visited California? Where did you go last weekend?* Encourage Ss to use the present perfect in their answers.

PRESENTATION

- Books open. Direct Ss' attention to Exercise **4A** and read the instructions aloud.

- ▶ **CD1, Track 5** Model the task. Play or read the audio for number 1 (see audio script, page T-176). Pause the audio after the first sentence. Ask: *What word did you hear?*

- Hold up the Student's Book. Point to the example answer in number 1. Say: *Listen and write the words you hear for the rest of the sentences. Use the words from the word bank.*

- ▶ **CD1, Track 5** Play or read the rest of the audio. Ss listen and complete the exercise individually.

- ▶ **CD1, Track 5** Play or read the audio again. Ss listen and check their answers.

Learner persistence *(individual work)*

▶ **CD1, Track 5** Ss can listen to the audio for Exercise **4A** at home for reinforcement and review. They can also listen to the audio for self-directed learning when class attendance is not possible.

PRACTICE

- Direct Ss' attention to Exercise **4B** and read the instructions aloud.

- Model the task. Ask a pair of Ss to read the first question and answer aloud.

- Ss complete the exercise individually. Walk around and help as needed.

- Direct Ss' attention to the second part of the instructions for Exercise **4B**.

- ▶ **CD1, Track 6** Play or read the audio again (see audio script, page T-176). Ss listen and check their answers.

- Ask Ss to read the questions and answers in pairs. Ask other Ss if the answers are correct. Make corrections as needed.

Learner persistence *(individual work)*

▶ **CD1, Track 6** Ss can listen to the audio for Exercise **4B** at home for reinforcement and review. They can also listen to the audio for self-directed learning when class attendance is not possible.

APPLICATION

- Direct Ss' attention to Exercise **4C**. Read the instructions aloud.

- Model the task. Ask for a volunteer to answer the first question. Review any new vocabulary words. Have Ss repeat.

- Ss work in small groups to complete the activity. Walk around and help as needed.

- Have several Ss ask and answer the questions for the rest of the class. Make sure that Ss use the correct verb form when responding to the questions.

4 Verb tense review (3 uses of the present perfect)

A **Listen** and write the words you hear. Use the words from the word bank.

◀)) CD1, Track 5

| a few times | already | lately | ~~recently~~ | several times | since | yet |

1. _____recently_____
2. _____a few times_____
3. _____lately_____
4. _____several times_____

5. _____yet_____
6. _____already_____
7. _____since_____
8. _____already_____

9. _____since_____
10. _____already_____

Use	Example	Clue words
Events that began in the past and are still happening now	Jaime has studied for two years.	for, since
Events that have happened before now but the time is not clear	Sara has already seen that movie.	already, yet, recently, lately
Events that were repeated before now	Boun has flown on a plane many times.	many times, a few times, several times

Listen and check your answers.

B **Read.** Complete the conversations. Use the present perfect form of the verb in parentheses.

1. A _____Have_____ you _____practiced_____ English outside of class lately? (practice)
   B No, I _____haven't_____. I'm too shy.
2. A How many times _____have_____ you _____texted_____ your friends today? (text)
   B I _____have texted_____ my friends at least seven times so far today.
3. A How many times _____have_____ you _____eaten_____ Mexican food? (eat)
   B I _____have eaten_____ Mexican food many times. I love it!
4. A _____Has_____ Daniel _____done_____ his homework yet? (do)
   B No, he _____hasn't_____. He needs to finish it before tomorrow.
5. A How long _____have_____ you _____studied_____ at this school? (study)
   B I _____have studied_____ at this school for three months.

Listen and check your answers.

◀)) CD1, Track 6

C **Talk** with your classmates. Ask and answer the questions.

1. Have you ever volunteered? What did you do?
2. Have you gone dancing recently? If yes, where did you go dancing?
3. Have you ever asked a stranger a question in English? What did you ask?
4. How long have you been a student at this school?
5. How many times have you flown in an airplane?

Lesson A Listening

1 Before you listen

A What do you see?

B What is happening?

UNIT 1

Teaching objectives
- Introduce students to the topic
- Find out what students know about the topic
- Preview the unit by talking about the pictures
- Provide practice of key vocabulary
- Provide practice that develops listening skills

WARM-UP AND REVIEW

- Before class. Write today's lesson focus on the board.
  Lesson A:
  Ask about aptitudes
  Discuss multiple intelligences
  Give opinions
- Begin class. Books closed. Point to *Ask about aptitudes* in the lesson focus. Say the words aloud. Tell Ss that *aptitudes* are personal strengths. Ask: *What are some examples of aptitudes?* This language may be new to Ss, so start them off with some examples, such as *artistic, athletic, mechanical, mathematical, musical*. On the board, write these words and any other examples that Ss brainstorm.
- Point to each word on the board and say the words aloud. Make sure that all Ss understand the meaning of each word.
- Ask: *What are your personal strengths? Are you _____?* (Point to each word on the board in turn.) Ss can say *yes* or *no* in response.

PRESENTATION

- Books open. Set the scene. Direct Ss' attention to picture 1 on page 6. Ask the question from Exercise **1A**: *What do you see?* Elicit and write on the board as much vocabulary about the picture as possible: *jogging clothes, neighborhood*. Continue eliciting words to describe the remaining pictures.
- Direct Ss' attention to the question in Exercise **1B**. Read it aloud. Ask individual Ss to describe what is happening in each of the pictures. Elicit appropriate responses, such as: *Emily is jogging. Nina is cooking in the kitchen. The girl is doing her homework. The boy is playing the guitar. The other boy is fixing the car.*

Teaching tip

Encourage Ss to be creative. At this point, there is no single correct answer.

PRACTICE

- Direct Ss' attention to Emily in the first picture and again ask what she has just been doing.
- Ask Ss: *Does anyone like to jog?* If some Ss answer *yes*, find out where and how often they like to run. Ask Ss who say they jog if they are athletic.
- Direct Ss' attention to Nina in picture 3. Ask Ss: *Do you like to cook?* Ask Ss who answer *yes* what they like to make and how often they cook. Write *gifted in cooking* on the board. Ask Ss what that means, and try to elicit the definition.
- Direct Ss' attention to the young woman in picture 4. Ask Ss: *What is she doing?* (She's studying.) *Do you like to study English?* When your Ss say *yes*, tell them that if they like to study – or study frequently – then we would say they are *studious*. Write *studious* on the board.
- Direct Ss' attention to the boy playing the guitar. Say: *If someone is good at playing music, we say that he or she is musical.*
- Direct Ss' attention to the picture of the young man fixing a car. Ask Ss: *What is this young man doing?* (He's working on a car.) Tell Ss that when someone is talented at fixing things, we say that the person is *mechanical*. Tell Ss that another word for *mechanical* is *handy*.

Expansion activity *(student pairs)*

- Have Ss work in pairs. Direct Ss' attention to the six pictures on page 6. Tell Ss that they are going to think of and practice a conversation between any two of the people in the pictures. Ss should use information from the picture, and each person should speak at least five times. Encourage Ss to use the different verb forms they reviewed in the Welcome unit.
- Model the activity. Ask Ss to come up with the beginning of the conversation as a class. Write the beginning of the conversation on the board.
- Ss finish the conversation in pairs. Walk around and help as needed.
- If you have enough class time, ask several pairs to role-play the conversation for the rest of the class.
- As a follow-up (either in class or at home), have Ss choose one of the people in any of the pictures and write a description of his or her day, again recycling information from the verb review in the Welcome unit.

LESSON A Listening

PRESENTATION

- Books open. Direct Ss' attention to Exercise **2A**. Read the instructions aloud. Tell Ss that they are going to hear a conversation between Nina and Emily, the two women in pictures 1 and 3 on page 6. Have Ss listen for the main ideas.
- ▶ **CD1, Track 7** Play or read the audio (see audio script, page T-176).
- Ask Ss if they understood everything in the listening exercise. Write any unfamiliar words on the board, and help Ss understand the meaning of each of the new words.
- Elicit answers to the questions.
- Focus Ss' attention on Exercise **2B**. Read the instructions aloud. Tell Ss to listen and complete the chart based on the information they hear.
- ▶ **CD1, Track 7** Play or read the audio again. Tell Ss to listen for details about Emily, Nina, and Nina's children. Model the task. Pause the audio after Nina says: *Yes, it's true! She's really good at math. She just loves it.* Call on a S to read the example answers in the chart (*math, got first place in a math contest*). Tell Ss to listen and complete the chart individually.
- Play or read the rest of the audio.
- ▶ **CD1, Track 7** Play or read the audio again. Ss listen and check their answers. Repeat the audio as needed.
- Write the chart on the board. Ask Ss to come to the board to write the answers. Correct as needed.

Learner persistence *(individual work)*
- ▶ **CD1, Track 7** Ss can listen to the audio for Exercises **2A** and **2B** at home for reinforcement and review. They can also listen to the audio for self-directed learning when class attendance is not possible.

PRACTICE

- Focus Ss' attention on Exercise **3A**. Read the instructions aloud. Tell Ss that the story in this exercise is a summary of what happened in the pictures on page 6. Review with Ss the idea that a summary contains the most important points of a story.
- Direct Ss' attention to the words or phrases in the word bank. Say each word or phrase aloud. Ask Ss to repeat. Correct pronunciation as needed.

- Ask Ss if they know the meaning of each word in the word bank. Explain any new words. Explain the similarities between *aptitude for* (we say someone *has* an aptitude for a particular subject), *gifted in*, and *talented in*, and how we use them. Write the phrases on the board. Underline the prepositions. Have Ss note the different propositions used with each word.
- Ss complete the exercise individually. Help as needed.

COMPREHENSION CHECK

- ▶ **CD1, Track 8** Play or read the audio (see audio script, page T-176). Ss listen and check their answers. Repeat the audio as needed.
- Write the numbers *1–10* on the board. Ask individual Ss to come to the board to write their answers.
- Ask the class: *Are these answers correct?* Make any corrections on the board.

Learner persistence *(individual work)*
- ▶ **CD1, Track 8** Ss can listen to the audio for Exercise **3A** at home for reinforcement and review. They can also listen to the audio for self-directed learning when class attendance is not possible.

APPLICATION

- Focus Ss' attention on Exercise **3B**. Read the instructions aloud.
- Model the task. Ask a S the first question in the exercise. Have Ss listen to the answer.
- Ss complete the exercise in pairs. Help as needed.
- Ask several pairs to ask and answer the questions for the rest of the class.

EVALUATION

- Direct Ss' attention to the lesson focus on the board. Ask individual Ss to tell you about Nina and her aptitudes as well as those of her children. Ask other Ss to tell you about their own aptitudes.
- Check off each part of the lesson focus as Ss demonstrate an understanding of what they have learned in the lesson.

More Ventures, Unit 1, Lesson A	
Workbook, 15–30 min.	
Multilevel Worksheets, 30–45 min.	www.cambridge.org/ ventures/resources/
Collaborative Worksheets, 30–45 min.	
Student Arcade, time varies	www.cambridge.org/ venturesarcade/

UNIT GOALS
Identify multiple intelligences   **Identify** one's primary intelligence
Recognize right-brain and left-brain functions

2 Listen

A Listen and answer the questions.

1. Who are the speakers?   2. What are they talking about?

🔊 CD1, Track 7

B Listen again. Complete the chart.

🔊 CD1, Track 7

Family member	Good at	Example
1. Brenda	*math*	*got first place in a math contest*
2. Gerry	*music*	*plays four instruments; sings really well*
3. Danny	*mechanics*	*fixed up an old car*
4. Nina	*cooking*	*cooking dinner for 14 people*

3 After you listen

A Read. Complete the story.

aptitude	bright	fixing	mathematical	musical
brain	contest	gifted in	mechanical	well

Emily stops by Nina's house on her way home from jogging. They talk about Nina's three

children. Brenda is very ___*mathematical*___ . She's just won a math ___*contest*___ at school.
   1   2

When Emily calls Brenda a ___*brain*___ , Nina says that all her children are ___*bright*___ ,
   3   4

but in different ways. Gerry isn't ___*gifted in*___ math, but he's very ___*musical*___ . He
   5   6

plays and sings very ___*well*___ and even writes music. Danny is the ___*mechanical*___
   7   8

one in the family. He's good at ___*fixing up*___ old cars. Emily thinks that Nina is also
   9

smart because she is such a good cook. Emily has no ___*aptitude*___ for cooking.
   10

Listen and check your answers.

🔊 CD1, Track 8

B Discuss. Talk with your classmates.

1. How are the three children different?

2. Do you think that one child is more intelligent than the others? Why or why not?

3. Do you think that Nina is a good parent? Why or why not?

Lesson B Parts of speech

1 Grammar focus: nouns, verbs, adjectives, and adverbs

Adjectives describe nouns and answer the question *What kind of?* (*What kind of driver is he?*). Adverbs describe verbs and answer the question *How?* (*How does he drive?*). Most adverbs end in *-ly*, but some adverbs are irregular.

Watch

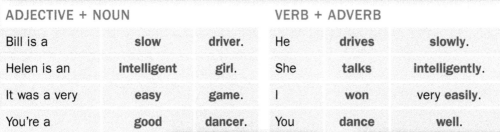

ADJECTIVE + NOUN			VERB + ADVERB		
Bill is a	slow	driver.	He	drives	slowly.
Helen is an	intelligent	girl.	She	talks	intelligently.
It was a very	easy	game.	I	won	very easily.
You're a	good	dancer.	You	dance	well.

Regular		Irregular	
Adjective	**Adverb**	**Adjective**	**Adverb**
bad	badly	fast	fast
easy	easily	good	well
intelligent	intelligently	hard	hard

2 Practice

A Write. Complete the sentences with adjectives or adverbs. Underline the nouns and verbs that they describe.

1. Carol speaks very __intelligently__ . She's a __bright__ girl.
   (intelligent)   (bright)

2. That isn't a __bad__ guitar, but he's playing it __badly__ .
   (bad)   (bad)

3. Benny is an __excellent__ cook. His dinner last night was __fantastic__ .
   (excellent)   (fantastic)

4. The mechanic did a __good__ job on my car. Now it runs __perfectly__ .
   (good)   (perfect)

5. You danced very __skillfully__ in the dance contest. You're a __wonderful__ dancer!
   (skillful)   (wonderful)

6. I don't type very __fast__ . I can't move my fingers very __quickly__ .
   (fast)   (quick)

7. That writing test was __hard__ . Writing isn't an __easy__ subject for me.
   (hard)   (easy)

8. You sang that song __beautifully__ ! I didn't know you could sing so __well__ !
   (beautiful)   (good)

9. Your report is __great__ . You wrote it very __clearly__ .
   (great)   (clear)

10. I work __slowly__ . I'm a __careful__ worker.
    (slow)   (careful)

Listen and check your answers.

◀)) CD1, Track 9

Teaching objectives
- Introduce noun clauses with *that*
- Provide practice with expressing opinions

WARM-UP AND REVIEW

- Before class: Write the lesson focus on the board.

  Lesson B:
  Contrasting adjectives and adverbs

- Begin class. Books closed. Review parts of speech. Write these four sentences on the board:

  The singer sang beautifully.
  She sang slowly.
  The singer was good.
  I love beautiful music.

- Ask Ss to identify the adjectives (*good, beautiful*) and the adverbs (*beautifully, slowly*).

PRESENTATION

Focus on meaning / personalize

- Direct Ss' attention to the lesson focus on the board. Read it aloud.

- Books closed. Ask: *What kind of dancer are you?* Write on the board:

  I'm a _____ dancer. Elicit answers, such as *I'm a good dancer.*, *I'm a clumsy dancer.*, and write the adjectives on the board.

- Then ask: *How well do you dance?* Write on the board: *I dance _____.* Elicit adverbs, such as *I dance well.* and *I dance poorly.* and write them on the board. Point out that an adjective tells you more about a noun and an adverb more about a verb.

Focus on form

- Use the animated grammar presentation in one or more of the following ways:
  - Preview it before class
  - Show in class
  - Encourage Ss to watch outside of class.

- Books open. Direct Ss' attention to the Adjective and Adverb charts in Exercise **1**. Read aloud each statement. Ask Ss to repeat. Have Ss identify and underline the adjective and adverb in each sentence. Ask: *Do adverbs always end in -ly?* (No.)

- Use the chart headings to explain that adjectives generally come before a noun, and adverbs come after a verb.

- Direct Ss' attention to the *Irregular* chart in Exercise **1**. Give example sentences for the first irregular adjective / adverb, and write them on the board, for example: *I'm a fast driver. I drive fast.* Have S volunteers make sentences using the other words in the irregular adjective / adverb box, for example: *She's a good speaker. She speaks well. He's a hard worker. He works hard.*

Useful language

Read the tip box aloud. Explain that we ask *How?* to identify adverbs and *What kind of?* to identify adjectives.

PRACTICE

- Direct Ss' attention to Exercise **2A**. Read the instructions aloud.

- Ask a S to read aloud the example sentence. Make sure Ss understand the exercise.

- Ss complete the exercise individually. Walk around and help as needed.

COMPREHENSION CHECK

▶ **CD1, Track 9** Play or read the audio (see audio script, page T-176). Ss listen and check their answers. Repeat the audio as needed.

- Write the numbers *1–10* on the board. Ask several Ss to come to the board to write their answers in complete sentences. Make corrections on the board as needed.

- Say sentences that contain an adjective or adverb, such as the following:

  She's an excellent student. (adjective)
  The traffic was moving slowly this morning. (adverb)
  Don't walk so fast. (adverb)
  He's a fast talker. (adjective)
  Ask Ss to tell you if they hear an adjective or an adverb.

PRACTICE

Focus on form

- Books open. Direct Ss' attention to the pictures in Exercise **2B**. Read the instructions aloud.

- Explain that Ss will use the words in the word bank as adjectives or adverbs. They will use these and the words below the pictures to talk about the pictures. Make sure that Ss understand the exercise.

- Model the task. Ask two Ss to read aloud the example conversations. Then have Ss complete the exercise in pairs.

- Read aloud the second part of the instructions for Exercise **2B**. Ask a S to read the example sentences to the class.

- Ss complete this part of the exercise individually. Walk around and help as needed.

- Ask individual Ss to write their sentences on the board. Ask other Ss to read aloud each sentence. Ask: *Is this sentence correct?* Make corrections on the board as needed.

APPLICATION

- Direct Ss' attention to Exercise **3A**. Read the instructions aloud.

- Model the task. Ask one S to read aloud the first question and another S to answer.

- Ss complete the exercise in small groups. Walk around and help as needed.

- Direct Ss' attention to Exercise **3B**. Read the instructions aloud.

- Ask different Ss to share information about their classmates with the class.

Expansion activity (small groups)

- **Materials needed** A set of index cards for each group, with a list of jobs, such as: *dancer, carpenter, mechanic, teacher, artist, dentist, truck driver.*

- Review occupations, if needed.

- Model the activity. Ask a S to choose one of the cards and use that information to make a sentence about himself or herself or a friend or family member. (*I am a dancer.*) Then call on another S to make a statement about the first S using an adjective or adverb, for example: *You're an excellent dancer. You dance beautifully.*

- Ss in small groups. Have each group sit in a circle. Give each group a set of index cards, and ask Ss to distribute them. One S begins by making a sentence with the word on his or her card, and the next S in the circle should comment on the first S's sentence using both an adjective and an adverb. (*He's a good carpenter. He works carefully.*)

- Continue for several minutes or until each S has had a chance to create sentences. Call on groups to share sample sentences. Write them on the board.

Learner persistence (whole group)

- Brainstorm different ways of keeping up with English lessons when Ss miss a class. Write ideas on the board, for example: *Practice the last lesson. Do Workbook exercises. Call a classmate and ask about class. Listen and repeat exercises on the CD. Call or e-mail your teacher for help.*

EVALUATION

- Direct Ss' attention to the lesson focus on the board. Ask Ss to tell you something about their skills and talents (or those of their classmates) using adjectives and adverbs.

- Check off each part of the lesson focus as Ss demonstrate an understanding of what they have learned in the lesson.

More Ventures, Unit 1, Lesson B	
Workbook, 15–30 min.	
Multilevel Worksheets, 30–45 min. **Collaborative Worksheets,** 30–45 min.	www.cambridge.org/ ventures/resources/
Student Arcade, time varies	www.cambridge.com/ venturesarcade/

B **Talk** with a partner. Ask and answer questions about the pictures. Use the adjective or adverb form of the words in the box.

A What kind of artist is he?

B He's a skillful artist.

A How does he paint?

B He paints beautifully.

beautiful	effective	fast	professional	terrible
careful	excellent	good	skillful	wonderful

1. artist / paint   2. seamstress / sew   3. driver / drive   4. swimmer / swim

5. carpenter / work   6. singer / sing   7. dancers / dance   8. speaker / speak

Write sentences about the people.

He's a skillful artist. He paints beautifully.   *Answers will vary.*

❸ Communicate

A **Work** in a small group. Ask and answer the questions.

1. What kind of student are you?
2. How do you speak English?
3. What can you do very well?
4. What is something you do badly?

5. What kind of worker are you?
6. What can you do perfectly?
7. What do you do very fast?
8. What kind of shopper are you?

B **Share** information about your classmates.

Armando says he's an excellent student.

Lesson C Noun clauses

1 Grammar focus: *that* clauses as objects

A clause is a group of words that has a subject and a verb. Sometimes a noun clause is used as the object of a sentence. It is called an *object clause*. An object clause follows an introductory clause and has the form *that* + subject + verb.

👁 Watch

INTRODUCTORY CLAUSE	OBJECT CLAUSE
Emily realizes	that Brenda has a good brain.
People say	that Gerry plays the guitar very well.
Do you think	that people are smart in different ways?
Do you feel	that you're smart?

USEFUL LANGUAGE
When speaking, we frequently omit *that* before a noun clause.
People think that she's smart.
People think she's smart.

Introductory clauses

I think . . .	Do you think . . . ?	I feel . . .	Do you feel . . . ?
He realizes . . .	Does he realize . . . ?	People believe . . .	Do people believe . . . ?

2 Practice

A **Write.** Write the words in the correct order. Make a sentence with an object clause. Circle the object clause in your sentence.

1. there/ intelligence / that / are / Do / many / you / of / kinds / believe / ?
   Do you believe (that there are many kinds of intelligence)?

2. think / interesting / has / I / an / Nina / family / .
   I think (that Nina has an interesting family.)

3. that / teachers / she / very / Brenda's / gifted / agree / is / .
   Brenda's teachers agree (that she is very gifted in math.)

4. Do / Nina / think / very / cooks / you / that / well / ?
   Do you think (that Nina cooks very well?)

5. become / Gerry / Many / famous / believe / a / will / people / musician /.
   Many people believe (that Gerry will be a famous musician someday.)

6. didn't / Danny / for / has / that / I / aptitude / cars / fixing / an / realize / .
   I didn't realize (that Danny has an aptitude for fixing cars.)

7. are / you / Do / that / very / skills / feel / important / mechanical / ?
   Do you feel (that mechanical skills are very important?)

8. her / that / Nina / very / children / are / knows / different / .
   Nina knows (that her children are very different.)

Listen and check your answers.

🔊 CD1, Track 10

WARM-UP AND REVIEW

- Before class: Write the lesson focus on the board.
  Lesson C:

  Noun clauses with "that"
  Express opinions
- Begin class. Books open. Review Lesson A vocabulary.

PRESENTATION

Focus on meaning / personalize

- Direct Ss' attention to the lesson focus on the board. Read it aloud.
- Ask: *What's an "opinion"?* Write student answers on the board. Explain that an opinion is what someone thinks about a particular person, thing, or situation.
- Books closed. Write as a heading on the board: *What people in other countries think about the United States.* Have Ss think of some opinions that people in other countries might have about people in the United States, and write them on the board. For example: *It's easy to get a job in the United States. People in the United States are friendly.*
- Write *True* and *False* to the right of the heading on the board. Tell Ss that, by a show of hands, you are going to find out how many Ss think the statements are true or false. Assure them that there is no right or wrong answer. Read each opinion and tally the answers on the board.
- After voting, summarize the information, for example: *Five students believe that it's easy to get a job in the United States. Most students think that people in the United States are friendly.*
- Write one of the opinion sentences on the board, such as: *Five students believe that it's easy to get a job in the United States.* Ask: *Which part of the sentence expresses the opinion?* (the part after *that*.) Circle the word *believe*. Ask what other words we could substitute for believe (*think, feel, say.*).

Focus on form

- Use the animated grammar presentation in one or more of the following ways:
  - Preview it before class
  - Show in class
  - Encourage Ss to watch outside of class.
- Books open. Direct Ss' attention to the Statements and questions chart in Exercise **1**. Review the meaning of *clause* (a group of words containing a subject and a verb). Read aloud each statement and question. Ask Ss to repeat.
- Write the following sentence on the board: *Gerry plays the guitar.*

  Ask: *What's the subject of the sentence?* (Gerry.)
  What's the verb? (plays.)
  What's the object? (the guitar.)
  How many clauses does the sentence have? (one.)
- Read aloud the *Introductory clauses* list. Ask Ss to repeat. Model each one by reading the opinions on the board, each with a different introductory clause.

Useful language

Read the tip box aloud. Ask Ss to repeat the two example sentences. Tell them that we sometimes omit *that* in questions, too. Ask Ss to restate the four statements and questions in Exercise **1**, omitting the word *that*.

PRACTICE

- Direct Ss' attention to Exercise **2A**. Read the instructions aloud. Ask a S to read aloud the example, and make sure that Ss understand the exercise.
- Ss complete the sentences individually. Walk around and help as needed.

COMPREHENSION CHECK

- Direct Ss' attention to the second part of Exercise **2A**.
- ▶ *CD1, Track 10* Play or read the audio (see audio script, page T-176). Ss listen and check their answers. Repeat the audio as needed.
- Write the numbers *1–8* on the board. Ask Ss to come to the board to write their answers. Make corrections on the board as needed.

LESSON C Noun Clauses

PRESENTATION

- Direct Ss' attention to the picture in Exercise **2B**. Ask Ss to look at the people in the picture. Ask: *What can you say about the man next to the car?* Elicit appropriate responses, such as: *I think he's athletic. I think he's about 30 years old.*
- Read the instructions aloud. Read the words in the word bank, and have Ss repeat.
- Model the exercise. Ask two Ss to read aloud the first example conversation.
- Have Ss work in pairs to talk about the picture. Walk around and help as needed.
- Call on pairs to share their conversations with the class.

Teaching tip

Ss may need clarification about the usage of these expressions. Explain that *I suppose* and *I'd say* are similar to saying *maybe*. Using them is a bit "softer" than *I'm sure, I believe,* and *I think*.

PRACTICE

- Read aloud the second part of the instructions for Exercise **2B**.
- Ask a S to read the example sentence.
- Have Ss work individually to write their opinions. After several minutes, have Ss compare their sentences with a partner.
- Call on Ss to share their sentences with the class.

APPLICATION

- Direct Ss' attention to Exercise **3A**. Read the instructions aloud.

Useful language

Read the tip box aloud. Ask Ss to repeat the statements after you. Explain that *totally* and *strongly* make the statements much stronger. You can ask Ss if they have heard other adverbs like this that make opinions stronger (*definitely, completely*).

Teaching tip

Ss from certain cultures may be unaccustomed to expressing opinions aloud, especially strong opinions. For these Ss, writing opinions is sometimes easier. Allow Ss the option of not using adverbs for emphasis if they do not feel comfortable doing so.

- After several minutes, read the instructions aloud for Exercise **3B**.
- Model the task. Ask Ss what they learned in Exercise **3A** about the opinions of the people in their group, for example: *(Stefan) doesn't believe that . . .*

Culture note

Read the culture note aloud. Ask Ss what they think happens concerning girls' and boys' aptitudes for math and science *after* elementary school. Ask Ss to share their opinions about this information.

Expansion activity (individual work, small groups)

- Tell Ss that they are going to give a presentation based on one of the beliefs they discussed in Exercise **3A**.
- Ask Ss to write down their "belief" statement and then several sentences to support their belief.
- Ask Ss to work in small groups to present their information to their classmates. After each presentation, Ss can agree or disagree with the presenter.
- When the groups are finished with the presentations, have some Ss share their belief statements with the class.

EVALUATION

- Direct Ss' attention to the lesson focus on the board.
- Write on the board: *I believe, I think, I'd say, I'm sure.* Then write: *mathematical, mechanical, musical,* and *gifted in art.* Then write: *I think that, I believe that, I strongly agree that, I disagree that.* Ask each S to make a sentence describing someone's aptitude or skill using the words on the board. Write some Ss' sentences on the board.
- Check off each part of the lesson focus as Ss demonstrate an understanding of what they have learned in the lesson.

More Ventures, Unit 1, Lesson C	
Workbook, 15–30 min.	
Multilevel Worksheets, 30–45 min.	www.cambridge.org/ ventures/resources/
Collaborative Worksheets, 30–45 min.	
Student Arcade, time varies	www.cambridge.org/ venuresarcade/

B **Talk** with a partner. Look at the picture. Answer the questions. Use introductory clauses from the box.

> I believe ...   I suppose ...   I think ...   I'd say ...   I'm sure ...

 A I think (that) Robert is about 26 years old.

B I'd say (that) Robert is only 20.

1. How old are they?
2. Where are they going?
3. Where are they coming from?
4. What do they do for a living?
5. What do they like to do?
6. What are they thinking about?
7. What are they good at?
8. What aren't they good at?

Write sentences about your opinions.

I think that Robert is about 26 years old.

③ Communicate

A **Work** in a small group. Give your opinions. Use *I believe, I think, I'd say, I don't believe,* and other introductory clauses.

1. Are women more talkative than men?
2. Are boys better at math and science than girls?
3. Are men more mechanical than women?
4. Are women more musical than men?
5. Are men more interested in sports than women?
6. Can women do the same jobs as men?

B **Share** your classmates' opinions.

> Marta thinks that women are more
> talkative than men.

> **USEFUL LANGUAGE**
> *I (totally) agree with you.*
> *I (strongly) disagree.*

> **CULTURE NOTE**
> Studies have shown that girls and boys in the United States have a similar aptitude for math and science when they start elementary school.

Lesson D Reading

1 Before you read

Talk with a partner. Look at the reading tip. Answer the questions.

1. What is this article about?
2. According to the article, how many ways are there to be smart?

> Before you begin reading, **skim**. Look at the title, headings, pictures, and boldfaced words to get a general idea of what the reading is about.

2 Read

Read the magazine article. Listen and read again.

 CD1, Track 11

Many Ways to be SMART

Josh is a star on the school baseball team. He gets Ds and Fs on all his math tests. His brother Frank can't catch, throw, or hit a baseball, but he easily gets As in math. Which boy do you think is more intelligent? Howard Gardner, a professor of education at Harvard University, would say that Josh and Frank are both smart, but in different ways. His theory of multiple intelligences identifies nine different "intelligences" to explain the way people understand, experience, and learn about the world around them.

Verbal / Linguistic

 Some people are good with words. They prefer to learn by reading, listening, and speaking.

Visual / Spatial

 These "picture people" are often good at drawing or painting. They are sensitive to colors and designs.

Intrapersonal

 Some people are "self smart." They can understand their own feelings and emotions. They often enjoy spending time alone.

Logical / Mathematical

 These people have an aptitude for math. They like solving logic problems and puzzles.

Bodily / Kinesthetic

 Some people are "body smart." They are often athletic. Kinesthetic learners learn best when they are moving.

Naturalist

 These people are skilled in working with plants and animals in the natural world.

Musical / Rhythmical

 These people are sensitive to sound, melodies, and rhythms. They are gifted in singing, playing instruments, or composing music.

Interpersonal

 Certain people are "group smart." They easily understand other people. They are good at communicating and interacting with others.

Existential

 Certain people are gifted in exploring deep questions about the meaning of life and death and ways to find inner peace.

According to Gardner, many people have several or even all of these intelligences, but most of us have one or two intelligences that are primary, or strongest.

Teaching objectives

- Introduce a magazine article about multiple intelligences
- Provide practice with recognizing the meaning of prefixes and roots
- Provide practice with skimming to predict what a reading is about
- Discuss multiple intelligencers

WARM-UP AND REVIEW

- **Before class.** Write today's lesson focus on the board.
  Lesson D:
  Read and understand "Many Ways to Be Smart"
  Recognize meaning of prefixes and roots
  Learn to skim to predict
- **Begin class.** Books closed. Write *intelligent* on the board. Draw a circle around it to create a word web. Ask Ss to brainstorm other words that explain or mean the same thing as *intelligent*. Write the words on the board around the circle, for example: *smart, talented, skillful, able to solve problems.*

PRESENTATION

- Books open. Direct Ss' attention to Exercise **1**. Read the instructions aloud.

> Read the tip box aloud. Make sure that Ss understand the reading term *skim*.

- Direct Ss' attention to the first question in Exercise **1**. Ask a S to read it aloud. Have the S read the title of the article. Ask Ss what they think the article is about. Elicit appropriate responses, such as: *It's about how people are smart. It's about different ways that people are intelligent.*
- Ask a different S to read question number 2. Encourage Ss to skim the article and pay attention to the boldfaced headings in the reading before answering the question.

PRACTICE

- Read aloud the instructions for Exercise **2**. Ask Ss to read the article silently before listening to the audio program.
- ▶ **CD1, Track 11** Play or read the audio, and ask Ss to read along (see audio script, pages T-176–T-177). Repeat the audio as needed.

- While Ss are listening to and reading the article, ask them to write in their notebooks any new words they don't understand. When the audio is finished, ask Ss to write the new vocabulary words on the board.
- Point to each word on the board. Say each word aloud and have Ss repeat. Give a brief explanation of each word, or ask Ss to explain the words if they are familiar with them. If Ss prefer to look up the new words in their dictionaries, allow them to do so.

Teaching tip

If Ss come from the same language background, ask them to help each other translate unfamiliar words into their own language. This encourages a sense of community and ownership in the learning process.

- Encourage Ss to find the meaning of each new word from the context of the article. For example, if a S writes *kinesthetic* on the board, show how the meaning of the word is explained in the article: *Some people are "body smart." They are often athletic. Kinesthetic learners learn best when they are moving.*
- You may need to review the pronunciation of several of the vocabulary words, such as *kinesthetic* and *intrapersonal* versus *interpersonal.*

Learner persistence (individual work)
▶ **CD1, Track 11** Ss can listen to the audio for Exercise **2** at home for reinforcement and review. They can also listen to the audio for self-directed learning when class attendance is not possible.

Expansion activity (small groups)

- Tell Ss that they are going to discuss their opinions about the articles. Recycle the language learned in Lesson B, and review ways to begin a sentence that expresses an opinion. Write examples on the board: *I think that . . . , I believe that . . . , I strongly agree . . . ,* etc.
- Ss in small groups. Tell Ss that they should each take turns expressing their opinions about the article to other members of their group. They should support their opinions with examples.

LESSON D Reading

COMPREHENSION CHECK

- Direct Ss' attention to Exercise **3A**. Read the instructions aloud.

- Ask individual Ss to read the statements aloud, one at a time. Make sure that all Ss understand them.

- Ss in pairs. Ask Ss to work with a partner to identify the primary intelligence of each person in the chart. Tell them that they can refer to the reading on page 12.

- Check answers by writing the numbers *1–6* on the board. Ask Ss to tell you the answers, and write each one next to the corresponding number. Make corrections as needed.

- Review pronunciation as needed.

Teaching tip

Using the dictionary may be new to some Ss. If so, spend some time reviewing dictionary usage. You can copy a dictionary page, review the components of each entry, and give a separate dictionary assignment for further practice if necessary.

PRACTICE

- Direct Ss' attention to Exercise **3B**. Ask a S to read the instructions aloud. Make sure each S has a dictionary (or can share one with a partner).

- Write the words *prefix* and *root* on the board. Say each word aloud and have Ss repeat. Ask Ss if they have heard these words before. Tell Ss that a *prefix* is a letter or group of letters added to the beginning of a word to change the meaning or make a new word. Tell Ss that a *root* is the basic form of a word, and that we can add prefixes to roots to make new words.

- Model the exercise. Call on a S to read aloud the prefix for number 1 (*intra-*). Ask the S to read the information in the corresponding columns.

- Ss complete the exercise in pairs. Walk around and help as needed.

- Write a grid on the board as it appears on Student's Book page 13. Call on pairs to fill in the information. Correct as needed.

Expansion activity *(student pairs)*

- **Materials needed** One dictionary for each pair of Ss.

- Ask some pairs to find examples of words with the prefixes presented in Exercise **3B**. Ask other pairs in the class to find examples of words with the roots presented in Exercise **3B**.

- Write the words Ss find on the board.

  Option Follow up by having Ss write sentences with the new words discussed. Have Ss share their sentences with a partner or with the whole class.

APPLICATION

- Focus Ss' attention on Exercise **3C**. Read the instructions aloud.

- Ask a S to read aloud the questions in Exercise **3C**.

- Ss ask and answer the questions in pairs. Walk around and help as needed.

Expansion activity

- Refer Ss to "Promoting Multiple Intelligences in the Classroom," another reading on the same topic on pages 136–138.

- Have Ss complete the activity either in class or outside of class.

- Provide feedback to Ss such as through whole-class discussion, partners comparing their worksheets, or T reviewing each S's worksheets.

EVALUATION

- Books closed. Direct Ss' attention to the lesson focus on the board.

- Write on the board the intelligences from the article on page 12 (*Verbal / Linguistic, Logical / Mathematical*, etc.) Ask Ss to make sentences about the meaning of these words. For example: *Someone who is verbal / linguistic learns by reading, listening, and speaking.*

- Have Ss share their sentences with the class.

- Check off each part of the lesson focus as Ss demonstrate an understanding of what they have learned in the lesson.

More Ventures, Unit 1, Lesson D	
Workbook, 15–30 min.	
Multilevel Worksheets, 30–45 min.	www.cambridge.org/ventures/ resources/
Collaborative Worksheets, 30–45 min.	
Student Arcade, time varies	www.cambridge.org/ venturesarcade/

3 After you read

A Check your understanding.

1. The main idea of this article is that there are many ways to be smart.
2. Howard Gardener is a professor of education at Harvard University. The name of his theory is different "intelligences."

1. What is the main idea of this article?

3. The nine intelligences that Professor Gardener identifies are Verbal / Linguistic, Visual / Spatial, Intrapersonal, Logical / Mathematical, Bodily / Kinesthetic, Naturalist, Musical / Rhythmical, Interpersonal, and Existential.

2. Who is Howard Gardner and what is the name of his theory?

3. What are the nine intelligences that Professor Gardner identifies?

4. Explain how the illustrations in the article help the reader to understand each intelligence.

4. The illustrations help the reader understand the words in the article because they provide a visual image of the words.

5. Susana is a vocational counselor at a community college. She volunteers at a senior center every Saturday. What do you think is her primary intelligence? Cite evidence in the reading to support your answer. 5. Susana's primary intelligence is Interpersonal. According to the evidence in the article, people who have the primary intelligence of Interpersonal are good at communicating and interacting with groups of people.

6. What words in the article help you to understand the meaning of *kinesthetic*?

6. Body, athletic, and moving are all words that help you understand the meaning of kinesthetic.

B Build your vocabulary.

Understanding prefixes and roots of words will help you learn new words.

1. Find an example of each prefix or root in the reading. Write it on the chart.

2. Use a dictionary. Write the meaning of the words.

3. Guess the meaning of the prefixes and roots on the chart.

Prefixes	Example from reading	Meaning of word	Meaning of prefix
1. intra-	*intrapersonal*	*inside a person's mind or self*	*in, inside*
2. inter-	*interpersonal*	*relationships between people*	*between*
3. multi-	*multiple*	*many things, people, or events*	*many*
Roots			**Meaning of root**
4. kine	*kinesthetic*	*related to movement*	*motion, movement*
5. log	*logical*	*reasonable*	*word, reason*
6. prim	*primary*	*more important than anything else*	*first*
7. vis	*visual*	*related to seeing*	*see*

C Talk with a partner.

1. What is your primary intelligence?

2. What are good jobs for people with each of the following intelligences: intrapersonal, interpersonal, kinesthetic, logical, and visual?

3. In your opinion, are some intelligences more important than others? Explain your answer.

4. Which intelligence would you like to develop more in yourself?

For college and career readiness practice, see pages 136–138.

Lesson E Writing

1 Before you write

A **Write** *1* through *4* next to your strongest intelligences. (Your primary intelligence should be number 1.) Compare with your classmates. *Answers will vary.*

_____ Verbal / Linguistic   _____ Visual / Spatial   _____ Intrapersonal

_____ Logical / Mathematical   _____ Bodily / Kinesthetic   _____ Naturalist

_____ Musical / Rhythmical   _____ Interpersonal   _____ Existential

B **Read** the writing tip. Then read the two paragraphs below. Circle the topic sentence and the concluding sentence in each paragraph.

> The topic sentence tells what the paragraph is about. A good paragraph has a topic sentence, supporting sentences and a concluding sentence.

1.

(My strongest intelligence is mathematical.) My parents say that I started counting before I was two years old. I've always liked to play games with numbers. I never forget my friends' birthdays or telephone numbers. I like to keep track of my monthly expenses so that I stay within my budget. Other people complain that balancing their checkbooks is hard, but I enjoy it. (My aptitude for mathematics helps me in every part of my life.)

2.

(My strongest intelligence is kinesthetic.) Since I was a child, I have loved to move my body. I've taken many types of dance classes, including ballet, modern, jazz, swing, salsa, and African. I can dance to any kind of music that I hear. My friends say that I'm a great dancer. (I think I was born to move.)

Teaching objectives
- Prepare Ss for writing a paragraph about a primary intelligence
- Provide practice developing topic sentences and supporting details

WARM-UP AND REVIEW

- Before class. Write today's lesson focus on the board.
  Lesson E:
  Discuss and write about personal intelligences
  Use a topic sentence and supporting details
  Write a paragraph about a primary intelligence
- Begin class. Books closed. Review vocabulary and grammar from the unit. Ask questions about the reading from Lesson D, for example: *What are the different types of intelligences?* (Verbal / Linguistic, Logical / Mathematical, Musical / Rhythmical, Visual / Spatial, Bodily / Kinesthetic, Interpersonal, Intrapersonal, Naturalist, Essentialist.)
- Write the terms on the board, and ask Ss to give definitions of each.

PRESENTATION

- Books open. Direct Ss' attention to Exercise **1A**. Read the instructions aloud.
- Ask Ss to work individually to complete the exercise.
- Have Ss work in pairs to compare their answers with their classmates.

PRACTICE

- Direct Ss' attention to Exercise **1B**. Read the instructions aloud.

  Read the tip box aloud. Tell Ss that a topic sentence presents the main idea of a paragraph.

- Ss read the two paragraphs silently. Help them with vocabulary as needed.

- Give Ss time to choose the appropriate topic sentences.
- Call on two Ss to read aloud each paragraph and share the topic sentences they chose. Ask Ss why one choice is better than the other one for each paragraph. (*For paragraph 1, choice "a" is a supporting sentence, whereas choice "b" is the topic sentence. For paragraph 2, choice "a" is the topic sentence, and choice "b" is a supporting sentence.*)

Expansion activity (small groups)

- **Materials needed** Nine index cards, one for each type of intelligence.
- Form seven groups. Tell Ss that each group is going to develop a four-question questionnaire based on one of the intelligences to determine if it is their primary intelligence.
- Give each group an index card with one of the primary intelligences written on it. Ask Ss: *What kinds of questions can you ask your classmates to find out if this intelligence is their primary intelligence?* Elicit suggestions, and write a few on the board. Tell Ss to write four different questions on the group's index card. Write the following model on the board:

  Bodily / Kinesthetic
  Do you regularly participate in a sport or some physical activity?
  Do you enjoy working with your hands to create things?
  Do you like working with tools?
  Do you find it difficult to sit still?

- Walk around and help as needed.
- Ask each group to share its questions with the class.
- Tell Ss to think about the questions as they listen to them. This will help them to determine their own primary intelligence.

LESSON E Writing

PRESENTATION

- Direct Ss' attention to Exercise **1C**. Read the instructions aloud.
- Ask five Ss to read each of the five sentences under *Supporting details*.
- Have Ss work individually to write a topic sentence.
- Ask Ss to share what they wrote. Write their answers on the board. For example: *My primary intelligence is kinesthetic. My strongest intelligence is kinesthetic.*

PRACTICE

- Direct Ss' attention to Exercise **1D**. Read the instructions aloud.
- Tell Ss they can start their outline by writing their topic sentence and then their supporting details.
- Have Ss work individually. Walk around and help as needed.

APPLICATION

- Focus Ss' attention on Exercise **2**. Read the instructions aloud.
- Ss complete the task individually. Walk around and help as needed.

Learner persistence (individual or pair work)

- If you have Ss who have difficulty writing, sit with them and help them while the other Ss are writing. Encourage them to review previous exercises to get ideas. If other Ss finish early, have them sit with and help the Ss who may be having difficulty with their writing.

COMPREHENSION CHECK

- Direct Ss' attention to Exercise **3A**. Read the instructions aloud. Ask a S to read the three checklist sentences to the class.
- This exercise asks Ss to review and edit their own writing. Ss check their own paragraphs individually. Walk around and help as needed. If any Ss check *No* for one or more of the checklist items, ask them to revise their paragraphs to include the missing information.

EVALUATION

- Focus Ss' attention on Exercise **3B**. Read the instructions aloud.
- This exercise asks Ss to work together to edit their writing. Reading aloud enables the writer to review his or her own writing and to understand the need to write clearly for an audience.

Teaching tip

Self-editing may be difficult for some Ss. To help them, read aloud or write on the board the following tips for self-editing:
- Read your writing aloud. Sometimes reading aloud – even to yourself – will help you to find errors.
- Read your writing to a friend. This will also help you become aware of points that need more work.
- When in doubt, look it up! If you are not sure of how to spell a word, use your dictionary. Don't rely only on computer spell-checkers, which cannot correct the meaning of a word.

- Ss in pairs. Tell Ss to take turns reading their paragraphs to each other. Walk around and help as needed.
- Listen to Ss as they ask their partners questions about the paragraph and about one thing they learned.
- Remind Ss that even professional writers need to self-edit. Writing, like playing a sport or a musical instrument, is a skill – the more you do it, the better you will become.
- Books closed. Direct Ss' attention to the lesson focus on the board. Ask Ss what two key points of paragraph writing were discussed (topic sentences and supporting details).
- Check off each part of the lesson focus as Ss demonstrate an understanding of what they have learned in the lesson.

More Ventures, Unit 1, Lesson E	
Workbook, 15–30 min.	
Multilevel Worksheets, 30–45 min. **Collaborative Worksheets,** 30–45 min.	www.cambridge.org/ventures/ resources/

C **Work** with a partner. Complete the outlines of the two model paragraphs on page 14.

1. **Topic sentence** of 1st paragraph: _My strongest intelligence is mathematical._

   Supporting details:

   - _started counting before age 2_
   - _like games with numbers_
   - _don't forget birthdays or phone numbers_
   - _keep track of expenses_
   - _enjoy balancing checkbook_

   Concluding sentence of 1st paragraph: _My aptitude for mathematics helps me in every part of my life._

2. **Topic sentence** of 2nd paragraph: _My strongest intelligence is kinesthetic._

   Supporting details:

   - _have loved to move my body since a child_
   - _have taken many types of dance classes_
   - _can dance to any kind of music I hear_
   - _my friends say that I am a great dancer_

   Concluding sentence of 2nd paragraph: _I think I was born to move._

D **Plan** a paragraph about your primary intelligence. Make an outline like the ones in Exercise 1C to make notes on your ideas. _Answers will vary._

2 Write

Write a paragraph about your primary intelligence. Include a topic sentence, specific details to support it, and a concluding sentence. Use the paragraphs in Exercise 1B and the outlines in Exercise 1C and 1D to help you. _Answers will vary._

3 After you write

A **Check** your writing.

	Yes	No
1. My topic sentence tells what my paragraph is about.	☐	☐
2. I gave specific details to support my topic sentence.	☐	☐
3. My paragraph has a concluding sentence.	☐	☐

B **Share** your writing with a partner.

1. Take turns. Read your paragraph to a partner.

2. Comment on your partner's paragraph. Ask your partner a question about the paragraph. Tell your partner one thing you learned.

Lesson F Another view

1 Life-skills reading

Left-brain functions   **Right-brain functions**

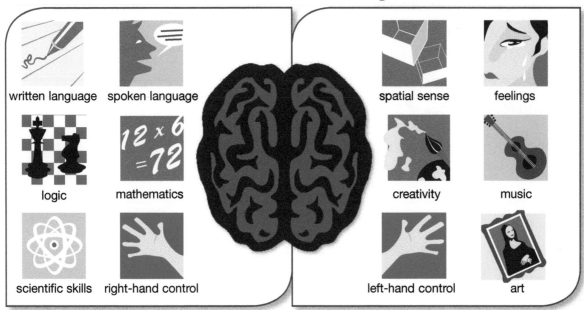

written language   spoken language   spatial sense   feelings

logic   mathematics   creativity   music

scientific skills   right-hand control   left-hand control   art

A **Read** the questions. Look at the diagram. Fill in the answer.

1. Which side of the brain controls verbal ability?

   ● left side

   B right side

   C both sides

   D none of the above

2. What can you say about *left-brained* people?

   A They are left-handed.

   B They are very musical.

   C They are artistic.

   ● They are logical.

3. Which abilities are right-brain functions?

   A art

   B music

   C creativity

   ● all of the above

4. Which sentence is true?

   A The left brain controls the left hand.

   B The right brain controls the right hand.

   ● The left brain controls the right hand.

   D none of the above

B **Solve** the problem. Give your opinion.

Jason is 17. He plays three musical instruments and is in a band with his friends. He wants to study music in college. His parents want him to be an engineer or a doctor. What should he do?

Answers will vary.

Teaching objectives
- Introduce reading a diagram about the brain
- Provide practice using *so* and *that* in questions and answers

WARM-UP AND REVIEW

- Before class. Write today's lesson focus on the board.
  Lesson F:
  Read a diagram and answer questions about the brain
  Use so and that in questions and answers
- Begin class. Books closed. Write *the brain* on the board. Then write *left side* on one side and *right side* on the other. Ask Ss if they know which side of the brain is in charge of which functions. If they have any ideas, write them under the appropriate heading. (The left brain is responsible for written and spoken language, mathematics, logic, scientific skills, and right-hand control. The right brain is responsible for spatial sense, feelings, creativity, music, art, and left-hand control.)
- Say: *We are going to look at a diagram about the brain and answer questions about it.*

PRESENTATION

- Books open. Direct Ss' attention to the diagram of the brain in Exercise **1**. Ask: *What do you see?* Elicit descriptions, such as: *left brain and right brain.*
- Have Ss focus on the icons and labels.
- Call on Ss to read the labels aloud.
- Ask other Ss to describe how each icon helps them to understand the brain function it represents.

PRACTICE

- Read the instructions aloud for Exercise **1A**. This exercise helps prepare Ss for standardized-type tests they may have to take. Be sure that Ss understand the task and the vocabulary in the labels. Have Ss individually scan for and fill in the answers.
- Check answers with the class. Ask Ss to read the questions and answers aloud. Ask: *Is that answer correct?* Make any necessary corrections.

APPLICATION

- Direct Ss' attention to Exercise **1B**. Read the instructions aloud. Make sure Ss understand the task. Have Ss individually sovle the problem.
- Ss discuss the problem in small groups. Walk around and help as needed.
- After Ss have discussed the problem, open up the discussion to the entire class. Accept all plausible answers.

Expansion activity (individual work)

- Have Ss write a paragraph about whether they are left-brained or right-brained people and why.
- Remind Ss to use topic sentences to start their paragraphs. They can refer to page 15 in the Student's Book for help in outlining their paragraphs.
- Have Ss complete the writing in class or at home.
- Ask Ss to use the checklist in Exercise **3A** on page 15 to review their paragraphs prior to submitting them or sharing them with the class.

Expansion activity (student pairs)

- Write *left-brained person* and *right-brained person* on the board in two columns. Ask Ss to give you several examples of brain side functions based on the diagram (e.g. right-brained = artistic, left-brained = logical).
- Ask Ss: *How do left-brained or right-brained people react to certain situations? How would they talk about something like the weather?* Elicit appropriate responses, for example: a left-brained person might quote a weather report that he or she read or saw on television, whereas a right-brained person might say that he or she "feels" like rain is in the air.
- Ss in pairs. Ask pairs to create a short dialog between two people, one left-brained and one right-brained. The conversation can be about anything: home, school, the weather, or a combination of a few things. However, it should show the differences in right-brain and left-brain personalities based on what Ss learned from studying the diagram as well as any background knowledge they have about the subject. Encourage Ss to be creative and have fun with the activity.
- Ss work together. Walk around and help as needed.
- After several minutes, ask different pairs to share their dialogs with the class.

LESSON F Another view

WARM UP AND REVIEW

- Books closed. Write a few questions on the board. Ask Ss the questions, and encourage them to reply using complete sentences, for example: *Do you think that it's important to study history? Yes, I think it's important to study history. Do you believe that musical intelligence is important? Yes, I believe musical intelligence is important.*

PRESENTATION

Focus on form

- Use the animated grammar presentation in one or more of the following ways:
  - Preview it before class
  - Show in class
  - Encourage Ss to watch outside of class.
- Books open. Direct Ss attention to the chart in **2A**. Read the two questions aloud. Ask S volunteers to read the *yes* and *no* answers (*I think so. I don't think so. She hopes so. She hopes not.*) Explain that *so* and *not* can be used as short answers in place of clauses after verbs like *think*, *hope*, and *believe*. Point to the warm up questions on the board. Ask Ss to reply using the short form, for example: *Do you think it's important to study history? Yes, I think so.*
- Write on the board: *I think that math is essential to succeed at school.* Underline the clause (math is essential to succeed at school). Ask Ss to point out the subject (*I*), verb (*think*), and object (*that it's essential to succeed at school*).
- Write *I think so.* below the first sentence. Underline *so.* Explain that *so* communicates the same meaning as the clause in the first sentence. Make sure Ss understand *so* is a short answer, not a clause.
- Direct Ss' attention to instructions for Exercise **2A**. Read the instructions aloud.
- Divide the class into small groups. Tell them to ask and answer the questions and complete the chart.
- Ss share information from their discussions with the class.

APPLICATION

- Direct Ss' attention to Exercise **2B**. Read the instructions aloud.
- Ss complete the activity with a partner. Help as needed.
- Check answers with the class. Call on individual Ss to share information about their classmates.

EVALUATION

- Do a quick review of the unit. Have Ss turn to Lesson A. Ask the class to talk about what they remember about this lesson. Prompt Ss, if necessary, with questions, for example: *What is the conversation about on this page? What vocabulary is in the pictures?* Continue in this manner to review each lesson quickly.

Expansion activity

- Before class. Print, for each student, one copy of the Self-assessment for this unit.
- Have Ss complete the Self-assessment either in class or outside of class.
- Provide feedback to Ss such as through a whole-class discussion, partners comparing their worksheets, or T reviewing each S's worksheet.
- If Ss are ready, administer the unit test on pages T-186–T-188 of this Teacher's Edition. The audio script for the test is on page T-222.

More Ventures, Unit 1, Lesson F	
Workbook, 15–30 min.	
Multilevel Worksheets, 30–45 min.	
Collaborative Worksheets, 30–45 min.	www.cambridge.org/ventures/resources/
Self-assessment, 10 min.	
CASAS Test Prep Worksheet, 5–10 min.	

Grammar connections: *so* and *that*

Use *so* after certain verbs (*think, hope, believe, guess*) when you don't want to repeat the object clause.

👁 Watch

	Yes answer	No answer
Do you think **that** math is essential to succeed at school?	Yes, I think **so**. (I think **that** math is essential to succeed at school.)	No, I don't think **so**. (I don't think **that** math is essential to succeed at school.)
Does Maria hope **that** robots will do most of the work in the future?	Yes, she hopes **so**. (She hopes **that** robots will do most of the work in the future.)	No, she hopes **not**. (She hopes **that** robots won't do most of the work in the future.)

A **Work** in a small group. Ask and answer the questions. Give reasons. Then complete the chart with your classmates' answers.

Answers will vary.

A Do you think that there will be only one world language in the future?

B No, I don't think so. There are too many people in small villages around the world. It would be difficult to get everyone to learn the same language.

C Yes, I hope so . . .

Do you think that . . .	Lina (name)	___ (name)	___ (name)	___ (name)
1. it's easy to find a job?	No			
2. people waste too much time on the Internet?	Yes			
3. there will be only one world language in the future?	No			
4. more women will study science in the future?	Yes			
5. most people will live to be 100 in the future?	Yes			
6. smartphones will get cheaper?	No			

B **Talk** with a new partner. Ask and answer questions about your classmates.

A Does Lina think that there will be only one world language?

B No, she doesn't think so.

📖 Scan a diagram for key details about brain function; use *so* in answers to replace object clauses

Lesson A Listening

1 Before you listen

A What do you see?

B What is happening?

1

2

La Costa Community College Course Schedule
Hospitality and Tourism Certificate Program

HOSP 100: Introduction to Hospitality and Tourism	**BUS 137:** Customer Service
Requirement: Pass English placement test.	**Requirement:** Pass HOSP 100.
Fall and spring T / Th 10:00–11:30 a.m. M / W 6:00–7:30 p.m.	Spring T / Th 8:00–9:30 a.m. (Online course also available.)
Room: T130	**Room:** B480

3 Vasili

Mrs. Ochoa

4

UNIT 2

Teaching objectives
- Introduce students to the topic
- Find out what students know about the topic
- Preview the unit by talking about the pictures
- Provide practice of key vocabulary
- Provide practice that develops listening skills

WARM-UP AND REVIEW

- Before class. Write today's lesson focus on the board.
  Lesson A:
  Ask about courses and classes
  Discuss how to continue one's education
  Discuss obstacles and successes

- Begin class. Books closed. Direct Ss' attention to the lesson focus. Point to *Ask about courses and classes.* Ask Ss: *What classes have you taken? What classes are you taking now?* List Ss' responses on the board, for example: *I've taken several engineering classes in my country. I'm taking an English class right now.*

- Ask Ss: *What courses are you going to take in the future?* Elicit appropriate responses, such as: *I'm going to take another English course. I'm going to study nursing.*

Teaching Tip
By asking questions about the courses and classes they have taken, you can find out what your Ss' educational backgrounds are and, from time to time, call on their expertise.

PRESENTATION

- Books open. Set the scene. Direct Ss' attention to the four pictures on page 18. Ask the question from Exercise **1A**: *What do you see?* Elicit and write on the board any vocabulary that Ss know, such as: *car, counselor, class schedules, computer, poster test.*

- Ask individual Ss to look at the pictures and talk about them: *There's a course schedule in the second picture. There is a young man meeting with a woman in the third picture. The young man is taking a test in the fourth picture.*

- Direct Ss' attention to the question in Exercise **1B**: *What is happening?* Read it aloud. Hold up the Student's Book. Point to the first picture. Ask: *What's he doing?* (He's meeting with someone to take college classes.)

- Hold up the Student's Book, and point to the young man in the third picture. Ask: *What's Vasili doing here?* (He's sitting in Mrs. Ochoa's office.) Ask Ss to describe what is happening in the third picture. Write Ss' responses on the board. (They are probably talking about classes and schedules, etc.) Ask Ss who they think Mrs. Ochoa is. (a counselor.)

Teaching Tip
Encourage Ss to be creative. At this point, there is no single correct answer.

Culture Tip
Tell Ss that in most colleges and universities, Ss can talk to counselors or advisors who can help them plan their class schedules. Tell Ss that counselors are specifically trained to help them figure out what classes they should take in order to achieve their educational and career goals.

- If you have counselors at your school, invite them to come to your class to talk to Ss about course selection and goal-setting. Have Ss prepare questions about their areas of interest prior to the guests' visit.

Expansion activity *(student pairs)*
- Tell Ss to work in pairs to create a dialog between Vasili and Mrs. Ochoa. Elicit that the characters are probably talking about classes Vasili should take. Ask Ss to include in their conversations different suggestions about classes he should take.

- Ask for volunteers to role play their conversations for the class.

LESSON A Listening

PRESENTATION

- Tell Ss that they are going to hear two different audio segments. Direct Ss' attention to Exercise **2A**. Read the instructions aloud. Ask a S to read the questions to the class. Tell Ss to listen for the answers as the audio program is played or read.
- ▶ **CD1, Track 12** Play or read the audio (see audio script, page T-177).
- Ask Ss if they understood everything in the listening exercise. Write any unfamiliar words on the board and help Ss understand their meanings. Be sure that Ss understand the meaning of *certificate program* (an academic program, usually a series of classes, in which completion is recognized by the receipt of a certificate).
- Elicit answers to the questions; for example: *The speakers are a radio announcer, Mrs. Ochoa, and Vasili. They're talking about a Hospitality and Tourism certificate program at La Costa Community College.*
- Ask: *What do you think Vasili will do?* Elicit appropriate responses and write them on the board; for example: *I think Vasili will enroll in the program.*
- Focus Ss' attention on Exercise **2B**. Read the instructions aloud.
- ▶ **CD1, Track 12** Tell Ss to listen for details about the certificate program. Model the task. Play or read the audio again. Pause the audio after the announcer says in Part 1: *Then La Costa Community College's Hospitality and Tourism certificate program is for you.* Elicit: *Hospitality and Tourism.* Show Ss where on the chart *Hospitality and Tourism* is written. Encourage Ss to listen and complete the chart. Play or read the rest of the audio program.
- ▶ **CD1, Track 12** Play or read the audio again. Ss listen and check their answers.
- Write the numbers *1–6* on the board. Ask Ss to come to the board to write the answers. Have other Ss make corrections on the board as needed.

Learner persistence *(individual work)*
- ▶ **CD1, Track 12** Ss can listen to the audio for Exercises **2A** and **2B** at home for reinforcement and review. They can also listen to the audio for self-directed learning when class attendance is not possible.

PRACTICE

- Focus Ss' attention on Exercise **3A**. Read the instructions aloud. Tell Ss that the story in this exercise is a summary of the events shown in the pictures on page 18.

- Focus Ss' attention on the words in the word bank. Say each word aloud. Ask Ss to repeat. Correct pronunciation as needed. Explain any unfamiliar words.
- Ss complete the exercise individually. Walk around and help as needed.

COMPREHENSION CHECK

- ▶ **CD1, Track 13** Play or read the audio (see audio script, page T-177). Ss listen and check their answers. Repeat the audio as needed.
- Write the numbers *1–10* on the board. Ask Ss to come to the board to write their answers.

Learner persistence *(individual work)*
- ▶ **CD1, Track 13** Ss can listen to the audio for Exercise **3A** at home for reinforcement and review. They can also listen to the audio for self-directed learning when class attendance is not possible.

APPLICATION

- Focus Ss' attention on Exercise **3B**. Read the instructions aloud.
- Ss complete the exercise in pairs. Help as needed.
- Ask several pairs to ask and answer the questions for the class. Discuss why Ss in the class would or would not like this type of job.

EVALUATION

- Direct Ss' attention to the lesson focus on the board. Ask individual Ss to look at the pictures on page 18 and make sentences using the words from the word bank in Exercise **3A**.
- Check off each part of the lesson focus as Ss demonstrate an understanding of what they have learned in the lesson.

More Ventures, Unit 2, Lesson A	
Workbook, 15–30 min.	
Multilevel Worksheets, 30–45 min.	www.cambridge.org/ ventures/resources/
Collaborative Worksheets, 30–45 min.	
Student Arcade, time varies	www.cambridge.org/ venturesarcade/

UNIT GOALS
Make educational plans   **Write** a descriptive paragraph about a successful person
Scan a chart for the location of classes

2 Listen

A Listen and answer the questions.

1. Who are the speakers?

2. What are they talking about?

◀)) CD1, Track 12

B Listen again. Complete the chart.

1. Type of certificate	*Hospitality and Tourism*
2. Places of employment	*hotels, restaurants, airlines, travel agencies*
3. Number of required classes	*six, plus an internship*
4. Time to complete the program	*between one and two years*
5. Cost per unit	*$50 per unit*
6. Estimated cost to earn the certificate	*$1600*

◀)) CD1, Track 12

3 After you listen

A Read. Complete the story.

bilingual	deadline	industry	internship	qualify
business	high-paying	interpersonal	motivated	requirements

Vasili hears a radio ad about the Hospitality and Tourism Certificate Program at La Costa Community College. The ad says graduates can find *high-paying* jobs in the
1
tourism *industry*. Vasili goes to see his ESL counselor, Mrs. Ochoa. She tells him
2
about the program *requirements*, which include an *internship* in a local tourism
3   4
business. She also tells him about the *deadline* for registration, and she
5   6
says there is financial aid for students who *qualify*. Vasili is concerned about
7
his English, but Mrs. Ochoa tells him not to worry. Vasili is *bilingual*, he's very
8
motivated, and he has good *interpersonal* skills.
9   10

Listen and check your answers.

◀)) CD1, Track 13

B Discuss. Talk with your classmates. Is hospitality and tourism a good industry for Vasili? Would you like this type of career? Why or why not?

Lesson B The passive

1 Grammar focus: present passive

Use the passive voice to change the focus from *who* is doing something to *what* is being done. If the person or thing doing the action is important, use a *by* phrase.

ACTIVE	PRESENT PASSIVE
The college **gives** a placement test.	A placement test **is given** (by the college).
The college **offers** online classes every semester.	Online classes **are offered** (by the college) every semester.
Does the college **offer** financial aid?	**Is** financial aid **offered** (by the college)?
When **does** the college **arrange** internships?	When **are** internships **arranged** (by the college)?

👁 Watch

2 Practice

A Write. Complete the sentences. Use the present passive.

1. **A** When _____*is*_____ the English placement test _____*given*_____ to new students?
   (give)

   B The English placement test ___*is administered*___ a week before the first day of class.
   (administer)

2. **A** _____*Is*_____ a math placement test also ___*required*___?
   (require)

   B No, a math placement test _____*is*_____ not ___*needed*___.
   (need)

3. **A** Where _____*is*_____ the financial aid office ___*located*___?
   (locate)

   B It ___*is located*___ next to the admissions office.
   (locate)

4. **A** Where _____*are*_____ the classes ___*held*___?
   (hold)

   B Most of the classes ___*are held*___ in the business building.
   (hold)

5. **A** ___*Are*___ classes ___*offered*___ at different times?
   (offer)

   B Yes. Both day and evening classes ___*are offered*___.
   (offer)

6. **A** ___*Are*___ job placement services ___*provided*___ to graduates?
   (provide)

   B Yes. Job help ___*is offered*___ to students who qualify.
   (offer)

Listen and check your answers. Then practice with a partner.

 ◀)) CD1, Track 14

Teaching objective
- Introduce and provide practice with the present passive voice

WARM-UP AND REVIEW

- Before class: Write the lesson focus on the board.
  Lesson B:
  Present passive voice
- Begin class. Books open. Direct Ss' attention to the pictures on page 18. Ask questions such as the following about Vasili: *What is Vasili interested in studying?* (hospitality and tourism.) *What does Mrs. Ochoa tell Vasili when he says he's worried about the cost of the program?* (There's financial aid for students who qualify.)

PRESENTATION

Focus on meaning / personalize

- Books closed. Direct Ss' attention to the lesson focus on the board. Read it aloud.
- Ask: *Does our school require a placement test?* Write on the board, *Our school requires / does not require a placement test.* Beneath that sentence, write *A test is required / is not required.*
- Explain to Ss that there are two voices in English – the *active* and the *passive*. In the active voice, an action is completed by the subject. Point to the first sentence and underline the subject (school). Tell Ss that the school does the action (requires). Point to the second sentence and underline the object (a test).
- Tell Ss we use the passive voice when we don't want to name the subject, we don't know the subject, or it is not important to name the subject.

Focus on form

- Use the animated grammar presentation in one or more of the following ways:
  - Preview it before class
  - Show in class
  - Encourage Ss to watch outside of class.
- Books open. Direct Ss' attention to the Active chart in Exercise **1**. Have Ss read the first sentence. Ask: *What's the subject?* (college.) *What's the verb?* (gives.) *What's the object?* (a placement test.) *Is the object necessary?* (Yes.)

- Direct Ss' attention to the Passive chart. Have Ss read the first sentence. Ask: *What's the subject?* (a placement test.) *What's the verb?* (is given.) *What's the object?* (by the college.) *Is the object necessary?* (No.)
- Elicit or explain that active sentences have the form *subject + verb + object* and that passive sentences have the form *subject + be + past participle*. The object of an active sentence becomes the subject of a passive sentence. An active verb is used to say what the subject does. A passive verb is used to say what happens to the subject.
- Direct Ss' attention to the two questions in the Active chart. Review question formation in the Passive. Ask: *How do you form a "Yes / No" question in the present passive voice?* (is + object + past participle). *How do you form a "Wh-" question in the present passive with Wh- words?* (Wh- + be + object + past participle).

Useful Language

Read the tip box aloud. Then direct Ss' attention again to the passive sentences in the chart. Tell Ss that we include a *by* phrase when we want to clarify information or add emphasis but that it is not always necessary.

PRACTICE

- Direct Ss' attention to Exercise **2A**. Read the instructions aloud. Have two Ss read the example aloud, and make sure that Ss understand the exercise.
- Ss complete the exercise individually. Walk around and help as needed.

COMPREHENSION CHECK

- ▶ **CD1, Track 14** Play or read the audio (see audio script, page T-177). Ss listen and check their answers. Repeat the audio as needed.
- Write the numbers *1–6* on the board. Ask several Ss to come to the board to write their answers in complete sentences. Make corrections on the board as needed.
- Have pairs practice the questions and answers.

LESSON B The passive

PRESENTATION

- Books open. Direct Ss' attention to Exercise **2B**. Read the instructions aloud.
- Direct Ss' attention to the La Costa Community College Course Schedule. Have a S read the HOSP 100 entry.
- Ask another S to read the BUS 137 entry.
- Guide Ss to see that most listings in course catalogs consist of an abbreviation and a course number.

Teaching Tip

Ss may be unfamiliar with course-name abbreviations. Write HOSP and BUS on the board. Ask Ss what they stand for (hospitality and business). Ask Ss if they have seen other examples of abbreviations and what they were. If Ss have not seen others, write the following on the board: ENG, MAT, BIO. Ask Ss what they stand for (English, mathematics, biology). Have Ss look for other abbreviations in catalogs and on the Internet.

- Model the task. Ask two pairs of Ss to read the sample questions and answers to the class.
- Ss continue by asking and answering questions in pairs. Walk around and help as needed.

PRACTICE

- Read aloud the second part of the instructions for Exercise **2B**.
- Ask a S to read the sample sentence to the class.
- Ss complete the exercise individually. Walk around and help as needed.

COMPREHENSION CHECK

- Ask individual Ss to come to the board to write their sentences. Ask Ss if the sentences are written correctly. Make corrections on the board as needed.

APPLICATION

- Direct Ss' attention to Exercise **3A**. Read aloud the instructions and the topics.
- Model the task. Ask two Ss to read the example conversation to the class.

- Ss work in pairs to complete the exercise. Help as needed.
- Direct Ss' attention to Exercise **3B**. Read the instructions aloud.
- Call on pairs to perform their role play for the class.

Expansion activity (small groups)

- Ask Ss: *What kinds of courses are you interested in?* Write student answers on the board.
- Use your college / program's course listings, or find listings for these classes from online sources. Give printouts or catalogs to each group and have Ss find listings for classes they'd be interested in.
- Ask Ss to ask and answer questions about the classes as they did in Exercise **2B**.
- Ss work in small groups to complete the activity. Walk around and help as needed.
- Call on groups to share the information they learned.

EVALUATION

- Direct Ss' attention to the lesson focus on the board.
- Write the following sentence on the board: *The college offers four different levels of ESL classes.*
- Ask a S whether the statement is in the active or the passive voice (*active*), and then ask the S to come to the board to write the sentence in the passive voice. (*Four different levels of ESL classes are offered by the college.*) If you have time, repeat this activity, but call on Ss to give you examples (in either voice) for other Ss to write on the board.
- Check off each part of the lesson focus as Ss demonstrate an understanding of what they have learned in the lesson.

More Ventures, Unit 2, Lesson B	
Workbook, 15–30 min.	
Multilevel Worksheets, 30–45 min. Collaborative Worksheets, 30–45 min.	www.cambridge.org/ ventures/resources
Student Arcade, time varies	www.cambridge.org/ venturesarcade/

B **Talk** with a partner. Ask and answer questions about the two courses on the flyer. Use the sentence prompts.

La Costa Community College Course Schedule
Hospitality and Tourism Certificate Program

HOSP 100: Introduction to Hospitality and Tourism	**BUS 137:** Customer Service
Requirement: Pass English placement test.	**Requirement:** Pass HOSP 100.
Fall and spring T / Th 10:00–11:30 a.m. M / W 6:00–7:30 p.m.	Spring T / Th 8:00–9:30 a.m. (Online course also available.)
Room: T130	**Room:** B480

Wh questions	**Yes / No questions**
Where / held	placement test / required

A Where is Hospitality 100 held?	A Is a placement test required for Hospitality 100?
B It's held in room T130.	B Yes, a placement test is required.
B Where Is Business 137 held?	B Is a placement test required for Business 137?
A It's held in room B480.	A No, a placement test is not required for Business 137.

1. Where / hold
2. Which days / give
3. What time / schedule
4. When /offer
5. What /require

6. placement test / require
7. online course / offer
8. spring classes / hold
9. evening classes /give
10. prerequisite / require

❸ Communicate

A **Work** with a partner. Role-play a conversation between a counselor and a student who wants to enroll in a certificate program at your school. Ask and answer questions about the topics below. Predict the answers a counselor would give.

- online courses
- required courses
- English or math placement tests
- location of classes

- internships
- financial aid
- job counseling

Student	Are online courses offered in the certificate program?
Counselor	No. Online courses are not offered in that program.
Student	What about internships?
Counselor	Internships are arranged for each student in the program.

B **Perform** your role play for the class.

Lesson C The passive

1 Grammar focus: infinitives after the passive

Some passive verbs are followed by infinitives.

Students **are told to arrive** early on the first day of class.

Everyone **is encouraged to attend** class regularly.

Are students **required to do** homework every night?

How often **are** students **expected to meet** with their counselors?

Verbs often followed by infinitives	
advise	expect
allow	require
encourage	tell

👁 Watch

2 Practice

A **Write** complete statements or questions. Use the present passive with infinitives.

1. applicants / expect / meet / all application deadlines.

   Applicants are expected to meet all application deadlines.

2. new students / tell / come early / for registration.

   New students are told to come early for registration.

3. all new students / require / take / a writing test?

   Are all new students required to take a writing test?

4. some students / advise / enroll / in an English composition class.

   Some students are advised to enroll in an English composition class.

5. students / expect / attend / every class?

   Are students expected to attend every class?

6. students / encourage / meet / with a counselor regularly.

   Students are encouraged to meet with a counselor regularly.

7. when / participants / expect / complete / their internships?

   When are participants expected to complete their internships?

8. students / require / earn / a grade of C or better in each course.

   Students are required to earn a grade of C or better in each course.

9. students / tell / study / with a partner and to go to tutoring often.

   Students are told to study with a partner and to go to tutoring often.

10. students / allow / retake / course / if they don't pass?

    Are students allowed to retake a course if they don't pass?

Listen and check your answers.

🔊 CD1, Track 15

WARM-UP AND REVIEW

• Before class: Write the lesson focus on the board.
Lesson C:
Infinitives after passive verbs

• Begin class. Books open. Direct Ss' attention to the advertisement on page 21, Exercise **2B**. Have Ss ask and answer questions using the past participles in the box, for example: *Where is HOSP 100 located?* (HOSP 100 is located in room T130.) *Is an English placement test required?* (Yes, an English placement test is required by the college.)

• Write a passive statement on the board and elicit its form, for example:

A placement test	is required	by the college.
subject	verb	
receiving action	(*be* + past participle of *require*)	giving action

PRESENTATION

Focus on meaning / personalize

• Books closed. Direct Ss' attention to the lesson focus on the board. Write on the board: *What can you do to learn more English?* Write Ss' responses on the board in the active voice. *I can come to class every day. I can speak only English in class.*

• Next, write sentences in the present passive voice on the board: *Students are expected to come to class every day. Students are encouraged to speak only English in class.*

• Ask S volunteers to come to the board and underline the passive verb and circle the infinitive. Ask: *Students are expected to do what?* (come to class every day.) *Students are encouraged to do what?* (speak only English in class.)

• Remind Ss that we use the passive voice when the object is more important than the subject. In these sentences, the students are more important than the teacher. Point out that many passive verbs can have infinitives after them.

Focus on form

• Use the animated grammar presentation in one or more of the following ways:
  • Preview it before class
  • Show in class
  • Encourage Ss to watch outside of class.

• Books open. Direct Ss' attention to the chart in Exercise **1**. Read the statements. Ask Ss to repeat.

• Point out the verb + infinitive in each statement. Elicit that some passive verbs require an infinitive (*to* + base verb). Review the verbs in the grammar box that are often followed by infinitives. Give examples of sentences, such as: *You are expected to speak English in the classroom.*

• Write the first two statements on the board. Ask Ss to come to the board and underline the complete passive: verb *to be* + past participle (*are told, is encouraged*) and circle the infinitive: *to* + base form of verb (*to arrive, to attend*).

• Write the two questions from Exercise **1** on the board. Have Ss identify the verb + infinitive and write answers to the questions. (Yes, *students are required to do homework every night. Students are expected to meet with their counselors every semester.*)

PRACTICE

• Direct Ss' attention to Exercise **2A**. Read the instructions aloud.

• Model the task. Ask a S to read aloud the example sentence. Remind Ss that the present passive is formed by using the present tense of *be* + the past participle and that the infinitive is formed by *to* + the base form of the verb. Tell Ss to continue the exercise by using the present passive with infinitives.

• Ss complete the exercise individually. Walk around and help as needed.

COMPREHENSION CHECK

• Read aloud the second part of the instructions for Exercise **2A**.

▶ **CD1, Track 15** Play or read the audio (see audio script, page T-177). Ss listen and check their answers.

• Ask individual Ss to come to the board to write their answers. Make corrections on the board as needed.

LESSON C The passive

PRESENTATION

- Books closed. Write on the board: *college credit*. Ask Ss if they know what this means. Elicit appropriate responses, such as: *College credit is what you earn when you take certain courses. College certificate and degree programs require a specific amount of college credit.*

PRACTICE

- Books open. Focus Ss' attention on Exercise **2B**. Read the instructions aloud.
- Direct Ss' attention to the flyer. Ask a S to read the ad aloud. Explain vocabulary as needed, and write any new words on the board.
- Ss complete the exercise in pairs. Walk around and help as needed.
- Ask several Ss to write their sentences on the board. Ask other Ss to read aloud each of the sentences on the board. Ask: *Is this sentence correct?* Have different Ss make corrections on the board as needed.

Culture Note

Read the culture note aloud. Ask Ss if they have heard of work experience programs. Explain that these programs are designed to encourage Ss – especially adult Ss – to go to college or, in some cases, to return to college. Tell Ss that each college has its own rules regarding work for credit and that in most cases, evidence of work (either volunteer or paid) must be provided.

Expansion activity (student pairs)

- Role-play. Ask Ss to practice role-playing the activity of a S asking a school counselor information about work experience credit. Write an example of a conversation on the board, such as:

  S: *I would like to try to get college credit for my work experience.*

  Counselor: *What kind of work experience do you have?*

  S: *I volunteered at the library last year. I gave people information about the library's programs.*

  Counselor: *Very interesting! This is perfect because it's related to the program you are interested in.*

  S: *If I get a letter from my boss, can I get credit for my work?*

  Counselor: *I think so, but we need to know how many hours you worked.*

- Ask two Ss to read the example conversation.
- Have pairs write and practice their own conversation. Walk around and help as needed.
- Ask several pairs to act out their conversation for the rest of the class.

APPLICATION

- Direct Ss' attention to Exercise **3A**. Read the instructions aloud. Call on a pair of Ss to read the dialog twice to practice both answers (positive and negative).
- Ask Ss to read aloud the items on the chart. Remind Ss that *must* means something is necessary. Model the task by asking the whole class questions about the chart.
- Ss complete the exercise. Walk around and help as needed.
- Direct Ss' attention to Exercise **3B**. Read the instructions aloud.
- Model the task. Ask a S from each pair to tell what he or she learned. Ask the S to make a sentence about the course requirements, for example: *Students are expected to sign up for a placement test.*
- Continue the exercise by asking different Ss to share information about the course requirements.

EVALUATION

- Direct Ss' attention to the lesson focus on the board. Ask individual Ss to look at the ad on Student's Book page 23 and to make sentences using *allowed, encouraged, expected, required,* and *told.* Ask Ss to share their answers with the class.
- Check off the lesson focus as Ss demonstrate an understanding of what they have learned in the lesson.

More Ventures, Unit 2, Lesson C	
Workbook, 15–30 min.	
Multilevel Worksheets, 30–45 min. Collaborative Worksheets, 30–45 min.	www.cambridge.org/ ventures/resources/
Student Arcade, time varies	www.cambridge.org/ venturesarcade/

B **Talk** with a partner. Read the flyer. One student asks a question in the passive about the flyer. Another answers in the passive.

Work Experience Program at La Costa Community College

Earn up to 4 units of college credit by participating in the program.

The program:
- requires you to attend an orientation session.
- allows you to work and get college credit at the same time.
- expects you to work at least 75 paid hours or 60 volunteer hours.
- encourages you to visit the website for more information.
- tells students to consider this opportunity.
- advises you to call the Career Center at 777-555-2222
- permits you to enroll at the orientation session.
- reminds you to call to reserve a spot at the orientation.
- asks you to tell other students about this opportunity.

CULTURE NOTE
Work experience programs exist in many U.S. colleges to help adult students get credit for past and present work experience.

USEFUL LANGUAGE
One meaning of *you* is *people in general.*

What are you required to attend?

You are required to attend an orientation session.

1. What / require / attend
2. What / allow / do
3. How long / expect / work
4. What / encourage / visit
5. What / tell / consider

6. Who / advise / call
7. What / permit / do
8. What / remind / do
9. Who / ask / tell

3 Communicate

A **Work** with a partner. Read the announcement below. Ask and answer questions about the enrollment information.

A Are students required to register early?

B No, but students are encouraged to register early.

Do you want to enroll this fall?

You must:	It's a good idea to:
• Meet with a counselor	• Register early (space is limited)
• Sign up for a placement test	• Find out about tutoring
• Choose courses	support
• Buy books	• Inquire about financial aid

B **Share** information with your classmates.

Lesson D Reading

1 Before you read

Talk with a partner. Look at the reading tip. Answer the questions.

1. Who is the newspaper article about?
2. What places are mentioned in the newspaper article?
3. How old is their son now?

 Scan a reading to find specific information such as names, places, and key words.

2 Read

Read the newspaper article. Listen and read again.

www.newyorknews.com

 CD1, Track 16

New York News

An Immigrant Family's Success Story

Choi and Lili Wei left China with their baby boy in the early 1990s. They were poor field workers in their native country, and they wanted their child to have the opportunities they <u>lacked</u>. They arrived in New York and found a one-bedroom apartment in a poor, <u>unstable</u> area. They could only afford a bicycle for transportation, yet they felt <u>fortunate</u> to have the chance to begin a new life in the United States.

Choi and Lili <u>faced</u> many <u>obstacles</u> because they couldn't speak English and had no skills. They found night work cleaning businesses and restaurants. They saved every penny, and after six years, they were able to buy a small restaurant of their own.

They were <u>determined</u> to learn English, get an education, and make a good life for their son. The couple sacrificed a great deal. They never went to the movies, never ate out, and hardly ever bought anything extra. In their free time, they attended English and citizenship classes. Both of them eventually earned their GED certificates. Choi then enrolled in college

while Lili worked in the restaurant.

This past spring, Choi fulfilled a lifelong dream of graduating from college. Now he is registered in a master's degree program in business beginning this fall. And what about their "baby" boy? Their son, Peter, now 21, received a scholarship to a private university, where he is working on his own dream to become an architect.

Choi and Lili are proud to be models of the "American dream." Choi has this advice for other new immigrants: "Find your <u>passion</u>, make a plan to succeed, and don't ever give up."

Teaching objectives
- Introduce a newspaper article about an immigrant family's success story
- Provide practice using new topic-related vocabulary
- Provide practice scanning a reading to find specific information
- Provide practice identifying words to describe obstacles and successes

WARM-UP AND REVIEW

- Before class. Write today's lesson focus on the board.
  Lesson D:
  Read and understand "An Immigrant Family's Success Story"
  Practice new vocabulary related to obstacles and successes

- Begin class. Books closed. Focus Ss' attention on the word *success* in the lesson focus. Write *success* on the board. Ask Ss: *How do you think most people define "success"? How do you define success?* Elicit appropriate responses and write them on the board. (Answers will vary.)

- Ask Ss to read the title of the newspaper article and tell what they think this article is about. Elicit responses, such as: *It's about a family from another country coming to the United States and achieving their goals.* Write some of the Ss' predictions on the board.

- Some Ss may mention the "American dream." Ask Ss what they think this expression means.

PRESENTATION

- Books open. Direct Ss' attention to Exercise **1**. Read the instructions aloud.

  Read the tip aloud. Write *scan* on the board. Say it and have Ss repeat. Ask Ss: *What is the difference between "skim" and "scan"?* Write on the board: *To skim = to find general information. To scan = to find specific information.* Tell Ss that both are important reading skills.

- Direct Ss' attention to the questions in Exercise **1**. Ask three Ss to read the questions aloud.

- Ss in pairs. Guide Ss to scan the article individually. Then ask Ss to answer the three questions with their partners. Have Ss indicate where in the article they found each of the three answers.

PRACTICE

- Read the instructions aloud for Exercise **2**. Ask Ss to read the article silently before listening to the audio program.

- ▶ *CD1, Track 16* Play or read the audio and ask Ss to read along (see audio script, page T-177). Repeat the audio as needed.

- While Ss are listening and reading the article, ask them to write any words in their notebooks that they don't understand. When the audio is finished, have Ss write the new vocabulary words on the board.

- Point to each word on the board. Say it and ask Ss to repeat. Give a brief explanation of each word, or ask Ss to explain the word if they know it. If Ss prefer to look up the new words in their dictionaries, allow them to do so.

- Encourage Ss to guess the meaning of unfamiliar words from the context of the article. For example, if a S writes *faced*, read the sentence aloud (*Choi and Lili faced many obstacles because they couldn't speak English and had no skills.*). Ask Ss to think about the meaning of the word *faced* based on the other information in the sentence. Tell Ss that *faced* is another way of saying *had to deal with* or *had to overcome obstacles.*

Learner persistence *(individual work)*
- ▶ *CD1, Track 16* Ss can listen to the audio for Exercise **2** at home for reinforcement and review. They can also listen to the audio for self-directed learning when class attendance is not possible.

Expansion activity *(student pairs)*
- Have Ss create a scanning exercise for their partners.
- Bring in articles from a newspaper written in language that will not be too difficult for Ss to follow. Pass out the articles to Ss. Ask them to make up three questions about the article.
- Ss in pairs. Ask partners to exchange articles and questions. Ss scan the articles for answers.
- Call on pairs to share the information they learned with the class.

LESSON D Reading

COMPREHENSION CHECK

- Books open. Direct Ss' attention to Exercise **3A**. Read the instructions aloud.

- Ask individual Ss to read the questions aloud, one at a time. Make sure that all Ss understand the questions.

- Ss in pairs. Have partners ask and answer the questions. Tell Ss that they can refer to the article on page 24.

- Discuss the answers to the questions with the class. Ask where in the reading the answers are found.

PRACTICE

- Direct Ss' attention to Exercise **3B**. Ask a S to read aloud the instructions in number 1.

- Tell Ss to look at the chart in **3B**. Say each word and ask Ss to repeat. Give a brief explanation of each word, or ask Ss to explain the word if they know it.

- Model the task. Read aloud the word *lacked*, and have Ss scan the article on page 24 to find it. (It's in the first paragraph.) Call on a S to read the sentence with this word. Then ask Ss to find and underline the rest of the words from the chart.

- Ss complete the exercise individually. Help as needed.

- Direct Ss to number 2 in Exercise **3B**. Ask a S to read the instructions aloud. Ask Ss for examples of parts of speech. Elicit: *verb, noun, adjective*.

Useful Language

Read the tip box aloud. Explain that synonyms are words that have the same meaning. For example, *big / large, nice / kind*. Ask Ss to think of other examples of synonyms. Write their answers on the board.

Teaching Tip

Remind Ss that when they look up a word in a dictionary, the word will appear in its base form, and there may be more than one definition for the word.

- Model the exercise by writing *fortunate* on the board. Ask a S what part of speech the word is (adjective), and write it on the board. Review the definition of *fortunate* and elicit synonyms: *lucky, successful*.

- Ss complete the exercise individually. Walk around and help as needed.

- Direct Ss to number 3 in Exercise **3B**. Ask a S to read the instructions aloud. Tell Ss to work in small groups to write sentences using the words in the chart.

- Ask each group to share a sentence from the chart until you have reviewed each word a few times.

APPLICATION

- Read the instructions aloud for Exercise **3C**.

- Ask three Ss to read the questions to the class.

- Ss complete the exercise in pairs. Help as needed.

- Ask several pairs to ask and answer the questions for the class.

Expansion activity *(small groups)*

- Write *100 years ago* and *Today* on the board as headings for each of two separate columns. Write *Similarities* and *Differences* to the left of the columns. Ask Ss what the similarities and differences are between immigrants who come to the United States today and those who came 100 years ago. Write examples under each heading, such as: *Both groups followed / are following their dreams for a better life*.

- Using the words from the chart in Exercise **3B**, as well as those from the reading, Ss discuss the similarities and differences between the two immigrant groups. Ss should share information they discussed with the class.

- Have Ss make a vocabulary card for each word. On one side of the card, have Ss write the word and the part of speech. On the other side, have Ss write the definition and their own sentence using the word.

Expansion activity

- Refer Ss to "Rafael Salazar," another reading on the same topic on pages 139–141.

- Have Ss complete the activity either in class or outside of class.

- Provide feedback to Ss such as through whole-class discussion, partners comparing their worksheets, or T reviewing each S's worksheets.

EVALUATION

- Books closed. Direct Ss' attention to the lesson focus on the board.

- Ask individual Ss to retell the main points of the article, "An Immigrant Family's Success Story."

- Focus Ss's attention on the words and synonyms from Exercise **3B**. Ask Ss to make a new sentence for each of these words to show that they understand the meaning.

- Check off each part of the lesson focus as Ss demonstrate an understanding of what they have learned in the lesson.

More Ventures, Unit 2, Lesson D	
Workbook, 15–30 min.	
Multilevel Worksheets, 30–45 min.	www.cambridge.org/ ventures/resources/
Collaborative Worksheets, 30–45 min.	
Student Arcade, time varies	www.cambridge.org/ venturesarcade/

3 After you read

A Check your understanding.

1. The main idea of this article is overcoming obstacles and attaining the American Dream. Supporting examples from the article: They were determined to learn English, get an education, and make a good life for their son. This past spring, Choi fulfilled a lifelong dream of graduating from college. Choi and Lili are proud to be models of the "American Dream."

1. What is the main idea of this newspaper article? Support your choice with two examples from the text.

2. What obstacles did Choi and Lili face in the United States?
2. Choi and Lili faced obstacles because they couldn't speak English, and they had no skills.

3. Explain the expression *saved every penny* as it is used in paragraph 2.
3. Saved every penny means that they saved every extra amount of money they had.

4. What were five specific things the Wei family did to make a better life for their son?
4. The things the Wei family did for their son were that they never went to the movies, never went out, and hardly bought anything extra.

5. Read Choi's advice for new immigrants. How do you think his advice influenced his son?
5. Mr. Wei influenced his son who is following his own dream of becoming an architect.

B Build your vocabulary.

> **USEFUL LANGUAGE**
> A synonym is a word that has the same meaning.
> *big - large*
> *nice - kind*
> *job - occupation*

1. In the reading passage, underline the words from the chart.

2. Use a dictionary or a thesaurus. Write the part of speech. Write a synonym for each word.

Word	Part of speech	Synonym
lacked	*verb*	*missed; didn't have*
unstable	*adjective*	*not balanced; uneven*
fortunate	*adjective*	*lucky*
faced	*verb*	*look toward; confront*
obstacles	*noun*	*difficulties; barriers*
determined	*verb*	*decided*
passion	*noun*	*devotion; fondness*

3. Work in a small group. Write sentences with the synonyms.

- _____
- _____
- _____
- _____
- _____
- _____
- _____

C Talk with a partner.

1. What is your definition of the "American Dream"? *Answers will vary.*

2. Do you know a family like the Wei family? What is their success story?

3. What is your passion? What is your plan for success?

For college and career readiness practice, see pages 139–141.

📖 Read closely to determine what the text says explicitly and to make logical inferences from the text; use a dictionary or thesaurus to identify synonyms

Lesson E Writing

1 Before you write

A **Talk** with your classmates. Answer the questions.

1. What is success? Is it only money?
2. Do you know a successful person?
3. What did the person do to become successful?
4. What was one obstacle to this person's success?

B **Read** the paragraph.

My Successful Cousin

My cousin, Daniel, is the most successful person I know, even though he has had many obstacles on his road to success. First of all, his parents died in an automobile accident when he was 17 years old. Daniel needed to take care of his two younger brothers, so he quit school and found a job at a local supermarket. When his brothers were in school, he worked. At night, he helped them with homework and did all the chores. Even with all his responsibilities, Daniel was a very reliable worker. His boss decided to help him go to college. It took Daniel eight years, but finally he graduated. Now Daniel plans to enroll in a business management course. If he is accepted, he hopes to open his own business someday. Daniel has a dream, and he is working hard to achieve his dream. He is my hero!

C **Talk** with a partner.

1. What are two facts given in the paragraph?
2. What are two examples given in the paragraph?
3. What is Daniel's dream?

 Use specific details such as facts, examples, and reasons to support your topic sentence.

Teaching objectives
- Prepare students for writing a paragraph about a successful person
- Provide practice using specific details about obstacles and successes to support the main idea

WARM-UP AND REVIEW

- Before class. Write today's lesson focus on the board.
  Lesson E:
  Write a paragraph about a successful person
  Use facts, examples, and reasons to support ideas
- Begin class. Books closed. Review vocabulary from the unit. Write the words *success* and *obstacle* on the board. Ask Ss what the difference is between a success and an obstacle. Elicit appropriate responses, such as: *A success is something that you accomplish or do well. An obstacle is an event or situation that makes it harder to succeed.*
- Remind Ss about the Wei family story. Ask Ss:
  Did Choi and his wife face many obstacles? (Yes, they did.)
  What were they? (They lacked money and English skills. They didn't have job skills.)
  Did they have successes? (Yes, they did.)
  What were they? (They were able to save enough money to buy a small restaurant. They earned their GED certificates. Their son, Choi graduated from college and he is still studying. He received a scholarship to a private university, where he is studying to become an architect.)
  What advice does Choi give to new immigrants? (He says that they should find their passion, make a plan to succeed, and never give up.)

PRESENTATION

- Books open. Direct Ss' attention to Exercise **1A**. Read the instructions aloud.
- Ask individual Ss to read aloud the questions in Exercise **1A**.
- Ss ask and answer the questions with a partner. Help as needed.

PRACTICE

- Direct Ss' attention to Exercise **1B**. Read the instructions aloud.
- Ss read the paragraph silently. Ask Ss to underline any unfamiliar words in the paragraph.
- Have Ss tell you the words they underlined. Write them on the board. Go over the meaning of each word.

Read the tip box aloud. Tell Ss that the topic sentence is the main idea of the paragraph and that the other sentences they write should support the topic sentence. Ask Ss why it is important to use facts, examples, and reasons to support the topic sentence. Elicit responses, such as: *Facts, examples, and reasons that support the topic sentence make a paragraph more interesting and convincing.*

APPLICATION

- Focus Ss' attention on Exercise **1C**. Read the instructions aloud.
- Ask individual Ss to read the questions in Exercise **1C**.
- Ss ask and answer the questions with a partner. Help as needed.
- Call on pairs to share their answers with the class.

Expansion activity (student pairs)

- Ask Ss to brainstorm a list of obstacles that immigrants face today and write them on the board.
- Ss in pairs. Tell Ss to write down the personal qualities people need to have in order to overcome each of these obstacles.
- Model the activity. Ask: *What qualities are most important for new immigrants to have?* Elicit appropriate responses, such as: *New immigrants need to be patient because it can take a long time to achieve goals and success.*
- Ask Ss to share their examples with the class.

LESSON E Writing

PRESENTATION

- Direct Ss' attention to Exercise **1D**. Read the instructions aloud.

- Ask a S to read the headings in the chart and the example answers.

- Remind Ss of the strategy they learned in the last lesson. Ask Ss to scan the paragraph for facts, examples and supporting information.

- Ss complete the chart individually.

- Write a chart on the board similar to the one in the Student's Book.

- Call on Ss to come to the board, one at a time, to fill in the chart. Make corrections on the board as needed.

Teaching Tip

Before Ss begin to write, have them talk about the topic in a prewriting activity. Speaking about the topic with a partner will help Ss to focus on the person they are going to write about in Exercise **2**.

PRACTICE

- Direct Ss' attention to Exercise **1E**. Read the instructions aloud.

- Point out to Ss that a graphic organizer, such as a chart, will help them organize their ideas for writing.

- Ss complete the exercise individually. Walk around and help as needed.

- Focus Ss' attention on Exercise **2**. Read the instructions aloud.

- Ss complete the task individually. Walk around and help as needed.

Learner persistence *(individual work)*

- If you have any Ss who have difficulty writing, sit with them and help them as the other Ss are writing. Encourage them to use their notes from Exercise **1E** to add facts and other details to support their topic sentence.

COMPREHENSION CHECK

- Direct Ss' attention to Exercise **3A**. Read the instructions aloud.

- Ss complete the task individually. Walk around and help as needed.

- Ss check their own paragraphs against the writing checklist. If any Ss check *No* for one or more of the checklist items, ask them to revise and edit their paragraphs to include the missing information.

EVALUATION

- Focus Ss' attention on Exercise **3B**. Read the instructions aloud. Make sure that Ss understand the task.

- This exercise enables Ss to work together to peer-correct their writing. Reading aloud enables the writer to review his or her own writing and to understand the need to write clearly for an audience.

- Ss complete the exercise in pairs. Tell Ss to take turns reading their paragraphs to each other. Walk around and help as needed.

- Listen to Ss as they ask their partner a question about the paragraph and tell their partner one thing they learned from the paragraph.

- Ask several Ss to read aloud the paragraphs they wrote for Exercise **2**. Have other Ss ask questions and tell the class something they learned from the paragraph.

- Direct Ss' attention to the lesson focus on the board.

- Check off each part of the lesson focus as Ss demonstrate an understanding of what they have learned in the lesson.

More Ventures, Unit 2, Lesson E	
Workbook, 15–30 min.	
Multilevel Worksheets, 30–45 min.	www.cambridge.org/ ventures/resources/
Collaborative Worksheets, 30–45 min.	

D **Complete** the chart with Daniel's obstacles and successes.

Topic sentence: *My cousin, Daniel, is the most successful person I know,*
even though he has had many obstacles on his road to success.

Daniel's obstacles	Daniel's successes
His parents died.	He found a job in a local supermarket.
He had to quit school.	He was a reliable worker.
He needed to take care of his brothers.	He graduated from college.

Concluding sentence: *He is my hero!*

E **Plan** a paragraph about a successful person you know. Use the chart to make notes on your own ideas.

Topic sentence: *Answers will vary.* _____

_____'s obstacles	_____'s successes

Concluding sentence: _____

2 Write

Write a paragraph about someone you know who is successful. Include a topic sentence, examples of obstacles and successes, and a concluding sentence. Use the paragraph in Exercise 1B and the charts in Exercises 1D and 1E to help you.

Answers will vary.

3 After you write

A **Check** your writing.

	Yes	No
1. My topic sentence identifies a successful person.	☐	☐
2. I included examples of obstacles and successes.	☐	☐
3. I wrote a concluding sentence.	☐	☐

B **Share** your writing with a partner.

1. Take turns. Read your paragraph to a partner.

2. Comment on your partner's paragraph. Ask your partner a question about the paragraph. Tell your partner one thing you learned.

Lesson F Another view

1 Life-skills reading

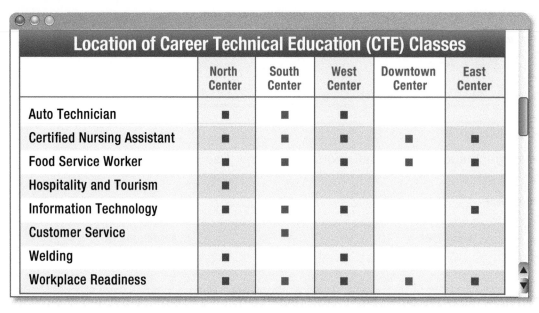

Location of Career Technical Education (CTE) Classes	North Center	South Center	West Center	Downtown Center	East Center
Auto Technician	■	■	■		
Certified Nursing Assistant	■	■	■	■	■
Food Service Worker	■	■	■	■	■
Hospitality and Tourism	■				
Information Technology	■	■	■		■
Customer Service		■			
Welding	■		■		
Workplace Readiness	■	■	■	■	■

A **Read** the questions. Look at the chart. Fill in the answer.

1. Which program is *not* offered at all five centers?
   - (A) Certified Nursing Assistant
   - (B) Workplace Readiness
   - (C) Food Service Worker
   - **(D) Information Technology**

2. Which centers offer fewer than five programs?
   - (A) South Center and Downtown Center
   - (B) North Center and East Center
   - **(C) Downtown Center and East Center**
   - (D) none of the above

3. Which center offers more than six programs?
   - (A) West Center
   - (B) East Center
   - **(C) North Center**
   - (D) South Center

4. Which programs are offered at only one center?
   - **(A) Hospitality and Tourism and Customer Service**
   - (B) Welding and Customer Service
   - (C) Auto Technician and Information Technology
   - (D) Hospitality and Tourism and Welding

B **Solve** the problem Give your opinion.

Ahmed works 4 days and 2 nights at a computer store. He wants to study Information Technology. The closest class is at the East Center. However, the class meets on the same two nights he works. What should he do?

Answers will vary.

Teaching objectives
- Introduce reading and understanding a chart about the location of classes
- Introduce and provide practice contrasting *be supposed to* and *be not supposed to* to show expectations about behavior

WARM-UP AND REVIEW

- Before class. Write today's lesson focus on the board.
  Lesson F:
  Read and understand a chart about course locations
  Contrast be supposed to and be not supposed to to show expectations about behavior
- Begin class. Books closed. Write *location* on the board. Say the word and ask Ss to repeat.
- Ask Ss: *What does "location" mean?* Elicit answers, such as: *Location is a place where something happens.*
- Ask Ss: *When and why do you need to check information about course locations?* Elicit responses, such as: *You should check the course locations so you know where to go on the first day of class. This is important to do before the first day.*

PRESENTATION

- Write *CTE* on the board. Explain the abbreviation (career technical education) and say that another word is "vocational" education. If Ss don't know, tell them that *vocation* means the same thing as *job or occupation*, and write that word on the board. Ask Ss what *vocational classes* are (classes for specific training in an occupation).
- Tell Ss that they will practice reading and understanding a chart of course locations for vocational classes.
- Books open. Call on individual Ss to read the names and locations of the eight vocational classes. Explain new vocabulary as needed.

PRACTICE

- Direct Ss' attention to Exercise **1A**. Read the instructions aloud. This task helps prepare Ss for standardized-type tests they may have to take. Be sure that Ss understand the task. Have Ss individually scan for and fill in the answers.

COMPREHENSION CHECK

- Check answers to Exercise **1A** with the class. Make sure that Ss have followed the instructions and filled in their answers.
- Have Ss read aloud the questions and the answers they filled in. Ask Ss: *Is that answer correct?* Make corrections as needed.

APPLICATION

- Direct Ss' attention to Exercise **1B**. Read the instructions aloud. Make sure Ss understand the task. Have Ss individually solve the problem.
- Ss discuss the problem in small groups. Walk around and help as needed.
- After groups have discussed the problem, call on individual Ss to share their answers with the class. Have other Ss share their answers. Accept all plausible answers.

LESSON F Another view

WARM-UP AND REVIEW

- Books closed. Ask Ss questions using the passive plus infinitives. What are students expected to do in English class? Ensure Ss reply using the passive, for example: *Students are expected to attend class regularly. Students are expected to do their homework.*

PRESENTATION

Focus on form

- Use the animated grammar presentation in one or more of the following ways:
  - Preview it before class
  - Show in class
  - Encourage Ss to watch outside of class.
- Books open. Direct Ss' attention to the grammar chart in Exercise 2. Ask two Ss to read the sentences. Explain that *be + supposed to* is an idiom we use in English to describe behavior that is expected of someone.
- Ask Ss for other examples of things people are not supposed to do in a park. Elicit answers, such as: *You're not supposed to spend the night in the park. You're supposed to leave the park when it gets dark.*

PRACTICE

- Direct Ss' attention to the instructions in Exercise **2A**. Read the instructions aloud. Ensure Ss understand the activity. Ask a pair of Ss to read the dialog aloud.
- Ss work in pairs and play the game. Walk around and help as needed.
- Direct Ss' attention to the instructions in Exercise **2B**. Read the instructions aloud. Encourage Ss to share their answers with the class.

EVALUATION

- Do a quick review of the unit. Have Ss turn to Lesson A. Ask the class to talk about what they remember about this lesson. Prompt Ss, if necessary, with questions, for example: *What are the conversations about on this page? What vocabulary is in the pictures?* Continue in this manner to review each lesson quickly.

Expansion activity

- Before class. Print, for each student, one copy of the Self-assessment for this unit.
- Have Ss complete the Self-assessment either in class or outside of class.
- Provide feedback to Ss such as through a whole-class discussion, partners comparing their worksheets, or T reviewing each S's worksheet.
- If Ss are ready, administer the unit test on pages T-189–T-191 of this Teacher's Edition. The audio script for the test is on page T-222.

More Ventures, Unit 2, Lesson F	
Workbook, 15–30 min.	
Multilevel Worksheets, 30–45 min.	
Collaborative Worksheets, 30–45 min.	www.cambridge.org/ventures/resources
Self-assessment, 10 min.	
CASAS Test Prep Worksheet, 5–10 min.	

2 Grammar connections: *be + supposed to* and *be + not supposed to*

Watch

Be + supposed to and *be + not supposed to* can show expectations about behavior.

You**'re supposed to come** early to register for the class.

You**'re not supposed to miss** class without an appropriate excuse.

A **Talk** with a partner. Choose one of the places in the box. Describe expectations about behavior there. Your partner guesses the place. Take turns.

the bookstore	the classroom	the counseling office	the library
the cafeteria	the computer lab	the gymnasium	the tutoring office

A You're supposed to be quiet in this place. You're not supposed to eat here.

B Is it the computer lab?

A No, it isn't. You're supposed to do research and borrow books here.

B Is it the library?

A Yes, it is.

A You're supposed to use cash or credit cards here. You're not supposed to use personal checks.

B Is it the cafeteria?

A No, it isn't. You're not supposed to eat here. You're supposed to buy materials for your class here.

B Is it the bookstore?

A Yes, it is.

B **Share** information with the class.

> You're supposed to be quiet in a library. You're not supposed to use your cell phones, and you're supposed to return books on time.

📖 Scan a chart listing class locations to locate key details; contrast *be supposed to* and *be not supposed to* to show expectations about behavior

REVIEW

1 Listening

Listen. Take notes on the conversation.

🔊 CD1, Track 17

1. Type of certificate	*Automotive Technology*
2. Number of required classes	*eight*
3. Total number of courses	*ten*
4. Time to complete the program	*four semesters*
5. Cost per course	*$60*

Talk with a partner. Check your answers.

2 Grammar

A Write. Complete the story.

A Famous Athlete

Albert Pujols _____*is considered*_____ one of the world's great baseball players. Raised in the
　　　　　　　1. considers / is considered

Dominican Republic, he immigrated to the United States in 1996. He demonstrated his hitting skills

_____*quickly*_____ by batting over .500 in his first season of baseball in high school. By 2001,
　　　2. quick / quickly

he was playing in the major leagues for the St. Louis Cardinals. He played so _____*well*_____
　　　　　　　　　　　　　　　　　　　　　　　　　　　　　　3. good / well

that in 2006 he became the fastest player in history to reach 19 home runs in a season. On June 3, 2017,

playing for the Los Angeles Angels, he became the 9th player to hit at least 600 home runs. In 2007 he

became a citizen of the United States, getting a _____*perfect*_____ score on his citizenship test.
　　　　　　　　　　　　　　　　　　　　4. perfect / perfectly

Pujols _____*is admired*_____ for his support of people with Down syndrome and other disabilities.
　　　5. admires / is admired

A center for adults with Down syndrome, opened in 2009, _____*is named*_____ for Pujols.
　　　　　　　　　　　　　　　　　　　　　　　6. names / is named

B Write. Look at the words that are underlined in the answers. Write the questions.

1. A _Where did Albert Pujols grow up?_

   B Albert Pujols grew up <u>in the Dominican Republic</u>.

2. A _When did he become a U.S. citizen?_

   B He became a citizen of the United States <u>in 2007</u>.

3. A _What is he admired for?_

   B He is admired <u>for his support of people with Down syndrome</u>.

Talk with a partner. Ask and answer the questions.

Teaching objectives
- Review vocabulary and grammar from Units 1 and 2
- Introduce and provide practice with pronunciation of -ed endings on verbs

WARM-UP AND REVIEW

- Before class. Write today's lesson focus on the board.
  Review unit:
  Review vocabulary and grammar from Units 1 and 2
  Pronounce "ed" verb endings

- Begin class. Books closed. Review vocabulary and grammar from Units 1 and 2. Ask Ss:

  Do you think that you have an aptitude for learning languages?
  What are the names of some of the intelligences?
  How do you define success?

- Review the passive voice. Ask a S: *Where is this class held?* Elicit: *This class is held in _____.* Ask another S: *Is a placement test required to take this class?* Elicit: *Yes, a placement test is required to take this class. / No, a placement test is not required to take this class.*

PRESENTATION

- Books open. Direct Ss' attention to Exercise **1**. Read the instructions aloud. Tell Ss that they will hear a conversation between two friends, Faisal and Angela.

- ▶ **CD1, Track 17** Model the task. Play or read the first part of the conversation on the audio (see audio script, page T-177). Pause the audio after Faisal says, *He gave me some information about a certificate program in automotive technology.*

- Direct Ss' attention to number 1 in the chart (*Type of certificate*) and ask: *What is the type of certificate Faisal spoke to his career counselor about?* (Automotive Technology.)

- Have four Ss read the remaining phrases in the chart. Say: *Now listen and fill in the information in the chart.*

- ▶ **CD1, Track 17** Play or read the complete audio. Ss listen and complete the chart. Repeat the audio as needed.

Culture Tip

Automotive technology is an important and changing industry in the United States. It includes many types of certificate programs in areas such as transmission (automatic and manual), brakes, electronics, and much more. Because the average American family owns at least two vehicles, and because there is so much to learn as the automotive industry rapidly changes, many schools offer specialized automotive certificate programs.

COMPREHENSION CHECK

- Read aloud the second part of the instructions for Exercise **1**.

- Ss complete the exercise in pairs. Walk around and help as needed.

PRACTICE

- Direct Ss' attention to Exercise **2A**. Ask: *What is the title of this story?* ("A Famous Athlete")

- Read the instructions aloud for Exercise **2A**.

- Ask a S to read aloud the first sentence in the story and to explain the choice of word needed to complete the sentence. Tell Ss to continue reading the story and filling in the blanks.

- Ss complete the exercise individually. Help as needed.

Teaching Tip

In multilevel classes, some Ss may have little difficulty with this review of grammar. Others may find this review more challenging. Create small groups of mixed ability. Encourage the Ss who are comfortable with these grammar points to help those who are less comfortable.

- Write the numbers *1–6* on the board. Ask Ss to come to the board to write only the answers.

- Read the story aloud using Ss' answers. Correct on the board as needed.

COMPREHENSION CHECK

- Direct Ss' attention to Exercise **2B**. This exercise reviews question formation by asking questions related to the story "A Famous Athlete."

- Read the instructions aloud. Model the exercise. Ask a S to read the answer to number 1. Ask: *What is the question for this answer?* Elicit: *Where did Albert Pujols grow up?*

- Ss complete the exercise individually. Help as needed.

- Check answers with the class. Ask for volunteers to read their questions. Write the correct questions on the board.

- Read aloud the second part of the instructions for Exercise **2B**.

- Ss ask and answer the questions in pairs. Walk around and help as needed.

REVIEW

PRESENTATION

- Write on the board: -ed verb endings. Explain that the regular past tense in English has three different- sounding endings. Write /t/, /d/, and /id/ as column heads in a chart on the board. Pronounce each sound.
- Write several words on the board that have different -ed verb endings (e.g., watched, lived, and wanted) and ask Ss to add additional verbs that end in -ed. Say each word. Have Ss repeat and indicate in which column each verb belongs.
- Direct Ss' attention to Exercise **3A**. Read the instructions aloud.
- ▶ **CD1, Track 18** Play or read the complete audio (see audio script, page T-177).
- Have a S read aloud the second part of the instructions for Exercise **3A**.
- ▶ **CD1, Track 18** Play the audio again. Pause after each phrase to give Ss time to repeat. Play the audio as many times as needed. Focus Ss' attention on the pronunciation of the words in bold in Exercise **3A**.

Teaching Tip

Some Ss may find it difficult to think beyond the spelling of words with final d when working on pronunciation for these exercises. If possible, take extra time with these Ss to review the sounds. Exaggerate the final sounds.

PRACTICE

- Direct Ss' attention to Exercise **3B**. Read the instructions aloud.
- ▶ **CD1, Track 19** Model the task. Play or read the first sentence on the audio (see audio script, page T-178). Ask Ss to tell you the -ed word (located) and in which column the word belongs (/id/).
- Tell Ss to pay attention to the sounds of the verbs with the -ed endings as they listen and repeat. Play or read the audio program, stopping as needed for Ss to repeat the sentences.
- ▶ **CD1, Track 19** Play or read the complete audio again. Ss identify the pronunciation of the -ed endings by marking the appropriate column.
- Read aloud the second part of the instructions for Exercise **3B**.
- Ss complete the exercise in pairs. Listen to Ss' pronunciation. Help Ss pronounce the -ed endings correctly.

APPLICATION

- Direct Ss' attention to Exercise **3C**. Read the instructions aloud.
- Ss complete the exercise in pairs. Walk around and listen to Ss' pronunciation. Write any words on the board that Ss had trouble pronouncing. Point to each word. Say it and ask Ss to repeat.
- Ask Ss to write the words with -ed verb endings on the board in the appropriate columns: /t/, /d/, or /id/. Correct pronunciation and have Ss repeat as needed.
- Focus Ss' attention on Exercise **3D**. Read the instructions aloud.
- Model the exercise. Ask a S to make up a question using administered and write it on the board. Ask another S to answer the question. Correct pronunciation as needed.
- Ss complete the exercise in pairs. Listen to Ss' pronunciation as they ask and answer the questions.

EVALUATION

- Direct Ss' attention to the lesson focus on the board.
- Write on the board:
  Venus Williams is a great athlete.
  Mathematical skills are very important.
- Ask Ss to make up questions using that and a noun clause and the statements on the board. (Do you think that Venus Williams is a great athlete?)
- Write adjectives and adverbs on the board. Ask Ss to give you examples of each (e.g., quick / quickly, skillful / skillfully, good / well).
- Write the following on the board:
  The college gives a placement test to all new students.
  Does the college arrange internships for students?
- Ask Ss to read each sentence and then change the sentences into the present passive voice. (A placement test is given to all new students. Are internships arranged for students?)
- Ask Ss to make sentences about their school's program using the following past participles and the infinitive: encouraged, expected, required, and told. (Students are encouraged to arrive early, etc.)
- Focus Ss' attention on the sentences in Exercise **3A**. Ask Ss to read the sentences aloud, and check that they pronounce the final -ed verb endings correctly.
- Check off each part of the lesson focus as Ss demonstrate an understanding of what they have learned in the lesson.

3 **Pronunciation:** *-ed* verb endings

A **Listen** to the *-ed* verb endings in these sentences.

🔊)) **CD1, Track 18**

/t/

1. He has always **liked** playing number games.

2. She has **worked** as an accountant for ten years.

/d/

3. Emily has **realized** that Brenda has a good brain.

4. Naturalists are **skilled** in working with plants.

/ɪd/

5. The little boy **started** counting when he was two.

6. She is **gifted** in singing and dancing.

Listen again and repeat. Pay attention to the *-ed* verb endings.

B **Listen and repeat.** Then check (✓) the correct pronunciation for each *-ed* verb ending.

🔊)) **CD1, Track 19**

	/t/	/d/	/ɪd/
1. Classes are **located** at various elementary schools.			✓
2. All students are **advised** of the school rules.		✓	
3. An application is **required** for admission.		✓	
4. A math test is **needed** as well.			✓
5. The test is **administered** once a week.		✓	
6. The students are **expected** to pay their fees soon.			✓
7. Lucas hasn't **talked** with a counselor yet.	✓		
8. But he is **finished** with all his tests.	✓		

Talk with a partner. Compare your answers.

C **Talk** with a partner. Practice the conversations. Pay attention to the pronunciation of the *-ed* verb endings: /t/, /d/, or /ɪd/.

1. A Are classes offered on Saturday?

   B Yes, they are offered from 9:00 to 12:00.

2. A What are we expected to bring to class?

   B We are expected to bring a notebook, the textbook, and a pen.

3. A How did she cook?

   B She cooked very well.

4. A How did he paint?

   B He painted skillfully.

D **Write** five past tense questions. Use the following words: *administer, expect, finish, locate, provide, require* and *talk*. Then talk with a partner. Ask and answer your questions.

UNIT 3 FRIENDS AND FAMILY

Lesson A Listening

1 Before you listen

A What do you see?

B What is happening?

UNIT 3

Teaching objective
- Introduce students to the topic
- Find out what students know about the topic
- Preview the unit by talking about the pictures
- Provide practice of key vocabulary
- Provide practice that develops listening skills

WARM-UP AND REVIEW

- Before class. Write today's lesson focus on the board.
  Lesson A:
  Ask about rules at home and at school
  Ask questions indirectly
  Talk about past events and experiences
- Begin class. Books closed. Direct Ss' attention to the lesson focus. Point to the first item: *Ask about rules at home and at school.* Write *rules* on the board. Ask Ss: *What are rules?* Elicit appropriate responses, such as: *Rules are statements that tell what is allowed or not allowed in a certain place or situation.* Ask: *What's an example of a school rule?* List Ss' responses on the board, for example: *Eating in the classroom is against the rules. Ss are not allowed to miss more than three classes per semester.*
- Ask Ss: *What happens if you don't follow rules?* (You will be asked to leave class.)

PRESENTATION

- Books open. Set the scene. Direct Ss' attention to the first picture on page 32. Ask the question from Exercise **1A**: *What do you see?* Elicit and write on the board as much vocabulary about the picture as possible. Explain any unfamiliar words. Continue eliciting words to describe the four remaining pictures.
- Direct Ss' attention to the question in Exercise **1B**: *What is happening?* Read it aloud. Focus on picture 1. Hold up the Student's Book. Point to the first picture. Ask: *What are Lan and Mary doing?* (They're leaving school.)
- Have Ss focus on picture 2. Hold up the Student's Book and point to the second picture. Ask: *What are they doing in this picture?* (They're walking around a shopping mall.)
- Direct Ss' attention to picture 3. Ask Ss to describe what is happening in the picture. (An older woman, probably Lan's mother, received a phone call.)
- Have Ss focus on picture 4. Ask Ss to describe what is happening in the picture. (The woman in picture 3, Lan's mother, is arguing with Lan.)
- Brainstorm and list on the board things that Lan and Mrs. Lee might be saying to each other.

- Have Ss focus on picture 5. As Ss: What is happening in this picture? (Lan probably didn't follow the rules, so her birthday party was cancelled.)

> ### Teaching Tip
> Encourage Ss to be creative. At this point, there is no single correct answer.

> ### Culture Tip
> Explain to Ss that in high schools in the United States, Ss are expected to be present every day that school is in session. In many places it is against the law to miss school, and in some schools Ss cannot return to classes without a note from a parent or a doctor explaining the reason for the absence. Many school systems now have computer phone systems that notify parents when children are not in school. You may wish to compare school attendance rules in the United States with those in your Ss' home countries.

PRACTICE

- Ss in pairs. Have Ss develop their visual literacy skills by working with a partner to create a story from the pictures. One S writes the story as pairs work together.

> ### Teaching Tip
> If you have a multilevel class, this would be a good time to pair a S who feels more confident with speaking skills with a S who feels more comfortable with writing skills. Encourage pairs to be supportive as they work together to create a story.

- Invite a S to begin the story. Write several suggestions or sentence-starters on the board. Then have partners work together to continue the story.
- Ask Ss from several pairs to share their stories with the class.

Expansion activity (student pairs)

- Tell Ss to work in pairs to create conversations. Divide the class into three groups: the first group should work on the conversation between the girls leaving the school, the second group should work on the conversation between the girls at the mall, and the third group should work on the conversation between the mother and her daughter.
- Have several pairs role play their conversations for the class.

LESSON A Listening

PRESENTATION

- Books open. Direct Ss' attention to Exercise **2A**. Tell Ss that they are going to listen to three audio segments, one for each of the pictures on page 32. Ss should listen for the main ideas. Read the instructions aloud.
- ▶ **CD1, Track 20** Play or read the audio (see audio script, page T-178). Ask a S to read the questions in Exercise **2A**. Tell Ss to listen for the answers.
- Elicit answers to the questions, for example: *In the first segment, there's a recorded message from the school for Mrs. Lee. The message from the school states that Lan was absent from her 7th period class.*
- Focus Ss' attention on Exercise **2B**. Read the instructions aloud. Tell Ss to listen and complete the chart based on the information they hear.
- ▶ **CD1, Track 20** Have Ss listen for details about Lan, her absence, and what her mother says. Model the task. Play or read the audio again. Pause it after the person calling from Lan's school in Part 1 says: *Please call the office at 619-555-2300 to explain why your daughter missed class. Thank you.* Call on a S to read the example under Part 1 of the chart (*Lan absent from class*). Tell Ss to listen to the audio and complete the chart based on the information they hear. Play or read the rest of the audio.
- ▶ **CD1, Track 20** Play or read the audio again. Ss listen and check their answers. Repeat as needed.
- Write the chart on the board. Have several Ss come to the board to write their answers.

Learner persistence *(individual work)*
- ▶ **CD1, Track 20** Ss can listen to the audio for Exercises **2A** and **2B** at home for reinforcement and review. They can also listen to the audio for self-directed learning when class attendance is not possible.

PRACTICE

- Focus Ss' attention on Exercise **3A**. Read the instructions aloud. Tell Ss that the story in this exercise is a summary of what happened in the three pictures on page 32.
- Direct Ss' attention to the words or expressions in the word bank. Say each and have Ss repeat. Correct pronunciation as needed. Explain the meaning of any words that are new to Ss.
- Model the exercise. Ask a S to read aloud the first three sentences of the story, including the answer in the example blank. Have Ss fill in the remaining blanks with the words from the word bank.
- Ss complete the exercise individually. Help as needed.

COMPREHENSION CHECK

- ▶ **CD1, Track 21** Play or read the audio (see audio script, page T-178). Ss listen and check their answers. Repeat the audio as needed.
- Write the numbers *1–10* on the board. Have Ss come to the board to write only the answers.
- Ask Ss: *Are the answers correct?* Have Ss make corrections on the board as needed.

Learner persistence *(individual work)*
- ▶ **CD1, Track 21** Ss can listen to the audio for Exercise 3A at home for reinforcement and review. They can also listen to the audio for self-directed learning when class attendance is not possible.

> **Culture Note**
>
> Read the culture note aloud. Ask Ss if they have ever heard of a school calling parents to talk about a problem with a student. Explain that this is common practice in many schools in the United States and that sometimes the school will request that the parents come to school for a meeting to discuss the problem. Ask Ss how parents might respond to such a meeting.

APPLICATION

- Focus Ss' attention on Exercise **3B**. Read the instructions aloud.
- Model the task. Ask a S the question: *Do you think Lan's mother is too strict?* Call on another S to respond, who should support his or her answer with reasons.
- Ss complete the exercise in pairs. Walk around and help as needed.

EVALUATION

- Direct Ss' attention to the lesson focus on the board. Ask individual Ss to look at the pictures on page 32 to tell you the story about Lan. Encourage Ss to make sentences using the words and expressions from the word bank in Exercise **3A**.
- Check off each part of the lesson focus as Ss demonstrate an understanding of what they have learned in the lesson.

More Ventures, Unit 3, Lesson A	
Workbook, 15–30 min.	
Multilevel Worksheets, 30–45 min.	www.cambridge.org/ventures/resources/
Collaborative Worksheets, 30–45 min.	
Student Arcade, time varies	www.cambridge.org/venturesarcade/

UNIT GOALS
Recognize appropriate school behavior   **Compare** parents and children
Identify barriers between generations

2 Listen

A **Listen** and answer the questions.

1. Who are the speakers?

2. What are they talking about?

◀)) CD1, Track 20

B **Listen again.** Take notes.

◀)) CD1, Track 20

Part 1	Part 2	Part 3
Reason for call: *Lan absent from class*	Mother's rules: *can't go anywhere alone*	Reason mother is upset: *Lan broke the rules*
Action mother should take: *call school office*	*can't go on a date without a chaperone until she is 18*	Lan's punishment: *on restriction for next two weekends*

3 After you listen

CULTURE NOTE
When a child gets into trouble at school, the school staff calls the parents to help enforce the school rules.

A **Read.** Complete the story.

argument	broke (the) rules	missed	permitted	strict
bring (someone) up	chaperone	on restriction	raised	trust

Mrs. Lee received a phone message from her daughter's school saying Lan

_____*missed*_____ her 7th period class. Lan left school early to go to the mall with her friend
   1

Mary. At the mall, Lan tells Mary that her mother is too _____*strict*_____. Lan thinks it's
   2

because her mother wants to ___*bring*___ her ___*up*___ the same way she was
   3   3

___*raised*___ in China. That's why Lan needs a ___*chaperone*___ to go out on a date.
   4   5

At home, Lan and her mother have an ___*argument*___. Lan is angry because she's not
   6

___*permitted*___ to go to the mall alone. She thinks her mother doesn't ___*trust*___ her.
   7   8

Mrs. Lee is upset because Lan ___*broke*___ the ___*rules*___. As a punishment, she
   9   9

says Lan is *on restriction* for two weeks.
   10

Listen and check your answers.

◀)) CD1, Track 21

B **Discuss.** Talk with your classmates.

Do you think Lan's mother is too strict? Give reasons for your opinion.

Lesson B Indirect questions

1 Grammar focus: indirect *Wh-* questions

An indirect question is a question inside a statement or another question. Indirect *Wh-*questions begin with a question word (*who, what, when*) and use subject-verb word order (*why she is so strict*). We do not use the auxiliary *do, does* or *did* with indirect questions.

👁 Watch

DIRECT *WH-* QUESTIONS	INDIRECT *WH-* QUESTIONS
Why is she so strict?	I wonder **why she is** so strict.
How is everything at home?	I'd like to know **how everything is** at home.
Where did you **go?**	Can you tell me **where** you **went?**
When did they **leave?**	Do you know **when** they **left?**
What did they **do?**	I don't know **what they did.**

Introductory clauses

I'd like to know . . .   Could you tell me . . . ?   Can you tell me . . . ?
I don't know . . .   I wonder . . .   Do you know . . . ?

CULTURE NOTE
Indirect questions are often more polite than direct questions. Add "please" to make the questions even more polite.

2 Practice

A **Write.** Change the direct questions to indirect *Wh-* questions. Circle the indirect *Wh-* questions.

1. What is the student's name?

   A Do you know (what the student's name is?)

   B Her name is Lan.

2. What class did she miss?

   A Can you please tell me (what class she missed) ?

   B Mr. Latham's 7th period English class.

3. Who did Lan go to the mall with?

   A I wonder (who Lan went to the mall with)

   B She went to the mall with Mary.

4. Why did she break the rules?

   A I would like to know (why she broke the rules).

   B I don't know why. Perhaps she was bored in class.

5. When did she and her friend leave the school?

   A Can you tell me (when she and her friends left the school)

   B They left after 6th period.

6. What did they do at the mall?

   A I want to know (what they did at the mall).

   B They talked and went window-shopping.

7. When did they come home from the mall?

   A Do you know (when they came home from the mall)?

   B I don't know when they came home.

8. What was Lan's punishment?

   A Could you please tell me (what Lan's punishment was)

   B Her mother put her on restriction for two weeks.

Listen and check your answers. Then practice with a partner.

🔊 CD1, Track 22

WARM-UP AND REVIEW

● Before class: Write the lesson focus on the board.
Lesson B:
Indirect "Wh-" questions?

● Begin class. Books open. Direct Ss' attention to the pictures on page 32. Ask questions about Lan: *What did Lan and her friend do at one o'clock?* (They left school.) *Where did they go?* (to the mall.) *Why is Lan's mother upset?* (because her daughter broke the rules.) *How does Lan's mother punish her?* (Lan is on restriction for the next two weeks.)

PRESENTATION

Focus on meaning / personalize

● Books closed. Direct Ss' attention to the lesson focus on the board. Read it aloud. Say to the class: *Listen to these two questions: What time is it? Can you tell me what time it is?* Repeat the two questions and ask: *What is different between these two questions?* (One is nicer.) *Which one sounded more polite?* (the second question.) *What made it more polite?* (Answers may vary. Point out that by asking *Can you tell me*, you are asking the listener for permission.)

● Say: *Listen to two more questions. Tell me which one sounds more polite: I would like to know what time you came home last night. What time did you come home last night?* (the first one.) Say: *By adding words before a direct question, we soften the question and make it more polite.*

Focus on form

● Use the animated grammar presentation in one or more of the following ways:

  ● Preview it before class

  ● Show in class

  ● Encourage Ss to watch outside of class.

● Books open. Direct Ss' attention to the top two charts in Exercise **1**. Read aloud the first direct and indirect question in each chart. Ask Ss to repeat. Ask: *How is the word order in the indirect Wh- question different from the word order in the direct Wh- question?* (The subject is before the verb instead of after the verb.)

● Read and have Ss repeat the other direct and indirect questions in the chart. Elicit the changes in word order (*is everything* becomes *everything is*; *did you go* becomes *you went*; *did they leave* becomes *they left*).

● Point out that with the *be* verb, only the word order changes, whereas with other verbs, the auxiliary (*do, does, did, will*) disappears, and the verb form also changes, for example: *Where did you go? Can you tell me where you went?*

● Read aloud the introductory clauses. Ask Ss to repeat. Ask: *When these introductory clauses come before questions, is the word order in the dependent clause statement word order or question word order?* (statement word order.)

● Direct Ss' attention to the *Culture note.* Have a S volunteer to read the culture note aloud. Ask: *What does adding "please" do to an indirect question?* (makes it even more polite.)

PRACTICE

● Focus Ss' attention on Exercise **2A**. Read the instructions aloud.

● Model the task. Ask two Ss to read aloud the first conversation. Make sure that Ss understand the exercise.

● Ss complete the exercise individually. Walk around and help as needed.

COMPREHENSION CHECK

● Focus Ss' attention on the second part of the instructions for Exercise **2A**, and read it aloud.

▶ *CD1, Track 22* Play or read the audio (see audio script, page T-178). Ss listen and check their answers. Repeat the audio as needed.

● Have Ss practice the conversation in pairs. Correct pronunciation as needed.

● Write the numbers *1–8* on the board. Ask several Ss to come to the board to write the correct sentences. Make corrections on the board as needed.

● Point out the use of *please* in questions 2 and 8.

Learner persistence (individual work)

▶ *CD1, Track 22* Ss can listen to the audio for Exercise **2A** at home for reinforcement and review. They can also listen to the audio for self-directed learning when class attendance is not possible.

LESSON B Indirect questions

PRESENTATION

- Direct Ss' attention to the school report card in Exercise **2B**. Ask Ss what information is on the card. (The semester, the name of the student, the advisor's name, the subject, the grade, and the teacher.)
- Ask a S to read the school subjects. Define or explain any unfamiliar subjects.

Teaching Tip

Ss may be unfamiliar with report cards and with grading systems in the United States. Tell Ss that grading systems vary according to schools and states. Some high schools, for example, don't use letters but number equivalents from 1 to 100. (An A might equal 90% to 100%.) Many high schools include short evaluations along with the grades. (If you have a sample report card, bring it to class.) Ask Ss about grading systems in their countries. You might also want to talk about grades and evaluations for noncredit adult programs.

PRACTICE

- Read the instructions aloud for Exercise **2B**.
- Model the task. Ask two Ss to read the example question and answer to the class.
- Ss complete the exercise with a partner. Walk around and help as needed.
- Call on pairs to share the indirect questions they asked each other.
- Read aloud the instructions for the second part of Exercise **2B**. Refer Ss to the introductory clauses in the chart on page 34 of the Student's Book.
- Call on a S to read the example question.
- Ss complete the exercise individually. Walk around and help as needed.

COMPREHENSION CHECK

- Ask several Ss to come to the board to write their indirect questions.
- Have other Ss read the questions aloud. Ask Ss if the indirect questions are written correctly.

APPLICATION

- Direct Ss' attention to Exercise **3A**. Read the instructions aloud.
- Model the task. Invite two Ss to read the example conversation between the parent and the teenager.

- Call on Ss to read Situations 1 and 2 to the class.
- Ask Ss to think of some direct questions they could ask for Situation 1, such as: *Why are you so late? Where were you? Write Ss'* questions on the board.
- Have Ss think of some indirect questions they could ask for Situation 1, such as: *Can you tell me why you are so late? I'd like to know where you were.* Write Ss' suggestions on the board.
- Ss work in pairs to complete the exercise. Walk around and help as needed.
- Direct Ss' attention to Exercise **3B**. Read the instructions aloud.
- Call on pairs to perform their role play for the class.

Expansion activity (student pairs)

- Have Ss role-play conversations outside of the school context. Suggest that they role-play the following conversations using indirect questions with *who, what, where, when, why,* and *how.*

  Situation 1
  A driver gets lost while trying to find the mall.
  The driver stops at a gas station and asks the gas station attendant for detailed directions.

  Situation 2
  A customer in a bookstore can't find the book that he or she wants.
  The customer asks the salesperson for help.

- Ss work in pairs to complete the activity. Walk around and help as needed.
- Call on pairs to perform their role play for the class.

EVALUATION

- Direct Ss' attention to the lesson focus on the board.
- Write the following questions on the board: *Where were you last night? Why didn't you go to class?* Ask Ss if these are direct or indirect *Wh-* questions (direct). Have three Ss come to the board to write the indirect form for each of the questions.
- Check off the lesson focus as Ss demonstrate an understanding of what they have learned in the lesson.

More Ventures, Unit 3, Lesson B	
Workbook, 15–30 min.	
Multilevel Worksheets, 30–45 min.	www.cambridge.org/ ventures/resources
Collaborative Worksheets, 30–45 min.	
Student Arcade, time varies	www.cambridge.org/ venturesarcade/

B **Talk** with a partner about Lan's report card. Ask indirect questions.

   A Do you know what grade Lan got in World History?

   B She got a B.

School Report Card – First Semester

Student's name: **Lan Suzi Lee**　　　　　　Advisor: **Mr. Green**

Subject	Grade	Teacher
World History	B	Lopez
Advanced English	A	Latham
Algebra	B+	Smith
P.E.	C	Chin
Chemistry	C	Hogan
Ceramics	A	Azari

Write indirect questions about Lan's report card.

Do you know what grade Lan got in World History?

Answers will vary.

❸ Communicate

A **Work** with a partner. Role-play conversations between a parent and a teenager. Use indirect questions with *who*, *what*, *where*, *when*, and *why*.

Parent	I'd like to know why you're late.
Teenager	I stayed after class to talk to my math teacher.
Parent	OK. But next time, call me if you're going to be late. All right?

Situation 1: The teenager is two hours late coming home from school.
The parent is worried.

Situation 2: The teenager's teacher called to say the teenager was cheating on a test.
The parent is shocked.

Situation 3: The teenager's report card arrived in the mail. He or she got one A, two Bs, two Cs, and a D. Normally, the teenager gets all As and Bs. The parent is angry.

Situation 4: The parent received a $70 ticket in the mail for parking in a "no parking" area.
The teenager got the ticket when she parked her parent's car, but she forgot to tell her parents about it. The parent is angry.

Situation 5: Make up your own conversation between a parent and a teenager.

B **Perform** your role play for the class.

Lesson C Indirect questions

1 Grammar focus: indirect *Yes / No* questions

Watch

An indirect *Yes / No* question is a question inside a statement or another question. Indirect *Yes / No* questions begin with *if* or *whether* and use subject-verb word order (*if you finished your homework.*) *If* is more common and *whether* is more formal. We do not use the auxiliary *do, does* or *did* with indirect questions.

DIRECT YES / NO QUESTIONS	INDIRECT YES / NO QUESTIONS
Did you finish your homework?	I'd like to know **if you finished** your homework.
Is her mother strict?	I wonder **if her mother is** strict.
Will they go to college?	Could you tell me **if they will go** to college?

2 Practice

A Write. Complete the conversation. Use indirect *Yes / No* questions with *if*.

Son   Can I go to a party at Joe's house?

Father   Maybe. First I need to know *if you finished your homework* .
        1. Did you finish your homework?

Son   Yes, I finished it an hour ago.

Father   Do you know *if the party starts at 5:00 or 6:00*
        2. Does the party start at 5:00 or 6:00?

Son   It starts at 6:00.

Father   OK. Can you tell me *if his parents will be home* ?
        3. Will his parents be home?

Son   Yes, his parents will be there.

Father   That's good. I wonder *if you need to take a birthday gift*
        4. Do you need to take a birthday gift?

Son   No, I don't. It's not a birthday party.

Father   I wonder *if they're going to serve dinner* .
        5. Are they going to serve dinner?

Son   Yes. They're going to grill chicken for us.

Father   What about your friend John?

        Do you know *if he's invited to the party* ?
        6. Is he invited to the party?

Son   Yes, I think so.

Father   Do you know *if John's parents can bring you home*
        7. Can John's parents bring you home?

Son   I'll ask them.

Father   I am wondering *if you can text us when you are on your* way home
        8. Can you text us when you are on the way home?

Son   Sure. I'll do that.

Listen and check your answers. Then practice with a partner.

CD1, Track 23

WARM-UP AND REVIEW

• Before class: Write the lesson focus on the board.
Lesson C:
Indirect Yes / No questions

• Begin class. Books closed. Review indirect *Wh-* questions. Write questions such as the following on the board: *What did she do yesterday? Can you tell me what she did yesterday?* Ask: *What is the difference between these two questions?* (The first is direct; the second is indirect.)

• Underline *Can you tell me* . . . Ask: *What other introductory clauses can go before indirect questions?* Write the responses on the board, for example: *Do you know, I wonder, I'd like to know.* Ask Ss how to change a question from direct to indirect. (The word order changes to statement word order. The word *do* disappears.)

PRESENTATION

Focus on meaning / personalize

• Books closed. Direct Ss' attention to the lesson focus on the board. Read it aloud.

Say: *Listen to these two questions:* 1. *Are you single?* 2. *Can you please tell me if you are single? Do these questions mean the same?* (Yes.) *Which question is softer and more polite?* (the second one.) Write the following two questions on the board: 1. *Can you please tell me if you are single?* 2. *Can you please tell me whether you are single?* Ask: *How are these sentences different?* (One has *if*, and one has *whether*.) Explain that indirect questions with *if* and *whether* have the same meaning.

• Elicit some *Yes / No* questions, for example: *Are you married? Do you have children?* Write the questions on the board. Point out that these are all direct *Yes / No* questions. Explain that we can also ask indirect *Yes / No* questions by using the same introductory clauses we use with indirect *Wh-* questions.

• Elicit the introductory clauses in Lesson *B*, Exercise **1** (*I'd like to know, Can you tell me, Do you know, I wonder*). Say an indirect question for each of the *Yes / No* questions on the board, for example: *I wonder if you are married? I'd like to know if you have children?*

Focus on form

• Use the animated grammar presentation in one or more of the following ways:
  • Preview it before class
  • Show in class
  • Encourage Ss to watch outside of class.

• Books open. Direct Ss' attention to the Direct *Yes / No* questions chart in Exercise **1**. Ask a S to read the sentences. Then have another S read the sentences under Indirect *Yes / No* questions.

PRACTICE

• Direct Ss' attention to Exercise **2A**. Read the instructions aloud.

• Model the task. Ask two Ss to read the first two lines of the conversation between a father and son.

• Ss complete the exercise individually. Walk around and help as needed.

COMPREHENSION CHECK

• Read aloud the second part of the instructions for Exercise **2A**.

▶ **CD1, Track 23** Play or read the audio (see audio script, page T-178). Ss listen and check their answers.

• Write the numbers *1–8* on the board. Ask individual Ss to come to the board to write their answers. Make corrections on the board as needed.

Option Have Ss read aloud the answers to Exercise **2A** using *whether* instead of *if*.

Learner persistence (individual work)

▶ **CD1, Track 23** Ss can listen to the audio for Exercise **2A** at home for reinforcement and review. Using the QR code, they can also listen to the audio for self-directed learning when class attendance is not possible.

LESSON C Indirect questions

PRESENTATION

- Books closed. Ask Ss about their relationships with their parents. Ask if they got along well with their parents when they were young. Ask whether they argued often, sometimes, or rarely.

PRACTICE

- Books open. Direct Ss to Exercise **2B**. Read the instructions aloud. Direct Ss' attention to the pictures. Ask: *What do you see?* Elicit appropriate responses, such as: *The girl's parents are meeting her new friend for the first time. They want to learn more about her friend.* They're asking her questions.
- Model the task. Ask two Ss to read the sentences. Ask other Ss to read aloud the bulleted points. Explain vocabulary as needed.

Teaching Tip

Review introductory clauses from the previous lesson, such as:
I'd like to know . . . Tell me . . .
I wonder . . .   Do you know . . . ?
Remind Ss that they can use these introductory clauses to make indirect *Yes / No* questions.

- Ss complete the exercise in pairs. Walk around and help as needed.
- Direct Ss' attention to the second part of the instructions for Exercise **2B**, and read it aloud. Call on a S to read the example indirect question to the class.
- Ss complete the exercise individually. Walk around and help as needed.
- Ask several Ss to come to the board to write their indirect questions. Ask other Ss to read aloud each of the sentences on the board. Ask: *Is this sentence correct?* Work with the class to correct the indirect questions as needed.

Useful Language

Read the tip box aloud. Remind Ss that in indirect *Yes / No* questions, *if* and *whether* share the same meaning, so either one can be used. Ask: *What is the purpose of using "if" or "whether"?* (to join the main clause with the dependent clause.)

Expansion activity (student pairs)

- Tell Ss to imagine that they are going to have a conversation with their teenage son or daughter's new friend. Have Ss use the questions they wrote in Exercise **2B** and any other indirect questions they think of to create a conversation between a parent and the new friend.

- Ss work together in pairs. One S plays the parent, and the other S plays the new friend.
- Walk around and help as needed.
- Ask several pairs to act out their conversations for the rest of the class.

APPLICATION

- Direct Ss' attention to Exercise **3A**. Read the instructions aloud. Call on a S to read the items listed.
- Have one S read the first bulleted item. Ask three Ss to read the example conversation.
- Ss complete the exercise in small groups. Walk around and help as needed.
- Direct Ss' attention to Exercise **3B**. Read the instructions aloud.
- Have volunteers share information about their classmates with the rest of the class.

EVALUATION

- Direct Ss' attention to the lesson focus on the board. Write the following *Yes / No* questions on the board: *Do you have plans this weekend? Will you be home late tonight?*
- Ask a S to read the questions aloud. Then ask Ss to write the same questions as indirect *Yes / No* questions. (*I'd like to know if you have plans this weekend. Can you tell me if you will be home late tonight?*, etc.)
- Check off the lesson focus as Ss demonstrate an understanding of what they have learned in the lesson.

More Ventures, Unit 3, Lesson C	
Workbook, 15–30 min.	
Multilevel Worksheets, 30–45 min.	www.cambridge.org/ ventures/resources/
Collaborative Worksheets, 30–45 min.	
Student Arcade, time varies	www.cambridge.org/ venturesarcade/

B **Talk** with a partner. Imagine you are a parent. Read the information you want to ask your daughter about her new friend from school. Make indirect questions using *if* or *whether*. Use a variety of introductory clauses.

Can you tell me if she's a good student?

I'd like to know whether she lives at home.

- is a good student
- has a job
- has nice friends
- has a good relationship with her parents

- lives alone or at home
- is polite
- drives carefully
- has brothers or sisters

USEFUL LANGUAGE
In indirect *Yes / No* questions, *whether* = *if*.

Write the parents' indirect questions.

Can you tell me if she's a good student?
Answers will vary.

3 Communicate

A **Work** in a small group. Ask and answer questions about your lives when you were teenagers. Use indirect *Yes / No* questions. Discuss the items listed below.

- relationship with parents
- grades in school
- school activities
- things you were required to do at home
- things you were permitted to do
- things you weren't permitted to do

   A I'd like to know if you got along well with your parents.

   B Yes, I did. But sometimes I argued with them.

   C I argued with my parents a lot.

B **Share** information about your classmates.

Elena sometimes argued with her parents.
Manny argued with his parents a lot.

Lesson D Reading

1 Before you read

Talk with your classmates. Answer the questions.

1. How many generations of your family are living in the United States? Which generation are you?

2. What are some of the differences between you and the other generations in your family?

3. Look at the reading tip. Look up the meaning of *barrier*, and predict what the story will be about.

> Pay attention to words that repeat in a reading. They often give you an idea of what the reading is about.

2 Read

Read the magazine article. Listen and read again.

)) **CD1, Track** 24

BARRIERS between GENERATIONS

In immigrant families, language differences and work schedules often create barriers to communication between the generations. Dolores Suarez, 42, and her son Diego, 16, face both kinds of barriers every day. Dolores is an immigrant from Mexico who works seven days a week as a housekeeper in a big hotel. She doesn't use much English in her job, and she has never had time to study it. Consequently, her English is limited. Her son, on the other hand, was raised in the United States. He understands Spanish, but he prefers to speak English. When his friends come over to visit, they speak only English. "They talk so fast, I can't understand what they are saying," says Dolores. To make the situation more complicated, Diego and Dolores live with Dolores's father, who speaks Nahuatl, a native language spoken in Mexico. Diego can't understand anything his grandfather says.

Dolores's work schedule is the second barrier to communication with Diego. Because she rarely has a day off, Dolores isn't able to spend much time with him. She doesn't have time to help him with his homework or attend parent-teacher conferences at his school. In 1995, when Dolores immigrated to the United States, her goal was to bring up her son with enough money to avoid the hardships her family suffered in Mexico. Her hard work has permitted Diego to have a comfortable life and a good education. But she has paid a price for this success. "Sometimes I feel like I don't know my own son," she says.

Teaching objectives

- Introduce a magazine article about barriers between generations
- Provide practice using new topic related vocabulary
- Provide practice locating words that repeat in a reading
- Provide practice identifying word families

WARM-UP AND REVIEW

- Before class. Write today's lesson focus on the board.
  Lesson D:
  Read and understand "Barriers Between Generations"
  Practice new vocabulary related to word families
- Begin class. Books closed. Direct Ss' attention to the title of the reading in the lesson focus.
- Write *generations* on the board. Ask Ss: *What is a generation?* Elicit responses, such as: *All the people of about the same age within a particular family or society.*
- Write *barriers* on the board. Ask: *What do you think "barriers" are?* Remind Ss of the word *obstacle* they learned in Unit 2. Say: *"Barrier" is a synonym of "obstacle."*

PRESENTATION

- Books open. Direct Ss' attention to Exercise **1**. Read the instructions aloud.
- Direct Ss' attention to the three questions in Exercise **1**. Ask three Ss to read them aloud.
- Ss in small groups. Have Ss discuss the questions together. Call on a S from each group to share some of the information their group discussed.

Read the tip box aloud. Write *words that repeat* on the board. Tell Ss that words that repeat can be an aid to reading comprehension. Point out that repeating words may include words in the title as well.

- Guide Ss to scan the article for words that repeat. Point out that *barriers* repeats in the title, in the first and second sentences of the first paragraph, and in the first sentence of the second paragraph.
- Ask Ss to tell you what other repeating words they found (*immigrant, communication, English*, etc.). Write the words on the board.

PRACTICE

- Read the instructions aloud for Exercise **2**. Ask Ss to read the magazine article silently before listening to the audio program.

▶ **CD1, Track 24** Play or read the audio, and ask Ss to read along (see audio script, page T-178). Repeat the audio as needed.

- While Ss are listening and reading the article, ask them to write any words they don't know in their notebooks. When the audio is finished, have Ss write the new vocabulary words on the board.
- Point to each word on the board. Say it and ask Ss to repeat. Give a brief explanation of each word, or ask Ss who are familiar with the word to explain it. Allow Ss to look up new words in their dictionaries.
- Encourage Ss to guess the meaning of the unfamiliar words from the context clues in the article. For example, if a S writes *hardships*, show how the S can figure out the meaning of the word from context clues in the article. Read this sentence aloud: *In 1995, when Dolores immigrated to the United States, her goal was to bring up her son with enough money to avoid the **hardships** her family suffered in Mexico.* Ask Ss to think about the meaning of *hardships* based on the surrounding words, such as *suffered*, and information in the sentence. Tell Ss that *hardships*, such as the lack of money, cause people to suffer.

Learner persistence (individual work)

▶ **CD1, Track 24** Ss can listen to the audio for Exercise **2** at home for reinforcement and review. They can also listen to the audio for self-directed learning when class attendance is not possible.

Expansion activity (whole group)

- Books closed. Point to the new vocabulary words from Exercise **2** that you elicited from Ss and wrote on the board. Say each word and have Ss repeat.
- Ask Ss to summarize the article in Exercise **2**, using the new vocabulary words on the board as a guide to citing only the most important points.
- Ask as many Ss as possible to say at least one sentence about the article. Listen closely to monitor how well Ss have comprehended the reading.

LESSON D Reading

COMPREHENSION CHECK

- Read the instructions aloud for Exercise **3A**.

- Ask individual Ss to read the questions aloud, one at a time. Make sure that Ss understand all the questions.

- Ss complete the exercise individually. Instruct Ss to write their answers on a separate piece of paper. Ss should answer in complete sentences. Walk around and help as needed.

- Ss in pairs. Ask Ss to compare answers with their partner.

- Discuss the answers with the class. Ask Ss to say where in the reading they found each of the answers.

PRACTICE

- **Materials needed** A dictionary for each S.

- Direct Ss' attention to Exercise **3B**. Have a volunteer read the instructions for number 1.

- Ss complete the task individually.

- Direct Ss to number 2 of Exercise **3B**, and read it aloud.

- Model the task. Find *immigrant* in the dictionary and show Ss how to find the part of speech of the word. (The word is a noun and an adjective.)

- Ss complete the task individually. Walk around and help as needed.

- Write the chart in number 2 on the board. Call on Ss to fill in the missing words in the word families and write these words on the board. Say each word and have Ss repeat.

- Ask Ss if they notice patterns in certain word-form endings (e.g., noun endings with *-tion*, verb endings with *-ate*, adjective endings with *-ive*, *-ful*, or *-al*).

- Call on a S to read aloud the three categories in the chart. Have another S read the examples in the top row. Point out that most words will change depending on their part of speech, but in this case, *immigrant* is the same in its noun and adjectival form. Ask Ss: *If "immigrant" looks the same when it is a noun and an adjective, how can you tell what part of speech it is?* Elicit appropriate responses, such as: *You have to look at the word in a sentence to figure out the part of speech.*

- Direct Ss' attention to number 3 in Exercise **3B**. Ask a S to read the instructions aloud.

- Ss complete the exercise individually by filling in the correct form of the word from the chart in number 2 of Exercise **3B**. Walk around and help as needed.

- Ask individual Ss to read their answers aloud. As they do, point to the chart on the board to indicate which word form the S used. Have other Ss make corrections on the board as needed.

APPLICATION

- Direct Ss' attention to Exercise **3C**, and read the instructions aloud.

- Ask a S to read the questions in Exercise **3C** to the class.

- Ss complete the exercise in pairs. Walk around and help as needed.

- Ask several pairs to ask and answer the questions for the rest of the class.

Expansion activity (individual work)

- Refer Ss to the questions in Exercise **3C**. Ask them to choose one of the questions and write a paragraph based on it. Remind them to start with a topic sentence and to use facts, examples, reasons, and other details to support their topic sentence and ideas.

Expansion activity

- Refer Ss to "Communication Tips for Immigrant Parents and Teens," another reading on the same topic on pages 142–144.

- Have Ss complete the activity either in class or outside of class.

- Provide feedback to Ss such as through whole-class discussion, partners comparing their worksheets, or T reviewing each S's worksheets.

EVALUATION

- Direct Ss' attention to the lesson focus on the board.

- Books closed. Ask individual Ss to summarize the article, "Barriers Between Generations."

- Write on the board several of the words from the chart in number 2 of Exercise **3B**. Ask Ss to identify whether each word is a noun, verb, adjective, or noun and adjective.

- Check off each part of the lesson focus as Ss demonstrate an understanding of what they have learned in the lesson.

More Ventures, Unit 3, Lesson D	
Workbook, 15–30 min.	
Multilevel Worksheets, 30–45 min. Collaborative Worksheets, 30–45 min.	www.cambridge.org/ventures/resources/
Student Arcade, time varies	www.cambridge.org/venturesarcade/

3 After you read

A **Check** your understanding.

1. What is the main idea of this article?
   1. Language is often a barrier between immigrant generations.
2. What are the two barriers to communication between Dolores and her son?
   2. The two barriers are language and Dolores's work schedule.
3. Why is Dolores's English limited?
   3. Dolores's English is limited because she doesn't use it in her job, and she never had time to study it.
4. According to the author, why does Diego prefer to speak English instead of Spanish?
   4. Diego's friends speak only in English.
5. Why can't Diego communicate with his grandfather?
   5. Diego's grandfather speaks a native language spoken in Mexico, and Diego speaks English.
6. What was Dolores's goal when she came to the United States?
   6. Her goal was to bring up her son with enough money to avoid the hardships that she had growing up.
7. Explain the expression *paid a price* as it is used in paragraph 2.
   7. Paid the price means that Dolores had to give up something in return for giving her son a better life.

B **Build** your vocabulary.

1. In the reading passage, underline the words from the chart.

2. Use a dictionary. Fill in the chart with the missing word forms.

Noun	Verb	Adjective
immigrant	*immigrate*	*immigrant*
differences	*differ*	*different*
creation	create	creative
communication	*communicate*	*communicative*
education	*educate*	*educated*
success	*succeed*	*successful*

3. Complete the sentences. Write the correct form of the word from Exercise B2.

   a. My family decided to ___*immigrate*___ to the United States because there was a war in my country.

   b. Parents and teenagers almost always ___*differ*___ in the kind of music they prefer.

   c. Shosha paints beautiful and unusual oil paintings. She's very ___*creative*___.

   d. Debra's son isn't very ___*communicative*___. It's hard to know what he's thinking.

   e. It's a parent's responsibility to ___*educate*___ children about right and wrong behavior.

   f. You need two things to be ___*successful*___ in life: motivation and luck.

C **Talk** with a partner.

1. What are some ways that you and your parents are different?

2. How can people communicate if they don't speak the same language?

3. Is it necessary to go to school to be an educated person? Explain your answer.

For college and career readiness practice, see pages 142–144.

Lesson E Writing

1 Before you write

A Talk with a partner. What are some differences between you and your parents or you and your children? Write your information on the charts. *Answers will vary.*

Me	My parents	Me	My children
like salads and sandwiches	like lamb and rice	play cards	play video games

B Read the paragraph.

Transitions like *for example* and *on the other hand* show the relationship between sentences or ideas in a paragraph. Underline the transition words in the paragraph that separate the different eating habits.

www.myblog.com

Different Eating Habits

One difference between my parents and me is that we don't have the same eating habits. My family is Iranian, but I was brought up in the United States. Since most of my friends are American, I enjoy eating "American style." For example, I like to eat salads and sandwiches instead of meat and rice. Because of my job, I don't have time to cook, so I like fast food. I also love to eat in restaurants. On the other hand, my parents still eat like they did back home. They eat rice with every meal, and they eat a lot of lamb and vegetables. They don't like to eat in restaurants because my father thinks my mother is the best cook in the world. Actually, I agree with him. I still love my mother's cooking even though our eating habits are different.

Teaching objectives
- Prepare students for writing an expository paragraph about differences between them and their parents or them and their children
- Provide practice identifying transitions in a paragraph

WARM-UP AND REVIEW

- Before class. Write today's lesson focus on the board.
  Lesson E:
  Write a paragraph about differences between you and your parents or you and your children
  Use transitions to show the relationship among sentences and ideas
- Begin class. Books closed. Review vocabulary from the unit. Write the words *Barriers between generations* on the board. Ask Ss to give some examples of these barriers. Elicit appropriate responses, such as: *differences in language, schedules, or tastes.*

PRESENTATION

- Books open. Direct Ss' attention to Exercise **1A** and read the instructions aloud.
- Ask two Ss to read the column headings and the examples in the charts. Tell Ss that if they want, they can fill in both charts and then decide later which one they will use for their writing.

Teaching Tip

It is important to be sensitive to the fact that some Ss may not have parents and may have been raised by guardians and/or other family members.

- Ask Ss to discuss the information with a partner. Then have Ss work individually to complete the chart.
- Have volunteers share some of the differences between themselves and their parents or between themselves and their children.

PRACTICE

- Direct Ss' attention to Exercise **1B** and read the instructions aloud. Tell Ss that they are going to read about a man who has eating habits that are different from those of his parents.

- Focus Ss' attention on the photographs. Ask Ss what type of meal they prefer – fast food or home-cooked.
- Have Ss read the paragraph silently. Tell them to underline any unfamiliar words.
- Ask Ss to write any new words on the board. Have other Ss explain the words if they know them, or encourage Ss to try to guess the meaning of the words from context.

Read the tip box aloud. Tell Ss that transitions (or transitional words and phrases) are good for both the writer *and* the reader because they make the relationships among sentences and ideas clear. Ask Ss if they know other transitional words or phrases in English. Elicit responses, such as: *also, finally, in addition, in contrast.*

Expansion activity (student pairs)

- Write a chart on the board similar to the one on page 40 in the Student's Book but with the headings *My parents and my grandparents* and *My children and my grandchildren.*
- Tell Ss that they should choose the situation that is most appropriate for them. Encourage Ss to work independently to make a list of differences between their parents and their grandparents or between their children and their grandchildren.
- Model the activity. Ask: *What are some differences between your parents and your grandparents?* Elicit appropriate responses, such as: *My parents travel; my grandparents never left their native country.*
- Ss work individually at first. Tell Ss to write down their ideas.
- Ss then work in pairs. Have Ss take turns asking and answering questions about the information in their charts.
- If both Ss feel comfortable, have partners share with the class the information they learned in their discussions.

LESSON E Writing

PRACTICE

- Direct Ss' attention to Exercise **1C**. Read the instructions aloud.

- Ask a S to read the sample topic sentence to the class.

- Ask another S to read aloud Part A of the informal outline. Make sure that Ss understand that the outline is based on the model paragraph on the previous page.

- Direct Ss' attention to Part B of the outline. Explain to Ss that they are using the model paragraphs to compare and contrast the two points of view from the paragraph on page 40. Ss work individually to complete this part. Walk around and help as needed.

- Have Ss share the examples they wrote with the class. Write them on the board.

- Direct Ss' attention to Exercise **1D**. Read the instructions aloud. Suggest topics such as taste in music or daily schedules.

- Write the skeleton of an outline on the board:

  Topic Sentence:

  A (Me):
     1. Example:
     2. Example:
     3. Example:
  Transition: On the other hand

  B (My parents / my children)
     1. Example:
     2. Example:
     3. Example:

- Ss work independently to complete their outline before writing.

Teaching Tip

Before Ss begin to write, encourage them to discuss the topic with a partner or a small group. Such prewriting discussions will help Ss focus their ideas for writing and may give them additional ideas they may not have considered.

APPLICATION

- Focus Ss' attention on Exercise **2**. Read the instructions aloud.

- Guide Ss to see that they will be writing a contrast paragraph in which they will be showing the differences between two items – here, two groups of people.

- Ss complete the task individually. Walk around and help as needed.

Learner persistence (individual work)

- If you have any Ss who have difficulty writing, sit with them and help them as the other Ss are writing. Refer to the outline from Exercise **1D** to show Ss how to use it as a guide for their writing.

COMPREHENSION CHECK

- Direct Ss' attention to Exercise **3A**. Read the instructions aloud.

- This exercise asks Ss to develop skills to revise and edit their own writing.

- Ss check their own paragraphs against the writing checklist. Walk around and help as needed. If any Ss checked *No* for one or more of the checklist items, ask them to revise and edit their paragraphs to include the missing information.

EVALUATION

- Focus Ss' attention on Exercise **3B**. Read the instructions aloud. This exercise enables Ss to work together to edit their writing. Reading aloud enables the writer to review his or her own writing and to understand the need to write clearly for an audience.

- Ss complete the exercise in pairs. Tell Ss to take turns reading their paragraphs to each other. Walk around and help as needed.

- Listen to Ss as they ask their partner a question about the paragraph and tell their partner one thing they learned from it.

- Ask several Ss to read their paragraphs to the class. Have other Ss ask questions and mention something they learned from the paragraph.

- Have Ss tell you examples of transitions they used or heard.

- Direct Ss' attention to the lesson focus on the board.

- Check off each part of the lesson focus as Ss demonstrate an understanding of what they have learned in the lesson.

More Ventures, Unit 3, Lesson E	
Workbook, 15–30 min.	
Multilevel Worksheets, 30–45 min.	www.cambridge.org/ventures/ resources/
Collaborative Worksheets, 30–45 min.	

C **Work** with a partner. Complete the outline of the model paragraph.

Topic sentence: *One difference between my parents and me is that we don't have the same eating habits.*

1 Me: *I enjoy eating "American style."*

    a. Example: *I like to eat salads and sandwiches.*

    b. Example: *I don't eat a lot of meat and rice.*

    c. Example: *I like fast food.*

Transition: *On the other hand*   *Answers will vary.*

2 My parents: _____

    a. Example: _____

    b. Example: _____

    c. Example: _____

D **Plan** a paragraph about a difference between you and your parents or you and your children. Include at least three examples to support your main idea. Make an outline. Use your own paper.

Answers will vary.

2 Write

Write a paragraph about a difference between you and your parents or you and your children. Include a topic sentence that identifies the difference. Give examples to support the main idea, and use a transition between the two parts of your paragraph. Use the paragraph in Exercise 1B and the outlines in Exercises 1C and 1D to help you.

3 After you write

A **Check** your writing.

	Yes	No
1. My topic sentence states the difference between my parents and me or my children and me.	☐	☐
2. I gave examples to support the main idea.	☐	☐
3. I used a transition between the two parts of my paragraph.	☐	☐

B **Share** your writing with a partner.

1. Take turns. Read your paragraph to a partner.

2. Comment on your partner's paragraph. Ask your partner a question about the paragraph. Tell your partner one thing you learned.

Lesson F Another view

1 Life-skills reading

U.S. Census Bureau				
2015 American Community Survey – 1 year estimates | Total number of households: 118,208,250				
Subject	Married couple family households	Female householder, no spouse present	Male householder, no spouse present	Non-family household
Total number of households	56,715,795 48%	15,083,980 13%	5,730,981 5%	40,677,494 34%
Average family size	3.26	3.33	3.10	X
Households with one or more children under 18	42.1%	63.9%	56.1%	.9%
Households with one or more people 60+ years old	38.3%	27.2 %	27.8%	43.1%

source: U.S. Census Bureau - Households and Families

A **Read** the questions. Look at the survey results. Fill in the answer.

1. Which of the four types of households is the least common?

   (A) married couple households

   (B) female householder, no spouse

   (C) male householder, no spouse

   (D) a non-family household

2. In a 2010 study, the percent of married couple households with one or more people 60+ years old was 34.1%. Compare this to the 2015 study. What can you conclude?

   (A) The percent of older people in married couple households is growing.

   (B) Married couples are staying married longer.

   (C) The percent of older people in married couple households is decreasing.

   (D) The United States population is getting younger.

3. What percentage of households are non-family households?

   (A) 5%

   (B) 34%

   (C) 13%

   (D) 48%

4. What is true about households led by females with no spouse present?

   (A) They have a higher percentage of children than married couple households.

   (B) There are over 15,000,000 of these households.

   (C) More than 1/4 of them have one or more people 60+ years old

   (D) all of the above

B **Solve** the problem. Give your opinion.

Emma has 2 daughters. Last month her two nephews moved in with them. The Census Bureau is coming soon to survey Emma's household. She is afraid to say 5 people are in her house because she doesn't want her landlord to know. What should she do?

Answers will vary.

Teaching objectives
- Introduce reading a census chart
- Provide practice using *say* and *tell* with reported speech

WARM-UP AND REVIEW

- Before class. Write today's lesson focus on the board.
  Lesson F:
  Read and interpret a census chart
  Use say and tell with reported speech
- Begin class. Books closed. Write *survey* on the board. Say the word and ask Ss to repeat.
- Ask Ss: *What's a "survey"?* Elicit answers, such as: *A survey asks people questions to gather information (or data), usually to find out how people live or to get their opinion about different things.*
- Ask Ss: *When would you need to read a survey?* Elicit responses, such as: *You would need to read a survey if you were taking a business class, or if you were working in a business and trying to get information about a certain group or groups of people.*

PRESENTATION

- Books open. Direct Ss' attention to the chart in Exercise **1**.
- Tell Ss that they will practice reading and interpreting a chart filled with information from a *census*, a type of survey. Explain that a *census* is an official process of counting a population to find out more about the people. In this chart, the census information is focused on households. Explain that a *household* is all the people who live together in one house.
- Ensure Ss understand all the words in the chart. Explain the meaning of any words that are new to Ss. Write these words on the board.
- Ask a S to read the headings on the top of the chart. Ask another S to read the subject headings in the left-hand column. Ask Ss a few questions about the chart to familiarize Ss with searching the chart for answers, for example: *What was the total number of households surveyed?* (118,208,250.) *What percentage of Married couple family households have one or more children under 18?* (42.1%.).

PRACTICE

- Direct Ss' attention to Exercise **1A**. Read the instructions aloud. This exercise helps prepare Ss for standardized-type tests they may have to take. Make sure that Ss understand the exercise. Have Ss individually scan for and fill in the answers.

COMPREHENSION CHECK

- Check answers to Exercise **1A** with the class. Make sure that Ss have followed the instructions and filled in their answers.
- Have Ss read aloud the questions and the answers they filled in.

APPLICATION

- Direct Ss' attention to Exercise **1B**. Read the instructions aloud. Make sure that Ss understand the task. Have Ss individually solve the problem.
- Ss discuss the problem in small groups. Walk around and help as needed.
- After Ss have discussed the problem, open up the discussion to the entire class. Accept all plausible answers.

Expansion activity (small groups)

- Ss in small groups. Ss should develop their own surveys about their classmates' households. (If you have a small class, you can have Ss ask other Ss in the program or in the school.)
- Ask Ss to identify characteristics of households other than those presented in the chart in **1A**. For example, Ss could survey people about whether they have pets, grandparents, grandchildren, or other family members living at home.
- Walk around and help as needed.
- Have Ss work together to coordinate asking Ss in other groups the questions they prepared. Encourage them to speak with as many Ss as possible (ideally, at least ten).
- Once Ss have gathered their information, they should create a chart modeled after the chart in Exercise **1**. Walk around and help as needed.
- Ss present their charts to the class.
- Allow time for a question-and-answer session.

LESSON F Another view

- Books closed. Write a few questions on the board. Ask Ss the questions and encourage them to reply using complete sentences, for example: *Do you have pets? Where do you live? How many brothers or sisters do you have? Yes, I have two cats and a dog.*

PRESENTATION

Focus on form

- Use the animated grammar presentation in one or more of the following ways:
  - Preview it before class
  - Show in class
  - Encourage Ss to watch outside of class.
- Books open. Direct Ss' attention to the grammar chart in **2A**. Read the *Direct Speech* sentence. Ask three students to read the *Reported Speech* sentences. Ask Ss what they notice about each sentence. Elicit answers, such as: *The sentences are about what people said to other people.*
- Tell Ss that we use reported speech to describe what one person said to another. Usually someone is repeating what someone said at an earlier time. Point out that *that* is optional in reported speech sentences.
- Write *Tatiana said, "I have a cat."* on the board. Write *Tatiana said (that) she has a cat.* under the first sentence. Ask Ss to describe the differences between the two sentences. Underline *I* and *she* and point out that the pronoun changes between the two sentences. Elicit additional comparisons (The quotation marks disappear. The verb tense stays the same).
- Write under the two sentences on the board: *Tatiana told me she has a cat.* Ask Ss to compare how *say* and *tell* are used. Explain that people *say* something and *tell* someone something. The verb *tell* requires an object directly after it. In this case, the object is the pronoun *me*.
- Point to the warm up questions on the board, and ask Ss a few Ss to answer the questions. Then ask other Ss to turn their answers into reported speech. For example, *David said that he has two cats and a dog.*

PRACTICE

- Direct Ss' attention to the instructions in **2A**. Read the instructions aloud. Ensure Ss understand the activity. Ask a pair of Ss to read parts A and B in the dialog. Ask a different pair of Ss to read parts C and D.
- Split the class into small groups. Have Ss ask one another questions. Walk around and help as needed.
- Direct Ss' attention to the instructions in **2B**. Read the instructions aloud. Ask a S to read the example sentences. Ss share information about their classmates. Ensure Ss use the proper reported speech form.

EVALUATION

- Do a quick review of the unit. Have Ss turn to Lesson A. Ask the class to talk about what they remember about this lesson. Prompt Ss, if necessary, with questions, for example: *What are the conversations about on this page? What vocabulary is in the pictures?* Continue in this manner to review each lesson quickly.

Expansion activity

- Before class. Print, for each student, one copy of the Self-assessment for this unit.
- Have Ss complete the Self-assessment either in class or outside of class.
- Provide feedback to Ss such as through a whole-class discussion, partners comparing their worksheets, or T reviewing each S's worksheet.
- If Ss are ready, administer the unit test on pages T-192–T-194 of this Teacher's Edition. The audio script for the test is on page T-222.

More Ventures, Unit 3, Lesson F	
Workbook, 15–30 min.	
Multilevel Worksheets, 30–45 min.	
Collaborative Worksheets, 30–45 min.	www.cambridge.org/ ventures/resources
Self-assessment, 10 min.	
CASAS Test Prep Worksheet, 5–10 min.	

2 Grammar connections: *say* and *tell* with reported speech

Use *say* or *tell* to report what someone said. Use *tell* with an object (*He told me...*).
Use *say* when there is no object. We don't say ~~He said me...~~. Change the pronoun in
the reported speech from the first person (*I* or *we*) to the 3rd person (*he, she or they*).

 Watch

DIRECT SPEECH	REPORTED SPEECH
	Tatiana **said (that)** she has a cat.
"I have a cat."	She **told me (that)** she has a cat.
	She **told Andrew (that)** she has a cat.

A **Work** in a small group. One person asks a question from the list. One person answers. One person reports the answer with *say*. One person reports the answer with *tell*. Take turns.

> A Who do you live with?
>
> B I live with my cousin.
>
> C She said that she lives with her cousin.
>
> D She told him that she lives with her cousin.

Questions:

1. Who do you live with?
2. Where do you live?
3. What language do you speak at home?
4. What kind of car do you drive?
5. How many brothers and sisters do you have?
6. Do you have children? How many?
7. What kinds of foods does your family eat?
8. What is your favorite food?
9. What do you do for fun?
10. Why do you study English?
11. How often are you absent from class?
12. How often are you late to class?
13. What school subjects do you like?
14. Do you have a job? Where do you work?

B **Share** information about your classmates.

> Laura told Andrew that she lives with her cousin. She told him she lives downtown. She said that she speaks Spanish at home.

UNIT 4 HEALTH

Lesson A Listening

1 Before you listen

A What do you see?

B What is happening?

Mr. Stanley

Sara

Mike

Department of Motor Vehicles

UNIT 4

Teaching objectives
- Introduce students to the topic
- Find out what students know about the topic
- Preview the unit by talking about the pictures
- Provide practice of key vocabulary
- Provide practice that develops listening skills

WARM-UP AND REVIEW

- Before class. Write today's lesson focus on the board.
  Lesson A:
  Ask about stress
  Discuss ways to cope with stress
  Give advice about past actions
- Begin class. Books closed. Direct Ss' attention to the lesson focus. Point to the first item: *Ask about stress.* Ask Ss: *What is stress?* List Ss' responses on the board, for example: *nervousness, tension, uneasy feelings,* etc.
- Ask Ss: *What causes stress?* List Ss' responses on the board, for example: *lack of money, problems with spouse or children, problems with a boss or other job difficulties.*

PRESENTATION

- Books open. Set the scene. Direct Ss' attention to the first picture on page 44. Ask the question from Exercise **1A**: *What do you see?* Elicit and write on the board as much vocabulary about the picture as possible: *people walking, people carrying briefcases, people rushing,* etc. Explain any unfamiliar words. Continue eliciting words to describe the four remaining pictures.
- Ask individual Ss to look at the pictures and talk about the similarities: *He's angry because she is late. She is stressed out because she was late to work.*
- Direct Ss' attention to the question in Exercise **1B**: *What is happening?* Read it aloud. Focus on picture 1. Hold up the Student's Book. Ask: *What's happening?* (*Everyone is rushing to get to work.*)

- Focus on picture 2. Hold up the Student's Book and point to Sara in the third picture. Ask: *Why is Mr. Stanley angry?* (He is angry at Sara for being late to work.)
- Focus on picture 3. Ask Ss to describe what is happening. (Sara's stressed out because she was late to work.)
- As Ss to look at picture 4. Ask: *What are Mike and Sara doing?* (They are walking to the car.)
- Focus on picture 5. Ask Ss what is happening. (Sara is going to take her driving test.) Check if Ss understand the meaning of DMV (Department of Motor Vehicles). Ask how Ss felt when they took their road tests.

Teaching Tip
Encourage Ss to be creative. At this point, there is no single correct answer.

Culture Tip
Tell Ss that in the United States, punctuality is very important. Many bosses interpret lateness as a sign of lack of interest in a job – or even disrespect.

- Ask Ss what Sara should do if her bus is usually late and prevents her from getting to work on time. Elicit responses, such as: *Sara should leave home earlier / take an earlier bus / take a train / join a carpool.*

Expansion activity (student pairs)
- Ss in pairs. Assign pairs one of the pictures, and have them create a dialog between the people in the picture (i.e., between Sara and a person waiting for the bus; between Sara and her boss; or between Sara and her friend Mike after she's taken the test).
- Pairs should write and then practice their dialog until they know it well.
- Invite several pairs to role play their dialog for the class.

LESSON A Listening

PRESENTATION

- Books open. Direct Ss' attention to Exercise **2A**. Have Ss listen for the main ideas. Read the instructions aloud. Tell Ss that they are going to hear two different audio segments.
- ▶ **CD1, Track 25** Play or read the audio (see audio script, page T-178).
- Ask Ss if they understood everything in the listening exercise. Write any unfamiliar words on the board, and help Ss understand the meanings. Make sure that Ss understand the meaning of *unreliable*.
- Elicit answers to the questions. For example: *The speakers are Sara, Cindy (Sara's co-worker), Mr. Stanley (Sara's boss), and Mike (Sara's friend). In the first audio segment, Mr. Stanley asks Cindy where Sara is. Then, after Sara arrives, Mr. Stanley tells Sara that if she's late to work again, she'll be fired. In the second audio segment, Sara tells Mike about her nervousness as she waits to take her driving test.*
- Focus Ss' attention on Exercise **2B** and read the instructions aloud. Tell Ss to listen and complete the chart based on the information they hear. Ask Ss what *symptoms* means. Elicit responses, such as: *Symptoms are signs of illness that a person might show or feel.*
- ▶ **CD1, Track 25** Tell Ss to listen for details about Sara's symptoms and Mike's advice. Model the task. Play or read the audio again. Pause the audio after Sara says in Part 2: *I'm so worried about losing my job, I can't sleep.* Ask a S to read the example written under Sara's symptoms (*can't sleep*). Tell Ss to listen and complete the chart. Then play or read the rest of the audio.
- ▶ **CD1, Track 25** Play or read the audio again. Ss listen and check their answers. Repeat the audio as needed.
- Write the numbers *1–6* on the board. Ask Ss to come to the board to write the answers. Have other Ss make corrections on the board as needed.

Learner persistence *(individual work)*
- ▶ **CD1, Track 25** Ss can listen to the audio for Exercise **2A** and **2B** at home for reinforcement and review. They can also listen to the audio for self-directed learning when class attendance is not possible.

PRACTICE

- Direct Ss' attention to Exercise **3A**, and read the instructions aloud. Tell Ss that the story in this exercise is a summary of what happened in the pictures on page 44.
- Focus Ss' attention on the words or expressions in the word bank. Say each word and ask Ss to repeat. Correct pronunciation. Explain any new words.
- Model the task. Ask a S to read aloud the first two sentences in the story, including the example answer.

- Ss complete the exercise individually. Walk around and help as needed.
- ▶ **CD1, Track 26** Play or read the audio (see audio script, page T-179). Ss listen and check their answers. Repeat the audio as needed.
- Write the numbers *1–10* on the board. Ask Ss to come to the board to write their answers. Work with the class to correct any answers as necessary.

Learner persistence *(individual work)*
- ▶ **CD1, Track 26** Ss can listen to the audio for Exercise **3A** at home for reinforcement and review. They can also listen to the audio for self-directed learning when class attendance is not possible.

APPLICATION

- Focus Ss' attention on Exercise **3B** and read the instructions aloud.
- Ss complete the exercise in pairs. Help as needed.
- Ask several pairs to share their answers with the class.

Community building *(whole group)*
- Because Ss may face a wide range of stress-inducing situations, it is important to discuss resources in your community that may be available to help alleviate stress. If your program is affiliated with a college, find out what the college has to offer in the way of counseling or stress-management classes. Ask Ss if they can recommend any stress-reduction classes they may have taken. Compile a list of places in your community that offer such classes or techniques and distribute it to the class. Your local librarian may also be helpful in finding resources that you can pass on to Ss.

EVALUATION

- Direct Ss' attention to the lesson focus on the board. Ask individual Ss to look at the pictures on page 44 and make sentences using the words in Exercise **3A**.
- Check off each part of the lesson focus as Ss demonstrate an understanding of what they have learned in the lesson.

More Ventures, Unit 4, Lesson A	
Workbook, 15–30 min.	
Multilevel Worksheets, 30–45 min. Collaborative Worksheets, 30–45 min.	www.cambridge.org/ventures/resources/
Student Arcade, time varies	www.cambridge.org/venturesarcade/

UNIT GOALS
Recognize causes of stress   **Explain** strategies for coping with stress
Recognize the impact of stress on work

2 Listen

A   Listen and answer the questions.

1. Who are the speakers?   2. What are they talking about?

◀)) CD1, Track 25

B   Listen again. Complete the chart.

Sara's symptoms	Mike's advice
1. _can't sleep_	4. _think positive thoughts_
2. _can't eat_	5. _deep breathing_
3. _can't concentrate_	6. _meditate_

◀)) CD1, Track 25

3 After you listen

A   Read. Complete the story.

anxiety   calm down   cope with   positive   techniques
breathing   concentrate   meditation   stressed out   tense

> Mike is driving Sara to the Department of Motor Vehicles (DMV) to take her driving test. He notices that she's very ____tense____ . Sara says she's ___stressed out___
> 　　　　　　　　　　　　　　　　　　　　　　1　　　　　　　　　　　　　　　　　　　　2
> because she was late to work again. She's worried that her boss will fire her if she's late one more time. She's so afraid of losing her job that she can't eat, she can't sleep, and she can't ___concentrate___ . Mike says that she has to ___calm down___
> 　　　　　　　　　　　　　　　　3　　　　　　　　　　　　　　　　　　　　　　　4
> if she wants to pass her driving test. He suggests three ___techniques___ to help her
> 　　　　　　　　　　　　　　　　　　　　　　　　　　　　　　　5
> ___cope with___ her ___anxiety___ . One is deep ___breathing___ . The second
> 　　6　　　　　　　　　7　　　　　　　　　　　　　　　　8
> one is thinking ___positive___ thoughts, and the third one is ___meditation___ .
> 　　　　　　　　　　9　　　　　　　　　　　　　　　　　　　　　　10

Listen and check your answers.

B   Discuss. Talk with your classmates.

1. Do you ever feel stressed out? What makes you feel stressed out?

2. What helps you when you feel stressed out?

◀)) CD1, Track 26

Lesson B Modals

1 Grammar focus: *should, shouldn't, have to, don't have to*

👁 Watch

Use *should / shouldn't* to give advice. Use *have to / has to* to indicate it is necessary to do something. Use *don't have to / doesn't have to* to indicate it is not necessary to do something.

ADVISABLE = GOOD IDEA	NOT ADVISABLE = BAD IDEA
Sara **should learn** how to meditate.	She **shouldn't get** stressed out.

NECESSARY	NOT NECESSARY
Sara **has to take** public transportation because she doesn't have a car.	She **doesn't have to take** her driving test today. She can take it next week.

2 Practice

A Write. Complete the story. Use *should, shouldn't, have to,* and *don't have to*.

Ana and Bill just got engaged, and they are planning to get married in four weeks. Because the wedding is so soon, they are feeling a lot of pressure. Ana's mother wants a big wedding, but Ana and Bill don't. Because they are paying for the wedding themselves, they believe they ___*should*___ do what they want. Another

1

pressure is all the things Ana and Bill ___*have to*___ do before

2

the wedding. For example, Ana ___*has to*___ buy a dress, choose her bridesmaids,

3

and send out the invitations. Bill ___*has to*___ plan the reception and order the

4

food. Most importantly, they ___*have to*___ decide where the wedding will be. Ana

5

wants to get married outdoors, but Bill thinks they ___*shouldn't*___ plan an outdoor

6

wedding because it might rain. Now Bill has a different idea. He realizes that they

___*shouldn't*___ get married so soon. Maybe they ___*should*___ postpone the

7   8

wedding by a few months. That way, they ___*don't have to*___ feel so much pressure.

9

Listen and check your answers.

🔊 CD1, Track 27

46 UNIT 4

WARM-UP AND REVIEW

- Before class: Write the lesson focus on the board.
  Lesson B:
  "should," "shouldn't," "have to," "don't have to"

- Begin class. Books open. Review Lesson A vocabulary and how to give advice.

- Direct Ss' attention to the pictures on page 44. Ask: *Why is Sara tense?* (In picture 3: She was late for work. In picture 5: She's going to take a driving test.) *What advice does her friend Mike give her?* (deep breathing, thinking positive thoughts, meditating.)

PRESENTATION

Focus on meaning / personalize

- Books closed. Direct Ss' attention to the lesson focus on the board. Read it aloud.

- Tell a story such as the following, and point to the words on the board as they come up in the story: *My friend Binh came to the United States two years ago. He doesn't have to become a citizen, but he wants to. To become a citizen, he has to take a test. He should study for the test.*

- Ask: *Does Binh have to become a citizen?* (No.) *Does he have to take a test to become a citizen?* (Yes.) *Should he study for the test?* (Yes.)

- Elicit or explain the meaning of *should* (it is a good / right thing to do), *shouldn't* (it is not a good / right thing to do), *have to* (it is necessary to do), *don't have to* (it is not necessary to do).

- Elicit examples from two or three Ss about something they have to do or stop doing. For example: *I have to stop smoking.*

Focus on form

Use the animated grammar presentation in one or more of the following ways:

- Preview it before class
- Show in class
- Encourage Ss to watch outside of class.

- Books open. Focus Ss' attention on the charts in Exercise **1**. Read aloud the statement under *Advisable*. Ask Ss to repeat. Ask: *Is it necessary for Sara to meditate, or is it just a good idea?* (just a good idea.) Read aloud the statement under *Not advisable*. Ask Ss *Why shouldn't Sara get stressed out?* (because stress is unhealthy.).

- Read aloud the statement under *Necessity*. Ask Ss to repeat. Ask: *Does Sara have a choice about taking public transportation?* (No.) *Why not?* (She doesn't have a car.) Read the statements under *Lack of necessity*. Ask Ss to repeat. Ask: *Why doesn't Sara need to take her driving test today?* (because she can take it next week.)

- Have Ss identify the subject and verb in each of the four sentences in the chart. Point out that *should* and *shouldn't* remain the same with any subject, for example: *I should, she should.* However, *have to* changes with the subject, for example: *I have to, she has to.*

PRACTICE

- Direct Ss' attention to Exercise **2A** and read the instructions aloud.

- Model the task. Ask a S to read aloud the first four sentences, including the example sentence.

- Ss complete the exercise individually. Walk around and help as needed.

COMPREHENSION CHECK

- Direct Ss' attention to the second part of the instructions for Exercise **2A** and read it aloud.

- ▶ **CD1, Track 27** Play or read the audio (see audio script, page T-179). Ss listen and check their answers.

- Write the numbers *1–9* on the board. Ask several Ss to come to the board to write the answers in complete sentences. Call on other Ss to make corrections on the board as needed.

LESSON B Modals

PRESENTATION

- Tell Ss that they are going to read and talk about different situations in which people need advice. Read the instructions aloud for Exercise **2B**.

- Books open. Direct Ss' attention to the pictures in Exercise **2B**.

Useful Language

Read the tip box aloud. Explain that both *ought to* and *should* have the same meaning. They are both followed by the base form of a verb.

- Call on three Ss to read the descriptions under the pictures.

- Ask individual Ss to read one piece of advice from the box. Explain the meaning of any phrases that are unclear to Ss.

- Model the task with a S. Read the two examples above the pictures.

- Ss complete the exercise in pairs. Walk around and help as needed.

PRACTICE

- Direct Ss' attention to the second part of the instructions for Exercise **2B**. Read the instructions aloud.

- Ask a S to read the sample sentence to the class.

- Ss work individually to complete the exercise. Walk around and help as needed.

- Have Ss come to the board to write their sentences. Work with the class to make corrections on the board as needed.

APPLICATION

- Direct Ss' attention to Exercise **3A** and read the instructions aloud.

- Model the task. Ask a S to read the first situation aloud. Have another S read the sample advice.

- Ss work in small groups to complete the exercise. Walk around and help as needed.

- Direct Ss' attention to Exercise **3B** and read the instructions aloud.

- Have groups share with the class the advice they gave for each situation.

Expansion activity *(small groups)*

- Ask Ss if they have ever heard of "Dear Abby" or a similar advice column. If not, explain that "Dear Abby" is a newspaper column that advises people about how to handle personal problems or difficult situations.

- Have each group brainstorm ideas to create a list of personal problems that might make a person write a letter asking for advice. Write a sample letter on the board. For example:

Dear Abby,
*   My mother has been getting bad headaches and her eyesight has worsened. I'd like her to see a doctor, but she refuses. What should I do to convince my mom to see a doctor?*
Sincerely,
Worried Daughter

- Explain that sometimes the letter writer will use a descriptive name to sign the letter rather than his or her real name. Ask Ss why the person might do this (to hide his or her identity).

- Call on a S to use the grammatical structures they learned in this unit (*should, shouldn't, have to, don't have to*) to respond to *Worried Friend's* request for advice.

- Have Ss in each group work together to write a group letter of advice. Walk around and help as needed.

- When groups have finished, invite a member from each group to read the group letter to the class.

- Allow time for questions and answers so that Ss can discuss some of the advice that was given.

EVALUATION

- Books closed. Direct Ss' attention to the lesson focus on the board.

- Write the following sentences on the board:
  1. You <u>should</u> go to the meeting tonight.
  2. You <u>have to</u> go to the meeting tonight.

- Ask a S what the difference is in the meaning of the two sentences. Elicit an appropriate response: *The first sentence shows that something is advisable. The second sentence shows necessity, or what you must do.* Ask a S for another way to say the first sentence. (*You ought to go to the meeting tonight.*)

- Check off the lesson focus as Ss demonstrate an understanding of what they have learned in the lesson.

More Ventures, Unit 4, Lesson B	
Workbook, 15–30 min.	
Multilevel Worksheets, 30–45 min.	www.cambridge.org/ventures/resources/
Collaborative Worksheets, 30–45 min.	
Student Arcade, time varies	www.cambridge.org/venturesarcade/

B **Talk** with a partner. Make sentences about the people in the pictures. Use *should*, *shouldn't*, *ought to*, *have to*, and *don't have to*. Use the items from the box in your sentences.

> Carmela and Hugo ought to try to meet new people.

> Chul and Sun-mi have to find a new place to live.

Carmela and Hugo
- just got married
- just moved to a new town

Chul and Sun-mi
- just had a baby
- live in a studio apartment

Kevin
- just started his first job
- still lives with his parents

try to meet new people	ask lots of questions
call parents about every problem	find a new place to live
learn how to manage money	follow their (his) parents' advice
try to do everything perfectly	make decisions by themselves (himself)
buy baby furniture	be responsible
meet the neighbors	volunteer at a local organization

Write sentences about the people in the pictures.

Carmela and Hugo ought to try to meet new people.

3 Communicate

A **Work** in a small group. Discuss the following situations, and give advice. Use *should*, *shouldn't*, *ought to*, *have to*, and *don't have to*.

> They have to buy furniture.

> They should check the newspaper for furniture sales.

1. The Wong family just bought a house. The house has no furniture at all. Also, it is far from Mr. Wong's job, and the family doesn't have a car.

2. Etsuko and Hiro immigrated to the United States. They are anxious because there are so many things to do. They don't have a big enough place to live, they aren't enrolled in English classes, and their children aren't registered for school.

3. Boris just started a new job. He hasn't met his coworkers. He also has duties that he hasn't done before, and he doesn't know the company's policies and procedures.

B **Share** your group's advice with your classmates.

Lesson C Past modals

1 Grammar focus: *should have* and *shouldn't have*

Watch

Use past modals *should have / shouldn't have* for regrets or advice about something that happened in the past. Use the past participle form of a verb after *should have / shouldn't have*.

REGRET IN THE PAST	ADVICE IN THE PAST
I don't like my new job.	Robert is late to work.
I **should have kept** my old job.	He **should have left** the house earlier.
I **shouldn't have changed** jobs.	He **shouldn't have read** the newspaper before work.

Past Participles	
regular	**irregular**
called	eat / ate
stayed	go / went
studied	make / made
talked	sleep / slept

2 Practice

A Write. Read about Imelda. Write sentences with *should have* and *shouldn't have*.

> Imelda left the Philippines last year and immigrated to the United States. None of her family came with her. She got homesick and depressed.

1. She didn't talk to anyone about her problems.
   She should have talked to someone about her problems.

2. She didn't go out with friends.
   She should have gone out with friends.

3. She stayed home alone all the time.
   She shouldn't have stayed home alone all the time.

4. She didn't make new friends.
   She should have made new friends.

5. She didn't exercise.
   She should have exercised.

6. She didn't eat regular, balanced meals.
   She should have eaten regular, balanced meals.

7. She ate lots of junk food.
   She shouldn't have eaten lots of junk food.

8. She slept so much.
   She shouldn't have slept so much.

9. She didn't call her family.
   She should have called her family.

Listen and check your answers.

◀ CD1, Track 28

- Introduce and provide practice with the modals *should have* and *shouldn't have*

WARM-UP AND REVIEW

- *Before class: Write the lesson focus on the board.*
  Lesson C:
  "should have," shouldn't have"
- Begin class. Books open. Review *should* and *shouldn't*.
- Focus Ss' attention on the pictures on page 44. Tell Ss to work with a partner to brainstorm things Sara should and shouldn't say or do and things her boss should and shouldn't say or do. Elicit ideas, for example: *Sara should call her boss to tell him she is going to be late. She should get up earlier.* After partners have shared ideas, elicit some and write them on the board.

PRESENTATION

Focus on meaning / personalize

- Books closed. Direct Ss' attention to the lesson focus on the board. Read it aloud.
- Give an example of *should have* and *shouldn't have* from your own life, for example: *Last night I stayed up late. Today I am very tired. I shouldn't have stayed up late. I should have gone to bed earlier.*
- Ask: *Is this about now, the past, or the future?* (the past.) *Is it about something in the past that I am happy about or regret?* (regret.)
- Ask two or three Ss questions such as the following and write their responses on the board: *What about you? What is something you did in the past that you regret? Why do you regret it?* (I regret that I started smoking. Now I have health problems.)
- Write on the board sentences about one of the Ss, for example: *Carlos shouldn't have started smoking. He should have taken care of his health.*
- Elicit or explain that we use *should have* and *shouldn't have* to talk about regrets about something we did in the past. We also use it to give advice to others about something they did or didn't do in the past.

Focus on form

- Use the animated grammar presentation in one or more of the following ways:
  - Preview it before class
  - Show in class
  - Encourage Ss to watch outside of class.
- Books open. Focus Ss' attention on the charts in Exercise **1**. Read aloud the sentences under *Regret in the past*. Ask Ss to repeat. Ask: *What do I regret?* (changing jobs) *Why am I unhappy about changing jobs?* (because you don't like your new job.) *Should I have changed jobs?* (No.)
- Read aloud the sentences under *Advice in the past*. Ask Ss to repeat. Ask: *What did Robert do wrong?* (He was late to work.) *What advice can you give him so he won't be late again?* (Leave the house earlier. Do not to read the newspaper before work.)
- Have Ss underline the verbs that follow *should have* and *shouldn't have*. Elicit or point out the form of the verb that follows *should have* and *shouldn't have* (the past participle).

PRACTICE

- Direct Ss' attention to Exercise **2A** and read the instructions aloud.
- Ask a S to read the background information about Imelda.
- Model the task. Ask another S to read aloud the first sentence and the example sentence.
- Ss complete the exercise individually. Walk around and help as needed.

COMPREHENSION CHECK

- Read aloud the second part of the instructions in Exercise **2A**.
- ▶ **CD1, Track 28** Play or read the audio (see audio script, page T-179). Ss listen and check their answers.
- Write the numbers *1–9* on the board. Ask individual Ss to come to the board to write the two sentences for each item. While Ss are writing sentences on the board, seated Ss can check their answers with a classmate.

LESSON C Past Modals

PRACTICE

- Direct Ss' attention to the eight pictures in Exercise **2B**. Ask Ss: *What is the man doing in the first picture?* Elicit an appropriate response, such as: *The man stayed up too late.* Focus Ss' attention on the second picture and ask: *What happened?* Elicit an appropriate response, such as: *The man overslept (slept for too long).* Continue in this manner with the six remaining pictures.

- Read the instructions aloud.

- Ask a S to read the example sentence aloud.

- Ss complete the exercise in pairs. Walk around and help as needed.

- Read the instructions aloud for the second part of Exercise **2B**. Ask a S to read the sample sentence to the class.

- Ss complete the exercise individually. Walk around and help as needed.

- Ask several Ss to write their sentences on the board.

- Have other Ss read aloud each of the sentences on the board. Ask: *Is this sentence correct?* Make corrections on the board as needed.

Expansion activity *(student pairs)*

- Ask Ss to role-play Nikolai arriving late to his meeting. Write an example of a conversation on the board, such as:

  Nikolai: *Hello, everyone. I'm sorry to keep you waiting!*

  Boss: *Nikolai, you should have been here an hour ago!*

  Nikolai: *I know. I should have arrived earlier. It won't happen again.*

- Ask two Ss to role-play the example conversation.

- Ss in pairs. Have partners write and practice their own conversations. Walk around and help as needed.

- Ask several pairs to act out their role play for the class.

APPLICATION

- Direct Ss' attention to Exercise **3A**. Read the instructions aloud. Ask a S to read the three questions.

- Ss work in small groups to complete the exercise. Walk around and help as needed.

- Direct Ss' attention to Exercise **3B** and read the instructions aloud.

- Model the task. Ask a S to use *should have* or *shouldn't have* to share a situation discussed in his or her group. For example: *One day when Ted went to work, he forgot his uniform. He should have remembered it. He should have gone home to get it before he went to work.*

- Continue the exercise by asking Ss from each group to share information they learned about their classmates.

EVALUATION

- Direct Ss' attention to the lesson focus on the board.

- Write on the board:
  1. *I watched five hours of television last night.*
  2. *I went to bed at 3:00 a.m. I'm tired.*
  3. *I didn't eat breakfast this morning.*
  4. *I didn't take out the trash this morning.*

- Ask four Ss to read the sentences on the board. Ask other Ss to write sentences with *should have* and *shouldn't have*. For example: *You shouldn't have watched television for five hours last night. You should have gone to bed earlier. You should have eaten breakfast. You shouldn't have forgotten to take out the trash.*

- Check off the lesson focus as Ss demonstrate an understanding of what they have learned in the lesson.

More Ventures, Unit 4, Lesson C	
Workbook, 15–30 min.	
Multilevel Worksheets, 30–45 min. Collaborative Worksheets, 30–45 min.	www.cambridge.org/ventures/ resources/
Student Arcade, time varies	www.cambrdge.org/ venturesarcade/

B **Talk** with a partner. Look at the pictures. What should Nikolai and his boss have done differently? Use *shouldn't have*.

Nikolai shouldn't have overslept.

1.

stay up late

2.

oversleep

3.

forget (his) briefcase

4.

miss (his) bus

5.

arrive late

6.

criticize (someone) in public

7.

leave the meeting

8.

lose (their) temper

Write sentences about what Nikolai and his boss should have done instead.

Nikolai should have gotten up on time.

3 Communicate

A **Work** in a small group. Think about a past situation in your life that didn't go well. Take turns asking and answering questions about it.

1. What was the situation?

2. What did you do that you shouldn't have?

3. What didn't you do that you should have?

B **Share** information about your classmates.

Lesson D Reading

1 Before you read

Talk with your classmates. Answer the questions.

1. When you are in a stressful situation, what happens to your body?

2. Read the **boldfaced** questions (section heads) in the article. Talk with a partner. Share your answers to these questions before you read the article.

> Before you read an article, read the title and section heads. Relate them to your own background and experience.

2 Read

Read the magazine article. Listen and read again.

STRESS:
What You Ought to Know

CD1, Track 29

What is stress?

Stress is our <u>reaction</u> to changing events in our lives. The reactions can be mental – what we think or feel about the changes – and physical – how our body reacts to the changes.

What causes stress?

Stress often comes when there are too many changes in our lives. The changes can be positive, like having a baby or getting a better job, or they can be negative, such as an <u>illness</u> or a divorce. Some stress is healthy. It motivates us to push forward. But too much stress over time can make us sick.

What are the signs of stress?

There are both physical and emotional signs of stress. Physical signs may include tight muscles, elevated blood pressure, grinding your teeth, trouble sleeping, an upset stomach, and back pain. Common emotional symptoms are anxiety, <u>nervousness</u>, <u>depression</u>, trouble concentrating, and nightmares.

How can you manage stress?

To prevent stress, you should eat right and exercise <u>regularly</u>. When you know there will be a <u>stressful</u> event in your day – such as a test, a business meeting, or an encounter with someone you don't get along with – it is really important to eat a healthy breakfast and to limit coffee and sugar.

When you find yourself in a stressful <u>situation</u>, stay calm. Take a few deep breaths to help you relax. Roll your shoulders or stretch to <u>loosen</u> any tight muscles. And take time to think before you speak. You don't want to say something you will regret later!

We all have some stress in our lives. It's important for us to use strategies for handling it, so that the stress doesn't overwhelm us.

Teaching objectives

- Introduce a magazine article about stress
- Provide practice using new topic related vocabulary
- Provide practice with the reading strategy of relating what students read to their own experiences
- Provide practice identifying suffixes that change the part of speech of a word

WARM-UP AND REVIEW

- Before class. Write today's lesson focus on the board.
  Lesson D:
  Read and understand "Stress: What You Ought to Know"
  Practice new vocabulary related to stress and managing stress
  Identify suffixes that change the part of speech of a word

- Begin class. Books closed. Focus Ss' attention on the word *stress* in the lesson focus. Write *stress* on the board. Remind Ss about Sara and her situation at the DMV. Ask Ss: *Why is Sara so stressed?* Elicit appropriate responses, for example: *She's worried about losing her job.*

- Ask Ss if they are familiar with health magazines or newspaper columns that offer health advice. If possible, bring to class a few examples and show to Ss.

- Write on the board: *"Stress: What You Ought to Know."* Have Ss read the title and use it as a clue to predict what the magazine article is about. Elicit responses, such as: *The article is about things you should know about stress. It's about how to help yourself when you're stressed.* Write Ss' predictions on the board.

PRESENTATION

- Books open. Direct Ss' attention to Exercise **1**. Read the instructions aloud.

- Ask two Ss to read the questions to the class.

- Have Ss focus on the second question. Ask: *What does "boldfaced" mean?* Guide Ss to look at the boldfaced questions. Ask Ss: *Why do you think the questions in this magazine article are boldfaced?* Elicit appropriate responses, such as: *The questions are boldfaced because they introduce the topic of the information that follows. They also make the reader want to read the paragraph to learn the answer.* Readers can **predict** *what the article will be about if they read the boldfaced text.* Ask Ss what the benefit of boldfaced questions is. Elicit an appropriate response, such as: *It makes it easier for the reader to find specific information.*

- Ss in pairs. Ask Ss to answer the questions with a partner. Walk around and help as needed.

PRACTICE

- Read the instructions aloud for Exercise **2**. Ask Ss to read the article silently before listening to the audio program.

▶ **CD1, Track 29** Play or read the audio, and ask Ss to read along (see audio script, page T-179). Repeat the audio as needed.

- While Ss are listening to the audio and reading the article, ask them to write in their notebooks any words or expressions they don't understand. When the audio is finished, have Ss write the new vocabulary words on the board.

- Point to each new word on the board. Say it aloud and ask Ss to repeat. Give a brief explanation of each word, or ask other Ss to explain the word if they know it. If Ss prefer to look up the new words in their dictionaries, allow them to do so.

Read the tip aloud. Write *relate* on the board. Say it and have Ss repeat. Ask Ss what they think the word means. Write on the board: *relate = connect.* Tell Ss that good readers relate the information they read to their own experience to help them understand what they are reading. If Ss have experienced some kind of stress, or if they know of someone who has, they will find the article easier to understand if they relate it to their personal experiences.

Learner persistence *(individual work)*

▶ **CD1, Track 29** Ss can listen to the audio for Exercise **2** at home for reinforcement and review. They can also listen to the audio for self-directed learning when class attendance is not possible.

Expansion activity *(small groups)*

- **Materials needed** Poster board and markers.

- Have Ss work in small groups to create a poster entitled "Low-stress Lifestyle Tips."

- Encourage group members to brainstorm ideas to make a list of tips for their poster.

- Point out to Ss that the list should be based on what they have read in the article and their personal experiences.

- Suggest that Ss take notes during the brainstorming session and the group discussion. Guide Ss to use their notes and the grammar from the unit to discuss low-stress lifestyle tips with their group.

- Invite each group to present its poster to the class. Write some of the tips on the board, and engage in a class discussion.

LESSON D Reading

COMPREHENSION CHECK

- Direct Ss' attention to Exercise **3A**, and read the instructions aloud.
- Ask individual Ss to read the questions aloud, one at a time. Make sure that all Ss understand the questions.
- Ss complete the exercise in pairs. Remind Ss that they can refer to the magazine article on page 50.
- Discuss the answers to the questions with the class. Ask Ss to locate in the reading where some of the answers are found.

APPLICATION

- Direct Ss' attention to Exercise **3B** and read the instructions aloud.
- Ask Ss to read aloud each of the four questions in Exercise **3B**.
- Ss complete the exercise in pairs. Walk around and help as needed.
- Ask several pairs to share the answers they discussed with the class.

Expansion activity

- Refer Ss to "Winning the Lottery Can Be Stressful," another reading on the same topic on pages 145–147.

- Have Ss complete the activity either in class or outside of class.
- Provide feedback to Ss such as through whole-class discussion, partners comparing their worksheets, or T reviewing each S's worksheets.

EVALUATION

- Direct Ss' attention to the lesson focus on the board.
- Ask individual Ss to retell the main points of the article, "Stress: What You Ought to Know."
- Have Ss focus on the words they wrote in the chart for number 2 of Exercise **3B**. Ask Ss to make sentences with these words to show that they understand their meanings.
- Check off each part of the lesson focus as Ss demonstrate an understanding of what they have learned in the lesson.

More Ventures, Unit 4, Lesson D	
Workbook, 15–30 min.	
Multilevel Worksheets, 30–45 min. **Collaborative Worksheets,** 30–45 min.	www.cambridge.org/ventures/ resources/
Student Arcade, time varies	www.cambridge.org/ venturesarcade/

❸ After you read

A **Check** your understanding.

1. In the third paragraph, find the word *symptoms* and underline it. What other word do you find in the paragraph that is a synonym for *symptom*?

2. What examples does the author give of both positive and negative experiences that can cause stress?

3. According to the article, there can be physical and emotional reactions to stress. What examples does the article give?

4. The article says that some stress can be healthy. What example does it give to support that statement?

5. The article says that an encounter with someone you don't get along with can be stressful. What advice in the fifth paragraph may help you?

6. If you eat healthy and exercise regularly, can you expect that you will never have problems with stress? Cite evidence from the article to support your answer.

B **Build** your vocabulary.

1. English uses suffixes to change the part of speech of a word. Underline words in the reading that end with the suffixes in the left column.

2. Complete the chart. Use a dictionary if necessary.

Suffix	Example	Part of speech	Main word	Part of speech
-ful	*stressful*	*adj*	*stress*	*noun*
-en	*loosen*	*verb*	*loose*	*verb*
-ly	*regularly*	*adverb*	*regular*	*adjective*
-ness	*illness*	*noun*	*ill*	*adjective*
	nervousness	*noun*	*nervous*	*adjective*
-ion	*reaction*	*noun*	*react*	*verb*
	depression	*noun*	*depress*	*verb*
	situation	*noun*	*situate*	*verb*

C **Talk** with a partner.

1. Think of a time when there were many changes in your life. Were the changes positive or negative? How did you feel? How did your body react?

2. What's a stressful situation you've been in recently?

3. Do you have a favorite exercise that you do to reduce stress? If so what is it?

4. After reading this article, is there something you would do differently to handle stress? If so, what?

For college and career readiness practice, see pages 145–147.

📖 Read closely to determine what the text says explicitly and to make logical inferences from the text; recognize suffixes that change part of speech

Lesson E Writing

1 Before you write

A Talk with a partner. Look at the pictures. Answer the questions.

1. How do the people in the pictures cope with stress?
2. What are some healthy ways of coping with stress?
3. What are some unhealthy ways of coping with stress?
4. What makes you feel stressed?

B Read the paragraph.

How I Cope with Stress

When I feel stressed on a warm summer day, I like to work in the community garden in my neighborhood. The sun on my back as I pull weeds provides relief from hunching over a computer and lessens the muscle tension. The birds, sucking nectar from the flowers and splashing in the birdbath, relax me. Talking with the other volunteers makes me forget my troubles.

When I feel stressed on a cold winter day, I like to curl up with my cat, listen to classical music, and read an interesting book. Stroking my cat's soft fur helps my body relax, and soon I feel less tense. The sound of classical music with piano and string instruments shuts out the noises around me and reduces my anxiety. I like to listen with my eyes closed until my muscles start to relax. Then I open my eyes and pick up a book. I usually choose stories about people and the difficult events in their lives because they help me forget about all the stressful things I have to do in my own life.

> One way to organize details in a paragraph is to write about cause and effect.
>
> *I like to listen with my eyes closed* (cause) *until my muscles start to relax* (effect).

Teaching objectives
- Prepare Ss for writing a paragraph about coping with stress
- Provide practice identifying causes and related effects

WARM-UP AND REVIEW

- Before class. Write today's lesson focus on the board.
  Lesson E:
  Write a paragraph about coping with stress
  Use actions and their results to organize and support ideas
- Begin class. Books closed. Write the words *Cope with stress* on the board. Ask Ss to define the words. Elicit appropriate responses, such as: *"Cope" means "to deal with or to handle something."*
- Ask Ss to refer to the magazine article on page 50 and to use some of their own ideas to answer the following questions:
  How did the article define stress? (Stress is how we react to the changing events in our lives.)
  What are some signs of stress? (Physical signs: tight muscles, elevated blood pressure, teeth grinding, trouble sleeping, upset stomach, and back pain; emotional signs: anxiety, nervousness, depression, trouble concentrating, and nightmares.)
  What are some ways to manage stress? (Eat right and exercise regularly.)
  What are some suggestions for coping with stress? (Stay calm, take deep breaths, roll your shoulders and stretch, take time to think before you speak.)

PRESENTATION

- Books open. Direct Ss' attention to Exercise **1A**. Read the instructions aloud.
- Ask Ss to read aloud the questions in Exercise **1A**.
- Ss work in pairs to ask and answer the questions. Walk around and help as needed.
- Have partners share with the class some of the information they discussed.

PRACTICE

- Direct Ss' attention to Exercise **1B** and read the instructions aloud.
- Ss read the paragraph silently. Ask them to underline any unfamiliar words.
- Have Ss tell you the words that they underlined. Write them on the board. Go over the meaning of each of the words.

Read the tip aloud. Point out that there are also other ways to organize details in a paragraph (by chronological order, by comparing and contrasting, etc.). Tell Ss that organizing details will help the writer to write more clearly and the reader to follow the ideas more easily.

Expansion activity (whole group)

- Ask Ss to work in small groups to brainstorm ideas for a list of some of their goals (e.g., travel, become a teacher, own a business). Elicit Ss' goals and write them on the board. Ask Ss to tell the steps (actions) they would have to take in order to reach each of those goals (results); write some goal-setting examples on the board:
  save money ➔ *travel*
  take education courses ➔ *become a teacher*
  take business classes ➔ *own a business*
- Have groups discuss their goals and give advice related to the actions group members have to take in order to achieve their goals.
- Model the task. Write on the board and have two Ss role-play this dialog:
  A: *What's your goal?*
  B: *I want to travel abroad.*
  A: *You should (or ought to) get a job and then save some money!*
- Call on groups to write and perform role plays based on their goal-setting discussions.

LESSON E Writing

PRESENTATION

- Direct Ss' attention to Exercise **1C** and read the instructions aloud. Tell Ss that they will need to refer to the model paragraphs on page 52 in order to complete this exercise.
- Ask a S to read aloud the first part of the topic sentence for the first paragraph.
- Call on another S to read the next heading (*Ways of reducing stress*) and the sample action and result.
- Explain that Ss will also fill in the information on the topic sentence and the next heading for the second paragraph.
- Ss work with a partner to fill in the missing information in Exercise **1C**. Walk around and help as needed.
- Copy the outlines from the Student's Book on the board.
- Have Ss come to the board, one at a time, to fill in the chart. Make corrections on the board as needed.

PRACTICE

- Direct Ss' attention to Exercise **1D** and read the instructions aloud. Tell Ss that taking the time to plan a paragraph makes it easier for the writer to write the paragraph and easier for the reader to understand it.
- Ss complete their outlines individually. Walk around and help as needed.

Teaching Tip

Before Ss begin to write, encourage them to engage in a prewriting discussion about the topic of coping with stress. Talking about the topic with a partner or a small group will help Ss narrow their topic and brainstorm ideas for writing.

APPLICATION

- Direct Ss' attention to Exercise **2** and read the instructions aloud.
- Ss complete the task individually. Walk around and help as needed.

Learner persistence (individual work)

- If you have any Ss who have difficulty writing, sit with them and help them as the other Ss are writing. Encourage them to use their notes from Exercise **1D** to create supporting facts and details for their topic sentence.

Expansion activity (student pairs)

- Encourage Ss to speak with a partner about coping with illness. Using the same outline as in Exercise **1D**, have Ss talk to their partners about actions and results.
- Model the task. Ask Ss what action they might take if they had a cold and were trying to feel better. For example: *action: drink hot tea with lemon → result: throat feels better, body feels warmer*
- Have Ss discuss the task with a partner.
  Option Give Ss the option of writing a paragraph about ways of treating a specific physical illness. Remind Ss to write about actions and results.

COMPREHENSION CHECK

- Direct Ss' attention to Exercise **3A** and read the instructions aloud. This exercise asks Ss to develop skills to review and edit their own writing.
- Ss check their own paragraphs against the writing checklist. Walk around and help as needed. If any Ss check *No* for one or more of the checklist items, ask them to revise and edit their paragraphs to include the missing information.

EVALUATION

- Focus Ss' attention on Exercise **3B**, and read the instructions aloud. This exercise enables Ss to work together to edit their writing. Reading aloud enables the writer to review his or her own writing and to understand the need to write clearly for an audience.
- Listen to Ss as they ask their partner a question about the paragraph and tell their partner one thing they learned from it.
- Direct Ss' attention to the lesson focus on the board.
- Check off each part of the lesson focus as Ss demonstrate an understanding of what they have learned in the lesson.

More Ventures, Unit 4, Lesson E	
Workbook, 15–30 min.	
Multilevel Worksheets, 30–45 min.	www.cambridge.org/ventures/resources/
Collaborative Worksheets, 30–45 min.	

C **Work** with a partner. Complete the two outlines, one for each of the two model paragraphs.

Topic sentence for the first paragraph: When I feel stressed on a warm summer day,

I like to curl up with my cat, listen to classical music, and read an interesting book.

_____.

Ways of reducing stress:

cause: _sun on my back_ → effect: _lessens muscle tension_

cause: _stroke my cat's fur_ → effect: _body relaxes, feels less tense_

cause: _listen to music with eyes closed_ → effect: _shuts out noises, reduces anxiety_

Topic sentence for the second paragraph: When I feel stressed on a cold winter day,

_____

_____.

Ways of reducing stress:

cause: _read stories about people with difficult events in their lives_ → effect: _forget stress in own life_

cause: _____ → effect: _____

cause: _____ → effect: _____

D **Plan** a paragraph about how you cope with stress. Make an outline like the ones in Exercise 1C to make notes on your ideas.

Answers will vary.

2 Write

Write a paragraph about how you cope with stress. Identify at least three ways you reduce stress (causes) and the effect of each. Use details to describe each effect. Use the paragraphs in Exercise 1B and the outlines in Exercises 1C and 1D to help you.

3 After you write

A **Check** your writing.

	Yes	No
1. My topic sentence identifies three ways of reducing stress.	☐	☐
2. For each cause, I described an effect.	☐	☐
3. I used details to describe each effect.	☐	☐

B **Share** your writing with a partner.

1. Take turns. Read your paragraph to a partner.

2. Comment on your partner's paragraph. Ask your partner a question about the paragraph. Tell your partner one thing you learned.

Lesson F Another view

1 Life-skills reading

Many companies today recognize that stressed employees can impact the company's profit. Some hire consulting firms to survey employees about their stress and determine its effect on the company. Here is the report on one such survey.

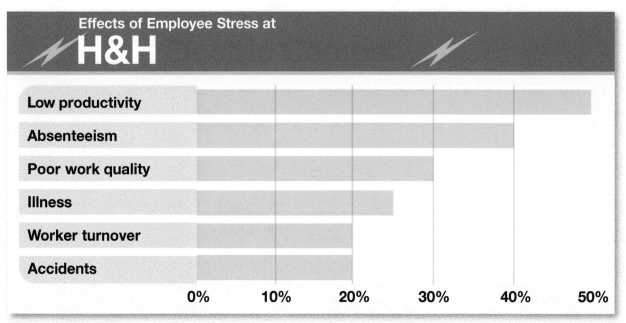

A Read the questions. Look at the bar graph. Fill in the answer.

1. This chart is about _____.

   A   how stress affects employees

   B   how stress affects a business

   C   both *a* and *b*

   D   neither *a* nor *b*

2. Employee stress is the cause of _____.

   A   30 percent of poor quality work

   B   20 percent of worker turnover

   C   both *a* and *b*

   D   neither *a* nor *b*

3. Employee stress contributes to worker turnover less than it contributes to _____.

   A   low productivity

   B   poor work quality

   C   illness

   D   all of the above

4. The chart does not show how stress affects _____.

   A   absenteeism

   B   illness

   C   tardiness

   D   accidents

B Solve the problem. Give your opinion.

You work in the accounting department of a medium-sized company. The quality of one of your coworkers has gone down. She has also called in sick quite a lot recently, which means you end up doing more work. What should you do?

Answers will vary.

Teaching objectives
- Introduce reading and understanding a graph related to employee stress
- Provide practice contrasting *must* and *may / might*

WARM-UP AND REVIEW

- Before class. Write today's lesson focus on the board.
  Lesson F:
  Read and understand a bar graph that shows the effects of employee stress
  Contrast must and may / might
- Begin class. Books closed. Write *Effects of employee stress* on the board. Say the words and have Ss repeat.
- Ask Ss: *What does "effects" mean?* Elicit: *consequences* or *results*.
- Say: *Today we will practice reading and understanding a bar graph about the effects of stress on workers and the company where they work.* Ask Ss: *What do you think the effects of employee stress are?* Elicit responses, such as: *poor quality of work, illness, frequent absences, job turnover, accidents.*

PRESENTATION

- Books open. Direct Ss' attention to the bar graph in Exercise **1**. Ask a S to read the names of six effects of employee stress on a business along the left side of the graph (the Y-axis). Explain new vocabulary as needed.
- Ask a S to read the different percentages listed along the bottom of the graph (the X-axis). Make sure that Ss understand what these percentages refer to. For example, employee stress is the cause of 40 percent of all worker absences.

Teaching Tip

Tell Ss that learning to read these kinds of graphs is a useful life skill. Explain that as technology increases in the workplace, Ss may have jobs in the future that will require them to create, read, interpret, and analyze graphs.

PRACTICE

- Read the instructions aloud for Exercise **1A**. This task helps prepare Ss for standardized-type tests they may have to take. Make sure that Ss understand the task. Have Ss individually scan for and fill in the answers.

COMPREHENSION CHECK

- Check the answers with the class. Make sure that Ss have followed the instructions and filled in their answers.
- Have Ss read aloud the answers they filled in. Ask Ss: *Is that answer correct?* Correct Ss' answers as needed.

APPLICATION

- Direct Ss' attention to Exercise **1B** and read the instructions aloud. Make sure that Ss understand the task.
- Ss discuss the problem in small groups. Walk around and help as needed.
- After Ss discuss the problem, open up the discussion to the entire class. Accept all plausible answers.

Expansion activity (small groups)

- Have Ss work together in small groups to write a list of suggestions for employers about how to relieve employee stress.
- Tell Ss to use *should, shouldn't, have to,* and *don't have to* in their recommendations. Refer Ss to page 46 in the Student's Book as needed.
- Model the activity. Write an example on the board:
  Employers should communicate with their employees in regular meetings.
  Employers should discuss any problems employees are having at work with their employees.
- Walk around and help groups as needed.
- Call on groups to write their recommendations on the board, and engage the class in a discussion.

LESSON F Another view

WARM-UP AND REVIEW

- Books closed. Write a few questions on the board. Ask Ss the questions and encourage them to reply using complete sentences, for example: *How much do you sleep each night? How often do you exercise?*

PRESENTATION

Focus on form

- Use the animated grammar presentation in one or more of the following ways:
  - Preview it before class
  - Show in class
  - Encourage Ss to watch outside of class.
- Books open. Direct Ss' attention to the grammar chart in **2A**. Read the situation aloud: *Sergio works 60 hours a week.* Ask Ss how many hours a week they work.
- Ask two Ss to read the sentences under *Conclusions*. Explain we use *must be* and *must not have* when we are fairly certain (80%) about something.
- Ask individual Ss to read the sentences under *Possibilities*. Explain we use *might be, may be, might not have,* and *may not have* when we are not certain (50%) about something. Underline the verbs after *must, might,* and *may.* Ask Ss what they notice about the verbs. Elicit answer, such as: *The verbs following must, might, and may remain in their base form (be, have).*
- Point to the warm up questions on the board, and ask Ss a few Ss to answer the questions. Then ask other Ss to turn their answers into *may, might,* or *must* sentences. For example: *David only sleeps four hours each night. He must be tired.*

PRACTICE

- Direct Ss' attention to the instructions in **2A**. Read the instructions aloud. Have Ss read the Stress Test. Ensure Ss understand the activity. Ask three Ss to read the dialog aloud.

- Split the class into small groups. Have Ss discuss the responses in the Stress Test. Walk around and help as needed.
- Direct Ss' attention to the instructions in **2B**. Read the instructions aloud. Encourage Ss' to share their sentences with the class.

  Option Tell Ss to add a column to the right of Larisa's answers in their books. Tell them to write their own answers to the questions. Ss share their answers with a partner.

EVALUATION

- Do a quick review of the unit. Have Ss turn to Lesson A. Ask the class to talk about what they remember about this lesson. Prompt Ss, if necessary, with questions, for example: *What are the conversations about on this page? What vocabulary is in the pictures?* Continue in this manner to review each lesson quickly.

Expansion activity

- Before class. Print, for each student, one copy of the Self-assessment for this unit.
- Have Ss complete the Self-assessment either in class or outside of class.
- Provide feedback to Ss such as through a whole-class discussion, partners comparing their worksheets, or T reviewing each S's worksheet.
- If Ss are ready, administer the unit test on pages T-195–T-197 of this Teacher's Edition. The audio script for the test is on pages T-222–T-223.

More Ventures, Unit 4, Lesson F	
Workbook, 15–30 min.	
Multilevel Worksheets, 30–45 min.	www.cambridge.org/ventures/resources/
Collaborative Worksheets, 30–45 min.	
Self-assessment, 10 min.	
CASAS Test Prep Worksheet, 5–10 min.	

2 Grammar connections: *must* and *may / might*

Use *must* and *must not* to make conclusions on the facts you know.
Use *may* and *might* when something is a possibility, but not for sure.

Situation: Sergio works 60 hours a week	
Conclusions	Possibilities
He **must be** tired	He **might be** tired, but he **may enjoy** the work.
He **must get** paid overtime.	He **may get** overtime, but I don't know.
He **must need** the money.	He **might need** the money. He just bought a new house!

After *must, must not, may,* and *might*, use the base form of a verb.

👁 Watch

A Work in a small group. Look at the results of the stress test. Say what you think about the people. Use *may, might,* and *must* in your answers.

A Tina eats only one meal a day.

B She must be on a diet.

C She may snack during the day.

D She might want to save money.

Stress Test

Name	Tina	Sergio	Larisa
1. How many meals do you eat a day?	One	Five	Three
2. Do you eat balanced meals?	No	No	Yes
3. How many cups of coffee do you drink a day?	Five	Two	None
4. How many hours do you sleep at night?	Five	Six	Nine
5. How often do you exercise?	Once a day	Never	Once a week
6. Do you worry about other people?	Yes	No	Yes
7. How often do you get angry?	Never	Every day	Rarely
8. Do you take time each day for yourself?	No	No	Yes
9. How often do you do fun things with friends or family?	Rarely	Once a week	Every day
10. How many hours a week are you at work or school?	45	60	25

B Share your group's ideas with the class.

Most of us think that Tina is on a diet although some of us think she may snack during the day or she might want to save money.

REVIEW

1 Listening

Listen to the phone conversation. Take notes.

🔊 CD1, Track 30

Yesenia's symptoms	Sue's suggestions
1. *tense*	4. *take a parenting class*
2. *too quiet*	5. *call Yesenia's school counselor*
3. *hard to concentrate*	6. *take an exercise class together*

Talk with a partner. Check your answers.

2 Grammar

A **Write.** Complete the story. Use indirect questions.

Ann's Night Out

Ann is 16 years old. It's midnight, and she isn't home yet. She went out with

her friend Liz. Ann's mom doesn't know ____*where they went*____ . She wonders
    1. Where did they go?

__*if Ann and Liz are safe*__ . Ann's mother wants to call Liz's house, but she
    2. Are Ann and Liz safe?

doesn't know __*what the number is*__ . Ann's father is worried, too. He wonders
    3. What is the phone number?

__*if he can find them*__ . Then he hears a sound downstairs. For a minute, he
    4. Can he find them?

doesn't know ____*who it is*____ . It's Ann! Her father says, "We had no idea
    5. Who is it?

__*where you were*__ , but we're glad you're home."
    6. Where were you?

B **Write.** Look at the words that are underlined in the answers. Write the questions.

1. A *When should Ann have been home?*

   B Ann should have been home <u>at 11:00</u>.

2. A *Who should Ann have called?*

   B She should have called <u>her parents</u>.

3. A *What should Ann's parents do?*

   B Ann's parents should <u>put her on restriction</u>.

Talk with a partner. Ask and answer the questions.

Teaching objectives
- Review vocabulary and grammar from Units 3 and 4
- Provide practice with intonation in questions

WARM-UP AND REVIEW

- Before class. Write today's lesson focus on the board.
  Review unit:
  Review vocabulary and grammar from Units 3 and 4
  Practice using intonation in questions

- Begin class. Books closed. Ask Ss questions to review vocabulary from Units 3 and 4, for example: *What are some barriers between generations of immigrant families? What are some differences between your parents and you? What is stress? What are some stressful situations? How can you cope with stress?*

PRESENTATION

- Books open. Direct Ss' attention to Exercise **1** and read the instructions aloud. Tell Ss that they will hear a conversation between two friends, Blanca and Sue.

- ▶ *CD1, Track 30* Model the task. Play or read only the first part of the conversation on the audio (see audio script, page T-179). Pause after Blanca says *I'm really worried about Yesenia. Lately she's been different. She seems tense and too quiet.*

- Direct Ss' attention to number 1 in the chart (*Yesenia's symptoms*), and ask: *How does Blanca describe Yesenia's behavior to her friend Sue?* Elicit: *tense.*

- Ask a S to read aloud the other chart heading (*Sue's suggestions*). Say: *Now listen and fill in the information in both columns of the chart.*

- ▶ *CD1, Track 30* Play or read the complete audio (see audio script, page T-179). Ss listen and complete the chart. Repeat the audio as needed.

COMPREHENSION CHECK

- Read aloud the second part of the instructions for Exercise **1**.

- Ss complete the exercise in pairs. Walk around and help as needed.

- Play the audio again if needed.

Culture Tip

Tell Ss that parenting classes are not uncommon in the United States. They are often held in schools or in local libraries. These classes help parents learn everything from helping children with homework to handling discipline issues. Point out that school counselors are also excellent resources for parents – and children – when it comes to coping with many different kinds of situations both inside and outside of school.

PRACTICE

- Direct Ss' attention to Exercise **2A**. Ask Ss: *What is the title of this story?* ("Ann's Night Out")

- Read the instructions aloud for Exercise **2A**. Point out that Ss should use the information below the blank to complete each sentence with an indirect question. Call on a S to read the first three sentences in the story, including the sample indirect question in the blank. Review how the sample direct question was changed into an indirect question. Have Ss continue reading the story and filling in the blanks.

- Ss complete the exercise individually. Walk around and help as needed.

- Write the numbers 1–6 on the board. Ask Ss to come to the board to write the answers. Have Ss write only the words that are missing from the blanks, not the entire sentence.

- Read the story aloud using Ss' answers. Make corrections on the board as needed.

Teaching Tip

In multilevel classes, some Ss may have little difficulty with this review of grammar. Others may find this review more challenging. Create small groups of mixed ability. Encourage the Ss who are comfortable with these grammar points to help those who are less comfortable.

COMPREHENSION CHECK

- Direct Ss' attention to Exercise **2B**. This exercise reviews question formation by asking questions related to the reading "Ann's Night Out."

- Read the instructions aloud. Model the task. Direct Ss' attention to Speaker B's answer in number 1. Ask Ss: *What question can you write to get this answer?* Elicit this response: *What time should Ann have been home?*

- Ss complete the exercise individually. Walk around and help as needed.

- Check answers with the class. Ask for volunteers to read their questions. Write the questions on the board and correct as needed.

- Read aloud the second part of the instructions for Exercise **2B**.

- Ss work in pairs to ask and answer the questions. Help as needed.

REVIEW

PRESENTATION

- Books closed. Write on the board: *intonation in questions*. Then write these two questions on the board: *How are you? Can you tell me if you did your homework?* Tell Ss that you are going to say these questions aloud and that you want them to pay attention to the tone, or intonation, of your voice at the end of each question. Explain that the tone – or *intonation* – is a change in pitch when speaking. Say: *In English, when we ask direct questions, our intonation falls: it goes down.* Draw a falling arrow above *you* in the first question. Then say: *In English, when we ask indirect questions, our intonation rises: it goes up.* Draw a rising arrow above *homework* in the second question.

- Write a few examples of direct and indirect questions on the board. Say each one aloud, and ask Ss to repeat. Ask Ss if the intonation rises or falls, and indicate the correct intonation with up-or-down arrows.

Teaching Tip

Some Ss may find it difficult to differentiate between rising and falling intonation. Exaggerate the intonation so that these Ss can hear the differences clearly.

- Books open. Direct Ss' attention to Exercise **3A**. Read the instructions aloud.

- ▶ **CD1, Track 31** Play or read the complete audio (see audio script, page T-179).

- Have a S read the second part of the instructions for Exercise **3A**.

- ▶ **CD1, Track 31** Repeat the audio. Pause after each sentence to give Ss time to repeat.

PRACTICE

- Direct Ss' attention to Exercise **3B** and read the instructions aloud.

- ▶ **CD1, Track 32** Model the task. Play or read the first sentence on the audio (see audio script, page T-179). Ask Ss to tell you whether the intonation is rising or falling (falling).

- Tell Ss to pay attention to the intonation in each question as they listen and repeat. Play or read the audio, stopping as needed for Ss to repeat the sentences.

- ▶ **CD1, Track 32** Play or read the complete audio again. Ss identify the intonation of each question by drawing rising or falling arrows. Repeat the audio as needed.

- Read aloud the second part of the instructions for Exercise **3B**.

- Ss complete the task in pairs. Listen to Ss' pronunciation, helping with intonation.

COMPREHENSION CHECK

- Direct Ss' attention to Exercise **3C**, and read the instructions aloud.

- Ss work in pairs to complete the exercise. Walk around and listen to Ss' intonation.

- Call on individual Ss to read aloud the questions. Ask Ss whether each question is direct or indirect. Also ask if the intonation is rising or falling.

APPLICATION

- Focus Ss' attention on Exercise **3D** and read the instructions aloud.

- Ask a S to read aloud the example question. Ask Ss if it is a direct or an indirect question (indirect). Ask Ss to repeat the question. Correct intonation as needed.

- Ss work in pairs to complete the exercise. Walk around and help as needed.

EVALUATION

- Direct Ss' attention to the lesson focus on the board.

- Write the following direct *Wh-* questions on the board: *Where did you go? When did he leave? How is everything at school? Why is she so strict?* Ask Ss to change the questions to indirect *Wh-* questions using introductory clauses.

- Write this question on the board: *Did you finish your homework?* Have Ss tell you what the indirect (Yes / No) form of the question is. For example: *I wonder if / whether you finished your homework.*

- Write on the board: *should, shouldn't, have to, don't have to.* Ask Ss to write four sentences, one for each modal.

- Write these two sentences on the board:
  1. *I don't like the way this soup tastes. It's too salty.*
  2. *Ed didn't do well on the test because he went to a party last night.*

- Ask Ss to read each sentence. Have Ss change number 1 into a sentence that shows regret (e.g., *I shouldn't have put so much salt in the soup. / I should have put less salt in the soup.*) and number 2 into a sentence that gives advice in the past (e.g., *Ed should have studied last night. He shouldn't have gone to the party*).

- Focus Ss' attention on the questions in Exercise **3B**. Ask Ss to read the questions aloud, using rising or falling intonation correctly.

- Check off each part of the lesson focus as Ss demonstrate an understanding of what they have learned in the lesson.

③ **Pronunciation:** intonation in *Wh-* questions

A **Listen** to the intonation in these *Wh-* questions.

Direct question

Where did he go?

Indirect question

Can you tell me where he went?

🔊 CD1, Track 31

Listen again and repeat. Pay attention to the intonation.

B **Listen and repeat.** Then draw arrows to show rising or falling intonation in the questions.

🔊 CD1, Track 32

1. **A** What does Ann do to reduce stress?

   B She listens to music.

2. **A** Why are you so tense?

   B I have my driver's test today.

3. **A** Do you know what Rodolfo does to calm down?

   B He walks or jogs.

4. **A** When did Ivan miss his class?

   B He missed his class on Tuesday.

5. **A** Can you tell me where Andy lives?

   B He lives on East Fifth Street.

6. **A** Do you know why they're always late?

   B No, I don't know.

Talk with a partner. Compare your answers.

C **Talk** with a partner. Ask and answer the questions. Use the correct intonation.

1. What is one thing you should have done today or yesterday?

2. What is a common punishment for teenagers when they come home late?

3. What were your favorite things to do when you were growing up?

4. Can you tell me what you do to reduce stress?

5. Do you know why it's important to exercise regularly?

6. Do you know if meditation is difficult to do?

D **Write** five questions. Make at least three indirect questions. Ask your partner.

Can you tell me how you cope with stressful situations?

1. *Answers will vary.* _____

2. _____

3. _____

4. _____

5. _____

Talk with a partner. Ask and answer the questions.

UNIT 5 AROUND TOWN

Lesson A Listening

1 Before you listen

A What do you see?

B What is happening?

Almaz

Steve Jones

VOLUNTEER APPLICATION

nformation

ddress

Code

UNIT 5

Teaching objectives
- Introduce students to the topic
- Find out what students know about the topic
- Preview the unit by talking about the pictures
- Provide practice of key vocabulary
- Provide practice that develops listening skills

WARM-UP AND REVIEW

- Before class. Write today's lesson focus on the board.
  Lesson A:
  Ask about volunteer activities
  Discuss personal experiences with volunteering or with helping people
- Begin class. Books closed. Direct Ss' attention to the lesson focus. Point to *Ask about volunteer activities.* Ask Ss: *What does "volunteer activities" mean?* List Ss' responses on the board, for example: *activities that help people, work that you don't receive money for.*
- Ask Ss: *What are some examples of volunteer activities?* List Ss' responses on the board, for example: *working in a homeless shelter, working at a school or a public library, helping in a soup kitchen, helping in a church program, helping at a community center.*

PRESENTATION

- Books open. Set the scene. Direct Ss' attention to the pictures on page 58. Ask the question from Exercise **1A**: *What do you see?* Elicit and write on the board as much vocabulary as possible: *elderly people, a desk, a volunteer application,* etc. Explain any unfamiliar words. Point to each word on the board and have Ss repeat.

Culture Tip

 Draw or show an example of this sign to your Ss. Ask Ss: *Where have you seen this sign?* Write Ss' responses on the board, for example: *on doors to public bathrooms, on parking spaces, in buses, at airports, on entrances to some public buildings.* Ask what the sign indicates (that a place can be used by – or is reserved for – handicapped people). Tell Ss that seating for the disabled and elderly is often indicated on public transportation. Emphasize that it is culturally understood that elderly people and people with physical disabilities have seating priority.

- Direct Ss' attention to the question in Exercise **1B**: *What is happening?*
- Hold up the Student's Book. Ask Ss to say a few sentences about each picture. Elicit responses such as: *Almaz is talking to Steve in an office. Almaz is applying to be a volunteer in a nursing home.*
- Brainstorm and list on the board things that Almaz and Steve might be saying to each other.
- Discuss Ss' ideas and make suggestions. For example, say: *What do you think Steve is asking Almaz about?*

Teaching Tip

Encourage Ss to be creative. At this point, there is no single correct answer.

Expansion activity (student pairs)

- Invite Ss to work in pairs to write and perform a dialog based on the situation they see in one of the two pictures. Ss' dialogs should be between two people; for example, between an elderly person and a volunteer in the first picture or between Almaz and Steve in the second picture.
- Encourage partners to develop their visual literacy skills by looking closely at the details in both pictures and talking about what they see.
- When partners have completed writing and practicing their dialog, call on several pairs to act it out for the class.

  Option Pairs may choose to write a story based on the situation they see in one of the pictures.

LESSON A Listening

PRESENTATION

- Books open. Direct Ss' attention to Exercise **2A** and read the instructions aloud.

- Ask a S to read aloud the two questions in Exercise **2A**. Tell Ss to listen for the answers as the audio is played or read.

- ▶ **CD1, Track 33** Play or read the audio (see audio script, page T-179). Repeat the audio as needed.

- Ask Ss if they understood everything in the listening exercise. Elicit any unfamiliar words and write them on the board. Help Ss understand the meanings. Be sure that they understand the definition of *worthwhile* (a good use of time or effort).

- Elicit answers to the questions in Exercise **2A**. For example: *The speakers are Almaz and Steve. They are talking about Almaz's interest in volunteering at the nursing home.*

- Focus Ss' attention on Exercise **2B** and read the instructions aloud. Tell Ss to listen to the audio and to complete the chart based on the information they hear. Ask Ss to define *responsibilities*. Elicit responses, such as: *Responsibilities are duties that a person has to do at work or at home.*

- ▶ **CD1, Track 33** Tell Ss to listen for details about Almaz's responsibilities when she volunteered at the public library and what her responsibilities will be at the nursing home. Model the task. Play or read the audio again. Pause the audio after Almaz says: *I worked with adults who wanted to learn how to read.* Ask a S to read the example in the chart, under the heading *Almaz's responsibilities at the library* (*worked with adults learning to read*). Play or read the rest of the audio. Ss listen and complete the chart.

- ▶ **CD1, Track 33** Play or read the audio again. Ss listen and check their answers.

- Write the numbers *1–6* on the board. Ask Ss to come to the board to write their answers.

Learner persistence (individual work)

- ▶ **CD1, Track 33** Ss can listen to the audio for Exercises **2A** and **2B** at home for reinforcement and review. They can also listen to the audio for self-directed learning when class attendance is not possible.

PRACTICE

- Focus Ss' attention on Exercise **3A**. Read the instructions aloud. Tell Ss that the story in this exercise is a summary of what happened in the pictures on the previous page.

- Direct Ss' attention to the words in the word bank. Say each word aloud and have Ss repeat. Correct pronunciation as needed. Explain any words that are new to Ss.

- Model the task. Ask a S to read aloud the first two sentences in the story. Point out that Ss need to fill in the remaining blanks with the words from the word bank.

- Ss complete the exercise individually. Walk around and help as needed.

COMPREHENSION CHECK

- ▶ **CD1, Track 34** Play or read the audio (see audio script, page T-179). Ss listen and check their answers. Repeat the audio as needed.

- Write the numbers *1–10* on the board. Ask individual Ss to come to the board to write only the answers. Have other Ss read the sentences using the words on the board to fill in the blanks.

Learner persistence (individual work)

- ▶ **CD1, Track 34** Ss can listen to the audio for Exercise **3A** at home for reinforcement and review. They can also listen to the audio for self-directed learning when class attendance is not possible.

Culture Note

Read the culture note aloud. Be sure that Ss understand the term *nursing home*. Ss may not be familiar with nursing homes since many may come from cultures in which elderly family members are cared for at home.

APPLICATION

- Read the instructions aloud for Exercise **3B**.

- Ss complete the exercise in pairs. Help as needed.

- Ask several pairs to share their ideas with the class.

EVALUATION

- Direct Ss' attention to the lesson focus on the board. Check Ss' understanding of the key vocabulary by asking them to use the words in the word bank in Exercise **3A** to write sentences about why Almaz wants to volunteer at the nursing home, Quiet Palms.

- Check off each part of the lesson focus as Ss demonstrate an understanding of what they have learned in the lesson.

More Ventures, Unit 5, Lesson A	
Workbook, 15–30 min.	
Multilevel Worksheets, 30–45 min. **Collaborative Worksheets**, 30–45 min.	www.cambridge.org/ventures/ resources/
Student Arcade, time varies	www.cambridge.org/ venturesarcade/

UNIT GOALS
Describe benefits of volunteering **Describe** someone who made a difference
Identify information in advertisements for volunteer positions

2 Listen

A **Listen** and answer the questions.

1. Who are the speakers?
2. What are they talking about?

🔊 CD1, Track 33

B **Listen again.** Complete the chart.

Almaz's responsibilities at the library	Volunteer responsibilities at Quiet Palms
1. *worked with adults learning to read*	4. *help residents with their meals*
2. *taught writing*	5. *deliver mail and flowers*
3. *read to children*	6. *take residents for walks*

🔊 CD1, Track 33

3 After you listen

A **Read.** Complete the story.

can't wait	compassionate	orientation	residents	volunteer
commitment	coordinator	patient	responsibilities	worthwhile

Last summer, Almaz volunteered at the public library downtown. She liked working with the older people because she felt that she was doing something ___*worthwhile*___ .
1

Today, she is meeting with Steve, the volunteer ___*coordinator*___ at Quiet Palms, a nursing
2

home. She wants to ___*volunteer*___ there to find out if she likes working in the health-
3

care field. Steve tells her about some of her *responsibilities* at Quiet Palms. He says it's
4

very important for volunteers to be ___*patient*___ and *compassionate* when they are
5   6

working with the ___*residents*___ . He asks Almaz to make a ___*commitment*___ to volunteer
7   8

at least three hours per week. Almaz agrees to attend an ___*orientation*___ . She
9

says she ___*can't wait*___ to start volunteering.
10

> **CULTURE NOTE**
> A *nursing home* is a place where elderly people live when their families can't take care of them.

🔊 CD1, Track 34

Listen and check your answers.

B **Talk** with your classmates.

What are some places in your community to volunteer? What are some benefits of volunteering?

Lesson B Time clauses

1 Grammar focus: clauses with *until* and *as soon as*

Watch

Dependent time clauses with *as soon as* and *until* can come at the beginning or end of a sentence. *As soon as* and *until* can be about the present, the past or the future.

AS SOON AS = RIGHT AFTER	*UNTIL* = UP TO A PARTICULAR TIME
Present: As soon as Mr. Shamash **finishes** his lunch, Almaz **leaves** Quiet Palms.	**Present:** Almaz **stays** with Mr. Shamash **until** he **finishes** lunch.
Past: As soon as Mr. Shamash **finished** his lunch, Almaz **left** Quiet Palms.	**Past:** Almaz **stayed** with Mr. Shamash **until** he **finished** his lunch.
Future: As soon as Mr. Shamash **finishes** his lunch, Almaz **will leave** Quiet Palms.	**Future:** Almaz **will stay** with Mr. Shamash **until** he **finishes** his lunch.

2 Practice

A Write. Complete the sentences with *until* or *as soon as*. Circle the time clause.

1. A Mr. Shamash is in pain. When will he start to feel better?

   B He'll feel better (*as soon as* he takes his medication.)

2. A How long will Mr. Shamash stay at Quiet Palms?

   B He'll stay (*until* his broken hip heals.)

3. A When can Mr. Shamash begin exercising again?

   B (*As soon as* Mr. Shamash feels stronger,) he can start doing moderate exercise.

4. A When does Mr. Shamash get ready for his walk?

   B He gets ready (*as soon as* Almaz arrives.)

5. A How long will Mr. Shamash and Almaz play cards?

   B They'll play cards (*until* it is time for lunch.)

6. A How long did Mr. Shamash nap yesterday?

   B He napped (*until* Almaz came to visit him.)

7. A When is Mr. Shamash going to go to sleep?

   B (*As soon as* his visitors leave,) he'll take his medicine and go to sleep.

8. A When did the nurse assistant help Mr. Shamash with his shower?

   B (*As soon as* Mr. Shamash woke up) the nurse assistant helped him with his shower.

Listen and check your answers. Then practice with a partner.

CD1, Track 35

WARM-UP AND REVIEW

- Before class: Write the lesson focus on the board.
  Lesson B:

  Time clauses with "until"
  Time clauses with "as soon as"

- Begin class. Books open. Review Lesson A vocabulary. Direct Ss' attention to the pictures on page 58. Ask questions about Almaz and Steve, such as: *What do you think Almaz will do immediately after the interview?* (call her mother to tell her about the interview.) *What do you think Steve will do immediately after the interview?* (check Almaz's references.)

- Ask Ss: *What will you do after class?* Elicit and write responses on the board, for example: *Ana will pick up her children. Samba will go to work. Maribel will buy groceries.*

PRESENTATION

Focus on meaning / personalize

- Books closed. Direct Ss' attention to the lesson focus on the board. Read it aloud.

- Add *as soon as* to one of the examples you wrote on the board in, for example: *Ana will pick up her children as soon as she leaves school.*

- Explain or elicit that *as soon as* emphasizes that one event will occur immediately after the other.

- Write on the board: *When will you stop studying English?* Elicit some examples, such as: *I will stop studying English when I speak very well.* Change the sentence to utilize *until*, for example: *Tony will study English until he speaks very well. Michiko will study English until she gets a job.*

- Explain or elicit that we use *until* to express how long an action will continue.

Focus on form

- Use the animated grammar presentation in one or more of the following ways:
  - Preview it before class
  - Show in class
  - Encourage Ss to watch outside of class.

- Books closed. Direct Ss' attention to the charts in Exercise **1**. Read the sentences in the chart aloud. Ask Ss to repeat. Write the first sentence on the board. Ask: *In this sentence, which clause is the main clause?* (Almaz leaves Quiet Palms.) Underline it. Ask: *Which clause is the dependent clause?* (as soon as Mr. Shamash finishes his lunch.) Circle it. Ask: *What is the verb in the main clause?* (leaves.) *What tense is it?* (present.) *What is the verb in the dependent clause?* (finishes.) *What tense is it?* (present.)

- Write the second sentence on the board. Ask: *In this sentence which clause is the main clause?* (Almaz left Quiet

Palms.) Underline it. Ask: *Which clause is the dependent clause?* (As soon as Mr. Shamash finishes his lunch.) Circle it. Ask: *What is the verb in the main clause?* (left.) *What tense is it?* (past.) *What is the verb in the main clause?* (finishes.) *What tense is it?* (present.)

- Write the third sentence on the board. Ask: *In this sentence, which clause is the main clause?* (Almaz will leave Quiet Palms.) Underline it. Ask: *Which clause is the dependent clause?* (As soon as Mr. Shamash finishes his lunch.) Circle it. Ask: *What is the verb in the main clause?* (finishes.) *What tense is it?* (present.) Explain that both sentences are about the future, but we use *will* only in the main clause.

- Do the same with the next three sentences in the chart with *until*. Point out that with *as soon as* the verb will be in the present tense in the dependent clause, even if the verb tense is past, present, or future in the independent clause. For until, the verb tenses change in the dependent and independent clauses.

- Ask: *Can you start a sentence with as soon as or until?* (Yes.) Write on the board:

  As soon as Ana leaves school, she will pick up her children. Until the class finishes, we will study English.
  Ask: *What's different when you start the sentence with "as soon as" or "until"?* (When *until* and *as soon as* clauses begin a sentence, we use a comma after the clause.)

Useful Language

Read the tip box aloud. Tell Ss that sentences utilizing *as soon as* and *until* are time clauses.

PRACTICE

- Direct Ss' attention to Exercise **2A** and read the instructions aloud.

- Model the task. Ask a S to read number 1 to the class. Make sure that Ss understand the task.

- Ss complete the exercise individually. Walk around and help as needed.

COMPREHENSION CHECK

- Focus Ss' attention on the second part of the instructions for Exercise **2A**.

- ▶ *CD1, Track 35* Play or read the audio (see audio script, pages T-179–T-180). Ss listen and check their answers. Then they practice the dialog with their partner.

- Write the numbers *1–8* on the board. Ask individual Ss to come to the board to write the questions and answers. Work with the class to make corrections on the board as needed.

- Invite partners to read aloud the A and B sentences on the board.

LESSON B Future time clauses

PRESENTATION

- Books open. Tell Ss they are going to read and talk about different volunteer activities. Read the instructions aloud for Exercise **2B**.
- Direct Ss' attention to the pictures and descriptions on page 61.
- Call on individual Ss to read the words under each picture.
- Model the task. Ask a S to read the example sentence.

Useful Language

Read the tip box aloud. Explain that *'til* is never used in formal writing.

- Ss complete the exercise with a partner. Walk around and help as needed.

PRACTICE

- Direct Ss' attention to the second part of Exercise **2B**. Read the instructions aloud.
- Ask a S to read the example sentence to the class.
- Ss work individually to complete the exercise. Walk around and help as needed.

Culture Note

Read the culture note aloud. Write on the board: *to volunteer* and *a volunteer*, explaining that the first is a verb and the second is a noun. Explain that Americans of all ages often use some of their free time to help people or to support a political campaign or a social cause. Ask Ss to list some example volunteer activities and write them on the board. Discuss each one.

COMPREHENSION CHECK

- Write the numbers *1–8* on the board. Ask individual Ss to come to the board to write their answers for Exercise **2B**.
- Have other Ss read the sentences aloud. Ask Ss if the sentences are written correctly. Have different Ss correct them on the board as needed.

APPLICATION

- Direct Ss' attention to Exercise **3A**. Read the instructions aloud.
- Ss work individually to make a list of activities. Walk around and help as needed.
- Direct Ss' attention to Exercise **3B**. Read the instructions aloud.

- Model the task. Ask a pair of Ss to read aloud the sample dialog.
- Ss work in pairs to complete the exercise, using *as soon as* and *until* to explain their activities. Walk around and help as needed.
- Read the instructions aloud for Exercise **3C**. Call on pairs to share information with the class about any volunteer activities in which their partners participated or participate.

Expansion activity *(student pairs)*

- Ask Ss to talk about their responsibilities at work or at home, using *until* and *as soon as*. Partners should begin by telling each other whether they want to talk about work or home so that their partner will know what questions to ask.
- Model the activity. Ask Ss: *What questions can you ask your partner about his or her responsibilities at home?* Write some examples on the board:

    What do you do as soon as you get home?
    What do you do until dinner is ready?
    What are some things you need to do as soon as you finish dinner?

- Tell Ss they can use these questions or make up others, depending on which situation they decide to discuss. Ss work in pairs to ask and answer each other's questions.
- Have pairs share the information they discussed.

EVALUATION

- Books closed. Direct Ss' attention to the lesson focus on the board.
- Write the following sentences on the board:

    He helps his brother with his homework as soon as he gets home.
    He helps his brother with his homework until it's time for dinner.

- Ask Ss: *What is the difference in the meaning of the two sentences?* Elicit an appropriate response, such as: *The first sentence means that when he gets home, he helps his brother. The second sentence means that he helps his brother before dinner, but once it's time for dinner, he stops.*
- Check off the lesson focus as Ss demonstrate an understanding of what they have learned in the lesson.

More Ventures, Unit 5, Lesson B	
Workbook, 15–30 min.	
Multilevel Worksheets, 30–45 min.	www.cambridge.org/ventures/ resources/
Collaborative Worksheets, 30–45 min.	
Student Arcade, time varies	www.cambridge.org/ venturesarcade/

B **Talk** with a partner. Discuss Charles's volunteer activities at a nursing home. Use *as soon as* or *until*. Use the present tense.

> As soon as Charles arrives at work, he puts on his name tag.

> Charles doesn't put on his name tag until he arrives at work.

1. arrive / put on name tag

2. get his assignment/ go to Mrs. Halliday's room

3. walk with Mrs. Halliday / feel tired

4. read to Mrs. Halliday / lunchtime

5. stop reading / lunch is delivered

6. stay with Mrs. Halliday / finish eating

7. watch TV with Mrs. Halliday / time to rest

8. go home / finish playing a game with Mrs. Halliday

Write sentences about Charles's volunteer activities.

As soon as Charles arrives at work, he puts on his name tag.

3 Communicate

A **Choose** one time when you helped someone or volunteered. Make a list of your activities. Use Exercise 2B to help you.

B **Work** with a partner. Ask questions about each other's activities. Use *as soon as* and *until*. Use the past tense.

> **A** I volunteered at an animal shelter.
>
> **B** What did you do as soon as you arrived?
>
> **A** I checked the board for my duties.
>
> **B** How late did you stay?
>
> **A** I stayed until the shelter closed for the day.

C **Share** information about your partner.

Lesson C Verb tense contrast

1 Grammar focus: repeated actions in the present and past

In sentences that talk about repeated actions, the correct word order is subject + verb + number of times + time expression. The number of times answers the question *How often?* The time expression answers the question *When?*

 Watch

		NUMBER OF TIMES	TIME EXPRESSIONS
PRESENT	This year, Sana **volunteers** at the homeless shelter		a week. each month.
	This year, Sana **is volunteering** at the homeless shelter	once twice	
PAST	Sana **volunteered** at the homeless shelter	three times several times many times	last year. two years ago. when she was 12.
PRESENT PERFECT	Sana **has volunteered** at the homeless shelter		so far. recently. in her life.

2 Practice

A Write. Complete the story with the present, present perfect, or past forms of the verbs.

Sharing with Sally

Sally Sutherland created "Sharing with Sally," a volunteer organization that helps seniors stay connected with the outside world. The organization *has delivered*
1. deliver
over 5,000 dinners to seniors so far. Sharing with Sally

_____*began*_____ six years ago. Several times a week,
2. begin

Sally and her volunteers _____*deliver*_____ meals, _____*talk*_____ to seniors on the phone,
3. deliver   4. talk

and _____*visit*_____ the ones who can't leave their homes. Over 200 people volunteer at
5. visit

Sharing with Sally. Jake, a college student, _____*volunteered*_____ all last year. He _____*called*_____
6. volunteer   7. call

elderly people on the phone once a week and _____*talked*_____ to each person. He said
8. talk

it was a very valuable experience. Betsy, a 35-year-old mother of

two, _____*volunteered*_____ for two years so far and loves it.
9. volunteer

Listen and check your answers.

🔊 CD1, Track 36

- Introduce and provide practice talking about repeated actions in the present and past

WARM-UP AND REVIEW

- Before class. Write the lesson focus on the board.
  Lesson C:
  Repeated actions in the present and past
- Begin class. Books closed. Review three tenses: the present, the past, and the present perfect. Ask several Ss questions utilizing the three tenses, for example: *What language do you study? When did you move to the United States? How long have you lived here?*

PRESENTATION

Focus on meaning / personalize

- Books closed. Direct Ss' attention to the lesson focus on the board. Read it aloud.
- Write on the board: *repeated actions.* Ask Ss what the phrase means (actions that are done over and over again).
- Write on the board: *In 2010, I studied English four times a week.* Ask: *Is the action over?* (Yes.) *How do you know?* (past tense.) *Was the action repeated in the past?* (Yes.) *How do you know?* (four times a week.)
- Ask: *What about this year? How often do you study now?* Elicit answers such as: *I study three days a week.* Ask: *Is the action over?* (No.) *How do you know?* (present tense.) *Is the action repeated?* (Yes.) *How do you know?* (three days a week.)
- Ask: *How many times have you gone to the library so far this month?* Elicit answers, for example: *So far, I have gone to the library several times this month.* Ask: *Is the action over?* (Yes.) *Was it repeated in the past?* (Yes.) *Do you think it will happen again?* (Yes.) *How do you know?* (So far.) *What verb tense is used?* (present perfect.)

Focus on form

- Use the animated grammar presentation in one or more of the following ways:
  - Preview it before class
  - Show in class
  - Encourage Ss to watch outside of class.

- Books open. Direct Ss' attention to the grammar chart in Exercise **1**. Tell Ss that when talking about repeated actions in the present and past, certain time expressions correspond to certain tenses. Read and have Ss repeat the first sentence in row 1: *This year, Sana volunteers at the homeless shelter.* Ask: *What tense is it?* (present) Repeat the sentence two times, once for each time expression: *Sana volunteers twice a day / week / year.* Note the second sentence: *This year, Sana volunteers at the homeless shelter.* We sometimes use the present continuous form with a future connotation. It does not mean that at the moment of speaking she is volunteering.
- Read and have Ss repeat the first sentence in row 2: *Sana volunteered at the homeless shelter twice last year.* Ask: *What tense is it?* (past) Repeat the sentence two times, once for each time expression, for example: *Sana volunteered at the homeless shelter twice last week / month / year.*
- Read and have Ss repeat the first sentence in row 3: *Sana has volunteered several times so far.* Ask: *What tense is it?* (present perfect) *How do you know?* (*has volunteered*) Repeat the sentence two times, once for each time expression.

PRACTICE

- Direct Ss' attention to Exercise **2A** and read the instructions aloud.
- Model the task. Call on a S to read the first two sentences, including the example answer.
- Ss complete the exercise individually. Walk around and help as needed.

COMPREHENSION CHECK

- Read aloud the second part of the instructions for Exercise **2A**.
- ▶ *CD1, Track 36* Play or read the audio (see audio script, page T-180). Ss listen and check their answers.
- Write the numbers *1–9* on the board. Invite individual Ss to come to the board to write the word or words they have written on the blanks. Ask other Ss to read the answers aloud. Make corrections on the board as needed.

LESSON C Verb tense contrast

PRACTICE

- Direct Ss' attention to Exercise **2B** and read the instructions aloud.

- Ask five Ss to read aloud the activities in the chart along with the corresponding numbers under the columns *Number of times last year* and *Number of times this year*. Explain vocabulary as needed, and write any new words on the board.

- Call on two Ss to read the two example sentences.

- Ss complete the exercise in pairs. Walk around and help as needed.

- Read the instructions aloud for the second part of Exercise **2B**. Call on a S to read the example sentence.

- Ss complete the exercise individually. Walk around and help as needed.

- Ask several Ss to write their sentences on the board.

- Call on other Ss to read each sentence on the board. Ask: *Is this sentence correct?* Make corrections on the board as needed.

APPLICATION

- Direct Ss' attention to Exercise **3A**. Read the instructions aloud. Ask a S to read aloud the first item in each list.

- Ss complete the chart individually. Walk around and help as needed.

- Direct Ss' attention to Exercise **3B**. Read the instructions aloud.

- Model the task. Ask two Ss to read the example conversation.

- Ss work with a partner to ask and answer each other's questions. Walk around and help as needed.

- Read the instructions aloud for Exercise **3C**. Ss take turns sharing information they learned from their partner.

Expansion activity (whole class)

- **Materials** Index cards.

- On separate index cards, write the words from the column of time expressions in the grammar chart on page 62. Make a set of cards for each group of three or four Ss in the class. Place the cards in two different piles.

- Have Ss look at the chart on page 62 and note which tenses correspond to which time expressions.

- Books closed. Form teams of three to four Ss. Have each S on a team choose a card from each pile (e.g., *each year* from the first pile, *in her life* from the second pile) and say the two phrases aloud. Ss write sentences on the board using the correct tense and phrases, and they check with their team to see if the sentence makes sense.

- Once Ss from all teams have finished writing their sentences on the board, each S then reads his or her sentence to the class. Each S who has written and read aloud a correct sentence earns a point for his or her team.

- Tally the number of points for each team. The team with the most points wins.

EVALUATION

- Direct Ss' attention to the lesson focus on the board.

- Ask Ss to refer to the grammar chart on page 62 and to write a sentence in the present tense using the time expression *a week*. Elicit responses, such as: *I work five days a week.* Call on individual Ss to read their sentences aloud.

- Ask Ss to write a sentence in the present perfect using the time expression *in my life*. Elicit responses, such as: *I have been on a plane twice in my life.* Call on individual Ss to read their sentences aloud.

- Then ask Ss to write a sentence in the past tense using *last year*. Elicit responses, such as: *I went to Riverside Park last year.* Call on individual Ss to read their sentences aloud.

- Check off the lesson focus as Ss demonstrate an understanding of what they have learned in the lesson.

More Ventures, Unit 5, Lesson C	
Workbook, 15–30 min.	
Multilevel Worksheets, 30–45 min. **Collaborative Worksheets,** 30–45 min.	www.cambridge.org/ventures/ resources/
Student Arcade, time varies	www.cambridge.org/ venturesarcade/

B Talk with a partner. Make sentences about Betsy's volunteer experience. Include the number of times and time expressions.

A Betsy visited seniors at their homes 30 times last year.

B She's also visited them 15 times so far this year.

Activity	Number of times last year	Number of times this year
Visit seniors at their homes	30	15
Call seniors on the phone	45	25
Help Sally put meals in the truck	5	1
Deliver meals	25	10
Return equipment to the truck	20	5
Take her children with her to the seniors' homes	10	3
Volunteer to read to seniors	5	2
Clean the truck	10	4

Write sentences about Betsy's activities.

Betsy visited seniors at their homes 30 times last year.

3 Communicate

A Make a list of your experiences volunteering or helping people.

Last year	This year
took my grandmother to the hairdresser	*volunteer at a homeless shelter*
Answers will vary.	

B Work with a partner. Share your lists. Ask questions about your partner's activities. Use *How often . . . ?* or *How many times . . . ?*

How often did you take your grandmother to the hairdresser last year?

Every week.

How often do you volunteer at a homeless shelter?

Several times a year.

How many times have you volunteered at the homeless shelter so far this year?

Three times.

C Share information about your partner.

Lesson D Reading

1 Before you read

Talk with your classmates. Answer the questions.

1. Look at the picture. What is unusual about it?

2. Read the title. What do you think the story will be about?

> Use titles and pictures to help predict what a reading is about.

2 Read

Read the newspaper article. Listen and read again.

◀)) CD1, Track 37

RUNNING WITH ROPES

Imagine running with your eyes closed. How do you feel? Insecure? Afraid? Justin Andrews knows these feelings very well. Justin is a former long-distance runner who lost his vision because of a grave illness. For the past six months, he has been running twice a week with the help of volunteer runners at Running with Ropes, an organization that assists blind and visually impaired runners. "Running with Ropes has changed my life," Justin says. "Until I heard about it, I thought I'd never run outside again."

Volunteers at Running with Ropes make a commitment to volunteer two to four hours a week. Scott Liponi, one of the running volunteers, explains what they do. "We use ropes to join ourselves to the blind runners and guide them around and over obstacles, such as holes in the road and other runners." Scott has learned how to keep the rope loose so the blind runner has more freedom. He deeply respects the blind runners' tenacity. "They are incredibly determined," he says. "It doesn't matter if it's hot, raining, or snowing – they are going to run." Scott says it is gratifying to share in the joy of the runners and to feel that they trust him. "The four hours I spend at Running with Ropes are the most rewarding part of my week," he says. "It's really a worthwhile commitment."

Teaching objectives

- Introduce a newspaper article about running with ropes
- Provide practice using pictures and titles to predict
- Provide practice using context clues to figure out the meaning of unfamiliar words
- Provide practice identifying conext clues to determine if the meaning of a word is positive or negative

WARM-UP AND REVIEW

- Before class. Write today's lesson focus on the board.
  Lesson D:
  Read and understand "Running with Ropes"
  Use pictures and titles to predict
  Identify positive and negative words

- Begin class. Books closed. Focus Ss' attention on the word *ropes* in the lesson focus. Write the word on the board. Ask: *What are ropes?*

- Point to *"Running with Ropes"* on the board and ask Ss what they think this title means. Write some of the Ss' ideas on the board.

PRESENTATION

- Books open. Direct Ss' attention to Exercise **1**. Read the instructions aloud.

- Have Ss focus on the two questions in Exercise **1**. Ask two Ss to read them aloud.

- Ss in pairs. Have Ss answer the questions with a partner.

Teaching Tip

Read the tip box aloud. Tell Ss that looking at pictures with a text or identifying any words they may know in the title is a good way to narrow down the possibilities of the subject matter of a reading.

PRACTICE

- Read the instructions aloud for Exercise **2**. Ask Ss to read the newspaper article silently before listening to the audio.

- ▶ **CD1, Track 37** Play or read the audio, and ask Ss to read along (see audio script, page T-180). Repeat the audio as needed.

- While Ss are listening and reading the article, ask them to write in their notebooks any words or expressions they don't understand. When the audio is finished, have Ss write the new vocabulary words on the board.

- Point to each word on the board. Say it aloud. Ask Ss to repeat. Give a brief explanation of each word, or ask Ss to explain the word if they know it. If Ss prefer to look up the new words in their dictionaries, allow them to do so.

- Encourage Ss to guess the meaning of unfamiliar words from the context of the article. For example, if a S writes *tenacity*, read aloud the sentence containing the word and any related sentences: *He deeply respects the blind runners' tenacity. "They are incredibly determined," he says.* Ask Ss to think about the meaning of the word *tenacity* based on the information in the surrounding sentences. Tell Ss that *tenacity* is another way of saying being determined, or of continuing to do something even when faced with obstacles.

Learner persistence (individual work)

▶ **CD1, Track 37** Ss can listen to the audio for Exercise **2** at home for reinforcement and review. They can also listen to the audio for self-directed learning when class attendance is not possible.

Community building (student pairs)

- Tell Ss to do some research about volunteer activities in their neighborhood. They can use the Internet, contact the Chamber of Commerce, or talk to storeowners or other people in their neighborhood.

- For each volunteer activity, Ss should find out what the responsibilities are and what kind of commitment is required. Ss should decide which activity they think would be a worthwhile commitment for them and present their research findings orally to the class.

- Write some of the volunteer activities on the board and discuss them with Ss.

LESSON D Reading

COMPREHENSION CHECK

- Direct Ss' attention to Exercise **3A** and read the instructions aloud.

- Ss work with a partner to ask and answer the questions. Walk around and help as needed.

- Discuss the answers with the class. Ask Ss to say where in the reading they found each of the answers.

PRACTICE

- Direct Ss' attention to Exercise **3B**. Ask a S to read aloud the instructions in number 1.

> Read the tip aloud. Write *positive* and *negative* on the board. Ask Ss for the meaning of *positive* and *negative*. Elicit an appropriate response, such as: *Positive means "good" or "happy," and negative means "bad" or "unhappy."* Remind Ss that looking at surrounding words or sentences can help them determine if a word has a positive or negative meaning, or connotation.

- Model the task. Ask Ss to find *grave* in the first paragraph of the article. Have a S read the sentence in which *grave* appears. Ask other Ss whether the word has a positive or negative meaning in the sentence. Tell Ss to place a check mark in the negative column and write the clue that helped them figure out the connotation of the word. Make sure that all Ss understand the task.

- Ss fill in the chart individually. Walk around and help as needed.

- Write the chart on the board and ask individual Ss to fill in their answers. Work with the class to make corrections on the board as needed.

- Direct Ss' attention to number 2 of Exercise **3B** and read the instructions aloud.

- Ss complete the task in a small group. Examples from the text include: *commitment* (P), *obstacles* (N), *determined* (P), *worthwhile* (P). Invite Ss to say their answers to the class. Correct as needed.

Expansion activity *(small groups)*

- Ss in small groups. Give Ss a time limit (3–5 minutes). Ask groups to brainstorm words to create a list of as many positive and negative words as they can think of without using a dictionary.

- Walk around and correct Ss' work if they have misspelled a word or categorized it incorrectly.

- Ask each group to write two sentences, one in which the word has a positive connotation or meaning, the other in which the word has a negative one. One representative from each group writes the group's two sentences on the board, underlining the positive or negative word without telling the class which is which.

- Ss from other groups have to guess whether the underlined word is positive or negative based on the words around it in the sentence.

APPLICATION

- Direct Ss' attention to Exercise **3C** and read the instructions aloud.

- Ask four Ss to read aloud the questions in Exercise **3C**.

- Partners take turns asking and answering the questions. Walk around and help as needed.

- Ask several pairs to share the answers they discussed with the class. (Ss discuss the response to number 1 only if they feel comfortable in doing so.)

Expansion activity

- Refer Ss to "Heifer International," another reading on the same topic on pages 148–150.

- Have Ss complete the activity either in class or outside of class.

- Provide feedback to Ss such as through whole-class discussion, partners comparing their worksheets, or T reviewing each S's worksheets.

EVALUATION

- Books closed. Direct Ss' attention to the lesson focus on the board. Write on the board the words in number 1 from Exercise **3B**. Ask Ss to use these words to retell the main points of the newspaper article "A Worthwhile Commitment."

- Check off each part of the lesson focus as Ss demonstrate an understanding of what they have learned in the lesson.

More Ventures, Unit 5, Lesson D	
Workbook, 15–30 min.	
Multilevel Worksheets, 30–45 min. **Collaborative Worksheets,** 30–45 min.	www.cambridge.org/ventures/ resources/
Student Arcade, time varies	www.cambridge.org/ venturesarcade/

3 After you read

A Check your understanding.

When you see a new word, look at the words around it to guess if the meaning is positive or negative.

*He lost his vision because of a **grave** illness.*

You can guess that *grave* has a negative meaning because loss of vision and illness are both negative events.

1. According to the author, why is *Running with Ropes* a worthwhile organization?

2. Who is Justin Andrews? What happened to him?

3. How is Justin able to run?

4. Compare what Justin says in paragraph 1 and what Scott says in the last paragraph about *Running with Ropes*. How are the statements similar?

5. Based on Justin and Scott's statements about their experiences, do you think they will continue to participate in the program? Why or why not?

B Build your vocabulary.

1. Look at the reading tip above. Then, in the reading passage, underline the words from the chart. Decide if their meanings are positive or negative. Fill in the clues that helped you guess.

Word	Positive	Negative	Clue
1. grave		✓	*He lost his vision because of an illness.*
2. insecure		✓	*afraid*
3. impaired		✓	*blind*
4. freedom	✓		*loose*
5. tenacity	✓		*incredibly determined*
6. gratifying	✓		*share in the runners' joy and feel that they trust him*
7. rewarding	✓		*Worthwhile commitment*

2. Work with your classmates. Write four more words from the reading that have positive or negative meanings. Indicate if their meanings are positive or negative. Fill in the clues that helped you guess. *Answers will vary.*

Word	Positive	Negative	Clue
a.			
b.			
c.			
d.			

C Talk with a partner.

1. When do you feel most insecure?

2. Tell about something that takes tenacity.

3. Describe a gratifying experience.

4. What is a commitment you have made in your life?

For college and career readiness practice, see pages 148–150.

Lesson E Writing

1 Before you write

A **Talk** with your classmates. Look at the picture. Answer the questions.

1. Who are the people in the picture? Where are they? What are they doing?

2. Do you think the young woman is doing something important? Why or why not?

B **Read** the paragraph.

Story Lady

My friend Vivianne is one of the most compassionate people I have ever met. After college, she wanted to do something truly worthwhile, so she spent a year working as a literacy volunteer in northeastern Brazil. At the time, this area didn't have any libraries, so Vivianne traveled to different schools in a mobile library van. As soon as she arrived at a school, the children would run outside and shout, "Story Lady! Story Lady!" Then everyone went inside, sat down, and listened quietly while she read them a story. Vivianne made a huge difference in these children's lives. She introduced them to literature and taught them to love reading. Today, she still gets letters from children who remember her generosity and kindness.

 Make your writing more interesting by including specific details that answer the questions *who, what, where, when, why,* and *how.*

Teaching objectives

- Prepare Ss for writing a paragraph about someone they know who made a difference
- Provide practice using specific details to make writing more interesting

WARM-UP AND REVIEW

- Before class. Write today's lesson focus on the board.
  Lesson E:
  Write a paragraph about someone you know who made a difference
  Use specific details to make your writing more interesting
- Begin class. Books closed. Review vocabulary from the unit. Write the words *someone who makes a difference*, and ask Ss what they think the expression means. Elicit an appropriate response, such as: *someone who changes something for the better.* Ask Ss if they can give you some examples of famous people who have made a difference (e.g., Mahatma Gandhi, Mother Teresa, Martin Luther King Jr., Cesar Chávez, Harriet Tubman).
- Ask Ss to explain to the class how the famous person they mentioned has made a difference.

PRESENTATION

- Books open. Focus Ss' attention on the picture in Exercise **1A**. Ask: *What do you see?* Elicit an appropriate response, such as: *a woman telling a story to children.*
- Read the instructions aloud for Exercise **1A**.
- Ask two Ss to read the two questions to the class.
- Ss work with a partner to ask and answer the questions. Walk around and help as needed.
- Have two pairs ask and answer the questions for the rest of the class.
- Ask Ss which stories they liked listening to when they were children, and why. Ask Ss: *Who used to tell you your favorite stories?* (Answers may include a teacher, a parent or another family member, a neighbor, or a friend.)
- If your Ss have children, ask those Ss whether they read to their children, and if so, what kinds of books or stories they read. Encourage Ss to read to their children in English or in their native language.

PRACTICE

- Direct Ss' attention to Exercise **1B** and read the instructions aloud.
- Have Ss focus on the title of the paragraph, "Story Lady." Ask Ss to use the title to predict what the story is about.
- Tell Ss to read the paragraph silently. Have Ss underline any words they don't know. Write the new words on the board. Encourage Ss to use context clues to try to figure out the meaning of each new word.

Read the tip aloud. Point out that specific details in a piece of writing can make the information more vivid, or colorful, by appealing to one or more of the reader's five senses. Also tell Ss that by including details that answer the questions *who, what, when, where, why,* and sometimes *how,* their writing will be clearer and more interesting. Explain that these question words are called the "five *Ws*" and that journalists use them when they write news articles. Guide Ss to see that the answers to these questions tell the reader *who* was involved in an event, *what* happened, *when* and *where* it happened, *why* it happened, and *how* it happened.

Expansion activity (small groups)

- Invite Ss to write a story for Vivianne, the Story Lady, to tell the Brazilian children. The story can be about any topic that the children might enjoy. Encourage Ss to be creative and to think of stories they liked to hear when they were young.
- Have Ss work in small groups to brainstorm a list of story ideas. Then encourage each group to choose a story idea as well as a recorder to write the group's story on a piece of paper.
- Walk around and help as needed.
- Have each group choose a reader (someone different from the recorder) to read the story aloud or to tell it to the class, using oral storytelling skills such as reading loudly and clearly and using appropriate emphasis, intonation, and gestures.
- After each group finishes reading its story aloud, ask Ss from other groups to assess the story they have just heard, evaluating it both for content and oral presentation.

LESSON E Writing

PRESENTATION

- Focus Ss' attention on Exercise **1C**. Read the instructions aloud. Tell Ss to refer to page 66 to complete this exercise.

- Model the task. Ask a S to read aloud the first detail from the paragraph and to read the example answer.

- Ss complete the exercise with a partner. Walk around and help as needed.

- Ask Ss to share their answers with the class. Make corrections as needed.

PRACTICE

- Direct Ss' attention to Exercise **1D** and read the instructions aloud.

- Ss complete their charts individually. Walk around and help as needed.

Teaching Tip

Before Ss get ready to write, encourage them to talk about their topics in a prewriting activity. Talking with a partner or a small group will help Ss focus on their subject and on the specific details they can use in the paragraph they will be writing in Exercise **2**.

APPLICATION

- Focus Ss' attention on Exercise **2**. Read the instructions aloud.

- Ss complete the task individually, using the model paragraph in Exercise **1B** on page 66 and the chart in Exercise **1D** on page 67 to help them write their own paragraph. Walk around and help as needed.

Learner persistence (pairs)

- If more proficient writers finish early, ask them to sit with Ss who need help with their writing.

COMPREHENSION CHECK

- Direct Ss' attention to Exercise **3A**.

- This exercise asks Ss to develop skills to review and edit their own writing.

- Ss check their own paragraphs against the writing checklist. Walk around and help as needed. If any Ss check *No* for one or more of the checklist items, ask them to revise and edit their paragraphs to include the missing information.

EVALUATION

- Direct Ss' attention to Exercise **3B** and read the instructions aloud. This exercise asks Ss to work together to edit their writing. Reading aloud enables the writer to review his or her own writing and to understand the need to write clearly for an audience.

- Ss complete the exercise in pairs. Have Ss take turns reading their paragraphs to each other. Walk around and help as needed.

- Listen to Ss as they ask their partner one question about the paragraph and tell their partner one thing they learned from it.

- Ask several Ss to read their paragraphs aloud. Tell the other Ss in the class to listen for descriptive details that appeal to one or more of their five senses. For example, ask Ss: *Which details in the story could you see, hear, touch, taste, and/or smell? How did these details make the writing more colorful and interesting?*

- Have Ss also listen for details that answer the questions: *who, when, where, why, what,* and *how*. The writer of the paragraph can confirm that the information is correct.

- Direct Ss' attention to the lesson focus on the board.

- Check off each part of the lesson focus as Ss demonstrate an understanding of what they have learned in the lesson.

More Ventures, Unit 5, Lesson E	
Workbook, 15–30 min.	
Multilevel Worksheets, 30–45 min.	www.cambridge.org/ventures/ resources/
Collaborative Worksheets, 30–45 min.	

C **Work** with a partner. Write the words *who, what, where, when, why,* or *how* next to the details from the paragraph.

1. _____*who*_____ my friend Vivianne
2. _____*when*_____ after college
3. _*what/who*_ a literacy volunteer
4. _____*where*_____ northeastern Brazil
5. _____*why*_____ because the area didn't have any libraries
6. _*how / where*_ in a mobile library van
7. _____*what*_____ read stories to the children
8. _____*what*_____ taught the children to love reading

D **Plan** a paragraph about someone you know who made a difference. Use the chart to make notes.

Who made a difference?	*Answers will vary.*
What did he or she do?	
Where did it happen?	
When did it happen?	
Why did this person do it?	

② Write

Write a paragraph about someone you know who made a difference in your life or someone else's life. Include specific details that answer *Wh-* questions. Use the paragraph in Exercise 1B and the chart in Exercise 1D to help you.
Answers will vary.

③ After you write

A **Check** your writing.

	Yes	No
1. My topic sentence names the person who made a difference.	☐	☐
2. I included specic details in my paragraph.	☐	☐
3. The details in my paragraph answer *Wh-* questions.	☐	☐

B **Share** your writing with a partner.

1. Take turns. Read your paragraph to a partner.
2. Comment on your partner's paragraph. Ask your partner a question about the paragraph. Tell your partner one thing you learned.

Lesson F Another view

1 Life-skills reading

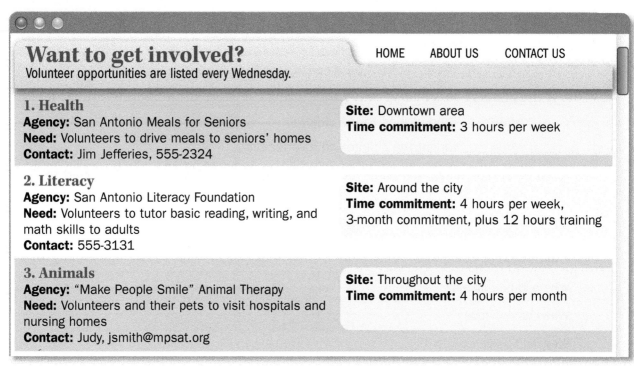

Want to get involved?
Volunteer opportunities are listed every Wednesday.

HOME   ABOUT US   CONTACT US

1. Health
Agency: San Antonio Meals for Seniors
Need: Volunteers to drive meals to seniors' homes
Contact: Jim Jefferies, 555-2324

Site: Downtown area
Time commitment: 3 hours per week

2. Literacy
Agency: San Antonio Literacy Foundation
Need: Volunteers to tutor basic reading, writing, and math skills to adults
Contact: 555-3131

Site: Around the city
Time commitment: 4 hours per week, 3-month commitment, plus 12 hours training

3. Animals
Agency: "Make People Smile" Animal Therapy
Need: Volunteers and their pets to visit hospitals and nursing homes
Contact: Judy, jsmith@mpsat.org

Site: Throughout the city
Time commitment: 4 hours per month

A Read the questions. Look at the advertisements for volunteer positions. Fill in the answer.

1. Which volunteer position requires the biggest time commitment?
   - (A) 1
   - **(B) 2**
   - (C) 3
   - (D) They are all the same.

2. Which position requires a driver's license?
   - **(A) 1**
   - (B) 2
   - (C) 3
   - (D) none of the above

3. Which word could replace *tutor* in the Literacy opportunity?
   - (A) know
   - (B) learn
   - **(C) teach**
   - (D) understand

4. Which statement is true?
   - (A) San Antonio Meals for Seniors has a bigger time commitment than the San Antonio Literacy Foundation.
   - **(B) San Antonio Literacy Foundation requires more training than the other places.**
   - (C) "Make People Smile" Animal Therapy has the biggest time commitment of the three places.
   - (D) San Antonio Meals for Seniors requires more training than the other places.

B Solve the problem. Give your opinion.

Ann volunteers at a day-care center. She thought she would be reading to the children and doing art projects with them, but the teachers ask her to organize the room and do clerical work for them. She doesn't spend very much time with the children. What should she do?
Answers will vary.

Teaching objectives
- Introduce reading and understanding ads for volunteer positions
- Provide practice contrasting *used to* and *be used to*

WARM-UP AND REVIEW

- Before class. Write today's lesson focus on the board.
  Lesson F:
  Read and understand ads for volunteer positions
  Contrast "used to" and "be used to"

- Begin class. Books closed. Ask Ss: *What does "get involved" mean?* Elicit responses, such as: *do something to make a difference, help a person or an organization.*

- Tell Ss that in this lesson, they will practice reading and understanding several advertisements looking for volunteers.

- Ask Ss where they can find ads for volunteer positions, for example: *in community newspapers, online, on bulletin boards at schools, in places of religious worship, in community centers, in supermarkets.*

- Ask Ss what kind of information they expect to see in an ad looking for volunteers. Elicit responses, such as: *the name of the company or organization looking for volunteers, where volunteers would work, how many hours a week or month they would work (time commitment), and who to contact for more information.*

PRESENTATION

- Books open. Direct Ss' attention to the three ads in Exercise **1**.

- Divide the class into three groups. Assign one of the advertisements to each group. Tell each group to read the advertisement and discuss the meaning of any new words. Allow Ss to use dictionaries to look up any words they don't understand. Walk around and help as needed.

- Tell Ss that they are going to explain their advertisement to another group without looking at the ad as they are talking. Ask each group to write down any key words that will help them remember the advertisement.

- Give each S a number according to how many Ss are in each group. For example, if there are three Ss in a group, number each S from 1 to 3.

- Ask all the ones, twos, and threes to get together in new groups.

- Books closed. Tell Ss to describe their ad to their new group.

- Walk around and help as needed. If Ss can't remember something about their advertisement, give them clues to help them recall the content.

PRACTICE

- Read aloud the instructions for Exercise **1A**. This exercise helps prepare Ss for standardized-type tests they may have to take. Be sure that Ss understand the task. Have Ss individually scan for and fill in the answers.

COMPREHENSION CHECK

- Check answers with the class. Make sure that Ss have followed the instructions and filled in their answers.

- Have Ss read aloud the questions and answers they filled in. Make corrections as needed.

APPLICATION

- Direct Ss' attention to Exercise **1B** and read the instructions aloud. Make sure that Ss understand the task. Have Ss individually solve the problem.

- Ss work in small groups to discuss the problem.

- Ask several Ss to share their opinions with the class. Accept all plausible answers.

Expansion activity (student pairs)

- Ss in pairs. Tell Ss that they are going to write the advertisement that motivated Almaz to apply for the volunteer job in the nursing home at the beginning of the unit.

- Encourage Ss to look at the pictures on page 58. Ask Ss: *What information should you include in the ad?* (name of the nursing home, responsibilities, time commitment, contact information, etc.).

- Tell Ss that they should talk about the information with their partner and then write the ad together. Have Ss use the ads on page 68 as models. Encourage Ss to be creative.

- Walk around and help as needed. When Ss have finished, have volunteers read their ads to the class.

LESSON F Another view

WARM-UP AND REVIEW

Focus on meaning / personalize

- Books closed. Ask several Ss *What did you use to do when you were a child?* Elicit several answers and write them on the board, for example: *I used to live in Colombia when I was a child. I used to play soccer.* Ensure Ss use the proper form of *used / use to* in positive and negative constructions.

PRESENTATION

Focus on form

- Use the animated grammar presentation in one or more of the following ways:
  - Preview it before class
  - Show in class
  - Encourage Ss to watch outside of class.
- Books open. Direct Ss' attention to the left-hand column of the grammar chart in **2A**. Write *used to + verb* on the board. Explain that we use this grammar structure to talk about things we did in the past and don't do anymore.
- Ask two Ss to read the sentences. Ask another S to read the question. Tell Ss to compare the sentences, and ask what the differences are. Elicit: *The base form of the verb "use" is used in questions and negative structures.*
- Direct Ss' attention to the right-hand column of the grammar chart in **2A**. Write *be used to + verb* on the board. Explain that we use this grammar structure to talk about things we are familiar with or accustomed to in our daily lives.
- Ask three Ss to read the sentences. Ask another S to read the question. Point out that *used* remains the same in positive / negative statements and questions.
- Ask several Ss *What are you used to doing every day?* Elicit several answers, and write them on the board, for example: *I am used to eating breakfast at 8 a.m. I am used to exercising every day.* Ask Ss to make sentences about their classmates changing the *I* pronoun to *he / she*. For example: *She is used to exercising every day.*

PRACTICE

- Direct Ss' attention to the instructions in **2A**. Read the instructions aloud. Ensure Ss understand the activity. Ask two pairs of Ss to read the dialogs aloud.

- Split the class into small groups. Pass out pennies to each S or have Ss use their own pennies. Have Ss ask one another the questions in the square. Walk around and help as needed. Ss should play the game until they have finished asking all the questions.
- Direct Ss' attention to the instructions in **2B**. Read the instructions aloud. Ask two Ss to read the example sentences. Encourage Ss to share information about their classmates.

EVALUATION

- Do a quick review of the unit. Have Ss turn to Lesson A. Ask the class to talk about what they remember about this lesson. Prompt Ss, if necessary, with questions, for example: *What are the conversations about on this page? What vocabulary is in the pictures?* Continue in this manner to review each lesson quickly.

Expansion activity

- Before class. Print, for each student, one copy of the Self-assessment for this unit.
- Have Ss complete the Self-assessment either in class or outside of class.
- Provide feedback to Ss such as through a whole-class discussion, partners comparing their worksheets, or T reviewing each S's worksheet.
- If Ss are ready, administer the unit test on pages T-198–T-200 of this Teacher's Edition. The audio script for the test is on page T-223.
- If Ss are ready, administer the midterm test on pages T-201–T-203 of this Teacher's Edition. The audio script for the test is on page T-223.

More Ventures, Unit 5, Lesson F	
Workbook, 15–30 min.	
Multilevel Worksheets, 30–45 min.	www.cambridge.org/ventures/ resources/
Collaborative Worksheets, 30–45 min.	
Self-assessment, 10 min.	
CASAS Test Prep Worksheet, 5–10 min.	

2 Grammar connections: *used to and be used to*

Use *used to* + base form of a verb for past situations that are not true now. Use *be used to* + gerund or noun for things a person is accustomed to.

I **used to eat** a lot of sandwiches as a child. I **didn't use to eat** meat.	I **am used to eating** fish for dinner. I **am not used to eating** dessert. Katia **is used to American food**.
What **did** you **use to eat** as a child?	What **are** you **used to eating** for dinner?

Watch

A **Work** in a small group. Play the game. Write your name on a small piece of paper. Flip a coin to move your paper. Then tell your group your answer to the question in the square. Use *used to* or *be used to* in your answer. Take turns.

= 1 space

= 2 spaces

This says, "What did you use to do for fun as a child?" Well, I used to play in the park with my sister. We had a lot of fun.

Start here →	What did you use to do for fun as a → child?	How often are you used to → going to the supermarket?	How did you use to get to school as a child?
Who are you used to helping in your family? ←	What kind of weather are you used to? ←	What did you use to do after school as a child? ←	What noises are you used to hearing in your neighborhood?
What time are you used to going to school? →	What time did you use to go to school as a child? →	What is something you used to do, but don't do now? →	What are you used to eating in the morning?
Finish! ←	What are you used to hearing (or seeing) in your neighborhood? ←	What is something you didn't use to do, but do now? ←	What kind of food did you use to eat as a child?

B **Share** information about your classmates.

Julia used to play in the park with her sister for fun.

Oswaldo is used to going to the supermarket once a week.

UNIT 6 TIME

Lesson A Listening

1 Before you listen

A What do you see?

B What is happening?

1

2
Mrs. Rosen

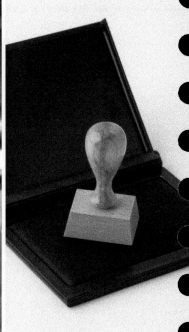

3

Mr. Chung

4
Ms. Morales

UNIT 6

Teaching objectives
- Introduce students to the topic
- Find out what students know about the topic
- Preview the unit by talking about the pictures
- Provide practice of key vocabulary
- Provide practice that develops listening skills

WARM-UP AND REVIEW

- Before class. Write today's lesson focus on the board.
  Lesson A:
  Talk about time-saving devices
  Discuss the advantages and disadvantages of technology

- Begin class. Books closed. Direct Ss' attention to the lesson focus. Point to *time-saving devices*. Ask Ss to guess the meaning of this phrase. Help Ss guess by asking: *What things do you use to help you save time?*

- Ask Ss: *What are some examples of time-saving devices?* List Ss' responses on the board, for example: *dishwashers, washing machines, copy machines, cell phones, computers.*

- Ask Ss: *What do the words "advantage" and "disadvantage" mean?* Elicit appropriate answers, such as: *positive and negative points about something.*

- Underline the prefix *dis-* in *disadvantages* in the lesson focus. Point out that *dis-* is a prefix meaning "not," so the literal meaning of the word is "not advantages." Ask Ss if they can think of other words that begin with *dis-*. Elicit appropriate answers, such as: *disrespect, disappear, dishonest, dislike, disagree, disorganized.*

PRESENTATION

- Books open. Set the scene. Direct Ss' attention to the pictures on page 70. Ask the question from Exercise **1A**: *What do you see?* Elicit and write on the board as much vocabulary as Ss know, such as: *reporter, journalist, microphone, cell phone, letters.* Explain any unfamiliar words.

- Direct Ss' attention to the question in Exercise **1B**: *What is happening?* Read it aloud. Hold up the Student's Book. Point to the picture of Mrs. Rosen. Ask: *What does Mrs. Rosen have?* (She has an address stamper.) Point out the object Mrs. Rosen is talking about. Explain that this is an address stamper. Tell Ss that an address stamper can be used to stamp the same address many times.

- Point to the picture of Mr. Chung. Ask: *What's Mr. Chung doing here?* (He's writing a letter.)

- Point to the picture of Ms. Morales. Ask: *What's Ms. Morales doing here?* (She's shopping with her daughter.)

Culture Tip

Ask Ss if they notice anything about the titles on the female characters' name labels (*Mrs.* and *Ms.*). Tell Ss that there are three possible titles for a woman in English: *Miss, Mrs.,* and *Ms.* Explain that *Miss* is used for an unmarried woman and that *Mrs.* is used for a married woman. Point out that unlike *Miss* and *Mrs.*, *Ms.* does not identify a woman's marital status. Tell Ss that the title *Ms.* is now the most common way to address a woman you don't know and that the best way to find out which title a woman prefers is to ask her.

PRACTICE

- Have Ss work in groups of three to write an interview between the person in each of the pictures and the reporter. Assign Ss in each group a number: *1, 2,* or *3.* Suggest that all the ones write an interview between Mrs. Rosen and the reporter; all the twos write an interview between Mr. Chung and the reporter; and all the threes write an interview between Ms. Morales and the reporter.

Teaching Tip

Encourage Ss to be imaginative. At this point, there is no single correct answer.

- Walk around and help as needed.

- Ask for volunteers to role play their interview for the class.

LESSON A Listening

PRESENTATION

- Books open. Direct Ss' attention to Exercise **2A**. Read the instructions aloud. Tell Ss that they are going to hear three different conversations. Have Ss listen for the main ideas.
- ▶ **CD2, Track 2** Play or read the audio (see audio script, page T-180).
- Ask Ss if they understood everything in the listening exercise. Write any unfamiliar words on the board and help Ss understand the meaning of each. Be sure that Ss understand the meaning of *spam* (junk e-mail, or unwanted e-mail advertising).
- Partners complete Exercise **2A**. Elicit answers to the questions in the exercise.
- Direct Ss to Exercise **2B**, and read the instructions aloud. Tell Ss to listen and complete the chart.
- ▶ **CD2, Track- 2** Model the task. Play or read the audio again. Pause the audio after Mrs. Rosen says in Conversation 1: *Let me see. . . . I guess it's this – my address stamper.* Ask a S to read the example written under *Time-saving device* (address stamper). Play or read the audio again. Pause after Mrs. Rosen says: *The address stamper just takes seconds, even though it's not electronic.* Ask Ss: *What would you fill in for Mrs. Rosen under "Opinion about time-saving device" in the chart?* (She thinks the address stamper is very useful.) Tell Ss that even though Mrs. Rosen's opinion is not stated directly, we can guess her opinion from what she says. Play or read the rest of the audio. Ss listen and complete the chart.
- ▶ **CD2, Track 2** Play or read the audio again. Ss listen and check their answers. Repeat the audio as needed.

Learner persistence *(individual work)*
- ▶ **CD2, Track 2** Ss can listen to the audio for Exercises **2A** and **2B** at home for reinforcement and review. They can also listen to the audio for self-directed learning when class attendance is not possible.

PRACTICE

- Direct Ss' attention to Exercise **3A**. Read the instructions aloud. Tell Ss that the story is a summary of what happened in the pictures on page 70. Remind Ss that a summary retells only the most important points of a story.
- Direct Ss' attention to the words in the word bank. Say each word aloud. Ask Ss to repeat. Correct pronunciation as needed. Make sure that Ss understand the meaning of each word. Explain any words that are new to Ss.
- Model the exercise. Call on a S to read the first sentence in the story, including the example answer.
- Ss complete the exercise individually. Walk around and help as needed.

COMPREHENSION CHECK

- ▶ **CD2, Track 3** Play or read the audio (see audio script, page T-180). Ss listen and check their answers. Repeat the audio as needed.
- Write the numbers *1–10* on the board. Ask individual Ss to come to the board to write their answers.
- Make corrections on the board as needed.

Learner persistence *(individual work)*
- ▶ **CD2, Track 3** Ss can listen to the audio for Exercise **3A** at home for reinforcement and review. They can also listen to the audio for self-directed learning when class attendance is not possible.

APPLICATION

- Focus Ss' attention on Exercise **3B**. Read the instructions aloud.
- Ss complete the exercise in pairs. Help as needed.
- Ask several pairs to ask and answer the questions for the class. Discuss Ss' opinions about technology.

Expansion activity *(small groups)*
- Ask Ss: *What's something that could be invented that would save you time and energy?*
- Ask small groups to brainstorm a list of time-saving devices that have not yet been invented (to the best of their knowledge) but that they would like to have. After each S has had a chance to share his or her device, the group should decide on the one device it will present to the class.
- One S in each group should present that group's favorite device to the class. The representative should say what it is, what it does, how it works, and why his or her group chose it.

EVALUATION

- Direct Ss' attention to the lesson focus on the board. Ask individual Ss to look at the pictures on page 70 and make sentences using the words in Exercise **3A**.
- Check off each part of the lesson focus as Ss demonstrate an understanding of what they have learned in the lesson.

More Ventures, Unit 6, Lesson A	
Workbook, 15–30 min.	
Multilevel Worksheets, 30–45 min. **Collaborative Worksheets**, 30–45 min.	www.cambridge.org/ventures/resources/
Student Arcade, time varies	www.cambridge.org/venturesarcade/

UNIT GOALS

Express opinions about technology   **Identify** advantages and disadvantages of technology
Predict how technology may change lives in the future

2 Listen

A **Listen** and answer the questions.

1. Who are the speakers?   2. What are they talking about?

◀)) CD2, Track 2

B **Listen again.** Complete the chart.

	Time-saving device	Opinion about time-saving device
1. Mrs. Rosen	*address stamper*	*saves time*
2. Mr. Chung	*computer*	*wastes more time than it saves*
3. Ms. Morales	*cell phone*	*saves time but not money*

◀)) CD2, Track 2

3 After you listen

A **Read.** Complete the story.

convenient	distracting	email	manual	technology
devices	electronic	innovative	spam	text message

Today, a reporter from KESL Radio asked three people about ___*technology*___
                                                                      1
and their favorite time-saving _____*devices*_____. Mrs. Rosen's favorite device is
                                        2
_____*manual*_____. She says it saves time, even though it isn't _____*electronic*_____.
        3   4
Mr. Chung isn't a fan of technology. In fact, he says technology *wastes* more time than

it saves. For example, he says he doesn't like _____*email*_____ because he gets lots
                                                        5
of _____*spam*_____. He also finds email ___*distracting*___. He doesn't think it is
        6   7
___*convenient*___. Ms. Morales loves technology. She uses the camera on her cell
        8
phone in a very _____*innovative*_____ way – to send her daughter pictures of clothes that
                          9
are on sale. Her daughter sends a _____*message*_____ back: "Buy." or "Don't buy."
                                              10

Listen and check your answers.

◀)) CD2, Track 3

B **Discuss.** Talk with your classmates.

1. Do you agree with the people interviewed? Why or why not?

2. In general, do you think technology saves time or wastes time? Give examples.

Lesson B Clauses of concession

1 Grammar focus: *although* clauses

Use *although* to connect two clauses that show a contrast. The information in one clause is surprising or unexpected because of the information in the other clause. *Although* goes with the information that is known or not surprising.

👁 Watch

KNOWN INFORMATION	UNEXPECTED INFORMATION	EXAMPLE
It takes thirty hours to drive from Denver to Los Angeles.	William refuses to fly.	**Although** it takes thirty hours to drive from Denver to Los Angeles, William refuses to fly.
Jake sets his alarm clock every day.	Jake often wakes up late and misses his bus.	Jake often wakes up late and misses his bus **although** he sets his alarm clock every day.

2 A Write. Which sentence is surprising or unexpected? Circle it. Then combine the two sentences. Use *although* in front of the sentence that is not surprising or unexpected.

1. Mrs. Sanchez can't operate her digital camera. She read the directions many times.
   (Mrs. Sanchez can't operate her digital camera) although *she read the directions many times*.

2. Mrs. White's car has a GPS system. She gets lost all the time.
   Although *Mrs. White's car has a GPS system,* (she gets lost all the time.)

3. Mr. Green doesn't use his microwave. He paid a lot of money for it.
   (Mr. Green doesn't use his microwave), although *he paid a lot of money for it*.

4. Mr. Chung doesn't like to use it. Email is fast.
   Although *email is fast*, (Mr. Chung doesn't like to use it)

5. I prefer to read paperback and hardcover books. E-books are very popular.
   Although E-books are very popular, (I prefer to read paperback and hardcover books).

6. Ms. Kaye had urgent business 1000 miles away. She refused to travel by plane.
   Although Ms. Kaye had urgent business in another state, (she refused to travel by plane)

7. I prefer to use a fan when it's hot. My house has central air-conditioning.
   Although my house has central air conditioning, (I prefer to use a fan when it's hot).

8. Ben never sets his alarm clock. He still gets to work on time.
   Although Ben never sets his alarm clock, (he still gets to work on time).

9. I play my CDs on my CD player at home. All my music is available online.
   Although all my music is available online, (I play my CDs on my CD player at home)

Listen and check your answers.

🔊 CD2, Track 4

WARM-UP AND REVIEW

• Before class: Write the lesson focus on the board.
Lesson B:
"although"

• Begin class. Books open. Review Lesson A charts. Ask two
Ss to read the example sentences aloud. Direct Ss attention
to the Language Use Statement and explain that we use
although to connect two clauses that show contrast.

PRESENTATION

Focus on meaning / personalize

• Books closed. Direct Ss' attention to the lesson focus on the
board. Read it aloud.

• Write on the board examples from your life of some unusual
"results" to an action, for example: *I sleep nine hours a night.*
I am always tired. My sister lives close by. I seldom see her.
Ask: *Is it unusual that I sleep so much, and I am still tired?*
(Yes.) *Is it surprising that my sister lives close by, but I rarely*
see her? (Yes.) Combine the sentences using *although*, for
example: *Although I sleep nine hours a night, I am always*
tired.

• Use the phrases on the board from the warm-up exercise to
give more examples of sentences with *although*: *Although Mr.*
Chung has a computer, he doesn't use it.

Ms. Morales loves her cell phone although it doesn't
save money.

• Ask: *Are timesaving devices usually manual or electronic?*
(electronic.) *Did the reporter expect Mrs. Morales to choose*
a manual device? (No.) *Is her choice of a manual device a*
surprise or expected? (a surprise.)

• Point out that the *although* clause describes a situation, and
the main clause describes a surprising contrast. We expect
that a timesaving device would be electronic, not manual.

• Elicit or explain that the purpose of dependent clauses
with *although* is to contrast two surprising, unexpected, or
opposing things.

Focus on form

• Use the animated grammar presentation in one or more of
the following ways:

• Preview it before class

• Show in class

• Encourage Ss to watch outside of class.

• Books open. Direct Ss' attention to the chart in Exercise **1**.
Read aloud the first sentence, and write it on the board. Ask
Ss to repeat. Ask: *Which clause is the dependent clause?*
(Although it takes thirty hours to drive from Denver to Los
Angeles.) Circle it. Ask: *Which clause is the main clause?*
(William refuses to fly.) Say: *Underline it.*

• Explain that we call *although* clauses "clauses of
concession."

• Ask: *What do you notice about using commas with although?*
(A comma is used when the *although* clause is at the
beginning of a sentence.)

PRACTICE

• Direct Ss' attention to Exercise **2A**. The purpose of this
exercise is to check comprehension of the grammar focus
and to combine sentences using *although*. Read the
instructions aloud.

• Call on a S to read the example. Make sure that Ss
understand the exercise.

• Ss complete the exercise individually. Walk around and help
as needed.

COMPREHENSION CHECK

• Focus Ss' attention on the second part of the instructions for
Exercise **2A**, and read it aloud.

▶ *CD2, Track 4* Play or read the audio (see audio script,
page T-180). Ss listen and check their answers. Repeat the
audio as needed.

• Write the numbers *1–9* on the board. Ask individual Ss to
come to the board to write their combined sentences. Make
corrections on the board as needed.

LESSON B Clauses of concession

PRESENTATION

- Books open. Direct Ss' attention to the pictures in Exercise **2B**. Hold up the Student's Book. Point to each picture and make sure that Ss know the vocabulary words for each illustration (e.g., *vacuum cleaner*, *laptop*, *dishwasher*.)
- Tell Ss that they are going to talk and write about which devices or technology Mr. Chung prefers.

PRACTICE

- Read the instructions aloud for Exercise **2B**.
- Ask a S to read the words in the word bank. Ask another S to read the example sentence above the pictures. Tell Ss that they should imagine which devices or technology Mr. Chung likes best.
- Ss complete the exercise in pairs. Walk around and help as needed.
- Direct Ss' attention to the second part of Exercise **2B**. Read the instructions aloud.
- Call on a S to read the example sentence. Tell Ss that their sentences must include a clause with *although* or *even though.*
- Ss work individually to complete the exercise. Walk around and help as needed.
- Ask Ss to come to the board to write their sentences. Make corrections on the board as needed.

APPLICATION

- Direct Ss' attention to Exercise **3A** and read the instructions aloud.
- Model the task. Ask two Ss to read the example dialog to the class.
- Ss work in small groups to complete the exercise. Walk around and help as needed.
- Direct Ss' attention to Exercise **3B** and read the instructions aloud.
- Ask Ss to share with the class information they learned about the time-saving devices and tools that their classmates own but don't use.

Culture Note

Call on a S to read the culture note to the class. Ask Ss if they have ever been to a garage, yard, or tag sale. Ss who have been to these sales can say what the sale was like and what items they bought. Have Ss suggest how they can find out about garage sales in their community (*by reading the local newspaper, by looking at signs that are posted around town,* etc.).

Expansion activity *(student pairs)*

- Ask Ss if they know somebody like Mr. Chung, who prefers to do things the "old-fashioned way." If so, they know it is sometimes difficult to convince someone to change his or her ways. Explain to Ss that in this activity, they will attempt to change Mr. Chung's mind.
- Tell Ss that they are going to write a conversation with a partner in which one of them is Mr. Chung, and the other is a friend. In the conversation, the other person should try to convince Mr. Chung to try a new way of doing something. Ss must use *even though* or *although* at least twice.
- Model the task. Write the following on the board:

  Ms. Morales: *Even though you prefer to listen to your cassette player, you should try an MP3 player!*

  Mr. Chung: *But why? Although I know they're very popular, I prefer my cassette player. It's less expensive.*

  Ms. Morales: *Even though it is less expensive, it's more difficult to carry.*

- Ss work in pairs to write their short dialog. Then have them practice their conversation a few times, taking turns to play each role. Walk around and help as needed.
- Ask several pairs to perform their dialog for the class.

EVALUATION

- Books closed. Direct Ss' attention to the lesson focus on the board.
- Write the following sentence on the board: *Although it's raining hard, I want to go to the football game.* Ask a S to say this sentence in another way. Tell the S that he or she can change the word order but not the words. Elicit an appropriate response: *I want to go to the football game although it's raining hard.*
- Ask a S to tell another way of saying that same sentence using a different word than *although*. Elicit: *Even though it's raining hard, I want to go to the football game. I want to go to the football game even though it's raining hard.*
- Check off the lesson focus as Ss demonstrate an understanding of what they have learned in the lesson.

More Ventures, Unit 6, Lesson B	
Workbook, 15–30 min.	
Multilevel Worksheets, 30–45 min. Collaborative Worksheets, 30–45 min.	www.cambridge.org/ventures/ resources/
Student Arcade, time varies	www.cambridge.org/ venturesarcade/

B **Talk** with a partner. Choose pairs of pictures and make sentences about Mr. Chung. Use *although* and *even though* with verbs from the box.

clean find information have listen use wash write

Even though Mr. Chung has a computer, he prefers to write letters by hand.

1.

2.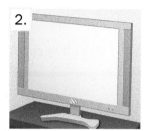

3.

4.

5.

6.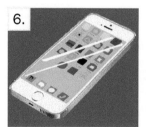

Write sentences about Mr. Chung.

Although Mr. Chung has a computer, he prefers to write letters by hand.

Answers will vary.

③ Communicate

A **Work** in a small group. Talk about time-saving devices or tools that you own but don't use. Give reasons. Use *although* and *even though*.

A Although I have a food processor, I almost never use it.

B Why?

A It's too hard to clean.

B **Share** information about your classmates.

Lesson C Clauses of reason and concession

1 Grammar focus: contrasting *because* and *although*

Use *because* to join two clauses in which one gives a reason for the other.
Use *although* to join two clauses that contrast with each other – one is surprising or unexpected based on the other.

Because cable Internet is fast, many people want it.

Although cable Internet is fast, many people cannot afford it.

👁 **Watch**

2 Practice

A Write. Complete the story. Use *because* or *although*.

Pam   Beth

> ___*Although*___ Pam and Beth are sisters, they are very different. Pam is very
>   1
>
> modern. She loves electrical appliances ___*because*___ they are fast and convenient. For
>   2
>
> example, she loves her microwave ___*because*___ she can use it to thaw meat quickly.
>   3
>
> She enjoys shopping for the latest kitchen devices ___*although*___ some of them are
>   4
>
> very expensive. Beth has a different attitude about modern technology. She prefers not
>
> to use electrical appliances. For instance, she never uses a microwave ___*because*___
>   5
>
> she thinks the radiation is bad. She dries her clothes outside on a line ___*because*___
>   6
>
> she likes their smell after they've been in the fresh air. She washes her dishes by hand
>
> ___*because*___ she says dishwashers waste energy. Pam doesn't understand why Beth is
>   7
>
> so old-fashioned. But ___*although*___ the sisters have different lifestyles, they appreciate
>   8
>
> and enjoy one another very much.

Listen and check your answers.

🔊 CD2, Track 5

WARM-UP AND REVIEW

- Before class: Write the lesson focus on the board.
  Lesson C:
  Contrasting "because" and "although"
- Begin class. Books open. Review *although*. Direct Ss' attention to page 73, Lesson B, Exercise **2B**. Write on the board: *although*. Have five S volunteers come to the board. Assign each volunteer a different set of pictures. Have them write sentences with *although*, for example: *Mr. Chung prefers to wash dishes by hand although he has a dishwasher. Although he has a vacuum cleaner, Mr. Chung prefers to use a broom.*
- For each sentence, elicit the surprising information by pointing to the sentence and asking: *What is surprising?* (Mr. Chung prefers to wash dishes by hand.) *Why?* (Most people prefer to use a dishwasher.) Make corrections as needed.

PRESENTATION

Focus on meaning / personalize

- Books closed. Direct Ss' attention to the lesson focus on the board. Read it aloud.
- Provide an example of a sentence with *although* and a sentence with *because* from your life, such as: *Although I have a food processor, I almost never use it. I don't use my food processor because it's so hard to clean.* Say sentence stems such as the following and have Ss finish them:

  I am studying English because . . . (I want to get a better job.)
  I am studying English although . . . (my English is very good.)
  I left my country because . . .
  I left my country although . . .
  I eat fast food because . . .
  I eat fast food although . . .

- Elicit or explain the difference in meaning between *because* clauses and *although* clauses. (*Because* clauses give the reason for something; they answer the question *Why . . . ?* In a sentence with an *although* clause, the main clause is a surprising or unexpected result from the situation described in the *although* clause. *I have a food processor* = the situation. *I almost never use it* = the surprise.)

Focus on form

- Use the animated grammar presentation in one or more of the following ways:
  - Preview it before class
  - Show in class
  - Encourage Ss to watch outside of class.
- Books open. Focus Ss' attention on the chart in Exercise **1**. Read aloud the sentence with *because*. Ask Ss to repeat. Ask: *What is the main clause?* (many people want it.) *What is the dependent clause?* (Because cable internet is fast.) Explain that we call *because* clauses "clauses of reason." They give the reason for the idea in the main clause.
- Elicit or explain why there are commas in the two sentences in the chart (when a dependent clause is at the beginning of a sentence, a comma separates it from the main clause). Elicit or show another way to order the sentence (reverse the two clauses).

PRACTICE

- Direct Ss' attention to Exercise **2A** and read the instructions aloud.
- Ask a S to read aloud the first sentence containing the sample answer.
- Ss complete the exercise individually. Walk around and help as needed.

COMPREHENSION CHECK

- Read aloud the second part of the instructions for Exercise **2A**.
- ▶ **CD2, Track 5** Play or read the audio (see audio script, page T-180). Ss listen and check their answers.
- Write the numbers *1–8* on the board. Ask individual Ss to come to the board to write and then read the sentences by filling in the answers. Make corrections on the board as needed.

LESSON C Clauses of reason and concession

PRACTICE

- Direct Ss' attention to the two pictures in Exercise **2B**. Ask Ss to compare what is happening in each picture. Elicit an appropriate response, such as: *The first man is sitting at his desk with a calculator, laptop, and chart. The second man is sitting with an adding machine holding a pencil and paper.*

- Direct Ss' attention to the two headings in the chart in Exercise **2B**. Ask: *What does "techie" mean?* Elicit an appropriate response: *"Techie" describes someone who familiar with the latest technology.* Then ask: *What does "nontech" mean?* Elicit: *"Nontech" describes someone who is not knowledgeable about the latest technology.*

- Read the instructions aloud. Call on two Ss to read the first item in each column of the chart. Call on two other Ss to read the example sentences above the two pictures.

- Have Ss complete the exercise with a partner. Be sure that each pair understands the task. Walk around and help as needed.

- Read the instructions aloud for the second part of Exercise **2B**. Call on two Ss to read the two example sentences.

- Ss complete the exercise individually. Remind Ss to use *because* or *although* in each sentence. Walk around and help as needed.

- Ask several Ss to come to the board to write their sentences.

- Have other Ss read aloud each of the sentences on the board. Ask: *Is this sentence correct?* Work with the class to make corrections on the board as needed.

Expansion activity *(student pairs)*

- Ask Ss to role-play a conversation between Mr. Speedy and Mr. Thrifty. Ss can ask and answer questions about Mr. Speedy's and Mr. Thrifty's preferences using the information from Exercise **2B** as a guide.

- Model the task. Write this example on the board.

  Mr. Speedy: *I just don't understand why you take the subway!*

  Mr. Thrifty: *I take the subway because it's convenient and inexpensive!*

- Encourage Ss to have fun with this activity. Ask several pairs to act out their conversations for the class, using appropriate stress, intonation, and gestures.

APPLICATION

- Direct Ss' attention to Exercise **3A** and read the instructions aloud.

- Ss in pairs. Model the task. Ask two Ss to read the example dialog aloud.

Useful Language

Read the tip box aloud. Ask two Ss to read the example dialog. Write the word *neither* on the board. Tell Ss that we can pronounce the *ei* in *neither* in two ways: /i/ and /aɪ/. Pronounce both ways and have Ss repeat. Ask Ss what the opposite of *neither* is (*both*).

- Ss complete the exercise in pairs. Walk around and help as needed.

- Direct Ss' attention to Exercise **3B**. Read the instructions aloud.

- Ask several Ss to share information they learned about their partner.

EVALUATION

- Direct Ss' attention to the lesson focus on the board. Ask Ss whether they drive or use public transportation. Tell Ss to answer using *although* and *because*.

- Check that Ss have used *although* and *because* correctly. Make corrections on the board as needed.

- Check off the lesson focus as Ss demonstrate an understanding of what they have learned in the lesson.

More Ventures, Unit 6, Lesson C	
Workbook, 15–30 min.	
Multilevel Worksheets, 30–45 min. **Collaborative Worksheets,** 30–45 min.	www.cambridge.org/ventures/ resources/
Student Arcade, time varies	www.cambridge.org/ venturesarcade/

B **Talk** with a partner. Compare Mr. Techie and Mr. Nontech. Use *because* and *although*.

> Mr. Techie uses a smartphone to calculate because it's convenient.

> Mr. Nontech uses an adding machine to calculate although it isn't always convenient.

Mr. Techie	Mr. Nontech
uses a smartphone to calculate	uses an adding machine to calculate
shops online	shops in stores
texts his lunch order	brings lunch from home
travels by plane	travels by train
looks up phone numbers on the Internet	uses the phone book
has prepared dinners delievered	cooks his own dinners
uses a cell phone	uses a landline
corresponds by "email"	corresponds by "snail mail"

Write sentences about Mr. Speedy and Mr. Thrifty.

Mr. Techie uses a smartphone to calculate because it is convenient.

Mr. Nontech uses an adding machine to calculate although it isn't always convenient.

❸ Communicate

A **Work** with a partner. Ask and answer questions about the activities in Exercise 2B. Give reasons for your answers.

   A Do you drive to work or take public transportation?

   B Well, although driving is faster, I take public transportation.

   A Why?

   B Because I don't have a car!

> **USEFUL LANGUAGE**
> Use *neither* when the answer to both choices in a question is negative.
> **A** *Do you drive to work or take public transportation?*
> **B** *Neither. I ride my bike.*

B **Share** information about your partner.

Lesson D Reading

1 Before you read

Talk with your classmates. Answer the questions.

1. How has technology changed transportation?
2. How has technology impacted the way we communicate with others?

> The first paragraph usually identifies the topic and the last paragraph often repeats the main idea. The paragraphs between provide details about the main idea. Before you read the entire article, **skim**. Read the first and last paragraph and the first sentence of the paragraphs between. This will give you an overview, or general idea, of the article.

2 Read

Read the article. Listen and read again.

The Impact of Technology

By Katelyn Houston

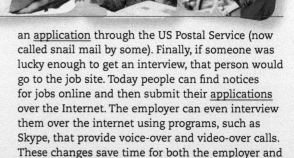

 CD2, Track 6

Changes in technology can change people's lives. The development of transportation — trains, cars, and planes — provides us with one example. Before the 19th century, most people lived within walking distance of work. In the 20th century many people began to <u>commute</u> between home and work because trains and cars connected cities with suburbs. Today, because of airplanes, many people travel great distances for their work. Some, because of the Internet, don't need to travel at all.

Technological changes have also impacted the media — for example, how we get the news. Newspapers were once people's primary <u>source</u> for the news: in 1965, 72% of Americans reported that they read a newspaper on an <u>average</u> day. By 2005, that number was down to 50%. In the past, a common way people got news was by listening to the radio. I suppose nearly everyone had a radio then. By the 1950s, television was overtaking radio. Now even the number of people watching the news on television has declined, dropping from 60% in 1993 to 28% in 2006. So what's the latest <u>source</u> for news? The web. The number of Americans who use the internet to get the news is increasing. Most people access the news on their smart phones.

Media has also changed the way people get jobs. People used to look for job openings in the <u>classified</u> ads of a newspaper. Then they would mail an <u>application</u> through the US Postal Service (now called snail mail by some). Finally, if someone was lucky enough to get an interview, that person would go to the job site. Today people can find notices for jobs online and then submit their <u>applications</u> over the Internet. The employer can even interview them over the internet using programs, such as Skype, that provide voice-over and video-over calls. These changes save time for both the employer and the applicant.

Another example of the <u>impact</u> of technology is how people pay for goods and services. Until the mid-1940s, people had to carry large amounts of cash in their purses and wallets. Then, one day in 1949, a man named Frank McNamara took some business associates to dinner, but he left his wallet at home. He had to call his wife to bring him money to pay the bill. Mr. McNamara vowed to find a way to avoid carrying cash. Although some stores already had their own charge cards, there was no single, multi-purpose credit card. A year later he returned to the same restaurant with the same people but paid with the credit card he had created, called "Diner's Club." Today, people don't even need to carry a credit card. They can pay with their smartphones.

In what other ways do you think technology may change people's lives in the future?

Teaching objectives
- Introduce an article about the impact of technology
- Provide practice using new topic related vocabulary
- Provide practice recognizing the difference between facts and opinions
- Provide practice using multiple meaning words

WARM-UP AND REVIEW

- Before class. Write today's lesson focus on the board.
  Lesson D:
  Read and understand "The Impact of Technology"
  Practice new vocabulary related to technology
  Understand the difference between facts and opinions
  Use multiple-meaning words

- Begin class. Books closed. Direct Ss' attention to the title of the reading, "The Impact of Technology," and ask Ss to predict what they think the reading is about. Write some of the Ss' predictions on the board.

PRESENTATION

- Books open. Direct Ss' attention to Exercise **1** and read the instructions aloud.
- Have two Ss read aloud the questions in Exercise **1**.
- Ss in small groups. Ss discuss their answers to the questions. Walk around and help as needed.
- Call on individual Ss to share their answers with the class.

PRACTICE

- Read the instructions aloud for Exercise **2**. Ask Ss to read the story silently before listening to the audio program.
- ▶ **CD2, Track 6** Play or read the audio and ask Ss to read along (see audio script, pages T-180–T-181). Repeat the audio as needed.
- While Ss are listening to and reading the article, ask them to underline any words they don't know. When the audio is finished, have Ss write the new vocabulary words on the board.
- Point to each word on the board. Say it and have Ss repeat. Give a brief explanation of each word, or ask Ss who know the word to explain it. If Ss prefer to look up the new words in their dictionaries, allow them to do so.

Learner persistence (individual work)
- ▶ **CD2, Track 6** Ss can listen to the audio for Exercise **2** at home for reinforcement and review. They can also listen to the audio for self-directed learning when class attendance is not possible.

Expansion activity (small groups)
- Split the class into small groups. Assign each group a mode of transportation, for example: *airplane, subway, car, boat.* Write the following questions on the board:

  How has technology changed this form of transportation over time?
  How do you think technology will affect this form of transportation in the future?
  How do you think technology could make this form of transportation faster, cheaper, or more efficient?

- Ask Ss to discuss the questions. One group member should take notes. Another group member should act as spokesperson and report the discussion notes to the class.
- Invite the spokesperson from each group to share the group's discussion notes with the class.

Community building (small groups)
- Ask Ss to work in small groups to design a questionnaire to ask their classmates or people outside the class about their technology use. You can start by brainstorming ideas with the class to create a list of questions for the questionnaire and then have Ss write questions with their groups. Write example questions on the board, such as: *How do you get the news every day? How often do you look at online newspapers? Do you typically pay for things with cash or credit cards? What do you like about using credit cards?*
- Ss work in small groups to prepare questionnaires of four to five questions.
- Have Ss interview their classmates or people outside of class about their technology use. Invite Ss to report their findings in a later class.
- Leave time for a question-and-answer session when Ss report their findings.

LESSON D Reading

COMPREHENSION CHECK

- Direct Ss' attention to Exercise **3A** and read the instructions aloud.

> Read the tip to the class. Write on the board: *critical reader*. Ask Ss what they think this term means. Elicit and write: *A critical reader is someone who reads carefully.* Tell Ss that all the tips in this book are designed to help them become better critical readers. Then write on the board: *facts* and *opinions*. Ask Ss: *Where do you usually find facts and opinions?* Elicit appropriate responses, such as: *Facts are usually found in news articles and encyclopedias. Opinions are found in editorial sections of newspapers or in blogs.* If Ss don't know what a *blog* is, tell them it's an online journal that is updated regularly.

- Ask a S to read the first question in Exercise **3A** to the class.
- Call on individual other Ss to read the remaining items, one at a time. Make sure that Ss understand the questions and task.
- Ss complete the exercise individually. Instruct Ss to write their answers on a separate piece of paper. Ss should answer in complete sentences. Walk around and help as needed.
- Check answers with the class.
- Ask Ss to share where they found the answers to the questions. Remind Ss that being a good critical reader means they read carefully.

PRACTICE

- **Materials needed** A dictionary for each S.
- Direct Ss' attention to number 1 of Exercise **3B**. Read the instructions aloud. Have a S read the sample dictionary entry. Ask Ss how many definitions there are in the entry. (two.)
- Have Ss focus on number 2 in Exercise **3B** and read the instructions aloud. Ask a S to read the three headings. Call on another S to read the example in the chart.
- Ss work individually to underline the words in the reading and then complete the chart. Walk around and help as needed.
- Encourage Ss to use their dictionaries.
- Copy the chart on page 77 on the board. Ask individual Ss to come to the board to complete the chart, writing the definition of each word as it is used in the reading and listing one other definition. Make corrections on the board as needed.

Learner persistence (individual work)

- Encourage Ss to use their notebook or vocabulary cards to write the definititions. Also encourage Ss to review new words daily and to practice them as much as possible.

APPLICATION

- Focus Ss' attention on Exercise **3C** and read the instructions aloud.
- Call on three Ss to read the questions.
- Ss complete the exercise in pairs, stating their opinions clearly.
- Ask several pairs to share their answers with the class.

Expansion activity

- Refer Ss to "Multitasking: Time saver or time waster?" another reading on the same topic on pages 151–153.
- Have Ss complete the activity either in class or outside of class.
- Provide feedback to Ss such as through whole-class discussion, partners comparing their worksheets, or T reviewing each S's worksheets.

EVALUATION

- Books closed. Direct Ss' attention to the lesson focus on the board.
- Ask individual Ss to retell the main points of the reading, "The Impact of Technology."
- Books open. Focus Ss' attention on the words that they wrote in the chart for number 2 in Exercise **3B**. Ask Ss to make sentences with these words to show that they understand the meanings.
- Check off each part of the lesson focus as Ss demonstrate an understanding of what they have learned in the lesson.

More Ventures, Unit 6, Lesson D	
Workbook, 15–30 min.	
Multilevel Worksheets, 30–45 min.	www.cambridge.org/ventures/resources/
Collaborative Worksheets, 30–45 min.	
Student Arcade, time varies	www.cambridge.org/venturesarcade/

❸ After you read

A Check your understanding.

1. In what four areas does the author provide examples for how technology has changed people's lives?

2. What statistics does the article give to support the statement that the number of people who get their news through the newspaper has declined?

3. According to the author, nearly everyone had a radio in the 1920s. What phrase does the article use that tells you whether this is fact or opinion?

4. Sometimes text provides examples that help us understand the meaning of a word. What examples does this text give for *media*? For *transportation*?

5. The article says some people refer to the US Postal Service as "snail mail." How are snails and the US mail similar?

6. Do you think the author believes that changes in technology have a positive or a negative impact on people's lives? Cite evidence from the article to support your opinion.

B Build your vocabulary.

1. Read the dictionary entry. How many definitions are there?

> **impact /n/ 1 force 2 effect**

2. Find the words in the story. Underline the sentence. Determine the part of speech and write it next to the word. Use a dictionary to find the definition that fits the reading.

Vocabulary	Definition that fits context	One other definition
1. impact *(n)*	*effect*	*force*
2. commute	*travel back and forth*	*ride or drive (v)*
3. source	*point of origin*	*sourced (v)*
4. average	*common*	*ordinary (adj)*
5. classified	*groups*	*categorized (adj)*
6. application	*formal request for something*	*document (n)*

C Talk with a partner.

1. What technological change has most impacted your life? How has it affected you?

2. Do you think paying for goods and services with smart phones is a good idea? Why or why not?

3. Recently companies have been developing and testing driverless cars. If they become popular, how do you think that will impact jobs?

For college and career readiness practice, see pages 151–153.

Lesson E Writing

1 Before you write

A **Work** in a small group. Make a list of time-saving devices you and your classmates use. Write one advantage and one disadvantage of each.

Device	Advantage	Disadvantage
calculator	does math quickly	breaks easily
1. Answers will vary.		
2.		
3.		
4.		
5.		
6.		
7.		
8.		

B **Read** the paragraph.

My Favorite Time-saving Device

My favorite time-saving device, voicemail, has many advantages, but it also has some disadvantages. Before I had voicemail, I used to answer my phone every time it rang, even if I was busy. But with voicemail, I don't have to interrupt my work. The caller can just leave a message, and I can get it later. Another benefit of voicemail is that it allows me to avoid talking to people I don't want to talk to. But, of course, that is also a disadvantage because they can avoid talking to me! Another problem is that not only friends leave messages. Sometimes there are voicemail messages from salespeople. So even though voicemail is very convenient, it has drawbacks as well.

> One way of organizing a paragraph is by describing advantages and disadvantages.

C **Work** with a partner. Complete the diagram of the model paragraph.

Teaching objective

- Prepare Ss for writing a paragraph about the advantages and disadvantages of a time-saving device or activity

WARM-UP AND REVIEW

- Before class. Write today's lesson focus on the board.
  Lesson E:
  Write a paragraph about the advantages and disadvantages of a time-saving device or activity

- Begin class. Books closed. Review vocabulary from the unit. Write the words *time-saving devices* on the board. Ask Ss for several examples. Elicit appropriate responses, such as: *dishwashers, washing machines, dryers, cars, calculators, cell phones, computers.*

- Ask Ss to recall the story they read in Lesson D. Ask: *What was "The Impact of Technology" about?* (advances in transportation; ways of getting the news; methods of paying for things.) *How do you get news every day?* (on the radio, TV, online newspapers.) *What other ways do you think technology may change our lives in the future?* (Answers may vary.)

PRESENTATION

- Books open. Direct Ss' attention to Exercise **1A**. Read the instructions aloud.

- Ask a S to read the three headings in the chart in Exercise **1A**: *Device, Advantage, Disadvantage.* Call on another S to read the example in the chart.

- Ss work in small groups to complete the chart. Walk around and help as needed.

- Write the chart from Exercise **1A** on the board. Call on Ss from each group to fill in one row at a time with an example from their group work.

PRACTICE

- Direct Ss' attention to Exercise **1B** and read the instructions aloud.

- Ss read the paragraph silently. Tell them to underline words they do not understand.

- Have Ss write the new words on the board. Point to each word. Say it and ask Ss to repeat.

- Remind Ss of the reading strategies they have learned for finding clues to help them figure out the meaning of an unfamiliar word. For example, if a S writes *drawbacks* on the board, ask the S to look at the sentence in which it appears (the last sentence of the paragraph). The words *even though* in the sentence indicate that there will be a contrast in the sentence. Something *convenient* is positive, so a *drawback* has to be something negative.

Read the tip aloud. Have Ss refer to the model paragraph in Exercise **1B**. Ask Ss: *According to the paragraph, how many advantages of voice mail are there? Read the examples from the paragraph.* (There are two: 1. *I don't have to interrupt my work.* 2. *It allows me to avoid talking to people I don't want to talk to.*) Ask Ss: *How many disadvantages are there? Tell what are they in your own words.* (There are two: 1. People can also avoid talking to the writer. 2. Salespeople, not just friends, leave messages.) Tell Ss that by showing both sides of a topic (advantages and disadvantages), their argument or opinion is presented in a more balanced and convincing way.

Expansion activity (student pairs)

- Ask Ss if they know some synonyms of the word *drawbacks* (e.g., disadvantages, problems, weak points, negative aspects, bad points). Write the synonyms on the board.

- Tell Ss that the concluding sentence of a paragraph can sometimes be more effective if it mentions that there are drawbacks as well as advantages.

- Direct Ss' attention to the concluding sentence in the paragraph in Exercise **1B**. Have a S read it aloud. Ask if there is another way that the sentence could have been worded. Elicit an appropriate response and write it on the board. For example: *Although voice mail is very convenient, it has drawbacks as well.*

- Ss in pairs. Have partners write several examples of possible concluding sentences for a paragraph about the advantages and disadvantages of a time-saving device, using *although* and *even though* to show that a contrast between advantages and drawbacks is being presented.

- Model the task. Ask a S to use the sample entry in the chart as the basis for a concluding sentence. Elicit an appropriate sentence and write it on the board. (*Although an electronic calculator does math quickly, it also has some drawbacks.*)

- When pairs have finished writing their sentences, have several volunteers write their concluding sentences on the board. Make corrections on the board as needed.

LESSON E Writing

PRESENTATION

- Focus Ss' attention on Exercise **1C** and read the instructions aloud. Tell Ss that using this kind of diagram or graphic organizer is a good way of organizing ideas before writing.
- Ask a S to read the example advantage of voice mail.
- Ss work in pairs to fill in the diagram with supporting information based on the model paragraph on page 78.
- Write a diagram or web on the board similar to the one in the Student's Book.
- Have Ss come to the board, one at a time, to fill in the diagram. Make corrections on the board as needed.

PRACTICE

- Direct Ss' attention to Exercise **1D** and read the instructions aloud. Guide Ss to see that the information they use to fill in this diagram will be useful for planning their own paragraphs.
- Ss complete their diagrams individually. Tell them that they can add more lines and bubbles to their diagrams if they have additional ideas. Walk around and help as needed.

APPLICATION

- Focus Ss' attention on Exercise **2** and read the instructions aloud.
- Ss complete the task individually. Walk around and help as needed.

Learner persistence *(individual work)*

- If you have Ss who have difficulty writing, sit with them and help them as the other Ss are writing. Help Ss use their notes from the model paragraph in Exercise **1B** on page 78 and the diagrams in Exercises **1C** and **1D** on page 79 to help them write a paragraph.

COMPREHENSION CHECK

- Direct Ss' attention to Exercise **3A**.
- This exercise asks Ss to develop skills to review and edit their own writing.
- Ss check their own paragraphs against the writing checklist. Walk around and help as needed. If any Ss check *No* for one or more of the checklist items, ask them to revise and edit their paragraphs to include the missing information.

EVALUATION

- Focus Ss' attention on Exercise **3B**. Read the instructions aloud. This exercise enables Ss to work together to peer-correct their writing. Reading aloud enables the writer to review his or her own writing and to understand the need to write clearly for an audience.
- Ss complete the exercise in pairs. Tell Ss to take turns reading their paragraphs to each other. Walk around and help as needed.
- Listen to Ss as they ask their partner one question about the paragraph and tell their partner one thing they learned from it.
- Ask several Ss to read their paragraphs aloud. Have other Ss ask questions and mention one thing they learned from the paragraph.
- Direct Ss' attention to the lesson focus on the board.
- Check off the lesson focus as Ss demonstrate an understanding of what they have learned in the lesson.

Expansion activity *(small groups)*

- **Materials needed** Several magazine pictures or online illustrations from advertisements for time-saving devices discussed in this unit (calculators, answering machines, cell phones, cars, washing machines, etc.).
- Tell Ss to imagine that they are having a garage sale and that they are trying to sell the devices in the pictures you give them. Remind Ss that people in the United States hold garage or yard sales to sell household items that they no longer use.
- Ss in small groups. Ss take turns being sellers and buyers. The sellers should present the advantages of the device, and the buyers can point out the disadvantages (especially if they want a lower price!).
- Distribute several pictures to each group. Tell Ss that there should be one seller, but there can be more than one buyer. Encourage Ss to use *although*, *even though*, and *because* in their conversations.
- Encourage several Ss to role play their conversations for the class.

More Ventures, Unit 6, Lesson E	
Workbook, 15–30 min.	
Multilevel Worksheets, 30–45 min.	www.cambridge.org/ventures/ resources/
Collaborative Worksheets, 30–45 min.	

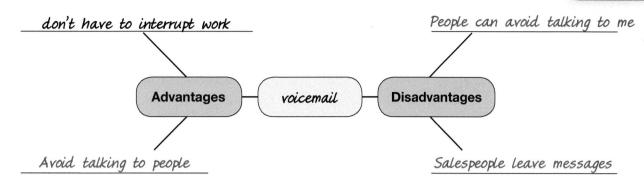

D **Plan** a paragraph that discusses the advantages and disadvantages of a time-saving device. Use the diagram to make notes on your ideas. *Answers will vary.*

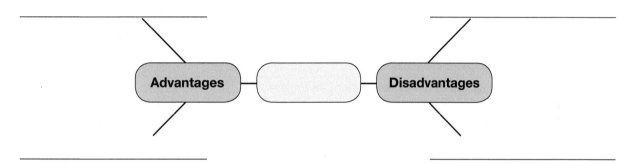

2 Write

Write a paragraph about a time-saving device. Give the paragraph a title, include a topic sentence, and describe at least two advantages and two disadvantages. Use the paragraph in Exercise 1B and the diagrams in Exercises 1C and 1D to help you.

Answers will vary.

3 After you write

A **Check** your writing.

	Yes	No
1. My paragraph has a title.	☐	☐
2. My topic sentence names the time-saving device.	☐	☐
3. I described at least two advantages and two disadvantages.	☐	☐

B **Share** your writing with a partner.

1. Take turns. Read your paragraph to a partner.

2. Comment on your partner's paragraph. Ask your partner a question about the paragraph. Tell your partner one thing you learned.

Lesson F Another view

1 Life-skills reading

Internet use has increased significantly since its beginnings in the 1960s. Reasons for using it have also increased. The following data show the results of one county's survey to compare its use by seniors with other adults.

Internet Activities of Adults* in Green County		
Activity	18-64 years	65+ years (Seniors)
Use the internet	97.50%	75.00%
Communication: e-mail, chats,	90.00%	72.25%
Social networks: share events, opinions	70.50%	45.75%
Consumer services: shop, make reservations, sell things	68.01%	64.00%
Financial services: bank, pay bills	64.00%	48.00%
Entertainment: stream / download music & videos; play games	53.40%	00.15%
Searches: information, people	48.00%	62.00%

* One hundred adults were interviewed. Twenty of those were seniors.

A **Read** the questions. Look at the chart. Fill in the answer.

1. How many seniors were interviewed?

   A 100

   B 75

   C 20

   D none of the above

2. Of those surveyed, how many were adults under 65?

   A 97.5%

   B 75%

   C 100%

   D 80%

3. Which internet activity is more popular with seniors than with other adults?

   A Consumer services

   B Searches

   C Communication

   D Social networks

4. In which area is there the biggest difference in how seniors and other adults use the internet?

   A Social networks

   B Consumer services

   C Financial services

   D Entertainment

B **Solve** the problem. Give your opinion.

Last year Juan gave his teenage son a computer for his birthday. It is in his bedroom. Now he spends a lot of time in his bedroom playing games online. His grades are not good, and his teachers report that he doesn't turn in his homework. What should Juan do?

Answers will vary.

Teaching objectives
- Introduce reading and understanding a table that shows adults' daily Internet activities
- Provide practice contrasting *so* and *such*

WARM-UP AND REVIEW

- Before class. Write today's lesson focus on the board.
  Lesson F:
  Read and understand a table that shows adults' daily Internet activities
  Contrast so and such

- Begin class. Books closed. Write on the board: *daily Internet activities.*

- Ask Ss: *What are examples of Internet activities?* Elicit: *banking, shopping, watching videos,* etc. Write the examples on the board.

- Say: *The table that you're going to read shows the Internet activities of adults and seniors living in Green County. What do you think are some differences between adults' and seniors' Internet activities?* Elicit: *Adults are more likely than seniors to use the Internet to pay bills, adults are more likely than seniors to use email,* etc.

PRESENTATION

- Books open. Call on individual Ss to read the listed activities. Explain vocabulary as needed.

- Make sure that Ss understand that the numbers are percentages of the total number of people who were asked. For example, say: *In the chart, 97.5 percent of adults 18 to 64 years of age used the Internet.*

PRACTICE

- Read the instructions aloud for Exercise **1A**. This task helps prepare Ss for standardized-type tests they may have to take. Make sure that Ss understand the task. Have Ss individually scan for and fill in the answers.

COMPREHENSION CHECK

- Check answers with the class. Be sure that Ss have followed the instructions and filled in their answers.

- Have Ss read aloud the questions and answers they filled in. Ask: *Is that answer correct?* Correct Ss' answers as needed.

APPLICATION

- Direct Ss' attention to Exercise **1B** and read the instructions aloud. Make sure that Ss understand the task. Have Ss individually solve the problem.

- Ss discuss the problem in small groups. Walk around and help as needed.

- Open up the discussion to the entire class. Accept all plausible answers.

Expansion activity (student pairs)

- Ask Ss: *Do you know someone who doesn't like the Internet or who has never tried to use it? How could you convince him or her to use the Internet?* Elicit: *By telling him or her about the advantages of using the Internet.*

- Ss in pairs. Ss fold a piece of paper in half. On one side they write a list of advantages of using the Internet, and on the other side they write a list of disadvantages.

- Invite Ss to perform a role play between a person who doesn't like to use the Internet and a person who likes it and is trying to convince the first person to change his or her opinion. Ss should support their statements with information from the unit as well as from their own experience.

- Have several pairs perform their conversation for the class.

- Invite Ss to discuss the advantages and disadvantages of the Internet as a class.

WARM-UP AND REVIEW

- Books closed. Write a few questions on the board. Ask Ss the questions and about the weather and how it affects their activities. Encourage them to reply using complete sentences, for example: *What was the weather like this past weekend? What did you do? The weather was sunny. I played tennis outside.*

PRESENTATION

Focus on meaning / personalize

- Use the animated grammar presentation in one or more of the following ways:
  - Preview it before class
  - Show in class
  - Encourage Ss to watch outside of class.
- Books closed. Write on the board: *It is hot today. I had to turn on my air conditioner.* Under this write: *It's so hot today (that) I had to turn on my air conditioner. It is such a hot day that I had to turn on my air conditioner.* Point out that *that* is optional in both sentences. Also point out that although *so* and *such* are both followed by adjectives, the difference between *so* and *such* is that *such* requires a noun to follow the adjective.
- Write on the board: *It is cold today. I had to turn on my heat.* Have Ss write two sentences with *so* and *such* like the example above.

Focus on form

- Books open. Direct Ss' attention to the grammar chart in **2A**. Ask two Ss to read the sentences in the left-hand column. Write *so + adjective* on the board. Tell Ss that we use this structure to emphasize something.
- Direct Ss' attention to the second column of the chart. Ask two Ss to read the sentences. Write *such + adjective + noun* on the board. Explain that *such* is also used for emphasis.
- Point to the warm-up questions on the board and ask Ss to answer the questions with *so* or *such*. For example, *It was so rainy I stayed inside all weekend.*

PRACTICE

- Direct Ss' attention to the instructions in **2A**. Read the instructions aloud. Ensure Ss understand the activity. Ask a pair of Ss to read the dialog aloud.
- Ss ask one another questions in pairs. Walk around and help as needed.
- Direct Ss' attention to the instructions in **2B**. Read the instructions aloud. Divide the class into small groups. Ss complete the exercise. Ask each group to share a sentence or two. Write the sentences on the board and make corrections as needed.

EVALUATION

- Do a quick review of the unit. Have Ss turn to Lesson A. Ask the class to talk about what they remember about this lesson. Prompt Ss, if necessary, with questions, for example: *What are the conversations about on this page? What vocabulary is in the pictures?* Continue in this manner to review each lesson quickly.

Expansion activity

- Before class. Print, for each student, one copy of the Self-assessment for this unit.
- Have Ss complete the Self-assessment either in class or outside of class.
- Provide feedback to Ss such as through a whole-class discussion, partners comparing their worksheets, or T reviewing each S's worksheet.
- If Ss are ready, administer the unit test on pages T-204–T-206 of this Teacher's Edition. The audio script for the test is on pages T-223–T-224.

More Ventures, Unit 6, Lesson F	
Workbook, 15–30 min.	
Multilevel Worksheets, 30–45 min.	www.cambridge.org/ventures/resources/
Collaborative Worksheets, 30–45 min.	
Self-assessment, 10 min.	
CASAS Test Prep Worksheet, 5–10 min.	

2 Grammar connections: *so* and *such*

So and *such* make the meaning stronger. Use *so* before an adjective. Use *such (a)* before a noun.

SO + ADJECTIVE	SUCH + ADJECTIVE + NOUN	OPTIONAL *THAT* CLAUSE
That clock is **so small**	That's **such a small clock**	**that** it's hard to see the time
Those cars are **so nice**	Those are **such nice cars**	**that** I want to drive them

👁 Watch

A **Talk** with a partner. Describe the pictures with *so* and *such*. Take turns.

A That watch is so old
(that no one would use it).

B That is such an old watch
(that no one would use it).

> **USEFUL LANGUAGE**
> In conversation people often omit the "that" clause. Formal writing usually includes the "that" clause.

B **Work** in a small group. Describe items in the word box with your own information. Use *so* and *such*. Take turns.

your Internet connection at home	your commute to work / school
your house / apartment / room	your cell phone
your television	your watch

A I have such a fast Internet connection at home that I can watch videos online easily.

B You're lucky! My Internet connection at home is so slow that I don't use it very often.

REVIEW

1 Listening

Listen. Take notes on a radio interview.

Characteristics of tutors	Requirements to be a tutor
1. *compassionate – care about helping*	4. *12 hours of training*
2. *Generous with their time*	5. *meet with student for at least 1.5 hours per week*
3. *Patient*	6. *minimum commitment of 6 months*

◄)) CD2, Track 7

Talk with a partner. Check your answers.

2 Grammar

A Write. Complete the story.

A Love of Technology

My friend Bob loves technology. ____*As soon as*____ a new computer

1. As soon as / Until

comes out, he buys it. The same is true with his cell phone. He doesn't wait

____*until*____ the end of his contract. ____*Even though*____ his

2. as soon as / until   3. Because / Even though

cell phone is still good, he buys a new one. ____*Because*____ he loves the

4. Because / Even though

latest technology, his house is filled with new devices. ____*Although*____ he

5. Although / Until

has the newest devices, he keeps the old ones. His wife is unhappy. She has told him,

"No more electronic gadgets ____*until*____ you get rid of the old ones."

6. as soon as / until

____*Although*____ Don really wants a new phone, he can't bear to discard his

7. Although / Until

older devices.

B Write. Look at the words that are underlined in the answers. Write the questions.

1. A *Who loves technology?*

   B <u>Bob</u> loves technology.

2. A *When does he buy a new cell phone?*

   B He buys a new cell phone <u>as soon as a new one comes out</u>.

3. A *What's his house filled with?*

   B His house is filled with <u>new devices</u>.

4. A *Why is Bob's wife unhappy?*

   B <u>Because of all the electronic gadgets</u>, Bob's wife is unhappy.

Talk with a partner. Ask and answer the questions.

Teaching objectives
- Review vocabulary and grammar from Units 5 and 6
- Provide practice with the pronunciation of stressed and unstressed words

WARM-UP AND REVIEW

- Before class. Write today's lesson focus on the board.
  Review unit:
  Review vocabulary and grammar from Units 5 and 6
  Practice pronouncing stressed and unstressed words

- Begin class. Books closed. Ask Ss questions to review vocabulary and grammar from Units 5 and 6, for example: *What do you do as soon as you get home? What do you do until dinner is ready?*

- Review repeated actions in the present and past. Ask Ss questions about their activities using *How often . . . ?* or *How many times . . . ?*

- Review *although* and *even though*. Encourage Ss to talk about time-saving devices or tools that they own but don't use, using *although* and *even though*.

- Review the difference between *although* and *because*. Write these two sentences on the board, and ask Ss to fill in each blank with *Although* or *Because*. _____ *it was a beautiful day, we stayed inside and watched TV.* _____ *we stayed inside, we didn't get to enjoy the sunny weather.*

PRESENTATION

- Books open. Direct Ss' attention to Exercise **1** and read the instructions aloud. Tell Ss that they will hear a radio interview between an interviewer and Rebecca Ford, a woman who works with volunteer literacy tutors.

- ▶ *CD2, Track 7* Model the task. Play or read only the first part of the conversation on the audio (see audio script, pages T-181). Pause after Rebecca says: *But in one way, they're all the same: they're very compassionate. They really care about helping other people.*

- Direct Ss' attention to the first heading in the chart (*Characteristics of tutors*). Tell Ss that *characteristics* is another word for *personal qualities*. Ask Ss: *How does Rebecca describe the tutors?* (She says that they're compassionate, which means that they care about helping other people.)

- Ask a S to read aloud the second chart heading (*Requirements to be a tutor*). Say: *Now listen and complete the information in the chart.*

- ▶ *CD2, Track 7* Play or read the complete audio. Ss listen and complete the chart individually. Repeat the audio as needed.

COMPREHENSION CHECK

- Read aloud the second part of the instructions for Exercise **1**.

- Ss check their answers with their partner. Walk around and help as needed.

PRACTICE

- Direct Ss' attention to Exercise **2A**. Ask Ss: *What is the title of this story?* ("A Love of Technology")

- Read the instructions aloud for Exercise **2A**. Point out that Ss should select one of the choices below each blank to complete each sentence. Ask a S to read aloud the first two sentences in the story, including the example. Tell Ss to continue reading the story and filling in the blanks to complete the story.

- Ss complete the exercise individually. Walk around and help as needed.

- Write the numbers *1–7* on the board. Have individual Ss come to the board to write only the answers.

- Invite other Ss to read the story aloud, filling in the blanks with the answers on the board. Make corrections as needed.

Teaching Tip

Encourage the Ss who are comfortable with these grammar points to help those who are less comfortable. Have Ss turn to the appropriate lessons in the book to work together to review the grammar presentation and exercises.

COMPREHENSION CHECK

- Direct Ss' attention to Exercise **2B**. This exercise reviews question formation related to the reading, "A Love of Technology."

- Read the instructions aloud. Model the task. Direct Ss to speaker B's answer in number 1. Say: *What question can you ask to get this answer?* Tell Ss that the underlined word is their clue for the *Wh-* question word they need to use. Ask Ss to think about the question word they would use for a person (Who).

- Ss complete the exercise individually. Walk around and help as needed.

- Check answers with the class. Ask for volunteers to read their questions. Write the questions on the board. Work with the class to make corrections on the board as needed.

- Read aloud the second part of the instructions for Exercise **2B**.

- Ss work in pairs to ask and answer the questions. Walk around and help as needed.

REVIEW

PRESENTATION

- Books closed. Write on the board: *stressed and unstressed words*. Then write this sentence on the board: *Bob buys a new cell phone as soon as a new one comes out.* Ask Ss if they can tell which words are *stressed* (have more emphasis) and which are *unstressed* (have less emphasis). Tell Ss that you are going to say the sentence aloud, and you want them to pay attention to the stresses.

- Write on the board:

  content words = stressed   function words = unstressed

- Say this sentence, stressing the underlined words: *Bob buys a new cell phone as soon as a new one comes out.*

Teaching Tip

Some Ss may find it difficult to differentiate between stressed and unstressed words when working on pronunciation. If possible, take extra time with these Ss to review the sounds. Exaggerate the stress in stressed words so that Ss can clearly hear the difference between words that are stressed and unstressed.

- Books open. Direct Ss' attention to the top of page 83. Call on a S to read the information about content and function words.

- Read the instructions aloud for Exercise **3A**.

- ▶ *CD2, Track 8* Play or read the complete audio (see audio script, page T-181).

- Have a S read aloud the second part of the instructions for Exercise **3A**.

- ▶ *CD2, Track 8* Repeat the audio. Pause after each phrase to give Ss time to repeat. Play the audio as many times as needed. Focus Ss' attention on the pronunciation of the underlined words in Exercise **3A**.

PRACTICE

- Direct Ss' attention to Exercise **3B**. Read the instructions aloud.

- ▶ *CD2, Track 9* Model the task. Play or read the first sentence on the audio (see audio script, page T-181). Ask Ss to tell you which words are stressed, and have them underline those content words in the sentence.

- Tell Ss to pay attention to the stressed words in each sentence as they listen and repeat. Play or read the audio, stopping as needed for Ss to repeat the sentences.

- Play or read the complete audio again. Ss identify the stressed words by underlining them. Repeat the audio as needed.

- Read aloud the second part of the instructions for Exercise **3B**.

- Ss complete the exercise in pairs. Walk around and listen to Ss' pronunciation. Help Ss pronounce the stressed words correctly.

COMPREHENSION CHECK

- Direct Ss' attention to Exercise **3C** and read the instructions aloud.

- Ss complete the exercise individually. Walk around and help as needed.

- Read aloud the second part of the instructions for Exercise **3C**.

- Ss work in pairs to compare their answers. Ss take turns reading the paragraph to each other.

- Call on individual Ss to read the paragraph aloud. Ask Ss which words are stressed in the paragraph.

APPLICATION

- Focus Ss' attention on Exercise **3D** and read the instructions aloud.

- Have Ss write five sentences from Units 5 and 6 to complete the exercise. Suggest Ss refer to the readings in Lesson D of both units.

- Ss work individually to write the sentences but then exchange papers to underline the stressed words in their partner's sentences.

EVALUATION

- Direct Ss' attention to the lesson focus on the board.

- Write these two sentences on the board, and ask Ss to fill in the blanks with *until* or *as soon as*.

  He'll feel better _____ he takes his medicine.

  The volunteer will stay with him _____ his family comes to visit.

- Write the words *advantage* and *disadvantage* on the board. Ask Ss to describe one advantage and one disadvantage of a time-saving device. Have Ss use *even though*, *although*, or *because* in their sentences.

- Check off each part of the lesson focus as Ss demonstrate an understanding of what they have learned in the lesson.

3 **Pronunciation:** stressed and unstressed words

> Content words (nouns, main verbs, adverbs, adjectives, negatives, and question words) are usually stressed. Function words (pronouns, prepositions, conjunctions, articles, *be* verbs, and auxiliary verbs) are usually not stressed.

A **Listen** to the stressed and unstressed words in each sentence. The stressed words are underlined.

🔊 CD2, Track 8

1. <u>Pam</u> <u>loves</u> <u>electrical</u> <u>appliances</u> because they <u>save</u> her <u>time</u>.
2. She <u>wants</u> to <u>volunteer</u> in the <u>health-care</u> <u>field</u>.
3. Even though <u>computers</u> are <u>time-savers</u>, <u>some</u> <u>people</u> <u>don't</u> <u>use</u> them.
4. Will he <u>go</u> to <u>sleep</u> as soon as his <u>visitors</u> <u>leave</u>?

Listen again and repeat. Stress the underlined content words.

B **Listen and repeat.** Then underline the stressed content words.

🔊 CD2, Track 9

1. She <u>delivers</u> <u>meals</u> to <u>seniors</u>.
2. <u>Volunteers</u> should be <u>patient</u> and <u>compassionate</u>.
3. Do you walk to <u>work</u> or <u>drive</u>?
4. <u>Mr.</u> <u>Chung</u> isn't a <u>fan</u> of <u>e-mail</u>.

Read your sentences to a partner. Compare your answers.

C **Read** the paragraph. Underline the stressed words.

>   <u>Ingrid</u> <u>worked</u> with <u>computers</u> in her <u>native</u> <u>country</u>, so she <u>wants</u> a <u>job</u> <u>working</u> with <u>computers</u> in the U.S. She's been <u>looking</u> for <u>several</u> <u>months</u>, but she hasn't <u>found</u> a <u>job</u> <u>yet</u>. Finally, she <u>decided</u> to do some <u>volunteer</u> <u>work</u> until she could <u>find</u> a <u>paying</u> <u>job</u>. <u>Ingrid</u> <u>volunteers</u> at the <u>local</u> <u>zoo</u>. She does <u>office</u> <u>work</u> on the <u>computer</u>.

Talk with a partner. Compare your answers. Read the paragraph to your partner.

D **Write** five sentences from Units 5 and 6. Then work with a partner. Underline the stressed words in your partner's sentences.

1. *Answers will vary.* _____
2. _____
3. _____
4. _____
5. _____

UNIT 7 SHOPPING

Lesson A Listening

1 Before you listen

A What do you see?

B What is happening?

Rosa

Katrina

UNIT 7

Teaching objectives

- Introduce students to the topic
- Find out what students know about the topic
- Preview the unit by talking about the pictures
- Provide practice of key vocabulary
- Provide practice that develops listening skills

WARM-UP AND REVIEW

- Before class. Write today's lesson focus on the board.
  Lesson A:
  Ask about returning merchandise
  Ask about store policies
  Talk about shopping mistakes
  Identify store personnel
  Describe people, places, and things
- Begin class. Books closed. Direct Ss' attention to the lesson focus. Point to *Ask about returning merchandise.* Ask Ss: *What is merchandise?* List Ss' responses on the board, for example things people buy such as: *clothes*, *shoes*, *electronic devices*.
- Point to *Ask about store policies.* Ask Ss: *What are store policies?* List Ss' responses on the board, for example: *rules for store employees and customers.*
- Point to *Identify store personnel.* Ask Ss: *What does "store personnel" mean?* List Ss' responses on the board, for example: *staff*, *people who work in the store*, *salesclerks*, *managers.*

PRESENTATION

- Books open. Set the scene. Direct Ss' attention to the pictures on page 84. Ask the question from Exercise **1A**: *What do you see?* Elicit and write on the board as much vocabulary about the pictures as possible: *cameras*, *customers*, *clerks*, *gift receipt*, etc. Explain any unfamiliar words. Ask: *What kind of cameras do you see here?* (They're digital cameras.) Ask Ss what type of store is featured in the second picture (electronics store).
- Direct Ss' attention to the question in **1B**: *What is happening?* Read it aloud. Hold up the Student's Book. Point to the first picture. Ask: *What's Rosa doing here?* (She's holding a camera.)
- Brainstorm and list on the board possible reasons why Rosa wants to return the camera.

Teaching Tip

Encourage Ss to be creative. At this point, there is no single correct answer.

Culture Tip

Tell Ss that in the United States, they can return or exchange items that don't work. Usually, the store will require a receipt in order to take back the item, but different stores have different policies. Ask Ss what they would do if they were in Rosa's situation. Elicit responses, such as: *go to the customer service department of the store*; *call the store*; *bring the item, receipt, and packaging to the store*; *ask for a new camera.*

PRACTICE

- Ask Ss to work in pairs to write a role play between Rosa and Karine or between Rosa and Frank. In either role play, Rosa should explain the problem she is having, and the clerk should offer advice.
- Walk around and listen to Ss as they role-play the situation.
- Ask several pairs to perform their role play for the class.

Teaching Tip

Encourage Ss to avoid reading their lines when they act out their role play. Suggest that Ss first read the line to themselves, then look up and say the line. This strategy helps build fluency and confidence in speaking English.

PRESENTATION

- Books open. Direct Ss' attention to Exercise **2A**. Read the instructions and questions aloud. Explain that after listening to the conversation, Ss will ask and answer the two questions in the exercise in pairs. Tell Ss to listen for the answers to these two questions as the audio is played or read.

▶ **CD2, Track 10** Play or read the audio (see audio script, page T-181).

- Ask Ss if they understood everything in the listening exercise. Write any unfamiliar words on the board and help Ss understand the meaning of each new word. Be sure that Ss understand *defective*.

- Elicit answers to the questions. For example: *The speakers are Rosa and different store personnel. In Part 1, Rosa asks Karine who she should speak to about getting a refund. In Part 2, Rosa asks for a refund. Frank in customer service tells her about the store refund and exchange policy. In the end, Frank offers her a store credit.*

- Focus Ss' attention on Exercise **2B** and read the instructions aloud. Tell Ss to listen to the audio and complete the chart based on the information they hear.

▶ **CD2, Track 10** Tell Ss to listen for details about Rosa's conversation with Frank. Model the task. Play or read the audio again. Pause the audio after Rosa says in Part 1: *It's a camera, a digital camera.* Ask a S to read the example answer written next to *kind of camera Rosa bought* (*a digital camera*). Play or read the rest of the audio. Ss listen and complete the chart. Draw the chart on the board.

▶ **CD2, Track 10** Play or read the audio again. Ss listen and check their answers.

- Write the numbers *1–6* on the board. Ask Ss to come to the board to write their answers in the chart. Make corrections on the board as needed.

Learner persistence *(individual work)*

▶ **CD2, Track 10** Ss can listen to the audio for Exercises **2A** and **2B** at home for reinforcement and review. They can also listen to the audio for self-directed learning when class attendance is not possible.

PRACTICE

- Direct Ss' attention to Exercise **3A** and read the instructions aloud. Tell Ss that the story is a summary of what happened in the pictures on the previous page.

- Focus Ss' attention on the words in the word bank. Say each word and have Ss repeat. Correct pronunciation as needed. Explain any words that are new to Ss.

- Model the task. Ask a S to read aloud the first sentence in the story, including the example answer.

- Ss complete the exercise individually. Walk around and help as needed.

COMPREHENSION CHECK

▶ **CD2, Track 11** Play or read the audio (see audio script, page T-181). Ss listen and check their answers. Repeat the audio as needed.

- Write the numbers *1–10* on the board. Ask Ss to come to the board to write only the answers.

Learner persistence *(individual work)*

▶ **CD2, Track 11** Ss can listen to the audio for Exercise **3A** at home for reinforcement and review. They can also listen to the audio for self-directed learning when class attendance is not possible.

APPLICATION

- Focus Ss' attention on Exercise **3B** and read the instructions aloud.

- Ss complete the exercise in pairs. Help as needed.

- Ask several pairs to ask and answer the questions for the class. Discuss Ss' experiences with returning or exchanging merchandise.

Teaching Tip
Ss with limited confidence in speaking English may be reluctant to return defective products or merchandise they don't really want. However, it is important to encourage them to do so. Remind Ss to always keep their receipts so that they can get a refund or an exchange. Emphasize that it is important for returns or exchanges to be done as soon as possible.

EVALUATION

- Direct Ss' attention to the lesson focus on the board. Ask individual Ss to look at the pictures on page 84 to make sentences using the words from Exercise **3A**.

- Check off each part of the lesson focus as Ss demonstrate an understanding of what they have learned in the lesson.

More Ventures, Unit 7, Lesson A	
Workbook, 15–30 min.	
Multilevel Worksheets, 30–45 min.	www.cambridge.org/ventures/resources/
Collaborative Worksheets, 30–45 min.	
Student Arcade, time varies	www.cambridge.org/venturesarcade/

UNIT GOALS
Identify store policies for returning items   **Identify** pros and cons of online shopping
Interpret a returned-merchandise form

2 Listen

A Listen and answer the questions.

1. Who are the speakers?   2. What are they talking about?

■)) CD2, Track 10

B Listen again. Complete the chart.

■)) CD2, Track 10

1. kind of camera Rosa bought	*a digital camera*
2. problem	*doesn't like it*
3. date purchased	*the 5th*
4. today's date	*the 20th*
5. store policy for refunds	*return within 10 days*
6. store policy for exchanges	*return within 30 days*

3 After you listen

A Read. Complete the story.

camera	customer service	exchanges	policy	store credit
condition	defective	merchandise	refund	warranty

Rosa wants to return the ____*camera*____ that she bought and get a

____*refund*____. She is told that she needs to speak with someone in
     2

____*customer service*____. The clerk there asks Rosa if the camera is ____*defective*____,
          3   4

and she says it isn't. The clerk tells her about the store ____*policy*____ for returns
                                                                                           5

and ____*exchanges*____. It's too late for Rosa to return the camera, but she can
                  6

exchange it if the ____*merchandise*____ is in perfect ____*condition*____. Rosa still has the
                              7   8

camera box with the instruction book and the ____*warranty*____ card. Since Rosa is in
                                                                                9

a hurry, she decides to get a ____*store credit*____, and she will use it at a later time.
                                                   10

Listen and check your answers.

■)) CD2, Track 11

B Discuss. Talk with your classmates.

1. What are some reasons that people may want to return merchandise to a store?

2. What are some situations where it may be impossible to return merchandise?

3. Do you think people should get a refund for something they have used? Why or why not?

Lesson B Subject-pattern adjective clauses

1 Grammar focus: *who*, *that* and *which*

Adjective clauses come after a noun and begin with a relative pronoun. *Who, that* and *which* are examples of relative pronouns. Use *who* with people, *which* with things, and *that* with people or things.

Watch

The camera costs only $99.

(It) is on sale.

The camera **which** is on sale costs only $99.

The camera **that** is on sale costs only $99.

The clerk helped the customer.

(She) lost her receipt.

The clerk helped the customer **who** lost her receipt.

The clerk helped the customer **that** lost her receipt.

2 Practice

A **Write**. Circle the subject in the second sentence. Then combine the sentences by making the second sentence into an adjective clause and replacing the subject with *which* or *who*.

1. I want to buy a camera. (It)'s not too expensive.
   I want to buy a camera which is not too expensive.

2. I'd like to get a good camera. (It) will last for many years.
   I'd like to get a good camera which will last for many years.

3. Many people shop online. (They) are looking for cameras.
   Many people who are looking for cameras shop online.

4. My friend told me about a camera store. (It) sells used merchandise.
   My friend told me about a camera store which sells used merchandise.

5. Customers like to shop at Super Camera. (They) appreciate good service.
   Customers who appreciate good service like to shop at Super Camera.

6. The clerk is very helpful. (He) works in customer service.
   The clerk who works in customer service is very helpful.

7. These days, many people want an expensive camera. (It) has separate lenses.
   These days, many people want an expensive camera which has separate lenses.

8. Sometimes people need to return merchandise. (It) is defective.
   Sometimes people need to return merchandise which is defective.

9. Buyers may be sorry later. (They) don't ask about a store's return policy.
   Buyers who don't ask about a store's return policy may be sorry later.

10. Many people now have smart phones. (The phones) have excellent cameras.
    Many people now have smart phones which have excellent cameras.

Listen and check your answers.

CD2, Track 12

- Introduce *who*, *that*, and *which* as the subject of a dependent clause

WARM-UP AND REVIEW

- Before class: Write the lesson focus on the board.
  Lesson B:
  "who," "that," and "which" as the subject of a dependent clause

- Begin class. Books open. Review Lesson A vocabulary. Direct Ss' attention to the pictures and the story on page 84. Ask Ss to generate some sentences about the pictures, stating what they remember, for example: *Rosa wants to return her camera. Frank helps her exchange her camera.*

- Point to the word *clause* in the lesson focus. Ask Ss what a clause is (a group of words containing a subject and a verb). Write the following sentences on the board:
  1. *Rosa took her camera to the camera shop.*
  2. *She wanted to get her money back because she didn't like the camera.*

  Ask Ss to tell you how many clauses there are in each of the sentences on the board (first sentence: 1; second sentence: 2). Ask Ss to identify the subject of each clause as you circle the word (*Rosa*, *She*, *she*). Ask Ss to identify the verb in each clause as you underline the word(s) (*took*, *wanted*, *didn't like*).

PRESENTATION

Focus on meaning / personalize

- Books closed. Direct Ss' attention to the lesson focus on the board. Read it aloud.

- Ask two or three S volunteers to tell the class true sentences about themselves. Write a few sentences on the board using Ss' names, for example: *Tanya likes to play the guitar.* Repeat each sentence using the Ss' names.

- Next to the sentences about your students, write sentences using *who* or *that* clauses, for example: *Tanya is a person who likes to play the guitar. David is a person that likes to dance.*

- Ask: *Does anyone want a car? What kind of car do you want?* Elicit answers. Repeat each sentence using the Ss' names and a *that* or *which* clause, for example: *Jorge wants a car which has a sunroof. Ana wants a car that has a manual transmission.* Write two or three sentences on the board.

- Direct Ss' attention to the sentences on the board with a *who* clause. Ask: *What word follows the person in these sentences?* (who.) Direct Ss' attention to the sentences on the board with a *which* clause. Ask: *What word follows the thing in these sentences?* (which.) Explain that *who* refers only to a person, and *which* refers to a thing. *That* can refer to a person or a thing.

Focus on form

- Use the animated grammar presentation in one or more of the following ways:
  - Preview it before class
  - Show in class
  - Encourage Ss to watch outside of class.

- Books open. Direct Ss' attention to the Subject-pattern adjective clauses chart in Exercise **1**. Read aloud each statement. Ask Ss to repeat.

- Write on the board the first sentence in each column of the chart. Read the second sentence. Ask: *What is the adjective clause?* (which is on sale.) Circle it.

- Read and have Ss repeat the third sentence. Have Ss circle the adjective clause.

- Repeat the above steps for the three sentences in the second column.

PRACTICE

- Focus Ss' attention on Exercise **2A** and read the instructions aloud.

- Model the exercise. Ask a S to read the example answer to the class. Make sure that Ss understand the task of combining two sentences using an adjective clause.

- Ss complete the exercise individually. Walk around and help as needed. Tell Ss that the combined sentences for numbers 3, 5, 6, 8, and 9 have a change in word order. The adjective clauses in these sentences must immediately follow the nouns that they are modifying.

COMPREHENSION CHECK

▶ *CD2, Track 12* Play or read the audio (see audio script, page T-181). Ss listen and check their answers.

- Write the numbers *1–10* on the board. Call on Ss to write the combined sentence for each item. Make corrections on the board as needed.

LESSON B Subject-pattern adjective clauses

PRESENTATION

- Direct Ss' attention to the picture on page 87. Ask Ss: *Where does this scene take place?* Elicit an appropriate response, such as: *in a large electronics store.* Ask Ss: *What kind of merchandise is sold here?* (cameras, stereos, TVs, DVD players, video equipment, appliances, computers, etc.)

PRACTICE

- Read the instructions aloud for Exercise **2B**.
- Ask a S to read the verbs in the word bank. Ask two other Ss to read the example conversation to the class.
- Ss complete the exercise in pairs. Walk around and help as needed.
- Direct Ss' attention to the second part of Exercise **2B** and read the instructions aloud.
- Model the exercise. Call on a S to read the example sentence. Tell Ss that their sentences must include an adjective clause with *who* or *that* or *which*.
- Ss work individually to complete the exercise. Help as needed.
- Have individual Ss write their sentences on the board. Make corrections on the board as needed.

APPLICATION

- Direct Ss' attention to Exercise **3A** and read the instructions and topics aloud.
- Model the task. Ask three Ss to read the example dialog to the class.
- Ss work in small groups to complete the exercise. Tell Ss that for the topic *your idea*, they should choose a place that they go to frequently, or enjoy going to, such as a park, or the beach. Walk around and help as needed.
- Direct Ss' attention to Exercise **3B** and read the instructions aloud.
- Ask groups to share the information they discussed.

Expansion activity (small groups)

- Tell Ss that this activity is a guessing game in which they have to identify stores, movie theaters, restaurants, and other places in their neighborhood. You can also adapt this activity – especially if Ss are not familiar with the neighborhood surrounding the school – so that Ss identify movies, songs, music groups, or celebrities.
- Ss in groups. Model the activity. Say: *I like a store that sells Caribbean foods.* Ask a S to guess which store it is and then make a sentence with an adjective clause about a location that the next S has to identify. For example: *I like a*

restaurant that is very big and has a red sign above the door. If a S doesn't know the answer, the next person in the group tries to answer.

- Make sure that Ss are using adjective clauses correctly and that each S has several chances to ask and answer questions. Walk around and help as needed.
- Ask a S from each group to come to the board to write an example sentence. Make corrections on the board as needed.

Expansion activity (individual work)

- Ask Ss to draw a map of their neighborhood, marking the places where they usually go. For each place, Ss should write a sentence with an adjective clause.
- Model the task. Write the following example sentences on the board:
  This is the market that sells the best fruit.
  This is the movie theater that's always crowded.
- Ss share their maps with a partner. Call on Ss to share several of the sentences they wrote.

EVALUATION

- Books closed. Direct Ss' attention to the lesson focus on the board.
- Write four simple sentences on the board:
  My friend told me about a market. It sells many kinds of Asian foods.
  The clerk is very nice. She works at the first register.
- Ask a S to read and combine the sentences, changing the second sentence into an adjective clause. Elicit: *My friend told me about a market which / that sells many kinds of Asian foods.*
- Ask another S to read aloud the second set of sentences and to combine them. Elicit: *The clerk who / that works at the first register is very nice.*
- Check off the lesson focus as Ss demonstrate an understanding of what they have learned in the lesson.

More Ventures, Unit 7, Lesson B	
Workbook, 15–30 min.	
Multilevel Worksheets, 30–45 min.	www.cambridge.org/ventures/ resources/
Collaborative Worksheets, 30–45 min.	
Student Arcade, time varies	www.cambridge.org/ venturesarcade/

B **Talk** with a partner. Ask and answer questions to identify the following people in the picture: the cashier, the cleaning person, the customer, the greeter, the stock clerk, and the store manager. Use adjective clauses with *who, that* or *which*. Choose verbs from the box.

| carry | give | help | listen | smile | sweep |
| clean | have | hold | put | stand | wear |

A Which one is the cashier?

B He's the man who's putting the video camera into the bag.

A You mean the one that's standing behind the counter?

B Right.

Write sentences about the people in the picture.

The cashier is the man who's putting the video camera into the bag.

Answers will vary.

3 **Communicate**

A **Work** in a small group. Ask and answer questions about the topics. Use adjective clauses with *that, who,* or *which.*

A Nadia, what kinds of supermarkets do you like?

B I like supermarkets that are open 24 hours a day. What about you, Phuong?

C I like supermarkets that have lots of fresh fish.

- books
- clothing stores
- internet sites
- malls
- restaurants
- salesclerks
- supermarkets
- (your idea)

B **Share** information about your classmates.

Lesson C Object-pattern adjective clauses

1 Grammar focus: *that*

Adjective clauses come after a noun and begin with a relative pronoun. *That* is an example of a relative pronoun. Use *that* with people or things.

Watch

I like the car.

You bought (it.)

I like the car **(that)** you bought.

The mechanic has 20 years of experience.

I use (him.)

The mechanic **(that)** I use has 20 years of experience.

2 Practice

A Write. Circle the object in the second sentence. Then combine the sentences by changing the second sentence into an adjective clause with *that*.

1. A good friend needed a new car. I've known (her) for several years.

   A good friend that I've known for several years needed a new car.

2. She used to drive an old car. She got (it) from her father.

   She used to drive an old car that she got from her father.

3. Last January, the old car stopped working. She was driving (it.)

   Last January, the old car that she was driving stopped working.

4. The mechanic couldn't fix it. Her neighbor recommended (the mechanic.)

   The mechanic that her friend recommended couldn't fix it.

5. Finally, she decided to buy a used car from a man. She knew (the man) at work.

   Finally, she decided to buy a used car from a man that she knew at work.

6. He's an honest person. She trusts (him) completely.

   He's an honest person that she trusts completely.

7. The price was really good. He named (it.)

   The price that he named was really good.

8. The used car is only three years old. He sold (her) the car.

   The used car that he sold her is only three years old.

9. It's a reliable car. She can drive (it) for a long time.

   It's a reliable car that she can drive for a long time.

10. Suzy is happy to have a vehicle. She doesn't have to worry about (it.)

    Suzy is happy to have a vehicle that she doesn't have to worry about.

Listen and check your answers.

CD2, Track 13

WARM-UP AND REVIEW

- Before class: Write the lesson focus on the board.
  Lesson C:
  "that" as the object of a dependent clause

- Begin class. Books open. Review adjective clauses. Direct Ss' attention to the pictures and story on page 84. Ask questions, and write Ss' complete answers on the board. For example: *Which person is Rosa? She's the woman who is wearing glasses.*

- Direct Ss' attention to the first sentence on the board. Ask: *Which is the main clause?* (She's the woman.) *Which is the dependent clause?* (who is wearing glasses.) *What word in the main clause is the adjective clause describing?* (woman.) Do the same for the remaining sentences on the board.

PRESENTATION

Focus on meaning / personalize

- Books closed. Direct Ss' attention to the lesson focus on the board. Read it aloud.

- Ask three or four Ss to come to the front of the classroom. Give them each a small object, such as a paper clip, a penny, or a small eraser. Tell them to go outside the classroom and hide their object somewhere on their person, such as in a shirt pocket, a handbag, a fist, or a sock. Tell them to reenter the classroom when all the objects are hidden from sight.

- When Ss return to the classroom, have them line up in front of the class. Ask: *Where's the penny that* (Ricardo) *got?* Have individual Ss guess until the penny is located. Then write on the board: *The penny that Ricardo got was in his sock.* Continue in the same way until all the objects have been found and there are three or four similar sentences on the board.

- Focus Ss' attention on the first sentence on the board. Identify the two clauses. Ask: *What's the subject of the dependent clause?* (Ricardo.) *What's the verb in the dependent clause?* (got.) *What does "that" refer to?* (the penny.) Explain that the word *that* is the object of the dependent clause, not the subject.

- Elicit or explain why we use adjective clauses (to give additional information about the word they follow, describe, identify, or make more specific).

Focus on form

- Use the animated grammar presentation in one or more of the following ways:
  - Preview it before class
  - Show in class
  - Encourage Ss to watch outside of class.

- Books open. Direct Ss' attention to the charts in Exercise **1**. Read aloud each statement. Ask Ss to repeat.

- Write on the board the sentences from the chart. Read the second sentence. Ask Ss to repeat. Ask: *What is the main clause?* (I like the car.)

  Underline it. Ask: *What is the dependent clause?* (that you bought.) Circle it. Ask: *What word in the main clause does the dependent clause describe?* (car.)

- Read and have Ss repeat the other sentences. Have Ss underline the main clause and circle the dependent clause in each one.

PRACTICE

- Direct Ss' attention to Exercise **2A** and read the instructions aloud.

- Ask a S to read aloud the first sentence containing the sample answer.

- Ss complete the exercise individually. Walk around and help as needed.

COMPREHENSION CHECK

- Read aloud the second part of the instructions for Exercise **2A**.

- ▶ **CD2, Track 13** Play or read the audio (see audio script, page T-181). Ss listen and check their answers.

- Write the numbers *1–10* on the board. Ask individual Ss to come to the board to write their answers. Make corrections on the board as needed.

PRESENTATION

- Direct Ss' attention to the picture in Exercise **2B**. Have Ss look carefully at the picture and describe what is happening. Elicit an appropriate response, such as: *The young couple is opening gifts, but there is a problem.*

PRACTICE

- Read the instructions aloud. Call on three Ss in turn to read each of the columns in the chart (the item, where Ted and Lisa got it, and the problem).
- Explain vocabulary as needed and write any new words on the board. Ask a S to read the example sentence.
- Ss complete the exercise in pairs. Walk around and help as needed.
- Read the instructions aloud for the second part of Exercise **2B**. Ask a S to read the example sentence to the class.
- Ss complete the exercise individually. Walk around and help as needed.
- Ask several Ss to write their sentences on the board. Call on other Ss to read each of the sentences. For each sentence ask Ss: *Is this sentence correct?* Make corrections on the board as needed.

APPLICATION

- Direct Ss' attention to Exercise **3A** and read the instructions aloud. Ask a S to read the questions.

Useful Language

Read the tip box aloud. Explain any new adjectives as needed. Ask Ss if they know of any similar words or expressions (*ripped*, *wrong size*, *irregular*, etc.), and write them on the board.

- Model the task. Ask two Ss to read the example dialog.
- Ss complete the exercise in small groups. Walk around and help as needed.
- Direct Ss' attention to Exercise **3B** and read the instructions aloud.

- Ask a S from each group to tell what he or she learned about a classmate's shopping mistake. Ask the S to make a sentence about the information the S's partner shared, for example: *The book that Marta ordered online was damaged. It was raining really hard, and the box got wet. She called the company. They told her that they would send her another book as soon as she sent back the first one.*
- Continue the exercise by asking different Ss to share information they learned from their classmates. Encourage Ss to use adjective clauses.

Expansion activity (individual work)

- Have Ss use the situation they discussed in Exercise **3A** as the basis of a paragraph. Collect these paragraphs, or have Ss exchange papers with their partner and use this as an opportunity for peer-correction.
- You may wish to place these paragraphs in a class book called *Shopping Mistakes.*
- Any artists in the class may illustrate the book with amusing cartoons or illustrations.

EVALUATION

- Direct Ss' attention to the lesson focus on the board. Ask Ss to look at the picture on page 89 and make sentences about Ted and Lisa's wedding presents using adjective clauses (e.g., *The rug that Lisa's aunt ordered from a catalog was the wrong color*). Ss should say their sentences aloud. Make corrections as needed.
- Check off the lesson focus as Ss demonstrate an understanding of what they have learned in the lesson.

More Ventures, Unit 7, Lesson C	
Workbook, 15–30 min.	
Multilevel Worksheets, 30–45 min.	www.cambridge.org/ventures/ resources/
Collaborative Worksheets, 30–45 min.	
Student Arcade, time varies	www.cambridge.org/ venturesarcade/

B **Talk** with a partner. Ted and Lisa got married recently. Unfortunately, they have had some bad luck. Look at the chart and make sentences by choosing an item from each column.

The dishes Ted and Lisa received from Aunt May were broken.

dishes	found on the Internet	the wrong size
computer	bought on sale	scratched
car	ordered from a catalog	broken
camera	got as a wedding present	damaged
rug	received from Aunt May	torn
lamps	picked up at a garage sale	the wrong color
coffee table	purchased from a friend	too slow

Write sentences about Ted and Lisa.

The dishes that they received from Aunt May were broken.

Answers will vary.

3 Communicate

A **Work** in a small group. Tell about a shopping "mistake." Include the information below.

- What was the item?
- Where did you buy it?
- What did you do about it?
- When did you buy it?
- What was wrong with it?

A The chicken I bought last week at Paglia's Meats was spoiled.

B What did you do about it?

A I took it back to the store and asked them to give me a fresh package.

B **Share** information about your classmates.

Lesson D Reading

1 Before you read

Talk with your classmates. Answer the questions.

1. Have you ever tried to exchange an item or get a refund? Describe your experience.

2. In your native country, is it easy or difficult for people to get a refund for something that they purchased?

Sometimes an important word is replaced by a synonym. This makes the reading more interesting. For example, *seller* and *retailer* are two nouns that have the same meaning.

2 Read

Read the newspaper advice column. Listen and read again.

The Smart Shopper

◄)) CD2, Track 14

Dear Smart Shopper,

I'm a jewelry lover, and I enjoy shopping online. Unfortunately, I just bought a pair of gold earrings that I don't like. When I tried to return them, I learned that the seller has a no-return policy. Don't I have the right to get a refund?

Mad Madelyn

Dear Mad Madelyn,

If the merchandise is defective, the seller must return your money or make an exchange. However, if the merchandise was in good condition when you received it, and if the retailer has a no-return policy, there is nothing you can do. This is true for store purchases as well as Internet purchases. In the future, here are some questions you should ask before you buy anything:

- Does the seller say "satisfaction guaranteed or your money back"?

- Is there a time limit on returns, such as two weeks?

- Who pays the shipping costs on items that are returned?

- Do you need to return the merchandise in its original package?

- Is the original receipt required?

- Does the retailer give a store credit instead of a cash refund?

- If the retailer has a store in your area, can you return the merchandise to the store instead of shipping it?

Next time, find the return policy on the merchant's Web site and print it, or ask the merchant for the return policy in writing. It's important to get all the facts that you need before you buy!

Smart Shopper

Teaching objectives
- Introduce a newspaper advice column about smart shopping
- Provide practice using new topic related vocabulary
- Provide practice identifying and using compound nouns

WARM-UP AND REVIEW

- Before class. Write today's lesson focus on the board.
  Lesson D:
  Read and understand "The Smart Shopper"
  Practice new vocabulary related to buying and
  returning merchandise
  Identify and use compound nouns
- Begin class. Books closed. Direct Ss' attention to the words *Smart Shopper* in the lesson focus. Write them on the board. Ask Ss: *What do you think a smart shopper is?* Elicit appropriate responses, such as: *Someone who knows where to buy things at a good price, someone who uses coupons and finds sales.*
- Tell Ss that they are going to read a newspaper advice column about shopping. Ask Ss if they are familiar with magazines or newspaper columns that offer shopping advice or tips. If possible, show Ss a few examples from magazines, newspapers, or Web sites.
- Point to *"The Smart Shopper"* on the board and ask Ss to predict what this newspaper advice column is about. Elicit responses, such as: *It's about how to make good shopping decisions.* Write some of the Ss' predictions on the board.

PRESENTATION

- Books open. Direct Ss' attention to Exercise **1** and read the instructions aloud.
- Focus Ss' attention on the questions in Exercise **1** and ask two Ss to read them aloud.
- Ss in small groups discuss their answers to the questions. Walk around and help as needed.
- Call on individual Ss to share their answers with the class.

PRACTICE

- Read the instructions aloud for Exercise **2**. Ask Ss to read the advice column silently before listening to the audio.
- ▶ **CD2, Track 14** Play or read the audio and ask Ss to read along (see audio script, pages T-181–T-182). Repeat the audio as needed.
- While Ss are listening and reading the advice column, ask them to underline any words or expressions they don't know. When the audio is finished, write the new words on the board.

- Point to each word. Say it and have Ss repeat. Give a brief explanation of each word, or ask Ss who know the word to explain it. If Ss prefer to look up the new words in their dictionaries, allow them to do so.

Call on a S to read the tip aloud. Have Ss recall the definition of a *synonym* – a word that has the same meaning as another word. Explain that writers use synonyms to make an article or another piece of writing more lively and interesting. Also, remind Ss that when they read, they can use synonyms as context clues to figure out the meaning of unfamiliar words. Ask Ss if they know of synonyms for words used in this unit (e.g., *product = merchandise, purchase = buy, ripped = torn*). Write some of the synonyms on the board. Read each one aloud and have Ss repeat.

Learner persistence (individual work)
▶ **CD2, Track 14** Ss can listen to the audio for Exercise **2** at home for reinforcement and review. They can also listen to the audio for self-directed learning when class attendance is not possible.

Expansion activity (small groups)
- **Materials needed** Poster board and markers.
- Have Ss work in small groups to present a list of "Smart Shopping Tips" in the form of a poster.
- Tell Ss in each group to brainstorm ideas based on what they have read in the article, along with their personal experiences, and if possible, additional research. Encourage a group recorder to take notes and to read these notes after the brainstorming session.
- Have Ss discuss their tips with their group using the notes as a guide.
- Elicit some "smart shopping tips" from each group and write them on the board.
- Encourage groups to use the tips on the board as well as their own to create a poster of smart shopping tips.
- When groups have finished, have them display their posters around the room.
- Allow time for a representative from each group to read and explain the group's poster.

COMPREHENSION CHECK

- Direct Ss' attention to Exercise **3A** and read the instructions aloud.

- Ask individual Ss to read the questions aloud, one at a time. Make sure that Ss understand all the questions.

- Ss complete the exercise individually. Instruct Ss to write their answers on a separate piece of paper. Ss should answer in complete sentences. Walk around and help as needed.

- Check answers with the class. Ask where in the reading the answers are found.

Expansion activity (student pairs)

- Have Ss work together to imagine and role-play a sitaution between the Smart Shopper columnist and someone who has had a problem with a purchase or an exchange. Ss may refer to the reading on page 90 for some ideas.

- When pairs have finished writing their role play, encourage them to practice it.

- Ask several pairs to perform their role play for the class.

PRACTICE

- Direct Ss' attention to Exercise **3B**. Read the introductory information about compound nouns.

- Call on a S to read aloud the instructions in number 1.

- Have another S read the example and the adjective clause in the chart that explains the compound noun.

- Ask a S to read the other adjective clauses in the chart.

- Ss work individually to complete the chart. Walk around and help as needed.

- Focus Ss' attention on number 2 in Exercise **3B** and read the instructions aloud. Ss work individually to find two more compound nouns in the reading and fill in the corresponding adjective clauses.

- Direct Ss' attention to number 3 in Exercise **3B** and read the instructions aloud.

- Ss work in small groups to compile a list of compound nouns and explanations of each. Walk around and help as needed.

- Write the following headings on the board:

  Compound noun   Explanation

- Ask Ss to come to the board to write the nouns and corresponding adjective clauses they discussed with their group. Make corrections on the board as needed.

Learner persistence (individual work)

- Encourage Ss to use their notebook or index cards to write new vocabulary words. Suggest that Ss review new words daily and practice them as much as possible.

APPLICATION

- Focus Ss' attention on Exercise **3C** and read the instructions aloud.

- Ask four Ss to read the four questions, one at a time.

- Ss complete the exercise in pairs.

- Ask several pairs to share their answers with the class.

Expansion activity

- Refer Ss to "Amazing Bargains in Internet Auction Sites," another reading on the same topic on pages 154–156.

- Have Ss complete the activity either in class or outside of class.

- Provide feedback to Ss such as through whole-class discussion, partners comparing their worksheets, or T reviewing each S's worksheets.

EVALUATION

- Books closed. Direct Ss' attention to the lesson focus on the board.

- Ask individual Ss to retell the main points of the advice column, "The Smart Shopper."

- Books open. Focus Ss' attention on the words that they wrote in the chart for number 1 of Exercise **3B**. Ask Ss to write sentences with these words to show that they understand the meanings.

- Check off each part of the lesson focus as Ss demonstrate an understanding of what they have learned in the lesson.

More Ventures, Unit 7, Lesson D	
Workbook, 15–30 min.	
Multilevel Worksheets, 30–45 min. **Collaborative Worksheets,** 30–45 min.	www.cambridge.org/ventures/ resources/
Student Arcade, time varies	www.cambridge.org/ venturesarcade/

3 After you read

A Check your understanding.

1. What is the purpose of *The Smart Shopper* newspaper column?

2. What problem does Madelyn write about?

3. According to the article, when must a retailer return a customer's money?

4. Do you believe that Madelyn is happy with the answer to her question? Why or why not?

5. What should Madelyn have done before she bought the earrings?

6. What is another word in the reading with the same meaning as *seller* and *retailer*?

B Build your vocabulary.

Compound nouns are noun + noun combinations that have special meanings. Sometimes you can explain compound nouns with adjective clauses. For example, a *jewelry lover* is a person who loves jewelry.

1. Find compound nouns in the reading that match the meanings. Write them on the chart.

Compound noun	Meaning
1. *jewelry lover*	a person who loves jewelry
2. *time limit*	a limit that is related to time
3. *shipping costs*	costs that are related to shipping
4. *store credit*	a credit that is given by a store
5. *cash refund*	a refund that is made in cash
6. *return policy*	a policy that is related to returns
7. *Answers will vary.*	
8. *Answers will vary.*	

2. Find two more compound nouns in the reading. Write them on the chart. Use adjective clauses to explain what they mean. *Answers will vary.*

3. Work in a small group. Make a list of other compound nouns you know. Use adjective clauses to explain what they mean. *Answers will vary.*

C Talk with a partner.

1. Are you a jewelry lover? What do you love to buy?

2. Are you a smart shopper? Explain your answer.

3. Have you ever gotten a cash refund? For what? Why?

4. What is something you wanted to return, but didn't?

For college and career readiness practice, see pages 154–156.

Lesson E Writing

1 Before you write

A **Talk** with a partner. List some reasons people should or shouldn't shop online.

Reasons people should shop online	Reasons people shouldn't shop online
It's convenient.	It's hard to choose merchandise you can't touch.
Answers will vary.	

B **Read** the paragraph.

Reasons You Shouldn't Shop Online

There are some good reasons you shouldn't shop online. First, it's hard to choose merchandise that you can't touch. For example, a piece of jewelry might look very good on the computer screen, but after you buy it and look at it closely, you may find that it's very ugly and poorly made. Furthermore, shopping online is slow. It may take several days to receive the merchandise. If you are not satisfied, it may take weeks to exchange the merchandise or get your money back. Finally, shopping online can be dangerous. People can steal your credit card number and use it to buy expensive items. An irresponsible seller can take your money and never send you the merchandise. I'm going to do my shopping in stores!

 Use transition words such as *first, second, next, furthermore, moreover,* and *finally* to signal a list of reasons in a paragraph.

Teaching objectives
- Prepare Ss for writing a paragraph about shopping online
- Provide practice using transition words

WARM-UP AND REVIEW

- Before class. Write today's lesson focus on the board.
  Lesson E:
  Write a persuasive paragraph about shopping online
  Use transition words to organize a paragraph

- Begin class. Books closed. Review vocabulary from the unit. Write the words *shopping online* on the board. Ask Ss: *How many of you have shopped online?* Ask Ss where they have shopped and what kind of purchases they have made (e.g., books, clothing, shoes).

- Remind Ss about the newspaper advice column they read on page 90. Ask the following questions:
  What was Mad Madelyn's complaint? (She wanted a refund for earrings she bought online from a store that has a no-return policy.)
  What did the Smart Shopper tell her? (Unless the merchandise is defective, there's nothing she can do.)
  What does Smart Shopper suggest in the article? (Smart Shopper suggests that before making any purchases, the buyer should check the store's return policy.)
  Where can you find a store's return policy? (You can find it online or at the store. If you look at a merchant's Web site, you should be able to find it there. Often a return policy is printed on a store's receipt. If not, you can ask the merchant in person to give you a written copy of the return policy.)

PRESENTATION

- Books open. Direct Ss attention to Exercise **1A** and read the instructions aloud.
- Call on two Ss to read the two boldfaced headings: *Why people should shop online* and *Why people shouldn't shop online.*
- Ask two other Ss to read the example answers.
- Ss work in pairs to list their reasons in the appropriate column. Walk around and help as needed.

- Write the two headings on the board. Ask Ss to share with the class some of the information they talked about with their partner. Write Ss' reasons on the board.

PRACTICE

- Direct Ss' attention to Exercise **1B** and read the instructions aloud.
- Ss read the paragraph silently. Tell them to underline any words they don't understand.
- Have Ss write the new words on the board. Point to each word. Say it and ask Ss to repeat.

Read the tip aloud. Ask Ss to reread the paragraph and underline the transition words. Call on Ss to say and locate each of the transition words in the paragraph (e.g., *First* appears in the second sentence; *furthermore* appears in the fourth sentence). Point out that transition words help the writer to organize a paragraph and make it easier for the reader to follow the list of reasons in a persuasive paragraph. Tell Ss that there are many more transition words in English but that these are some of the most common.

Expansion activity (small groups)

- Tell Ss that they are going to work with a small group to share some online shopping tips.
- Direct Ss' attention to the advice column on page 90. Ask Ss: *What questions does the Smart Shopper say buyers should ask themselves?* Elicit the questions on page 90 in the Ss' own words.
- Invite members in each group to brainstorm a list of similar advice questions about online shopping. If you have computers in class, you can also have Ss look up online shopping tips, since there are several sites that offer them.
- Call on Ss to share their questions. Write several examples on the board.

LESSON E Writing

PRESENTATION

- Direct Ss' attention to Exercise **1C** and read the instructions aloud.
- Call on a S to read aloud the two boldfaced headings: *Transition words* and *Reasons and supporting details.*
- Call on another S to read the example answers.
- Ss work in pairs to complete the informal outline of the model paragraph on page 92.
- Write an outline on the board similar to the one in the Student's Book.
- Have Ss come to the board, one at a time, to fill in the outline with the information from the model paragraph. Make corrections on the board as needed.

PRACTICE

- Direct Ss' attention to Exercise **1D** and read the instructions aloud. Explain that it will be easier for Ss to write a paragraph if they plan it carefully.
- Ss complete their outline individually. Walk around and help as needed.

Teaching Tip

Before Ss begin to write, have them talk about the topic in a prewriting activity. Talking with a partner or a small group will help Ss focus on the reasons they are going to use to support their argument in Exercise **2**.

APPLICATION

- Focus Ss' attention on Exercise **2** and read the instructions aloud.
- Ss complete the task individually. Walk around and help as needed.

Learner persistence (individual work)

- If you have any Ss who have difficulty writing, sit with them and help them as the other Ss are writing. Help Ss use their notes from their outline in Exercise **1D** to add strong reasons to support their opinion of why you *should* shop online.

COMPREHENSION CHECK

- Direct Ss' attention to Exercise **3A**.
- This exercise asks Ss to develop skills to review and edit their own writing.
- Ss check their own paragraph against the writing checklist. Walk around and help as needed. If any Ss check *No* for one or more of the checklist items, ask them to revise and edit their paragraph to include the missing information.

EVALUATION

- Focus Ss' attention on Exercise **3B**. Read the instructions aloud. This exercise enables Ss to work together to edit their writing. Reading aloud enables the writer to review his or her own writing and to understand the need to write clearly for an audience.
- Ss complete the exercise in pairs. Tell Ss to take turns reading their paragraphs to each other. Walk around and help as needed.
- Listen to Ss as they ask their partner one question about the paragraph and tell their partner one thing they learned from it.
- Ask several Ss to read their paragraph aloud. Have other Ss ask questions and mention one thing they learned from the paragraph.
- Direct Ss' attention to the lesson focus on the board.
- Check off each part of the lesson focus as Ss demonstrate an understanding of what they have learned in the lesson.

Community building (small groups)

- Identify some people in the community who have stores nearby, and invite them to come to the class to talk about their business. Tell the storeowners that you have been talking about the advantages and disadvantages of online shopping and would like their views.
- Prepare Ss for the visits beforehand by having them work in small groups to brainstorm a list of five to seven questions to ask each guest speaker. Encourage Ss to incorporate as much new vocabulary as possible. Ss should write down their questions. Walk around and help as needed.
- Call on groups to say some of their questions aloud. Correct as needed.
- On the day of the event, have group members take turns asking the questions they discussed in their group.
- After the event, call on Ss to share ideas. Ask Ss questions, such as: *What was the most interesting thing you learned? Did anything surprise you? What was it?*

More Ventures, Unit 7, Lesson E	
Workbook, 15–30 min.	
Multilevel Worksheets, 30–45 min.	www.cambridge.org/ventures/ resources/
Collaborative Worksheets, 30–45 min.	

C **Complete** the outline with information from the model paragraph.

Transition words	Reasons and supporting details
First	First reason: _hard to choose merchandise you can't touch_
	Supporting detail: _might look good on screen, but you may find that it's ugly and poorly made._
Furthermore	Second reason: _is slow_
	Supporting detail: _may take several days to receive the merchandise_
	Supporting detail: _may take weeks to exchange or get a refund_
Finally	Third reason: _may be dangerous_
	Supporting detail: _people can steal credit card number and use it to buy expensive items_
	Supporting detail: _seller could take your money and not send merchandise_

D **Plan** a paragraph about why you *should* shop online. Think of two or more reasons and one or more supporting details for each reason. Make notes about your ideas in an outline like the one in Exercise 1C. Use your own paper.

Answers will vary.

2 Write

Write a paragraph about why you should shop online. Give at least two reasons and one supporting detail for each reason. Use transition words to signal your list of reasons. Use the paragraph in Exercise 1B and the outlines in Exercises 1C and 1D to help you.

3 After you write

A **Check** your writing.

	Yes	No
1. I wrote two or more reasons to shop online.	☐	☐
2. I gave one or more supporting details for each reason.	☐	☐
3. I used transition words like *first*, *furthermore*, and *finally* to signal my list of reasons.	☐	☐

B **Share** your writing with a partner.

1. Take turns. Read your paragraph to a partner.

2. Comment on your partner's paragraph. Ask your partner a question about the paragraph. Tell your partner one thing you learned.

Lesson F Another view

1 Life-skills reading

JedsSports.com

RETURNED-MERCHANDISE FORM

Please complete this form and send it with the returned merchandise within 21 days to JedsSports.com, 3209 W. Foster Ave., Chicago, IL 60625. Include a copy of the invoice and the original packaging. Call us for a Returned-Merchandise Authorization number (M–F, 8 a.m.–5 p.m., CST) at 800-555-4143.

Name: *Rita Miller*   **RMA#:** *98704370*

Address *271 Dade Drive* **City** *Largo* **State** *FL* **Zip** *33771*

Check one:
☐ Store Credit
☑ Exchange

List items for return:

Item #	Description	Size	Color	Reason	Additional Comments
P4103	*sweatshirt*	*medium*	*red*	*wrong size*	*I ordered a large.*

List items to receive in exchange:

Item #	Description	Size	Color
P4128	*sweatshirt*	*large*	*red*

A **Read** the questions. Look at the returned-merchandise form. Fill in the answer.

1. Why is the buyer using this form?
   - Ⓐ She wants her money back.
   - Ⓑ She wants a store credit.
   - **Ⓒ** She wants to exchange the merchandise.
   - Ⓓ none of the above

2. What does the buyer need to include with this form?
   - Ⓐ the invoice
   - Ⓑ the item that she is returning
   - Ⓒ the original packaging
   - **Ⓓ** all of the above

3. Which statement is true?
   - **Ⓐ** The buyer must return the items within 21 days.
   - Ⓑ The buyer is satisfied with her purchase.
   - Ⓒ The buyer needs a smaller sweatshirt.
   - Ⓓ The buyer lives in New Jersey.

4. Which statement is not true?
   - Ⓐ The buyer is returning one item.
   - Ⓑ The buyer needs a different size.
   - **Ⓒ** The merchandise was defective.
   - Ⓓ The buyer wants the same color.

B **Solve** the problem. Give your opinion.

Catherine lives in an apartment building where all the mailboxes are just inside the main door. The mail carrier usually leaves packages on the floor beside the mailboxes. Recently Catherine ordered a soccer uniform from JedsSports.com. She never received her package even though the store says that the package was delivered a few days ago. What should she do?

Answers will vary.

Teaching objectives
- Introduce reading and understanding a form for returning merchandise
- Provide practice with clarifying questions

WARM-UP AND REVIEW

- Before class. Write today's lesson focus on the board.
  Lesson F:
  Read and understand a returned-merchandise form
  Use clarifying questions
- Begin class. Books closed. Point to the words on the board: *returned-merchandise form.*
- Ask Ss: *What kind of information do you think this form would have?* Elicit appropriate answers, such as: *the item purchased, the store policy for returns, a description of the item, a reason for the return.*
- Ask Ss: *When would you use this form?* Elicit an appropriate response, such as: *You would use this form when you're unhappy with something you bought and want to exchange it or get a refund.*
- Tell Ss that in this lesson, they will practice reading and understanding a returned-merchandise form.

PRESENTATION

- Books open. Call on individual Ss to read the form and the filled-in information in Exercise **1**. Explain vocabulary as needed.

Teaching Tip

Tell Ss that learning to read these kinds of forms is a useful skill for everyday life. Ask Ss if they have used similar forms. If no one says *yes*, explain that they may be in situations in the future in which they will need to use a form like this.

PRACTICE

- Read the instructions aloud for Exercise **1A**. This task helps prepare Ss for standardized-type tests they may have to take. Be sure that Ss understand the task. Have Ss individually scan for and fill in the answers.

COMPREHENSION CHECK

- Check answers with the class. Make sure that Ss have followed the instructions and filled in their answers.
- Have Ss read aloud the questions and answers they filled in. Ask Ss: *Is this answer correct?* Correct Ss' answers as needed.

APPLICATION

- Direct Ss' attention to Exercise **1B** and read the instructions aloud. Make sure that Ss understand the task. Have Ss individually solve the problem.
- Ss discuss the problem in small groups. Walk around and help as needed.
- Open up the discussion to the entire class. Accept all plausible answers.

Expansion activity (small groups)

- **Materials needed** Samples of returned-merchandise forms (they can be found online) – one form for each group.
- Bring in samples of returned-merchandise forms. Although most of them are basically the same, it will be more interesting for Ss if you can find forms for different kinds of merchandise.
- Distribute one form to each small group of Ss. Review vocabulary as needed. Have Ss in each group think of an appropriate product to "return" to the store. Encourage Ss to be creative. Walk around and help as needed.
- Call on groups to share their completed returned-merchandise forms with the class.
- Leave time for a question-and-answer session.

LESSON F Another view

WARM-UP AND REVIEW

- Books closed. Write three sentences on the board.
  1. *I went to visit my friend yesterday.* (who)
  2. *We walked in the park.* (what)
  3. *We came home after lunch.* (when)
- Ask a volunteer to read Sentence 1, and say *Who did you visit?* Have Ss read sentences 2 and 3 aloud, and ask *What did you do?* and *When did you come home?* Ensure Ss reply using complete sentences.

PRESENTATION

Focus on form

- Use the animated grammar presentation in one or more of the following ways:
  - Preview it before class
  - Show in class
  - Encourage Ss to watch outside of class.
- Books open. Direct Ss' attention to the grammar chart in **2A**. Ask pairs of Ss to take turns reading the statements and questions. Review the meaning of the 5 Ws (*Who?, What?, Where?, Why?, When? [and How?]*). Tell Ss that they can use clarifying questions when they are unsure of what a person has said and would like to clarify something.
- Ask a S to read the first statement: *I went to the mall.* Ask the S the accompanying clarifying question. Explain that you asked this question because you were unsure of what the person said. You wanted to clarify that they said *mall*.
- Ask Ss: *How are clarifying questions different from regular questions?* Elicit appropriate answers like: *The question words* (Who, What, Where, Why, When, *and* How) *come at the end instead of at the beginning of the sentences. There are no helping words like* do *or* does.

PRACTICE

- Direct Ss' attention to the instructions in **2A**. Read the instructions aloud. Ensure Ss understand the activity. Ask a pair of Ss to read the dialog aloud.

- Ss complete activity **2A** in pairs. Walk around and help as needed.
- Direct Ss' attention to the instructions in **2B**. Read the instructions aloud. Ask two Ss to read the example sentences. Ask several Ss to share their partners' story with the class.

EVALUATION

- Do a quick review of the unit. Have Ss turn to Lesson A. Ask the class to talk about what they remember about this lesson. Prompt Ss, if necessary, with questions, for example: *What are the conversations about on this page? What vocabulary is in the pictures?* Continue in this manner to review each lesson quickly.

Expansion activity

- Before class. Print, for each student, one copy of the Self-assessment for this unit.
- Have Ss complete the Self-assessment either in class or outside of class.
- Provide feedback to Ss such as through a whole-class discussion, partners comparing their worksheets, or T reviewing each S's worksheet.
- If Ss are ready, administer the unit test on pages T-207–T-209 of this Teacher's Edition. The audio script for the test is on pages T-223–T-224.

More Ventures, Unit 7, Lesson F	
Workbook, 15–30 min.	
Multilevel Worksheets, 30–45 min.	www.cambridge.org/ventrures/resources/
Collaborative Worksheets, 30–45 min.	
Self-assessment, 10 min.	
CASAS Test Prep Worksheet, 5–10 min.	

2 Grammar connections: Clarifying questions

To ask for clarification of words not heard or understood, insert a question word into the statement.

Watch

STATEMENT	CLARIFYING QUESTIONS
I went to the mall.	You went **where**?
There was a sale last weekend.	There was a sale **when**?
I bought some shirts.	You bought some **what**?
They were $20 each.	They were **how much**?
I bought five of them.	You bought **how many**?
They're for my sister.	They're for **who**?

A **Complete** the paragraph to make a story. Then talk with a partner. Your partner will listen and ask a clarifying question after every sentence. Answer your partner's question.

   A I needed to buy a laptop case.

   B You needed to buy what?

   A A laptop case.

Answers will vary.

I needed to buy _____. So I went to _____. I got there
                  1   2
at _____ o'clock. I couldn't find any, so I talked to _____.
        3   4
That person told me to go _____. Finally I found one. It only cost
                              5
$ _____. I didn't buy just one. I bought _____! I took
    6   7
them home and showed them to _____. He / She / They said,
                                      8
"_____!"
  9

B **Share** your partner's story with the class. The class will ask clarifying questions.

   A Luis needed to buy a laptop case.

   B Class He needed to buy what?

   A A laptop case.

UNIT 8 WORK

Lesson A Listening

1 Before you listen

A What do you see?

B What is happening?

Yolanda

David

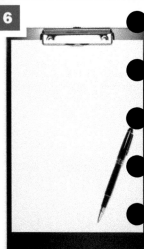

VANILLA SPRINKLE   CHOCOLATE SPRINKLE

UNIT 8

Teaching objectives
- Introduce students to the topic
- Find out what students know about the topic
- Preview the unit by talking about the pictures
- Provide practice of key vocabulary
- Provide practice that develops listening skills

WARM-UP AND REVIEW

- Before class. Write today's lesson focus on the board.
  Lesson A:
  Discuss work schedules
  Talk about workplace problems and solutions
  Ask questions about work experience
- Begin class. Books closed. Direct Ss' attention to the lesson focus. Point to *work schedules*. Ask Ss: *What are work schedules?* List Ss' responses on the board, for example: *part-time, full-time, seasonal, weekdays, weekends, 9 to 5.*
- Point to *workplace problems*. Ask Ss: *What are some examples of workplace problems?* List Ss' responses on the board, for example: *long hours, no days off, not enough sick days, not enough vacation time, difficult co-workers, demanding boss.*
- Point to *work experience*. Ask Ss: *What is work experience?* List Ss' responses on the board, for example: *previous jobs, past responsibilities, volunteer work.* Ask Ss: *When do you usually talk about work experience?* Elicit appropriate responses, such as: *in a job interview, when applying for a job.*

PRESENTATION

- Books open. Set the scene. Direct Ss' attention to the first picture on page 96. Ask the question from Exercise **1A**: *What do you see?* Elicit and write on the board as much vocabulary about the picture as possible: *donut shop, worker counter, apron, uniform,* etc. Explain any words Ss don't know. Continue eliciting words to describe the remaining pictures.
- Ask individual Ss to look at the six pictures and talk about the similarities (e.g., pictures one and four have donuts) and the differences (e.g., pictures one and four have donuts in them, and pictures two and three have a clock and a watch).

- Direct Ss' attention to the question in Exercise **1B**: *What is happening?* Hold up the Student's Book. Point to picture 1. Ask: *What's Yolanda doing here?* (She's serving a donut.)
- Point to picture 3. Ask: *What's David doing here?* (David is leaving work.)
- Point to picture 5. Ask: *What's Yolanda doing here?* (Yolanda is talking with her friends.) *How does she feel?* (She looks upset.)

Expansion activity (student pairs)

- Have Ss work with a partner. Ask pairs to create a role play between Yolanda and David or between Yolanda and her friends.
- Call on several pairs to perform their role play for the class.

> **Teaching Tip**
>
> Encourage Ss to be creative in their discussions of the opening pictures for the unit. At this point, there is no single correct answer.

Expansion activity (small groups)

- Ask Ss: *Have any of you ever worked in a restaurant? If you have, what is the most difficult part about restaurant work?*
- Write *Advantages* and *Disadvantages* on the board. Have Ss work in small groups to discuss and list on a sheet of paper the advantages and disadvantages of working in various places, such as a hospital, an office, a beauty shop, a school, a factory.
- After several minutes, ask each group to share its list with the class. On the board, write the name or type of job, and then write several examples under *Advantages* and *Disadvantages*. For example:

  <u>Restaurant work</u>
<u>Advantages</u>	<u>Disadvantages</u>
You can make tips.	You have to be on your feet for long periods of time.

- At the end of the activity, poll Ss to see which job they think is the hardest one.

LESSON A Listening

PRESENTATION

- Books open. Direct Ss' attention to Exercise **2A**. Read the instructions aloud. Tell Ss that they are going to hear two different conversations.
- ▶ **CD2, Track 15** Play or read the audio (see audio script, page T-182).
- Ask Ss if they understand everything in the listening exercise. Write any unfamiliar words on the board and help Ss understand the meaning of each.
- Partners complete Exercise **2A**. Elicit answers to the questions in the exercise.
- Have Ss focus their attention on Exercise **2B**. Read the instructions aloud. Tell Ss to listen and complete the diagram based on the information they hear.
- ▶ **CD2, Track 15** Tell Ss to listen for details about Yolanda's conversation with David and her friends' suggested solutions. Model the exercise. Play or read the audio again. Pause the audio after Yolanda says in Part 2: *It's really frustrating.*
- Model the first answer in the diagram. Draw the diagram on the board as it appears on page 97. Point to the blank in the web that says *Yolanda's problem* underneath it. Ask Ss: *What is Yolanda's problem?* Elicit appropriate responses, such as: *David is not doing his share of the work.* Write the answer on the line in the diagram on the board. Play or read the rest of the audio. Ss listen and complete the diagram.
- ▶ **CD2, Track 15** Play or read the audio again. Ss listen and check their answers. Repeat the audio as needed.
- Ask Ss to come to the board to write the answers in the diagram. Make corrections on the board as needed.

Learner persistence *(individual work)*
- ▶ **CD2, Track 15** Ss can listen to the audio for Exercises **2A** and **2B** at home for reinforcement and review. They can also listen to the audio for self-directed learning when class attendance is not possible.

PRACTICE

- Direct Ss' attention to Exercise **3A**. Read the instructions aloud. Tell Ss that the story in this exercise is a summary of what happened in the pictures on the previous page.
- Focus Ss' attention on the words in the word bank. Say each word aloud. Ask Ss to repeat. Correct pronunciation as needed. Make sure that Ss understand the meaning of each word. Explain any words that are new to Ss.
- Model the exercise. Ask a S to read aloud the first two sentences in the story, including the example answer.
- Ss complete the exercise individually. Walk around and help as needed.

COMPREHENSION CHECK

- ▶ **CD2, Track 16** Play or read the audio (see audio script, page T-182). Ss listen and check their answers. Repeat the audio as needed.
- Write the numbers *1–10* on the board. Ask Ss to come to the board to write only the answers. Have other Ss read the sentences, filling in each blank with the answer on the board. Make corrections as needed.

Learner persistence *(individual work)*
- ▶ **CD2, Track 16** Ss can listen to the audio for Exercise **3A** at home for reinforcement and review. They can also listen to the audio for self-directed learning when class attendance is not possible.

APPLICATION

- Focus Ss' attention on Exercise **3B** and read the instructions aloud.
- Ss complete the exercise with a partner. Walk around and help as needed.
- Ask several pairs to ask and answer the questions for the class. Discuss Ss' opinions about how to handle problems at work and at school.

Expansion activity *(small groups)*
- Ask Ss to work with a small group to imagine that David is their co-worker and that they are having the same problem with him that Yolanda is having. Have each group write a note, an email, or a letter to David in which Ss talk about the situation that is bothering them and propose a possible solution. Ss can use the ideas that Yolanda's friends presented or their own ideas.
- Have each group share its writing with the class.

EVALUATION

- Direct Ss' attention to the lesson focus on the board. Ask individual Ss to look at the pictures on page 96 and write sentences using the words from the word bank in Exercise **3A**.
- Check off each part of the lesson focus as Ss demonstrate an understanding of what they have learned in the lesson.

More Ventures, Unit 8, Lesson A	
Workbook, 15–30 min.	
Multilevel Worksheets, 30–45 min.	www.cambridge.org/ ventures/resources/
Collaborative Worksheets, 30–45 min.	
Student Arcade, time varies	www.cambridge.org/ venturesarcade/

UNIT GOALS
Identify problems at work and school   **Describe** hard and soft skills
Provide solutions and identify consequences to those solutions

2 Listen

A Listen and answer the questions.

1. Who are the speakers?   2. What are they talking about?

🔊 CD2, Track 15

B Listen again. Complete the diagram.

🔊 CD2, Track 15

co-worker not doing his share of the work
Yolanda's problem

1. _____quit job_____ ——— (Possible solutions) ——— 4. _____chart of tasks_____

2. _____talk to David_____   3. _____tell boss_____

Create a chart of tasks _for David. If David doesn't do his share, then tell the boss._
Yolanda's decision

3 After you listen

A Read. Complete the story.

advice	close up	exhausted	negotiate	tasks
chart	deal with	initials	share	work (something) out

Yolanda and David work at Daria's Donut Shop. Lately, David has been leaving work

early, and Yolanda has to _____close up_____ the shop by herself. Tonight, Yolanda
                                      1

is having coffee with her friends. She is _____exhausted_____. Her friends give her
                                                    2

_____advice_____. Teresa thinks she should talk to her boss, but Yolanda wants to
        3

try to _____work_____ things _____out_____ with David first. Julie thinks Yolanda
              4   4

should make a _____chart_____ of their duties. Then she should _____negotiate_____
                        5   6

with David and decide who is going to do which _____tasks_____. When they finish
                                                              7

a task, they should write their _____initials_____ on the chart. If David isn't doing his
                                            8

_____share_____ of the work, it will show in the chart. Then, Yolanda can show the
          9

chart to their boss and let her _____deal with_____ the situation.
                                          10

Listen and check your answers.

B Discuss. Talk with your classmates.

🔊 CD2, Track 16

Lesson B Verb tense contrast

1 Grammar focus: present perfect and present perfect continuous

The present perfect is formed by *have / has* + past participle. One use of the present perfect is to talk about recently finished actions (often with the word *just*) with no specific time of completion of those actions.

The present perfect continuous is formed by *have / has* + *been* + present participle (*-ing*). Use the present perfect continuous to talk about actions that started in the past, continue to now, and will probably continue in the future.

Watch

PRESENT PERFECT (RECENTLY FINISHED ACTION)	PRESENT PERFECT CONTINUOUS (CONTINUING ACTION)
Yolanda **has (just) mopped** the floor. It's clean now.	Yolanda **has been mopping** the floor **for** 15 minutes.

2 Practice

A Write. Complete the sentences. Use the present perfect or present perfect continuous forms of the verbs. Use *just* where possible.

1. Daria Thompson is the owner of Daria's Donut Shop. She ____*has been selling*____ donuts at this location for more than 20 years.
   (sell)

2. It's 7:00 a.m. Daria ____*has been making*____ donuts for three hours.
   (make)

3. It's 7:30 a.m. Daria ____*has just opened*____ the shop for customers.
   (open)

4. It's 10:30 a.m. Daria's son ____*has been helping*____ her all morning.
   (help)

5. He *has just finished clearing* cleaning the counters and shelves. Everything is spotless.
   (finish)

6. Daria needs more help in the shop. She ____*has decided*____ to hire Yolanda.
   (decide)

7. Yolanda's shift begins at 6:00 a.m. today. She ____*has been waiting*____ for the bus for 30 minutes. She's worried that she's going to be late.
   (wait)

8. It's 6:05 a.m. Yolanda ____*has just called*____ to say she will be late.
   (call)

9. It's 6:30 a.m. Yolanda ____*has just arrived*____ at the store. Daria is really glad to see her!
   (arrive)

10. It's noon. Yolanda ____*has been working*____ for several hours and she's ready to take a break.
    (work)

Listen and check your answers.

CD2, Track 17

Teaching objective
- Introduce, contrast, and provide practice using the present perfect and present perfect continuous

WARM-UP AND REVIEW

- Before class: Write the lesson focus on the board.
  Lesson B:
  Present perfect
  Present perfect continuous
- Write the following sentences on the board: *We have just begun Lesson B. We have been studying Unit 8 for two days.* Ask Ss: *What is the difference between the two sentences?* Elicit that the first sentence uses present perfect only, and the second sentence uses present perfect + a continuous verb (studying).

PRESENTATION

Focus on meaning / personalize

- Books closed. Direct Ss' attention to the lesson focus on the board. Read it aloud.
- Ask: *What time is it?* Imagine it is 8:30 a.m. Write 8:30 on the board. Tell Ss you ate breakfast after you got to school at about 8:15 a.m. and finished eating at 8:25 a.m. Say: *I have just eaten breakfast.* Ask: *Am I still eating?* (No.) *Did I finish breakfast a very short time ago?* (Yes.) Say and write on the board: *I have just eaten breakfast.*
- Now show Ss a cup of coffee or tea that is half full and say: *I started drinking this coffee at 8:00 a.m.* Take a sip. Ask: *Am I still drinking this coffee?* (Yes.) Say: *I started drinking at 8:00 a.m., and now it's 8:30 a.m.* Say and write on the board: *I have been drinking this coffee since 8:00 a.m.*
- Write *Present perfect* on the board above *I have just eaten breakfast*, and write *Present perfect continuous* on the board above *I have been drinking this coffee since 8:00 a.m.* Point to the present perfect sentence and ask: *Did this happen before?* (Yes.) *Is it still happening?* (No.) Point to the present perfect continuous sentence and ask: *Did this happen before?* (Yes.) *Is it still happening?* (Yes.)
- Elicit that both the present perfect and the present perfect continuous can express the idea of an action or situation that began in the past and continues into the present, but the present perfect continuous emphasizes the duration or continuous nature of an action.

Focus on form

- Use the animated grammar presentation in one or more of the following ways:
  - Preview it before class
  - Show in class
  - Encourage Ss to watch outside of class.
- Books open. Direct Ss' attention to the two charts in Exercise **1**. Read the two headings aloud: *Present perfect* and *Present perfect continuous*. Then read the explanation and the example sentences under the headings. Point out that *just* is not used with the present perfect continuous.
- Elicit how the present perfect is formed (verb + *have* [*have* or *has*] + the past participle) and how the present perfect continuous is formed (verb *have* [*have* or *has*] + *been* + the present participle ending in *-ing*).

PRACTICE

- Direct Ss' attention to Exercise **2A** and read the instructions aloud.
- Have a S read the example aloud, and make sure that Ss understand the exercise.
- Ss complete the exercise individually. Walk around and help as needed.

COMPREHENSION CHECK

- Read aloud the second part of the instructions for Exercise **2A**.
- ▶ **CD2, Track 17** Play or read the audio (see audio script, page T-182). Ss listen and check their answers. Repeat the audio as needed.
- Write the numbers *1–10* on the board. Ask individual Ss to come to the board to write the complete sentences. Work with the class to make corrections on the board as needed.

PRACTICE

- Books open. Direct Ss' attention to Yolanda's work schedule in Exercise **2B**. Tell Ss that they are going to read and talk about Yolanda's work schedule. Call on individual Ss to read each of the times and the corresponding activity.

- Read the instructions aloud for Exercise **2B**.

- Ask two Ss to read aloud the sample time and corresponding activities.

- Ss complete the exercise in pairs. Remind Ss that several of the past participles are irregular (*gone, taken, eaten*). Walk around and help as needed.

- Direct Ss' attention to the second part of Exercise **2B** and read the instructions aloud.

- Call on a S to read the example sentences.

- Ss work individually to complete the exercise. Walk around and help as needed.

- Ask individual Ss to come to the board to write their sentences. Make corrections on the board as needed.

APPLICATION

- Direct Ss' attention to Exercise **3A** and read the instructions aloud.

- Model the task. Ask two Ss to read the example dialog to the class.

- Ss work with a partner to complete the exercise. Walk around and help as needed.

- Direct Ss' attention to Exercise **3B** and read the instructions aloud.

- Have Ss take turns sharing information about their partner with the class.

Expansion activity *(small groups)*

- Have Ss take out a piece of notebook paper. They should draw a schedule, using Yolanda's schedule on page 99 as a model.

- Tell Ss to title the schedule with their name and to fill it in with information based on what they typically do during their day. Remind Ss to include information from their workday as well as any chores, errands, or school work.

- Collect all the schedules. Then redistribute them, making sure that each S receives someone else's schedule.

- Ss work in small groups. Write a time on the board and have Ss tell one another what their person has been doing and what he or she has just done.

- After a few minutes, change the time. Ss in each group continue to exchange information using the schedules and various verb tenses.

EVALUATION

- Books closed. Direct Ss' attention to the lesson focus on the board.

- Write the following on the board. (Note: Adjust the time to fit your class's schedule.)

  It's 3:00 p.m. We _____ English for three hours.
  (study)

  It's 3:05 p.m. We _____ our English lesson for the day.
  (finish)

- Ask Ss to tell you the correct form of each of the verbs, and fill in the blanks. Elicit: *have been studying* and *have just finished.*

- Ask a S to tell you the difference between the perfect tenses in these two sentences. Elicit an appropriate response: *In the first sentence, the emphasis is on a continuing action of studying for three hours. In the second sentence, the emphasis is on talking about something that has recently finished.*

- Check off the lesson focus as Ss demonstrate an understanding of what they have learned in the lesson.

More Ventures, Unit 8, Lesson B	
Workbook, 15–30 min.	
Multilevel Worksheets, 30–45 min. **Collaborative Worksheets,** 30–45 min.	www.cambridge.org/ ventures/resources/
Student Arcade, time varies	www.cambridge.org/ venturesarcade/

B **Talk** with a partner. Look at Yolanda's work schedule. Make sentences about the things she has just done and has been doing at the following times: 6:15, 6:30, 7:30, 11:00, 12:00, 2:00, and 4:00.

It's 6:15 a.m. Yolanda has just arrived.

It's 11:00 a.m. Yolanda has been serving customers for three and a half hours.

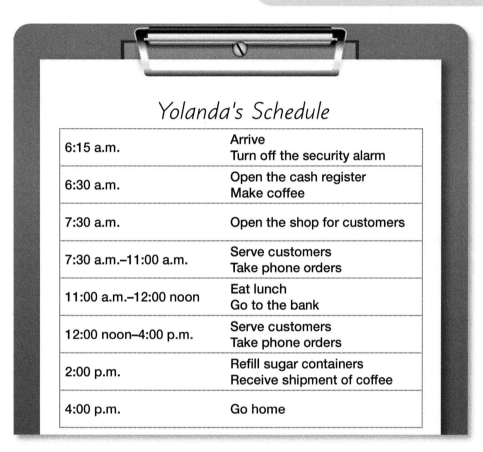

Yolanda's Schedule

6:15 a.m.	Arrive Turn off the security alarm
6:30 a.m.	Open the cash register Make coffee
7:30 a.m.	Open the shop for customers
7:30 a.m.–11:00 a.m.	Serve customers Take phone orders
11:00 a.m.–12:00 noon	Eat lunch Go to the bank
12:00 noon–4:00 p.m.	Serve customers Take phone orders
2:00 p.m.	Refill sugar containers Receive shipment of coffee
4:00 p.m.	Go home

Write sentences about Yolanda's schedule.

It's 6:15 a.m. Yolanda has just arrived.
It's 11:00 a.m. Yolanda has been serving customers for three and a half hours.
Answers will vary.

3 Communicate

A **Work** with a partner. Think about your own schedule. Your partner says a time. You say what you have been doing and what you have just done.

A Natalia, pretend it's 10:30 a.m.

B OK, it's 10:30 a.m. I've been working for two hours. I've just read my email.

B **Share** information about your partner.

It's 10:30 a.m. Natalia has been working for two hours. She has just read her email.

Lesson C Participles as adjectives

1 Grammar focus: adjectives ending in -ed and -ing

Participles are forms of verbs. They can end in -ed or -ing. Sometimes we use them as adjectives. Often the -ing form describes a thing or person and the -ed form describes the way someone feels.

Watch

-ed ADJECTIVES	-ing ADJECTIVES	
I'm **tired** of this job.	This is a **tiring** job.	This job is **tiring**.
He's **interested** in this task.	This is an **interesting** task.	This task is **interesting**.
They're **disappointed** about their grades.	These are **disappointing** grades.	These grades are **disappointing**.

2 Practice

A Write. Circle the correct adjective.

1. A I heard that Juan and his friends went to a party after work. How was the party?

   B It was really **(exciting)** / **excited**.

2. A What did Juan and his friends like the most about the party?

   B There was a lot of **(interesting)** / **interested** music from different countries.

3. A How did Juan feel the next day at work?

   B He was **exhausting** / **(exhausted)**.

4. A How long did he have to work?

   B He had to work from 9:30 to 6:30. It was a **(tiring)** / **tired** day.

5. A Does Juan usually start working at 9:30?

   B No, he overslept! He was **shocking** / **(shocked)** that he didn't hear the alarm clock.

6. A How did his boss react when he showed up late?

   B His boss was **irritating** / **(irritated)**.

7. A What did his boss say to him?

   B He told Juan that he was **disappointing** / **(disappointed)** in him.

8. A How did Juan feel after his boss told him that?

   B Juan felt **embarrassing** / **(embarrassed)**.

9. A Juan didn't have a good day, I guess. What did he do later that night?

   B He stayed home and had a **(relaxing)** / **relaxed** night in front of the TV.

10. A So, is Juan going to go out again on a weeknight?

    B I don't think so. He said it was an **(exhausting)** / **exhausted** experience.

Listen and check your answers. Then practice with a partner.

CD2, Track 18

Teaching objective

- Introduce and provide practice using participles as adjectives

WARM-UP AND REVIEW

- Before class. Write the lesson focus on the board.
  Lesson C:
  Participles as adjectives ending in "-ed" and "-ing"

- Begin class. Books closed. Review adjectives describing feelings. Ask Ss to share some of the activities they did over the weekend. Elicit answers, such as: *went to the beach, visited family, stayed home.* Have Ss work in pairs to describe how they felt when they were doing each activity, for example: *I went to the beach with some friends. It was fun.* or *I stayed home, and I was bored.* Write some of their adjectives on the board.

PRESENTATION

Focus on meaning / personalize

- Books closed. Direct Ss' attention to the lesson focus on the board. Read it aloud.

- Divide the board into three columns with *Boring activities, Interesting activities,* and *How did you feel?* as headings. Ask Ss about something they have done recently that was boring. Elicit responses and have those Ss come to the board and write the activities in the appropriate columns. For example:

Boring activities	Interesting activities	How did you feel?
cleaned house	went to a concert	bored
		interested

- Ask: *How did you feel when you were cleaning your house?* (bored.) *How did you feel when you went to the concert?* (interested, excited.)

- Write on the board *disappointed* and *disappointing.* Say: *You went to a party, and you didn't know anyone, and people were just sitting around. How would you describe the party?* (disappointing.) *How would you describe how you felt about the party?* (disappointed.) Write on the board *tiring* and *tired.* Say: *You flew from New York to Hawaii. It took nine hours. How would you describe the flight?* (tiring.) *How would you describe how you felt after the flight?* (tired.)

- Explain that only things can be described with the *-ing* form because things can't have emotions. For example, you can say, *The movie was boring* but not *The movie was bored.* (The movie can't have feelings.) On the other hand, people can be described using either *-ing* or *-ed* forms because they can produce emotions in other people as well as experience emotions themselves. For example, *The man is bored* is correct, but so is *The man is boring.* Point out that the sentences have different meanings. That is, in the first sentence, the man is bored by whatever he is doing; in the second sentence, the man is an uninteresting person.

- Explain that verb forms ending in *-ed* or *-ing* are called *participles.* When they are adjectives, they are called *participial adjectives.*

Focus on form

- Use the animated grammar presentation in one or more of the following ways:
  - Preview it before class
  - Show in class
  - Encourage Ss to watch outside of class.

- Books open. Direct Ss' attention to the three columns in Exercise **1**. Read aloud the first statement in each, then the second statements in each. Ask Ss to repeat.

PRACTICE

- Direct Ss' attention to Exercise **2A** and read the instructions aloud.

- Ask a S to read aloud the first example conversation, including the circled answer.

- Ss complete the exercise individually. Walk around and help as needed.

COMPREHENSION CHECK

- Read aloud the second part of the instructions for Exercise **2A**.

- ▶ *CD2, Track 18* Play or read the audio (see audio script, page T-182). Ss listen and check their answers.

- Have Ss sit in pairs to practice the conversations with a partner. Walk around and correct pronunciation as needed.

LESSON C Participles as Adjectives

PRACTICE

- Direct Ss' attention to the eight pictures in Exercise **2B**. Ask Ss to describe what they see in each picture.

- Read the instructions aloud in Exercise **2B**.

- Call on a S to read the two headings: *Positive* and *Negative*. Ask another S to read each of the adjectives under *Positive*. Ask another S to read each of the adjectives under *Negative*.

- Explain vocabulary as needed, and ask Ss to repeat any words they don't know.

- Have two Ss read the example sentences above the two adjective charts.

- Ss complete the exercise with a partner. Walk around and help as needed.

- Read the instructions aloud for the second part of Exercise **2B**. Ask two Ss to read the two example sentence to the class.

- Ss complete the exercise individually. Walk around and help as needed.

- Ask several Ss to come to the board to write their sentences.

- Call on other Ss to read each of the sentences on the board. Work with the class to make corrections on the board as needed.

Expansion activity *(student pairs)*

- Ask Ss to role-play a conversation between two of the people in the pictures. They can be on the phone or talking in person. Ss can ask and answer questions using the pictures and words in Exercise **2B** as a guide.

- Model the activity. Write this example on the board.

  S1: *Did you see this award I got? I'm so excited.*
  S2: *Yeah, well, that's great. I just had the most boring meeting at work!*

- Encourage Ss to have fun with this activity. Ask several pairs to act out their role play for the class.

APPLICATION

- Direct Ss' attention to Exercise **3A** and read the instructions aloud.

- Model the exercise. Ask two Ss to read the example dialog to the class.

- Ss complete the exercise in small groups. Walk around and help as needed.

- Direct Ss' attention to Exercise **3B** and read the instructions aloud.

- Model the task. Say: *I learned that Tan has an exciting job. He meets people from all over the world and practices his English every day.*

- Continue the exercise by asking several Ss to share information they learned about one another.

Expansion activity *(individual work)*

- Ask Ss to think about two experiences they have had, one positive, the other negative.

- Ss should choose one of their experiences and write a paragraph about it, using as many of the adjectives from the chart in **2B** as possible.

- Model the activity as needed. Write this (positive) example on the board:

  My bus trip to Niagara Falls was fascinating! Even though I thought the bus ride was going to be boring, it was very exciting. There was so much to see. My friends and I talked and told stories about what we did when we were younger. Some of our stories were amusing!

- Ask Ss to share their paragraphs with their partner. Call on several Ss to read their paragraphs aloud.

EVALUATION

- Direct Ss' attention to the lesson focus on the board. Ask Ss to look at the six pictures on page 101 and use participial adjectives to make new sentences about each one. Ask Ss to say their sentences aloud.

- Check off the lesson focus as Ss demonstrate an understanding of what they have learned in the lesson.

More Ventures, Unit 8, Lesson C	
Workbook, 15–30 min.	
Multilevel Worksheets, 30–45 min.	www.cambridge.org/ ventures/resources/
Collaborative Worksheets, 30–45 min.	
Student Arcade, time varies	www.cambridge.org/ venturesarcade/

B **Talk** with a partner. For each picture, describe the person and the activity. Choose participial adjectives from the boxes.

The man is excited.

Getting an award is exciting.

Positive	
amusing	amused
exciting	excited
interesting	interested
relaxing	relaxed

Negative	
annoying	annoyed
boring	bored
frightening	frightened
frustrating	frustrated

1.
2.
3.
4.

5.
6.
7.
8.

Write two sentences about each picture.

The man is excited.
Getting an award is exciting.

Answers will vary.

3 Communicate

A **Work** in a small group. Ask and answer questions about your experiences. Use the adjectives from Exercise 2B.

A What's an amusing experience that you have had at work?

B I was very amused when . . . it was amusing because . . .

B **Share** information about your classmates.

Lesson D Reading

1 Before you read

Talk with your classmates. Answer the questions.

1. What are some skills, such as following directions, that are necessary for most jobs?
2. What special skills do you have?

2 Read

Read the magazine article. Listen and read again.

CD2, Track 19

Hard and Soft Job Skills

Som Sarawong has been working as an automotive technician at George's Auto Repair for over five years. Today was a special day for Som, a 35-year-old Thai immigrant, because he received the Employee of the Year award. According to Ed Overton, Som's boss, Som received the award "because he's a great 'people person' and he has superb technical skills. I even have him work on my own car!"

Som has the two kinds of skills that are necessary to be successful and move up in his career: soft skills and hard skills. Soft skills are personal and social skills. Som gets along with his co-workers. He has a strong work ethic; in five years, he has never been late or absent from work. Customers trust him. Hard skills, on the other hand, are the technical skills a person needs to do a job. Som can repair cars, trucks, and motorcycles. He learned from his father, who was also a mechanic. Then he took classes and got a certificate as an auto technician.

Soft and hard skills are equally important, but hard skills are easier to teach and assess than soft skills. People can learn how to use a machine and then take a test on their knowledge. However, it's harder to teach people how to be cooperative and have a good work ethic.

George Griffith, the owner of George's Auto Repair, explains, "I've been working in this business for over 30 years, and most of the time when I've needed to fire someone, it was because of weak people skills, not because they didn't have technical abilities." Soft skills and good technical knowledge are a winning combination, and today, Som Sarawong was the winner.

Teaching objectives

- Introduce a magazine article about hard and soft job skills
- Provide practice recognizing reasons for using quotations
- Provide practice identifying and determining meaning of prefixes and roots

WARM-UP AND REVIEW

- Before class. Write today's lesson focus on the board.
  Lesson D:
  Read and understand "Hard and Soft Job Skills"
  Recognize reasons for using quotations
  Learn and use different prefixes and roots

- Begin class. Books closed. Ask Ss: *What are job skills?* Elicit: *abilities you need for a specific job.* Then ask: *What are some examples of job skills?* Elicit appropriate responses, such as: *A chef needs to know how to cook.*

- Direct Ss' attention to the title of the reading on the board: "Hard and Soft Job Skills." Ask Ss what they think this reading is about. Elicit responses, such as: *The reading is about different kinds of job skills.* Write Ss' predictions on the board.

PRESENTATION

- Books open. Direct Ss' attention to Exercise **1** and read the instructions aloud.

- Ask two Ss to read the questions in Exercise **1** to the class.

- Ss in small groups. Invite Ss to discuss their answers to the questions. Walk around and help as needed.

- Call on individual Ss to share their answers with the class.

PRACTICE

- Read the instructions aloud for Exercise **2**. Ask Ss to read the magazine article silently before listening to the audio program.

- ▶ **CD2, Track 19** Play or read the audio, and ask Ss to read along (see audio script, page T-182). Repeat the audio as needed.

- While Ss are listening and reading the magazine article, ask them to underline any words they don't know. When the audio program is finished, have Ss write the new vocabulary words on the board.

- Point to each word on the board. Say it and have Ss repeat. Give a brief explanation of each word, or ask Ss who know the word to explain it.

Read the tip on page 103 aloud. Write *quotations* on the board. Ask Ss what the word means. Write on the board: *Quotations are words or sentences that people have spoken or written.* Ask: *How do we indicate that something is a quotation?* Elicit: *by using quotation marks.* Draw quotation marks on the board. Have Ss identify the two quotations in the text. Lead Ss to see that these quotations not only explain or support the main idea but also make the article come alive. Point out, too, that *soft* and *hard* are in quotation marks. Explain that sometimes we use quotation marks to highlight words or terms. In this case, the quotation marks show that "hard" and "soft" are the adjectives we use to describe certain job skills, even though they may seem like unusual adjectives to use in this way. Point out that the term "people person" is in single quotes. Tell Ss that when there is a quote within a quote, we use single, not double, quotation marks.

Learner persistence (individual work)

▶ **CD2, Track 19** Ss can listen to the audio for Exercise **2** at home for reinforcement and review. They can also listen to the audio for self-directed learning when class attendance is not possible.

Expansion activity (small groups)

- Write the following list on the board:

Job	Skills required
librarian	good with people (S), knowledge of books (H), knowledge of how to look up information (H)

- Ss in small groups. Ask Ss to brainstorm ideas to create a list of jobs and then decide which skills are important for that job. Ss should identify each skill with an H for hard skills and an S for soft skills.

- Model the activity. Call on a S to read the example on the board.

- Ss work together to complete the exercise. Walk around and help as needed.

- Have Ss share the information they discussed with the class.

LESSON D Reading

COMPREHENSION CHECK

- Direct Ss' attention to Exercise **3A** and read the instructions aloud.

Culture Note

Call on a S to read the culture note aloud. Tell Ss that the word *ethic* means "a set of rules that someone lives by." A *work ethic* is something that many people in the United States believe in and follow. Ask Ss what the advantages and disadvantages might be of having a strong work ethic.

- Call on individual Ss to read the seven questions, one at a time.
- Ss complete the exercise individually. Instruct Ss to write their answers on a separate piece of paper. Ss should answer in complete sentences. Walk around and help as needed.
- Check answers with the class. Whenever possible, have Ss indicate where they found the answers in the reading.

PRACTICE

- **Materials needed** A dictionary for each S.
- Direct Ss' attention to number 1 of Exercise **3B**. Read the instructions aloud. Remind Ss that a prefix is a letter or group of letters added to the beginning of a word, base, or root; a root is the base of a word. Tell Ss that they should write each word with the prefix or root in the column under the heading: *Example from reading*.
- Call on a S to read the instructions aloud for number 2 of Exercise **3B**. Have Ss use a dictionary to write the meaning of the words in the column under the heading: *Meaning of word*.
- Ask a S to read aloud the instructions for number 3 of Exercise **3B**. Guide Ss to guess and then write the meaning of each prefix or root in the column under the heading: *Meaning of prefix or root*.
- Have another S read the first example in the chart.
- Ss work individually to find the words in the reading and then complete the chart. Walk around and help as needed.
- Read the instructions aloud for number 4 of Exercise **3B**. Ss work in small groups to make a list of other words they know with the same prefix or root. Walk around and help as needed.
- Review with the class. Write a chart on the board that is similar to the one on page 103. Call on six Ss to come to the board to fill in the chart. Make corrections on the board as needed. Ask Ss to share the additional words they discussed in their groups and their example sentences.

APPLICATION

- Direct Ss' attention to Exercise **3C**. Read the instructions aloud.
- Call on four Ss to read the questions in Exercise **3C**, one at a time. Ask Ss if they know what *superbly* means (extremely well). Explain additional vocabulary as needed.
- Ss ask and answer questions with a partner.
- Ask several pairs to share the answers they discussed.

Expansion activity (individual work)

- Ask partners to interview each other about their hard and soft job skills.
- Encourage Ss to take notes and to use their notes to write a brief article about their partner's job skills for an "Employee of the Week" newsletter. Ask Ss to include at least one quotation from their partner or from a co-worker, perhaps another S in the class.
- Have Ss share their articles with the class, calling on several Ss to read them aloud. If possible, have Ss take pictures of their partner and post the articles, along with the photos, on the bulletin board.

Expansion activity

- Refer Ss to "The Benefits of Telecommuting," another reading on the same topic on pages 157–159.
- Have Ss complete the activity either in class or outside of class.
- Provide feedback to Ss such as through whole-class discussion, partners comparing their worksheets, or T reviewing each S's worksheets.

EVALUATION

- Books closed. Direct Ss' attention to the lesson focus on the board.
- Ask individual Ss to retell the main points of the reading "Hard and Soft Job Skills."
- Books open. Focus Ss' attention on the words that they wrote in the chart in Exercise **3B**. Ask Ss to make sentences with these words to show that they understand the meanings.
- Check off each part of the lesson focus as Ss demonstrate an understanding of what they have learned in the lesson.

More Ventures, Unit 8, Lesson D	
Workbook, 15–30 min.	
Multilevel Worksheets, 30–45 min.	www.cambridge.org/ ventures/resources/
Collaborative Worksheets, 30–45 min.	
Student Arcade, time varies	www.cambridge.org/ venturesarcade/

❸ After you read

A **Check** your understanding.

1. What is the main idea of this article?

2. How does the quotation from Ed Overton support the main idea of the article?

3. What is the difference between a soft skill and a hard skill? Give examples from the article.

4. What are three examples of Som's soft skills?

5. According to the article, why are hard skills easier to evaluate than soft skills?

6. Which example shows that Som has a good work ethic?

7. According to George Griffith, do more workers lose their jobs because of weak soft skills or weak hard skills? Do you agree with George? Why or why not?

> Quotations are used to explain or support a main idea. They also make a reading more interesting.

> **CULTURE NOTE**
> The expression *work ethic* is the belief that if you work hard in life you will get ahead and become successful.

B **Build** your vocabulary.

1. Find an example in the reading of each prefix and root. Write it in the chart.

2. Use a dictionary. Write the meaning of the words.

3. Guess the meaning of the prefixes and roots in the chart.

Prefixes	Example from reading	Meaning of word	Meaning of prefix
1. re-	*repair*	*to fix what is torn or broken*	*again*
2. co-	*cooperative*	*working together*	*with; together*
3. auto-	*automotive*	*related to cars*	*self*
Roots			**Meaning of root**
4. tech	*technical*	*specialized knowledge or skills*	*skill; art*
5. super	*superb*	*excellent; best quality*	*over; above*
6. equ	*equally*	*in equal amounts or parts*	*equal*

4. Work in a small group. Make a list of other words you know with the same prefixes and roots. Write a sentence for each new word. *Answers will vary.*

C **Talk** with a partner.

1. What is something that you can do superbly?

2. What are some examples of technical skills?

3. What is a hobby or profession that requires good technical skills?

4. What are two hard skills and two soft skills that you have?

For college and career readiness practice, see pages 157–159.

Lesson E Writing

1 Before you write

A **Talk** with a partner. Answer the questions.

1. What is a cover letter? What information does it include?

2. Have you ever written a cover letter? Tell your partner about your experience.

3. Today, most people write email cover letters. Why do you think this is true?

B **Read** the cover letter.

New Message	
From:	Ester Yitbarek <eyitbarek@youmail.com>
Subject:	Teacher's assistant position
To:	lynn.stevens@osbornk12.edu
𝒫:	Resume_Ester Yitbarek

Dear Ms. Stevens:

I read your advertisement online for a position as a teacher's assistant. I am very interested in this position and have attached my résumé.

I have been working as a teacher's assistant at Hilltop Elementary School for three years. In this job, I have taught reading and math to students in small groups. I have also tutored individual students who were having problems with the lessons. I'm very interested in child development, and I love working with children. I get along very well with my co-workers, and I'm also skilled at dealing with parents.

I am planning to move to a new home in your district. I hope you will call me to schedule an interview. My phone number is 773-555-2673. I look forward to hearing from you.

Sincerely,

Ester Yitbarek

Ester Yitbarek
773-555-2673
eyitbarek@youmail.com

OBJECTIVE: To obtain a position as Teacher's Assistant

SUMMARY OF QUALIFICATIONS
- Teacher's assistant at Hilltop Elementary for three years
- Taught reading in small groups
- Tutored students who need extra help
- Bilingual English / Amharic

CULTURE NOTE
Applicants are usually expected to include a résumé — a written statement of their educational and work experience — with their cover letter.

WARM-UP AND REVIEW

• Before class. Write today's lesson focus on the board.
Lesson E:
Write an email cover letter to apply for a job

• Begin class. Books closed. Focus Ss' attention on the words *cover letter* in the lesson focus on the board. Say it aloud and have Ss repeat. Ask Ss if they have ever written a cover letter. If any Ss say yes, ask them when they wrote it. Elicit appropriate responses.

• Tell Ss that today's lesson is about writing an email cover letter in order to apply for a job.

PRESENTATION

• Books open. Direct Ss' attention to Exercise **1A** and read the instructions aloud.

• Ask three Ss to read aloud the questions in Exercise **1A**.

• Ss work with a partner to ask and answer the questions. Walk around and help as needed.

PRACTICE

• Direct Ss' attention to Exercise **1B** and read the instructions aloud.

• Ss read the cover letter silently. Ask Ss to underline any words in the letter with which they are unfamiliar.

• Have Ss tell you the words they underlined and write them on the board. Go over the meaning of each word.

Teaching Tip

Lead Ss to see that like a standard business letter, a cover letter is composed of five parts: the sender's address, the address of the person to whom you are writing, the greeting (or salutation), the body of the letter, and the closing. Ask Ss to look carefully at the sample cover letter as you go over each of these parts. You might want to bring in sample cover letters for Ss to examine and discuss.

Culture Note

Read the culture note aloud. Say the word *resume* and have Ss repeat. Tell Ss that the word comes from the French, meaning "summary." Some Ss may be familiar with the Latin term *curriculum vitae* (CV), which, like a resume, is a short account of someone's career and qualifications. Most employers in the United States require a resume or CV when a person applies for a job, so if any Ss are unfamiliar with resumes, show them examples. Point out that in English, the word *resume* can also be written as it is in French, with two accent marks: *résumé*.

Expansion activity (small groups)

• **Materials needed** Sample resumes, one for each small group. (These resumes can be found online or in a public library.)

• Write on the board these essential elements of a resume:
Contact information
Employment goal or job objective
Work experience and dates of jobs
Education
Any awards and organizations
Special skills, interests, and abilities

• Have Ss work in small groups to discuss the elements of the resume they are examining. Explain vocabulary as needed.

• Remind Ss that there is not just one way to write a resume and that often the contents of a resume are tailored to the job Ss are applying for and their experience.

LESSON E Writing

PRESENTATION

- Books open. Focus Ss' attention on Exercise **1C**. Read the instructions aloud.

- Ask individual Ss to read the questions, one at a time.

Call on a S to read the writing tip aloud. Ask Ss to look at the sample cover letter on page 104 to identify where the elements listed here can be found in the model. Tell Ss that including these elements in a cover letter is important in order to make a good first impression with a potential employer.

- Ss answer the questions with a partner.

- Check answers with the class.

PRACTICE

- Direct Ss' attention to Exercise **1D** and read the instructions aloud. Tell Ss that taking the time to plan their email cover letter carefully will make it easier to write the letter.

- Ss should work individually to complete their plan for an email cover letter. Walk around and help as needed.

APPLICATION

- Focus Ss' attention on Exercise **2**. Read the instructions aloud.

- Ss complete the task individually. Walk around and help as needed.

Learner persistence (individual work)

- If you have any Ss who have difficulty writing, sit with them and help them as the other Ss are writing. Encourage them to use their plan (or informal outline) from Exercise **1D** to help them.

Comprehension check

- Direct Ss' attention to Exercise **3A**. This exercise asks Ss to develop skills to review and edit their own writing.

- Ss check their own cover letters against the writing checklist. Walk around and help as needed. If any Ss check *No* for one or more of the checklist items, ask them to revise and edit their letters to include the missing information.

EVALUATION

- Focus Ss' attention on Exercise **3B**. Read the instructions aloud. This exercise enables Ss to work together to edit their writing. Reading aloud enables the writer to review his or her own writing and to understand the need to write clearly for an audience.

- Ss complete the exercise in pairs. Tell Ss to take turns reading their letters to each other. Walk around and help as needed.

- Listen to Ss as they ask their partner a question about the letter and tell their partner one thing they learned from it.

- Ask several Ss to read their letters aloud. Have other Ss ask questions and mention something they learned from the letter.

- Direct Ss' attention to the lesson focus on the board.

- Check off the lesson focus as Ss demonstrate an understanding of what they have learned in the lesson.

Expansion activity (student pairs)

- **Materials needed** Help-wanted ads from a local newspaper or an online Web site – one ad for each pair of Ss.

- Ss in pairs. Distribute a help-wanted ad to each pair and have partners review the ad together to find a job for which they would consider applying in a role play.

- Ss in each pair should take turns being the potential employer and employee. Using the information from their cover letters as a basis for discussion, partners should conduct simple interviews. Interviewers should ask about the potential employee's work experience and qualifications.

- Call on several Ss to perform their role play for the class.

More Ventures, Unit 8, Lesson E	
Workbook, 15–30 min.	
Multilevel Worksheets, 30–45 min.	www.cambridge.org/ ventures/resources/
Collaborative Worksheets, 30–45 min.	

C **Work** with a partner. Answer the questions.

1. Who wrote the email cover letter?
2. Who did she write it to?
3. What position is she applying for?
4. Where did she hear about the job?
5. How much experience does she have?
6. What are some of her skills?
7. What is the purpose of the last paragraph?

> In the body of a cover letter, include:
> • the title of the job you are applying for
> • how you found out about the job
> • information about your skills and experience
> • how the employer can contact you

D **Plan** a cover letter for a real or an imaginary job. Complete the information.

Paragraph 1: *Answers will vary.*

1. Title of the job you are applying for: _____

2. How you found out about it: _____

Paragraph 2:

3. Your skills and experience: _____

_____

_____

Paragraph 3:

4. How the employer can contact you: _____

2 Write

Write an email cover letter for a real or an imaginary job that you are interested in. Include the title of the job in the first sentence and say how you found out about it. Give at least two examples of your skills and experience. Use the cover letter in Exercise 1B and your outline in Exercise 1D to help you.

3 After you write

A **Check** your writing.

	Yes	No
1. My first sentence says the title of the job I am applying for.	☐	☐
2. I included how I found out about the job.	☐	☐
3. I gave two or more examples of my skills and experience.	☐	☐
4. I gave information about how to contact me.	☐	☐

B **Share** your writing with a partner.

1. Take turns. Read your letter to a partner.
2. Comment on your partner's letter. Ask your partner a question about the letter. Tell your partner one thing you learned.

📖 Write an email cover letter that includes information about skills and experience **UNIT 8** **105**

Lesson F Another view

1 Life-skills reading

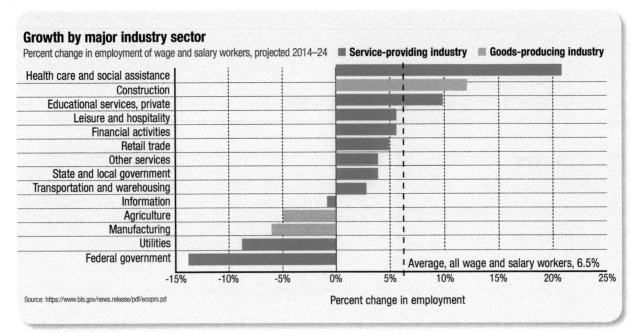

Growth by major industry sector

Percent change in employment of wage and salary workers, projected 2014–24   ■ Service-providing industry   ■ Goods-producing industry

Health care and social assistance
Construction
Educational services, private
Leisure and hospitality
Financial activities
Retail trade
Other services
State and local government
Transportation and warehousing
Information
Agriculture
Manufacturing
Utilities
Federal government

-15%   -10%   -5%   0%   5%   10%   15%   20%   25%

Average, all wage and salary workers, 6.5%

Source: https://www.bls.gov/news.release/pdf/ecopro.pd

Percent change in employment

A Read the questions. Look at the chart. Fill in the answer.

1. Which service-providing industry will most likely have the largest increase in employment?

   A Construction

   B Federal government

   C Health care and social assistance

   D Manufacturing

2. What percent of job growth will there be for teachers?

   A 5

   B 10

   C 15

   D 20

3. What is *not* true about manufacturing?

   A It's a goods-producing industry.

   B An increase in the percentage of change in employment is expected.

   C It will lose more jobs than Agriculture.

   D It will decrease by more than 5% by 2024.

4. According to the chart, which of the major industries listed below project the least growth from 2014–2024?

   A Agriculture

   B Federal government

   C Leisure and hospitality

   D none of the above

B Solve the problem. Give your opinion.

Kumio is a 40-year old man who was working as an electronic assembler at a large manufacturing company for 12 years. Last month Kumio and a large number of assemblers were laid off. He's thinking about getting a job in health care. He heard about a private training program that costs $2,500. He also heard about a low-cost program at a community college, but it takes longer. What should he do? *Answers will vary.*

- Introduce reading and understanding a chart about job growth
- Introduce and provide practice making requests and offers

WARM-UP AND REVIEW

- Before class. Write today's lesson focus on the board.
  Lesson F:
  Read and understand a chart about job growth in major careers
  Contrast requests and offers
- Begin class. Books closed. Write on the board: *job growth by major industry sector.* Explain that major industry sector means jobs in different categories. Give the example of health care: that's the name of the category. What are some specific jobs in that category? Elicit answers such as: *Nursing assistant, physical therapist, nurse,* etc.
- Ask Ss: *What are some job categories besides health care that are growing?* Elicit appropriate answers, such as: *hospitality, educational services,* etc.
- Ask Ss: *What do you think service-providing industry means?* Elicit appropriate responses, such as: categories of jobs in which people help others, such as nursing.
- Ask: *What do you think goods-producing industry means?* Elicit appropriate responses, such as categories of jobs where goods are made, such as agriculture.

PRESENTATION

- Books open. Read the title of the chart to the class.
- Call on a S to read the jobs listed in the left-hand column of the chart.
- Call on individual Ss in turn to read the jobs listed. Explain vocabulary as needed.

Teaching Tip

Tell Ss that learning to read these kinds of charts is a useful skill for everyday life. Ask Ss if they have seen similar types of charts. If no one says *yes,* explain that this is the kind of chart they may find in a newspaper or magazine article.

PRACTICE

- Direct Ss' attention to **1A** and read the instructions aloud. This task helps prepare Ss for standardized-type tests they may have to take. Be sure that Ss understand the task. Have Ss individually scan for and fill in the answers.

COMPREHENSION CHECK

- Check answers to Exercise **1A** with the class. Make sure that Ss have followed the instructions and filled in their answers.
- Have Ss read aloud the questions and answers they filled in. Ask: *Is that answer correct?* Make corrections as needed.

APPLICATION

- Direct Ss' attention to Exercise **1B** and read the instructions aloud. Make sure that Ss understand the task. Have Ss individually solve the problem.
- Ss discuss the problem in small groups. Walk around and help as needed.
- Open up the discussion to the entire class. Accept all plausible answers.

Expansion activity (small groups)

- **Materials needed** Stop by a career development office or center at your school or in the community to pick up any pamphlets or materials you can find about various service and professional occupations.
- Ss in small groups. Give each group a different set of materials about occupations. Write the following questions on the board. Tell Ss they may not be able to find answers to all the questions in the materials, but they should try to answer as many of the questions as possible:

  What kind of training does the occupation require?
  Is the occupation a service or professional job?
  What kind of skills does the occupation require?
  What hours does the occupation require?
  Where do people who have this occupation work (e.g., hospital, office)?
- Walk around and help Ss as needed.
- Ask a representative from each group to share their group's findings. They should come to the board and write any key vocabulary terms relating to the occupation.
- Leave time for a question-and-answer session.

LESSON F Another view

WARM UP AND REVIEW

- Books closed. Write a few examples of polite requests on the board. For example, *Would you mind helping me move this chair? May I borrow a pen?* Ask Ss the questions, and elicit answers using the polite forms *would*, *could*, or *may*. Write a few of the Ss' answers on the board.

PRESENTATION

Focus on form

- Use the animated grammar presentation in one or more of the following ways:
  - Preview it before class
  - Show in class
  - Encourage Ss to watch outside of class.
- Books closed. Write the words *request* and *offer* on the board. Ask Ss to define what each word means. Elicit or explain that a request is a polite or formal inquiry for something and that an offer is a statement a person makes if they are willing to do something for someone.
- Point to the questions and answers on the board. Ask Ss to label them as requests or offers. Ensure Ss understand the difference between the two.
- Books open. Direct Ss' attention to the grammar chart in Exercise **2A**. Ask a pair of Ss to read the questions and answers in the first row. Write the questions on the board and underline the words *would*, *could*, and *can*. Ask another pair of Ss to read the questions and answers in the second row. Write the sentences on the board and underline *why don't I*, *may*, *can*, and *let*.
- Tell Ss that the underlined words are used to make requests and offers more polite. Ask Ss to think of situations in which it would be important to be more polite. Elicit suggestions, such as: *at work, asking a stranger for help with something, when you want to seem friendly.*

PRACTICE

- Direct Ss' attention to the instructions in Exercise **2A**. Read the instructions aloud. Ensure Ss understand the activity. Ask two pairs of Ss to read the dialogs aloud.

- Have Ss complete Exercise **2A** in pairs. Walk around and help as needed.
- Ask several pairs to role play their dialogs for the class.
- Direct Ss' attention to the instructions in Exercise **2B**. Read the instructions aloud. Ask a pair to read the dialog aloud. Ask Ss where they think this dialog is taking place (a dark movie theater). Encourage Ss to use a similar dialog format and to complete Exercise **2B** in pairs.
- Ask several pairs to role play their dialogs for the class.

EVALUATION

- Do a quick review of the unit. Have Ss turn to Lesson A. Ask the class to talk about what they remember about this lesson. Prompt Ss, if necessary, with questions, for example: *What are the conversations about on this page? What vocabulary is in the pictures?* Continue in this manner to review each lesson quickly.

Expansion activity

- Before class. Print, for each student, one copy of the Self-assessment for this unit.
- Have Ss complete the Self-assessment either in class or outside of class.
- Provide feedback to Ss such as through a whole-class discussion, partners comparing their worksheets, or T reviewing each S's worksheet.
- If Ss are ready, administer the unit test on pages T-210–T-212 of this Teacher's Edition. The audio script for the test is on page T-224.

More Ventures, Unit 8, Lesson F	
Workbook, 15–30 min.	
Multilevel Worksheets, 30–45 min.	www.cambridge.org/ventures/resources/
Collaborative Worksheets, 30–45 min.	
Self-assessment, 10 min.	
CASAS Test Prep Worksheet, 5–10 min.	

2 Grammar connections: polite requests and offers

Polite requests ask someone to do something to help you. To make a polite request, use *Could you*, *Would you* or *Can you* with the base form of the verb. You can also use *Would you mind* with the gerund (verb + *-ing*) form of the verb.

Polite offers say you can do something to help someone. To make a polite offer, use *Could I*, *Can I*, *May I*, *Let me*, or *Why don't I* with the base form of the verb.

 Watch

	QUESTIONS	ANSWERS
Polite requests	**Would / Will you move** your chair? **Could / Can you help** me with this box? **Would you mind helping** me?	Sure. No problem. I'd be glad to.
Offers	**Why don't I move** this box for you? **May / Can / Could I help** you with that? **Let me open** that for you.	OK, thanks. I'd appreciate it. That'd be great.

I'd = I would
that'd = that would

A **Talk** with a partner. Use the pictures to make and respond to requests for the situation. Then use the pictures to make and respond to offers for the situation. Take turns.

A Could you help me with this box?

B Sure.

A Let me move those books out of your way.

B Thanks! That'd be great!

1.

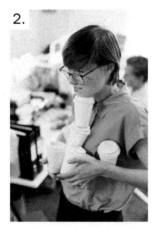
2.

3.

4.

B **Talk** with a partner. Look at the places in the box. Have a conversation in each place. Make a request or offer in each conversation. Take turns.

a bus	a grocery store	an airplane
a dark movie theater	a post office	an office

A It's dark in here. Would you mind helping me find my seat?

B I'd be glad to. Follow me.

A OK, thanks.

REVIEW

1 Listening

Listen. Take notes on a class lecture.

Job skills for an electronics store	Job skills for a restaurant
1. *good communication skills*	4. *good time management skills*
2. *good listening skills*	5. *good communication skills*
3. *good problem-solving skills*	6. *ability to train others*

◀))) CD2, Track 20

Talk with a partner. Check your answers.

2 Grammar

A Write. Complete the story.

Joanie's Problem

Joanie is at the electronics store. She ___*has been talking*___ with a clerk in
1. has talked / has been talking

customer service for the past 15 minutes. She wants to return a scanner. He told her she

could exchange the scanner. However, Joanie ___*has been looking*___ at scanners
2. has looked / has been looking

for several months, and she still ___*hasn't found*___ another one she likes.
3. hasn't found / hasn't been finding

She wants a refund. The clerk ___*has just called*___ his manager this minute
4. has just called / has been calling

to see if Joanie can get a refund, but the manager is not in his offi ce. This situation is

very ___*frustrating*___ for Joanie. She's ___*tired*___ and wants
5. frustrating / frustrated   6. tiring / tired

to go home.

B Write. Look at the words that are underlined in the answers. Write the questions.

1. A *What does Joanie want to return?*

   B Joanie wants to return her scanner.

2. A *How long has Joanie been talking to the clerk?*

   B Joanie has been talking to the clerk for 15 minutes.

3. A *Who says she can exchange the scanner?*

   B The customer-service clerk says that she can exchange the scanner.

4. A *When did Joanie go to the store?*

   B Joanie went to the store on Saturday afternoon.

Talk with a partner. Ask and answer the questions.

Teaching objectives
- Review vocabulary and grammar from Units 7 and 8
- Provide practice pronouncing stressed function words

WARM-UP AND REVIEW

- Before class. Write today's lesson focus on the board.
  Review unit:
  Review vocabulary and grammar from Units 7 and 8
  Practice pronouncing stressed function words
- Begin class. Books closed. Review vocabulary and grammar from Units 7 and 8. Ask Ss: *What are some of the qualities you consider when you are making an important purchase, such as a camera, a computer, or a car?* Encourage Ss to answer using adjective clauses, for example: *I want a camera that . . .*
- Review the present perfect and the present perfect continuous. Write these sentences on the board, and ask Ss to fill in the blanks with the appropriate form of the present perfect or the present perfect continuous. Then ask Ss to make up similar sentences.
  It's 3:00 p.m. We _____ English for three hours. (study)
  It's 3:05 p.m. We _____ our English lesson for the day. (finish)
- Review adjectives ending in *-ed* and *-ing*. Write the following words on the board: *excited, relaxing, exhausting, shocked, boring.* Ask Ss to make up sentences using these adjectives.

PRESENTATION

- Books open. Direct Ss' attention to Exercise **1** and read the instructions aloud. Tell Ss that they will hear a class lecture to which two business owners have been invited to speak.
- ▶ **CD2, Track 20** Model the task. Play or read only the first part of the lecture on the audio (see audio script, pages T-182–T-183). Pause after Mr. Sullivan says, *So, talking about job skills, I would say that first and most importantly, my employees need to have good communications skills.*
- Direct Ss' attention to number 1 in the chart under *Job skills for an electronics store,* and ask: *What does Mr. Sullivan say is one of the most important job skills for his employees in his electronics store?* (good communication skills.)
- Ask a S to read aloud the other chart heading (*Job skills for a restaurant*). Say: *Now listen and complete the chart.*
- ▶ **CD2, Track 20** Play or read the complete audio. Ss listen and complete the chart. Repeat the audio as needed.

COMPREHENSION CHECK

- Read aloud the second part of the instructions for Exercise **1**.
- Ss check their answers in pairs. Help as needed.

PRACTICE

- Direct Ss' attention to Exercise **2A**. Ask Ss: *What is the title of this story?* ("Joanie's Problem")
- Read the instructions aloud for Exercise **2A**.
- Ask a S to read aloud the first three sentences in the story, including the sample answer. Tell Ss to continue reading the story and filling in the blanks.
- If Ss are unfamiliar with scanners, explain that a scanner is a device that *optically scans* (similar to photographing) images, printed text, handwriting, or an object, and changes it to a digital image.
- Ss complete the exercise individually. Walk around and help as needed.
- Write the numbers *1–6* on the board. Ask Ss to come to the board to write the answers only.
- Call on several Ss to read the complete story using the answers on the board. Correct as needed.

Teaching Tip

Encourage the Ss who are comfortable with this grammar review to help those who are less comfortable with these key grammar points.

COMPREHENSION CHECK

- Direct Ss' attention to Exercise **2B**. This exercise reviews question formation related to the reading, "Joanie's Problem."
- Read the instructions aloud. Model the task. Focus Ss' attention on the answer to number 1. Ask: *What question can you ask to get this answer?*
- Ss complete the exercise individually. Walk around and help as needed.
- Check answers with the class. Call on Ss to read their questions to the class. Correct as needed.
- Read aloud the second part of the instructions for Exercise **2B**.
- Ss work in pairs to ask and answer the questions. Help as needed.

REVIEW

PRESENTATION

- Books closed. Write on the board: *stressing function words*. Ask Ss if they can recall from the review for Units 5 and 6 which words are usually stressed and which are unstressed. Elicit the response: *Content words are usually stressed, and function words are usually unstressed.*

- Ask Ss to tell you which words are the function words (pronouns, prepositions, conjunctions, articles, and auxiliary verbs).

- Say the following sentence, stressing the underlined words: *Bob buys a new cell phone as soon as a new one comes out*.

- Ask Ss which words are stressed and which ones are unstressed. Write the sentence on the board. Indicate the stressed words by underlining them.

- Erase the underlining from the sentence on the board. Tell Ss that you are going to say the sentence in a different way. Say the sentence again, stressing the underlined words: *Bob buys a new cell phone as soon as a new one comes out.*

- Ask Ss: *Which words were stressed?* (as soon as.) Underline *as soon as* on the board. Ask Ss: *Why would you stress these particular words?* Elicit an appropriate an swer, such as: *Because this time, you want to emphasize when something happened.*

- Tell Ss that although we typically stress content words, we sometimes stress function words, depending on the situation and how we feel about it.

Teaching Tip

Some Ss may find it difficult to differentiate between stressed and unstressed words. Take extra time to review the sounds. Exaggerate the stress in usually unstressed words so that Ss can hear the differences.

- Books open. Direct Ss to page 109, and call on a S to read the information at the top of the page.

- Focus Ss' attention on Exercise **3A** and read the instructions aloud.

- ▶ **CD2, Track 21** Play or read the complete audio (see audio script, page T-183).

- Read the second part of the instructions for Exercise **3A**.

- ▶ **CD2, Track 21** Repeat the audio. Pause after each phrase to give Ss time to repeat. Play the audio as many times as needed.

PRACTICE

- Direct Ss' attention to Exercise **3B** and read the instructions aloud.

- ▶ **CD2, Track 22** Model the activity. Play or read the first sentence on the audio (see audio script, page T-183). Ask Ss to tell you which words are stressed.

- Have Ss pay attention to the stressed words in each sentence as they listen and repeat. Play or read the audio, stopping as needed for Ss to repeat.

- Play or read the complete audio again. Ss identify the stressed words by underlining them.

- Read aloud the second part of the instructions for Exercise **3B**.

- Ss complete the task in pairs. Walk around and help Ss to pronounce the stressed words correctly.

COMPREHENSION CHECK

- Direct Ss' attention to Exercise **3C** and read the instructions aloud.

- Ss practice the conversations with a partner. Listen to Ss' pronunciation of the stressed function words.

APPLICATION

- Focus Ss' attention on Exercise **3D** and read the instructions aloud.

- Ss work with a partner to write new conversations.

- Call on Ss to share the conversations they wrote. Correct as needed.

EVALUATION

- Direct Ss' attention to the lesson focus on the board.

- Write these sentences on the board: *The DVD player was defective. I bought the DVD player at an electronics store last year.* Ask Ss to combine the sentences, using an adjective clause with *that*. (The DVD player that I bought at the electronics store last year was defective.)

- Write on the board:

  We _____ all afternoon. *(have been cooking)*
     (cook)
  It's 8:00 p.m. We ——— dessert. *(have just eaten)*
         (eat)

  Have Ss complete them with the correct form of the verb in parentheses. Tell Ss to use *just* where possible.

- Check off each part of the lesson focus as Ss demonstrate an understanding of what they have learned in the lesson.

③ Pronunciation: stressing function words

Normally, function words such as pronouns, prepositions, conjunctions, articles, *to be* verbs, and auxiliary verbs are not stressed. However, when strong feelings or disagreements are expressed, function words can receive strong stress.

🔊 CD2, Track 21

A Listen to the stressed function words in each conversation.

1. A Is the camera defective?
   B It's defective <u>and</u> too small!

2. A Don't you usually finish at 5:00?
   B I <u>do</u> usually finish at 5:00, but not today.

3. A Why aren't you applying for that job?
   B I <u>am</u>. I'll go there tomorrow

4. A I don't trust the man who sold you this car.
   B Well, I <u>do</u>! It's <u>my</u> decision, not <u>yours</u>.

5. A Is he excited about his new job?
   B No, but his wife <u>is</u>.

6. A Did you put the returned merchandise on my desk?
   B No, I put it <u>in</u> your desk.

Listen again and repeat. Stress the underlined function words.

B Listen and repeat. Then underline the stressed function words.

1. A I'd like to exchange this sweater.
   B Why?
   A It's too big, <u>and</u> it has a hole.

2. A You <u>can't</u> leave early again!
   B Yes, I <u>can</u> and I <u>will</u>.

3. A Why don't you clean the counters?
   B Why don't <u>you</u>?

4. A Let's talk about a raise after you've worked here for six months.
   B Can we talk <u>before</u> six months?

🔊 CD2, Track 22

Talk with a partner. Compare your answers.

C Talk with a partner. Practice the conversations. Pay attention to the stressed function words.

1. A We <u>don't</u> give refunds or exchanges on watches.
   B My warranty says you <u>can</u> if the merchandise is defective.
   A So, <u>is</u> it defective?
   B Yes, it <u>is</u>.
   A Then I <u>can</u> give you a refund.

2. A Who just mopped the floors, <u>you</u> or <u>Kevin</u>?
   B I did. <u>And</u> I cleaned the tables.
   A Good work. I <u>do</u> enjoy seeing a clean bakery.
   A And <u>I</u> love working here.

D Write two new conversations using stressed function words. Practice with a partner.

A Does Karen need more help?
B No, but <u>I</u> do.

UNIT 9 DAILY LIVING

Lesson A Listening

1 Before you listen

A What do you see?

B What is happening?

Global Warming
- record high temperatures
- drought / wild fires
- rising sea levels
- record high levels of CO₂
- melting ice caps
- expanding desert

Mei

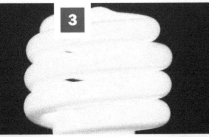

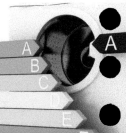

UNIT 9

Teaching objectives
- Introduce students to the topic
- Find out what students know about the topic
- Preview the unit by talking about the pictures
- Provide practice of key vocabulary
- Provide practice that develops listening skills

WARM-UP AND REVIEW

- Before class. Write today's lesson focus on the board.
  Lesson A:
  Ask questions about protecting the environment
  Discuss causes and effects of environmental problems
  Discuss human actions that could help the environment

- Begin class. Books closed. Direct Ss' attention to the words *environmental problems* in the lesson focus. Ask Ss: *What are some examples of environmental problems?* List Ss' responses on the board, for example: *pollution, global warming, rain-forest destruction (deforestation), endangered species, overpopulation.*

- Point to *human actions that could help the environment.* Ask Ss: *What are some actions we could take to help save the environment?* List Ss' responses on the board, for example: *cleaning up litter, recycling, saving energy, driving less, carpooling, using alternative forms of energy.*

- Ask Ss: *What do you think "global warming" means?* Answers will vary, but may include: *earth getting warmer, more storms, sea is rising, etc.* Write Ss' responses on the board.

PRESENTATION

- Books open. Set the scene. Direct Ss' attention to the first picture on page 110. Ask the question from Exercise **1A**: *What do you see?* Elicit and write on the board as much vocabulary about the picture as possible, for example: *teacher giving lecture on global warming.* Continue eliciting words to describe the remaining five pictures and write them on the board. Explain any unfamiliar words.

- Ask individual Ss to look at the pictures and talk about the similarities. Elicit appropriate responses, such as: *the pictures are showing different ways of saving energy with images of a carpool, recycling, energy saving lights, and energy efficient appliances.*

- Direct Ss' attention to the question in Exercise **1B**: *What is happening?* Read it aloud. Hold up the Student's Book. Point to the first picture. Ask: *What's Mei doing here?* (She's listening to the speaker.) Say: *What do you think the speaker is talking about?*

- Point to the second picture. Ask: *What's Mei doing here?* (She's working on her computer.)

Teaching Tip
Encourage Ss to be creative. At this point, there is no single correct answer.

Expansion activity (small groups)
- Ss in small groups. Assign each group one of the pictures in the Student's Book, and have Ss create a conversation between the people in the picture (either between Mei and the speaker, or Mei and her parents).

- Listen as two or three Ss practice their conversation. Walk around and help as needed.

- Ask several Ss to perform their role play for the class.

Expansion activity (small groups)
- Write the following on the board: *Your community's environmental activities.*

- Ask Ss: *Do you know of any activities in your community that are environmentally friendly?* Then say: *Talk with your classmates and make a list of these activities. If your community doesn't do anything right now, make a list of what it could do, such as saving water, cleaning up a park, or promoting a recycling program.*

- Ss work in small groups to discuss the question and make a list. Walk around and help as needed.

- After several minutes, invite Ss to share information they discussed with their groups.

- Write several examples on the board, for example: *reducing waste, reusing bottles, recycling paper and plastic, cleaning up a lake or beach, protecting wildlife.*

LESSON A Listening

PRESENTATION

- Books open. Direct Ss' attention to Exercise **2A**. Have Ss listen for the main idea. Read the instructions aloud.
- ▶ **CD2, Track 23** Play or read the audio (see audio script, page T-183).
- Ask Ss if they understood everything in the listening exercise. Write any unfamiliar words on the board and help Ss understand the meaning of each word.
- Elicit answers to the questions.
- Focus Ss' attention on Exercise **2B**. Read the instructions aloud.
- ▶ **CD2, Track 23** Tell Ss to listen for details about Mei's conversation with her parents and her suggestions for what they could try to do at home to conserve energy and protect the environment. Play or read the audio again. Pause the audio after Mei says: *OK, well, first of all, he said we need to cut down on driving, so we should walk, ride a bicycle, carpool, or take public transportation.*
- Point to "no" written in the chart. Tell Ss the family has decided that they can't cut down on driving. Tell Ss to listen and complete the chart with the ideas for protecting the environment. Play or read the rest of the audio.
- ▶ **CD2, Track 23** Play or read the audio again. Ss listen and check their answers.
- Copy the chart from Exercise **2B** on the board. Ask several Ss to come to the board and write their answers. Make corrections on the board as needed.

Learner persistence *(individual work)*
- ▶ **CD2, Track 23** Ss can listen to the audio for Exercises **2A** and **2B** at home for reinforcement and review. They can also listen to the audio for self-directed learning when class attendance is not possible.

PRACTICE

- Focus Ss' attention on Exercise **3A**. Read the instructions aloud. Tell Ss that the story in this exercise is a summary of what happened in the pictures on the previous page.
- Direct Ss' attention to the words in the word bank. Say each word aloud. Ask Ss to repeat. Explain any unfamiliar words.
- Model the exercise. Ask a S to read aloud the first two sentences in the story, including the sample answer for number 2. Point out that Ss need to fill in the remaining blanks with the words from the word bank.
- Ss complete the exercise individually. Walk around and help as needed.

COMPREHENSION CHECK

- ▶ **CD2, Track 24** Play or read the audio (see audio script, page T-183). Ss listen and check their answers. Repeat the audio as needed.
- Write the numbers *1–10* on the board. Ask individual Ss to come to the board to write their answers.

Learner persistence *(individual work)*
- ▶ **CD2, Track 24** Ss can listen to the audio for Exercise **3** at home for reinforcement and review. They can also listen to the audio for self-directed learning when class attendance is not possible.

APPLICATION

- Focus Ss' attention on Exercise **3B** and read the instructions aloud.
- Ss work in a small group to answer the questions. Walk around and help as needed.
- Open up the discussion to the class. Ask Ss to share the suggestions that are difficult for them, and have them tell why.

Expansion activity *(student pairs)*
- Have Ss imagine that they are having a conversation with their family similar to the one that Mei is having with her parents. What would they say? What would their parents (or children) say? Have Ss take turns in their group talking about their conversation about protecting the environment with a relative.
- Have Ss in each group form pairs. Ask pairs to write a dialog based on their conversation. Ss can use the ideas that Mei presented or their own.
- Ss practice their dialog with a partner. Walk around and help as needed.
- Ask several pairs to perform their dialogs for the class.

EVALUATION

- Direct Ss' attention to the lesson focus on the board. Ask individual Ss to look at the pictures on page 110 to make sentences using the words in Exercise **3**.
- Check off each part of the lesson focus as Ss demonstrate an understanding of what they have learned in the lesson.

More Ventures, Unit 9, Lesson A	
Workbook, 15–30 min.	
Multilevel Worksheets, 30–45 min. **Collaborative Worksheets,** 30–45 min.	www.cambridge.org/ventures/resources/
Student Arcade, time varies	www.cambridge.org/venturesarcade/

UNIT GOALS
Identify environmental issues and concerns   **Scan** a chart to determine reasons to save our planet
Write a cause-and-effect paragraph about an environmental problem

2 Listen

CD2, Track 23

A **Listen** and answer the questions.

1. Who are the speakers?   2. What are they talking about?

B **Listen again.** Complete the diagram.

Ideas for saving our planet	Will the family try?
1. *cut down on driving*	*no*
2. *Recycling bottles, cans, glass, paper*	*Yes*
3. *Turn off unnecessary lights*	*Yes*
4. *Wash clothes in cold water*	*Yes*
5. *Buy energy-efficient washing machine*	*No*
6. *Switch to energy-efficient light bulbs*	*Yes*

3 After you listen

A **Read.** Complete the story.

appliances	carpool	energy-efficient	global warming	recycle
Biology	cut down on	environment	planet	responsibility

Mei was late to dinner because she was looking at a website about saving the

_____*planet*_____ . She wants to take more _____*responsibility*_____ for saving the earth
            1   2

from _____*global warming*_____ . Mei tells her parents about the guest speaker who came to
            3

her _____*Biology*_____ class. The speaker suggested simple things people could do to
            4

reduce their energy use and protect the _____*environment*_____ . For example, they could
                                                      5

_____*carpool*_____ instead of driving alone, _____*recycle*_____ their bottles and cans,
            6   7

and use _*energy-efficient*_ lightbulbs. Mei's parents agree that it is important to
            8

_____*cut down on*_____ energy use since it would also help them save money. However, they
            9

can't afford to buy new _____*appliances*_____ right now.
                                      10

Listen and check your answers.

CD2, Track 24

B **Discuss.** Talk with your classmates. Which of the speaker's suggestions
can you try? Which are difficult for you? Why?

📖 Listen for and identify environmental problems and solutions   **UNIT 9   111**

Lesson B Conditionals

1 Grammar focus: present unreal

Watch

> Use the present unreal conditional to talk about what would happen in an imaginary (not real) situation. Use *if* with verb in past tense in the clause that describes the imaginary situation. Use *would* with the base form of the verb in the results clause.

If everybody **drove** smaller cars, we **would use** less gasoline.	**If** she **used** energy-efficient lightbulbs, she **would save** electricity
We **would use** less gasoline **if** everybody **drove** smaller cars.	She **would save** electricity **if** she **used** energy-efficient lightbulbs.

2 Practice

A Write. Complete the sentences. Use the present unreal conditional.

1. Many people put their newspapers in the trash can. If everybody ____recycled____
   (recycle)
   newspapers, we ____would save____ millions of trees.
   (save)

2. Noah never takes his car in for a tune-up. Noah's car ____would use____ less gas if he
   (use)
   ____tuned up____ his car regularly.
   (tune up)

3. Mr. Brown drives his own car to his job downtown. Mr. Brown ____could save____ money
   (save)
   on gas if he ____carpooled____ to work.
   (carpool)

4. Many items in the supermarket are packaged in plastic. If you ____bought____ products
   (buy)
   that are packaged with recycled paper, you ____would help____ to reduce global warming.
   (help)

5. Jessica always stays in the shower for a very long time. If Jessica ____took____
   (take)
   shorter showers, she ____could save____ water.
   (save)

6. Some kinds of fish contain large amounts of lead, a poisonous metal. You
   ____could be____ healthier if you ____stopped____ eating fish that contains lead.
   (be)   (stop)

7. Energy efficient appliances use less electricity. If Mei's family ____bought____ a new
   (buy)
   washing machine, they ____could save____ money on their electric bill.
   (save)

8. Kristina never puts enough air in her tires. If Kristina ____put____ more
   (put)
   air in her tires, she ____would buy____ less gasoline.
   (buy)

Listen and check your answers.

◀)) CD2, Track 25

Teaching objective
- Introduce and provide practice with the present unreal conditional

WARM-UP AND REVIEW

- Before class: Write the lesson focus on the board.
  Lesson B:
  Present unreal conditional
- Begin class. Books open. Review Lesson A vocabulary. Direct Ss' attention to the pictures on page 110. Ask them to identify some of the ideas Mei suggested to her parents to protect the environment (carpool, use energy-efficient lightbulbs and appliances, recycle). Ask questions about what protecting the environment means to Ss (doing things that help the environment).

PRESENTATION

Focus on meaning / personalize

- Books closed. Direct Ss' attention to the lesson focus on the board. Read it aloud.
- Tell Ss: *I think it is important to protect the environment. I always recycle bottles and cans.* Ask: *What else can people do to protect the environment?* Write answers on the board, for example: *turn off lights, use fewer plastic bags, drive less.* Write a sentence with one of the responses on the board, for example: *If everyone recycled bottles and cans, we would have less trash.*
- Ask: *Does everyone recycle?* (No.) *Is it possible that everyone will?* (No.) *What would happen if they did?* (We would have less trash.)
- Point to the sentence on the board with *if*. Tell Ss that these *if* clauses are conditional clauses and that conditional clauses can be real or unreal. *Real* means the situation in the sentence is possible. Explain that they will study "unreal" conditional sentences. The situation isn't possible; it's imaginary.

Focus on form

- Use the animated grammar presentation in one or more of the following ways:
  - Preview it before class
  - Show in class
  - Encourage Ss to watch outside of class.

- Books open. Focus Ss' attention on the left-hand side of the chart in Exercise **1**. Read the two statements aloud. Ask Ss to repeat. Ask Ss if everyone driving a smaller car is a real or unreal situation. (Unreal. Everyone does not drive a small car.) Direct Ss' attention to the column heading. Tell Ss that we use present unreal sentences with *would* when we are very sure of something.
- Elicit or explain how to form the present unreal conditional (*If . . . simple past, would + base form of verb*).
- Direct Ss' attention to the column on the left. Have a S read the second sentence aloud. Ask Ss to identify what is different from the first sentence in the chart. (The independent clause is second; no comma.)

PRACTICE

- Focus Ss' attention on Exercise **2A** and read the instructions aloud.
- Call on a S to read the first example. Make sure that Ss understand the exercise.
- Ss complete the exercise individually. Walk around and help as needed.

COMPREHENSION CHECK

- Direct Ss' attention to the second part of the instructions for Exercise **2A**.
- ▶ **CD2, Track 25** Play or read the audio (see audio script, page T-183). Ss listen and check their answers. Repeat the audio as needed.
- Write the numbers *1–8* on the board. Ask several Ss to come to the board to write their answers in complete sentences. Make corrections on the board as needed.

LESSON B Conditionals

PRACTICE

- Books open. Tell Ss that they are going to read and talk about the causes and effects of different activities related to protecting the environment. Read the instructions aloud for Exercise **2B**.
- Direct Ss' attention to the phrases under the two headings, *Actions* and *Results*. Call on one S to read the actions and another S to read the results.
- Model the task. Call on a S to read the example sentence.
- Ss complete the exercise in pairs, matching each action with an environmentally friendly result. Walk around and help as needed.
- Direct Ss' attention to the second part of Exercise **2B** and read the instructions aloud.
- Ask a S to read the example sentence to the class.
- Ss work individually to complete the exercise. Walk around and help as needed.
- Have individual Ss come to the board to write their sentences. Work with the class to make corrections on the board as needed.

APPLICATION

- Direct Ss' attention to Exercise **3A** and read the instructions aloud. Point out that *could* is used in this exercise because the sentences are about the possibility of something occurring.
- Model the task. Ask a S to read the example sentence.
- Ss work in a small group to complete the exercise. Walk around and help as needed.
- Direct Ss' attention to Exercise **3B** and read the instructions aloud.
- Have Ss take turns sharing information they discussed with their groups.

Expansion activity *(student pairs)*

- Ask partners to prepare a dialog in which they suggest that someone change his or her habits in order to protect the environment. Ss take turns being the one who convinces and the one who needs convincing. Instruct Ss to use the vocabulary from the unit as well as the grammar just discussed. Tell Ss that they are not required to write the dialog for their role play.

- Model the task. Write the following on the board:

  S1: *We can all take more responsibility for saving the earth.*

  S2: *I'm only one person! What can I do?*

  S1: *Well, if you recycled your garbage, you could reduce the amount of trash in landfills.*

  S2: *How can I do that? I'm so busy!*

  S1: *All you need to do is separate your cans, glass, plastic, newspapers, cardboard, and other paper products.*

- Call on two Ss to read the sample dialog. Ss complete the exercise in pairs.
- After a few minutes, call on several pairs to perform their role play for the class.

EVALUATION

- Books closed. Direct Ss' attention to the lesson focus on the board.
- Write the following on the board:

  If everybody _____ cans, bottles, and glass, we
          (recycle)

  _____ a lot less garbage.
    (have)

  We _____ millions of trees if everybody
      (save)

  _____ paper.
    (recycle)

- Ask Ss to tell you the correct form of the verbs and to fill in the blanks. Elicit: *recycled, would have; would save* or *could save, recycled.*
- Check off the lesson focus as Ss demonstrate an understanding of what they have learned in the lesson.

More Ventures, Unit 9, Lesson B	
Workbook, 15–30 min.	
Multilevel Worksheets, 30–45 min. **Collaborative Worksheets,** 30–45 min.	www.cambridge.org/ventures/resources/
Student Arcade, time varies	www.cambridge.org/venturesarcade/

B **Talk** with a partner. Match each action with a result. Some items have more than one correct answer. Use the present unreal conditional.

> If everybody bought energy-efficient appliances, we would save electricity.

Actions	Results
buy energy-efficient appliances	save gas
fix water leaks	cut down on energy use
replace lightbulbs with energy-efficient ones	save water
recycle cans, bottles, glass, and paper	reduce air-conditioning and heating use
put enough air in their tires	reduce the amount of trash in landfills
close off unused rooms	save electricity

Write sentences about the actions and results.

If everybody bought energy-efficient appliances, we would save electricity.
Answers will vary.

3 Communicate

A **Work** in a small group. Look at the picture of the beach. Talk about actions people could take to help the environment.

> If more people picked up the trash on the beach, everyone would enjoy a clean beach.

B **Share** ideas with your classmates.

Lesson C Connectors

1 Grammar focus: *since* and *so*

Connectors are words at the beginning of a sentence or clause. Use the connector *since* to introduce a cause (reason) clause. Use the connector *so* to introduce an effect (result) clause.

Watch

CONNECTOR OF CAUSE

Since the earth is getting warmer, the polar ice caps are melting.

The polar ice caps are melting **since** the earth is getting warmer.

CONNECTOR OF EFFECT

The earth is getting warmer, **so** the polar ice caps are melting.

The earth is getting warmer, **so** the sea water is getting warmer.

2 Practice

A Write. Combine the sentences. Use the connectors in parentheses.

1. There is a buildup of harmful gases in the atmosphere. Global warming is increasing.

    (since) *Since there is a buildup of harmful gases in the atmosphere, global warming is increasing.*

2. Warm water is expanding in the oceans. The sea level is rising.

    (so) *Warm water is expanding in the oceans, so the sea level is rising.*

3. The sea level is rising. Towns near oceans are in danger of flooding.

    (since) *Since the sea level is rising, towns near oceans are in danger of flooding.*

4. Global warming changes weather patterns. Many places will have less rainfall.

    (so) *Global warming changes weather patterns, so many places will have less rainfall.*

5. The mosquito population will increase. There will be an increase in diseases like malaria.

    (so) *The mosquito population will increase, so there will be an increase in diseases like malaria.*

6. The ocean water is getting warmer. Typhoons and hurricanes are becoming more frequent.

    (since) *Since the ocean water is getting warmer, typhoons and hurricanes are becoming more frequent.*

7. Cities are growing. Many plants and animals may lose their natural habitats.

    (since) *Since cities are growing, many plants and animals may lose their natural habitats.*

8. Summer temperatures will continue to rise. There will be longer periods of no rain and increased days of very high temperatures.

    (so) *Summer temperatures will continue to rise, so there will be longer periods of no rain and increased days of very high temperatures.*

Listen and check your answers. CD2, Track 26

Teaching objective

- Introduce and provide practice with the connectors *since, so*

WARM-UP AND REVIEW

- Before class: Write the lesson focus on the board.
  Lesson C:
  Connectors "since" and "so"
- Begin class. Books open. Review the present unreal conditional. Direct Ss' attention to the picture on page 113. Write on the board: *trash, bottles, cans, small cars, water leaks.* Have Ss make statements using the cues and the present unreal conditional. Begin with an example, such as: *If everybody picked up their trash, the beach would be clean. Amanda could use less gasoline if she drove a smaller car.*

PRESENTATION

Focus on meaning / personalize

- Books closed. Direct Ss' attention to the lesson focus on the board. Read it aloud.
- Divide the board into two columns with *Cause* and *Effect* as headings. Ask: *What do you do to learn more English words and grammar?* Write responses in the *Cause* column (write new words down; speak only English in class). Ask: *How does that help you learn more English?* Write responses in the *Effect* column (learn more English vocabulary; feel more comfortable using English).
- Write the first cause and effect in a sentence on the board: *Since I am writing down new words, I am learning more English vocabulary.* Ask: *What is the cause?* (write down new words.) *What is the effect of doing this?* (learn more vocabulary.)
- Do the same with the remaining items in the chart, eliciting the cause and its effect. Explain that we can make sentences about cause and effect by using connectors. We can use a connector, such as *since*, to signal cause. We can use a connector, such as *so*, to signal effect. Although the meanings of the words and phrases are similar, their grammar is different.

Focus on form

- Use the animated grammar presentation in one or more of the following ways:
  - Preview it before class
  - Show in class
  - Encourage Ss to watch outside of class.

- Books open. Focus Ss' attention on the top chart in Exercise **1**. Read the heading. Write the first statement on the board. Ask: *What is the main clause?* (the polar ice caps are melting.) *What is the dependent clause?* (Since the earth is getting warmer.) Put a box around the connector (since.). Ask: *What is the cause?* (the earth is getting warmer.) *What is the effect?* (polar ice caps are melting.)
- Read aloud the bottom chart's heading. Write the first sentence on the board. Ask: *Which sentence is the cause?* (The earth is getting warmer.) *Which sentence is the effect?* (polar ice caps are melting.) *What is the connector?* (so.)
- Write the second sentence on the board: *The earth is getting warmer, so the sea water is getting warmer.* Ask: *What is the cause?* (earth is getting warmer.) *What is the effect?* (the sea water is getting warmer.)

Useful Language

Read the tip box aloud. Ask: *If these connectors mean the same thing, why do we use them?* Elicit or give an appropriate answer, for example: *It helps writers make their writing more interesting and less repetitive.* Point out to Ss that *therefore* is different from *so* in that it requires a comma afterward. Remind Ss that if they use *therefore*, they must use a semicolon before and a comma after it.

- Direct Ss' attention to Exercise **2A** and read the instructions aloud.
- Ask a S to read aloud the first two sentences in number 1 and the example combined sentence. Call on another S to read number 2 and the example answer.
- Ss complete the exercise individually. Walk around and help as needed.

COMPREHENSION CHECK

- Read aloud the second part of the instructions for Exercise **2A**.
- ▶ *CD2, Track 26* Play or read the audio (see audio script, page T-183). Ss listen and check their answers.
- Write the numbers *1–8* on the board. Ask individual Ss to come to the board to write their answers. Make corrections on the board as needed.

- Read the instructions aloud for Exercise **2B**.
- Focus Ss' attention on the cause-and-effect chart. Call on a S to read the two headings: *Causes* and *Effects*. Ask individual Ss to read each of the causes and corresponding effects.
- Explain vocabulary as needed. Write any words on the board that are unfamiliar to Ss.
- Have two Ss read the example dialog above the chart. Ask Ss to identify the connectors in each sentence. (Since, so.)
- Ss complete the exercise with a partner. Walk around and help as needed.
- Read the instructions aloud for the second part of Exercise **2B**. Call on a S to read aloud the example sentence.
- Ss complete the exercise individually. Walk around and help as needed.
- Ask several Ss to write their sentences on the board. Ask other Ss to read aloud each of the sentences. Ask: *Is this sentence correct?* Make corrections on the board as needed. Ss may get confused about whether the clauses are cause or effect clauses. One way to support Ss is to have them underline the cause clauses with one line and the effect clauses with double lines.

Expansion activity *(small groups)*

- Ask Ss to talk about the causes and effects of air, land, or water pollution. Have them discuss the causes and effects using connectors.
- Ss work in groups to write several sentences on the topic of pollution using the connectors *since, because, so,* and *therefore.*
- Walk around and help as needed.
- Call on Ss from each group to write sentences on the board. Work with the class to make corrections on the board as needed.

APPLICATION

- Direct Ss' attention to Exercise **3A** and read the instructions aloud.
- Focus Ss' attention on the pictures in Exercise **3A**. Ask four Ss to read the headlines. Make sure that Ss understand what has happened in each picture.
- Call on another S to read the example sentence.

- Ss work in small groups to complete the exercise. Walk around and help as needed.
- Direct Ss' attention to Exercise **3B** and read the instructions aloud.
- Continue the exercise by asking each group to share information they discussed with another group of classmates.

Expansion activity *(small groups)*

- **Materials needed** Enough copies of one or more newspaper or magazine articles about habitat loss for each small group of Ss.
- Distribute to each small group a copy of the same (or a different) newspaper or magazine article about habitat loss and how it is endangering species and frightening people in communities.
- If possible, before reading, elicit from Ss the causes of habitat loss, including the suburbanization of rural areas, which is causing animals, such as alligators, coyotes, and deer, to lose their homes and invade populated areas.
- Encourage each group to make a cause-and-effect chart to organize the article as they take turns reading and to share their chart with the class, using connectors of cause and effect in their discussion.

EVALUATION

- Direct Ss' attention to the lesson focus on the board. Ask Ss to look at the pictures on page 115 and write sentences about each picture in **3A**. Call on Ss to read their sentences aloud.
- Check off the lesson focus as Ss demonstrate an understanding of what they have learned in the lesson.

More Ventures, Unit 9, Lesson C	
Workbook, 15–30 min.	
Multilevel Worksheets, 30–45 min. **Collaborative Worksheets,** 30–45 min.	www.cambridge.org/ventures/ resources/
Student Arcade, time varies	www.cambridge.org/ venturesarcade/

B **Talk** with a partner. Combine sentences in different ways using the connectors *since*, *because*, *therefore*, and *so*.

A Since people are building homes in forests, animals are losing their natural habitats.

B Animals are losing their natural habitats because people are building homes in forests.

> **USEFUL LANGUAGE**
> *Because* can replace *since*.
>
> *Therefore* can replace *so*.
>
> Use a semicolon before *therefore* and a comma after it.
>
> *The earth is getting warmer; therefore, the polar ice caps are melting.*

Causes	Effects
1. People are building homes in forests.	Animals are losing their natural habitats.
2. There is habitat loss.	Animals are moving into towns and cities.
3. Animals are moving into towns and cities.	The animals are frightened.
4. The animals are frightened.	Sometimes they attack people.
5. Wild animals sometimes attack people.	People are afraid of them.
6. People are afraid of wild animals.	They kill the animals.

Write sentences about the causes and effects. Use the connectors *since, because, therefore* and *so*.

Since people are building homes in forests, animals are losing their natural habitats.
Answers will vary.

❸ Communicate

A **Work** in a small group. Read the newspaper headlines. Discuss the possible causes and effects of each event. Think of other possible headlines to discuss.

> Coyotes are losing their natural habitats, so they're moving into towns.

> Coyotes are moving into towns because they're losing their natural habitats.

THE MESSENGER
ANOTHER COYOTE MOVES INTO TOWN

THE NEWS
WHALE WASHES UP ON SHORE

THE DAILY
POLAR BEARS DROWNING AS ICE CAPS MELT

DAILY FISH REPORT
WHERE HAVE ALL THE FISH GONE?

B **Share** information about your classmates.

> 📖 Use the connectors *since* and *because* to show cause and the connectors *so* and *therefore* to show effect

Lesson D Reading

 Before you read

Talk with your classmates. Answer the questions.

1. What is a *fable*?
2. Do you know any fables or folktales from your native country? Which ones?

> Ask yourself questions when you read to identify a cause-and-effect relationship.
> · To find an effect, ask, "What happened?"
> · To find a cause, ask, "Why did it happen?"

2 Read

Read the fable. Listen and read again.

All Things Are Connected

🔊 CD2, Track 27

Long ago, there was a village chief who never allowed anyone to disagree with him. Whenever he wanted to do something, he asked the members of his court for their advice. But whether the chief's idea was wise or foolish, his advisors always said the same thing, "Indeed, it is wise." Only one old woman dared to give a different answer. Whenever the chief asked for her advice, she always replied, "All things are connected."

One night, the chief was awakened by the sound of frogs croaking in the swamp. It happened again the next night and the next and the next. The chief decided to kill all the frogs in the swamp. When he consulted the members of his court, they replied as usual, "Indeed, it is wise." But the old woman kept silent. "And you, old woman, what do you think?" the chief demanded. "All things are connected," she replied. The chief concluded that the old woman was a fool, and he ordered his servants to kill all the frogs. Therefore, the chief slept peacefully.

But soon the mosquitoes in the swamp began to multiply since there were no frogs to eat them. They came into the village and made everyone miserable. The chief ordered his servants to go into the swamp and kill the mosquitoes, but it was impossible. Furious, the chief summoned the members of his court and blamed them, saying, "Why didn't you tell me that killing the frogs would make the mosquitoes multiply and everyone would be miserable? I should have listened to the old woman."

Because the mosquitoes were there, all the people of the village were forced to go away. Finally, the chief and his family left, too. Until he died, the chief never forgot the old woman's words, "All things are connected."

Teaching objectives

- Introduce a fable about how all things are connected
- Provide practice identifying cause and effect
- Provide practice using antonyms

WARM-UP AND REVIEW

- Before class. Write today's lesson focus on the board.
  Lesson D:
  Read and understand "All Things Are Connected"
  Identify cause and effect
  Use antonyms

- Begin class. Books closed. Focus Ss' attention on the title of the reading, "All Things Are Connected." Ask Ss these questions: *What do you think the title means? How do you think the reading will relate to the environment?* Elicit appropriate responses, for example: *The title means that everything we do has an effect on everything else on earth. If we cut down on pollution, we will help save the earth.*

PRESENTATION

- Books open. Direct Ss' attention to Exercise **1** and read the instructions aloud.

- Have Ss focus on the two questions in Exercise **1**. Ask two Ss to read them aloud.

- Ss answer the questions with a partner, citing fables or folktales they know from their home country.

- Call on pairs to share their answers with the class. Elicit a lively discussion of world folktales, guiding Ss to see that similarities exist among many folktales of different cultures or countries.

PRACTICE

- Read the instructions aloud for Exercise **2**. Ask Ss to read the fable silently before listening to the audio program.

- ▶ **CD2, Track 27** Play or read the audio and ask Ss to read along (see audio script, page T-183). Repeat the audio as needed.

- While Ss are listening and reading the fable, ask them to underline any words they don't know. When the audio is finished, have Ss write the new vocabulary words on the board.

- Point to each word on the board, say it, and have Ss repeat. Give a brief explanation of each word, or ask Ss to guess the meaning of each word from context clues in the fable. Allow Ss to look up new words in their dictionaries.

Learner persistence (individual work)

- ▶ **CD2, Track 27** Ss can listen to the audio for Exercise **2** at home for reinforcement and review. They can also listen to the audio for self-directed learning when class attendance is not possible.

Expansion activity (small groups)

- **Materials needed** A dictionary for each group of three to four Ss and a different Aesop's fable for each group. (Review the fables before class to familiarize yourself with the content and to preview any vocabulary that you may need to preteach to Ss.)

- Explain to Ss that all fables, such as the one they have just read, teach a lesson, or *moral*. Ask Ss: *What is the moral of "All Things Are Connected"?* Write Ss' answers on the board, such as: *All things in nature are connected. Everything in nature depends on everything else for its survival.*

- Ss in groups of three or four. Distribute a different fable to each group. Review unfamiliar or new vocabulary as needed. Have Ss in each group take turns reading the fable aloud and looking up any new words in the dictionary. Walk around and help as needed.

- Ss prepare a summary of their group's fable and the moral it teaches.

- Encourage a S from each group to summarize the group's fable for the class without telling the moral. Then invite Ss from other groups to guess the moral of the fable.

LESSON D Reading

COMPREHENSION CHECK

- Direct Ss' attention to Exercise **3A** and read the instructions aloud.
- Ask individual Ss to read the questions. Make sure that all Ss understand the questions.
- Ss complete the exercise individually. Instruct Ss to write their answers on a separate piece of paper. Ss should answer in complete sentences. Walk around and help as needed.
- Discuss the answers to the questions with the class. Have Ss indicate where they found the answers in the reading.

Read the tip box aloud. Write *cause* and *effect* on the board. Ask Ss: *What question would you ask if you wanted to know what caused the chief to kill the frogs?* Elicit: *Why did it happen?* Then ask: *What question would you ask if you wanted to know what the effect was of killing the frogs?* Elicit: *What happened?* Or *What happened as a result?* Invite Ss to give examples of cause-and-effect relationships from their own lives.

Expansion activity *(student pairs)*

- Draw a cause-and-effect chart on the board similar to the one on page 115.
- Tell Ss that they should refer to the fable in Exercise **2** on page 116 to complete the chart.
- Model the task. Write *Frogs were croaking in the swamp.* on the board and ask Ss: *What was the effect?* Elicit an appropriate response, such as: *The chief couldn't sleep.* Write the examples in the chart on the board.

Causes	*Effects*
Frogs were croaking in the swamp.	*The chief couldn't sleep.*

- Ss work in pairs to find three cause-and-effect relationships in the story. Call on pairs to share what they wrote. Write their answers in the chart on the board.

PRACTICE

- **Materials needed** A dictionary for each S.
- Direct Ss' attention to Exercise **3B**. Read the instructions aloud for number 1. Call on Ss to read each of the seven words in the chart in number 3.
- Ss work individually to underline the words from the chart in the reading, "All Things Are Connected."
- Call on a S to read the instructions for number 2 of Exercise **3B**.

Useful Language

Read the tip box aloud. Ask Ss' to define the word *synonym*. Explain or elicit that a *synonym* is a word for two words that have the same meaning, for example: *big / large*. Tell Ss that an *antonym* is the opposite of a synonym. It describes two words that have opposite meanings, for example: *good / bad; big / small*.

- Tell Ss that we use antonyms to make our writing or speech more lively or interesting and less repetitive.
- Focus Ss' attention on the headings in the chart. Read aloud the three headings. Call on a S to read the first example in the chart.
- Ss work individually to write the part of speech and an antonym for each word in the chart. Help as needed.
- Ss in pairs. Have Ss show their partner where they underlined the words in the reading and the antonym they chose for each of the words.
- Review with the class. Write the chart on the board from page 117. Call on individual Ss to come to the board to fill in the chart. Work with the class to make corrections on the board as needed.
- Call on a S to read the instructions for number 3 of Exercise **3B**.
- Ss work in small groups to write sentences with the antonyms in the chart. Walk around and help as needed.

APPLICATION

- Direct Ss' attention to Exercise **3C** and read the instructions aloud.
- Call on individual Ss to read the questions in Exercise **3C**.
- Ss ask and answer questions with a partner.
- Ask several pairs to share their answers with the class.

Expansion activity

- Refer Ss to "Plastic Bags – Convenience or Catastrophe?" another reading on the same topic on pages 160–162..
- Have Ss complete the activity either in class or outside of class.
- Provide feedback to Ss such as through whole-class discussion, partners comparing their worksheets, or T reviewing each S's worksheets.

EVALUATION

- Direct Ss' attention to the lesson focus on the board.
- Books closed. Ask individual Ss to retell the main points of the reading, "All Things Are Connected."
- Focus Ss' attention on the words from the reading passage in the first column of the chart in Exercise **3B**. Ask Ss to write a sentence for each word to show that they understand the meaning of each word.
- Check off each part of the lesson focus as Ss demonstrate an understanding of what they have learned in the lesson.

More Ventures, Unit 9, Lesson D	
Workbook, 15–30 min.	
Multilevel Worksheets, 30–45 min.	www.cambridge.org/ventures/ resources/
Collaborative Worksheets, 30–45 min.	
Student Arcade, time varies	www.cambridge.org/ venturesarcade/

3 After you read

A **Check** your understanding.

1. What is the overall meaning (moral) of this fable?

2. What was the chief's main problem?

3. When the chief wanted advice, what did almost all his advisors say? Why did they say that?

4. Why did the chief assume the old woman was a fool?

5. What two things were connected in this fable?

6. In paragraph 2, what does *croaking* mean? What words provide clues to the meaning?

7. Read the last paragraph. Do you think the chief understood the old woman's words? Why or why not?

> **USEFUL LANGUAGE**
> an **antonym** is a word that has the opposite meaning.
>
> *good – bad*
>
> *hard – easy*
>
> *tall – short*

B **Build** your vocabulary.

1. In the reading passage, underline the words from the chart.

2. Use a dictionary or a thesaurus. Write the part of speech. Write an antonym for each word.

Word	Part of speech	Antonym
wise	*adjective*	*foolish*
connected	*adjective*	*disconnected*
peacefully	*adverb*	*noisily*
multiply	*verb*	*decrease*
miserable	*adjective*	*cheerful*
furious	*adjective*	*pleased*
summoned	*verb*	*dismissed*
blamed	*verb*	*absolve*
swamp	*noun*	*desert*

3. Work in a small group. Write sentences with the words in the chart.

   ■ *Answers will vary.* _____

   ■ _____

   ■ _____

C **Talk** with a partner.

1. How can people who disagree solve their conflicts peacefully?

2. What do you do when you have a problem and you can't find a solution?

3. Do you think it is wise to follow other people's advice? Why or why not?

For college and career readiness practice, see pages 160–162.

> 📖 Analyze how the text makes connections among individuals, ideas and events; use a dictionary to identify antonyms

Lesson E Writing

1 Before you write

A **Talk** with a partner. Answer the questions.

1. What is the environmental problem in this photo?

2. Why is it a problem? (causes)

3. How does this problem hurt people and the environment? (effects)

B **Read** the paragraph.

> ### The Causes and Effects of Smog
>
> Smog is a serious environmental problem in my city. One cause is that there are too many cars on the roads and highways. Most of the cars have only one person – the driver. People seem to take a lot of unnecessary trips. They drive to the drugstore instead of walking two blocks. Another cause of smog in my city is that we use too much electricity. Since many homes are not energy-efficient, our city's power plant has to produce more electricity. The burning coal from the power plant produces more air pollution. The smog is thick, so the air is hard to breathe. Consequently, on many days it is unsafe for children and senior citizens to be outside. Smog also kills many trees and plants that produce oxygen and clean the air. If people drove less and used less electricity, I am sure our air quality would improve.

One way to organize a paragraph is to discuss the causes and effects of a problem.

C **Work** with a partner. Complete the graphic organizer with information from the model paragraph.

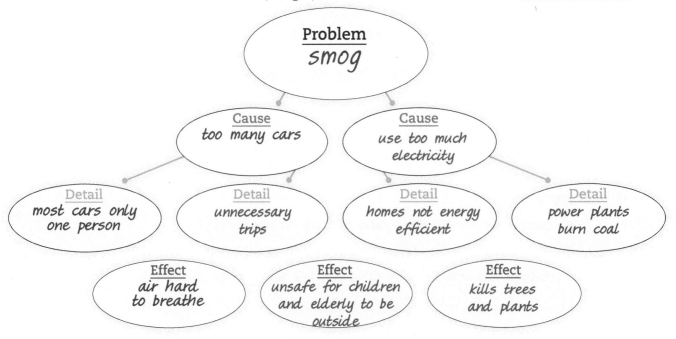

• Prepare Ss for writing a cause and effect paragraph about an environmental problem

WARM-UP AND REVIEW

• Before class. Write today's lesson focus on the board.
Lesson E:
Write a cause and effect paragraph

• Begin class. Books closed. Review cause and effect by asking Ss questions about the fable in Lesson D:

What was the fable "All Things Are Connected" about? (It was about what happens when you don't think carefully about how your actions will affect the environment.)
What was the cause of the chief's problem? (He couldn't sleep because of the sound of the frogs croaking in the middle of the night.)
What advice did the chief receive but decide not to follow? (He didn't listen to the wise old woman, who warned him not to kill all the frogs because in nature, "all things are connected.")
What was the effect of the chief's not listening to the old woman's advice? (The mosquitoes multiplied, and all the people in the village were forced to leave.)

PRESENTATION

• Books open. Direct Ss' attention to Exercise **1A** and read the instructions aloud.

• Ask three Ss to read the questions in Exercise **1A**.

• Ss work with a partner to answer the questions. Encourage partners to list the causes and effects of the environmental problem shown in the picture. Walk around and help as needed.

PRACTICE

• Direct Ss' attention to Exercise **1B** and read the instructions aloud.

• Ss read the paragraph silently. Ask Ss to underline any words with which they are unfamiliar.

• Have Ss tell you the words they underlined, and write them on the board. Go over the meaning of each word.

Teaching Tip

Tell Ss that this paragraph is an example of cause-and-effect writing. Point out the use of the connector *since* to signal a cause of smog. *Consequently* signals one of the effects of smog on people.

Read the tip aloud. Tell Ss that by organizing a paragraph or an essay by causes and effects, the writer makes the information clearer and easier for the reader to follow. Tell Ss that this method of cause-and-effect organization is often used in writing informational paragraphs or essays.

• Focus Ss' attention on Exercise **1C** and read the instructions aloud.

• Model the task. Direct Ss' attention to the second sentence in the graphic organizer that states that one cause of smog is that there are too many cars on the roads and highways. Call on a S to read the first example cause in the graphic organizer: *too many cars.*

• Ss work with a partner to complete the graphic organizer of the model paragraph, filling in the causes and effects of smog.

• Write the graphic organizer on the board.

• Call on individual Ss to fill in the information they discussed with their partners. Make corrections to the graphic organizer on the board as needed.

Expansion activity (whole class)

• Prepare Ss for the writing they will do in the next part of this lesson by having the class brainstorm a list of environmental problems in their city or community.

• Write Ss' responses on the board, or call on a S to come to the board to write Ss' responses.

• Tell Ss that they will be using one of the environmental problems listed on the board to plan, organize, and write their own paragraphs.

LESSON E Writing

PRACTICE

- Books open. Direct Ss' attention to Exercise **1D** and read the instructions aloud.
- Ask Ss to choose an environmental problem in their city or community as the topic of their paragraph.
- Tell Ss that the information they use here in planning will be helpful for them as they write their paragraph.
- Ss work individually to complete the graphic organizer with information for their paragraph. Walk around and help as needed.

APPLICATION

- Focus Ss' attention on Exercise **2** and read the instructions aloud.
- Ss complete the task individually. Walk around and help as needed.

Learner persistence (individual work)

- If you have any Ss who have difficulty writing, sit with them and help them while other Ss are writing. Encourage them to look at their graphic organizer of the model paragraph in Exercise **1C** on page 118. Ss should also use their graphic organizer from Exercise **1D** to help them write.

COMPREHENSION CHECK

- Direct Ss' attention to Exercise **3A**. This exercise asks Ss to develop skills to review and edit their own writing.
- Ss check their own paragraphs against the writing checklist. Walk around and help as needed. If any Ss checked *No* for one or more of the checklist items, ask them to revise and edit their paragraphs to include the missing information.

EVALUATION

- Focus Ss' attention on Exercise **3B** and read the instructions aloud. This exercise enables Ss to work together to peer-correct their writing. Reading aloud enables the writer to review his or her own writing and to understand the need to write clearly for an audience.
- Ss complete the exercise in pairs. Tell Ss to take turns reading their paragraphs to each other. Walk around and help as needed.

- Listen to Ss as they ask their partner a question about his or her paragraph and tell their partner one thing they learned from it.
- Ask several Ss to read their paragraphs aloud. Have other Ss ask questions and mention something they learned from the paragraph.
- Direct Ss' attention to the lesson focus on the board.
- Check off the lesson focus as Ss demonstrate an understanding of what they have learned in the lesson.

Expansion activity (individual work, whole class)

- **Materials needed** An example of a letter to the editor – ideally, one with an environmental theme.
- Ask Ss if they have ever read a letter to the editor in a newspaper or magazine. Ask Ss why they think people write these letters. Elicit an appropriate response, such as: *to complain about a problem, to show people another way to look at a situation, to express their opinion, to try to persuade others to agree with their point of view, to try to persuade others to take a certain course of action.*
- Distribute copies of an example letter to the editor to each S. Ss read the letter independently.
- Review the letter with the class, and call on Ss to read it aloud. Write new vocabulary on the board.
- Call on Ss to explain how the writer defends his or her opinion (through the use of persuasive words and phrases, such as *should, must, I feel, in my opinion*).
- Tell Ss to work individually to write their own letter to the editor about an environmental problem in the community that is different from the one they wrote about in Exercise **2**. Encourage Ss to use the vocabulary, grammar, and connectors learned in this unit. Walk around and help as needed.
- Call on individual Ss to read their letter to the editor to the class.

More Ventures, Unit 9, Lesson E	
Workbook, 15–30 min.	
Multilevel Worksheets, 30–45 min.	www.cambridge.org/ventures/resources/
Collaborative Worksheets, 30–45 min.	

D **Plan** a paragraph about an environmental problem in your city or community. Include the causes and effects of the problem. Use the graphic organizer to make notes on your ideas.

Answers will vary.

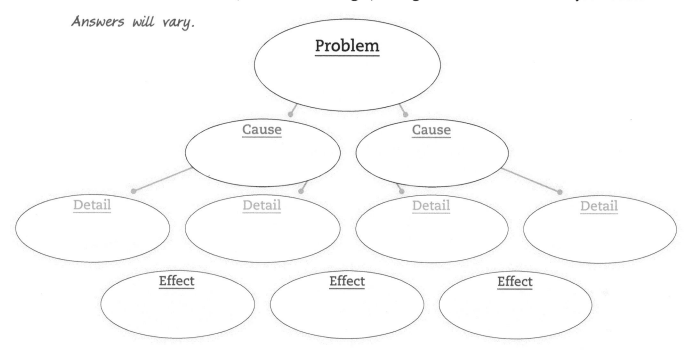

2 Write

Write a paragraph about an environmental problem in your city or community. Identify the problem in your topic sentence. explain the causes and their effects and provide supporting details for each cause. Use the paragraph in exercise 1B and the graphic organizers in exercises 1C and 1D to help you.

Answers will vary.

3 After you write

A **Check** your writing.

	Yes	No
1. My topic sentence identifies an environmental problem.	☐	☐
2. I clearly explained the causes and effects.	☐	☐
3. I provided supporting details for the causes of the environmental problem.	☐	☐

B **Share** your writing with a partner.

1. Take turns. Read your paragraph to a partner.

2. Comment on your partner's paragraph. Ask your partner a question about the paragraph. Tell your partner one thing you learned.

Lesson F Another view

1 Life-skills reading

Save our Planet: Our Choices Matter

150 percent more energy is used by regular lightbulbs than energy-efficient (compact fluorescent) bulbs.	**400** gallons of water are wasted every month when you have a leaky faucet.	**1,000** years is how long plastic bottles take to decompose in landfills.
1,200 pounds of organic garbage are thrown out by the average American in a year.	**95,000** pounds of pollution are produced by driving a car for one year.	**14,000,000** trees are cut down to produce the 10,000,000,000 paper bags that Americans use every year.

A Read the questions. Look at the handout. Fill in the answer.

1. What does the number 95,000 represent?

   (A) pounds of organic garbage thrown out

   (B) pounds of smog from factories

   (C) pounds of pollution from a car in one year

   (D) none of the above

2. According to the handout, why are plastic bottles bad?

   (A) require a lot of energy to make

   (B) take a long time to decompose

   (C) expensive to make

   (D) none of the above

3. In the sentence *400 gallons of water are wasted every month when you have a leaky faucet*, what does *wasted* mean?

   (A) used carefully

   (B) used carelessly

   (C) used wisely

   (D) used on purpose

4. The handout does not discuss _____.

   (A) plastic bottles in landfills

   (B) pollution from cars

   (C) pollution from airplanes

   (D) cutting down trees to make bags

B Solve the problem. Give your opinion.

Joshua rents an apartment. He has a leaky faucet in the bathroom sink. He hates to waste water, and he is worried the leak will get worse. He tried to fix it, but he couldn't stop the leak. He called the landlord, but the landlord hasn't returned his call. What should he do?

Answers will vary.

Teaching objectives
- Introduce reading and understanding a handout about reasons for environmental problems.
- Introduce the difference between and provide practice contrasting present real and present unreal conditionals

WARM-UP AND REVIEW

- Before class. Write today's lesson focus on the board.
  Lesson F:
  Read and understand a chart about reasons to protect the environment Contrast present real and present unreal conditionals
- Begin class. Books closed. Write on the board: *What would happen if people didn't try to protect the environment?* Read the question aloud. Elicit appropriate responses, for example: *The air, land, and water would become more polluted. The air would be so polluted that it would be hard for us to breathe.*
- Say: *Today we will practice reading and understanding a chart called "Save our Planet: Our Choices Matter."*

PRESENTATION

- Books open. Read the title of the chart aloud.
- Call on individual Ss to read each of the six reasons in the chart.
- Explain vocabulary as needed.

PRACTICE

- Direct Ss' attention to Exercise **1A** and read the instructions aloud. This task helps prepare Ss for standardized-type tests they may have to take. Make sure that Ss understand the task. Have Ss individually scan for and fill in the answers.

COMPREHENSION CHECK

- Check answers to Exercise **1A** with the class. Make sure that Ss have followed the instructions and filled in their answers.
- Have Ss read aloud the questions and answers they filled in. Ask: *Is that answer correct?* Make corrections as needed.

APPLICATION

- Direct Ss' attention to Exercise **1B** and read the instructions aloud. Make sure that Ss understand the task. Have Ss individually solve the problem.
- Ss discuss the problem in smaill groups. Walk around and help as needed.
- After Ss discuss the problem, open up the discussion to the entire class. Accept all plausible answers.

Expansion activity (small groups)

- **Materials needed** Poster board and colored markers. (If possible, bring in a collection of magazines that have pictures related to the environment and nature.)
- Provide each group with poster board, markers, and magazines, if available.
- Ss should work in a small group to choose from the chart one of the reasons to protect the environment and make a poster or ad designed to convince people that they should do something related to that point.
- Encourage Ss to use pictures from the magazines or draw their own to make their poster visually appealing.
- Model the task. Write the following on the board:
  It's time to make a change!
  Problem: Due to the lack of recycling, there are too many plastic bottles in our landfills.
  Fact: It takes 450 to 1,000 years for plastic bottles to decompose in landfills.
  What we can do:
  If we saved our bottles and reused them, we wouldn't need to buy new ones.
  If we recycled our plastic bottles, we would create less trash.
  We would help the environment if we used less plastic.
- Tell Ss to work together to write three conditional sentences in their poster about what people can do related to the environmental point they chose. Walk around and help as needed.
- Call on groups to present and explain their poster to the class. Display the posters in the classroom if possible.
- Leave time for a question-and-answer session.

LESSON F Another view

WARM-UP AND REVIEW

- Books closed. Write the structure of present unreal conditional on the board (*If . . . simple past, would / could +* base form of verb). Tell Ss that the habitat of black bears is shrinking in Florida. Ask: *What would prevent the habitat of black bears from shrinking?*
- Ask Ss to respond using *could* or *would*. *If cities stopped expanding, the black bear's habitat would stop shrinking. If Florida made new laws, the black bear's habitat could stop shrinking.* Remind Ss that we use *would* when we are 100 percent certain about something and *could* when we are less sure.

PRESENTATION

Focus on form

- Use the animated grammar presentation in one or more of the following ways:
  - Preview it before class
  - Show in class
  - Encourage Ss to watch outside of class.
- Books open. Direct Ss' attention to the grammar chart in **2A**. Ask a S to read the sentences in the left column. Ask another S to read the two sentences in the right column. Ask Ss to compare the sentences. Elicit the answer *The sentences on the left are in the present tense and the sentences on the right combine past + conditional.*
- Explain we use the present real conditional when something is possible or always true. We use the present unreal conditional when something is not possible or not likely.

PRACTICE

- Direct Ss' attention to the instructions in **2A**. Read the instructions aloud. Ensure Ss understand the activity. Ask two pairs of Ss to read the example sentences aloud.

- Split the class into small groups. Pass out pennies to each S or have Ss use their own pennies. Have Ss ask one another the questions in the square. Walk around and help as needed. Ss should play the game until they have finished asking all the questions.
- Direct Ss' attention to the instructions in **2B**. Read the instructions aloud. Ask two Ss to read the example sentences. Encourage Ss to share information about their classmates.

EVALUATION

- Do a quick review of the unit. Have Ss turn to Lesson A. Ask the class to talk about what they remember about this lesson. Prompt Ss, if necessary, with questions, for example: *What are the conversations about on this page? What vocabulary is in the pictures?* Continue in this manner to review each lesson quickly.

Expansion activity

- Before class. Print, for each student, one copy of the Self-assessment for this unit.
- Have Ss complete the Self-assessment either in class or outside of class.
- Provide feedback to Ss such as through a whole-class discussion, partners comparing their worksheets, or T reviewing each S's worksheet.
- If Ss are ready, administer the unit test on pages T-213–T-215 of this Teacher's Edition. The audio script for the test is on page T-224.

More Ventures, Unit 9, Lesson F	
Workbook, 15–30 min.	
Multilevel Worksheets, 30–45 min.	www.cambridge.org/ventures/resources/
Collaborative Worksheets, 30–45 min.	
Self-assessment, 10 min.	
CASAS Test Prep Worksheet, 5–10 min.	

2 **Grammar connections:** present real conditional vs. present unreal conditional

Use present real conditional when something is possible or always true.
Use present unreal conditional when something is not possible or not likely.

PRESENT REAL	PRESENT UNREAL
If I **have** time, I **walk** to school.	**If** I **found** a large bag of money, I **would give** it to charity.
If you **heat** water to 212° F, it **boils**.	**If** I **were** a bird, I'**d fly** all over the world.

👁 Watch

A **Work** in a small group. Play the game. Write your name on a small piece of paper. Flip a coin to move your paper. Then tell your group about the topic in the square. Use the present real or present unreal conditional to finish the sentence. Take turns.

> If I'm late to English class, I come in quietly.

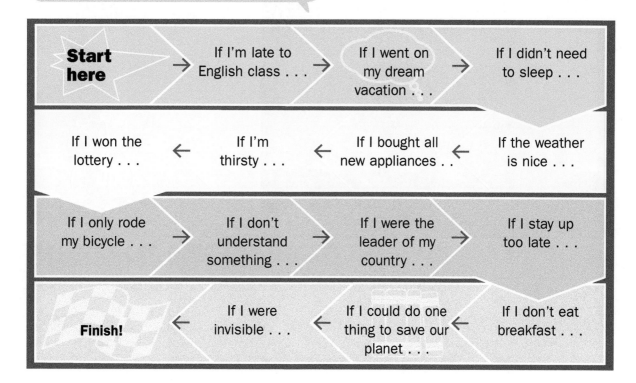

Start here → If I'm late to English class . . . → If I went on my dream vacation . . . → If I didn't need to sleep . . .

If I won the lottery . . . ← If I'm thirsty . . . ← If I bought all new appliances . . ← If the weather is nice . . .

If I only rode my bicycle . . . → If I don't understand something . . . → If I were the leader of my country . . . → If I stay up too late . . .

Finish! ← If I were invisible . . . ← If I could do one thing to save our planet . . . ← If I don't eat breakfast . . .

B **Share** information about your classmates.

> If Pedro is late to English class, he comes in quietly.

> If Sally went on her dream vacation, it would be in a warm and sunny place.

📖 Scan a lecture handout to identify information about key environmental problems; contrast present real and present unreal conditionals

UNIT 10 FREE TIME

Lesson A Listening

1 **Before you listen**

A What do you see?

B What is happening?

UNIT 10

Teaching objectives
- Introduce students to the topic
- Find out what students know about the topic
- Preview the unit by talking about the pictures
- Provide practice of key vocabulary
- Provide practice that develops listening skills

WARM-UP AND REVIEW

- Before class. Write today's lesson focus on the board.

  Lesson A:
  Ask about and compare wedding customs

- Begin class. Books closed. Direct Ss' attention to the lesson focus. Point to *wedding customs*. Ask Ss: *What are some examples of wedding customs in the United States?* List Ss' responses on the board, for example: *The bride wears a white gown. The groom wears a tuxedo. The couple cuts the wedding cake. Usually, the couple hosts a dinner the night before the wedding.*

Culture Tip

Tell Ss that another wedding custom in the United States, although less popular today, is the bride's wearing of "something old, something new, something borrowed, something blue." To fulfill this tradition, the bride may borrow an older family member's wedding dress and wear a new blue garter or ribbon.

PRESENTATION

- Books open. Set the scene. Direct Ss' attention to the third picture on page 122. Ask the question from Exercise **1A**: *What do you see?* Elicit and write on the board as much vocabulary about the picture as possible: *bride and groom, traditional wedding dress*, etc. Explain any unfamiliar words. Continue eliciting words to describe the remaining pictures.

- Tell Ss that it used to be traditional to throw rice at a bride and groom, in the United States. However, these days many couples choose not to do so because birds can get sick from eating rice left on the ground. Today, it is not unusual for guests to throw birdseed (which is safe for birds to eat) or flower petals at the bride and groom after the wedding ceremony.

- Ask individual Ss to look at the pictures and talk about the similarities (e.g., pictures show wedding customs) and differences (e.g., in one picture, the wedding dress is red, and in the another the wedding dress is white.).

- Direct Ss' attention to the question in Exercise **1B**: *What is happening?* Hold up the Student's Book. Point to the first picture. Ask: *What are the bride and groom doing here?* (They're getting married.)

- Point to the second picture. Ask: *What is in the envelope?* (money)

- Point to the third picture. Ask: *What are the bride and groom doing here?* (They're leaving the ceremony.)

- Point to the fourth picture. Ask: *What is the table for?* (gifts.)

PRACTICE

- Invite Ss to work with a partner to create a story from one of the pictures on page 122. One S writes the story as pairs work together.

- Call on several pairs to share their story with the class.

Teaching Tip

Encourage Ss to be creative. At this point, there is no single correct story.

Expansion activity (small groups)

- Write the following questions on the board: *What is your idea of the perfect wedding? What is the ceremony like? What is the reception like? Where would you go on your honeymoon?*

- Ask Ss if they understand the meaning of the word *honeymoon*. Explain that it is a vacation that a newly married couple (newlyweds) takes after the wedding.

- Tell Ss that even if they are already married, they can imagine a different wedding from the one they had. Encourage Ss to use their imagination to come up with an idea for their "dream wedding." Tell them that they have unlimited money to spend.

- Ss work in small groups to discuss their dream wedding.

- Call on each group to share information from their group discussion.

- If any Ss in the class are married, ask them what they liked most about their own wedding. Ss may wish to bring their wedding album to class to share pictures with their group.

LESSON A Listening

PRESENTATION

- Books open. Direct Ss' attention to Exercise **2A**. Have Ss listen for the main idea. Read the instructions aloud.
- ▶ **CD2, Track 28** Play or read the audio (see audio script, pages T-183–T-184).
- Ask Ss if they understand everything in the listening exercise. Write any unfamiliar words on the board and help Ss understand the meaning of each.
- Elicit answers to the questions, for example: *The speakers are Cathy and Thanh. They're talking about wedding customs. Cathy says she doesn't know what to get Bao and An for their wedding gift. Thanh tells her about Vietnamese wedding customs. Thanh explains that according to Vietnamese customs, the ceremony is usually a private one just for the family, but the reception is a huge party with a lot of people and food.*
- Focus Ss' attention on Exercise **2B** and read the instructions aloud. Have Ss listen and complete the chart based on the information they hear.
- ▶ **CD2, Track 28** Tell Ss to listen for details about Cathy's conversation with Thanh. Model the task. Play or read the audio again. Pause the audio after Cathy says: *They make a list of what they want, and then people can go to the store or the store's Web site and buy something on the couple's list.*
- Model the first answer in the chart. Draw the chart on the board as it appears on page 123. Point to the heading that says *American customs*. Call on a S to read the sample answer (*register in a store*). Write it on the board. Play or read the rest of the audio. Ss listen and complete the chart.
- ▶ **CD2, Track 28** Play or read the audio again. Ss listen and check their answers. Repeat the audio as needed.
- Ask Ss to come to the board to write the answers in the chart. Make corrections on the board as needed.

Learner persistence *(individual work)*
- ▶ **CD2, Track 28** Ss can listen to the audio for Exercise **2A** and **2B** at home for reinforcement and review. They can also listen to the audio for self-directed learning when class attendance is not possible.

PRACTICE

- Direct Ss' attention to Exercise **3A** and read the instructions aloud. Tell Ss that the story in this exercise is a summary of what happened in the pictures on the previous page.
- Focus Ss' attention to the words in the word bank. Say each word and ask Ss to repeat. Correct pronunciation as needed. Make sure that Ss understand the meaning of each word.
- Model the task. Ask a S to read aloud the first two sentences in the story, including the example answer.
- Ss complete the exercise individually. Help as needed.

COMPREHENSION CHECK

- ▶ **CD2, Track 29** Play or read the audio (see audio script, page T-184). Ss listen and check their answers. Repeat the audio as needed.
- Write the numbers *1–10* on the board. Ask Ss to come to the board to write only the answers. Have other Ss read the sentences, filling in each blank with the answer on the board. Make corrections as needed.

Learner persistence *(individual work)*
- ▶ **CD2, Track 29** Ss can listen to the audio for Exercise **3A** at home for reinforcement and review. They can also listen to the audio for self-directed learning when class attendance is not possible.

APPLICATION

- Focus Ss' attention on Exercise **3B** and read the instructions aloud.
- Call on two Ss to read the questions.
- Ss complete the exercise in small groups. Walk around and help as needed.
- Ask Ss to share information they learned with the class.

Expansion activity *(individual work)*
- Have Ss choose a wedding custom from their culture to write about in a paragraph. Tell Ss that their paragraph should contain a topic sentence that introduces the main idea of the paragraph.
- Ss in pairs. Have Ss read their paragraph to a partner.
- You may also choose to assign the writing task as homework.

EVALUATION

- Direct Ss' attention to the lesson focus on the board. Ask individual Ss to look at the pictures on page 122 and make sentences using the words in Exercise **3**.
- Check off the lesson focus as Ss demonstrate an understanding of what they have learned in the lesson.

More Ventures, Unit 10, Lesson A	
Workbook, 15–30 min.	
Multilevel Worksheets, 30–45 min.	www.cambridge.org/ventures/resources/
Collaborative Worksheets, 30–45 min.	
Student Arcade, time varies	www.cambridge.org/venturesarcade/

UNIT GOALS
Compare celebration customs   **Read** a recipe
Write about a favorite holiday

2 Listen

◀)) CD2, Track 28

A **Listen** and answer the questions.

1. Who are the speakers?   2. What are they talking about?

B **Listen again.** Complete the chart.

◀)) CD2, Track 28

	American customs	Vietnamese customs
1. gifts	*register in a store*	*cash in an envelope*
2. use of rice	*throw rice at bride and groom*	*eat red sticky rice*
3. dress color	*white*	*red*

3 After you listen

A **Read.** Complete the story.

acquaintances	courses	fortune	reception	symbolizes
bride	customs	looking forward	registered	tradition

Cathy and Thanh are talking about wedding ___*customs*___ . Cathy is invited

to a Vietnamese wedding, and she is surprised that the bride and groom are not

___*registered*___ for gifts at any stores. In contrast, Thanh is surprised by the

American ___*tradition*___ of throwing rice at the bride and groom. Next, they

talk about clothes. Thanh says a Vietnamese ___*bride*___ wears a red dress

because the color red ___*symbolizes*___ good ___*fortune*___ . Then Cathy

asks why she was invited only to the wedding ___*reception*___ , not the ceremony.

Thanh explains that traditionally the ceremony is only for the family. The couple's friends

and ___*acquaintances*___ are invited to the evening reception. In fact, Thanh says the

evening party will include seven or eight ___*courses*___ of food. Cathy says she is

___*looking forward*___ to the wedding.

Listen and check your answers.

◀)) CD2, Track 28

B **Discuss.** Talk with your classmates. Share some special wedding customs from your culture.

Lesson B Conditionals

1 Grammar focus: future real and future unreal

Use the future real conditional to talk about a result that will likely happen if a certain condition is true. Use the future unreal conditional to talk about a future result that is unlikely to happen because the condition is not true or possible at this time.

FUTURE REAL (POSSIBLE)	FUTURE UNREAL (NOT POSSIBLE)
If I **go** to the wedding, I **will wear** my new shoes.	If I **went** to the wedding, I **would wear** my new shoes. (But I'm not going.)
If Jane **isn't working** on Saturday, she **will go** to the wedding.	If Jane **weren't working** on Saturday, she **would go** to the wedding. (But Jane will be working on Saturday.)

👁 Watch

USEFUL LANGUAGE
The future unreal conditional form of the verb *be* is *were*.

2 Practice

A Write. Complete the sentences. Use the future real or future unreal conditional.

1. The Patels are from India, but they live in the United States now. They are planning a
   wedding for their daughter, Parveen. If they _____*lived*_____ in India, the groom's family
   _____*would pay*_____ for the wedding.
   (live)
   (pay)

2. The wedding will be in the United States. If the Patels _____*had*_____ the wedding in
   India, the wedding celebration _____*would last*_____ three days. Here it will last for one day.
   (have)
   (last)

3. The Patels don't have a lot of money. If they _____*were*_____ rich, they
   _____*would invite*_____ 300 people; instead, they will invite about 150.
   (be)
   (invite)

4. The Patels are planning to have music for the reception. If a band _____*doesn't*_____ too
   much, they _____*will have*_____ live music.
   (not / charge)
   (have)

5. It's possible that the weather will be nice on the day of the wedding. If the weather
   _____*is*_____ nice, they _____*will have*_____ the ceremony outside.
   (be)
   (have)

6 It is possible Parveen and her husband will get some vacation time from work. If Parveen
   and her husband _____*get*_____ enough time off from work, they _____*will take*_____
   (get)
   (take)
   a trip to Hawaii for their honeymoon.

7. They don't have a lot of time off from work. If they _____*had*_____ more time off, they
   _____*would go*_____ to India for their honeymoon.
   (have)
   (go)

8. Parveen and her new husband will live in their own apartment. If they
   _____*were*_____ in India, they _____*would live*_____ with the groom's parents.
   (be)
   (live)

Listen and check your answers.

🔊 CD2, Track 30

124 UNIT 10

WARM-UP AND REVIEW

• Before class: Write the lesson focus on the board.

Lesson B:
Future real and future unreal

• Begin class. Books closed. Review Lesson A vocabulary. Direct Ss' attention to the pictures on page 122. Ask Ss to give examples of American and Vietnamese wedding customs, for example: *People give cash at Vietnamese weddings. An American custom is to register for gifts before the wedding.*

PRESENTATION

Focus on meaning / personalize

• Books closed. Direct Ss' attention to the lesson focus on the board. Read it aloud.

• Ask a S: *Are you going to a Vietnamese wedding next weekend?* Find a S that says no, then ask: *Is there any possibility you will go to a Vietnamese wedding next weekend?* (No.) *If you went to a Vietnamese wedding next weekend, what kind of gift would you take?* Elicit the answer *I would take cash.* Write the full sentence on the board: *If I went to a Vietnamese wedding, I would take cash as a gift.*

• Say: *Tu Nguyen is Vietnamese. He has a lot of Vietnamese friends who are planning to get married soon. Is there a chance that Tu will go to a Vietnamese wedding next weekend?* (Yes.) Write the following sentence under the one on the board: *If Tu goes to a Vietnamese wedding, he will take cash as a gift.* Underline *went / would* and *goes / will* in the two sentences.

• Ask: *What do you think is the difference in meaning between these two sentences?* Point to the first sentence. Say: *This sentence has an unreal condition. There is no chance he / she is going to a Vietnamese wedding next weekend.* Point to the second sentence. Say: *This sentence has a real condition. There is a chance he is going to a Vietnamese wedding next weekend.*

Focus on form

• Use the animated grammar presentation in one or more of the following ways:
  • Preview it before class
  • Show in class
  • Encourage Ss to watch outside of class.

• Books open. Direct Ss' attention to the two charts in Exercise **1**. Ask a S to read the first examples in each chart. Ask Ss to repeat. Ask in which example the person might go to the wedding (first), and in which example the person will definitely not be going to the wedding (second). Point out that the words in parentheses under Unreal conditional are there to emphasize that the situations are not possible. However, the information in parentheses isn't usually stated because it is understood.

• Write on the board: *If* + subject + present tense, subject + future tense = possible

If + subject + past tense, subject + *would* + simple form of verb = not possible

• Explain that *were* is used for all persons (*I, he, she, we, you, they*) with the unreal conditional.

PRACTICE

• Focus Ss' attention on Exercise **2A** and read the instructions aloud.

• Have a S read number 1 aloud, including the two example answers. Make sure that Ss understand the exercise.

• Ss complete the exercise individually. Walk around and help as needed.

COMPREHENSION CHECK

• Read aloud the second part of the instructions for Exercise **2A**.

▶ *CD2, Track 30* Play or read the audio (see audio script, page T-184). Ss listen and check their answers. Repeat the audio as needed.

• Write the numbers *1–8* on the board. Ask several Ss to come to the board to write the complete sentences. Work with the class to make corrections as needed.

Expansion activity (student pairs)

• Ask Ss: *What would you do if you won the lottery?* Then say: *Name five activities that you couldn't do before that you would now be able to do. Share your ideas with a partner.*

• Model the activity. Write the following on the board and ask a S to read it aloud: *If I won the lottery, I would take a long trip to Egypt.*

• Ss discuss the question with a partner. Walk around and help as needed.

• Invite pairs to share their "wish list" of activities with the class.

LESSON B Conditionals

PRACTICE

- Books open. Direct Ss' attention to Exercise **2B** and read the instructions aloud.

- Direct Ss' attention to the chart of future real and future unreal plans for New Year's Eve. Call on two Ss to read aloud Victor's real and imaginary plans.

- Call on two Ss to read the sample dialog aloud.

- Ss use the real and unreal situations from the chart to complete the exercise with a partner. Walk around and help as needed.

- Direct Ss' attention to the second part of Exercise **2B** and read the instructions aloud.

- Ask a S to read aloud the example sentences.

- Ss work individually to complete the exercise. Walk around and help as needed.

- Ask individual Ss to come to the board to write their sentences. Work with the class to make corrections on the board as needed.

APPLICATION

- Direct Ss' attention to Exercise **3A** and read the instructions aloud. Explain any unfamiliar vocabulary.

- Call on a S to read the three headings and the words under *Holiday or event*.

- Model the task. Ask two Ss to read the examples in the chart.

- Ss talk with a partner and then individually complete the chart. Tell Ss that in the chart where it says *your idea*, they should add their own choices or reasons for celebration. Tell Ss they could be holidays from their own culture or country or important occasions (job promotion, engagement, etc.). Walk around and help as needed.

- Direct Ss' attention to Exercise **3B** and read the instructions aloud.

- Call on two Ss to read aloud the example dialog about real and unreal plans.

- Ss in small groups. Ss ask and answer questions about each other's plans.

- Read aloud the instructions in Exercise **3C**.

- Invite Ss to take turns sharing with the class information they learned about their partner. Have Ss use the future real conditional and the unreal conditional in their discussions.

Expansion activity *(individual work)*

- Tell Ss to write about the plans they discussed in Exercise **3B**. They should write one paragraph either about a real plan or an unreal plan for New Year's Eve.

- Walk around and help as needed.

- Ss exchange paragraphs with a partner. Ss discuss the paragraphs they wrote.

- Call on Ss to share their partner's plans with the class.

EVALUATION

- Books closed. Direct Ss' attention to the lesson focus on the board.

- Write the following on the board:
  1. *If I go to the party, I _____.*
  2. *If he doesn't go to his friend's house on Friday night, he _____.*
  3. *If I went to the movies, I _____.*
  4. *If he didn't go to a restaurant for dinner, he _____.*
  5. *If she weren't working that evening, she _____.*
  6. *If I were rich, I _____.*

- Ask Ss to write the numbers *1–6* in their notebooks and to complete the sentences using the future real conditional or the unreal conditional.

- Ss work individually to complete the sentences. Walk around and help as needed.

- Ask Ss which sentences express the future real conditional (the first two) and which express the unreal conditional (the last four). Ask Ss how they could tell (1 and 2 begin in the present tense; 3–6 begin in the past tense).

- Call on individual Ss to write their sentences on the board and read them aloud. Make corrections on the board as needed.

- Check off the lesson focus as Ss demonstrate an understanding of what they have learned in the lesson.

More Ventures, Unit 10, Lesson B	
Workbook, 15–30 min.	
Multilevel Worksheets, 30–45 min. Collaborative Worksheets, 30–45 min.	www.cambridge.org/ventures/resources/
Student Arcade, time varies	www.cambridge.org/venturesarcade/

B Talk with a partner. Take turns making sentences about Victor's real and unreal plans for New Year's Eve.

A If Victor stays home on New Year's Eve, he will have a party with his friends.

B But if he traveled to Florida, he would spend New Year's Eve near the beach.

Future real (possible)	Future unreal (not possible)
stay home / have a party with his friends	travel to Florida / spend New Year's Eve near the beach
have a party at his house / cook for his friends	have a lot of money / take his friends to a nice restaurant in Florida
go to his parents' house / have a quiet celebration with family	be in Mexico / eat 12 grapes at midnight
travel to New York / celebrate New Year's Eve in Times Square	travel to Brazil / watch fireworks on the beach at midnight
go to a club / dance all night	be in France / have a special dinner

Write sentences about Victor's real and unreal plans.

If Victor stays home on New Year's Eve, he will have a party with his friends. If he traveled to Florida, he would spend New Year's Eve near the beach.

Answers will vary.

3 Communicate

A Work with a partner. Complete the chart with your real and unreal plans for some future holidays or special events. *Answers will vary.*

Holiday or event	Real	Unreal
New Year's Eve	*stay home*	*be in my native country*
birthday		
(your idea)		
(your idea)		

B Work in a small group. Share your charts. Ask and answer questions about each other's plans.

A If you stay home on New Year's Eve, how will you celebrate?

B If I stay home, i'll invite my friends to come over and celebrate with me.

A If you were in your native country on New Year's Eve, how would you celebrate?

B If I were in my native country, I would watch fireworks at midnight.

B Share information about your classmates.

Lesson C *Hope* and *wish*

1 Grammar focus: possible and impossible

Use *hope* to talk about something you want that is possible in the present or future. Use *wish* to talk about situations that are not possible in the present or future.

Possible situations	Situations that are not possible
Samira **hopes** her cousin **will come** to her wedding.	Samira **wishes** her cousin **would come** to her wedding.
Samira **hopes** her cousin **comes** to her wedding.	Samira **wishes** she had more money.
Nick and Mia **hope** they **can go** to the party.	Nick and Mia **wish** they **could go** to the party.

👁 Watch

2 Practice

A Write. Complete the sentences. Use *hope* or *wish* and the correct form of the verb or modal.

1. Paul's high school graduation is tomorrow. His friend Luis has to work. Luis
   _____*wishes*_____ he ____*could go*____ to Paul's graduation.
   (can go)

2. Paul's father has asked for the day off so that he can attend his son's graduation. He
   _____*hopes*_____ he _____*can get*_____ the day off.
   (get)

3. Paul's grandfather has been sick. He's not sure if he will attend the graduation. Paul
   _____*hopes*_____ his grandfather _____*will attend*_____ the ceremony.
   (will attend)

4. Paul's sister is out of the country, so she cannot come to the ceremony. Paul
   _____*hopes*_____ his sister _____*will be*_____ here to attend his graduation.
   (be)

5. The graduation ceremony will be outside. Paul _____*hopes*_____ it _____*will not rain*_____.
   (will not / rain)

6 Paul's parents would like to buy him a new car, but they can't afford it. They
   _____*wish*_____ they _____*could buy*_____ him a new car.
   (can buy)

7. Paul wasn't accepted to the university, so he will go to a community college. Paul
   _____*wishes*_____ he _____*could go*_____ to the university.
   (can go)

8. Paul has applied for financial aid. Paul _____*hopes*_____ he _____*can get*_____ financial
   (get)
   aid to help pay for his books.

9. It's possible that Paul will be able to transfer to the university in two years.
   He _____*hopes*_____ he _____*can transfer*_____ in two years.
   (can transfer)

   Listen and check your answers.

🔊 CD2, Track 31

WARM-UP AND REVIEW

- Before class: Write the lesson focus on the board.

  Lesson C:
  "hope" and "wish"

- Begin class. Books closed. Review the future real conditional and unreal conditional.

- Write the following two sentences on the board: 1. *If I have time, I will take a walk in the park next weekend.* 2. *If I had time, I would take a walk in the park next weekend.*

  Ask: *Which sentence means it might happen?* (1) *Which sentence means it can't happen?* (2)

PRESENTATION

Focus on meaning / personalize

- Books closed. Direct Ss' attention to the lesson focus on the board. Read it aloud.

- Say: *I hope I can go to the movies next weekend, but I may have too much work. What do you hope you can do next weekend?* Elicit and write answers on the board, for example: *Maria hopes to spend time with her sister.*

- Say: *I wish I could buy a house, but houses are too expensive.* Ask: *What do you wish you could do?* Elicit and write answers on the board.

- Write these two sentences on the board: 1. *I hope I have time to walk in the park this evening.* 2. *I wish I had time to walk in the park this evening.* Say: *Both of these sentences are about the future. One is possible, and one is not possible. Which one is possible?* (1) *Which one is not possible?* (2)

- Elicit or explain that we use *hope* to talk about possible situations, and we use *wish* to talk about situations that are not possible.

Focus on form

- Use the animated grammar presentation in one or more of the following ways:
  - Preview it before class
  - Show in class
  - Encourage Ss to watch outside of class.

- Books open. Direct Ss' attention to the two charts in Exercise **1**. Read each heading and the two sentences under each heading. Ask Ss to repeat.

- Ask: *In the first example, will Samira's cousin come to her wedding?* (Yes, it is possible.) *In the second example, can Samira's cousin come to the wedding?* (No, it is not possible.)

- Write these two sentences on the board and underline the verbs: 1. *Nick hopes he can go to the party.* 2. *Nick wishes he could go to the party.*

- Point to the verbs *hopes* and *wishes*. Ask: *What is the verb tense?* (present.) Point to *can*. Ask: *What is the verb tense of can?* (present.) Point to *could*. Ask: *What is the verb tense here?* (past.) *In the possible situations, what verb tenses are used?* (present or future.) *In the not possible situations, what verb tenses are used?* (present tense of *wish* with *could* or *would*.)

- Ask: *Do you have to use will in sentences with with* hope? (No.) *Can you omit the helping verb –* would, could *– with* wish? (No.)

PRACTICE

- Direct Ss' attention to Exercise **2A** and read the instructions aloud.

- Ask a S to read aloud the sentences in number 1, including the example answers.

- Ss complete the exercise individually. Walk around and help as needed.

COMPREHENSION CHECK

- Read aloud the second part of the instructions for Exercise **2A**.

- ▶ **CD2, Track 31** Play or read the audio (see audio script, page T-184). Ss listen and check their answers.

- Write the numbers *1–7* on the board. Ask several Ss to come to the board to write their answers. Make corrections on the board as needed.

Expansion activity *(small groups)*

- Write *wish* and *hope* on the board.

- Have small groups of Ss sit in a circle and take turns saying something they want to do. The first S makes a statement, and the second S decides whether it is a hope or a wish. The second S makes a sentence about the first S and then says a new sentence beginning with I want for the next S in the circle.

- Model the activity. Write the following on the board:

  S1: *I want to visit Rome some day.*

  S2: *(Maria) hopes to visit Rome someday. I want to live on the moon for a month.*

  S3: *(Ben) wishes he could live on the moon for a month. I want to have a conversation with the president.*

- Encourage Ss to have fun with this activity. Walk around and help as needed.

LESSON C *Hope* and *wish*

PRACTICE

- Direct Ss' attention to Exercise **2B** and read the instructions aloud.
- Call on individual Ss to read each of the statements to the class.
- Ask Ss to read the sample sentences.
- Ss complete the exercise with a partner. Walk around and help as needed.
- Read aloud the instructions for the second part of Exercise **2B**. Call on a S to read the example sentence.
- Ss complete the exercise individually. Walk around and help as needed.
- Ask several Ss to write their sentences on the board.
- Call on other Ss to read each of the sentences. Work with the class to make corrections on the board as needed.

APPLICATION

- Direct Ss' attention to Exercise **3A** and read the instructions aloud.
- Model the exercise. Ask a S to read the example answer.
- Ss work individually to complete the exercise. Walk around and help as needed.
- Direct Ss' attention to Exercise **3B** and read the instructions aloud.
- Call on three Ss to read the example conversation to the class.

Useful Language

Read the tip box aloud. Call on two Ss to read the example sentences. Ask Ss if they can think of other expressions using *hope* that are used to end conversations. Elicit appropriate responses, such as: *I hope to see you soon. I hope to talk to you soon.*

- Ss work in a small group to complete the exercise. Walk around and help as needed.
- Read the instructions aloud for Exercise **3C**. Model the task. Say: *I learned that Juan wishes he could visit his parents in Mexico on his birthday.*

- Continue the exercise by asking Ss to share information they learned about one another with the class.

Expansion activity *(individual work)*

- Write the following on the board: *I wish I could _____.*
- Tell Ss that they should complete this sentence and then use it as the topic sentence for a written paragraph. Instruct Ss to use conditional sentences and sentences with *hope* or *wish*.
- Model the activity. Write this example on the board:

  I wish I could fly! If I were able to fly, I would spend a lot of my time traveling. I would visit my family in Brazil. Then I would travel to Argentina to eat a delicious steak. After that, I would fly to . . .

- Ss work on their paragraphs individually. After they've finished, ask Ss to share their paragraph with a partner.
- After Ss have had time to share their writing with a partner, call on several Ss to read their paragraph to the class.

EVALUATION

- Direct Ss' attention to the lesson focus on the board.
- Encourage Ss to look at the photo on page 126 and make sentences about the photo using *hope* and *wish*. Elicit appropriate responses, such as: *Paul wishes he could go to the university this fall. Paul hopes he can transfer to the university in the future.*
- Check off the lesson focus as Ss demonstrate an understanding of what they have learned in the lesson.

More Ventures, Unit 10, Lesson C	
Workbook, 15–30 min.	
Multilevel Worksheets, 30–45 min. **Collaborative Worksheets,** 30–45 min.	www.cambridge.org/venures/ resources/
Student Arcade, time varies	www.cambridge.org/ venuresarcade/

B **Talk** with a partner. Read the situations. Make statements with *hope* or *wish*.

Ryan wants to get a new cell phone soon.

> Ryan hopes he can get a new cell phone soon.

Soraya can't go home for Thanksgiving.

> Soraya wishes she could go home for Thanksgiving.

1. Ryan wants to get a new cell phone soon.
2. Soraya can't go home for Thanksgiving because she has to work.
3. Marla wants to have a big graduation party, but her apartment is too small.
4. Avi is trying to get a plane reservation so he can attend his cousin's wedding in Las Vegas.
5. Karl plans to ask Marta to marry him next weekend. He doesn't know if she will say yes.
6. Maria wants to go to Spain, but she can't afford it.
7. Anton and Ilsa are expecting a baby. They want the baby to be healthy.
8. Jose's wife is in Mexico. He has applied for her to immigrate to the United States. He wants her to come soon.
9. Farid's brother and sister are living in Iran. They cannot come to the United States now. Farid misses them.

Write a sentence for each situation.

Ryan hopes he can get a new cell phone soon.
Answers will vary.

3 Communicate

A **Write** three holidays or celebrations that you observe. Think about something you wish you could change about each one.

    Mother's Day : *I wish I could have the day off to be with my children.*

1. _____ : _____

2. _____ : _____

3. _____ : _____

B **Work** in a small group. Talk about your wishes. Listen to your classmates' hopes for you.

  A I don't have Mother's Day off. I wish I could have the day off to be with my children.

  B I hope you get the day off next year.

  A I hope your children will do something special for you.

> **USEFUL LANGUAGE**
> Expressing hope is a common way of ending a conversation.
> *I hope you feel better soon.*
> *I hope you have a good time.*

C **Share** information about your classmates.

Lesson D Reading

1 Before you read

Talk with your classmates. Answer the questions.

1. How are birthdays usually celebrated in your culture?

2. Are some birthdays more special than others? Which ones?

> Punctuation can be a clue to meaning. For example, parentheses, commas, and dashes are all used to mark definitions, examples, or explanations. Find two examples in the reading where dashes or commas help define key words.

2 Read

Read the blog. Listen and read again.

www.blogaddress.com

◄)) CD2, Track 32

Special Birthdays Around the World

In most cultures, there are certain birthdays that are especially important in a young person's life. If you were an American teenager, for example, you would eagerly look forward to your 16th birthday because in most states that is the age to get a driver's license. Other cultures also have birthdays with special meanings:

Mexico   For Mexican girls, the 15th birthday – the "Quinceañera" – symbolizes a girl's transition into adulthood. To celebrate, the girl's family throws a huge party. The girl wears a ball gown similar to a wedding dress. The girl performs a waltz, a formal dance, with her father. A similar custom is celebrated in Brazil.

China   On a child's first birthday, parents place their baby in the center of a group of objects, such as a shiny coin, a book, and a doll. Then they watch to see which object the baby picks up first. Most parents hope their child will pick up the coin because, according to tradition, it means the child will be rich.

A girl's Quincaeñera

Nigeria   The 1st, 5th, 10th, and 15th birthdays are considered extremely important. Parties are held with up to 100 people. The guests enjoy a feast of a roasted cow or goat.

Saudi Arabia   In some countries, such as Saudi Arabia, people don't observe birthdays at all because of spiritual beliefs. According to Muslim traditions, the only celebrations allowed are Eid al Fitr, a feast that signifies the end of Ramadan, and Eid al Adha, which celebrates the end of the annual pilgrimage to Mecca.

Israel   A boy's 13th and a girl's 12th birthdays are serious as well as happy occasions. On these birthdays, children become responsible for their own religious and moral behavior.

Adult birthdays also have special significance in many cultures. In the United States, for example, birthdays ending in "0" – 30, 40, 50, etc. – are especially meaningful.

Teaching objectives
- Introduce a magazine article about special birthdays around the world
- Provide practice recognizing punctuation that signals definitions
- Provide practice finding multiple meanings of words

WARM-UP AND REVIEW

- Before class. Write today's lesson focus on the board.

  Lesson D:
  Read and understand "Special Birthdays Around the World"
  Recognize punctuation that signals definitions
  Learn and use words with more than one meaning

- Begin class. Books closed. Write *birthday celebrations* on the board. Ask Ss: *What do you think of when you think about birthday celebrations?* Elicit appropriate responses, such as: *candles, birthday cake, cards, gifts, balloons, streamers, party.* Write Ss' responses on the board.

- Direct Ss' attention to the title on the board: "Special Birthdays Around the World." Ask Ss to predict what they think this reading is about. Elicit appropriate responses, such as: *I think it's about different birthday celebrations in different cultures.* Write some of the Ss' predictions on the board.

PRESENTATION

- Books open. Direct Ss' attention to Exercise **1** and read the instructions aloud.

- Have Ss focus on the questions, and ask two Ss to read them to the class.

- Ss in small groups. Ss discuss their answers to the questions. Walk around and help as needed.

- Call on individual Ss to share their answers with the class.

PRACTICE

- Read the instructions aloud for Exercise **2**. Ask Ss to read the magazine article silently before listening to the audio.

- ▶ **CD2, Track 32** Play or read the audio and ask Ss to follow along (see audio script, page T-184). Repeat the audio as needed.

- While Ss are listening and reading the magazine article, ask them to underline any words they don't know. When the audio is finished, have Ss write the new vocabulary words on the board.

- Point to each new vocabulary word on the board. Say it aloud and have Ss repeat. Give a brief explanation of each word, or ask Ss who know the word to explain it. If Ss prefer to look up the new words in their dictionaries, allow them to do so.

Learner persistence (individual work)
▶ **CD2, Track 32** Ss can listen to the audio for Exercise **2** at home for reinforcement and review. They can also listen to the audio for self-directed learning when class attendance is not possible.

Expansion activity (whole group, small groups)
- Tell Ss that they're going to develop a "birthday questionnaire" with the class.

- Write some example questions on the board, such as: *What was your favorite birthday celebration? How do you choose birthday gifts for your friends and family members?*

- Ask the class to brainstorm a list of approximately 12 to 15 birthday-related questions, and write them on the board. Have the class choose ten of the questions for the class questionnaire.

- Ss in small groups. Ss discuss their answers to the questions. Have one S take notes. Walk around and help as needed.

- Once all the groups have finished answering the questions, encourage Ss to share their results with the class.

- Ask Ss: *Was there anything you learned about your classmates that surprised you? Explain. What did the majority of Ss say was their favorite way to spend their birthday?*

- You can follow up this activity by having a class birthday celebration. Choose a day to celebrate everyone's birthday at once, and decide as a class how you will celebrate.

COMPREHENSION CHECK

- Books open. Direct Ss' attention to Exercise **3A** and read the instructions aloud.

> Read the tip box aloud. Write *punctuation* on the board. Ask Ss to refer to the reading on page 128 to find examples of the different punctuation marks mentioned in the tip and circle them. Call on Ss to share their findings. For each set of dashes and parentheses, ask Ss if the punctuation mark is being used to signal definitions, examples, or explanations.

- Call on Ss to read the questions, one at a time.
- Ss complete the exercise individually. Instruct Ss to write their answers on a separate piece of paper. Ss should answer in complete sentences. Walk around and help as needed.
- Check answers with the class. Whenever possible, have Ss indicate where they found the answers in the reading.

PRACTICE

- **Materials needed** A dictionary for each S.
- Direct Ss' attention to number 1 of Exercise **3B** and read the instructions aloud.
- Focus Ss' attention on the headings in the chart below number 3. Read the three headings aloud. Call on a S to read the words in the left-hand column.
- Ask another S to read the first example definition in the chart, under *Meaning in story*.
- Ss work individually to underline the words in the reading and then write in the second column of the chart the meaning of the word as it is used in the story. Walk around and help as needed.
- Call on a S to read the instructions for number 2 of Exercise **3B**. Tell Ss that they should look in the dictionary to write a different meaning of the word, under *Other meaning* in the chart.
- Have a S read the instructions aloud for number 3 of Exercise **3B**. Ss should write sentences using the other meaning of each of the seven words in the chart.
- Review with the class. Write the chart on the board from page 129. Call on individual Ss to come to the board to fill in the chart. Work with the class to make corrections on the board as needed.

Learner persistence (individual work)

- Encourage Ss to use their notebook or index cards to write new vocabulary words. Suggest that Ss review new words and practice them as much as possible.

APPLICATION

- Focus Ss' attention on Exercise **3C** and read the instructions aloud.
- Ask individual Ss to read aloud the questions in Exercise **3C**, one at a time.
- Ss ask and answer the questions with a partner.
- Ask several pairs to share the answers they discussed.

Expansion activity (student pairs)

- Ss in pairs. Have Ss work together to write a conversation using as many of the words from the chart in Exercise **3B** as possible. They can choose the meaning of the words that best fits their conversation.
- Ask Ss to practice their conversation with their partner until they know it well.
- Call on several pairs to perform their conversations for the class.

Expansion activity

- Refer Ss to "Kwanzaa," another reading on the same topic on pages 163–165.
- Have Ss complete the activity either in class or outside of class.
- Provide feedback to Ss such as through whole-class discussion, partners comparing their worksheets, or T reviewing each S's worksheets.

EVALUATION

- Books closed. Direct Ss' attention to the lesson focus on the board.
- Ask individual Ss to retell the main points of the reading "Special Birthdays Around the World."
- Books open. Focus Ss' attention on the words in the first column of the chart in Exercise **3B**, under *Word in story*. Ask Ss to make sentences with these words to show that they understand the meaning of each word as it is used in the story.
- Check off each part of the lesson focus as Ss demonstrate an understanding of what they have learned in the lesson.

More Ventures, Unit 10, Lesson D	
Workbook, 15–30 min.	
Multilevel Worksheets, 30–45 min. Collaborative Worksheets, 30–45 min.	www.cambridge.org/ventures/ resources/
Student Arcade, time varies	www.cambridge.org/ venturesarcade/

❸ After you read

A Check your understanding.

1. What is the writer's purpose in writing this article?

2. Why do American teenagers look forward to their 16th birthdays?

3. Birthdays in some cultures symbolize important transitions in one's life. Provide two examples of this from the article.

4. Why are birthdays not celebrated in Saudi Arabia?

5. Underline the word *eagerly* in the first paragraph. Does this word have a positive or negative meaning? What words help you to understand the meaning of this word?

6. Are any of the special birthdays described in the reading similar to traditions in your culture? Which ones?

7. What would be a good concluding sentence to this article?

B Build your vocabulary.

1. In the reading passage, underline the words from the chart. Write the meaning from the story.

2. Use a dictionary and write a different meaning for each word.

word in story	Meaning in story	Other meaning
1. states	*areas that are part of a country*	*conditions of the mind*
2. object	*item*	*purpose or goal*
3. rich	*have a lot of money*	*food with a lot of oil, butter, or cream*
4. transition	*move from one stage of life to another*	*words connecting two topics*
5. throw	*give*	*toss*
6. ball	*formal dance*	*spherical object; toy*
7. pick up	*touch; lift*	*to continue*
8. observe	*recognize; celebrate*	*to watch*

3. Write sentences using the other meaning of each word on your own paper. *Answers will vary.*

C Talk with a partner.

1. How many states or provinces are there in your native country?

2. Do you have a favorite object? What is it? Why do you like it?

3. What transitions have you made in your life?

4. What does *being rich* mean to you?

5. What holidays do you observe?

For college and career readiness practice, see pages 163–165.

Determine the purpose of the text and how it is conveyed through key details and examples; use a dictionary to identify multiple meanings of a word

Lesson E Writing

1 Before you write

A Talk with a partner. Answer the questions.

1. Look at the pictures. Can you guess where the people are from and what holiday they are celebrating?

2. What is your favorite holiday or celebration? Why?

B Read the paragraph.

> ### My Favorite Celebration
>
> My favorite celebration is the Iranian New Year, *Norouz* ("new day"). This holiday begins on the first day of spring and lasts 13 days. On the Wednesday before Norouz, people build bonfires and jump over them. Iranian people believe that if they do this, they will get rid of their illnesses and misfortunes. On Norouz Eve, the family gathers around a table with seven items that begin with the letter "s" in Persian: an apple, wheat pudding, dried berries, vinegar, a coin, a beautiful flower, and garlic. A bowl of goldfih, a Koran, colored eggs, and a mirror are also on the table. These items symbolize beauty, health, prosperity, and fertility. On Norouz Day, people kiss each other and say, "I hope you will live for one hundred years." We spend the next 13 days visiting each other and eating sweets. Finally, on the last day of the celebration, everyone goes to a park for a big picnic. I wish my whole family lived with me here so that we could celebrate Norouz together.

> The conclusion – the last sentence of a paragraph – is an important part of a paragraph. One way to conclude a paragraph is to relate the topic to your personal life.

Teaching objective
- Prepare Ss for writing a descriptive paragraph about a favorite holiday or celebration

WARM-UP AND REVIEW

- Before class. Write today's lesson focus on the board.
  Lesson E:
  Write a descriptive paragraph about a favorite holiday or celebration
- Begin class. Books closed. Review vocabulary from the unit. Write *holidays* and *celebrations* on the board. Ask Ss for several examples. Elicit appropriate responses, such as: *New Year's Eve, birthdays, weddings.*
- Ask Ss: *What are some examples of significant birthdays around the world?* (In Nigeria, the 1st, 5th, 10th, and 15th birthdays are very important. In Mexico, a girl's 15th birthday – Quinceañera – is very important. In Israel, a boy's 13th and a girl's 12th birthday are considered important.)
- Ask Ss: *What's an important birthday for American teenagers?* (The 16th birthday is important because in most states it marks a teenager's ability to get a driver's license.)

PRESENTATION

- Books open. Direct Ss' attention to Exercise **1A** and read the instructions aloud.
- Ask two Ss to read the questions in Exercise **1A** to the class.
- Ss work with a partner to ask and answer the questions. Walk around and help as needed.

PRACTICE

- Direct Ss' attention to Exercise **1B** and read the instructions aloud.
- Ss read the paragraph silently. Ask Ss to underline any words in the paragraph with which they are unfamiliar.
- Have Ss tell you the words they underlined, and write them on the board. Go over the meaning of each word.

> Ask a S to read the tip box aloud. Call on another S to read the last sentence of "My Favorite Celebration." Tell Ss that just as the topic sentence introduces the topic, the concluding sentence wraps up the topic and often summarizes the key points. Explain that there are many ways to conclude a paragraph and that ending on a personal note is one option, especially for a paragraph that expresses the writer's opinion or tells an event from the writer's own life.

Expansion activity (student pairs)

- Have Ss compare the celebration in the model paragraph with a celebration from their home culture or country, or with a celebration they have attended in the United States. Write the following on the board: *How does this celebration compare with another celebration you have attended? How are they the same? How are they different?*
- Ss discuss the questions with a partner.
- Write a list of words and phrases on the board that Ss could use to compare and contrast celebrations such as: *similar, both, like, alike, in the same way.* Words or phrases used to contrast, or show differences, include: *unlike, difference, but, while, on the other hand, in a different way.*
- Ask Ss to use words of comparison and contrast to share information they discussed with their partner with the class.
- As a follow-up activity, have Ss bring in photos of celebrations they have attended either in the United States or in their home countries.

Expansion activity (small groups)

- **Materials needed** Photographs or magazine clippings of different kinds of celebrations.
- Ss in small groups. Distribute one photograph to each group.
- Have Ss in each group look carefully at the photograph and describe what they see.
- Encourage Ss to describe the details of the celebration, such as the food, clothing, and decorations. Ss should also compare the celebration they see in the photograph with a similar one they have celebrated.
- Call on groups to share the information they learned with the class.
- To conclude the activity and help Ss develop their visual literacy skills, ask: *Why do you think the photographer took the picture in the way he (or she) did? Would you have focused on the same people and details? Why or why not?*

LESSON E Writing

PRESENTATION

- Books open. Focus Ss' attention on Exercise **1C** and read the instructions aloud.
- Ask a S to read aloud the headings in the outline.
- Call on another S to read the sample topic.
- Ss work with a partner to complete the outline of the model paragraph on page 130.
- Share answers as a class. Make corrections as needed.

PRACTICE

- Direct Ss' attention to Exercise **1D** and read the instructions aloud. Tell Ss that the information that they use here in writing their outline will help them plan, organize, and write their paragraphs.
- Ss should work individually to complete their outlines. Walk around and help as needed.

Teaching Tip

Before Ss begin to write, invite them to talk with a partner about the topic. Talking about the topic will help Ss narrow the topic and focus on the details, facts, and examples that they are going to use to support their ideas and opinion in Exercise **2**.

APPLICATION

- Focus Ss' attention on Exercise **2** and read the instructions aloud.
- Ss complete the task individually. Walk around and help as needed.

Learner persistence (individual work)

- If you have any Ss who have difficulty in writing, sit with them and help them as the other Ss are writing. Work with Ss to use the model paragraph in Exercise **1B** on page 130 and the outlines in Exercises **1C** and **1D** on page 131 to help them plan, organize, and write their paragraphs. Also help Ss write a conclusion that relates the topic to their personal life and experiences (as illustrated in the model).

COMPREHENSION CHECK

- Direct Ss' attention to Exercise **3A**. This exercise asks Ss to develop skills to review and edit their own writing.

- Ss check their own paragraphs against the writing checklist. Walk around and help as needed. If any Ss check *No* for one or more of the checklist items, ask them to edit their paragraphs to include the missing information.

EVALUATION

- Focus Ss' attention on Exercise **3B** and read the instructions aloud. This exercise enables Ss to work together to edit their writing. Reading aloud enables the writer to review his or her own writing and to understand the need to write clearly for an audience.
- Ss complete the exercise in pairs. Guide Ss to take turns reading their paragraphs to each other. Walk around and help as needed.
- Listen to Ss as they ask their partner one question about the paragraph and tell their partner one thing they learned from it.
- Ask several Ss to read their paragraphs aloud. Have other Ss ask questions and tell the class something they learned from the paragraph.
- Direct Ss' attention to the lesson focus on the board.
- Check off the lesson focus as Ss demonstrate an understanding of what they have learned in the lesson.

Expansion activity (small groups)

- First, have the class work together to brainstorm a list of questions for a survey on favorite holidays or celebrations in the United States. Then have small groups of Ss ask several people outside the class, in English, about their favorite holiday or celebration in the United States.
- Model the activity. Write the following questions on the board: *What's your favorite American holiday? Why?*
- Encourage each group to look at the headings in the outline in Exercise **1C** to come up with additional questions to ask, for example: *What is the meaning of this holiday or celebration? When is it? How long does it last? What customs are related to the celebration? Who participates?* Have Ss take notes.
- Ask each group to share the results of its findings with the class.

More Ventures, Unit 10, Lesson E	
Workbook, 15–30 min.	
Multilevel Worksheets, 30–45 min.	www.cambridge.org/
Collaborative Worksheets, 30–45 min.	ventures/resources/

C **Work** with a partner. Complete the outline of the model paragraph.

    I. Topic: _My Favorite Celebration - Norouz_

    II. Meaning or symbolism: _Iranian New Year ("new day")_

    III. When celebrated: _first day of spring; lasts 13 days_

    IV. Customs:

        A. _Build bonfires and jump over them_

        B. _Family gathers at table with thirteen items that begin with "s" in Persian_

        C. _Kiss each other and say, "I hope you will for one hundred years."_

        D. _Visit each other and eat sweets_

        E. _Go to park for a big picnic_

    V. Conclusion: _I wish my whole family lived with me here so that we could celebrate Nouroz together._

D **Plan** a paragraph about your favorite holiday or celebration. Make an outline like the one in Exercise 1C. Include at least three customs. Use your own paper.

Answers will vary.

2 Write

Write a paragraph about your favorite holiday or celebration. Describe its meaning or symbolism. Include at least three customs. Write a conclusion that relates the celebration to your personal life. Use the paragraph in Exercise 1B and the outlines in Exercises 1C and 1D to help you.

Answers will vary.

3 After you write

A **Check** your writing.

	Yes	No
1. My paragraph describes the meaning or symbolism of my favorite holiday	☐	☐
2. I described at least three customs for my favorite holiday or celebration.	☐	☐
3. I wrote a conclusion relating the celebration to my personal life.	☐	☐

B **Share** your writing with a partner.

    1. Take turns. Read your paragraph to a partner.

    2. Comment on your partner's paragraph. Ask your partner a question about the paragraph. Tell your partner one thing you learned.

Lesson F Another view

1 Life-skills reading

Mother's Thanksgiving **Pumpkin Pie**
Preparation time: 15 minutes / Cooking time: 50 minutes

Ingredients

1 pre-made pie crust
1 (8-ounce) package
   cream cheese, softened
2 cups canned pumpkin,
   mashed

¼ teaspoon salt
1 cup sugar
1 egg plus 2 egg yolks,
   lightly beaten
1 cup heavy cream

¼ cup (½ stick) melted butter
1 teaspoon vanilla extract
½ teaspoon ground cinnamon
¼ teaspoon ground ginger,
   optional

1. Preheat the oven to 350 degrees Fahrenheit.
2. Beat the softened cream cheese.
3. Add the pumpkin and beat until blended.
4. Then add the salt and sugar, and beat until blended.
5. Then add the egg mixed with the yolks, cream, and melted butter, and beat until blended.
6. Finally, mix in the vanilla, cinnamon, and ginger.

7. Pour the filling into the pre-made pie crust, and bake for 50 minutes, or until the center is firm.
8. Set the pie on a wire rack, and cool until it is room temperature. Cut into slices and serve with whipped cream or ice cream.

Serves 6–8 people.

A Read the questions. Look at the recipe. Fill in the answer.

1. Which ingredient do you need one cup of?

   A heavy cream
   B sugar
   C vanilla
   D both *a* and *b*

2. What should you do after you blend the cream cheese and pumpkin?

   A Add the salt and sugar.
   B Bake the pie.
   C Add the eggs.
   D Pour the filling into the pie crust.

3. Which ingredient is not required?

   A vanilla
   B ginger
   C cinnamon
   D cream cheese

4. According to the recipe, what would be a good synonym for the word *blended*?

   A cooked
   B beat
   C melted
   D mixed

B Solve the problem. Give your opinion.

Ana's class is having a *potluck*. Everyone is supposed to bring something. Her classmates are asking her to bring a dish from her country. Ana has very little time and money now and can't afford to make the dish for the potluck. What should she do?

Answers will vary.

Teaching objectives
- Introduce reading and understanding a recipe
- Provide practice using tag questions

WARM-UP AND REVIEW

- Before class. Write today's lesson focus on the board.

  Lesson F:
  Read and understand a recipe
  Use tag questions

- Begin class. Books closed. Write the word *recipe* on the board. Explain or elicit that a recipe is a set of instructions for preparing a particular kind of food.

- Ask Ss: *How many of you like to cook? What do you like to make? Do you like to follow a recipe or cook without following directions?*

- Ask Ss: *What information do you find in a recipe?* Elicit appropriate responses, such as: *ingredients, measurements, cooking time, how-to directions or steps, how many people the recipe is for.* Write the Ss' answers on the board.

- Tell Ss that they will be reading a recipe for pumpkin pie. Ask Ss if they know when this pie is typically prepared and eaten in the United States (on Thanksgiving). Ask if anyone in the class has ever tasted pumpkin pie.

PRESENTATION

- Books open. Read the title of the recipe aloud, as well as the preparation and cooking time.

- Call on Ss to read each of the recipe ingredients aloud. Explain any new words.

- Ask individual Ss to read the eight steps, one at a time. Explain vocabulary as needed.

Teaching Tip

Tell Ss that learning to read a recipe is a useful skill for everyday life. Ask Ss if they have ever followed recipes, either in their native language or in English. Explain to Ss that they may need to read recipes in the future, or they may have jobs in which they will need to read, understand, and follow recipes or directions, like those used in a recipe.

PRACTICE

- Read the instructions aloud for Exercise **1A**. This exercise helps prepare Ss for standardized-type tests they may have to take. Be sure that Ss understand the task. Have Ss individually scan for and fill in the answers.

COMPREHENSION CHECK

- Check answers to Exercise **1A** with the class. Make sure that Ss have followed the instructions and filled in their answers.

- Have Ss read aloud the questions and answers they filled in. Make corrections as needed.

APPLICATION

- Direct Ss' attention to Exercise **1B** and read the instructions aloud. Make sure that Ss understand the task. Have Ss individually solve the problem.

- Ss discuss the problem in small groups. Walk around and help as needed.

- After Ss discuss the problem, open up the discussion to the entire class. Accept all plausible answers.

Expansion activity (small groups)

- Tell Ss that they are going to write a recipe for a holiday dish from their native culture or country. Write this chart on the board:

Typical dish	Holiday
pumpkin pie	Thanksgiving (U.S.)

- Call on a S to read the two headings. Ask another S to read the example.

- Invite Ss in small groups to talk about a specific dish from their culture or country and the holiday for which it is usually prepared.

- Have Ss come to the board to add their examples to the chart.

- Tell groups that they should choose a dish that they have just discussed, or one that they especially enjoy, and write it in recipe format as in the model on page 132.

- Ask each group to share its recipe with the class. Walk around and help as needed.

- Collect the recipes and put them together in a class cookbook that all Ss can consult.

- If possible, have Ss prepare the recipe at home and then bring it to class to celebrate the completion of *Ventures Student's Book 4.*

  Option You can give Ss the option of preparing the pumpkin pie recipe presented in Exercise **1**.

LESSON F Another view

WARM-UP AND REVIEW

- Books closed. Write a few questions about Ss on the board, for example: *Do you have any brothers or sisters? Are you from Vietnam? Have you been to New York City?* Ask the Ss the questions and write a few of their answers on the board, for example: *Maria has two sisters. Tu is from Vietnam. Donna has not been to New York City.*
- Books closed. Direct Ss' attention to the sentences and answers on the board. Point to *Do you have any brothers or sisters?* Ask Ss to identify the subject (you) and main verb (have). Review basic question structure with Ss. Write [*Do / Are / Have*] + subject + main verb on the board.

PRESENTATION

Focus on form

- Use the animated grammar presentation in one or more of the following ways:
  - Preview it before class
  - Show in class
  - Encourage Ss to watch outside of class.
- Books open. Direct Ss' attention to the grammar chart in **2A**. Ask a pair of Ss to read the questions and possible answers in the first row. Point out that the words in parentheses are optional. Ask individual Ss to read the rest of the questions. Write *affirmative sentence + negative tag* and *negative sentence + affirmative tag* on the board.
- Ask Ss to compare the two sentences. Elicit that the sentences are composed of positive or negative statements followed by opposite questions. Tell Ss that we use tag questions frequently in English. We use them to check or verify information we think is true.
- Point to the sentences on the board. Turn them into tag questions, and ask the Ss tag questions, for example: *Maria, you're a home health aide, aren't you?*

PRACTICE

- Direct Ss' attention to the instructions in **2A**. Read the instructions aloud. Ask a pair of Ss to read the dialog aloud. Ensure Ss understand the activity.

- Tell the class to stand up and to pick up their books. Ask Ss to walk around the classroom interviewing their classmates about the items in the chart using tag questions. Ss continue asking one another questions until they have completed the chart. Walk around and help as needed.
- Direct Ss' attention to the instructions in **2B**. Read the instructions aloud. Ask two Ss to read the example sentences. Ss complete the exercise in pairs.

EVALUATION

- Do a quick review of the unit. Have Ss turn to Lesson A. Ask the class to talk about what they remember about this lesson. Prompt Ss, if necessary, with questions, for example: *What are the conversations about on this page? What vocabulary is in the pictures?* Continue in this manner to review each lesson quickly.

Expansion activity

- Before class. Print, for each student, one copy of the Self-assessment for this unit.
- Have Ss complete the Self-assessment either in class or outside of class.
- Provide feedback to Ss such as through a whole-class discussion, partners comparing their worksheets, or T reviewing each S's worksheet.
- If Ss are ready, administer the unit test on pages T-216–T-218 of this Teacher's Edition. The audio script for the test is on pages T-224–T-225.
- If Ss are ready, administer the final test on pages T-219–T-221 of this Teacher's Edition. The audio script for the test is on page T-225.

More Ventures, Unit 10, Lesson F	
Workbook, 15–30 min.	
Multilevel Worksheets, 30–45 min.	www.cambridge.org/ventures/resources/
Collaborative Worksheets, 30–45 min.	
Self-assessment, 10 min.	
CASAS Test Prep Worksheet, 5–10 min.	

2 Grammar connections: tag questions

👁 Watch

A tag question is a small question at the end of a statement. Use tag questions to confirm what you think is true or not true. A positive statement is followed by a negative question tag, and a negative statement is followed by a positive question tag.

AFFIRMATIVE SENTENCE + NEGATIVE TAG	NEGATIVE SENTENCE + AFFIRMATIVE TAG
You **like** to dance, **don't** you? –Yes, I do. (I like to dance.) –Actually, no. I don't like to dance.	You **don't like** to dance, **do** you? –No, I don't. (I don't like to dance.) –Actually, I do. I like to dance.
You**'re** tired, **aren't** you?	You **aren't** tired, **are** you?
You **went** to a restaurant, **didn't** you?	You **didn't go** to a restaurant, **did** you?

A **Work** with your classmates. Use tag questions. Complete the chart.

A Ivan, you don't like chocolate, do you?

B Actually, I do. I like chocolate.

A Fabiana, you don't like chocolate, do you?

B No, I don't.

Find someone who . . .	Name
doesn't like chocolate	*Fabiana*
ate at a restaurant last night	*Answers will vary.*
isn't tired today	
didn't go on vacation last month	
is good at math	
didn't study last night	
has a birthday in June	

B **Talk** with a partner. Ask questions about your partner's life. Use tag questions. Take turns.

A You like to fish, don't you?

B Yes, I do.

REVIEW

1 Listening

Listen. Take notes on a street interview.

🔊 CD2, Track 33

Things that bring good luck	Things that bring bad luck
1. *wear bright colors like red*	4. *sweep the house*
2. *open doors and windows at midnight*	5. *buy a pair of shoes*
3. *eat a lot of candy*	6. *use knives or scissors*

Talk with a partner. Check your answers.

2 Grammar

A Write. Complete the story.

A New Year's Eve Celebration

Sergei _____*wishes*_____ his friend Olga could visit him in New York over the holidays, but
       1. hopes / wishes

she can't get the time off. _____*Therefore*_____, they won't be together on New Year's Eve. If she
                              2. Therefore / Since

_____*were*_____ in New York, he would take her to Times Square _____*because*_____
    3. is / were   4. so / because

there is a big celebration there. Every year at one minute before midnight, a large crystal ball

starts to drop slowly from high above the street. When it reaches the bottom, everybody goes crazy

_____*since*_____ it's the beginning of the New Year. Sergei really _____*hopes*_____
    5. since / so   6. hopes / wishes

that Olga can come next year. If she comes, she _____*will*_____ have a great time.
                                               7. will / would

B Write. Look at the words that are underlined in the answers. Write the questions.

1. A *Where would Sergei take Olga if she were in New York?*

   B Sergei would take Olga <u>to Times Square</u> if she were in New York.

2. A *What starts to drop at one minute before midnight?*

   B <u>The crystal ball</u> starts to drop at one minute before midnight.

3. A *When does Sergei hope Olga can come?*

   B Sergei hopes that Olga can come <u>next year</u>.

Talk with a partner. Ask and answer the questions.

Teaching objectives
- Review vocabulary and grammar from Units 9 and 10
- Provide practice identifying thought groups

WARM-UP AND REVIEW

- Before class. Write today's lesson focus on the board.
  Review unit:
  Review vocabulary and grammar from Units 9 and 10
  Practice identifying thought groups in sentences

- Begin class. Books closed. Review vocabulary and grammar from Units 9 and 10. Write these sentences on the board. Have Ss complete the sentences using the present unreal conditional and the words in parentheses.

  If you _____ energy-efficient appliances, you _____ on energy use. (buy, cut down)
  We _____ millions of trees if everyone _____ their newspapers. (save, recycle)

- Say this sentence to Ss: *Because of global warming, the sea levels are rising.* Ask: *What are some other consequences of global warming?* If your Ss don't know the answer, lead them to see that many scientists think global warming is causing climate changes as well as extreme weather, such as hurricanes and other storms. Encourage Ss to use the connectors of cause (*since, because*) and the connectors of effect (*therefore, so*).

- Review the future real conditional and the unreal conditional. Write these sentences on the board.

  Future real conditional: If you don't stay home on New Year's Eve, what will you do?
  Unreal conditional: What would you do if you won a lot of money?

- Encourage Ss to answer each question using *if* + the future real or the unreal conditional form of the verb.

- Review *hope* and *wish*. Write the following sentences on the board. Have Ss read the situations and make statements using *hope* and *wish*.

  Jenny can't go home for Thanksgiving because she doesn't have enough money. (Jenny wishes she could go home for Thanksgiving.)
  Gustavo wants to get a new TV as a birthday gift. (Gustavo hopes he will get a new TV as a birthday gift.)

PRESENTATION

- Books open. Direct Ss' attention to Exercise **1** and read the instructions aloud. Tell Ss that they will hear an interview between an interviewer and two different people.

- ▶ *CD2, Track 33* Model the task. Play or read only the first part of the interview on the audio (see audio script, page T-184). Pause after Angela says, *Well, it's traditional to wear bright colors, such as red.*

- Direct Ss' attention to number 1 in the chart (*Things that bring good luck*) and ask: *What does Angela say is one of the things that people can do to bring good luck?* (wear bright colors like red.)

- Ask a S to read aloud the other chart heading (*Things that bring bad luck*). Say: *Now listen and complete the chart.*

- ▶ *CD2, Track 33* Play or read the complete audio. Ss listen and complete the chart. Repeat the audio as needed.

COMPREHENSION CHECK

- Read aloud the second part of the instructions for Exercise **1**.

- Ss complete the exercise in pairs. Walk around and help as needed.

- Ask several Ss to make sentences about things that bring good luck and bad luck, using the information in the chart.

PRACTICE

- Direct Ss' attention to Exercise **2A**. Ask: *What is the title of this story?* ("A New Year's Eve Celebration")

- Read the instructions aloud in Exercise **2A**. Point out that in this exercise, Ss choose the correct word(s) to complete each sentence.

- Ask a S to read aloud the first sentence in the story, including the sample answer. Explain any unfamiliar vocabulary as needed.

- Ss complete the exercise individually. Help as needed.

- Write the numbers *1–7* on the board. Ask Ss to come to the board to write the answers only.

- Call on Ss to read the complete story using the answers on the board. Make corrections as needed.

COMPREHENSION CHECK

- Direct Ss' attention to Exercise **2B**. This exercise reviews question formation related to the reading, "A New Year's Eve Celebration."

- Read the instructions aloud. Model the exercise. Focus Ss' attention on the answer to number 1. Ask: *What question can you ask to get this answer?*

- Ss complete the exercise individually. Help as needed.

- Check answers with the class. Call on three Ss to read their questions. Make corrections as needed.

- Read aloud the second part of the instructions for Exercise **2B**.

- Ss work in pairs to ask and answer the questions. Help as needed.

REVIEW

PRESENTATION

- Books closed. Write on the board: *linking consonant-vowel sounds*.
- Ask Ss to list the vowels in English, eliciting *a, e, i, o, u*. Elicit or explain to Ss that consonants are the letters in the English alphabet that aren't vowels.
- Tell Ss that when a word ends in a consonant sound, we sometimes move the consonant sound to the beginning of the following word if that word starts with a vowel sound. By linking two sounds, we eliminate the pause between them. Linking consonant and vowel sounds helps us to control pauses and the rhythm of sentences.
- Write on the board: *Smaller cars would use less energy.* Ask Ss which words start with vowel sounds (use, energy). Ask Ss if the words in front of *use* and *energy* end in consonants (Yes). Draw arrows to link these sounds. *Smaller cars would→use less→energy.*
- Pronounce this sentence a few times putting extra emphasis on the linked consonant-vowel sounds. Ask Ss to repeat the sentence a few times.
- Books open. Direct Ss to page 135, and call on a S to read the information at the top of the page.
- Focus Ss' attention on Exercise **3A** and read the instructions aloud.
- ▶ *CD2, Track 34* Play or read the complete audio (see audio script, page T-184).
- Read aloud the second part of the instructions for Exercise **3A**.
- ▶ *CD2, Track 34* Repeat the audio. Play the audio as many times as needed. Focus Ss' attention on the linked consonant-vowel sounds.

PRACTICE

- Direct Ss' attention to Exercise **3B** and read the instructions aloud.
- ▶ *CD2, Track 35* Model the exercise. Play or read the first sentence on the audio (see audio script, page T-184). Ask Ss to tell you which sounds they underlined.
- Tell Ss to pay attention to the linked consonant-vowel sounds in each sentence as they listen. Play or read the audio, stopping as needed for Ss to repeat the sentences.
- Play or read the complete audio again. Repeat the audio as needed.
- Read aloud the second part of the instructions in Exercise **3B**.
- Ss complete the task in pairs. Help as needed.

COMPREHENSION CHECK

- Direct Ss' attention to Exercise **3C** and read the instructions aloud.
- Ss work in pairs to practice the dialogs and underline consonant-vowel sounds. Walk around and listen to Ss' pronunciation of consonant-vowel sounds. Help as needed.
- Ask several partners to read the conversations aloud. Call on other Ss to identify the consonant-vowel sounds. Write any sentence on the board with which Ss had trouble identifying the consonant-vowel sounds. Say the sentence and emphasize the consonant-vowel sounds. Have Ss repeat.

APPLICATION

- Read the instructions aloud in Exercise **3D**.
- Ss work individually to complete the exercise.
- Ss work with their partner to practice emphasizing the linked consonant-vowel sounds in the sentences they chose.

EVALUATION

- Direct Ss' attention to the lesson focus on the board.
- Write this sentence on the board, and ask Ss to complete it using the correct form of the present unreal conditional and the words in parentheses. *If you _____ eating fish that contains lead, you _____ healthier. (stop, be)*
- Ask Ss to give examples of sentences using these connectors: *since, because, so,* and *consequently.*
- Write these sentences on the board: *If I go to Mexico this summer, I will visit my family. If she traveled to Brazil, she would spend time at the beach.* Ask Ss to make up similar sentences about themselves or their classmates using the future real conditional or the unreal conditional.
- Write these sentences on the board: *Ana really wants to go out to dinner with her husband on Valentine's Day. Ana has to work at night on Valentine's Day.* Ask Ss to read the two sentences and make a statement with *hope* or *wish.* (Ana wishes she could have dinner with her husband on Valentine's Day.)
- Check off each part of the lesson focus as Ss demonstrate an understanding of what they have learned in the lesson.

3 Pronunciation: linking consonant-vowel sounds

When a word ends in a consonant sound and the next word begins with a vowel sound, the words sound like they are linked together. Move the final consonant sound of the first word to the beginning of the second word.

A **Listen** to the following sentences.

🔊 CD2, Track 34

1. Smaller cars would use less energy.
2. Smog is a big environmental problem.
3. If everyone drove less, our air quality would improve.
4. In the future, we will see more electric cars and trucks on our roads.
5. We should all have efficient appliances.
6. We need to protect our environment.

Listen again and repeat. Pay attention to the linked consonant-vowel sounds.

B **Listen and repeat.** Then underline the linked consonant-vowel sounds.

🔊 CD2, Track 35

1. All things in this world are connected.
2. People are concerned about saving this earth.
3. Most of the cars on the highway have only one person in them.
4. People make a lot of unnecessary trips.
5. We should close off unused rooms in our homes.
6. The Internet is a good source of information about global warming.

Talk with a partner. Compare your answers.

C **Read** the questions and answers. Underline the linked consonant-vowel sounds.

1. A What do you think about global warming?
   B Well, I haven't read a lot about it.

2. A How can I help clean up the beach?
   B You can pick up trash and put it in garbage cans.

3. A What can all of us do to protect our environment?
   B We can all cut down on our energy use.

4. A What is an easy way to save energy?
   B Turn off lights when you leave a room.

Talk with a partner. Practice the questions and answers.

D **Write** four sentences from Units 9 and 10. Underline the linked consonant-vowel sounds. Then work with a partner. Read your sentences using linked consonant-vowel sounds. *Answers will vary.*

Reading Tip: Read the first paragraph. What is the focus of the article? Then read the first sentence in each of the following paragraphs. How is each different?

Promoting Multiple Intelligences in the Classroom

Frank Kimmel's 4th grade class in Seattle, Washington buzzes with activity. Kimmel is a strong believer in Howard Gardner's theory of multiple intelligences. This is the idea that there are several different kinds of intelligence, and people can be intelligent in different ways. "My job as a teacher is to provide my students a variety of learning experiences that will help them use and develop all of their intelligences," he explains. In Kimmel's classroom, students spend part of each day moving around to various learning centers – places where they can work on different skills, individually or in small groups.

For example, in one corner of the classroom there is the "visual center," with art supplies, photo books, building blocks, and a computer that's connected to a 3-D printer. Students can look at photos and use their imagination to draw, paint, build, and create things.

Along one side wall is the "music center" where students can listen to music and nature sounds, look at musical scores, and use a computer program to write their own musical compositions. There are also some simple musical instruments that students can check out and practice at home.

There's the "STEM corner" – Science, Technology, Engineering and Mathematics – where students come to work on math problems and scientific experiments. This area has games and puzzles that require logic and Kimmel sometimes brings in old appliances that students take apart and put back together.

On the back wall is the "word center" with adventure stories and biographies, books on tape, and poetry. In addition, there are crossword puzzles and other word games, dictionaries, and writing materials. This is a popular gathering place for group storytelling.

In one front corner is the "quiet zone" where students can go for quiet reflection and meditation. Here, students can also write in their journals and complete self-assessments.

Finally, the "nature center" is outside, in a corner of the playground. It's a small garden area with raised beds where students can dig in the dirt and learn about planting and caring for vegetables and flowers.

At the end of a busy day, one of the 4th graders summed it up when she said enthusiastically, "I really like Mr. Kimmel's class because there are lots of interesting things to do and I'm never bored!"

1 Check your understanding

1. What is special about Mr. Kimmel's class?
2. How many learning centers does the article describe?
3. What can students do in the visual center?
4. What can students do in the nature center?
5. Read the last paragraph. Do you think the author agrees with Mr. Kimmel's way of teaching? Explain your answer.

2 Build your vocabulary

A Find the words in Column 1 in the paragraph indicated and underline them. Then write the clue that helped you know the meaning. Finally, write the dictionary definition that matches the meaning in the article.

Word	Clue	Dictionary definition
1. buzzes, ¶1	*class... buzzes with activity*	*Makes a low humming sound like bees, machinery, or people talking.*
2. learning center, ¶1		
3. check out, ¶3		
4. meditation, ¶6		
5. nature center, ¶7		
6. enthusiastically, ¶8		

B Find each of the following academic words in the article and underline the sentence.

> create   individually   journals   logic   theory

Then, on another piece of paper, copy and complete the chart.

Academic word	Phrase or sentence from article	Part of speech	Dictionary definition	My sentence
create	*Students can . . . use their imagination to create things.*	*verb*	*to make something new or imaginative*	*I like to create my own greeting cards.*

3 Talk with a partner

Answer each question with evidence from the reading. Use one of the phrases in the Useful Language box.

1. What does Mr. Kimmel say about his job as a teacher?
2. What is a popular place for storytelling?
3. What does one student say about Mr. Kimmel's class?

> **USEFUL LANGUAGE**
> Phrases to cite evidence:
> (name of person) states that . . .
> The article states that . . .

Objective: **CCR Anchor 9:** Analyze how two or more texts address similar themes or topics in order to build knowledge or to compare the approaches the authors take.

4 Analyze the texts

Review the following texts to answer the questions below: (1) p. 12, *Many Ways to be Smart;* and (2) p. 136, *Promoting Multiple Intelligences in the Classroom.*

1. What main idea do both articles share?
2. What intelligence does the "STEM corner" address? What activities take place there?
3. What intelligences does the "word center" address? What activities take place there?
4. What intelligence does the "quiet zone" address? What activities take place there?
5. Do you think that teachers should use a variety of activities in order to address multiple intelligences? Support your answer with examples from your personal experience.

5 Before you write

Copy and complete the graphic organizer on another piece of paper. Fill it in with (1) the main idea, (2) the types of intelligence, and (3) examples of materials in the learning center that support that intelligence. Use information from Exercises 1–4 and evidence from the two articles. Finally, (4) fill in the conclusion with your answer to question five in Exercise 4.

Main Idea:	
Types of Intelligence in *Many Ways to be Smart*	**Supporting Teaching Methodology in** *Promoting Multiple Intelligences in the Classroom*
Conclusion:	

6 Write

Write one paragraph explaining multiple intelligences. Include examples for three different intelligences. Use information from your graphic organizer.

7 After you write

A Check your writing. Did you include all the ideas in your graphic organizer?
B Share your writing with a partner.
  a. Take turns. Read your writing to your partner.
  b. Read your partner's writing to yourself. Compare it to your partner's graphic organizer.
  c. Comment on your partner's writing: Ask one question; share one thing you learned.

Reading Tip: Look at the picture. Then read the title and the first sentence in each paragraph. Who is this article about? What happened? Read and find out.

Rafael Salazar

Rafael Salazar was born in 1986 on a small farm in southern Mexico. His family was very poor. He remembers waking up at 5:30 a.m. and going with his father to milk cows before breakfast, then walking one hour to his local elementary school. "I was fortunate because my parents always pushed me to study," Rafael says. "They weren't educated, but they knew that education is the only way out of poverty."

Rafael's parents encouraged him to move to the United States. He arrived in 2004 and moved in with his aunt in San Diego, California. He spoke no English, but he knew he had to learn English to be successful. Right away, he registered for ESL classes at San Diego City College. He started with morning classes, then he joined the afternoon classes and even attended evening classes. Everyone was glad to see Rafael's passion for learning. "I never saw such a determined student," said Amanda Yellin, Rafael's teacher in ESL 1. "He practically lived at the school."

Rafael's career counselor helped him obtain a weekend job as a houseman in a local hotel, where he moved furniture and prepared rooms for banquets, or large dinner parties.

His boss noticed his passion to succeed and encouraged him to consider a career in the hospitality industry. Soon, Rafael was promoted to the position of lead houseman, then banquet waiter. Now, he's banquet captain.

Rafael believes strongly in setting goals. "Set a goal and make it happen. When you reach that goal, set another one," he suggests. His next goal is to become a food and beverage manager. He plans to begin a certificate program in hotel management in the fall. Eventually, he wants to be the general manager of a major hotel.

At a recent banquet honoring hospitality employees, Rafael received his hotel's Outstanding Hospitality Worker Award. Speaking fluent English, he gave an encouraging speech in which he thanked his parents, his aunt, his ESL teachers, and his boss at the hotel. He encouraged others like him to set goals, work hard, and, above all, learn English. "Don't allow language to be an obstacle to your success," he told them. "If a poor farmer like me can succeed in America, so can you."

UNIT 2

1 Check your understanding

1. Look at the reading tip again. What is the article about?
2. Why did Rafael's teacher, Amanda Yellen, say, "I have never seen a more dedicated student?"
3. What was Rafael's first job? What other jobs has he had at the hotel?
4. What is Rafael's goal? How does he plan to achieve his goal?
5. Read the last paragraph. Why do you think the author wrote this article?

2 Build your vocabulary

A Find the words in Column 1 in the paragraph indicated and underline them. Identify the part of speech: noun, verb, adjective, or adverb. Then use a dictionary to complete the chart with other forms of the word and their parts of speech.

Word in Article	Part of speech	Other forms of the word	Part of speech
1. educated, ¶1	*verb*	*education* *educational*	*noun* *adjective*
2. encouraged, ¶2			
3. passion, ¶2, ¶3			
4. succeed, ¶3, ¶5			
5. strongly, ¶4			
6. believes, ¶4			

B Find each of the following academic words in the article and underline the sentence.

> eventually   major   obtain   promoted   registered

Then, on another piece of paper, copy and complete the chart.

Academic word	Phrase or sentence from article	Part of speech	Dictionary definition	My sentence
eventually	*Eventually he wants to be the general manager of a major hotel.*	*adverb*	*in the end*	*Eventually she wants to be a doctor.*

3 Talk with a partner

Answer each question with evidence from the reading. Use one of the phrases in the Useful Language box.

1. How did Rafael show that education was important to him when he was a child in Mexico?
2. How do you know Rafael was determined to learn English in the United States?
3. Why did Rafael's boss encourage him to consider a career in the hospitality industry?

> **USEFUL LANGUAGE**
> Phrases to cite an example:
> One example from the article is . . .
> One example the author gives is . . .

> **Objective: CCR Anchor 9:** Analyze how two or more texts address similar themes or topics in order to build knowledge or to compare the approaches the authors take.

4 Analyze the texts

Review the following texts to answer the questions below: (1) p. 24, *An Immigrant Family's Success Story;* and (2) p. 139, *Rafael Salazar.*

1. What do both articles describe?
2. What is one example from each article about learning English?
3. What is one example from each article about hard work and sacrifice?
4. What is one example from each article about eventual success?
5. Read the quotes from Choi and Rafael from the last paragraphs in each article. Restate your favorite quote in your own words.

5 Before you write

Copy and complete the graphic organizer on another piece of paper. Fill it in with (1) the topic and (2) two examples for each key point. Use information from Exercises 1–4 and evidence from the two articles. Finally, (3) fill in the conclusion with your answer to question five in Exercise 4.

Topic:		
Learning English	**Hard Work and Sacrifice**	**Plan for Success**
Examples	Examples	Examples
1.	1.	1.
2.	2.	2.
Conclusion:		

6 Write

Write one paragraph that explains how immigrants overcome obstacles to become successful. Use information from your grahic organizer.

7 After you write

A Check your writing. Did you include all the ideas in your graphic organizer?

B Share your writing with a partner.

    a. Take turns. Read your writing to your partner.

    b. Read your partner's writing to yourself. Compare it to your partner's graphic organizer.

    c. Comment on your partner's writing: Ask one question; share one thing you learned.

Reading Tip: Read the title and first paragraph. Identify one problem between immigrant parents and their teens.

Communication Tips for Immigrant Parents and Teens

Parents in the United States face challenges in communicating with their teenage children as the teens struggle to establish their own identities. When the parents are immigrants whose teenagers came to the U.S. at a young age, these challenges are magnified. There are a couple of reasons for this. First of all, the teenagers may have a greater identification with American culture than their parents have. In addition, the teenagers often speak more English than their parents. Trying to be traditional children at home and all-American children at school, the teenagers may feel they lead double lives and the parents may feel they no longer know their children. This leads to conflict and stress.

Professional experts offer several tips to immigrant parents for improving communication with their teenagers.

1. Learn as much English as you can. Free English as a Second Language classes are offered at adult schools, community colleges, and libraries as well as at community-based organizations. For those whose work or family schedules prevent attending classes, there are also online programs, many of them free. Your children will respect you for trying to learn more English.

2. Set regular times for conversation and interaction. Eating meals together is a great way to listen and talk with each other. You can discuss experiences in adapting to the new culture as well as how the new culture is different from the home culture. The more you listen to your teenager the more your teenager will have a sense of self-respect and respect for you.

3. Provide praise. Most teenagers want to be independent, but they also need feedback. Compliment them for their good behavior. For example, even if a report card has a bad grade, before you ask about the bad grade, give a compliment on the good grades.

4. Allow some privacy. As teenagers become young adults, they may not share everything with their parents. For safety reasons, you always need to know where they are, and who they are with, but you don't need to know every detail.

The role parents play in their children's lives is especially important during the teenage years. Teenagers can be difficult as they try to find out who they are and who they want to be. Keep open communication channels with teens so that they don't feel isolated. And remember, the most important way to help your teens is to express your love and appreciation for them as they struggle to adapt to adulthood in a new culture.

UNIT 3

1 Check your understanding

1. What is the purpose of this article?
2. According to the article, what are two ways parents can learn more English?
3. Why is it important for parents to set regular times for conversation with their teens?
4. Why is it important to praise teenagers?
5. Of the four tips suggested to improve communication between immigrant parents and their teens, which two tips do you think are the most effective? Why?

2 Build your vocabulary

A Find the words in Column 1 in the paragraphs indicated and underline them. Then complete the chart by writing the phrase in which the word occurs and your guess of its meaning as used in the article. Finally, write the dictionary definition.

Word	Phrase	Guess the meaning	Dictionary definition
1. struggle, ¶1	*struggle to establish their own identities*	*try*	*to make great efforts*
2. magnified, ¶1			
3. respect, ¶3			
4. praise, ¶5			
5. compliment, ¶5			
6. express, ¶7			

B Find each of the following academic words in the article and underline the sentence.

> adapt   conflict   establish   isolated   stress

Then, on another piece of paper, copy and complete the chart.

Academic word	Phrase or sentence from article	Part of speech	Dictionary definition	My sentence
adapt	*adapt to a new culture*	*verb*	*to adjust to new circumstances*	*Soon you will adapt to the cold weather.*

3 Talk with a partner

Answer each question with evidence from the reading.
Use one of the phrases in the Useful Language box.

> **USEFUL LANGUAGE**
> Phrases to cite evidence:
> The article states that . . .
> According to the article, . . .

1. Why are the challenges of communication between immigrant parents and teens greater than those between non-immigrant parents and teens?
2. What causes teenagers of immigrant parents to feel they are leading double lives?
3. What is the most important way for parents to help teens?

Objective: CCR Anchor 9: Analyze how two or more texts address similar themes or topics in order to build knowledge or to compare the approaches the authors take.

4 Analyze the texts

Review the following texts to answer the questions below: (1) p. 38, *Barriers Between Generations*; and (2) p. 142, *Communication Tips for Immigrant Parents and Teens*.

1. What is the topic of both articles?
2. What is the first barrier described in *Barriers between Generations*? What is a solution for it from *Communication Tips for Immigrant Parents and Teens*?
3. What is the second barrier described in *Barriers between Generations*? What is a solution for it from *Communication Tips for Immigrant Parents and Teens*?
4. Which tips for opening communication channels suggested in the article *Communication Tips for Immigrant Parents and Teens* might help Dolores communicate more effectively with her son?
5. Which tip do you think is the most effective for solving communication barriers between parents and their teens? Use evidence from both articles and your experience to support your answer.

5 Before you write

Copy and complete the graphic organizer on another piece of paper. Fill it in with (1) the topic, (2) one communication problem between immigrant parents and teens, (3) three solutions to the problem, and (4) two details for each solution. Use information from Exercises 1–4 and evidence from the two articles. Finally, (5) fill in the conclusion with your answer to question five in Exercise 4.

Topic:		
Problem	**Solution 1**	**Detail** **Detail**
	Solution 2	**Detail** **Detail**
	Solution 3	**Detail** **Detail**
Conclusion:		

6 Write

Write one paragraph that identifies one communication problem between immigrant parents and teens and two or three solutions for it. Use information from your graphic organizer.

7 After you write

A Check your writing. Did you include all the ideas in your graphic organizer?

B Share your writing with a partner.
  a. Take turns. Read your writing to your partner.
  b. Read your partner's writing to yourself. Compare it to your partner's graphic organizer.
  c. Comment on your partner's writing: Ask one question; share one thing you learned.

Ventures 4

Reading Tip: Look at the title, first sentence, and last sentence of the article. What do you think is the main idea of this article? Is it surprising?

Winning the Lottery Can Be Stressful

Stress is defined as our body's reaction to changing events in our lives. We usually think of change as negative, but positive events also produce stress. Here are three stories about people who experienced stress as a result of a positive event – winning the lottery.

Money demand upsets couple. John and Susan Patel couldn't believe their good luck when they won $92 million in their state's lottery. A short time later, however, they were shocked and upset by a demand from a clerk at the convenience store where they bought their lottery tickets. The clerk shouted angrily that the Patels promised to give her $500,000 as a reward for selling them the winning ticket. John Patel says he pledged to "take care of" the clerk, but he never promised her a specific dollar amount. He also says that right after winning the jackpot, he gave the clerk $20,000.

No money left for this winner. Robert Novak, who won almost $14 million in the Pennsylvania state lottery, discovered that it can be very difficult to cope with sudden success. He used the money to start several businesses, including a restaurant and a used-car lot, but they all failed. His own brother tried to steal money from him. Novak's landlady said that Novak owed her half the lottery money. In the end, a court gave her one-third of Novak's winnings. By 1999, Novak was broke and stressed out. Without money, he was living with his parents and seeing a doctor for depression.

Rich man, poor man. The life of Calvin Ross changed overnight when he won $5.6 million in the lottery. He divorced his wife, bought expensive cars, and spent huge sums of money on gifts for his friends. But because of bad investments and excessive spending, Ross always ran out of money before his $191,000 annual checks arrived every October. He now lives by himself and works to pay off his debts.

Of course, most people who win the lottery say that winning has had a positive effect in their lives. The three stories in this article are unusual. However, they show that even a happy event like winning the lottery may bring about new and stressful problems.

1 Check your understanding

1. Look at the reading tip again. What is the article about?
2. How does this article define *stress*?
3. According to the article, do people usually have positive or negative ideas about stress? Underline the sentence that answers this question and restate it in your own words.
4. Who won the most money? What problem did they face?
5. Read the last paragraph. Why do you think the author wrote this article?

2 Build your vocabulary

A Find the words in Column 1 in the paragraphs indicated and underline them. For each, find clues in the words around them to guess their meaning. Then match the words with their meanings.

Word		Clue	Meaning
1. produce, ¶1	_b_	*as a result*	
2. demand, ¶2	____		a. strong request
			b. cause
3. pledged, ¶2	____		c. huge amount of something
4. jackpot, ¶2	____		d. without money
			e. promise
5. broke, ¶3	____		f. lottery winnings
6. excessive, ¶4	____		

B Find each of the following academic words in the article and underline the sentence.

> annual   defined   investments   reaction   specific

Then, on another piece of paper, copy and complete the chart.

Academic word	Phrase or sentence from article	Part of speech	Dictionary definition	My sentence
annual	*before his $191,000 annual checks arrived*	*adjective*	*every year*	*It's important to get an annual health check-up.*

3 Talk with a partner

Answer each question with evidence from the reading.
Use one of the phrases in the Useful Language box.

1. Why was the paragraph about Calvin Ross called "Rich man, poor man?"
2. Why did Robert Novak end up living with his parents after he won the lottery?
3. Does winning the lottery usually have a positive or negative effect?

> **USEFUL LANGUAGE**
> Phrases to cite evidence:
> The article pointed out . . .
> The author states that . . .

> **Objective: CCR Anchor 9:** Analyze how two or more texts address similar themes or topics in order to build knowledge or to compare the approaches the authors take.

4 Analyze the texts

Review the following texts to answer the questions below: (1) p. 50, *Stress: What You Ought to Know* and (2) p. 145, *Winning the Lottery Can Be Stressful*.

1. What is the topic of both articles?
2. Are the definitions of stress the same or different in both articles? Use information from both texts to support your answer.
3. Reread "What are the signs of stress" in *Stress: What You Ought to Know*. Provide two examples of physical or emotional stress from *Winning the Lottery Can Be Stressful*.
4. Reread "How can you manage stress" in *Stress: What You Ought to Know*. Does this paragraph provide solutions to the people in the three stories in *Winning the Lottery Can Be Stressful*? Why or why not?
5. If you were to win the lottery, do you think it would be stressful? Why or why not? Use evidence from both articles to support your opinion.

5 Before you write

Copy and complete the graphic organizer on another piece of paper. Fill it in with (1) your topic, (2) two examples of how the articles are the same, and (3) two examples of how the articles are different. Use information from Exercises 1–4 and evidence from the two articles. Finally, (4) fill in the conclusion with your answer to question five in Exercise 4.

Topic:	
Stress: What You Ought to Know	**Winning the Lottery Can Be Stressful**
HOW THE SAME?	
HOW DIFFERENT?	
Conclusion:	

6 Write

Write one paragraph that compares and contrasts the two articles that discuss stress. Use the information from your graphic organizer.

7 After you write

A Check your writing. Did you include all the ideas in your graphic organizer?
B Share your writing with a partner.
  a. Take turns. Read your writing to your partner.
  b. Read your partner's writing to yourself. Compare it to your partner's graphic organizer.
  c. Comment on your partner's writing: Ask one question; share one thing you learned.

Reading Tip: Read the proverb. What do you think it means? Can you guess how it is connected to the picture?

"Give a man a fish, and you have fed him for today. Teach a man to fish, and you have fed him for a lifetime."

∼ Heifer International ∼

A well-known Chinese and English proverb says, "Give a man a fish, and you have fed him for today. Teach a man to fish, and you have fed him for a lifetime." This proverb, or statement that gives advice, represents the beliefs of Heifer International, an organization that gives gifts of live animals to poor families all over the world.

Heifer International was started by an American farmer named Dan West. West was a volunteer relief worker in Spain during its civil war, from 1936 to 1939. His job was to decide who would  receive the small amount of food aid offered to them. Because there was not enough food, many people died. West realized that it was good to give people food, but it was more important to help them find a way to produce or create their own food. With this simple idea, West founded Heifer International as soon as he returned to America.

The first group of heifers — young female cows -- was shipped to Puerto Rico in 1944. Families used the animals to produce milk, fertilizer (food for plants), and calves, which are baby cows. Also, each family agreed to give its heifer's first female calf to another family. West called this "passing on the gift." In this way, an entire community would benefit from the gift of one heifer.

Today, Heifer International gives gifts of heifers, sheep, goats, and many other animals. Since 1944, it has helped more than 8 million people in 125 countries. The story of Christine Makahumure from Rwanda is typical. After her husband died in a war, Christine had no way to support her parents and young daughter. She applied to Heifer International and received a cow. She used some of the milk to feed her family and sold the rest. With the money she made by selling milk, she was able to buy a small house for her parents. To meet her commitment of "passing it on," she gave her cow's first calf to a neighbor as a gift. She also adopted and took care of four orphans -- local children whose parents had died. According to the Heifer International Web site, "Christine is living proof of the life-changing difference an animal from Heifer can make" to the people of a community.

UNIT 5

1 Check your understanding

1. Look at the reading tip again. Restate the proverb in your own words.
2. Explain the saying "passing on the gift" in your own words.
3. What gave Dan West the idea to start Heifer International?
4. How did Christine survive after her husband died in the war?
5. How does Christine's story illustrate the way Heifer International can change the lives of more than one person in a community?

2 Build your vocabulary

A English often uses punctuation, such as dashes and commas, with synonyms and phrases to signal definitions. Find the words in Column 1 in the paragraphs indicated and underline them. Then complete the chart with the punctuation that signaled the meaning, and the definition, explanation or example.

Word	Signal	Definition, explanation or example
1. proverb, ¶1	comma	*statement that gives advice*
2. Heifer International, ¶1		
3. heifers, ¶3		
4. fertilizer, ¶3		
5. calves, ¶3		
6. orphans, ¶4		

B Find each of the following academic words in the article and underline the sentence.

> aid   civil   commitment   community   founded

Then, on another piece of paper, copy and complete the chart.

Academic word	Phrase or sentence from article	Part of speech	Dictionary definition	My sentence
aid	*who would receive the small amount of food aid offered to them*	*noun*	*help, assistance*	*The Red Cross gives aid to people who need help after a disaster.*

3 Talk with a partner

Answer each question with evidence from the reading. Use one of the phrases in the Useful Language box.

1. What can a heifer provide a family?
2. What other gifts does Heifer International give needy people?
3. What are two examples from the reading of "passing on the gift"?

> **USEFUL LANGUAGE**
> Phrases to cite evidence:
> According to the author, . . .
> The author states that . . .

> **Objective: CCR Anchor 9:** Analyze how two or more texts address similar themes or topics in order to build knowledge or to compare the approaches the authors take.

4 Analyze the texts

Review the following articles to answer the questions below: (1) p. 64, *Running with Ropes*; and (2) p. 148, *Heifer International*.

1. What is the main idea of both articles?
2. Both articles describe people who need help and people who give help. Who needed help? Who gave help?
3. Both articles describe people who have received help from others. What help did they need? Why did they need it?
4. For each article, describe the reason for giving help and the benefits the giver identified.
5. The articles describe how Scott, Justin, Dan and Christine's lives changed. Describe in your own words how their lives changed. Who do you think benefited more, the giver or the receiver? Explain why.

5 Before you write

Copy and complete the graphic organizer on another piece of paper. Fill it in with (1) the main idea and (2) answers to the questions for each organization. Use information from Exercises 1–4 and evidence from the two articles. Finally, (3) fill in the conclusion with your answer to question five in Exercise 4.

Main Idea:		
	Running With Ropes	*Heifer International*
1. Who experienced a problem?		
2. What was the problem?		
3. Who helped to solve the problem?		
4. What was the solution?		
5. How did the receiver benefit?		
6. How did the giver benefit?		
Conclusion:		

6 Write

Write one paragraph about the life-changing events described in the articles and the benefits to both giver and receiver. Use information from your graphic organizer.

7 After you write

A Check your writing. Did you include all the ideas in your graphic organizer?

B Share your writing with a partner.
   a. Take turns. Read your writing to your partner.
   b. Read your partner's writing to yourself. Compare it to your partner's graphic organizer.
   c. Comment on your partner's writing: Ask one question; share one thing you learned.

Reading Tip: Look at the picture. Identify the different things in the picture. Read the title. What do you think the article is about?

Multitasking: Time saver or time waster?

Are you a multitasker? Do you watch TV and cook dinner at the same time? Do you often interrupt your work to check your email? Do you talk on your phone while you're driving? If you do these or similar things, then you are one of many multitaskers. According to a survey, or study, by the magazine *Scientific American MIND*, 90 percent of American adults multitask regularly.

Most people say they multitask because they are too busy, and multitasking saves time. Popular electronic devices like tablets and smart phones make it convenient to do several tasks at once, so people feel like they are getting more done. Melissa Brown of Evanston, Illinois, says she has no trouble listening to music, surfing the Internet, and sending text messages to friends while she does her homework.

Recent studies, however, show that Melissa and others like her are perhaps getting less done than they think they are. That's because with multitasking, there are actually many "microinterruptions" in which people stop one task, start another, and eventually return to the first one. These stops and starts make it difficult to concentrate, and so multitaskers actually waste time, according to a study at Microsoft Corporation. In the study, workers who interrupted their work to answer an email or text message took an average of 15 minutes to return to the work they were doing before the interruption.

Some psychologists say that the human brain just isn't good at concentrating on two things at the same time. This doesn't matter if you're only preparing a salad and listening to the radio, they say. But if you're doing a difficult task that requires thinking, like writing a report, then multitasking can slow you down and cause mistakes. It can even be dangerous, as in the case of people who talk on the phone, eat, or even apply makeup while driving.

In short, even though most people believe multitasking saves time, studies show that the opposite is true. Experts, or people who know a lot about saving time, offer some basic advice: try to focus on one task at a time. Check email just once an hour, turn off distracting noise while you're working, and most importantly, avoid talking on the phone while you're driving.

UNIT 6

1 Check your understanding

1. Look at the reading tip again. Did you guess correctly? Restate what the article is about.
2. According to the article, why do people multitask?
3. What did the Microsoft Corporation study find out about workers who stopped their work to check emails?
4. Find what some psychologists say about multitasking and difficult tasks. Underline the sentence. Restate it in your own words.
5. Read the last paragraph. What do experts advise about multitasking?

2 Build your vocabulary

A Many English words are based on Latin or Greek prefixes. Find the prefixes in Column 1 in the paragraphs indicated and underline the words that contain them. Then complete the chart by writing the word and your guess of its meaning.

Prefix	Signal	Example from article	Meaning
1. multi, ¶1	many	*multitasker*	*Someone who does several things at once*
2. micro, ¶3	small		
3. inter, ¶3	between		
4. pre, ¶4	before		
5. psycho, ¶4	mind		
6. mis, ¶4	wrong		

B Find each of the following academic words in the article and underline the sentence.

> experts   concentrate   focus   requires   survey

Then, on another piece of paper, copy and complete the chart.

Academic word	Phrase or sentence from article	Part of speech	Dictionary definition	My sentence
experts	*Experts, or people who know a lot about saving time, offer some basic advice*	*noun*	*specialists*	*It's important to get financial advice from experts.*

3 Talk with a partner

Answer each question with evidence from the reading. Use one of the phrases in the Useful Language box.

1. How many Americans multitask?
2. How does Melissa Brown feel about multitasking?
3. What did the Microsoft Corporation study show?

> **USEFUL LANGUAGE**
> Phrases to report ideas or research:
> _____ (name of person) indicated that . . .
> _____ (name of company or study) reported that . . .

Objective: CCR Anchor 9: Analyze how two or more texts address similar themes or topics in order to build knowledge or to compare the approaches the authors take.

4 Analyze the texts

Review the following texts to answer the questions below: (1) p. 76, *The Impact of Technology*; and (2) p. 151, *Multitasking: Time saver or time waster?*

1. What topic do both articles address?
2. Both articles mention different kinds of technology. Identify two from each article.
3. New technology can have a negative as well as a positive impact. Cite the example of a negative outcome described in the article *"Multitasking: Time saver or time waster?"* and the example of a positive outcome described in the article *"The Impact of Technology."*
4. Both articles provide research or statistics. Give one example from each article.
5. Do you think the technology featured in these articles makes your life better or causes you more problems? Use your own experience and information from the articles to support your answer.

5 Before you write

Copy and complete the graphic organizer on another piece of paper. Fill it in with (1) the topic and (2) two examples for each key point. Use the information from Exercises 1–4 and evidence from the two articles. Finally, (3) fill in the conclusion with your answer to question five in Exercise 4.

Topic:		
Kinds of Technology	**Research about Technology**	**Advantages / Disadvantages of using Technology**
Examples	Examples	Examples
Conclusion:		

6 Write

Write one paragraph that discusses different kinds of technology, research about technology, and advantages and disadvantages of using technology. Use information from your graphic organizer.

7 After you write

A Check your writing. Did you include all the ideas in your graphic organizer?

B Share your writing with a partner.
   a. Take turns. Read your writing to your partner.
   b. Read your partner's writing to yourself. Compare it to your partner's graphic organizer.
   c. Comment on your partner's writing: Ask one question; share one thing you learned.

Reading Tip: Look at the title. Then read the first sentence in each paragraph. What is the article about? Read and find out.

Amazing Bargains on Internet Auction Sites

Would you like to buy a new pair of sneakers for $6.99? How about headphones for $3.50 or a leather coat for $20? In the past, you could only find bargains, or discounts, like these at thrift stores, flea markets, and garage sales. Nowadays, however, you can find them easily and conveniently at an Internet auction Web site.

In an auction, people who want to buy the same item bid against each other. That is, they compete, or try to win the item, by offering more and more money. The "winner" is the person who offers the highest price. In 1995, a clever immigrant to the United States named Pierre Omidyar had the brilliant idea of starting an auction site on the Internet. He named it eBay. And eBay has become one of the largest and most successful online auction sites, although there are many others.

You can buy almost anything at an online auction. There is practical everyday merchandise like car parts, children's clothing, laptops, books, and sports equipment. There are collectors' items like rare and unusual stamps, glass animals, valuable old photographs, or comic books. And then there are the strange, off-the-wall items that have sold on Internet auction sites: a ten-year-old grilled cheese sandwich that showed the head of the Virgin Mary, which sold for $28,000 in 2004; and the entire town of Albert, Texas, which sold for $3.8 million in 2007.

You can also sell almost anything at an Internet auction site. Is your garage full of worthless old junk? Sell it online to the highest bidder! Do you have an old smart phone or computer that you aren't using anymore? Price them cheaply and someone is sure to bid on them. Millions of people utilize online auction sites every day to sell their "unwanted items". Many people have even started lucrative online auction businesses that earn hundreds or even thousands of dollars each month.

Since 1995, online auction sites have become enormously popular. As an example, eBay has almost 150 million registered users in 30 countries. Of course, there are some disadvantages to shopping at online auctions. You cannot touch the merchandise you are buying, and after you buy something, there is often a limited refund period. However, the convenience of the sites and the possibility of finding bargains are the reasons why millions of people buy and sell regularly at Internet auctions.

1 Check your understanding

1. What is the main idea of the article?
2. How do Internet auction sites work?
3. Describe one well-known auction site that the article talks about.
4. What are some of the things that people can buy on Internet auction sites?
5. Read the last paragraph. Do you think the author is in favor of Internet auction sites? Explain your answer.

2 Build your vocabulary

A Find the words in Column 1 in the paragraphs indicated and underline them. Which words are positive? Which words are negative? Write the clue that helped you guess.

Word	Clue	Positive	Negative
1. conveniently, ¶1	*easily*	☑	☐
2. brilliant, ¶2		☐	☐
3. practical, ¶3		☐	☐
4. off-the-wall, ¶3		☐	☐
5. junk, ¶4		☐	☐
5. lucrative, ¶4		☐	☐

B Find each of the following academic words in the article and underline the sentence.

enormously   equipment   immigrant   items   utilize

Then, on another piece of paper, copy and complete the chart.

Academic word	Phrase or sentence from article	Part of speech	Dictionary definition	My sentence
enormously	*auction sites have become enormously popular*	*adverb*	*to a large degree; extremely*	*He ate an enormously large dinner.*

3 Talk with a partner

Answer each question with evidence from the reading. Use one of the phrases in the Useful Language box.

1. When did Pierre Omidyar get his idea for eBay?
2. What are some practical things that people can buy on Internet auction sites?
3. What are some of the disadvantages to shopping at online auctions?

> **USEFUL LANGUAGE**
> Phrases to cite evidence:
> According to the article, . . .
> The article states that . . .

UNIT 7

> **Objective: CCR Anchor 9:** Analyze how two or more texts address similar themes or topics in order to build knowledge or to compare the approaches the authors take.

4 Analyze the texts

Review the following texts to answer the questions below: (1) p. 90, *The Smart Shopper*; and (2) p. 154, *Amazing Bargains on Internet Auction Sites*.

1. What is the topic shared by the articles?
2. What are some ways that the articles are similar?
3. What are some ways that the articles are different?
4. Which article is more positive about online shopping? Explain your answer.
5. Based on what you have read or based on your experience, do you recommend online shopping? Cite examples from both articles to support your answer.

5 Before you write

Copy and complete the graphic organizer on another piece of paper. Fill it in with: (1) the topic shared by the articles, (2) two examples of how the articles are the same, and (3) two examples of how they are different. Use information from Exercises 1–4 and evidence from the two articles. Finally, (4) fill in the conclusion with your answer to question five in Exercise 4.

Topic:	
The Smart Shopper	*Amazing Bargains on Internet Auction Sites*
HOW THE SAME?	
HOW DIFFERENT?	
Conclusion:	

6 Write

Write one paragraph that compares and contrasts the two articles about online shopping. Use information from your graphic organizer.

7 After you write

A Check your writing. Did you include all the ideas in your graphic organizer?

B Share your writing with a partner.
   a. Take turns. Read your writing to your partner.
   b. Read your partner's writing to yourself. Compare it to your partner's graphic organizer.
   c. Comment on your partner's writing: Ask one question; share one thing you learned.

Reading Tip: Read the last paragraph of the article. What is the article about? What is the main idea?

The Benefits of Telecommuting

Gloria Alvarez gets up at 6:30 a.m. each weekday morning and goes into her kitchen. There, she makes coffee and prepares breakfast for her two teenagers. After the children take off for school, she heads for work. Most days, she gets dressed first, but once in a while, she works in her pajamas. However, no one cares, because Ms. Alvarez is one of a growing number of Americans who telecommute, or telework. That is, they work from home, and they use technology – a computer, phone, and fax machine – to stay in touch with their workplace.

According to Global Workplace Analytics, 3.7 million employees (2.8% of the workforce) now work from home at least half the time. Many commuters are mothers like Alvarez, who work from home full-time as a customer service representative for a major clothing company.

Telecommuting has great advantages for both workers and employers. For workers, the best benefit is the time they save because they don't have to travel. Parents who telecommute can spend more time with their children. Likewise, they are available to take care of additional family responsibilities. Furthermore, working at home is also convenient for disabled people and others who have difficulty traveling. In addition, telecommuting gives workers more opportunities because, thanks to technology, they can work for companies that are not near their homes.

Employers also benefit when workers telecommute. They save money because they don't need as much office or parking space. Moreover, their workers are less likely to leave the company and look for another job because they are more motivated. Also, studies show that telecommuters can often complete more work in less time, because they don't have to deal with office interruptions.

Research shows that almost half of U.S. workers have jobs that they can do at home at least part of the time. Examples are managers, telephone salespeople, writers, computer programmers, artists, and customer service representatives. In the future, if all these people are able to work at home, they can avoid miles of driving and save millions of gallons of gasoline. In this way, telecommuting could help not just workers and companies, but also the earth.

1 Check your understanding

1. What is the main idea of the text?
2. According to the article, what are the benefits of telecommuting for workers?
3. According to the article, what are the benefits of telecommuting for employers?
4. Where do people who telecommute usually do their work?
5. Do you agree that telecommuting is beneficial? Support your opinion with examples from the article.

2 Build your vocabulary

A Transitions are words and phrases that link ideas between sentences and paragraphs as well as within sentences. Some transitions signal addition of ideas — such as *also*. Other transitions signal contrast between ideas — such as *but*. Find the transition words and phrases in Column 1 in the paragraphs indicated and underline them. Then complete the chart by identifying the two ideas they connect. Finally, identify the purpose of the transition by checking the correct box.

Transition word	First idea	Second idea	Purpose	
			Adds an idea	Contrasts two ideas
1. however, ¶1	*she works in her pajamas*	*no one cares*	☐	☑
2. likewise, ¶3			☐	☐
3. furthermore, ¶3			☐	☐
4. in addition, ¶3			☐	☐
5. moreover, ¶4			☐	☐

B Find each of the following academic words in the article and underline the sentence.

available   benefit   major   motivated   research

Then, on another piece of paper, copy and complete the chart.

Academic word	Phrase or sentence from article	Part of speech	Dictionary definition	My sentence
available	*and are available to take care of family responsibilities*	*adjective*	*free, uncommitted*	*I am available to meet with you tomorrow.*

3 Talk with a partner

Answer each question with evidence from the reading.
Use one of the phrases in the Useful Language box.

1. What do studies show about the productivity of telecommuters versus employees at the workplace?
2. Who are some of the people who benefit the most from telecommunicating?
3. What equipment do telecommuters need to have at home to do their work?

> **USEFUL LANGUAGE**
> Phrases to cite evidence:
> According to the author, . . .
> The author states that . . .

> **Objective: CCR Anchor 9:** Analyze how two or more texts address similar themes or topics in order to build knowledge or to compare the approaches the authors take.

4 Analyze the texts

Review the following texts to answer the questions below: (1) p. 102, *Hard and Soft Job Skills*; and (2) p. 157, *The Benefits of Telecommuting*.

1. What is the topic of both articles?
2. Both articles describe people who work. How is Som's job different from Gloria's job? Give two examples of differences.
3. How is Som's job similar to Gloria's job? Give two examples of similarities.
4. What are a few reasons Som thrives at his job in the workplace and Gloria enjoys telecommuting?
5. The two articles are about working in the actual workplace and telecommuting. Which way do you think is more beneficial? Explain why. Use examples from both articles.

5 Before you write

Copy and complete the graphic organizer on another piece of paper. Fill it in with (1) your opinion based on your answer to question five in Exercise 4, (2) three key arguments and (3) evidence to support each argument. Use the information from Exercises 1–4 and evidence from the two articles. Finally, (4) fill in a conclusion based on your opinion.

Opinion:	
3 Key Arguments	**Evidence to Support Arguments**
1.	1.
2.	2.
3.	3.
Conclusion:	

6 Write

Is working in the workplace more or less beneficial than telecommuting? Write one paragraph that gives your opinion, arguments and supporting evidence. Use information from your graphic organizer.

7 After you write

A Check your writing. Did you include all the ideas in your graphic organizer?

B Share your writing with a partner.
   a. Take turns. Read your writing to your partner.
   b. Read your partner's writing to yourself. Compare it to your partner's graphic organizer.
   c. Comment on your partner's writing: Ask one question; share one thing you learned.

Reading Tip: Before you read, look at the title and headings. What is the article about?

Plastic Bags – Convenience or Catastrophe?

Prior to the invention of plastic bags, shoppers used paper bags. Often these bags would tear easily, and they were not easy to carry from store to store. The first plastic bags were developed in the 1950s. Their simple design with built-in handles offered a strong carrying bag with a high load capacity. Store owners liked plastic bags because they were cheaper to purchase than paper bags, and shoppers thought they were easy to use and much stronger than paper bags. By the 1980s, plastic bags had completely replaced paper shopping bags in grocery chains and stores.

So why are they a catastrophe?
Although other countries use plastic bags, in the United States they are almost an institution. People in the United States throw away almost 100 billion plastic bags every year. Unfortunately, many of these plastic bags fly off garbage trucks and landfills and go into waterways or spoil the landscape. These plastic bags are not biodegradable, so it takes 10 to 20 years for them to disintegrate in landfills. Eventually, they break down into smaller pieces, which then pollute the land and water. Another problem is they are a serious danger to birds and marine mammals that mistake them for food. For example, sea turtles regularly try to eat floating plastic bags because they think they are jellyfish.

What can be done about the problem?
Many businesses have stopped offering customers plastic bags and even some communities have banned them. There are two things that can be done immediately to reduce the use of plastic bags.
1. Switch to reusable shopping bags.
These bags are convenient and come in a variety of sizes, styles and materials. When they aren't using being used, they can be folded up and put into a pocket or purse.
2. Recycle plastic bags.
If people have to use some plastic bags, they need to be sure to recycle them. Many grocery stores have places to recycle plastic bags. More and more people are questioning whether the convenience of using plastic bags is outweighed by the catastrophe that these bags create for our planet. One frequent shopper concludes, "Sure plastic bags are convenient, but they are not worth the trouble! Every time I carry something in plastic, I think of the plastic littering our parks, the years and years it takes for plastic to decompose, and those poor turtles eating them and dying."

1 Check your understanding

1. Look at the reading tip again. Did you guess correctly? What is the main idea of this article?
2. Why does the author say plastic bags are so convenient?
3. According to the article, why are plastic bags a catastrophe? Underline the three reasons given.
4. What are two suggestions from the article to reduce the use of plastic bags?
5. Read the last sentence of the article. Restate it in your own words. Why do you think the author put that quote in the article?

2 Build your vocabulary

A Many English words are based on Latin or Greek prefixes. Find the prefixes in Column 1 in the paragraphs indicated and underline the full word. Use a dictionary to complete the chart with the meaning of each word.

Prefix	Meaning of Prefix	Word from reading	Meaning of word
1. dis-, ¶2	away	*disintegrate*	*break into fragments*
2. un-, ¶2	not		
3. re-, ¶3	again		
re-, ¶3			
4. re-, ¶1	back backward		
re-, ¶3			
5. de-, ¶4	not		

B Find each of the following academic words in the article and underline the sentence.

capacity   concludes   design   institution   prior

Then, on another piece of paper, copy and complete the chart.

Academic word	Phrase or sentence from article	Part of speech	Dictionary definition	My sentence
capacity	*a strong carrying bag with a high load capacity*	*noun*	*the amount that a container can hold*	*I need a pitcher with one quart capacity.*

3 Talk with a partner

Answer each question with evidence from the reading.
Use one of the phrases in the Useful Language box.

1. Why do turtles try to eat plastic bags?
2. Which country uses the most plastic bags?
3. How long does it take plastic bags to disintegrate in landfills?

USEFUL LANGUAGE
Phrases to cite evidence:
The author reports that . . .
The author points out that . . .

Objective: CCR Anchor 9: Analyze how two or more texts address similar themes or topics in order to build knowledge or to compare the approaches the authors take.

4 Analyze the texts

Review the following texts to answer the questions below: (1) p. 116, *All Things Are Connected*; and (2) p. 160, *Plastic Bags: Convenience or Catastrophe?*

1. What is the topic of both the fable and the article?
2. Both the fable and the article describe a problem. Identify the problem in the fable and the article.
3. Both the fable and the article explain what caused the problem. What are the causes for each problem identified in question #2?
4. What are the effects of the causes identified in question #3?
5. The old woman in the fable always told the chief, "All things are connected." Do you agree or disagree? Use evidence from both the fable and the article to support your opinion.

5 Before you write

Copy and complete the graphic organizer on another piece of paper. Fill it in with (1) the topic, (2) the problems, (3) the causes of each problem and (4) the effect (or what happened) for the fable and the article. Use information from Exercises 1–4 and evidence from the two articles. Finally, (5) fill in the conclusion with your answer to question five in Exercise 4.

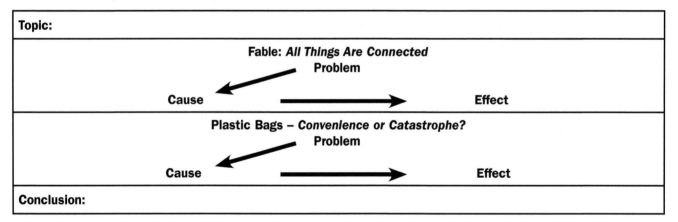

Topic:
Fable: *All Things Are Connected*
Problem — Cause → Effect
Plastic Bags – *Convenience or Catastrophe?*
Problem — Cause → Effect
Conclusion:

6 Write

Write one paragraph that identifies two main problems, one in the fable and one in the article, and the causes and effects of each of those two problems. Use the information in your graphic organizer.

7 After you write

A Check your writing. Did you include all the ideas in your graphic organizer?

B Share your writing with a partner.
   a. Take turns. Read your writing to your partner.
   b. Read your partner's writing to yourself. Compare it to your partner's graphic organizer.
   c. Comment on your partner's writing: Ask one question; share one thing you learned.

Reading Tip: Read the title and the first and last paragraphs to find the meaning of the topic. What is the article about?

Kwanzaa

Americans celebrate several holidays in December. These are: Christmas, Hanukkah, Kwanzaa, and depending on the year, Eid al-Adha. But unlike Christmas, Hanukkah, and Eid al-Adha, Kwanzaa is not a religious holiday. It celebrates African–American culture, community, and family.

Dr. Maulana Karenga, a professor at California State University, Long Beach, created Kwanzaa in 1966. For many years, he looked for a way to bring African–American people together by connecting them with their African roots, or beginnings. *Kwanzaa* comes from a phrase in Kiswahili, a language spoken in eastern and central Africa, for "first fruits." So the holiday combines traditions from different African harvest festivals.

The number seven is important in Kwanzaa. The holiday lasts seven days, from December 26 to January 1, and there are seven principles, or rules, to follow. The Nguzo Saba, or seven principles, are:

1. *Umoja* (unity): Joining together to form and maintain unity in the family, community, and as African–Americans;
2. *Kujichagulia* (self-determination): To speak for, create for, and take care of ourselves;
3. *Ujima* (collective work and responsibility): Building the community and solving its problems together;
4. *Ujamaa* (cooperative economics): A community building and profiting from its own businesses;
5. *Nia* (purpose): The goal of building and developing African–American communities;
6. *Kuumba* (creativity): Using new ideas to make the community beautiful and successful;
7. *Imani* (faith): Belief in the importance of African and African–American culture, history, family, and leaders.

Each family celebrates Kwanzaa in its own way. Celebrations often include songs and dances, African drumming, storytelling, poetry, and traditional foods. Many people enjoy wearing brightly colored African clothes. On each of the seven nights, the family gathers and a child lights a candle. Then the family discusses one of the seven principles. Kwanzaa also has seven basic symbols that symbolize values and ideas from African culture. The symbols include an ear of corn, a cup, candles, a candleholder, crops (fruits, nuts, and vegetables), a mat, and gifts. A feast of African or African–American foods, called *karamu*, is held on December 31.

Kwanzaa is growing in popularity around the world. It is now celebrated by almost 20 million people with African ancestry in the United States, the United Kingdom, the Bahamas, and Brazil, as well as in Kenya and Zimbabwe.

1 Check your understanding

1. What is the purpose of this article?
2. Why and when was Kwanzaa created?
3. How is Kwanzaa different from the other American holidays in December?
4. What is done on each of the seven nights of Kwanzaa?
5. Which of the seven principles of Kwanzaa do you think is the most important? Explain why.

2 Build your vocabulary

A Suffixes are letter(s) added to the end of a word to change its meaning or part of speech. The suffix *–ity* is added to adjectives to change them to nouns. Find the nouns that end in *-ity* in the paragraph indicated and underline them. Write the words into Column 1 in the chart. Then use a dictionary to complete the chart with the definition of the noun and the adjective form of the word.

Nouns	Definition	Adjective
1. ¶**1**, community	*Any group living in the same area or having common interests.*	*communal*
2. ¶**2**, _____		
3. ¶**3**, _____		
4. ¶**3**, _____		
5. ¶**3**, _____		
6. ¶**5**, _____		

B Find each of the following academic words in the article and underline the sentence.

> cooperative   maintain   principles   symbolize   traditions

Then, on another piece of paper, copy and complete the chart.

Academic word	Phrase or sentence from article	Part of speech	Dictionary definition	My sentence
cooperative	*cooperative economics*	*adjective*	*acting or working together with others*	*Cleaning up after the party was a cooperative effort.*

3 Talk with a partner

Answer each question with evidence from the reading.
Use one of the phrases in the Useful Language box.

1. What is *umoja*?
2. What is *karamu*?
3. How many people around the world celebrate Kwanzaa?

> **USEFUL LANGUAGE**
> Phrases to cite evidence:
> The article defines . . . as . . .
> The article estimates that . . .

Objective: CCR Anchor 9: Analyze how two or more texts address similar themes or topics in order to build knowledge or to compare the approaches the authors take.

4 Analyze the texts

Review the following texts to answer the questions below: (1) p. 128, *Special Birthdays Around the World;* and (2) p. 163, *Kwanzaa.*

1. What topic do the two articles share?
2. What are two similar activities that happen during Kwanzaa and birthday celebrations around the world?
3. Both articles describe symbols used in celebrations. Give an example from each article.
4. Give an example from each article about the significance of numbers in the celebrations.
5. Both articles describe holidays or celebrations that bring families or communities together. What holiday or celebration in your culture brings families or communities together? How is it similar or different from those described in the two articles?

5 Before you write

Copy and complete the graphic organizer on another piece of paper. Fill it in with (1) the topic and (2) details about Kwanzaa and birthday celebrations in two different countries. Use information from Exercises 1–4 and evidence from the two articles. Finally, (3) fill in the conclusion with your answer to question five in Exercise 4.

Topic:			
	Kwanzaa	**Birthday celebration**	**Birthday celebration**
1. Where is it celebrated?			
2. What is it?			
3. When is it celebrated?			
4. What are two customs?			
5. What are two symbols that are part of the celebration?			
Conclusion:			

6 Write

Write one paragraph that describes Kwanzaa and birthday celebrations from two different countries. Use information from your graphic organizer.

7 After you write

A Check your writing. Did you include all the ideas in your graphic organizer?

B Share your writing with a partner.
   a. Take turns. Read your writing to your partner.
   b. Read your partner's writing to yourself. Compare it to your partner's graphic organizer.
   c. Comment on your partner's writing: Ask one question; share one thing you learned.

Unit 1

Exercise 1

1. Mr. Kimmel's class buzzes with activity. Students move around to different learning centers.
2. The article describes six learning centers.
3. Students can look at photos, draw, paint, build, and create things.
4. Students can dig in the dirt and learn about planting and caring for vegetables and flowers.
5. Answers will vary.

Exercise 2 A

1. class. . . buzzes with activity; makes a low humming sound like bees, machinery, or people talking
2. places where they [students] can work on different skills; a section of a classroom for independent learning activities
3. practice at home; to borrow something for a period of time
4. quiet reflection; contemplation and reflection
5. outside, small garden; a place for educating people about nature
6. really like; having enthusiasm or excitement about something

Exercise 2 B

1. create, (¶2); Students can . . . use their imagination to create things; verb; to make something new or imaginative; Answers will vary.
2. individually, (¶1); work on different skills, individually or in small groups; adverb; separately; Answers will vary.
3. journals, (¶6); students can write in their journals; noun; personal records kept on a daily basis; Answers will vary.
4. logic, (¶4); This area has games and puzzles that require logic; noun; reasoned thought; Answers will vary.
5. theory, (¶1); Howard Gardner's theory of multiple intelligences; noun; an idea that explains something; Answers will vary.

Exercise 3

1. Mr. Kimmel states that his job as a teacher is to provide his students a variety of learning experiences that will help them use and develop all of their intelligences.
2. The article states that the "word center" is a popular place for storytelling.
3. One student states that she likes Mr. Kimmel's class because there are lots of interesting things to do and she's never bored.

Exercise 4

1. The main idea in both articles is that people are intelligent in different ways and that they experience and learn about the world around them differently.
2. The "STEM" corner addresses Logical/Mathematical intelligence. There students can work on math problems, scientific experiments, games and puzzles that require logic, and take apart and put back together old appliances.
3. The word center addresses Verbal/Linguistic intelligence. There students read and listen to stories, biographies, and poetry, do crossword puzzles and word games, use dictionaries, and write.
4. The quiet zone addresses Intrapersonal intelligence. There students can spend time in quiet reflection and meditation, write in their journals, and complete self-assessments.
5. Answers will vary.

Exercise 5

Answers will vary.

Exercise 6

Answers will vary.

Unit 2

Exercise 1

1. The article is about the importance of education.
2. The reason that Rafael's teacher said Rafael was a dedicated student is because Rafael took morning, afternoon and evening classes.
3. Rafael's first job was a houseman at a hotel. Other job's he's had at a hotel are lead houseman, banquet manager, banquet waiter and banquet captain.

4. Rafael's goal is to become a food and beverage manager. To achieve his goal he plans to begin a certificate program.

5. Answers will vary.

Exercise 2 A

1. verb; education – noun; educational - adjective

2. verb; encouraging – adjective;

3. noun; passionate – adjective; passionately, adverb

4. verb; success – noun; successful - adjective

5. adverb; strong – adjective; strength - noun

6. verb; belief – noun; believable – adjective; believer - noun

Exercise 2 B

1. eventually (¶4); Eventually he wants to be the general manager of a major hotel; adverb; after a lot of delays or problems; Answers will vary.

2. major (¶4); Eventually he wants to be the general manager of a major hotel; adjective; main or most important; Answers will vary.

3. obtain (¶3); Rafael's career counselor helped him obtain a weekend job; verb; get; Anwers will vary.

4. promoted (¶3); Soon, Rafael was promoted to the position of lead houseman, then banquet waiter; verb; to be given a better job or to advance on a job; Answers will vary.

5. registered (¶2); Right away he registered for ESL classes at San Diego City College; verb; to put a name on an official list; Answers will vary.

Exercise 3

1. One example the author gives is that he walked one hour to his elementary school.

2. One example the article gives is that Rafael took morning, afternoon, and evening classes.

3. One example the article gives is that he noticed Rafael's passion to succeed.

Exercise 4

1. Both articles describe immigrant stories of obstacles and successes.

2. In the article *An Immigrant Family's Success Story,* both the husband and wife attended English and citizenship classes and eventually earned their GED certificates. The husband also enrolled in college, graduated, and then registered in a master's degree

program. In the article *Rafael Salazar,* Rafael attended ESL classes in the morning, the afternoon and the evening.

3. Both articles provide examples of hard work and sacrifice. Choi and Lili Wei found night work cleaning businesses and restaurants, saved their money, and after six years were able to buy a small restaurant of their own. Rafael had a weekend job as a houseman in a local hotel while he was also studying.

4. Both articles provide examples of eventual success. The Weis saved their money and bought a small restaurant. Mr. Wei has graduated college and enrolled in a master's degree program in business. Rafael received the Outstanding Hospitality Worker Award at his hotel. He also plans to begin a certificate program in hotel management.

5. Answers will vary.

Exercise 5

Answers will vary.

Exercise 6

Answers will vary.

Unit 3

Exercise 1

1. The purpose of this article is to provide tips to immigrant parents for improving communication with their teens.

2. According to this article, parents can learn more English by attending free English classes in the community or studying English online for free.

3. It is important to set regular times for conversation because you can discuss experiences in adapting to the new culture and how the new culture is different from the home culture.

4. It is important to praise teenagers because they need positive feedback.

5. Answers will vary.

Exercise 2 A

1. struggle to establish their own identities; try; to make great efforts

2. these challenges are magnified; made bigger; to increase the apparent size of

3. Your children will respect you for trying to learn more English; look up to you; show honor for

4. provide praise; compliment; to express admiration and respect

5. Compliment them for their good behavior; say good things; something said in praise

6. express your love and appreciation for them; show; to put into words

Exercise 2 B

1. adapt (¶4); adapt to a new culture; verb; to adjust to new circumstances; Answers will vary.

2. conflict (¶1); this leads to conflict and stress; noun; sharp disagreement; Answers will vary.

3. establish (¶1); teens struggle to establish their own identities; verb; to bring about; Answers will vary.

4. isolated (¶7); keep open communication channels with teens so that they don't feel isolated.; adjective; to be set apart from others; Answers will vary.

5. stress (¶1); this leads to conflict and stress; noun; mental or physical strain, or difficulty caused by pressure; Answers will vary.

Exercise 3

1. The article states that the challenges of communication between immigrant parents and their teens are greater because teenagers have a greater identification with American culture than their parents have and teenagers speak more English than their parents.

2. The article states that the teens feel they lead double lives because they are trying to be traditional children at home and all-American children at school.

3. According to the article, the most important way for parents to help teens is to express their love and appreciation for their teens.

Exercise 4

1. The topic is communication barriers between immigrant parents and their teens.

2. The first barrier is language differences between parents and their teens. A solution for this is for the parent to study English at a free school in the community or study English online.

3. The second barrier is the demanding work schedule of an immigrant parent, which prevents the parent from spending time with their children. A solution would be to set regular times for conversation between the parents and children, such as eating meals together.

4. Any of the following might help: learning more English; setting regular times for conversation and interaction; and providing praise for a child as much as possible.

5. Answers will vary.

Exercise 5

Answers will vary.

Exercise 6

Answers will vary.

Unit 4

Exercise 1

1. The main article is about how a happy event, such as winning the lottery, can be stressful.

2. The article defines stress as our body's reaction to changing events in our lives.

3. According to the article, people usually have negative ideas about stress. The sentence that answers this question is "We usually think of change as negative, ..." The author is saying that when events produce change that change can create stress.

4. John and Susan Patel won the most money. They faced a problem when the store clerk who sold them the lottery ticket claimed that the Patels promised to give her $500,000 as a reward for selling them the winning ticket.

5. Answers will vary.

Exercise 2 A

1. *b*; as a result of

2. *a*; shouted angrily

3. *e*; promised

4. *f*; lottery winnings

5. *d*; without money

6. *c*; expensive cars, huge sums of money

Exercise 2 B

1. annual (¶4); adjective; happening once every year; Answers will vary.

2. defined (¶1); verb; to explain the meaning of; Answers will vary.

3. investments (¶4); noun; money spent on something in the hope of making more money; Answers will vary.

4. reaction (¶1); noun; something you do or say because of something that has been done or said; Answers will vary.

5. specific (¶2); adjective; exact, particular; Answers will vary.

Exercise 3

1. The article pointed out that Calvin Ross went from winning $5.6 million to working to pay off debts because of bad investments and excessive spending.

2. The author states that stress is our body's reaction to changing events in our lives.

3. The article pointed out that most people who win the lottery say it has had a positive effect on their lives and it says the three stories in the article are unusual.

Exercise 4

1. The topic of both articles is stress.

2. The definitions of stress in the two articles are the same.

3. All three stories in *Winning the Lottery Can Be Stressful* have examples of emotional stress. The Patels were shocked and upset by a demand for money from a clerk. For Robert Novak, failed businesses, a brother who tried to steal money from him, and a claim from Novak's landlady that Novak owed her half the lottery winnings resulted in his being broke and seeing a doctor for depression. Calvin Ross always ran out of money before he received his annual checks so now he is working to pay off debts.

4. The suggestions for managing stress include eating right, exercising regularly, and staying calm when in stressful situations. I don't believe the people in the three stories in *Winning the Lottery Can Be Stressful* followed the suggestions.

5. Answers will vary.

Exercise 5

Answers will vary.

Exercise 6

Answers will vary.

Unit 5

Exercise 1

1. If you give food to someone, you can feed him for one day. If you teach someone to grow or produce food, you can feed him for his whole life.

2. "Passing on the gift" means that when a family gets a female cow (heifer) as a gift, that family gives the first female baby (calf) to another family so that the whole community benefits from the gift of one heifer.

3. During West's volunteer relief work in Spain, he had to decide who would receive the small amount of food aid that they had. Since there wasn't enough food for everyone, he realized it was more important for them to learn how to produce or create their own food.

4. She applied to Heifer International and received a cow. She used some milk to feed her family and sold the rest.

5. Because when she got one cow from Heifer International, she was able to sell the milk to sustain herself and her family. She was also able to adopt four orphans. Christine gave her cow's first calf to a neighbor who could use that cow to help support herself and her family.

Exercise 2 A

1. comma; statement that gives advice

2. comma; an organization that gives gifts of live animals to poor families all over the world

3. dash; young female cows

4. parentheses; food for plants

5. comma; baby cows

6. dash; local children whose parents had died

Exercise 2 B

1. aid (¶2); who would receive the small amount of food aid offered to them; noun; help, assistance; Answers will vary.

2. civil (¶2); in Spain during its civil war; adjective; of or relating to the ordinary people of a country; Answers will vary.

3. commitment (¶4); To meet her commitment of "passing it on"; noun; a promise; Answers will vary.

4. community (¶3); an entire community would benefit; noun; all the people who live in a particular area; Answers will vary.

5. founded (¶2); West founded Heifer International as soon as he returned to America; verb; to bring something into existence; Answers will vary.

Exercise 3

1. According to the author, a heifer can provide a way for families to produce their own food.

2. The author states that Heifer International gives sheep, goats and other animals as gifts.

3. According to the author, two examples of "passing on the gift" are giving the baby's first calf to a neighbor so she could produce food and adopting children whose parents had died.

Exercise 4

1. The main idea in both articles is the benefit of giving and the joy of receiving.

2. Justin needed help. Scott gave help as the volunteer. Christine needed help. Heifer International (Dan West's company) gave a cow to help her produce food.

3. Justin needed help running because he was blind. Christine needed help because she didn't have any food for her family.

4. In *Running with Ropes,* Scott helped Justin run by holding on to a rope and guiding him while they were running. The giver, Scott, said that it was gratifying to share in the joy of the runners and to feel that they trusted him. He said those hours were the most rewarding part of his week and a worthwhile commitment. Dan West at Heifer International knew that it was good to give people food, but he felt that it was better to give the animal so that people could produce food, and then pass on the gift to help an entire community.

5. Scott's life changed because he was doing something rewarding and worthwhile; Justin's life changed because he got to run again. Christine's life changed because she got to feed and support her family; Dan West's life changed because he founded Heifer International and helped many communities. Answers will vary for the second part of this question.

Exercise 5

Answers will vary.

Exercise 6

Answers will vary.

Unit 6

Exercise 1

1. The article is about people multi-tasking, people who do more than one thing at a time.

2. According to the article, most people say they multitask because it saves time.

3. The Microsoft Corporation study found out that workers who stopped their work to check emails took an average of 15 minutes to return to the work they were doing before the interruption.

4. Some psychologists say that it is dangerous to to multitask when you are doing difficult tasks because it can result in errors and it can take longer to do the task.

5. Experts say that multitasking does not save time. They recommend that people focus on one task at a time. The article gives two examples: (1) don't check your email while you are doing something else; schedule a time to check your email and when you do that, don't do something else, too; and (2) when you are driving don't talk on the telephone.

Exercise 2 A

1. multitasker; someone who does more than one task at the same time

2. microinterruptions; short stops from a task and then returning to the task

3. interruptions; something that makes an activity stop for a short time

4. psychologists; someone who studies the mind and how it affects behavior

5. preparing; to get ready for something

6. mistakes; something wrong or incorrect

Exercise 2 B

1. experts (¶5); Experts, or people who know a lot about saving time, offer some basic advice; noun; specialists; Answers will vary.

2. concentrate (¶3); These stops and starts make it difficult to concentrate; verb; to think hard about something; Answers will vary.

3. focus (¶5); Try to focus on one task at a time; verb; to center one's attention; Answers will vary.

4. requires (¶4); But if you are doing a difficult task that requires thinking, like writing a report, then multitasking can slow you down and cause mistakes; verb; to need; Answers will vary.

5. survey (¶1); According to a survey, or study, by the magazine Scientific American MIND, 90 percent of American adults multitask regularly; noun; a set of questions designed to measure opinions; Answers will vary.

Exercise 3

1. A survey by the magazine *Scientific American MIND* indicated that 90 percent of American adults multitask regularly.

2. Melissa Brown reported that she has no trouble multitasking.

3. The Microsoft study indicated that 90 percent of American adults multitask regularly. It also indicated that workers who stopped their work to check emails took an average of 15 minutes to return to the work they were doing before the interruption.

Exercise 4

1. Both articles address the topic of technology.

2. Both articles mention different kinds of technology. The article on multitasking mentions electronic devices like tablets and smartphones. The article about the impact of technology mentions cars, radios, television, the Web, and credit cards.

3. The article about multitasking argues that technology has a negative impact when people multitask. One example is that it can make it difficult to concentrate. Another example the article gives is that multitasking can slow you down and cause mistakes. The article about the impact of technology focuses on how technology can change people's lives, especially in a positive way. One example the article gives is the use of the Web to access news. Another example the article gives is the development of credit cards, which means people can avoid carrying large amounts of cash.

4. The article about the impact of technology cites statistics on ways people get the news: in 1965, 72 percent of American got it from reading the newspaper; by 2005, that number was down to 50 percent. In 1993, 60 percent watched the news on television but by 2006, that number had dropped to 28 percent. It also provides statistics about credit cards: a year after the multi-purpose

credit card was developed, 42,000 people in the United States had the card. Two years after that, the card was used in four more countries – Canada, Cuba, Mexico and the United Kingdom. Research in the article about multitasking cites a survey by the magazine *Scientific American MIND* and a study by the Microsoft Corporation. The survey reported that 90 percent of American adults multitask regularly. The study reported that workers who interrupt their work to answer an e-mail or text message took an average of 15 minutes to return to the work they were doing before the interruption.

5. Answers will vary.

Exercise 5

Answers will vary.

Exercise 6

Answers will vary.

Unit 7

Exercise 1

1. The main idea of the article is that online auctions are popular.

2. The way Internet auction sites work is that sellers post items for sale, potential buyers bid against each other and the seller sells to the highest bidder.

3. E-Bay, one well-known auction site that the article talks about, has 150 registered users in 30 countries.

4. Things that people can buy on Internet auction sites include practical everyday merchandise like car parts, children's clothing, laptops, books and sports equipment; collectors' items like rare and unusual stamps, glass animals, valuable old photographs, or comic books; and strange items.

5. Answers will vary.

Exercise 2 A

1. easily; positive
2. clever; positive
3. everyday; positive
4. strange; negative
5. worthless; negative
6. earn hundreds or even thousands of dollars each month; positive

Exercise 2 B

1. enormously (¶5); Since 1995, online auction sites have become enormously popular; adverb; hugely; Answers will vary.

2. equipment (¶3); There is practical everyday merchandise like car parts, children's clothing, laptops, books, and sports equipment; noun; items needed for a purpose; Answers will vary.

3. immigrant (¶3); In 1995, a clever immigrant to the United States named Pierre Omidyar had the brilliant idea of starting an auction site on the Internet; noun; a person who moves to another country to live; Answers will vary.

4. items (¶3); There are collectors' items like rare and unusual stamps; adjective; a thing, an object; Answers will vary.

5. utilize (¶4); Millions of people utilize online auction sites every day to sell their "unwanted items"; verb; to use; Answers will vary.

Exercise 3

1. According to the article, Pierre Omidyar got his idea for eBay in 1995.

2. According to the article, people can buy practical things like car parts, children's clothing, laptops, books, and sports equipment on the Internet.

3. The article states that not being able to touch the merchandise and a limited refund period are two disadvantages to shopping at online auctions.

Exercise 4

1. The topic shared by the two articles is shopping online.

2. One way the articles are similar is that each mentions a disadvantage – the policy about refunds.

3. In some ways the articles are different. For example, *The Smart Shopper* is only about buying online, whereas the article about Internet auction sites discusses selling as well as buying online. Another difference is the focus of the two articles: *The Smart Shopper* focuses on a problem and advice on how to avoid the problem in the future; the article about Internet auction sites focuses on describing what an Internet auction site is. Finally, the information in *The Smart Shopper* applies to shopping in stores as well as online, whereas the article about Internet auction sites doesn't apply to stores.

4. The article about Internet auction sites is more positive than the article *The Smart Shopper*. The article about Internet auction sites only mentions a couple of disadvantages at the end. Most of the information in *The Smart Shopper* is about how to avoid problems; it lists seven questions to ask to avoid problems.

5. Answers will vary.

Exercise 5

Answers will vary.

Exercise 6

Answers will vary.

Unit 8

Exercise 1

1. The main idea of the text is that telecommuting is beneficial for employers and employees.

2. The benefits of telecommuting for workers are that employees can work from home and spend more time with their families and not have to spend time traveling to work; workers have more time to take care of additional family responsibilities; it's more convenient for disabled people; and people can work and live far from each other.

3. The benefits of telecommunicating for employers are that they save more on office and parking space, employees are more productive because they aren't interrupted in the office; workers probably won't leave the company and look for another job because they are more motivated.

4. People who telecommute usually do their work from home.

5. Answers will vary.

Exercise 2 A

1. she works in her pajamas; no one cares, contrasts two ideas

2. people can spend more time with their children; they are available to take care of additional family responsibilities; adds an idea

3. they are available to take care of additional family responsibilities; working at home is also convenient for disabled people; adds an idea

4. working at home is also convenient for disabled people and others who have difficulty traveling; telecommuting gives workers more opportunities; adds an idea

5. they save money because they don't need as much office or parking space; their workers are less likely to leave the company; adds an idea

Exercise 2 B

1. available (¶3); and are available to take care of family responsibilities; adjective; free, uncommitted. Answers will vary.

2. benefits (¶3); the best benefit is the time they save because they don't have to travel; noun; a helpful or good effect. Answers will vary.

3. major (¶2); for a major clothing company; adjective; more important or bigger. Answers will vary.

4. motivated (¶4); because they are more motivated; adjective; a reason for doing something. Answers will vary.

5. research (¶5); Research shows that almost half of U.S. workers have jobs; noun; a detailed study of a subject in order to discover information. Answers will vary.

Exercise 3

1. According to the author, studies show that telecommuters are more productive because they don't have office interruptions.

2. The author states that parents, disabled people, workers who don't live near their workplace, and employers who save money on office and parking space are some of the people who benefit the most from telecommunicating.

3. According to the author, telecommuters need to have a computer, phone and fax machine in order to do their work at home.

Exercise 4

1. The topic in both articles is work.

2. Some examples of how Som's job is different from Gloria's job are that Gloria works at home in her pajamas and Som goes to a workplace. Som has a lot of interaction with his co-workers. Gloria works alone and talks to customers over the phone or through the computer.

3. Som's job is similar to Gloria's job because they are both responsible for completing their work and they both work full time. They both seem to enjoy their jobs.

4. Som thrives at his job in the workplace because he has good people and technical skills. He gets along with his co-workers and his customers trust him. Gloria enjoys telecommuting because she can spend additional time with her family and she doesn't waste time driving to work.

5. Answers will vary.

Exercise 5

Answers will vary.

Exercise 6

Answers will vary.

Unit 9

Exercise 1

1. The main idea of the article is that although plastic bags are convenient, they can be a catastrophe if we don't do something about the problem.

2. The authors says that plastic bags are convenient because they are strong and they can hold a lot.

3. The article gives the following three reasons why plastic bags are a catastrophe: (1) they are not biodegradable, (2) they pollute the land and water, and (3) they're a danger to birds and marine life.

4. The article says we can reduce the use of plastic bags in two ways: (1) switch to reusable bags and (2) recycle the plastic.

5. The person quoted at the end of the article says that plastic bags are more trouble than they are worth. I believe the author used this quotation because it reflects his own opinion.

Exercise 2 A

1. disintegrate; break into fragments

2. unfortunately; sadly

3. reusable; able to use again

4. recycle; to process used items so they can be reused

5. replaced; to use one thing in place of another

6. reduce; to make something smaller or less important

7. decompose; to be slowly destroyed by a natural process such as decay

ANSWER KEY

Exercise 2 B

1. capacity (¶1); Their simple design with built-in handles offered a strong carrying bag with a high load capacity; noun; the amount something can hold; Answers will vary.

2. concludes (¶4); One frequent shopper concludes, "Sure plastic bags are convenient, but they are not worth the trouble!"; verb; to bring to an end; Answers will vary.

3. design (¶1); Their simple design with built-in handles offered a strong carrying bag with a high load capacity; noun; the way something is planned or made; Answers will vary.

4. institution (¶2); Although other countries use plastic bags, in the United States they are almost an institution; noun; a common custom in society; Answers will vary.

5. prior (¶1); Prior to the invention of plastic bags, shoppers used paper bags; adjective; before; Answers will vary.

Exercise 3

1. The author points out that turtles eat plastic bags because they mistake them for food.

2. The author points out that the United States is the country that uses the most plastic bags.

3. The author reports that it takes 10 to 20 years for plastic bags to disintegrate in landfills.

Exercise 4

1. The main topic of both articles is the connection between what we do and what happens because we do it. In the fable, killing frogs resulted in too many mosquitoes; in the article, using plastic bags results in ruining the environment.

2. Both the fable and the article describe a problem. The problem in the fable is too many mosquitoes. The problem in the article is what plastic bags do to the environment – filling up landfills, polluting land and water, and killing birds and animal.

3. Both the fable and the article explain what caused the problem. In the fable, the problem was caused because the king, who couldn't sleep because of the croaking of the frogs, had the frogs killed. In the article, people who wanted something more convenient to carry than paper or cloth bags caused the problem.

4. In the fable, the first result of killing the frogs was that there was nothing to kill the mosquitoes. The second result was that people had to leave the village because of the mosquitoes. In the

article, the result of plastic bags was that they are destroying the planet because they don't disintegrate like paper bags do.

5. Answers will vary.

Exercise 5

Answers will vary.

Exercise 6

Answers will vary.

Unit 10

Exercise 1

1. The purpose of this article is to describe the holiday Kwanzaa.

2. The holiday was created in 1966 by a professor at a university who wanted to find a way to bring African–American people together to celebrate their African roots.

3. Kwanzaa is different because it is not a religious holiday.

4. On each of the seven nights the family gathers and a child lights a candle. Then the family discusses one of the 7 principles or rules to follow.

5. Answers will vary.

Exercise 2 A

1. community; any group living in the same area or having common interests; communal

2. university; a 4-year college; universal

3. unit; oneness; united

4. responsibility; obligation; responsible

5. creativity; causing something to come into existence; creative

6. popularity; state of being liked by many people; popular

Exercise 2 B

1. cooperative (¶3); cooperative economics; adjective; acting or working together with others; Answers will vary.

2. maintain (¶3); maintain unity in the family; verb; to keep up; Answers will vary.

3. principles (¶3, ¶4); seven principles or rules to follow; noun; a fundamental truth; Answers will vary.

4. symbolize (¶4); seven basic symbols that symbolize; verb; to represent; Answers will vary.

5. traditions (¶2); holiday combines traditions from different African harvest festivals; noun; the handing down of customs; Answers will vary.

Exercise 3

1. The article defines *umoja* as unity.
2. The article defines *karamu* as a feast of African or African-American foods.
3. The article estimates that 20 million people around the world celebrate Kwanzaa.

Exercise 4

1. The two articles share the topic of celebrations.
2. Similar activities include songs, dances, and parties.

3. For Kwanzaa, symbols include an ear of corn, a cup, candles, crops, a mat, and gifts. In China on a child's first birthday, symbols of importance are a shiny coin, a book, and a doll.
4. In the article on Kwanzaa, the number 7 is important, as there are 7 important principles; In Nigeria, the 1st, 5th, 10th, and 15th birthdays are important. In Mexico a girl's 15th birthday is important.
5. Answers will vary.

Exercise 5

Answers will vary.

Exercise 6

Answers will vary.

AUDIO SCRIPT

Welcome

Page 3, Exercise 2A – CD1, Track 2

A Hi, Mark. I see you're studying for the vocabulary test. You did so well on the last one. What's your secret?

B I make vocabulary cards. I write the vocabulary words on one side of the card and then write the definition on the other side. I also write an example sentence with the word in it and draw a picture for some words. I test myself and ask others to test me, too.

A Oh, that's a creative way to study, and I can see that you're artistic, too.

B Thanks! And you always do well on math tests. What strategies do you use for studying math?

A I like to study with other people. We form a small group and test each other on equations and formulas. We have fun while we study so the time goes by fast.

B You're so outgoing and fun-loving – I can see how that fits your personality. Who do you study with?

A I often study with Juan. He's an active person and likes to study while moving – sometimes we memorize formulas while bouncing a basketball. It's a good way to remember something.

Page 4, Exercise 3A – CD1, Track 3

1. Mohammed was listening to the radio.
2. Yoko heard a loud noise.
3. Last night at 8:00 p.m., the Martinez family was watching television.
4. I woke up at 6:00 a.m. this morning.
5. Merin was playing her violin this morning.
6. Isabella and Jeremy were doing their homework.
7. Marcos drove to the supermarket.
8. Nur vacuumed the house yesterday.

Page 4, Exercise 3B – CD1, Track 4

Last summer, my sister and I drove from Tucson to Phoenix. On our way, it was very windy, and there were dark clouds in the sky. We were traveling slowly when suddenly we saw huge clouds of dust in the air. The sky turned brown, and we couldn't see anything. It was very scary. While we were driving, we were looking for a place to turn off the road. Finally we came to an exit and got off the main road. We went into a restaurant. The dust finally went away while we were waiting at the restaurant.

Page 5, Exercise 4A – CD1, Track 5

1. Angelica hasn't been to Mexico recently.
2. I've been to Niagara Falls a few times.
3. Claudia and Paul haven't gone camping lately.
4. Sabrina has volunteered at the Humane Society several times.
5. She hasn't cooked Korean food yet.
6. My father has already shown his confidence.
7. Peter has enjoyed socializing since his graduation.
8. Roberta has already traveled all over the United States.
9. Monica has spoken Spanish since preschool.
10. Manuel has already taken several English classes

Page 5, Exercise 4B – CD1, Track 6

1. **A** Have you practiced English outside of class lately?
   B No, I haven't. I'm too shy.
2. **A** How many times have you texted your friends today?
   B I have texted my friends at least seven times so far today.
3. **A** How many times have you eaten Mexican food?
   B I have eaten Mexican food many times. I love it!
4. **A** Has Daniel done his homework yet?
   B No, he hasn't. He needs to finish it before tomorrow.
5. **A** How long have you studied in this school?
   B I have studied at this school for three months.

Unit 1: Personal information

Page 7, Exercises 2A and 2B – CD1, Track 7

A Come on in. The door's open!

B Hi, Nina!

A Emily! Come on in. Have you been jogging?

B Yeah, I was just coming back from my run, and I thought I'd see what you're – whoa! Look at this kitchen!

A Yeah, it's a mess, isn't it? We're having 14 people for dinner tonight, and I'm going to be in the kitchen all afternoon!

B It smells great already! Hey, I just heard that Brenda got first place in the high school math contest. Is it true?

A Yes, it's true! She's really good at math. She just loves it.

B Brenda's such a "brain." I'm sure you're really proud of her!

A Yeah, she's very intelligent. But I have to say that Gerry and Danny are bright, too – they're just smart in different ways.

B What do you mean?

A Well, take Gerry. He's not mathematical like Brenda, but he's really musical. He plays four different instruments, he sings really well – he's even writing some of his own songs.

B I guess that's Gerry?

A Yeah.

B So Brenda's gifted in math, and Gerry's good at music. What about Danny? What's he good at?

A Well, he's good at fixing cars. He's the mechanical one in the family.

B Oh, I remember he bought that old, old car when he was 16. How's that coming? Is he still working on it?

A Emily, you should see that car now! It's gorgeous! He fixed everything, and it runs perfectly!

B Amazing! You know, it's really interesting how your kids are all smart in different ways. And, Nina, you're pretty smart, too!

A Me?

B Well, look at you! Maybe it's easy for you to cook for 14 people, but I could never do it. I have absolutely no aptitude for cooking!

A Gee, Emily. No one ever told me that I'm smart!

B Well, Nina, you are smart! And the smart thing for me to do is to go home and let you do your work. I'll talk to you tomorrow.

A Bye, Emily. Thanks for stopping by!

Page 7, Exercise 3A – CD1, Track 8

Emily stops by Nina's house on her way home from jogging. They talk about Nina's three children. Brenda is very mathematical. She's just won a math contest at school. When Emily calls Brenda a brain, Nina says that all her children are bright, but in different ways. Gerry isn't gifted in math, but he's very musical. He plays and sings very well and even writes music. Danny is the mechanical one in the family. He's good at fixing old cars. Emily thinks that Nina is also smart because she is such a good cook. Emily has no aptitude for cooking.

Page 8, Exercise 2A – CD1, Track 9

1. Carol speaks very intelligently. She's a bright girl.
2. That isn't a bad guitar, but he's playing it badly.
3. Benny is an excellent cook. His dinner last night was fantastic.
4. The mechanic did a good job on my car. Now it runs perfectly.
5. You danced very skillfully in the dance contest. You're a wonderful dancer!
6. I don't type very fast. I can't move my fingers very quickly.
7. That writing test was hard. Writing isn't an easy subject for me.
8. You sang that song beautifully! I didn't know you could sing so well!
9. Your report is great. You wrote it very clearly.
10. I work slowly. I'm a careful worker.

Page 10, Exercise 2A – CD1, Track 10

1. Do you believe that there are many kinds of intelligence?
2. I think Nina has an interesting family.
3. Brenda's teachers agree that she is very gifted.
4. Do you think that Nina cooks very well?
5. Many people believe Gerry will become a famous musician.
6. I didn't realize that Danny has an aptitude for fixing cars.
7. Do you feel that mechanical skills are very important?
8. Nina knows that her children are very different.

Page 12, Exercise 2 – CD1, Track 11

Many Ways to Be Smart

Josh is a star on the school baseball team. He gets Ds and Fs on all his math tests. His brother, Frank, can't catch, throw, or hit a baseball, but he easily gets As in math. Which boy do you think is more intelligent? Howard Gardner, a professor of education at Harvard University, would say that Josh and Frank are both smart, but in different ways. His theory of multiple intelligences identifies nine different "intelligences" to explain the way people understand, experience, and learn about the world around them.

Verbal / Linguistic Some people are good with words. They prefer to learn by reading, listening, and speaking.

Logical / Mathematical These people have an aptitude for math. They like solving logic problems and puzzles.

Musical / Rhythmical These people are sensitive to sound, melodies, and rhythms. They are gifted in singing, playing instruments, or composing music.

Visual / Spatial These "picture people" are often good at drawing or painting. They are sensitive to colors and designs.
Bodily / Kinesthetic Some people are "body smart." They are often athletic. Kinesthetic learners learn best when they are moving.
Interpersonal Certain people are "group smart." They easily understand other people. They are good at communicating and interacting with others.
Intrapersonal Some people are "self smart." They can understand their own feelings and emotions. They often enjoy spending time alone.
Naturalist These people are skilled in working with plants and animals in the natural world.
Existential Certain people are gifted in exploring deep questions about the meaning of life and death and ways to find inner peace.

According to Gardner, many people have several or even all of these intelligences, but most of us have one or two intelligences that are primary, or strongest.

Unit 2: At school

Page 19, Exercises 2A and 2B – CD1, Track 12

Part 1

Do you like to work with people? Do you enjoy traveling? Are you bilingual?
Then La Costa Community College's Hospitality and Tourism certificate program is for you. Our graduates find high-paying jobs with hotels, restaurants, airlines, travel agencies, and more! This growing industry needs leaders – it needs you!
For more information about La Costa's certificate program in Hospitality and Tourism, call 866-555-6868 today!

Part 2

A Mrs. Ochoa?
B Oh, hi, Vasili. How's it going?
A Pretty well. Um, I was in my car this morning, and I heard an advertisement about a certificate program in hospitality and tourism.
B Yes, it's a great program. Are you interested?
A Yeah, but I have some questions.
B Well, I'll try to answer them for you.
A OK. So first, what are the requirements for the certificate? How many courses are required?
B There are six required courses, plus an internship.
A An internship? What's that?
B You work at a local tourism business for three months. There's no pay, but it's a great way to learn about the industry – you know, see if you like it.
A I see. Are the classes in the daytime or at night? Because you know, I can't quit my job, and . . .
B No problem, Vasili. Classes are scheduled at different times, and some of them are even offered online.
A Oh, yeah? That's great. Um, how long does it take to complete the program?
B Well, it depends. I'd say – with the internship – between one and two years. Some people just take one class at a time, so it takes them longer.
A OK, that's good. How much does the program cost?
B Well, let's see. There are six classes, and they're three units each. It's $50 a unit, so that's $900 for the certificate. Books are another $100 per class, and then there's parking and health fees. So the total is about $1,600.
A $1,600? Wow! That's a lot of money.
B Don't worry. There's financial aid for students who qualify.

A OK. You know, I think I'd like to apply. When's the registration deadline?
B Let's see. Looks like it's December fifteenth for the winter semester. You have time.
A But my English, is it good enough?
B Well, you're required to take an English placement test, but I'm sure you'll do fine, Vasili. You're bilingual, you're very motivated, and you have good interpersonal skills. Hospitality and tourism could be a really good career for you.

Page 19, Exercise 3A – CD1, Track 13

Vasili hears a radio ad about the Hospitality and Tourism certificate program at La Costa Community College. The ad says graduates can find high-paying jobs in the tourism industry. Vasili goes to see his ESL counselor, Mrs. Ochoa. She tells him about the program requirements, which include an internship in a local tourism business. She also tells him about the deadline for registration, and she says there is financial aid for students who qualify. Vasili is concerned about his English, but Mrs. Ochoa tells him not to worry. Vasili is bilingual, he's very motivated, and he has good interpersonal skills.

Page 20, Exercise 2A – CD1, Track 14

1. **A** When is the English placement test given to new students?
   B The English placement test is administered a week before the first day of class.
2. **A** Is a math placement test also required?
   B No, a math placement test is not needed.
3. **A** Where is the financial aid office located?
   B It is located next to the admissions office.
4. **A** Where are the classes held?
   B Most of the classes are held in the business building.
5. **A** Are classes offered at different times?
   B Yes. Both day and evening classes are offered.
6. **A** Are job placement services provided to graduates?
   B Yes. Job help is offered to students who qualify.

Page 22, Exercise 2A – CD1, Track 15

1. Applicants are expected to meet all application deadlines.
2. New students are told to come early for registration.
3. Are all new students required to take a writing test?
4. Some students are advised to enroll in an English composition class.
5. Are students expected to attend every class?
6. Students are encouraged to meet with a counselor regularly.
7. When are participants expected to complete their internships?
8. Students are required to earn a grade of C or better in each course.
9. Students are told to study with a partner and to go to tutoring often.
10. Are students allowed to retake the course if they don't pass?

Page 24, Exercise 2 – CD1, Track 16

An Immigrant Family's Success Story
Choi and Lili Wei left China with their baby boy in the early 1990s. They were poor field workers in their native country, and they wanted their child to have the opportunities they lacked. They arrived in New York and found a one-bedroom apartment in a poor, unstable area. They could only afford a bicycle for transportation, yet they felt fortunate to have the chance to begin a new life in the United States.
Choi and Lili faced many obstacles because they couldn't speak English and had no skills.

They found night work cleaning businesses and restaurants. They saved every penny, and after six years, they were able to buy a small restaurant of their own.
They were determined to learn English, get an education, and make a good life for their son. The couple sacrificed a great deal. They never went to the movies, never ate out, and hardly ever bought anything extra. In their free time, they attended English and citizenship classes. Both of them eventually earned their GED certificates. Choi then enrolled in college while Lili worked in the restaurant.
This past spring, Choi fulfilled a lifelong dream of graduating from college. Now he is registered in a master's degree program in business beginning this fall. And what about their "baby" boy? Their son, Peter, now 21, received a scholarship to a private university, where he is working on his own dream to become an architect.
Choi and Lili are proud to be models of the "American dream." Choi has this advice for other new immigrants: "Find your passion, make a plan to succeed, and don't ever give up."

Review: Units 1 and 2

Page 30, Exercise 1 – CD1, Track 17

A Hey, Faisal! I haven't seen you in a while. What's new?
B Hi, Angela. Um, I just talked to Mr. Ortiz, my career counselor. He gave me some information about a certificate program in automotive technology.
A Is that like car repair?
B Well, yeah, but these days, you know, cars are a lot more complicated than they used to be. Everything is computerized now. I've always liked fixing up cars, but . . .
A I remember back in high school when you fixed the transmission on my dad's truck. He said you had a real aptitude for mechanical things.
B Yeah, I guess so. But I need more education if I want to get a high-paying job in the auto industry.
A So what did Mr. Ortiz tell you?
B Well, there are eight required courses, plus two more courses that you're allowed to choose.
A That's a lot of classes. How long will it take to complete them all?
B Four semesters. It's pretty fast. And the classes are scheduled at all different times, you know – daytime and evening, and even on weekends.
A How much will it cost?
B Each course is $60. And I need ten courses. So the total is $600, not including books and tools. Plus financial aid is offered to students who qualify.
A You sound really motivated.
B I am. I think this is the right program for me.

Page 31, Exercise 3A – CD1, Track 18

/t/
1. He has always liked playing number games.
2. She has worked as an accountant for ten years.

/d/
3. Emily has realized that Brenda has a good brain.
4. Naturalists are skilled in working with plants.

/ɪd/
5. The little boy started counting when he was two.
6. She is gifted in singing and dancing.

Page 31, Exercise 3B – CD1, Track 19

1. Classes are located at various elementary schools.
2. All students are advised of the school rules.
3. An application is required for admission.
4. A math test is needed as well.
5. The test is administered once a week.
6. The students are expected to pay their fees soon.
7. Lucas hasn't talked with a counselor yet.
8. But he is finished with all his tests.

Unit 3: Friends and family

Page 33, Exercises 2A and 2B – CD1, Track 20

Part 1

A You have one new message.
B This call is for Mrs. Wen Lee. This is the attendance office from Central High School calling on Tuesday, March 10th, at 2:00 p.m. We're calling to report an unexcused absence for your daughter, Lan, from her 7th period class today. Please call the office at 619-555-2300 to explain why your daughter missed class. Thank you.

Part 2

C I can't believe we're at the mall on a school day!
D Yeah. Do you think anyone at school is going to miss us?
C No way. There's a substitute teacher in my last period class.
D Mine, too! So, how's everything at home?
C It's the same old thing. I'm so frustrated. My mother won't let me do anything! She is so strict.
D Strict? Like how?
C Well, I'm not permitted to go anywhere without my parents or my brother. And my mom says I can't go out on a date without a chaperone until I'm 18!
D That's so unfair! I wonder why your mother's so strict.
C I don't know. I think she's trying to bring me up like she was raised in China. She just doesn't understand the customs here in the United States.

Part 3

C Hi, Mom.
E Hi, Lan. How was school today?
C Um, fine. Is something wrong?
E The school called and said you were absent from your 7th period class. Where did you go?
C Come on, Mom. Don't get excited.
E Tell me where you went!
C Mary and I just went to the mall right across the street from school, OK?
E But what about your last class?
C There was a substitute teacher, OK? I didn't miss anything!
E I don't understand how you could do this!
C Well, it's your fault! You're so strict that I had no choice. Everybody's allowed to go to the mall except for me. Why can't you trust me?
E This is not about trust. You broke the school rules. You're on restriction for the next two weekends.
C On restriction?! What about Celia's birthday party next Saturday?
E I'm afraid you'll have to miss it. Next time, maybe you'll think before you act.

Page 33, Exercise 3A – CD1, Track 21

Mrs. Lee received a phone message from her daughter's school saying Lan missed her 7th period class. Lan left school early to go to the mall with her friend Mary. At the mall, Lan tells Mary that her mother is too strict. Lan thinks it's because her mother wants to bring her up the same way she was raised in China. That's why Lan needs a chaperone to go out on a date. At home, Lan and her mother have an argument. Lan is angry because she's not permitted to go to the mall alone. She thinks her mother doesn't trust her. Mrs. Lee is upset because Lan broke the rules. As a punishment, she says Lan is on restriction for two weeks.

Page 34, Exercise 2A – CD1, Track 22

1. A Do you know what the student's name is?
   B Her name is Lan.
2. A Can you please tell me what class she missed?
   B Mr. Latham's 7th period English class.
3. A I wonder who Lan went to the mall with.
   B She went to the mall with Mary.
4. A I would like to know why she broke the rules.
   B I don't know why. Perhaps she was bored in class.
5. A Can you tell me when she and her friend left the school.
   B They left after 6th period.
6. A I want to know what they did at the mall.
   B They talked and went window-shopping.
7. A Do you know when they came home from the mall?
   B I don't know when they came home.
8. A Could you please tell me what Lan's punishment was?
   B Her mother put her on restriction for two weeks.

Page 36, Exercise 2A – CD1, Track 23

A Can I go to a party at Joe's house?
B Maybe. First I need to know if you finished your homework.
A Yes, I finished it an hour ago.
B Do you know if the party starts at 5:00 or 6:00?
A It starts at 6:00.
B OK. Can you tell me if his parents will be home?
A Yes, his parents will be there.
B That's good. I wonder if you need to take a birthday gift.
A No, I don't. It's not a birthday party.
B I wonder if they're going to serve dinner.
A Yes. They're going to grill chicken for us.
B What about your friend John? Do you know if he's invited to the party?
A Yes, I think so.
B Do you know if John's parents can bring you home?
A I'll ask them.
B I am wondering if you can text us when you are on the way home.
A Sure. I'll do that.

Page 38, Exercise 2 – CD1, Track 24

Barriers Between Generations

In immigrant families, language differences and work schedules often create barriers to communication between the generations. Dolores Suarez, 42, and her son, Diego, 16, face both kinds of barriers every day. Dolores is an immigrant from Mexico who works seven days a week as a housekeeper in a big hotel. She doesn't use much English in her job, and she has never had time to study it. Consequently, her English is limited. Her son, on the other hand, was raised in the United States. He understands Spanish, but he prefers to speak English. When his friends come over to visit, they speak only English. "They talk so fast, I can't understand what they are saying," says Dolores. To make the situation more complicated, Diego and Dolores live with Dolores's father, who speaks Nahuatl, a native language spoken in Mexico. Diego can't understand anything his grandfather says. Dolores's work schedule is the second barrier to communication with Diego. Because she rarely has a day off, Dolores isn't able to spend much time with him. She doesn't have time to help him with his homework or attend parent-teacher conferences at his school. In 1995, when Dolores immigrated to the United States, her goal was to bring up her son with enough money to avoid the hardships her family suffered in Mexico. Her hard work has permitted Diego to have a comfortable life and a good education. But she has paid a price for this success. "Sometimes I feel like I don't know my own son," she says.

Unit 4: Health

Page 45, Exercises 2A and 2B – CD1, Track 25

Part 1

A Cindy, have you seen Sara?
B No. I don't think she's here yet.
A She should have been here 25 minutes ago. Did she call to say she'd be late?
B No, she didn't.
C Oh! Uh, good morning, Mr. Stanley.
A Good morning, Sara.
C I'm sorry, I know I'm late, but the buses are so unreliable.
A I don't know about the buses, Sara, but I do know that if you're late one more time, I'm going to have to fire you.

Part 2

C Thanks for picking me up, Mike.
D No problem.
C We have to hurry – my driving test is in half an hour.
D We have plenty of time. The DMV is just ten minutes from here.
C All right.
D Are you OK? You seem tense.
C Yeah, I'm pretty stressed out.
D How come?
C I was late to work again this morning . . .
D Oh, no!
C And the boss said that if it happens again, he's going to fire me.
D No wonder you're stressed out.
C I'm so worried about losing my job, I can't sleep, I can't eat, I can't concentrate . . .
D You know, Sara, if you're not feeling well, you don't have to take the driving test today.
C Yes, I do, Mike. I have to pass this driving test so I can get my license and buy a car and stop depending on buses.
D OK, OK, I understand. But if you want to pass the test, then you have to calm down. Try to relax. Take a few deep breaths.
C OK.
D Now think positive thoughts. Tell yourself, "I'm a good driver. I'm going to pass my driving test."
C "I'm a good driver, I'm going to pass my driving test."
D Seriously, Sara. You ought to learn some techniques for coping with anxiety.
C Like what?
D Simple stuff. Like I said, deep breathing is good, um, thinking positive thoughts. And I find that it helps me to meditate every day.
C Meditation. Let's talk about it later. Here's the DMV.
D Good luck, and don't forget: You're a good driver!
C Thanks, Mike. You're a good friend.

Page 45, Exercise 3A – CD1, Track 26

Mike is driving Sara to the Department of Motor Vehicles (DMV) to take her driving test. He notices that she's very tense. Sara says she's stressed out because she was late to work again. She's worried that her boss will fire her if she's late one more time. She's so afraid of losing her job that she can't eat, she can't sleep, and she can't concentrate. Mike says that she has to calm down if she wants to pass her driving test. He suggests three techniques to help her cope with her anxiety. One is deep breathing. The second one is thinking positive thoughts, and the third one is meditation.

Page 46, Exercise 2A – CD1, Track 27

Ana and Bill just got engaged, and they are planning to get married in four weeks. Because the wedding is so soon, they are feeling a lot of pressure. Ana's mother wants a big wedding, but Ana and Bill don't. Because they are paying for the wedding themselves, they believe they should do what they want. Another pressure is all the things Ana and Bill have to do before the wedding. For example, Ana has to buy a dress, choose her bridesmaids, and send out the invitations. Bill has to plan the reception and order the food. Most importantly, they have to decide where the wedding will be. Ana wants to get married outdoors, but Bill thinks they shouldn't plan an outdoor wedding because it might rain. Now Bill has a different idea. He realizes that they shouldn't get married so soon. Maybe they should postpone the wedding by a few months. That way, they don't have to feel so much pressure.

Page 48, Exercise 2A – CD1, Track 28

1. She should have talked to someone about her problems.
2. She should have gone out with friends.
3. She shouldn't have stayed home alone all the time.
4. She should have made new friends.
5. She should have exercised.
6. She should have eaten regular, balanced meals.
7. She shouldn't have eaten lots of junk food.
8. She shouldn't have slept so much.
9. She should have called her family.

Page 50, Exercise 2 – CD1, Track 29

Stress: What You Ought to Know
What is stress?
Stress is our reaction to changing events in our lives. The reactions can be mental – what we think or feel about the changes – and physical – how our body reacts to the changes.
What causes stress?
Stress often comes when there are too many changes in our lives. The changes can be positive, like having a baby or getting a better job, or they can be negative, such as an illness or a divorce. Some stress is healthy. It motivates us to push forward. But too much stress over time can make us sick.
What are the signs of stress?
There are both physical and emotional signs of stress. Physical signs may include tight muscles, elevated blood pressure, grinding your teeth, trouble sleeping, an upset stomach, and back pain. Common emotional symptoms are anxiety, nervousness, depression, trouble concentrating, and nightmares.
How can you manage stress?
To prevent stress, you should eat right and exercise regularly. When you know there will be a stressful event in your day – such as a test, a business meeting, or an encounter with someone you don't get along with – it is really important to eat a healthy breakfast and to limit coffee and sugar. When you find yourself in a stressful situation, stay calm. Take a few deep breaths to help you relax. Roll your shoulders or stretch to loosen any tight muscles. And take time to think before you speak. You don't want to say something you will regret later! We all have some stress in our lives. It is important for us to use strategies to handle it, so that the stress doesn't overwhelm us.

Review: Units 3 and 4

Page 56, Exercise 1 – CD1, Track 30

A Hi, Sue. This is Blanca.
B Hi! How are you?
A Well, to be honest, not so good.
B Why? What's wrong?
A I'm really worried about Yesenia. Lately she's been different. She seems tense and too quiet. It's hard for her to concentrate on her schoolwork.
B She's 13 now, isn't she?
A Yeah. She just had a birthday last week.
B That's a hard age.
A You know, we raised her to always talk to us about her problems, but last night, I got angry at her. I shouldn't have shouted at her, but she wouldn't answer my questions.
B Do you know if she's having any problems at school?
A That's what I was asking her about. I don't know what's going on with her.
B You know, Blanca, when my daughter was 13, I took a parenting class at the middle school. It really helped me learn how to cope with teenagers.
A A parenting class? I don't know. I'll have to think about that.
B I also think you ought to call Yesenia's counselor at school. The counselor can talk to Yesenia and to her teachers and find out how she's doing.
A OK.
B And one more thing. You sound pretty stressed out, too. Why don't you and Yesenia take an exercise class together? It will help both of you to calm down and relax.
A That's a great suggestion, Sue. I'll ask her tonight. Thanks a lot.

Page 57, Exercise 3A – CD1, Track 31

A Where did he go?
B Can you tell me where he went?

Page 57, Exercise 3B – CD1, Track 32

1. A What does Ann do to reduce stress?
   B She listens to music.
2. A Why are you so tense?
   B I have my driver's test today.
3. A Do you know what Rodolfo does to calm down?
   B He walks or jogs.
4. A When did Ivan miss his class?
   B He missed his class on Tuesday.
5. A Can you tell me where Andy lives?
   B He lives on East Fifth Street.
6. A Do you know why they're always late?
   B No, I don't know.

Unit 5: Around town

Page 59, Exercises 2A and 2B – CD1, Track 33

A Hi! Are you the volunteer coordinator?
B Yup, Steve Jones. And you're Almaz? Did I say it right?
A Yes, exactly, Almaz Bekele. Nice to meet you.
B You, too. Please have a seat. I was just looking over your application to volunteer here at Quiet Palms, and it looks really good. Is it OK if I ask you some questions?
A Of course. Go ahead.
B OK, let's see. You wrote that you've been a volunteer before. Can you tell me about that?
A Sure. I volunteered last summer at the public library downtown.
B What did you do there?
A I worked with adults who wanted to learn how to read. I also taught a little writing, and on Saturdays, I read stories to the kids.
B Did you enjoy that?
A Yeah, but what I really liked was working with the older people. It felt like I was doing something really worthwhile.
B Uh-huh. So now tell me why you want to volunteer in a nursing home.
A Well, I think I might want to work in the healthcare field someday, but I won't know for sure until I get some experience.
B I see. Well, we'd love to have you volunteer here.
A Great! When can I start?
B I like your enthusiasm, but we have some health requirements. First, you need to take a blood test and a TB test. You can start as soon as we get the results. It usually takes two or three days.
A OK. I'll take care of that right away. Also, um, I was wondering – can you tell me what my responsibilities will be?
B Sure. One thing volunteers do is, uh, they help residents with their meals. You might encourage them to eat, or just keep them company during mealtime.
A Yeah, my grandmother always eats more when I'm with her. She likes having people around.
B Then I'm sure you understand that you need to be patient and compassionate with the residents.
A I know.
B Volunteers also deliver mail and flowers, and they take residents for walks. You'll get more responsibilities as soon as you feel more confident.
A Sounds good.
B There's an orientation next Monday at 8:30.
A I'll be there!
B One more thing. You'll need to make a commitment to volunteer at least three hours per week.
A No problem! I can't wait to start.

Page 59, Exercise 3A – CD1, Track 34

Last summer, Almaz volunteered at the public library downtown. She liked working with the older people because she felt that she was doing something worthwhile. Today, she is meeting with Steve, the volunteer coordinator at Quiet Palms, a nursing home. She wants to volunteer there to find out if she likes working in the healthcare field. Steve tells her about some of her responsibilities at Quiet Palms. He says it's very important for volunteers to be compassionate and patient when they are working with the residents. He asks Almaz to make a commitment to volunteer at least three hours per week. Almaz agrees to attend an orientation. She says she can't wait to start volunteering.

Page 60, Exercise 2A – CD1, Track 35

1. A Mr. Shamash is in pain. When will he start to feel better?
   B He'll feel better as soon as he takes his medication.
2. A How long will Mr. Shamash stay at Quiet Palms?
   B He'll stay until his broken hip heals.
3. A When can Mr. Shamash begin exercising again?
   B As soon as Mr. Shamash feels stronger, he can start doing moderate exercise.

4. **A** When does Mr. Shamash get ready for his walk?
   B He gets ready as soon as Almaz arrives.
5. **A** How long will Mr. Shamash and Almaz play cards?
   B They'll play cards until it is time for lunch.
6. **A** How long did Mr. Shamash nap yesterday?
   B He napped until Almaz came to visit him.
7. **A** When is Mr. Shamash going to go to sleep?
   B As soon as his visitors leave, he'll take his medicine and go to sleep.
8. **A** When did the nurse assistant help Mr. Shamash with his shower?
   B As soon as Mr. Shamash woke up, the nurse assistant helped him with his shower.

Page 62, Exercise 2A – CD1, Track 36
Sharing with Sally

Jake, a college student, volunteered all last year. He called elderly people on the phone once a week and talked to each person. He said it was a very valuable experience. Betsy, a 35-year-old mother of two, has volunteered for two years so far and loves it.

Page 64, Exercise 2 – CD1, Track 37
Running with Ropes
Imagine running with your eyes closed. How do you feel? Insecure? Afraid? Justin Andrews knows these feelings very well. Justin is a former long-distance runner who lost his vision because of a grave illness. For the past six months, he has been running twice a week with the help of volunteer runners at Running with Ropes, an organization
that assists blind and visually impaired runners. "Running with Ropes has changed my life," Justin says. "Until I heard about it, I thought I'd never run outside again."
Volunteers at Running with Ropes make a commitment to volunteer two to four hours a week. Scott Liponi, one of the running volunteers, explains what they do. "We use ropes to join ourselves to the blind runners and guide them around and over obstacles, such as holes in the road and other runners." Scott has learned how to keep the rope loose so the blind runner has more freedom. He deeply respects the blind runners' tenacity. "They are incredibly determined," he says. "It doesn't matter if it's hot, raining, or snowing – they are going to run." Scott says it is gratifying to share in the joy of the runners and to feel that they trust him. "The four hours I spend at Running with Ropes are the most rewarding part of my week," he says. "It's really a worthwhile Commitment."

Unit 6: Time
Page 71, Exercises 2A and 2B – CD2, Track 2

Part 1

A Excuse me, ma'am?
B Yes?
A I'm a reporter for KESL Radio, and today we're asking people for their opinions about technology and timesaving devices. Do you have a minute to answer some questions for me?
B Sure.
A May I have your name?
B Jean Rosen. Mrs. Rosen.
A Do you have a favorite time-saving device?
B Let me see. . . . I guess it's this – my address stamper.
A Oh. I expected something electronic, not manual! Does it really save you time?
B Absolutely. It takes about a minute to handwrite a return address. The address stamper just takes seconds, even though it's not electronic.
A Thank you for your time, Mrs. Rosen.

Part 2

A Excuse me, sir. Do you have a minute?
C Well, I'm in a bit of a hurry.
A I'm a reporter for KESL Radio. I'm asking people for their opinions about how technology helps them save time.
C Technology – a time-saver? I'm afraid you're talking to the wrong man. I'm not a fan of technology.
A Why is that?
C Well, take email, for example. Half the time it's spam. And it's distracting, too. It interrupts my work.
A But isn't it convenient?
C Not that I can see. If you ask me, most of this electronic stuff wastes more time than it saves. I still write letters by hand although I have a perfectly good computer at home.
A I see. Could I get your name before you go?
C Ronald Chung.
A Thank you for your time, Mr. Chung.

Part 3

A Good morning, ma'am. I'm a reporter for KESL Radio.
D Yes?
A I'm asking people their opinions about technology and time-saving devices.
D Oh, that sounds interesting.
A Do you have a favorite time-saving device?
D Oh, yes. I just love my cell phone.
A I guess it saves you lots of time because you can use it anywhere.
D That's right. You see, I go to lots of sales to buy clothes for my daughter. I take pictures with my camera phone of clothes I think she might like.
A Really?
D Yeah. Then I send her the pictures while I'm still in the store. She sends me a text message back. It says "Buy" or "Don't buy."
A Now that's innovative.
D Yeah. Not a bad idea, huh?
A I'm sure our listeners will enjoy hearing about such an unusual use.
D Happy to share. It really is a time-saver. But not a money-saver.
A I see what you mean! Oh, I didn't get your name.
D Patricia Morales.
A Well, thank you, Ms. Morales, for sharing your favorite time-saving device.

Page 71, Exercise 3A – CD2, Track 3
Today, a reporter from KESL Radio asked three people about technology and their favorite time-saving devices. Mrs. Rosen's favorite device is manual. She says it saves time, even though it isn't electronic. Mr. Chung isn't a fan of technology. In fact, he says technology wastes more time than it saves. For example, he says he doesn't like email because he gets lots of spam. He also finds email distracting. He doesn't think it is convenient. Ms. Morales loves technology. She uses the camera on her cell phone in a very innovative way – to send her daughter pictures of clothes that are on sale. Her daughter sends a text message back: "Buy" or "Don't buy. "

Page 72, Exercise 2A – CD2, Track 4
1. Mrs. Sanchez can't operate her digital camera although she read the directions many times.
2. Although Mrs. White's car has a GPS system, she gets lost all the time.
3. Mr. Green doesn't use his microwave although he paid a lot of money for it.
4. Although email is fast, Mr. Chung doesn't like to use it.
5. I prefer to read paperback and hardcover books although e-books are very popular.
6. Although Ms. Kaye had urgent business 1000 miles away, she refused to travel by plane.
7. I prefer to use a fan when it's hot although my house has central air-conditioning.
8. Although Ben never sets his alarm clock, he still gets to work on time.
9. I play my CDs on my CD player at home although all my music is available online.

Page 74, Exercise 2A – CD2, Track 5
Although Pam and Beth are sisters, they are very different. Pam is very modern. She loves electrical appliances because they are fast and convenient. For example, she loves her microwave because she can use it to thaw meat quickly. She enjoys shopping for the latest kitchen devices, although some of them are very expensive. Beth has a different attitude about modern technology. She prefers not to use electrical appliances. For instance, she never uses a microwave because she thinks the radiation is bad. She dries her clothes outside on a line because she likes their smell after they've been in the fresh air. She washes her dishes by hand because she says dishwashers waste energy. Pam doesn't understand why Beth is so old-fashioned. But although the sisters have different lifestyles, they appreciate and enjoy one another very much.

Page 76, Exercise 2 – CD2, Track 6

Changes in technology can change people's lives.
The development of transportation— trains, cars, and planes - provides us with one example. Before the 19th century, most people lived within walking distance of work. In the 20th century many people began to commute between home and work because trains and cars connected cities with suburbs. Today, because of airplanes, many people travel great distances for their work. Some, because of the Internet, don't need to travel at all.
Technological changes have also impacted the media – for example, how we get the news. Newspapers were once people's primary source for the news: in 1965, 72 percent of Americans reported that they read a newspaper on an average day. By 2005, that number was down to 50 percent. In the past, a common way people got news was by listening to the radio. I suppose nearly everyone had a radio then. By the 1950s, television was overtaking radio. Now even the number of people watching the news on television has declined, dropping from 60 percent in 1993 to 28 percent in 2006. So what's the latest source for news? The Web. The number of Americans who use the Internet to get the news is increasing. Most people access the news on their smartphones.
Media has also changed the way we get jobs. We used to look for job openings in the classified ads of a newspaper. Then we'd mail an application through the US Postal Service (now called snail mail by some). Finally, if we were lucky enough to get an interview, we'd go to the job site. Today we can find notices for jobs online and we can submit our applications over the Internet. The employer can even interview us over the Internet using programs, such as Skype, that provide voice over and video over calls. These changes save time for both the employer and the applicant.

Another example of the impact of technology is how we pay for goods and services. Until the mid-1940s, people had to carry large amounts of cash in their purses and wallets. Then, one day in 1949, a man named Frank McNamara took some business associates to dinner, but he left his wallet at home. He had to call his wife to bring him money to pay the bill. Mr. McNamara vowed to find a way to avoid carrying cash. Although some stores already had their own charge cards, there was no single, multi-purpose credit card. A year later he returned to the same restaurant with the same people but paid with the credit card he had created, called "Diner's Club." Today, people don't even need to carry a credit card. They can pay with their smartphones. In what other ways do you think technology may change our lives in the future?

Review: Units 5 and 6

Page 82, Exercise 1 – CD2, Track 7

A Good afternoon, listeners. Today we're talking with Rebecca Ford, Coordinator of Adult Literacy Services at our downtown library. Thank you for joining us, Ms. Ford.

B It's a pleasure to be here.

A To start off, could you describe your job for us?

B Sure. I'm responsible for training and supervising all the volunteer literacy tutors at the library.

A How many tutors are there?

B We have between 20 and 30 volunteer tutors at a time.

A And who are the students that they work with?

B The students are adults who don't have good reading and writing skills. Some of them are immigrants who can't read and write very well, even though they've been in this country for many years.

A I see. Could you tell us more about your tutors? What kind of people are they?

B Well, our tutors are all different ages, and they have different backgrounds. Some of them are volunteering for the first time, and some have volunteered many times in their lives. But in one way, they're all the same: they're very compassionate. They really care about helping other people. Also, they're very generous with their time.

A I suppose they also have to be very patient if they're teaching adults to read.

B Yes, that's right.

A What are the requirements for becoming a literacy tutor?

B OK. First, they're required to have 12 hours of training in tutoring techniques. Then, as soon as they complete their training, we match each tutor with a student. They're required to meet their student for at least one and a half hours per week, and the library requires a minimum commitment of six months.

A That's good to know. Ms. Ford, if any of our listeners are interested in volunteering, who should they contact?

B They can call my office. The number is 914-555-6700.

A OK, listeners, that number again is 914-555-6700 if you want to volunteer. We appreciate your taking the time to talk with us today, Ms. Ford.

B I enjoyed it. Thank you for having me.

Page 83, Exercise 3A – CD2, Track 8

1. Pam loves electrical appliances because they save her time.
2. She wants to volunteer in the healthcare field.

3. Even though computers are timesavers, some people don't use them.
4. Will he go to sleep as soon as his visitors leave?

Page 83, Exercise 3B – CD2, Track 9

1. She delivers meals to seniors.
2. Volunteers should be patient and compassionate.
3. Do you walk to work or drive?
4. Mr. Chung isn't a fan of e-mail.

Unit 7: Shopping

Page 85, Exercises 2A and 2B – CD2, Track 10

Part 1

A Excuse me. Do you work here?

B Yes. Do you need some help?

A Where do I take this thing?

B What have you got there?

A It's a camera, a digital camera. I'd like to get my money back, if possible.

B OK, if you want a refund, you need to talk to somebody in Customer Service. See that guy who's wearing a red tie over there? He'll help you.

A Thank you.

Part 2

C Who's next?

A Hi. I want to return this camera that I bought. I'd like to get my money back.

C You bought it here? Do you have the receipt?

A The receipt? Just a minute. Here it is.

C OK. That's good. Is the camera defective?

A What do you mean – "defective"?

C Well, is there something wrong with it? Doesn't it work?

A Oh, no – it's not broken or anything. I just don't like it.

C What's the problem?

A It's the screen.

C The screen?

A Yeah. The screen is too small. A few days ago, I was taking pictures. It was a sunny day, and I couldn't see the picture in the screen! Maybe it's my eyes.

C No, I don't think it's your eyes. That screen is kind of small. So, did you want to exchange it for another camera?

A I'm not sure. Is it possible to get my money back?

C Well, let me look at that receipt again. You got this on the 5th, and today is the 20th. So it's been 15 days. Our policy for a refund is that you have to bring it back within 10 days. So, sorry – no refund.

A Oh. I didn't know about the 10 days.

C Now, for an exchange: You have 30 days – if the merchandise is in perfect condition.

A Oh, it's just like new! I only used it a couple of times. Here, see for yourself.

C Yeah, you're right. Looks OK to me. Is everything in the box?

A I think so. Like I said, I hardly used the camera. Here's the case that came with it. And here's the instruction book, and the warranty card, and all the papers that –

C OK, great. Why don't I keep this camera here while you look around the store?

A You mean, I have to choose another camera today? I'm kind of in a hurry.

C Well, if you want, I could just give you a store credit instead. With a store credit, you can come back and shop anytime.

A Oh, that's a good idea. Maybe I can bring my nephew with me next time I come. He knows a lot about cameras.

C OK, let me get you a store credit.

A I really appreciate all your help.

C No problem.

Page 85, Exercise 3A – CD2, Track 11

Rosa wants to return the camera that she bought and get a refund. She is told that she needs to speak with someone in customer service. The clerk there asks Rosa if the camera is defective, and she says it isn't. The clerk tells her about the store policy for returns and exchanges. It's too late for Rosa to return the camera, but she can exchange it if the merchandise is in perfect condition. Rosa still has the camera box with the instruction book and the warranty card. Since Rosa is in a hurry, she decides to get a store credit, and she will use it at a later time.

Page 86, Exercise 2A – CD2, Track 12

1. I want to buy a camera which is not too expensive.
2. I'd like to get a good camera which will last for many years.
3. Many people who are looking for cameras shop online.
4. My friend told me about a camera store which sells used merchandise.
5. Customers who appreciate good service like to shop at Super Camera.
6. The clerk who works in customer service is very helpful.
7. These days, many people want an expensive camera which has separate lenses.
8. Sometimes people need to return merchandise which is defective.
9. Buyers who don't ask about a store's return policy may be sorry later.
10. Many people now have smart phones which have excellent cameras.

Page 88, Exercise 2A – CD2, Track 13

1. A good friend that I've known for several years needed a new car.
2. She used to drive an old car that she got from her father.
3. Last January, the old car that she was driving stopped working.
4. The mechanic that her neighbor recommended couldn't fix it.
5. Finally, she decided to buy a used car from a man that she knew at work.
6. He's an honest person that she trusts completely.
7. The price that he named was really good.
8. The used car that he sold her is only three years old.
9. It's a reliable car that she can drive for a long time.
10. Suzy is happy to have a vehicle that she doesn't have to worry about.

Page 90, Exercise 2 – CD2, Track 14

The Smart Shopper

Dear smart shopper,

I'm a jewelry lover, and I enjoy shopping online. Unfortunately, I just bought a pair of gold earrings that I don't like. When I tried to return them, I learned that the seller has a no-return policy. Don't I have the right to get a refund?
– Mad Madelyn

Dear Mad Madelyn,

If the merchandise is defective, the seller must return your money or make an exchange. However, if the merchandise was in good condition when you received it, and if the retailer has a no-return policy, there is nothing you can do. This is true for store purchases as well as Internet purchases. In the future, here are some questions you should ask before you buy anything:

- Does the seller say "satisfaction guaranteed or your money back"?
- Is there a time limit on returns, such as two weeks?
- Who pays the shipping costs on items that are returned?
- Do you need to return the merchandise in its original package?
- Is the original receipt required?
- Does the retailer give a store credit instead of a cash refund?
- If the retailer has a store in your area, can you return the merchandise to the store instead of shipping it?

Next time, find the return policy on the merchant's Web site and print it, or ask the merchant for the return policy in writing. It's important to get all the facts that you need before you buy!

– Smart Shopper

Unit 8: Work

Page 97, Exercises 2A and 2B – CD2, Track 15

Part 1

A David, can I talk to you for a second?

B Yeah, sure.

A Um, you know, you've been leaving early a lot lately, and when you do that, I have to stay later and close up the shop by myself.

B Oh, come on, Yolanda. That doesn't happen very often.

A Well, it happened twice last week, and it's happened once so far this week. I'd say that's pretty often. Plus, sometimes the shop is full of customers, and you're in the back room talking on your cell phone. So I feel like I've been doing my job and yours, too. It's not fair. Something's wrong here. We have to figure out a better system here so we divide the work more equally.

B OK, whatever – but I have to go now. See you!

Part 2

C Yolanda, over here!

A Hi, guys.

D Whoa, Yolanda – what's wrong?

A I'm exhausted. I've just finished work.

D Don't you usually finish at 4:00?

A Yeah, but the other guy on my shift, David, he's going to night school, and lately he's been leaving early a lot. So then I have to clean up the shop and close up by myself. Sometimes I don't get out of there until 4:45 or 5:00. It's really frustrating.

D That's really unfair.

C I think you should quit that job!

D Quit? That's crazy, Julie. She can't quit – it's hard to find another job!

C Well, have you tried talking to David?

A Yeah, I talked to him, but it didn't help.

D What about your boss? Have you told her?

A No, not yet. I'd really like to try to work something out with David first.

C Listen, I have an idea. What about making a chart?

A A chart? How does that work?

C It's simple. You make a list of all the duties in your shift. You know – open up, make coffee, whatever. Then you negotiate with David and decide who's going to do which tasks.

A OK . . .

C And then, every day, as soon as you finish a task, you write your initials on the chart.

A I get it. So then if David isn't doing his share, it's easy to see.

C And if the problem continues, you can show the chart to your boss and let her deal with it.

A I like that idea, Julie. Especially the part about negotiating with David. I really hope we can work this out together.

Page 97, Exercise 3A – CD2, Track 16

Yolanda and David work at Daria's Donut Shop. Lately, David has been leaving work early, and Yolanda has to close up the shop by herself. Tonight, Yolanda is having coffee with her friends. She is exhausted. Her friends give her advice. Teresa thinks she should talk to her boss, but Yolanda wants to try to work things out with David first. Julie thinks Yolanda should make a chart of their duties. Then she should negotiate with David and decide who is going to do which tasks. When they finish a task, they should write their initials on the chart. If David isn't doing his share of the work, it will show in the chart. Then Yolanda can show the chart to their boss and let her deal with the situation.

Page 98, Exercise 2A – CD2, Track 17

1. Daria Thompson is the owner of Daria's Donut Shop. She has been selling donuts at this location for more than 20 years.
2. It's 7:00 a.m. Daria has been making donuts for three hours.
3. It's 7:30 a.m. Daria has just opened the shop for customers.
4. It's 10:30 a.m. Daria's son has been helping her all morning.
5. He has just finished cleaning the counters and shelves. Everything is spotless.
6. Daria needs more help in the shop. She has decided to hire Yolanda.
7. Yolanda's shift begins at 6:00 a.m. today. She has been waiting for the bus for 30 minutes. She's worried that she's going to be late.
8. It's 6:05 a.m. Yolanda has just called to say she will be late.
9. It's 6:30 a.m. Yolanda has just arrived at the store. Daria is really glad to see her!
10. It's noon. Yolanda has been working for several hours and she's ready to take a break.

Page 100, Exercise 2A – CD2, Track 18

1. **A** I heard that Juan and his friends went to a party after work. How was the party?
   B It was really exciting.
2. **A** What did Juan and his friends like the most about the party?
   B There was a lot of interesting music from different countries.
3. **A** How did Juan feel the next day at work?
   B He was exhausted.
4. **A** How long did he have to work?
   B He had to work from 9:30 to 6:30. It was a tiring day.
5. **A** Does Juan usually start working at 9:30?
   B No, he overslept! He was shocked that he didn't hear the alarm clock.
6. **A** How did his boss react when he showed up late?
   B His boss was irritated.
7. **A** What did his boss say to him?
   B He told Juan that he was disappointed in him.
8. **A** How did Juan feel after his boss told him that?
   B He felt embarrassed.
9. **A** Juan didn't have a good day, I guess. What did he do later that night?
   B He stayed home and had a relaxing night in front of the TV.
10. **A** So, is Juan going to go out again on a weeknight?
    B I don't think so. He said it was an exhausting experience.

Page 102, Exercise 2 – CD2, Track 19

Hard and Soft Job Skills

Som Sarawong has been working as an automotive technician at George's Auto Repair for over five years. Today was a special day for Som, a 35-year-old Thai immigrant, because he received the Employee of the Year award. According to Ed Overton, Som's boss, Som received the award "because he's a great 'people person' and he has superb technical skills. I even have him work on my own car!" Som has the two kinds of skills that are necessary to be successful and move up in his career: soft skills and hard skills. Soft skills are personal and social skills. Som gets along with his co-workers. He has a strong work ethic; in five years, he has never been late or absent from work. Customers trust him. Hard skills, on the other hand, are the technical skills a person needs to do a job. Som can repair cars, trucks, and motorcycles. He learned from his father, who was also a mechanic. Then he took classes and got a certificate as an auto Technician. Soft and hard skills are equally important, but hard skills are easier to teach and assess than soft skills. People can learn how to use a machine and then take a test on their knowledge. However, it's harder to teach people how to be cooperative and have a good work ethic. George Griffith, the owner of George's Auto Repair, explains, "I've been working in this business for over 30 years, and most of the time when I've needed to fire someone, it was because of weak people skills, not because they didn't have technical abilities." Soft skills and good technical knowledge are a winning combination, and today, Som Sarawong was the winner.

Review: Units 7 and 8

Page 108, Exercise 1 – CD2, Track 20

A Good evening, class. I've invited two business owners to our class to describe job skills that are important for their businesses. I'd like to introduce Len Sullivan, the owner of Sullivan's Electronics, and Cora Zimmer, the owner of Zimmer's Restaurant. First, let's hear from Mr. Sullivan.

B Thanks. It's a pleasure to be here. So, talking about job skills, I would say that first and most importantly, my employees need to have good communication skills. That's true for the salespeople on the floor as well as the ones working in customer service. And at the same time, I expect my people to be good listeners. I've been working in this business for 25 years, and I've hired a lot of people in that time. And I can tell you, my best employees are the ones who really know how to listen to customers and respond to their needs. And now the third important skill is that my employees need to be good problem solvers. They have to deal with all sorts of problems every day, and I expect them to work things out and find good solutions.

A Thank you, Mr. Sullivan. Now let's listen to Ms. Zimmer and find out what skills are important in the restaurant business.

C Thank you so much for inviting me. One important skill my employees need is to manage their time effectively. Restaurant work is very fast-paced and exhausting, so the waiters and also the cooks have to be good time managers. Another important job skill for my employees is good communication skills, just as Mr. Sullivan said. I want my employees to understand instructions and also be able to talk to our

customers. Finally, I need employees who
can train others in their job duties.

A Thank you both. I know the class is very
interested in your comments. And now, I'd like
to open this up for questions. Class, do you
have questions that you would like to ask?

Page 109, Exercise 3A – CD2, Track 21

1. **A** Is the camera defective?
   B It's defective and too small!
2. **A** Don't you usually finish at 5:00?
   B I do usually finish at 5:00, but not today.
3. **A** Why aren't you applying for that job?
   B I am. I'll go there tomorrow.
4. **A** I don't trust the man who sold you this
   car.
   B Well, I do! It's my decision, not yours.
5. **A** Is he excited about his new job?
   B No, but his wife is.
6. **A** Did you put the returned merchandise on
   my desk?
   B No, I put it in your desk.

Page 109, Exercise 3B – CD2, Track 22

1. **A** I'd like to exchange this sweater.
   B Why?
   C It's too big, and it has a hole.
2. **A** You can't leave early again!
   B Yes, I can and I will.
3. **A** Why don't you clean the counters?
   B Why don't you?
4. **A** Let's talk about a raise after you've
   worked here for six months.
   B Can we talk before six months?

Unit 9: Daily living

**Page 111, Exercises 2A and
2B – CD2, Track 23**

A Mei! Dinner!
B I'll be right there! Sorry I'm late. I was just
checking something on the computer.
A OK. Sit down. We've been waiting for you.
B I know. I'm sorry, but I was looking at a
website that describes ways to save our
planet.
C Save our planet? What does that mean?
What's the matter with our planet?
B Dad, it means taking responsibility for saving
the earth.
C Saving it from what?
B From global warming! We had a guest
speaker today in biology class, and he
mentioned a whole bunch of stuff – simple
steps we can take to reduce our energy use
and protect the environment.
A Like what?
B OK, well, first of all, he said we need to cut
down on driving, so we should walk, ride a
bicycle, carpool, or take public transportation.
C I'd do those things if I could. But my job is
an hour away, and there's no bus service
that goes there. And there's nobody for me
to carpool with.
B I see your point, but how about recycling? I
think we could do a better job of recycling
bottles, cans, glass, paper . . .
A You're right. We could do that if we tried.
B Another idea was to turn off unnecessary
lights. Look at this house: lights on in every
room.
C I like that idea. It'll help cut down on the
electric bill.
A What else did the speaker suggest?
B Let me think. Oh, he said that we should
wash our clothes in cold water.
A Really? I'm not sure the clothes will get
clean, but I suppose we can try.
C That'll save money on the electric bill, too.

B But isn't our washing machine really old? If
we bought a new one that's more energy-
efficient, it could help the environment and
our electric bill!
A I don't think we can afford to buy new
appliances right now.
B OK. But what about energy-efficient light
bulbs? We could switch to those, right?
A That sounds pretty simple, Mei.
B Cool!
C I have to say, I love your enthusiasm. I never
realized how simple it can be to . . . what
did you say. . . save our planet?
B Yeah, the speaker said that if everyone did
even one of these things every day, it would
do a lot to reduce global warming.
C Speaking of warming, can we eat before the
food gets cold?

Page 111, Exercise 3A – CD2, Track 24

Mei was late to dinner because she was looking
at a website about saving the planet. She wants
to take more responsibility for saving the earth
from global warming. Mei tells her parents about
the guest speaker who came to her biology
class. The speaker suggested simple things
people could do to reduce their energy use and
protect the environment. For example, they could
carpool instead of driving alone,
recycle their bottles and cans, and use energy-
efficient light bulbs. Mei's parents agree that it
is important to cut down on energy use since it
would also help them save money. However, they
can't afford to buy new appliances right now.

Page 112, Exercise 2A – CD2, Track 25

1. Many people put their newspapers in the trash
   can. If everybody recycled newspapers, we
   would save millions of trees.
2. Noah never takes his car in for a tune-up.
   Noah's car would use less gas if he tuned
   up his car regularly.
3. Mr. Brown drives his own car to his job
   downtown. Mr. Brown would save money on
   gas if he carpooled to work.
4. Many items in the supermarket are packaged
   in plastic. If you bought products that are
   packaged with recycled paper, you would
   help to reduce global warming.
5. Jessica always stays in the shower for a very
   long time. If Jessica took shorter showers,
   she would save water.
6. Some kinds of fish contain large amounts
   of lead, a poisonous metal. You would be
   healthier if you stopped eating fish that
   contains lead.
7. Energy-efficient appliances use less
   electricity. If Mei's family bought a new
   washing machine, they would save money on
   their electric bill.
8. Kristina never puts enough air in her tires. If
   Kristina put more air in her tires, she would
   buy less gasoline.

Page 114, Exercise 2A – CD2, Track 26

1. Since there is a buildup of harmful gases in
   the atmosphere, global warming is increasing.
2. Warm water is expanding in the oceans, so
   the sea level is rising.
3. Since the sea level is rising, towns near
   oceans are in danger of flooding.
4. Since global warming changes weather
   patterns, many places will have less rainfall.
5. The mosquito population will increase, so
   there will be an increase in diseases like
   malaria.
6. Since the ocean water is getting warmer,
   typhoons and hurricanes are becoming more
   frequent.

7. Cities are growing, so many plants and
   animals may lose their natural habitats.
8. Summer temperatures will continue to rise,
   so there will be longer periods of no rain and
   increased days of very high temperatures.

Page 116, Exercise 2 – CD2, Track 27
All Things Are Connected

Long ago, there was a village chief who never
allowed anyone to disagree with him. Whenever
he wanted to do something, he asked the
members of his court for their advice. But whether
the chief's idea was wise or foolish, his advisors
always said the same thing: "Indeed, it is wise."
Only one old woman dared to give a different
answer. Whenever the chief asked for her advice,
she always replied, "All things are connected."
One night, the chief was awakened by the sound
of frogs croaking in the swamp. It happened
again the next night and the next and the next.
The chief decided to kill all the frogs in the
swamp. When he consulted the members of his
court, they replied as usual: "Indeed, it is wise."
But the old woman kept silent. "And you, old
woman, what do you think?" the chief demanded.
"All things are connected," she replied. The
chief concluded that the old woman was a fool,
and he ordered his servants to kill all the frogs.
Therefore, the chief slept peacefully.
But soon the mosquitoes in the swamp began to
multiply since there were no frogs to eat them.
They came into the village and made everyone
miserable. The chief ordered his servants to go
into the swamp and kill the mosquitoes, but it
was impossible. Furious, the chief summoned
the members of his court and blamed them,
saying, "Why didn't you tell me that killing the
frogs would make the mosquitoes multiply and
everyone would be miserable? I should have
listened to the old woman."
Because the mosquitoes were there, all the
people of the village were forced to go away.
Finally, the chief and his family left, too. Until
he died the chief never forgot the old woman's
words: "All things are connected."

Unit 10: Free time

Page 123, Exercises 2A and 2B – CD2, Track 28

A Hi, Cathy. What are you doing this weekend?
B Oh, Thanh. I'm glad you asked. I was
invited to Bao and An's wedding. It's
Saturday night, and I haven't bought them
a gift yet.
A So?
B Well, I don't know what to get them. They
aren't registered at any stores.
A Registered? What's that?
B Well, for many American weddings, the bride
and groom sign up with a gift registry service
at a store. They make a list of what they
want, and then people can go to the store
or the store's website and buy something on
the couple's list.
A I've never heard of that custom. At a
Vietnamese wedding, guests just bring cash
in an envelope.
B Really?
A Yeah, and during the reception, the bride and
groom walk from table to table, greet the
guests, and collect the envelopes. If I were
you, I would just take an envelope.
B OK. Thanks for the advice. I guess customs
are really different- across cultures, aren't
they?
A That's for sure. Do you know what really
surprised me the first time I went to an
American wedding?
B No, what?

A As the bride and groom were leaving the reception, the guests threw rice at them. What a waste of food! Where does that custom come from?

B Oh, that's a really old tradition. Rice is a symbol of fertility and longevity, so throwing rice represents the hope that the couple will have children and live a long life together.

A That's really interesting.

B Yeah. So, Thanh, what else happens at a Vietnamese wedding?

A Well, for one thing, it's traditional for a Vietnamese bride to wear a red dress.

B Red? Not white, like in this country?

A That's right. In our culture, red symbolizes good fortune. In fact, one of the traditional foods at a Vietnamese wedding is red sticky rice.

B Interesting. Let me ask you something else. My invitation was just for the wedding reception in the evening. What about the ceremony?

A Well, traditionally, the ceremony takes place at the bride's home, with just the family and close relatives. It's usually held in the morning. The reception in the evening is actually a huge party, with all the couple's friends and acquaintances, lots of dancing, and lots of food. Be prepared for a seven- or eight-course dinner.

B Wow! I guess I won't eat anything beforehand. So, will I see you at Bao and An's wedding?

A I wish I could go, but I have to go to my nephew's graduation party. I hope you have a great time.

B I hope so, too. I'm really looking forward to it.

Page 123, Exercise 3A – CD2, Track 29

Cathy and Thanh are talking about wedding customs. Cathy is invited to a Vietnamese wedding, and she is surprised that the bride and groom are not registered for gifts at any stores. In contrast, Thanh is surprised by the American tradition of throwing rice at the bride and groom. Next, they talk about clothes. Thanh says a Vietnamese bride wears a red dress because the color red symbolizes good fortune. Then Cathy asks why she was invited only to the wedding reception, not the ceremony. Thanh explains that traditionally the ceremony is only for the family. The couple's friends and acquaintances are invited to the evening reception. In fact, Thanh says the evening party will include seven or eight courses of food. Cathy says she is looking forward to the wedding.

Page 124, Exercise 2A – CD2, Track 30

1. The Patels are from India, but they live in the United States now. They are planning a wedding for their daughter, Parveen. If they lived in India, the groom's family would pay for the wedding.

2. The wedding will be in the United States. If the Patels had the wedding in India, the wedding celebration would last three days. Here it will last for one day.

3. The Patels don't have a lot of money. If they were rich, they would invite 300 people; instead, they will invite about 150.

4. The Patels are planning to have music for the reception. If a band doesn't charge too much, they will have live music.

5. It's possible that the weather will be nice on the day of the wedding. If the weather is nice, they will have the ceremony outside.

6. It's possible Parveen and her husband will get some vacation time from work. If Parveen and husband get enough time off from work, they will take a trip to Hawaii for their honeymoon.

7. They don't have a lot of time off from work. If they had more time, they would go to India for their honeymoon.

8. Parveen and her new husband will live in their own apartment. If they were in India, they would live with the groom's parents.

Page 126, Exercise 2A – CD2, Track 31

1. Paul's high school graduation is tomorrow. His friend Luis has to work. Luis wishes he could go to Paul's graduation.

2. Paul's father has asked for the day off so that he can attend his son's graduation. He hopes he gets the day off.

3. Paul's grandfather has been sick. He's not sure if he will attend the graduation. Paul hopes his grandfather will attend the ceremony.

4. Paul's sister is out of the country, so she can't come to the ceremony. Paul wishes his sister were here to attend his graduation.

5. The graduation ceremony will be outside. Paul hopes it will not rain.

6. Paul's parents would like to buy him a new car, but they can't afford it. They wish they could buy him a new car.

7. Paul wasn't accepted to the university, so he will go to a community college. Paul wishes he could go to the university.

8. Paul has applied for financial aid. Paul hopes he gets financial aid to help pay for his books.

9. It's possible that Paul will be able to transfer to the university in two years. He hopes he can transfer in two years.

Page 128, Exercise 2 – CD2, Track 32
Special Birthdays Around the World

In most cultures, there are certain birthdays that are especially important in a young person's life. If you were an American teenager, for example, you would eagerly look forward to your 16th birthday because in most states, that is the age to get a driver's license. Other cultures also have birthdays with special meanings:

Mexico For Mexican girls, the 15th birthday – the "Quinceañera" – symbolizes a girl's transition into adulthood. To celebrate, the girl's family throws a huge party. The girl wears a ball gown similar to a wedding dress. The girl performs a waltz, a formal dance, with her father. A similar custom is celebrated in Brazil.

China On a child's first birthday, parents place their baby in the center of a group of objects, such as a shiny coin, a book, and a doll. Then they watch to see which object the baby picks up first. Most parents hope their child will pick up the coin because, according to tradition, it means the child will be rich.

Nigeria The 1st, 5th, 10th, and 15th birthdays are considered extremely important. Parties are held with up to 100 people. The guests enjoy a feast of a roasted cow or goat.

Saudi Arabia In some countries, such as Saudi Arabia, people don't observe birthdays at all because of spiritual beliefs. According to Muslim traditions, the only celebrations allowed are Eid al Fitr, a feast that signifies the end of Ramadan, and Eid al Adha, which celebrates the end of the annual pilgrimage to Mecca.

Israel A boy's 13th and a girl's 12th birthdays are serious as well as happy occasions. On these birthdays, children become responsible for their own religious and moral behavior. Adult birthdays also have special significance in many cultures. In the United States, for example, birthdays ending in "0" – 30, 40, 50, etc. – are especially meaningful.

Review: Units 9 and 10

Page 134, Exercise 1 – CD2, Track 33

A This is Grace Leong, for KPFX News. I'm standing on the busy corner of Pacific Avenue and Grant Avenue in San Francisco's Chinatown. Tomorrow is the beginning of Chinese New Year, and with me I have two people who can give us some interesting information related to good luck in the coming year. Could you tell us your name, please?

B Angela Kwan.

A Angela, what are some things we can do to bring good luck?

B Well, it's traditional to wear bright colors, such as red. Red is a very bright and happy color, so it symbolizes a bright and happy future. Another thing is, at midnight on New Year's Eve, you should open all the doors and windows of your house. That's to let the old year out and make room for the new. And on New Year's Day, one good thing to do is to eat a lot of candy. If you do that, the new year will be very sweet.

A Very interesting, Angela. I think I'll go shopping for a new red dress, and I'm definitely looking forward to eating all that candy! And what's your name, sir?

C Hi. My name's Martin Chan.

A Martin, Angela told us some things that bring good luck. What are some things that we should not do on New Year's?

C Well, you shouldn't sweep the house on New Year's Day because you might sweep away your family's good fortune. That's why people sweep the house very carefully before the start of the holiday. And it's bad luck to buy a pair of shoes, because . . .

A Not even red shoes?

C No. The word for "shoes" sounds like the word for "evil" in Mandarin, so you don't want to buy shoes. And you shouldn't use knives or scissors on New Year's Day because if you do, you might cut off your good fortune.

A Thank you, Martin and Angela, and I hope you both have a very happy new year.

Page 135, Exercise 3A – CD2, Track 34

1. Smaller cars would use less energy.
2. Smog is a big environmental problem.
3. If everyone drove less, our air quality would improve.
4. In the future, we will see more electric cars and trucks on our roads.
5. We should all have efficient appliances.
6. We need to protect our environment.

Page 135, Exercise 3B – CD2, Track 35

1. All things in this world are connected.
2. People are concerned about saving this earth.
3. Most of the cars on the highway have only one person in them.
4. People make a lot of unnecessary trips.
5. We should close off unused rooms in our homes.
6. The Internet is a good source of information about global warming.

TESTS

Overview

The unit tests, midterm test, and final test help teachers assess students' mastery of the material in the *Ventures 4* 2nd Edition Student's Book.

- Each of the ten unit tests covers one unit.
- The midterm test covers Units 1–5.
- The final test covers Units 6–10.
- Each test assesses listening, grammar, reading, and writing.

Students' performance on the tests helps to determine what has been successfully learned and what may need more attention. Successful completion of a test can also give students a sense of accomplishment.

Getting ready for a test

- Plan to give a unit test shortly after students have completed a unit and have had time for a review. The midterm should follow completion of Unit 5 and the review lesson for Units 5 and 6. The final test should follow completion of Unit 10 and the review lesson for Units 9 and 10. Tell students when the test will be given. Encourage students to study together and to ask you for help if needed.
- Explain the purpose of the test and how students' scores will be used.
- Prepare one test for each student. The tests may be photocopied from the Teacher's Edition, starting on page T-186, or printed from the *Ventures* online teacher's resources.
- Schedule approximately 45 minutes to 1 hour for the tests. Allow more time if needed.
- Locate the audio program for each test's listening section in the online teacher's resources.

Giving a test

- During the test, have students use a pencil and an eraser. Tell students to put away their Student's Books and dictionaries before the test.
- Hand out one copy of the test to each student.
- Encourage students to take a few minutes to look through the test without answering any of the items. Go through the instructions to make sure students understand them.

- Customizable tests and test audio are available via a secure download site. Contact your Cambridge ESL Specialist (www.cambridge.org/cambridgeenglish/contact) for more information.
- Tell students that approximately 10 minutes of the tests will be used for the listening section.
- When playing the audio for the listening section of the test, you may choose to pause or repeat the audio program if you feel that students require more time to answer. The audio script appears in the Teacher's Edition on pages T-222–T-225. The script can also be printed from the online teacher's resources and read aloud in class.

Scoring

- You can collect the tests and grade them on your own. Alternatively, you can have students correct their own tests by going over the answers in class or by having students exchange tests with a partner and correcting each other's answers. The answer key for the tests is located in the Teacher's Edition on pages T-226–T-230. It can also be printed from the online teacher's resources.
- Each test has a total score of 100 points. Each unit test has five sections worth 20 points each. The midterm and final tests have five sections worth 12.5 or 25 points each.

Track list for test audio program

Track 2:   Unit 1 Test
Track 3:   Unit 2 Test
Track 4:   Unit 3 Test
Track 5:   Unit 4 Test
Track 6:   Unit 5 Test
Track 7:   Midterm Test
Track 8:   Unit 6 Test
Track 9:   Unit 7 Test
Track 10: Unit 8 Test
Track 11: Unit 9 Test
Track 12: Unit 10 Test
Track 13: Final Test

TEST
UNIT 1 PERSONAL INFORMATION

A Listening

Track 2   1 Listen. Circle the correct answer.

1. What are they planning?
   a. a class trip   b. a party   c. a menu

2. Carol and George are
   a. classmates   b. co-workers   c. teachers

3. Who will pay for the party?
   a. the school   b. the teacher   c. the students

Track 2   2 Listen again. Complete the chart.

Name	Task	Reason
1. Carol		
2. George		
3. Leonard		
4. Elena		
5. Jonathan		
6. Ming		
7. Marina		

B Grammar

Complete the sentences with adjectives or adverbs.

1. Math is _____ for him. He has learned _____.
   (easy)   (quick)

2. That song was _____! Do you sing _____?
   (beautiful)   (professional)

3. I need a _____ mechanic. My car is running _____ now.
   (skillful)   (slow)

4. She used to be a _____ driver. Now she drives _____.
   (fast)   (careful)

5. He's a _____ communicator. He doesn't listen _____.
   (bad)   (good)

C Grammar

Write the words in the correct order. Make a sentence with a noun clause as an object.

1. girls / than boys / learning / better at / you / languages / Do / believe / are / ?

   _____

2. aptitude / has / parents / art / he / realize / for / Samuel's / an / .

   _____

3. that / math / son / class / help / you / your / needs / feel / in / Do / ?

   _____

4. Everyone / gifted / is / dance / Naomi / agrees / in / that / .

   _____

5. know / aptitude / you / for / Karen / Do / that / has / an / cooking / ?

   _____

D Reading

Read the magazine article. Then read the sentences. Circle *T* (true) or *F* (false).

Multiple Intelligences in the Classroom

Harold Gardner's theory of multiple intelligences has impacted education across the United States. He has identified nine different "intelligences" to show that people understand, experience, and learn in different ways. Educators in the United States have carefully considered Gardner's theory. Many educators think that students gifted in the verbal / linguistic and logical / mathematical intelligences do better in traditional classrooms than those with other intelligences. This is because many traditional teachers teach by using textbooks, giving lectures, checking written homework, and giving written tests. Their methods of teaching are based on verbal / linguistic and logical / mathematical coursework.

Some teachers are changing the way they teach their students. These teachers think that if students think and learn in different ways, then teachers should think and teach in different ways. Their idea is to reach all students by using different intelligences in their classrooms. Teachers who are trained in multiple intelligences might use a visual / spatial activity to teach math. For example, they might ask students to take pictures of objects as they study geometry. Teachers may have students with interpersonal intelligence lead a discussion or teach new terms to other students. These teachers feel that teaching to each student's aptitude and getting each student to learn on his or her own is more important than teaching course subjects in the traditional way.

1. Educators have paid attention to Gardner's theory.   T   F

2. Traditional teachers in the United States often base their
   teaching methods on two intelligences.   T   F

3. It is impossible to teach multiple intelligences in one classroom.   T   F

4. A teacher might ask a student with visual / spatial intelligence
   to lead a group discussion.   T   F

5. Teachers who teach to multiple intelligences try to reach all students.   T   F

E Writing

1 Plan a paragraph about the primary intelligence of someone you know. Use
  the outline to make notes on your ideas.

   Topic sentence: _____
   Supporting details:

   • _____

   • _____

   • _____

   • _____

   Concluding sentence: _____

2 Write a paragraph about the primary intelligence of someone you know. Use a
  separate piece of paper.

TEST

UNIT 2 AT SCHOOL

A Listening

Track 3   1 Listen. Circle the correct answer.

1. What are they talking about?
   a. an academic program   b. a job opening   c. setting up a small business

2. What is their relationship?
   a. teacher and student   b. two friends   c. student and counselor

3. Where are they?
   a. at home   b. at school   c. at work

Track 3   2 Listen again. Complete the chart.

1. Type of certificate	
2. Location of certificate program	
3. Reason for getting a certificate	
4. One thing you cannot do with a certificate	
5. Number of courses	
6. Cost	
7. Length of time to complete	

B Grammar

Complete the sentences. Use the present passive voice.

1. **A** _____ bilingual skills _____ by many employers in

   (expect)

   this country?

   B Yes, bilingual skills _____ for many jobs in this country.

   (need)

2. **A** _____ an internship _____ to graduate from

   (require)

   the program?

   B Yes. Internships _____ by the school.

   (arranged)

3. **A** Where _____ the admissions office _____?

   (locate)

   B It _____ next to the business building.

   (locate)

4. **A** _____ most of the classes _____ in the morning?
(hold)

   B Actually, many of the classes _____ in the evening.
(offer)

5. **A** _____ scholarships _____ for students.
(provide)

   B Yes, scholarships _____ to students by the financial aid office.
(give)

C Grammar

Write complete statements or questions. Use the present passive with infinitives.

1. graduates / require / complete / their courses by May 4th.

   _____

2. all interns / expect / be on time for every meeting.

   _____

3. students / encourage / participate in work experience programs?

   _____

4. applicants / tell / meet with a counselor.

   _____

5. students / allow / earn credit for work experience?

   _____

D Reading

Read the story. Then read the sentences. Circle *T* (true) or *F* (false).

Kate Shelley

In 1865, when Kate Shelley was a baby, her family immigrated to the United States from Ireland. As a child, Kate faced many obstacles. When she was 12, her father and her brother died in separate accidents. These unfortunate events caused Kate's mother to become unhappy. Kate had to become the responsible member of the family. As a young girl, Kate was expected to take care of the household and the family farm.

Kate's life changed on March 25, 1881. A thunderstorm started to flood the farm and surrounding areas. At first, Kate went out to save the animals in the barn. On the way back to the house, she heard a loud crash. The bridge over Honey Creek fell. Kate knew a midnight train was scheduled to cross the bridge. She was determined to get to the station in time. She took a lantern and ran through the winds, rain, thunder, and lightning to warn the train station employees to stop the midnight train. Strong winds blew out Kate's lantern, so she had to find her way across a different bridge in the dark to reach the station. Kate arrived at the station in time. The midnight train stopped before its passengers crashed into the river. Everyone on the train was fortunate to have Kate's help that night.

For her courage, the railroad company gave Kate a free railroad pass for the rest of her life. Even now, people in Iowa remember the young girl when they use the Kate Shelley Bridge in Moingona, Iowa.

---

1. Kate grew up in Ireland.   T   F
2. Kate's father and brother died when she was a baby.   T   F
3. The bridge over Honey Creek fell after Kate's lantern blew out.   T   F
4. Kate succeeded in stopping the midnight train.   T   F
5. Kate was rewarded for her courage and determination.   T   F

E Writing

1 Plan a paragraph about your obstacles and successes. Use the chart to make notes on your ideas.

My obstacles	My successes

2 Write a paragraph about your obstacles and successes. Use a separate piece of paper.

TEST

UNIT 3 FRIENDS AND FAMILY

A Listening

Track 4 1 Listen. Circle the correct answer.

1. What are they talking about?
   a. school   b. a dance   c. countries

2. What is their relationship?
   a. parent and child   b. brother and sister   c. two friends

3. How do you think Mike feels about Vanna?
   a. he likes her   b. he's not interested   c. she annoys him

4. What is a good description of Vanna?
   a. obedient   b. independent   c. angry

Track 4 2 Listen again. Complete the chart.

1. Day of the event	
2. Reason she can't go	
3. Country her parents are from	
4. Who she is going to the dance with	
5. Two things she is allowed to do	
6. Where her parents will be that night	

B Grammar

Change the direct questions to indirect *Wh-* questions.

1. Why is he on restriction?

   A I'd like to know _____.

   B I think his grades were bad.

2. When did she start to trust him again?

   A I wonder _____.

   B She started to trust him again after he apologized.

3. How can I get a better job?

   A Can you tell me _____?

   B First, you can continue to improve your English.

4. What time does the class start?

   A Do you know _____?

   B It starts at 5:30.

5. What grade did Lidia get in chemistry?

A Can you tell me _____?

B I think she got a B+.

C Grammar

Write indirect *Yes / No* questions with *whether*.

1. Do you know _____?
   (Did he break the school rules?)

2. Can you tell me _____?
   (Is there a bus stop nearby?)

3. I'd like to know _____.
   (Is he on restriction this weekend?)

4. Can you tell me _____?
   (Did she leave school early?)

5. I wonder _____.
   (Can she come to the party?)

D Reading

Read the article. Answer the questions.

Teenagers and Spending

Teenagers in the United States generally spend money on clothing, entertainment, food, computers, and even cars. Many teens get their spending money as an allowance from their parents or as paychecks for part-time jobs. Studies have shown that parents' attitudes toward their children and money may influence their spending habits. For example, some parents try to teach their children how to spend responsibly at a young age by giving their children weekly allowances. They may connect a weekly allowance to the child's age. In other words, a parent will give $15 a week to his or her 15-year-old. Other parents offer payment to children for chores they do around the house. For example, a teen may earn money for babysitting younger siblings or cleaning the house.

Parents also encourage teenagers to get part-time jobs for their spending money. Recent studies have shown that 33 to 44 percent of teenagers have jobs while in school. They often work 15 to 20 hours per week. Teens like these, who have jobs or whose parents limit the amount of money they receive, may spend more responsibly.

However, problems with spending occur when teenagers have poor money-management skills. These teens will often choose to spend their money rather than save it. And they spend money on the latest fashions or the latest technology without thinking beyond the present. However, as these teens become more responsible adults, they will need to reconsider their spending habits.

1. What types of things do teens in the United States spend their money on?
   Name at least three. _____
   _____

2. What is one way teens in the United States get their spending money? _____
   _____

3. What is one way that parents in the United States try to teach their teenagers how to spend
   responsibly? _____
   _____

4. What do teens with poor money-management skills do? _____
   _____

5. What will teens who spend a lot of money need to do when they become adults? _____
   _____

E Writing

1 Plan a paragraph about the differences between you and your best friend. Use the outline to make
  notes on your ideas.

Topic sentence: _____

A. Me:

    1. Example: _____

    2. Example: _____

    3. Example: _____

Transition: *On the other hand*

B. My best friend:

    1. Example: _____

    2. Example: _____

    3. Example: _____

2 Write a paragraph about the differences between you and your best friend. Use a separate piece
  of paper.

TEST

UNIT 4 HEALTH

A Listening

Track 5   1 Listen. Circle the correct answer.

1. What are they talking about?
   a. schools   b. an apartment   c. bills

2. What is their relationship?
   a. parent and child   b. landlord and tenant   c. husband and wife

3. Where are they?
   a. at home   b. at work   c. at school

4. How do they feel?
   a. happy   b. confused   c. stressed

Track 5   2 Listen again. Complete the chart.

1. What is going to happen?	
2. How did they find out?	
3. What do they have to decide?	
4. How long do they have?	
5. What is the most important factor?	
6. Why is Marcus sorry?	

B Grammar

Match the sentences with the advice.

1. She's often late for class. _____
2. She is worried that her boss will fire her. _____
3. She gets tense during tests. _____
4. She has no time for herself. _____
5. The rent is due today. _____

a. She has to learn to calm down and concentrate.
b. She has to pay today.
c. She doesn't have to do everything for her family!
d. She shouldn't lose her temper.
e. She should take an earlier bus.

C Grammar

Write sentences with *should have* and *shouldn't have*.

1. He couldn't concentrate during the test.

_____

(go to bed on time)

Name: _____

Date: _____

2. They spent too much money.

_____
(use a credit card every day)

3. She was late to work.

_____
(turn off her alarm clock)

4. He didn't understand the rules.

_____
(ask someone to explain them)

5. We lost our jobs.

_____
(be more responsible)

D Reading

Read the article. Answer the questions.

Stress and Music

Music can help you to calm down when you are stressed out. But it is important to find the best kind of music for you. You might assume that you should choose quiet music to help you to relieve stress. However, many doctors think that different types of music affect people differently. They say that each person's reaction to sounds and noises is unique and complicated. This means that the music that helps you to calm down may make another person anxious.

To discover the right music to help you relax, you ought to experiment. You should start by listening to music that you like. If you like loud music, you should start by seeing how loud music affects you. If you prefer quiet music, you should choose a calmer piece. To begin your experiment, feel for your pulse with your first and second fingers by pressing down on your wrist. Count the number of beats you feel in one minute. Write down the number. Next, pay attention to your muscles. Write down if they are tense or relaxed. A stressed-out person often has tense muscles and a fast pulse. Then, listen to the music for 20 minutes. React to the music in your own way. Relax, dance, sing along – do whatever your body wants to do. After 20 minutes, check your pulse and muscles again. Write down the changes that you have noticed. Is your pulse slower? Are your muscles less tense? If not, try the experiment again with another type of music.

1. How does music help someone who is stressed out? _____

_____

2. Do all people react to music in the same way? Why or why not? _____

_____

3. Why should you do an experiment with music? _____

_____

4. What are some of the physical signs that a person is stressed out? _____

_____

5. What are some of the physical signs that a person is relaxed? _____

_____

🅴 Writing

1 Plan a paragraph about how you coped with a stressful situation in your past. Use the outline to make notes on your ideas.

Topic sentence: _____

_____

Actions you took	Results of your actions
_____	_____
_____	_____
_____	_____

2 Write a paragraph about how you coped with a stressful situation in your past. Use a separate piece of paper.

TEST

UNIT 5 AROUND TOWN

A Listening

Track 6 1 Listen. Circle the correct answer.

1. Where are they?
   - a. at school
   - b. at an Internet cafe
   - c. at the library

2. What is their relationship?
   - a. teacher and student
   - b. volunteer and coordinator
   - c. librarian and visitor

3. What are they talking about?
   - a. computers
   - b. family problems
   - c. research

Track 6 2 Listen again. Answer the questions.

1. What is Jackie's job?

   _____

2. Who encouraged Yousef to go to the library?

   _____

3. What skills does Yousef have?

   _____

4. What experience does Yousef have in helping people use computers?

   _____

5. What is one characteristic Yousef has?

   _____

6. What languages does Yousef speak?

   _____

7. What time commitment does Yousef make?

   _____

B Grammar

Complete the sentences with *until* or *as soon as*.

1. **A** When will the party begin?
   B The party will begin _____ the first guests arrive.

2. **A** How long will Raul volunteer at the animal shelter?
   B He will volunteer there _____ he finds a full-time job.

3. **A** When will Samah eat lunch?
   B _____ she finishes her homework, she will eat lunch.

4. **A** How long will you and your wife live in the city?

   B We will live in the city _____ we have children.

5. **A** When will you take a vacation?

   B I will take a vacation _____ I have enough money!

Ⓒ Grammar

Complete the sentences with the present, present perfect, or past forms of the verbs.

1. My husband _____ our neighbors several times last year.
                       (help)

2. Jun-Ming _____ once last week.
               (oversleep)

3. My daughter _____ her grandmother twice a week.
                (visit)

4. I _____ with our new neighbors once so far.
         (speak)

5. Solange _____ her cousins many times in her life.
           (babysit)

Ⓓ Reading

Read the article. Answer the questions.

Community Gardens

Members of communities in cities across the nation are changing the physical appearance and social setting of their neighborhoods. They are transforming unused, empty parking lots into community gardens. In these gardens, the residents of the neighborhoods grow their own vegetables, fruits, herbs, and flowers. The empty parking lots change into colorful, productive gardens, shared by different members of the community.

Community gardens don't just make neighborhoods more beautiful. They are worthwhile for residents in many ways. Some people use the gardens to save money on bills by growing their own fruits and vegetables. Others like the taste of their own fruits and vegetables. Immigrant families often grow fruits and vegetables from their native countries that they cannot find in supermarkets. Residents also go to the gardens for light exercise and fresh air.

When neighbors plant a garden together, they can create positive changes in a neighborhood. Community gardens bring neighbors closer together. In some neighborhoods, there has been less crime because neighbors work together to create, maintain, and harvest their community gardens. Community gardens offer safe, green space in city neighborhoods with few public parks. Finally, community gardens can help the environment. They help keep city air clean. No wonder there are about 100,000 community gardens in cities around the country! With all the great things gained from community gardens, we can expect to see many more in the near future!

---

1. Who is responsible for creating community gardens? _____

_____

2. Where do people build community gardens? _____

_____

3. Why are community gardens worthwhile for residents? Give two reasons. _____

_____

4. How do community gardens result in less crime? _____

_____

5. Why can we expect to see more community gardens in the future? _____

_____

E Writing

1 Plan a paragraph about a famous person who has made a difference. Use the chart to make notes.

Who made a difference?	
What did he or she do?	
Why did this person do it?	
Where did it happen?	
When did it happen?	
How did this person make a difference?	

2 Write a paragraph about a famous person who has made a difference.
Use a separate piece of paper.

MIDTERM TEST

UNITS 1–5

Name: _____

Date: _____   Score: _____

A Listening

Track 7   **1** Listen. Circle the correct answer.

1. Where are they?
   a. at school   b. at home   c. at the hospital

2. What is their relationship?
   a. parent and child   b. student and teacher   c. counselor and parent

3. What are they talking about?
   a. a teenager's problems   b. college opportunities   c. social difficulties

Track 7   **2** Listen again. Complete the chart.

1. Who made the appointment?	
2. What is Mrs. Patterson's job?	
3. What do teenagers have to cope with?	
4. What is Mrs. Brown worried about?	
5. What does Sam say?	
6. What solution have Sam's parents tried?	
7. What does Mrs. Patterson suggest?	

B Grammar

Complete the sentences.

have to   shouldn't   that   until   whether

1. Molly can't have dessert _____ she turns off the television.

2. You _____ calm down before you lose your temper.

3. I wonder _____ John had a basketball game today.

4. My teachers realized _____ I was really good at math.

5. His parents _____ have let him go to the movies.

C Grammar

Complete the sentences.

1. We found the shopping mall _____ .
   (easy / easily)

2. Students are encouraged _____ college credit for work experience.
   (earn / to earn)

3. He _____ learn how to manage his money.
   (ought to / shouldn't)

4. She will read to the children _____ they fall asleep.
   (as soon as / until)

5. We _____ at Running with Ropes three times last year.
   (volunteered / have volunteered)

D Reading

Read the article. Then read the sentences. Circle *T* (true) or *F* (false).

Resolving Conflict

In workplaces, school settings, and homes, conflict resolution techniques have been helping people to solve conflicts, or arguments, in better ways. In the workplace, co-workers may encourage teamwork and discussion, and in schools, children may be trained to become mediators, or peacekeepers, in order to help with conflicts among their fellow students.

People who help to resolve conflict learn about other people's interpersonal skills. They look at how people communicate with words and how people communicate with their bodies – their body language. When they look at how people communicate with words, they look at the words people choose to speak or write to others. For body language, they look at how people "say" things with their body's gestures, voice tone, and eye contact. From doing this, they understand how people communicate best.

Not being able to communicate clearly, or miscommunication, is one of the main reasons conflicts happen. So mediators often learn how to prevent miscommunication with good communication techniques. They do this by learning how to speak clearly and how to give feedback. They also learn how to listen carefully to understand another person's message. Once they've learned the best ways to communicate, they share them with their co-workers or classmates.

Conflict resolution techniques are not just used in offices and classrooms. They are used to solve arguments between parents and children and husbands and wives. They are also used for conflicts between companies, organizations, and countries. If conflict resolution techniques are used well, they can help change the outcome of many arguments and conflicts.

1. Conflicts occur in offices, schools, and homes.   T   F
2. Conflict resolution techniques are not usually successful.   T   F
3. Mediators help to resolve conflicts.   T   F
4. Children are too young to use conflict resolution techniques.   T   F
5. People who resolve conflicts learn about other people's intrapersonal skills.   T   F
6. Gestures, eye contact, and voice tone are examples of body language.   T   F
7. Miscommunication is a common reason conflicts occur.   T   F
8. People who help with conflicts don't know how to communicate well.   T   F
9. Conflict resolution techniques are not helpful between husbands and wives.   T   F
10. Conflict resolution techniques are also used for conflicts between countries.   T   F

E Writing

1 Plan a paragraph about a conflict you had with a family member or friend. How did you resolve the problem? Use the chart to make notes on your ideas.

Who did you have a conflict with?	
What happened?	
Why did the conflict happen?	
Where did it happen?	
When did it happen?	
How did you resolve the conflict?	

2 Write a paragraph about a conflict you had with a family member or friend. Use a separate piece of paper.

TEST
UNIT 6 TIME

A Listening

Track 8 1 Listen. Circle the correct answer.

1. What is their relationship?
   a. parent and child   b. husband and wife   c. student and teacher

2. What are they talking about?
   a. getting cell phones   b. getting smartphone   c. expenses

Track 8 2 Listen again. Answer the questions.

1. Who wants a smartphone?

   _____

2. What does Linda think is a problem with smartphone?

   _____

3. What happens in Chris's English class?

   _____

4. What is one feature that smartphone have that other cell phones don't?

   _____

5. Why is this a good feature for Chris?

   _____

6. What are two other advantages?

   _____

7. Why doesn't Linda think the children should get smartphone?

   _____

8. How will they pay for the smartphone?

   _____

B Grammar

Combine the sentences. Use *although*.

1. She doesn't understand the instructions. She read the manual many times.

   _____

2. There are free computer classes at the community center. My parents still don't know how to use email.

_____

3. I rarely use my microwave. Microwaves help me to make dinner quickly.

_____

4. He can take the subway to work. He prefers to walk for the exercise.

_____

5. She never used to write letters to her brother. She enjoys sending him emails now.

_____

C Grammar

Complete the sentences. Use *because* or *although*.

1. A Why is Julie always so busy?

   B _____ she has a full-time job, she volunteers at the senior center three times a week.

2. A Why doesn't David ever answer his phone?

   B Well, he rarely answers his cell phone _____ he forgets to turn it on.

3. A They don't often use their video camera _____ they have had it for years.

   B Maybe they'll let us borrow it!

4. A Why is Jason's mom concerned about his grades?

   B He has stopped reading books _____ he prefers to play video games.

5. A _____ Lana wants to try videoconferencing, she's worried about the cost.

   B Maybe she can look online for an affordable videoconferencing center.

D Reading

Read the article. Then read the sentences. Write *A* for advantage or *D* for disadvantage, based on the reading.

Saving Time with Microwaves

Do you look for ways to save time, especially in the kitchen? One of the most commonly used time-saving devices in homes today is the microwave. Because using a microwave can cut dinner preparation time from two or three hours to a half hour, they are used by many American families.

But microwaves aren't just used in the home. They're everywhere – in restaurants, trains, cafeterias, college dormitories, and lunch or break rooms in workplaces, for example. It's not surprising that microwaves are popular. Workers and students can put leftovers from last night's dinner in the microwave, heat them for a few minutes, and eat a delicious lunch. Supermarkets also add to the convenience of microwaves because they sell different types of "microwaveable" meals. These frozen dinners are packaged in microwave-safe containers.

Some people have health concerns about food cooked in a microwave. Others feel strongly that food cooked in a microwave does not taste as good as food cooked in a regular oven. They say that using a microwave takes away from the pleasure of cooking. Luckily for people who do not believe cooking is fun, microwaves can make their lives a lot easier.

_____ 1. Microwaves cut down on the time it takes to prepare meals.

_____ 2. Microwaves can be used in different places, such as homes, restaurants, and cafeterias.

_____ 3. Food cooked in microwaves may not taste as good as food cooked in regular ovens.

_____ 4. Microwaves make it easy for workers and students to bring leftovers for lunch.

_____ 5. Microwaves take away from the pleasure of cooking.

E Writing

1 Plan a paragraph that discusses the advantages and disadvantages of your favorite time-saving or technological device. Use the diagram to make notes on your ideas.

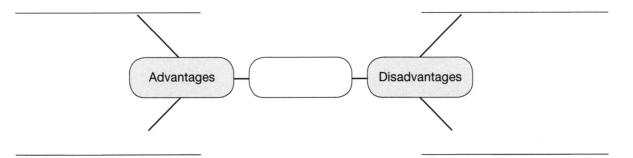

2 Write a paragraph that discusses the advantages and disadvantages of your favorite time-saving or technological device. Use a separate piece of paper.

Name: _____

Date: _____   Score: _____

A Listening

Track 9 1 Listen. Circle the correct answer.

1. Where are they?
   a. in a store   b. in an office   c. on the phone

2. What is their relationship?
   a. salesclerk and   b. service representative   c. operator and long-distance
      customer   and customer   caller

3. What is the reason for the conversation?
   a. a phone bill   b. a defective phone   c. a new phone

Track 9 2 Listen again. Answer the questions.

1. What is wrong with the phone?

   _____

2. When did she buy it?

   _____

3. What two ways can the woman return the phone?

   _____

4. What are the two choices Jack offers?

   _____

5. What does Jack mean by an upgrade?

   _____

6. Which costs more, the upgrade or getting the same phone?

   _____

7. Which choice does the woman make?

   _____

B Grammar

Combine the sentences. Change the second sentence into an adjective clause
with *which* or *who*.

1. Our merchandise comes with a warranty. It is good for two years.

   _____

2. Customers can order from our online store. They are looking for discounts.

   _____

3. Cellular phones are popular. They have Internet access.

   _____

4. The clerk is looking for the customer. She had a question about a product.

_____

5. Store managers solve problems. They happen between clerks and customers.

_____

C Grammar

Combine the sentences. Change the second sentence into an adjective clause with *that*.

1. He's a manager. I've worked with him for years.

_____

2. The car is great! You recommended it to us.

_____

3. The computer is defective. We bought it yesterday.

_____

4. The sweater was too small. I gave it to her.

_____

5. We bought it from a retailer. We trusted him.

_____

D Reading

Read the article. Answer the questions.

Thrift Stores

Shoppers who are looking for the lowest priced items don't usually go to the large shopping malls or the shopping centers in town. Instead, many bargain shoppers go to neighborhood thrift stores. At thrift stores, shoppers can buy used clothing, household items, books, jewelry, and furniture. The merchandise for sale is donated, or given, to the stores, and the salesclerks are volunteers. Because of this, thrift stores are able to offer used items that cost very little money.

However, thrift stores sell merchandise "as is," which means that the items for sale may or may not be defective. In most cases, if an item has small defects, such as small tears or stains, shoppers usually don't mind. But, in all cases, shoppers have to make sure the merchandise is in good condition because there are no refunds, exchanges, or warranties at thrift stores. Even so, shoppers usually consider shopping at thrift stores worthwhile because they often find valuable items that they can afford.

Finally, for many people, thrift stores are great places to give items that they no longer need. When people donate to thrift stores, they can be sure that their old clothes or furniture will be used again. Also, thrift stores are run by organizations that help people who need shelter, food, clothing, or money, like charities and churches. So those who donate know that the profits will help people in their communities as well.

1. Where do bargain shoppers go for the lowest prices? _____

_____

2. What kind of items can you buy at a thrift store? _____

_____

3. Why are prices so low at thrift stores? _____

_____

4. Do thrift stores sometimes sell defective items? Why? _____

_____

5. What benefits do thrift stores offer? _____

_____

E Writing

1 Plan a paragraph about your favorite place to shop. Use the chart to make notes on your ideas.

Transition words	Reasons and supporting details	
	First reason:	
	Example:	
	Second reason:	
	Fact:	
	Fact:	
	Third reason:	
	Fact:	
	Fact:	

2 Write a paragraph about your favorite place to shop. Use a separate piece of paper.

TEST

UNIT 8 WORK

A Listening

Track 10 **1** Listen. Circle the correct answer.

1. Where are they?
   a. at work   b. at home   c. at school

2. What is their relationship?
   a. friends   b. co-workers   c. both friends and co-workers

3. What are they talking about?
   a. finding a new job   b. communication problems   c. job responsibilities

Track 10 **2** Listen again. Answer the questions.

1. Who helped Dan get the job?

   _____

2. How does Dan feel about the job?

   _____

3. What is Tom's job?

   _____

4. How does Tom feel about Dan's performance?

   _____

5. How does Tom know Dan has not been completing his duties?

   _____

6. What is one reason Dan gives for not completing his duties?

   _____

7. Why does Tom think the job isn't that hard for Dan?

   _____

B Grammar

Complete the sentences. Use the present perfect or present perfect continuous forms of the verbs. Use *just* where possible.

1. It's 7:00 a.m. Joe _____ making coffee.
   (finish)

2. Marie is exhausted. She _____ overtime all week.
   (work)

3. This book is so interesting! I _____ it all afternoon.
   (read)

4. I'm so excited. The clothes I ordered online _____.
   (arrive)

5. Mike's not home. He _____ to work.
   (go)

C Grammar

Circle the correct adjective.

1. I thought the movie was very **amusing / amused**.
2. My boss was **shocking / shocked** when I told him I was leaving.
3. After working so hard all day, Ricardo was **exhausting / exhausted**.
4. Everyone was in a bad mood because of the **disappointing / disappointed** results.
5. Jane's co-workers are **irritating / irritated** because she takes long lunches.

D Reading

Read the article. Answer the questions.

The "Hottest" Jobs in the Future

Every few years, the United States government issues a report on what the "hottest" jobs will be in the future. These reports suggest which jobs will have the largest growth and popularity in years to come. Based on information provided by the biggest job industries, they predict how quickly certain industries will need new employees. Students and workers who look at these reports can find out the most popular and fastest-growing jobs. They can use this information to help them decide which careers will be the most promising or which programs to study.

Recently, reports have said that some of the "hottest" jobs are service industry occupations. Jobs in the service industry include jobs in health care, hospitality, and food services, for example. There are many reasons why certain industries will have more jobs available in the future. One reason is a growing need for more people to do similar jobs.

Since people are living longer, more people are needed to take care of the elderly. Therefore, nurses, nursing aides, and home health aides are expected to be some of the "hottest" jobs in the near future. For jobs in health care, some hard skills are necessary, such as a certificate or a degree. However, the soft skills of having a good work ethic and patience are also just as important.

For all of the fastest-growing occupations, employers will look for hard and soft skills. Will you be ready for one of the "hottest" jobs in the future?

1. What does the article mean by the "hottest" jobs?

_____

2. How can students and workers use job reports?

_____

3. What are some service industry occupations?

_____

4. What are some of the fastest growing health-care jobs?

_____

5. What will employers look for?

_____

E Writing

1 Plan a cover letter for a job in one of the service industries discussed in the article, such as health care, hospitality, or food services. Use the outline to make notes on your ideas.

1. Inside address: Mary Freeman mfreeman@bestjob.com

2. Position you are applying for:

   Job title: _____

3. Your skills and experience: _____

   _____

   _____

4. How the employer can contact you: _____

2 Write a cover letter for a job in one of the service industries discussed in the article, such as health care, hospitality, or food services. Use a separate piece of paper.

Name: _____

Date: _____ Score: _____

UNIT 9 DAILY LIVING

A Listening

Track 11 1 Listen. Circle the correct answer.

1. What are they talking about?
   a. the environment　　　　　b. a new car　　　　　c. the price of gas

2. Why does Ed talk to George?
   a. George knows a lot.　　　b. George is his father.　　　c. George listens well.

Track 11 2 Listen again. Complete the chart.

1. What kind of car does George suggest?	
2. What is a hybrid?	
3. What powers the car?	
4. How are the batteries charged?	
5. What does it reduce?	
6. Why is gasoline bad?	
7. Where does acid rain come from?	
8. How does the government help?	

B Grammar

Complete the sentences. Use the present unreal conditional.

1. If more people _____ public transportation, we _____ on
   (take)   (cut down)
   air pollution.

2. We _____ energy if we _____ the air conditioning.
   (save)   (turn down)

3. If we _____ enough air in the tires, we _____ gas.
   (put)   (save)

4. There _____ less trash if everyone _____.
                                              (recycle)

5. If we _____ unused rooms, we _____ air conditioning and
   (close off)   (reduce)
   heating use.

C Grammar

Combine the sentences. Use the connectors in parentheses.

1. There has been a drought. There are fewer crops this season.

   (so) _____

2. Air pollution is trapping the sun's heat. The atmosphere is warming up.

   (since) _____

3. Global warming changes weather. Hurricanes are stronger and more dangerous.

   (therefore) _____

4. There are new laws. We may be forced to change our routines.

   (because) _____

5. I have learned more about the environment. I have become more responsible.

   (since) _____

D Reading

Read the article. Answer the questions.

Carpool Slugs

Cities have been dealing with rush hour traffic problems for a long time. One way they have cut down on traffic jams has been to create High Occupancy Vehicle (HOV) lanes. In these lanes, also known as carpool lanes, drivers must have two or more people in their cars to enter. Neighbors and co-workers often carpool to gain access to these HOV lanes. With fewer cars and more people in each car, carpool lanes have helped rush hour traffic to run smoother and commuters to get to their destinations faster.

In recent years, commuters have started a new kind of carpooling. In this type of carpooling, a driver drives past bus stops or well-known parking lots and offers a free ride to people he doesn't know. This is so that the driver and the passenger can take the HOV lanes to work. The passengers are called carpool slugs, and they commute to work by *slugging*, or carpooling with strangers.

Both drivers and the carpool slugs are happy with slugging. Every day, slugs save up to $12 in transportation fares and parking fees. And drivers save up to $5,000 a year in gas. In addition, both drivers and slugs save from 30 to 60 minutes of travel time daily.

After many years of slugging, carpool slugs and drivers have become a community. Many of them know each other and have become friends. They look out for each other and may know each other by face, if not by name. Slugging has become an efficient way to commute in large cities and help the environment. Fewer cars on the road means less gas to pollute the air.

1. What is one way that many cities have dealt with rush hour traffic? _____

   _____

2. What is an HOV lane? _____

   _____

3. What is a carpool slug? _____

_____

4. What are two benefits of carpool slugging? _____

_____

5. What has started to happen between carpool slugs and drivers? _____

_____

E Writing

1 Plan a paragraph about one of these environmental problems: global warming, air pollution, or smog. Use the outline to make notes on your ideas.

Problem:	
Causes	**Effects**
1.	1.
(detail) a.	
(detail) b.	2.
2.	
(detail) a.	3.
(detail) b.	

2 Write a paragraph about one of these environmental problems: global warming, air pollution, or smog. Use a separate piece of paper.

TEST
UNIT 10 FREE TIME

A Listening

1 Listen. Circle the correct answer.

1. What are they talking about?
   a. France   b. a vacation   c. a wedding

2. What is the speakers' relationship?
   a. cousins   b. friends   c. bride and groom

2 Listen again. Complete the chart.

1. location of event	
2. fiance's country	
3. day of event	
4. guests at the ceremony	
5. items served at reception	
6. event at castle	
7. where they spend the night	
8. when the event ends	

B Grammar

Complete the sentences. Use the future real or future unreal conditional forms of the verbs.

1. **A** I'm looking forward to the party tonight!

   B I am, too. If everyone _____, we _____ a lot of fun!
   (come)   (have)

2. **A** I heard that you're taking a trip to China! Do you speak Chinese?

   B No. If we _____ the language, we _____ more comfortable.
   (knew)   (feel)

3. **A** What will her family think about the wedding ceremony?

   B If she _____ the cultural traditions, she _____ her family.
   (not / follow)   (disappoint)

4. **A** What should I wear to the reception?

   B If I _____ you, I _____ a nice dress.
   (be)   (wear)

© Cambridge University Press 2018 **Photocopiable**

5. **A** Will Roberto be invited to the wedding ceremony?

   B If he _____ an acquaintance, the couple _____ him to the
   _____(be)_____ _____(not / invite)_____
   ceremony.

C Grammar

Complete the sentences. Use *hope* or *wish* and the correct form of the verb or modal.

1. He _____ he _____, but he's too busy right now.
   _____(can visit)_____

2. They _____ the weather _____ nice for their picnic next Saturday.
   _____(will be)_____

3. She _____ her son _____ married. He doesn't seem interested in
   _____(get)_____
   getting married.

4. I _____ I _____ to Japan next summer. I'm saving money now for
   _____(can travel)_____
   the trip.

5. We _____ we _____ on vacation, but we don't have any free time.
   _____(can go)_____

D Reading

Read the article. Answer the questions.

New Year's in China

New Year's celebrations in China start with the New Moon, the first day of the New Year, and continue for 15 days. Celebrations involve family gatherings and visiting friends. During these days, many Chinese people put up special decorations, eat symbolic food, and participate in traditional activities.

During New Year's celebrations in China, many houses are decorated with vases of flowers, bowls of fruit, and a tray with dried fruit, candies, and sweets. Many Chinese people believe that flowers make the house beautiful and that they symbolize wealth and good luck. In addition, bowls of oranges and tangerines are placed around the home to represent happiness. The walls and doors are decorated with short poems written on red paper. In addition to decorating homes, many Chinese people visit friends and relatives. When they visit, they often bring gifts of

fruit or red envelopes with money for children.

Traditional meals are prepared for the whole family, including those who cannot be there and ancestors – family members who have died. Ancestors are remembered and honored with respect during the celebrations. In addition, certain foods symbolize different things. Noodles represent a long life, and fish represent success. A chicken is served with all of its parts – the head, the legs, and the tail – to represent completeness.

Finally, everyone looks forward to the end of the celebration, the Lantern Festival. This is a fun night. Many people participate in parades with lanterns, while others watch as young men perform a dragon dance with dragons made of bamboo, silk, and paper. And everyone watches the fireworks and firecrackers.

1. When does the Chinese New Year begin? How long is it celebrated?

   _____

2. What do flowers symbolize?

   _____

3. What is done for ancestors during New Year's celebrations?

   _____

4. How is chicken served during Chinese New Year, and why?

   _____

5. What happens at the end of New Year's celebrations in China?

   _____

E Writing

1 Plan a paragraph about a ceremony you attended or a tradition you observed. Use the outline to help you make notes on your ideas.

   I. Ceremony / tradition: _____

   II. Reason for the ceremony / tradition: _____

   _____

   III. Where: _____

   IV. When: _____

   V. Special traditions / activities:

       A. _____

       B. _____

       C. _____

   VI. Conclusion: _____

   _____

2 Write a paragraph about a ceremony you attended or a tradition you observed. Use a separate piece of paper.

FINAL TEST
UNITS 6–10

A Listening

Track 13 1 Listen. Circle the correct answer.

1. What are they talking about?
   a. an event   b. a problem   c. new equipment

2. What is the speakers' relationship?
   a. friends   b. customer and salesperson   c. student and teacher

3. How does Jenny feel?
   a. excited   b. annoyed   c. nervous

Track 13 2 Listen again. Complete the chart.

1. number of calls to Jenny last night	
2. purpose of calls	
3. Michelle's solution	
4. what you register	
5. cost	
6. number of calls Michelle gets	
7. time it takes	

B Grammar

Circle the correct word.

1. Salina **has / has been** negotiating with her co-worker for two days.
2. If I **was / were** you, I would take a vacation.
3. He **wishes / hopes** he could go to his cousin's quinceañera, but he didn't get the day off.
4. If we carpooled to work, we **will / would** save a lot of money on gas.
5. They were **amusing / amused** when they read Mike's blog.

C Grammar

Complete the sentences.

although   because   because of   just   which

1. _____ traditional customs, only family members will be invited to the wedding ceremony.

2. My mother has _____ learned how to use a smartphone.

3. The store manager refused to give the customer a refund _____ the customer didn't have a receipt.

4. Omar is interested in electronic devices _____ are innovative and energy-efficient.

5. _____ wireless technology is amazing, I cannot afford it.

D Reading

Read the article. Circle *T* (true) or *F* (false).

Habitat for Humanity

Habitat for Humanity is an international organization that brings volunteers together to help change the lives and living conditions of people around the world. The goal of the organization is to help homeless families worldwide. Because of donations of money and supplies and the help of volunteers, Habitat for Humanity houses are often built and repaired at very low cost.

To get started, poor and needy families apply to local programs to become "partner families" with Habitat for Humanity. Partner families may have to pay a down payment and monthly payments for their homes, but they also pay in "sweat equity." "Sweat equity" means that partner families have the responsibility of building and repairing their homes with the help of volunteers. So, partner families often spend many hours on the construction of their house and on houses for other families, too. In this way, partner families and volunteers from small businesses, large corporations, church groups, and individuals work together to build and repair many new homes.

Many of the building materials are donated by construction companies, and no one gets paid for their work. Professional construction workers offer their skills to build the foundation and the outside of the houses. Non-professional volunteers with no experience in housing construction learn skills from the professionals and work on the inside of the houses. In addition, all houses that are repaired and built are made to be more energy-efficient.

Even though the central office of Habitat for Humanity is in Atlanta, Georgia, the organization has been building homes in more than 90 countries around the world. In each country, people work together to strengthen communities, to unite cultures, and to give opportunities for affordable homes to more than one million people worldwide.

Source: http://www.habitat.org

---

1. Habitat for Humanity is a worldwide housing program.   T   F

2. Professional construction workers get paid for their work with Habitat for Humanity.   T   F

3. The organization succeeds because of donations of money and volunteers.   T   F

4. Families need to apply to get help from Habitat for Humanity.   T   F

5. Partner families have no financial responsibilities for their houses.   T   F

6. People who work on the exterior of the houses have hard skills.   T   F

7. Volunteers without construction skills can work on the inside of houses.   T   F

8. If you are unskilled, you may receive training from a professional.   T   F

9. It's too expensive for Habitat for Humanity to build energy-efficient houses.   T   F

10. There are Habitat for Humanity houses in more than 90 countries.   T   F

E Writing

1 Plan a paragraph about a time you helped someone. Use the chart to make notes on your ideas.

Who did you help?	
What was the problem or situation?	
What did you do?	
When did this happen?	
How did you feel?	

2 Write a paragraph about a time you helped someone. Use a separate piece of paper.

AUDIO SCRIPTS FOR TESTS

These audio scripts contain the listening portions of the *Ventures 4* unit tests, midterm test, and final test. A customizable copy is available in the *Ventures* online teacher's resources. You can play the audio using the audio files in the online teacher's resources, or you can read the script aloud.

Unit 1: Personal information

Track 2

A Listening

A Well, Carol, having a class party is an excellent idea. But now we have to plan it. Where do we start?

B Why don't we start with the food and drinks? Any ideas, George?

A How about pizza and soda? Leonard works at Pizza Joe's. Maybe he can get a discount for us.

B Great. So let's ask Leonard to order the pizza and soda. Uh, how many pizzas should we order? How much will they cost with the discount?

A Sounds like a problem for Elena. She's really good at math. Let's ask her to figure out the total cost. Then she can tell us the cost for each classmate.

B OK. Now what about music?

A Did you know that Jonathan is a disk jockey? He's the DJ at the dance club downtown. I'm sure he has a lot of different kinds of music!

B You're right. He's got music from all around the world. He can choose the music. Oh, and we'll need some activities. George, you're a great organizer. Can you organize them?

A What do you mean? Like a dance contest? Something like that?
Sure! I think I can organize a few things pretty easily. And what about decorations, Carol? You're creative and artistic – can you do those?

B Yeah, George, I'll decorate. Hey, this planning isn't very hard. Now, what are we missing? Who else can we ask to help?

A Well, maybe Ming could bring the cups, plates, and napkins. She has a car so she could transport everything easily.

B Good idea. And let's ask Marina to bring a cake. She's a fabulous baker!

Unit 2: At school

Track 3

A Listening

A Come in. Oh, hello, Joy! How are you doing?

B Good morning, Mrs. Almada. I need some advice.

A How can I help you?

B Well, I really need to start thinking about my future. I need a job where I can help my family.

A Do you have any ideas?

B Yes! I was talking to my teacher, Mrs. Ash. You know I'm taking that class in child care, right?

A Yes, I know. Do you like it?

B I love it! I love working with young kids! And yesterday, Mrs. Ash told me that there's a certificate program in child care at the community college. Do you know how I can learn more about the program?

A I have information about it. What would you like to know?

B Well, first of all – with a certificate, does it mean that I can open my own child care business?

A Not exactly, Joy. It means that you are certified to work in child care. There are other requirements for opening a child care business, and you'll need to have a lot of work experience before you do that.

B But the certificate is the first step, right? Can you tell me about the program requirements? How many courses are required?

A There are seven required courses.

B And how much is each course?

A Well, let's see. There are seven courses, and each course is three units. That's 21 units, and it costs $35 a unit. So, the total cost of the courses is $735.

B $735? Whoa! That's more than I expected. How long does it take to complete the child care program?

A It depends. Have a seat – let's look at the possibilities.

Unit 3: Friends and family

Track 4

A Listening

A Hey! Vanna! How are you doing?

B I'm OK. Thanks.

A Listen, there's a dance Friday night. I was wondering if you plan to go.

B Well, I *might* go . . .

A What's the matter? Don't you like to dance?

B Yeah, sure. I like to dance.

A Well, then, would you like to go to the dance with me?

B Oh, Mike, I like to dance, and I'm planning to go to the dance – but I can't go with you.

A Yeah, that's cool. I understand.

B No, you don't understand, Mike. Listen, I have very strict parents. I'm not permitted to go anywhere alone with a boy.

A Well, can you tell them that we won't be alone? That we'll be at a dance?

B No, that won't work. My parents are from "the old country." Do you know what I mean? They are bringing me up the same way they were brought up in Cambodia.

A Wow. They don't trust you at all, huh?

B They do trust me. It's just that they only know one way to raise a daughter. Going out alone with a boy is against the rules!

A Well, you can still go to the dance, right?

B Yeah, I'm going with some other girls.

A And you're permitted to dance, right?

B Yes, I'm allowed to dance.

A So, will you save a dance for me?

B Yeah, of course, but . . . I guess I should tell you . . . my parents are going to be chaperones at the dance!

A Oh, no!

Unit 4: Health

Track 5

A Listening

A Oh, no! This letter is bad news!

B Why? What's the matter, Marcus?

A It's from the landlord. He's sold the building. The new owner is going to make these apartments into condos!

B What does that mean?

A It means we have to make a decision, Sylvia: We have to buy this apartment, or we have to move out.

B But we don't want to buy this place! It's old, and it needs fixing up! We'll have to move out. How much time do we have?

A We have 60 days. We ought to start looking immediately. Oh, I should have listened to Charlie.

B Why? What did Charlie say?

A Well, a few months ago, Charlie mentioned that the landlord was trying to sell the place, but I didn't really pay attention.

B You should have told me! Now we have to start thinking and acting – fast! We have to find a place in this neighborhood. The kids shouldn't change schools.

A Let's calm down, honey. We don't have to panic yet. I'll take tomorrow off.

B No, Marcus, you shouldn't miss work. Let me think. . . . Tomorrow I'll look in the newspaper and start making a list of available apartments.

A OK. And we can start looking at apartments next weekend.

B That's right. But, listen, we have to stay in this area. I don't want the kids to be stressed out about changing schools. You should have told me.

A You're right. I'm sorry.

Unit 5: Around town

Track 6

A Listening

A Hi! I'm Jackie, the volunteer coordinator. Are you Yousef?

B Yes. Nice to meet you, Jackie.

A Well, I'm so happy you came by! I am glad that you are interested in volunteering here at the library. How would you like to help?

B Well, my English teacher told me that the library is looking for volunteers to help with the new computer lab.

A Oh, yes! Do you know a lot about computers?

B I know how to use a lot of software and how to do research on the Internet . . . that kind of stuff.

A Great. We have a lot of older people who come here. They know we have computers and want to learn how to use them, but they don't really know where to begin.

B Yes, I know. That's why my teacher encouraged me to come. She knows that I have been helping my parents and my aunts and uncles. I taught them how to use email. They had no idea where to begin until I set up the computer and showed them how. As soon as I showed them, they sent a message to our family in Lebanon! It seems easy to me, but – as you said – they didn't know where to start. I had to be very patient with them.

A I understand. Sometimes it's harder to be patient with family members.

B That's true. Anyway, it was really worthwhile. They are so happy to be able to communicate so often and so cheaply!

A Exactly. And, Yousef, do you speak another language?

B Yes, I speak Arabic at home.

A Oh, that's great. We have a lot of people who could use your help. Now let's talk about your schedule. Can you make a commitment of three hours a week?

B Yes, if I can come on Saturday mornings.

A Terrific. We open at 10:00. Should we say, 10:00 to 1:00? Does that work?

B Yes, that works for me. Should I start this Saturday?

A Yes. I can't wait to get you started!

Midterm Test Units 1–5

Track 7

A Listening

A Hello, Mrs. Brown. Come into my office. I'm glad you made an appointment with me.

B Thank you, Mrs. Patterson. My husband and I are so worried about Sam. He is so bright and gifted in many areas. But we just don't know what his problem is. We really don't know why he's doing so poorly in high school. Do you think that you can help us figure out what's wrong with Sam?

A Well, Mrs. Brown, as a counselor with many years of experience working with teenagers, I can tell you – high school is difficult! Teenagers have to cope with a lot of things these days – new social situations, more difficult schoolwork, extracurricular activities, fitting in with others.

B Yes, I'm sure you're right. But I have no idea why his attendance is so bad. Or why he is missing so many classes. I'm really worried.

A Have you talked with Sam? What does he say?

B Actually, he doesn't say much. When he does talk, he says we're too strict. But recently his grades have been bad because he misses deadlines for homework assignments. He forgets a lot! He forgets his books, he forgets his keys, and he forgot his lunch twice last week!

A What solutions have you tried so far?

B Well, we put him on restriction a few times last month for not going to school and for bad grades. I think we were more stressed out than he was! He just stayed in his room and listened to music.

A Hmm. That doesn't seem to work. Does he have friends?

B Yes, he's very social. He has a large group of friends.

A Does he oversleep?

B No, that doesn't seem to be a problem.

A Does he seem to be stressed out about his grades at all?

B Yes, he does.

A Well, maybe he's just frustrated. He ought to get some help with his schoolwork. Maybe you should get a tutor for Sam. The school has professional tutors available. Do you think he would be interested in meeting with a tutor?

B I'll definitely ask him to go, and then we'll see what happens. Is there a fee?

A No, the school offers free tutoring three days a week after school.

B Well, that's a start! I'll talk to my husband and Sam about the tutor.

Unit 6: Time

Track 8

A Listening

A Linda, I've been thinking about getting smartphones for all of us.

B But Chris, the cell phones we have work just fine.

A Yes, but I was thinking. . . . It would be nice to be able to check my email during the day.

B Well, I think it's nice to get away from email and everything else for a while. It's bad enough that people can call and text me all the time!

A Yes, I know what you mean. In my English class, even though the teacher always reminds students to turn off their cell phones, someone always forgets. It's distracting.

B Well, then why do you want to be even more distracted?

A Well, they're very convenient, especially when we travel. I like the GPS feature on smartphones.

B That's true. You don't like to ask for directions. And you do get lost sometimes.

A Yeah, and also, a smartphone would let us check weather and find out where good restaurants are.

B Hmm. Smartphones make sense for you and me, but I think the kids are fine with regular cell phones. I don't want them to spend all their time on their phones. And with smartphones, they might waste too much time playing games.

A Yeah, and the data plan for all of us might be expensive.

B Have you looked into plans yet? How much is it going to cost?

A Well, we're eligible for two upgrades, so you and I could each get a phone for $99. And I think our data plan would add about $30 to our current bill.

B I guess we could use our tax refund to cover the new phones and the increase in charges.

A Let's go take a look at them today.

Unit 7: Shopping

Track 9

A Listening

A You have reached Swift Customer Service. My name is Jack. How can I help you?

B Well, I bought a cell phone for my daughter a few months ago. And I think the phone is defective. She can't make or receive calls. So, she needs a new phone.

A Well, let's see what we can do. Can you tell me the account number?

B Is the account number the same as the telephone number?

A No, it's the number that's at the top of your monthly bill.

B Oh, here it is: 6494 6603.

A OK, ma'am. I have the account here on the computer. Here's what we can do. You will need to mail the defective phone to us or bring it to one of our stores. If we see that it really is defective, you have two choices. We can exchange it for the same kind of phone, or we can offer you an upgrade.

B An upgrade? What do you mean?

A I mean you can get a better, newer phone that has more features. The newer phone has Internet access and a music player – I'm sure your daughter would love that. The monthly fee is only $15 more than the fee you are paying now.

B But my phone is still under warranty, right?

A Yes, that's right.

B So I can get another phone that is similar to the phone my daughter has for free, right?

A Well, the phone is free, but you will need to pay a small service charge for us to send it to you.

B Let's go with that. I don't want an upgrade at this time. Just send me a phone that works.

A OK. As soon as we receive the broken phone from you, we will send you a new one. Let me confirm your address.

Unit 8: Work

Track 10

A Listening

A Hey, Dan. How do you like the job so far?

B I like it a lot, Tom. Thanks for helping me get it. I'm excited about making some money, finally!

A Yeah. Well, that's what friends are for, right?

B Right! The job isn't that hard, and it's cool that we're working together.

A Yeah, it's great that we get to work together. But, actually, Dan, since I'm the manager here, there's something I need to tell you. It's sort of uncomfortable for me because we're buddies, but . . . well, I hate having to remind you about your responsibilities all the time.

B Well, I'm just learning. I've only been working here for two weeks, you know.

A Yeah, I know. But, you know about the chart, right? I just looked, and I didn't see your initials after any of the duties. What happened?

B Come on, Tom, I've been dealing with customers all morning, and I'm exhausted. And anyway, aren't we supposed to share the duties? I don't see your initials up there!

A Dan, I'm the manager. I don't have to write my initials on the chart, but you do! And another thing. You say this job "isn't that hard," but the reason it isn't hard is because you haven't been doing your share of the work. There's a chart up there for a reason.

B All right, all right! I'll initial the stupid chart! Then will you leave me alone?

A Dan. We're good friends, but I have to make sure things get done around here. You have to try to understand that.

B All right. I'll do the best I can.

A Good. I hope we can work this out somehow.

Unit 9: Daily living

Track 11

A Listening

A Hey, George! Do you have a minute?

B Sure, Ed, what's up?

A Well, Rita and I have been talking about getting a new car.

B That's great!

A And since you know so much about cars, I was wondering if you could tell me more about hybrid cars.

B Sure. I love mine. It's so much more energy-efficient than a regular car.

A So a hybrid uses electricity and gas?

B Well, a hybrid uses two different sources of power. In most hybrids, both electricity and gasoline power the car. The car runs with an electric motor and a gas engine, but the engine is smaller, and it uses a lot less gasoline than a standard car. Car companies are also making other kinds of hybrids like diesel-electric cars, but most are gas-electric hybrids.

A Why don't they just make completely electric cars? They'd be more efficient, right?

B Well electric cars are definitely energy-efficient. But, to be practical, a car needs to go about 300 miles before refueling. And you'd have to recharge an all-electric car every 50 or 100 miles. It takes too long and is inconvenient. A hybrid has batteries that charge themselves with energy the car produces on its own. And it still cuts down on the gas you use, which means less air pollution.

A Well, that's the main reason the kids want to get rid of our old car. They've learned that pollution from oil products like gasoline damages the environment and causes global warming. And

we've started teaching them how to protect the environment and take responsibility. So the next thing you know, the kids are telling me that we have to replace our old car.

B Well, your kids are right, Ed! Since your car is so old, it uses a lot of gas, which is bad for the environment. Pollution from standard cars gets into the atmosphere and comes down as acid rain.

A So, driving a hybrid is better for the environment.

B Absolutely! Every little thing helps. And did you know the government gives you a tax credit for buying a hybrid?

A So, it's even good for our wallets!

Unit 10: Free time

Track 12

A Listening

A Sara, did I tell you my cousin, Marie, is getting married next month . . . in France? Her fiancé is from France.

B Really? Are you going?

A No, I wish I could go, but the trip is too far and too expensive. But Marie told me all about it. Weddings in France are a big deal, and sometimes they last for two days! And her family is planning a very special celebration.

B It sounds exciting! What are they planning?

A Well, Marie said her wedding ceremony will start on a Saturday afternoon at a small church. Only family and close friends are invited. The ceremony will last about an hour. Then after the ceremony, all her fiancé's neighbors and acquaintances are invited to a reception in the courtyard of the church.

B Wow, Elena. How many people will there be?

A Lots of people! The reception will last about two hours, and they'll serve champagne and snacks.

B Oh, that sounds fun!

A But, Sara, that's not all! After the reception, the family and close friends are going to go to a castle for a five-course meal.

B A five-course meal of French food sounds delicious! I absolutely love French food.

A And after the meal, the dancing begins.

B Elena, if I ate a five-course meal, I'd never be able to dance!

A Well, it's not uncommon for the French to celebrate all day. The dancing will probably continue until very late. And afterward, the family will spend the night at the castle.

B Oh my gosh!

A Then finally, the next day, in the late morning or early afternoon, the friends will come back to the castle and join the family for another meal. Oh, I really wish I could go!

B I wish you could go, too! All of those activities sound exhausting, but so exciting. If I were you, I'd find a way to go.

Final Test Units 6–10

Track 13

A Listening

A Oh, Michelle, I am so frustrated!

B Why, Jenny? What's wrong?

A Oh, it's those annoying telephone calls that I get all the time! Last night, I was making dinner and I received three phone calls from people trying to sell me something again. They always call at the worst times.

B Oh, you mean telemarketers. They used to drive me crazy, too. I absolutely hated dealing with them.

A Michelle, what do you mean when you say "they used to drive you crazy"?

B Well, Jenny, we've just registered for the National Do Not Call Registry. Have you heard of it?

A No, but I'm very interested.

B It's a government program that you can use to stop telemarketers from calling you. If you register your telephone number with the system, the telemarketers are not allowed to call you! It's easy!

A Wow. Do you need to pay to do this? Do you have to buy any special devices?

B No, you don't have to pay anything or buy any special equipment.

A Well, that's good. So does the Do Not Call Registry really work?

B Absolutely. Since we registered our telephone number, we haven't had even one phone call from someone trying to sell us something or asking us to donate money.

A OK, I'm convinced. How do I register?

B You can register by phone or online – it doesn't take long.

A Michelle, thanks so much for the tip. I'm going to register my phone number right now. I'm really looking forward to ending those annoying phone calls!

Each unit test section is worth 20 points, for a total of 100 points per unit test. Therefore, each listening item is 2 points. All other items are worth 4 points.

Unit 1: Personal information

A Listening
1 1. b   2. a   3. c
2 1. decorating; She is creative and artistic.
   2. organize the activities; He's a great organizer.
   3. order the pizza and soda; He works at Pizza Joe's.
   4. figure out the total cost; She's good at math.
   5. choose the music; He's a DJ and has a lot of different kinds of music.
   6. bring cups, plates, and napkins; She has a car.
   7. bring a cake; She's a fabulous baker.

B Grammar
1. easy; quickly
2. beautiful; professionally
3. skillful; slowly
4. fast; carefully
5. bad; well

C Grammar
1. Do you believe girls are better at learning languages than boys?
2. Samuel's parents realize he has an aptitude for art.
3. Do you feel that your son needs help in math class?
4. Everyone agrees that Naomi is gifted in dance.
5. Do you know that Karen has an aptitude for cooking?

D Reading
1. T   2. T   3. F   4. F   5. T

E Writing
Answers will vary.
Sample answer:
The primary intelligence of my brother, Daniel, is visual/spatial. All his life, he has drawn beautiful pictures. Everyone talks about his artistic aptitude. As a boy, he spent a lot of his free time drawing and painting. Now, as an adult, he uses his visual/spatial intelligence by painting and teaching art. He also has a fantastic sense of design. I wish I had his artistic aptitude.

Unit 2: At school

A Listening
1 1. a   2. c   3. b
2 1. childcare
   2. at the community college
   3. loves working with children/can work in childcare

4. open a childcare business
5. seven
6. $735
7. it depends

B Grammar
1. A Are bilingual skills expected by many employers in this country?
   B Yes, bilingual skills are needed for many jobs in this country.
2. A Is an internship required to graduate from the program?
   B Yes. Internships are arranged by the school.
3. A Where is the admissions office located?
   B It is located next to the business building.
4. A Are most of the classes held in the morning?
   B Actually, many of the classes are offered in the evening.
5. A Are scholarships provided for students?
   B Yes, scholarships are given to students by the financial aid office.

C Grammar
1. Graduates are required to complete their courses by May 4th.
2. All interns are expected to be on time for every meeting.
3. Are students encouraged to participate in work experience programs?
4. Applicants are told to meet with a counselor.
5. Are students allowed to earn credit for work experience?

D Reading
1. F   2. F   3. F   4. T   5. T

E Writing
Answers will vary.
Sample answer:
My wife and I immigrated to the United States. We had many obstacles and successes. Our first obstacle was money. I was a teacher in my country, but I had to find a job cleaning buildings. I wanted my wife to stay home with the children, but we needed to make enough money to pay the rent and buy things for our house. I am happy to say that we have succeeded in earning and saving our money. The second obstacle was learning English. I study English so that I can teach one day in this country. I am not fluent, but I am making a lot of progress.

Unit 3: Friends and famiily

A Listening
1 1. b   2. a   3. a   4. a
2 1. Friday
   2. her parents are strict
   3. Cambodia
   4. some other girls
   5. dance
   6. at the dance

B Grammar
1. I'd like to know why he is on restriction.
2. I wonder when she started to trust him again.
3. Can you tell me how I can get a better job?
4. Do you know what time the class starts?
5. Can you tell me what grade Lidia got in chemistry?

C Grammar
1. Do you know whether he broke the school rules?
2. Can you tell me whether there is a bus stop nearby?
3. I'd like to know whether he is on restriction this weekend.
4. Can you tell me whether she left school early?
5. I wonder whether she can come to the party.

D Reading
1. They spend their money on clothing, entertainment, food, computers, and cars.
2. They get their spending money from allowances from their parents, from part-time jobs, and from payment for chores.
3. Parents teach their teenagers how to spend responsibly by: giving their children weekly allowances connected to their age; giving their children weekly allowances connected to the chores they do around the house; and encouraging them to get part-time jobs.
4. They spend their money rather than save it. They spend money on the latest fashions or technology.
5. They will need to reconsider their spending habits.

E Writing
Answers will vary.
Sample answer:
One difference between me and my best friend, Dan, is that we spend our evenings after work very differently. I prefer quiet nights at home. For

example, when I get home, I cook a healthy dinner. Then, I like to watch a movie and go to bed early. On the other hand, Dan likes to go out after work. He loves fast food and enjoys eating in restaurants for dinner. He visits me and his other friends and then goes to bed very late. Dan and I are very different people, but he is still my best friend.

Unit 4: Health

A Listening
1 1. b   2. c   3. a   4. c
2 1. The new owner is going to make apartments into condos
   2. in a letter
   3. to buy the apartment or move
   4. 60 days
   5. children's school
   6. he didn't tell Sylvia

B Grammar
1. e   2. d   3. a   4. c   5. b

C Grammar
1. He should have gone to bed on time.
2. They shouldn't have used a credit card every day.
3. She shouldn't have turned off her alarm clock.
4. He should have asked someone to explain them.
5. We should have been more responsible.

D Reading
1. Music can help someone calm down or relax.
2. No. Many doctors think that a person's reaction to music is unique and complicated.
3. You should do an experiment with music to find out which kind of music helps you to relax.
4. A stressed-out person often has a fast pulse and tense muscles.
5. Some of the physical signs that a person is relaxed are a slower pulse and relaxed muscles.

E Writing
Answers will vary.
Sample answer:
I felt stressed out last summer when I spent too much on my credit card. I was anxious because I didn't have enough money to pay the bill. I stopped buying anything unnecessary, and I saved $40 each week. I worked for five more hours each week until I had enough money to pay the bill. I also decided to take a free yoga class at the community center. This class helped me to relax and to forget about all the stressful things in my life. I am going to take the yoga class again this summer!

Unit 5: Around town

A Listening
1 1. c   2. b   3. a
2 1. Volunteer coordinator at the library
   2. his English teacher
   3. He knows how to use software and do research on the Internet
   4. He helped his family set up and use email
   5. He is patient
   6. English and Arabic
   7. Saturday mornings from 10 to 1 p.m.

B Grammar
1. as soon as   4. until
2. until   5. as soon as
3. As soon as

C Grammar
1. helped   4. have spoken
2. overslept   5. has babysat
3. visits

D Reading
1. Residents of a neighborhood, members of a community, and neighbors are responsible for creating community gardens.
2. People build community gardens in unused, empty parking lots.
3. Residents can save money by growing their own vegetables, fruits, herbs, and flowers. / Residents can grow food from their native countries. / Residents can get exercise and fresh air. / The gardens help keep the air clean. / There might be less crime in the neighborhood because neighbors know each other better.
4. Neighbors get to know each other. Neighbors work together in the gardens. / Community gardens are safe and clean parks.
5. Community gardens help keep the air clean and do good things for city neighborhoods.

E Writing
Answers will vary.
Sample answer:
Bill Gates is famous for starting the Microsoft Corporation in the 1970s. In recent years, he has also helped many people around the world with the Bill and Melinda Gates Foundation. This organization helps people who need health care in poor countries. It also donates money and materials to schools across the United States. The organization has the goal of giving people equal chances to get health care and education. Bill Gates has helped to improve many lives with his organization.

Midterm Test Units 1–5

A Listening
1 1. a   2. c   3. a
2 1. Mrs. Brown
   2. a counselor
   3. new social situations, more difficult schoolwork, extracurricular activities, fitting in
   4. Sam's attendance, bad grades, forgetting
   5. his parents are too strict
   6. they put him on restriction
   7. that they get a tutor for him

B Grammar
1. until   4. that
2. have to   5. shouldn't
3. whether

C Grammar
1. easily   4. until
2. to earn   5. volunteered
3. ought to

D Reading
1. T   3. T   5. F   7. T   9. F
2. F   4. F   6. T   8. F   10. T

E Writing
Answers will vary.
Sample answer:
I had a conflict with my sister last year. While we were talking on the telephone, she told me about a problem she was having with her daughter. I gave her my opinion about the situation, and she got upset. She just wanted me to listen. She should have told me that! I was sad because my sister did not talk to me for the rest of the day. However, she called me back the next day and said she was sorry. We are now trying to communicate better with each other.

Unit 6: Time

A Listening
1 1. b   2. b
2 1. Chris
   2. People can email her.
   3. Someone always forgets to turn off the phone.
   4. They have GPS.
   5. He doesn't like to ask for directions and he sometimes gets lost.
   6. You can get the weather and find good restaurants.
   7. They would waste time playing games.
   8. They will use their tax refund.

B Grammar
1. She doesn't understand the instructions although she read the manual many times. / Although she read the manual many times, she doesn't understand the instructions.

2. Although there are free computer classes at the community center, my parents still don't know how to use email. / My parents still don't know how to use email although there are free computer classes at the community center.
3. I rarely use my microwave although microwaves help me to make dinner quickly. / Although microwaves help me to make dinner quickly, I rarely use my microwave.
4. Although he can take the subway to work, he prefers to walk for the exercise. / He prefers to walk for the exercise although he can take the subway to work.
5. Although she never used to write letters to her brother, she enjoys sending him emails now. / She enjoys sending her brother emails now although she never used to write letters to him.

C Grammar
1. Although
2. because
3. although
4. because
5. Although

D Reading
1. A   2. A   3. D   4. A   5. D

E Writing
Answers will vary.
Sample answer:
My computer is my favorite technological device. It has several advantages. When I want to look for jobs or find out information about something, it is easier to use my computer than to look through newspapers and books. Using a computer saves time because I don't have to go to the library for information. Another benefit of my computer is that it's very easy to communicate with my family. I can send my family an email at any time of day, and it's free. But, of course, there are disadvantages. Information online is not always correct. I also get a lot of spam. So even though my computer makes things easier, it has drawbacks as well.

Unit 7: Shopping

A Listening
1 1. c   2. b   3. b
2 1. It's defective – can't make or receive calls
   2. A few months ago
   3. She can mail it or bring it to a store
   4. She can exchange it for the same phone or get an upgrade.
   5. a newer better phone with more features (internet access and a music player)
6. The upgrade is $15 more a month
7. The same kind of phone

B Grammar
1. Our merchandise comes with a warranty which is good for two years.
2. Customers who are looking for discounts can order from our online store.
3. Cellular phones which have Internet access are popular.
4. The clerk is looking for the customer who had a question about a product.
5. Store managers solve problems which happen between clerks and customers.

C Grammar
1. He's a manager that I've worked with for years.
2. The car that you recommended to us is great!
3. The computer that we bought yesterday is defective.
4. The sweater that I gave her was too small.
5. We bought it from a retailer that we trusted.

D Reading
1. Bargain shoppers often go to neighborhood thrift stores for the lowest prices.
2. You can buy used items such as clothing, household items, books, jewelry, and furniture at a thrift store.
3. Prices are low at thrift stores because the merchandise is donated, and the salesclerks are volunteers.
4. Yes. Merchandise is sold "as is," so items may be defective. In most cases, if an item has small defects, shoppers usually don't mind.
5. Donors can be sure their donated items will be used, and the money from sales goes to people in need. / Thrift stores offer merchandise at low prices.

E Writing
Answers will vary.
Sample answer:
I like to shop at outlet malls. First, at outlet malls, there are many stores to choose from. There are discount clothing stores, shoe stores, drugstores, and music stores in one place. Furthermore, I like the convenience of outlet malls. I can park in the parking lot and spend a couple of hours getting my shopping done quickly. Finally, my husband and I like the discount prices! We were able to buy back-to-school clothing for our children for half the price of clothing at regular stores. There is also a big variety of clothing. Outlet malls are the best!

Unit 8: Work

A Listening
1 1. a   2. c   3. c
2 1. Tom
   2. excited about making money; the job isn't that hard
   3. manager
   4. uncomfortable
   5. he doesn't write his initials on the chart
   6. he's been dealing with customers and is exhausted
   7. because Dan hasn't been doing his share of the work

B Grammar
1. has just finished
2. has been working
3. have been reading
4. have just arrived
5. has just gone

C Grammar
1. amusing   4. disappointing
2. shocked   5. irritated
3. exhausted

D Reading
1. The hottest jobs are jobs that will have the largest growth and popularity in years to come.
2. Students and workers can use job reports to help them decide which careers will be the most promising or which programs to study.
3. Some service industry occupations are in health care, hospitality, and food services.
4. Some of the fastest growing health-care jobs are nurses, nursing aides, and home health aides.
5. Employers will look for hard and soft skills.

E Writing
Answers will vary.
Sample answer:
From: [Student's Name and Email]
To: mfreeman@bestjob.com
Subject: Nursing Aide Position

Dear Ms. Freeman:

I read your advertisement online for the nursing aide position. I am very interested in this position and have enclosed my résumé.

I have just received nursing assistant's certification and have been volunteering at the hospital every Saturday. I also worked as a nursing assistant before I arrived in Florida two years ago. I am very interested in health care, and I am studying to be a nurse at the community college. I get along very well with my co-workers, and I am skilled in dealing with patients.

I hope you will call me to schedule an interview. My phone number is 555-555-5555. I look forward to hearing from you.
Sincerely,
[Student's name]

Unit 9: Daily living

A Listening
1 1. b   2. a
2 1. A hybrid
   2. mix between and electric and standard car
   3. electricity and gasoline
   4. with energy the car produces on its own
   5. amount of gas used and air pollution
   6. damages the environment and causes global warming
   7. pollution in the atmosphere
   8. it gives a tax credit

B Grammar
1. If more people took public transportation, we would cut down on air pollution.
2. We would save energy if we turned down the air conditioning.
3. If we put enough air in the tires, we would save gas.
4. There would be less trash if everyone recycled.
5. If we closed off unused rooms, we would reduce air conditioning and heating use.

C Grammar
1. There has been a drought. As a result, there are fewer crops this season.
2. Since air pollution is trapping the sun's heat, the atmosphere is warming up.
3. Global warming changes weather. Consequently, hurricanes are stronger and more dangerous.
4. Due to new laws, we may be forced to change our routines.
5. Since I have learned more about the environment, I have become more responsible.

D Reading
1. Cities have dealt with rush hour traffic by creating HOV or carpool lanes.
2. An HOV lane is a High Occupancy Vehicle lane. Drivers must have two or more people in their cars in order to enter.
3. A carpool slug is a person who commutes to work in a car with strangers.
4. Slugs save on transportation fares and parking fees. / Drivers save on gasoline. / Both slugs and drivers save on travel time. / It's better for the environment if there are fewer cars on the road.
5. Carpool slugs and drivers have started to form a community. / Many of them have become friends.

E Writing
Answers will vary.
Sample answer:
Global warming is a serious environmental problem. One cause is air pollution. Burning gasoline and coal causes a lot of air pollution. People should drive less and use gas-efficient cars. Another cause of global warming is that people cut down trees to make paper and to build new homes. Trees produce oxygen and help clean the air. Since too many trees are cut down, there is a buildup of harmful gases in the atmosphere. Because of global warming, weather patterns change. Many places have less rainfall. Due to global warming, the sea level is rising. Towns near oceans are in danger of flooding. As a result of global warming, ocean water is also getting warmer. Typhoons and hurricanes are becoming more frequent. If we all took responsibility for saving the earth, we would help to reduce global warming.

Unit 10: Free time

A Listening
1 1. c   2. b
2 1. France
   2. France
   3. Saturday
   4. family and close friends
   5. champagne and snacks
   6. five-course meal and dancing
   7. at the castle
   8. the next day/Sunday

B Grammar
1. comes, will have
2. knew, would feel
3. doesn't follow, will disappoint
4. were, would wear
5. were, wouldn't invite

C Grammar
1. wishes, could visit
2. hope, will be
3. wishes, would get
4. hope, can travel
5. wish, could go

D Reading
1. The Chinese New Year begins with the New Moon, the first day of the New Year. / It is celebrated for 15 days.
2. Flowers symbolize wealth and good luck.
3. They are remembered and honored during the celebrations.
4. A chicken is served with all its parts to represent completeness.
5. At the end of New Year's celebrations in China, people celebrate at the Lantern Festival. There are parades, dancers, fireworks, and firecrackers.

E Writing
Answers will vary.
Sample answer:
On January 1, I was invited to a traditional Greek celebration in New York. Everyone was there to celebrate the New Year. When we arrived, the family wished us "many more years" – a traditional greeting on the first day of the year. For dinner we had roast lamb, rice, green beans with tomatoes, and roasted potatoes. After dinner, some men played the bouzoukia (a musical instrument), and the guests sang songs. For dessert, we had the Vasilopita, a special cake. The cake is baked with a coin in it. The host slices a piece of cake for each member of the family and any guest. If you're the person who receives the coin in your slice, you will have good luck for the entire year. I didn't get the coin in my slice, but we all hoped for a year of good luck!

Final Test Units 6–10

A Listening
1 1. b   2. a   3. b
2 1. three
   2. to sell something
   3. National Do Not Call Registry
   4. phone number
   5. free
   6. zero
   7. not long

B Grammar
1. has been   4. would
2. were   5. amused
3. wishes

C Grammar
1. Because of   4. which
2. just   5. Although
3. because

D Reading
1. T   3. T   5. F   7. T   9. F
2. F   4. T   6. T   8. T   10. T

E Writing
Answers will vary.
Sample answer:

Last summer, there was a knock on my apartment door. It was about 10:00 p.m., so I was not sure if I should open the door. I opened the door a little and saw Mrs. Kim, my neighbor from across the hall. She was upset. Her husband, who is 90 years old, was hurt. He fell in the bathroom, and Mrs. Kim needed help. First, I called 911. Then, I went to the Kims' apartment. Although Mr. Kim wanted me to help him get up, I just sat with him and tried to make him calm down. I explained that I called 911 and that professional medical staff were coming. Finally, professional medical staff arrived and helped Mr. Kim get up. They checked him and said that he was fine and just needed some rest. I hope I'll be that strong when I'm 90 years old!

AUTHORS' ACKNOWLEDGMENTS

The authors would like to acknowledge and thank focus-group participants and reviewers for their insightful comments, as well as Cambridge University Press editorial, marketing, and production staffs, whose thorough research and attention to detail have resulted in a quality product.

The publishers would also like to extend their particular thanks to the following reviewers and consultants for their valuable insights and suggestions:

Barry Bakin, Instructional Technology, Los Angeles Unified School District, Los Angeles, CA;

Jim Brice, San Diego Community College District Continuing Education, San Diego, CA;

Diana Contreras, West Valley Occupational Center, Los Angeles, CA;

Druci J. Diaz, Hillsborough Country Public Schools, Tampa, FL;

Linda Foster, Instructor, Hillsborough County Schools Adult Education Department, Tampa, FL;

Margaret Geiger, M.Ed., Dallas, TX;

Ana L. Herrera, San Jacinto Adult Learning Center, El Paso, TX;

Cindi Hartmen, ESL Instructor, San Diego Continuing Education, San Diego, CA;

Patrick Jennings, Tomlinson Adult Learning Center, St. Petersburg, FL;

Lori Hess-Tolbert, Frisco, TX;

AnnMarie Kokash-Wood, Tomlinson Adult Learning Center, St. Petersburg, FL;

Linda P. Kozin, San Diego Continuing Ed, San Diego Community College District, San Diego, CA;

Caron Lieber, Palomar College, San Marcos, CA;

Reyna P. Lopez, Southwest College, Los Angeles, CA;

Rosemary Lubarov, Palo Alto Adult School, Palo Alto, CA;

Lori K. Markel, Plant City Adult and Community School, Plant City, FL;

Mary Spanarke, Center for Applied Linguistics / Washington English Center, Washington, DC;

Rosalie Tauscher, Fort Worth ISD Adult Ed, Fort Worth, TX;

Timothy Wahl, Abram Friedman Occupation Center, Los Angeles, CA;

Delia Watley, Irving ISD Adult Education and Literacy, Irving, TX;

Andrea V. White, Tarrant County College, Arlington, TX;

Sandra Wilson, Fort Worth Adult Education, Fort Worth, TX

ACKNOWLEDGMENTS

The authors and publishers acknowledge the following sources of copyright material and are grateful for the permissions granted. While every effort has been made, it has not always been possible to identify the sources of all the material used, or to trace all copyright holders. If any omissions are brought to our notice, we will be happy to include the appropriate acknowledgments on reprinting and in the next update to the digital edition, as applicable.

Key: B = Below, BL = Below Left, BR = Below Right, C = Centre, L = Left, R = Right, T = Top, TC = Top Centre, TL = Top Left, TR = Top Right.

Photos
All images are sourced from Getty Images.

p. 2 (TL): Robert Daly/OJO Images; p. 2 (TR): samdiesel/E+; p. 2 (BL): Stuart O'Sullivan/Taxi; p. 2 (BR): XiXinXing; p. 6 (photo 1), p. 50: sturti/E+; p. 6 (photo 2): Purestock; p. 6 (photo 3): Sollina Images/Blend Images; p. 6 (photo 4): Gianni Diliberto/Caiaimage; p. 6 (photo 5), p. 55, p. 84 (photo 1, photo 4), p. 110 (photo 2), p. 128: Fuse/Corbis; p. 6 (photo 6): Gravity Images/Photographer's Choice; p. 9 (photo 1): MaaHoo Studio/The Image Bank; p. 9 (photo 2): Reza Estakhrian/Stone; p. 9 (photo 3): Glowimages; p. 9 (photo 4): Rosenberg Philip/Perspectives; p. 9 (photo 5): Monty Rakusen/Cultura; p. 9 (photo 6): Jose Luis Pelaez Inc/Blend Images; p. 9 (photo 7): Tony Anderson/Taxi; p. 9 (photo 8): Steve Debenport/E+; p. 18 (T), p. 107 (photo 3): Eric Audras/ONOKY; p. 18 (BR): Hill Street Studios/Blend Images; p. 18 (BL): Caiaimage/Sam Edwards; p. 24: Noel Hendrickson/DigitalVision; p. 26: Sportstock/E+; p. 29 (T): arabianEye arabianEye; p. 29 (B): GeorgeRudy/iStock/Getty Images Plus; p. 32 (photo 1): Kevin Dodge/Corbis; p. 32 (photo 2): XiFotos/iStock/Getty Images Plus; p. 32 (photo 3): RBFried/iStock/Getty Images Plus; p. 32 (photo 4): DragonImages/iStock/Getty Images Plus; p. 32 (photo 5 girl): ljubaphoto/E+; p. 32 (photo 5 birthday): Tim Macpherson/Cultura; p. 38: Hill Street Studios/Blend Images; p. 40 (T): Garry Gay/The Image Bank; p. 40 (B): Cheshmeh/iStock/Getty Images Plus; p. 43: Steve Debenport/E+; p. 44 (photo 1): ti-ja/E+; p. 44 (photo 2): jaycriss/iStock/Getty Images Plus; p. 44 (photo 3): Image Source; p. 44 (photo 4): Maskot; p. 44 (photo 5): KatSnowden/iStock/Getty Images Plus; p. 47 (L): Glowimages; p. 47 (C): Insung Jeon/Moment Open; p. 47 (R): Hero Images; p. 52 (L): franckreporter/E+; p. 52 (C): Eugenio Marongiu/Cultura; p. 52 (R): Image Source; p. 58 (photo 1): Westend61; p. 58 (photo 2): Hailshadow/iStock/Getty Images Plus; p. 58 (photo 3): avid_creative/E+; p. 58 (woman): Blend Images - JGI/Tom Grill/Brand X Pictures; p. 58 (photo 4: serving a meal): FredFroese/E+; p. 58 (photo 5): BURGER/Canopy; p. 60: fstop123/iStock/Getty Images Plus; p. 62: CasarsaGuru/E+; p. 66: FatCamera/iStock/Getty Images Plus; p. 70 (photo 1): PeopleImages/DigitalVision; p. 70 (photo 2): Betsie Van Der Meer/Stone; p. 70 (photo 3: Mr. Chung): XiXinXing; p. 70 (photo 3: letter): Yuri Nunes/EyeEm; p. 70 (photo 4): Hero Images; p. 75 (L): baona/iStock/Getty Images Plus; p. 75 (R): Hill Street Studios/Blend Images; p. 76 (L): Flashpop/DigitalVision; p. 76 (C): Dan Dalton/Caiaimage; p. 76 (R), p. 107 (photo 4): Dougal Waters/DigitalVision; p. 78, p. 110 (photo 3: light bulb): Tetra Images; p. 81 (watch): DmitryVPetrenko/iStock/Getty Images Plus; p. 81 (burger): Elena Pejchinova/Moment; p. 81 (car): John Lund/Blend Images; p. 81 (ring): Lena Mirisola/

Moment; p. 81 (televisions):VICTOR DE SCHWANBERG/SPL/Science Photo Library; p. 81 (crowd): Glowimages; p. 81 (collision): Matthias Clamer/Stone; p. 84 (photo 2): Juice Images/Cultura; p. 84 (photo 3): Lava; p. 84 (photo 5): Ceneri/E+; p. 90: Neustockimages/E+; p. 92: AndreyPopov/iStock/Getty Images Plus; p. 95: ozgurdonmaz/E+; p. 96 (photo 1): JackF/iStock/Getty Images Plus; p. 96 (photo 2): Lisa Kehoffer/EyeEm; p. 96 (photo 3): Yew! Images/Image Source; p. 96 (photo 4): Malcolm MacGregor/Moment Open; p. 96 (photo 5): KatarzynaBialasiewicz/iStock/Getty Images Plus; p. 96 (photo 6): blackred/E+; p. 101 (photo 1): ColorBlind Images/Iconica; p. 101 (photo 2): Asiaselects; p. 101 (photo 3): Karen Moskowitz/The Image Bank; p. 101 (photo 4): DragonImages/iStock/Getty Images Plus; p. 101 (photo 5): dolgachov/iStock/Getty Images Plus; p. 101 (photo 6): pzAxe/ iStock/Getty Images Plus; p. 101 (photo 7): CREATISTA/iStock/Getty Images Plus; p. 101 (photo 8): M Swiet Productions/Moment; p. 102: Ryouchin/DigitalVision; p. 107 (photo 1): Markus Altmann/Corbis; p. 107 (photo 2): Paul Bradbury/Caiaimage; p. 110 (photo 1): DonNichols/E+; p. 110 (photo 3: carpooling): Lawrence Manning/Corbis; p. 110 (photo 3: recycling): Mike Powles/Photolibrary; p. 110 (photo 3: washing machine): alxpin/E+; p. 110 (photo 4): RapidEye/E+; p. 118: Harrison Shull/Aurora; p. 122 (photo 1): DragonImages/iStock/Getty Images Plus; p. 122 (photo 2): Anna_Om/iStock/Getty Images Plus; p. 122 (photo 3):Caiaimage/Tom Merton/OJO+; p. 122 (photo 4): JB325/iStock/Getty Images Plus; p. 130 (L): AFP; p. 130 (C): Kaveh Kazemi/Hulton Archive; p. 130 (R): ATTA KENARE/AFP; p. 132: mphillips007/iStock/Getty Images Plus; p. 133 (chocolate): malerapaso/E+; p. 133 (restaurant):allensima/iStock/Getty Images Plus; p. 133 (man): drbimages/E+; p. 133 (boarding pass): lindwa/iStock/Getty Images Plus; p. 133 (hat): ScrappinStacy/iStock/Getty Images Plus; p. 139: Blend Images/Hill Street Studios/Brand X Pictures; p. 148: CSA Images/B&W Archive Collection; p. 151: LWA/Dann Tardif/Blend Images; p. 163: FrankRamspott/DigitalVision Vectors.

The following images are from other libraries:
p. 69, p. 121: United States coin images from the United States Mint.

Illustrations
p. 11, p. 49, p. 61 (2, 7), p. 73 (6), p. 119: QBS Learning; p. 12: Adrian D' Alimonte; p. 37, p. 46, p. 89: Nina Edwards; p. 49, p. 74: Chuck Gonzales; p. 61 (1, 3, 4, 5, 6, 8), p. 113: Monika Roe; p. 73 (1, 2, 3, 4, 5): Kenneth Betelman; p. 87: Brad Hamann.

Front Cover Photography by Betsie Van Der Meer/Taxi.

Back Cover Photography by pressureUA/iStock/Getty Images Plus; Adidet Chaiwattanakul/EyeEm; pixelfit/E+.

Audio produced by CityVox.